The Yale Edition of the Complete Works of St. Thomas More

VOLUME 1

ENGLISH POEMS

LIFE OF PICO

THE LAST THINGS

*Published by the St. Thomas More Project, Yale University,
under the auspices of Gerard L. Carroll and Joseph B. Murray,
Trustees of the Michael P. Grace, II, Trust,
and with the support of the Editing Program of the
National Endowment for the Humanities
and the Knights of Columbus*

Portrait of Giovanni Pico della Mirandola, Anonymous. Galleria Uffizi, Florence.

The Complete Works of
ST. THOMAS MORE

VOLUME 1

Edited by

ANTHONY S. G. EDWARDS

KATHERINE GARDINER RODGERS

and

CLARENCE H. MILLER

Yale University Press, New Haven and London

Set in Baskerville type by The Composing Room
of Michigan, Inc.
Printed in the United States of America by
Vail-Ballou Press, Binghamton, N.Y.

Library of Congress catalogue number: 63-7949
International standard book number: 0-300-06231-1

⊗ The paper in this book meets
the guidelines for permanence and durability
of the Committee on Production Guidelines
for Book Longevity of the Council on
Library Resources.

10   9   8   7   6   5   4   3   2   1

To the Other Editors of the More Volumes

To the Helpers Who Worked at the More Project
in Sterling Library

And to the Generous Patrons of the Yale Edition of the
Complete Works of St. Thomas More

We Gratefully Dedicate This Final Volume

ACKNOWLEDGMENTS

Professor Edwards gratefully acknowledges information and assistance from the following: Dr. Julia Boffey, Dr. Lotte Hellinga, Professor George Keiser, Dr. Carol Meale, Dr. Anne Sutton, the British Library, and Balliol College, Oxford. He wishes to extend particular gratitude to Clarence Miller, who, in his role as Executive Editor, has attended to every aspect of this work, constantly improving it in matters large and small; his vigilance in the pursuit of truth and the extirpation of error has offered a model of scholarly integrity. Professor Edwards wishes also to thank the University of Victoria for a sabbatical leave during which some preliminary work was done for this edition and for the subsequent award of a research grant.

Katherine G. Rodgers gratefully acknowledges the assistance of the following people: Clarence H. Miller, for his unstinting generosity as a scholar, mentor, and friend and for his inspiring enthusiasm for the editorial task at hand; Lawrence Manley, for his guidance in pursuing fruitful lines of inquiry and exposition; Harold Skulsky, for his helpful suggestions and comments, his learned example, and his friendship; and her husband, Peter Rodgers, for his support in countless ways, both scholarly and spousal.

Clarence Miller wishes to express his gratitude to Laura Jones Dooley, Judith Calvert, and Maureen Noonan for their expert assistance along the sometimes rocky road toward a handsome and usable volume; to Mary Ellen Curtain, who made the index and in doing so pointed out some errors and inconsistencies; to Anne Hawthorne, our copyeditor, whose learned, meticulous, and unflagging reading of the typescript was invaluable; to Ralph Keen, for his skilled and laborious checking of the typescript; to Daniel Kinney, for his generous and copious assistance with the addenda and corrigenda; to Joseph Trapp, who read the whole typescript and made helpful suggestions; and especially to Germain Marc'hadour, who not only read the Pico translations in the appendix carefully and helpfully but also read the whole volume in corrected page proof, giving us the benefit of his learning and judgment and enabling us to apply the file for the last time in many places. It is also appropriate that I should express my personal gratitude to all those thanked in the dedication of this volume, especially those with whom I have worked over the past two decades.

Finally, homage should be paid for the last time in these volumes to

Richard Sylvester and Louis Martz, the founders and furtherers of this great enterprise, which now, after almost forty years, has been brought to fulfillment and fruition. We may hope that Richard Sylvester, who intended to edit this volume himself, is pleased with the work we have done.

A. S. G. E., K. G. R., and C. H. M.

Victoria, B.C.; New Haven, Conn.; St. Louis, Mo.

• • •

Our series, for which actual work began in 1960, now at last has reached conclusion with the publication of Volume 1! The anomaly is explained by our practice of publishing volumes, not in any set order, but whenever any given volume was ready for the Press. We were often complimented for the timing of our three volumes of the Tower Works, the *Dialogue of Comfort,* the *Treatise on the Passion,* and the *De Tristitia,* all of which appeared in 1976, just in time to celebrate the quincentennial of More's birth, in 1977–78. But the timing was wholly accidental; two of the volumes had been delayed by illness and administrative duties. The triumphant appearance of this triple set of volumes and the numerous celebrations of the quincentennial left us ill-prepared for the blow that fell on July 9, 1978, when our dedicated Executive Editor, Richard Sylvester, died. Our tribute to his achievement appeared in the last volume prepared under his supervision, *The Apology,* in 1979. We did not know how his energy, his dedication, his zeal for accuracy, and his friendly but determined urging could ever be replaced.

But he had already chosen his successor, Clarence Miller, who had just completed what proved to be the most difficult task of editing in the entire series, the two-volume set of the *De Tristitia,* reproduced in facsimile from the recently discovered Valencia manuscript in More's own hand, and now accompanied by transcription, translation, collation, and commentary, performed in masterly fashion. This was a foreshadowing of the standard of scholarship that Clarence Miller would achieve in his post as Executive Editor for the remaining volumes, several of which required the superb command of Latin that Clarence possessed: the *Latin Poems* (1984), the volume headed by the *Letter to Bugenhagen* (1990), and the Latin letters published under the title *In Defense of Humanism* (1986), a volume edited by Dale Kinney, based upon his prize-winning doctoral dissertation fostered by Clarence Miller. Meanwhile, Clarence supervised the publication of the two-volume set *A Dialogue Concerning Heresies* (1981) and co-edited, with Stephen

Foley, *The Answer to a Poisoned Book* (1985). Finally, after so many years, he has been able to bring to publication the first volume of the series, a volume that Richard Sylvester had planned to edit. The wheel has come full circle: Clarence Miller has fulfilled in every way the confidence and hope of Richard Sylvester. This edition has been carried to completion by the skill and wisdom of two of the finest editors of Renaissance materials that the learned world has seen in this century.

L. L. M.

New Haven, Conn.

CONTENTS

ILLUSTRATIONS

INTRODUCTION

ENGLISH POEMS

M ore's English verse is a very small part of his oeuvre. It comprises
fewer than 1,500 lines: the Pageant Verses (56 lines in rhyme royal),
written to accompany some painted cloths belonging to More's father;
the "Lamytacyon off Quene Elyzabeth" (84 lines in rhyme royal), on the
death of Elizabeth of York, wife of Henry VII; the *Mery Gest How a
Sergeaunt Wolde Lerne to Be a Frere* (432 lines in tail rhyme); the Fortune
Verses (306 lines generally in rhyme royal); and the two rhyme royal
stanzas "Lewes yᵉ loste louer" and "Dauy the Diser." In addition, there
are segments of verse in More's *Life of Picus* (511 lines in rhyme royal),
which are edited and discussed elsewhere in this volume.

Nearly all of this verse was written early in More's life and circulated
anonymously: only one text before the *English Works* of 1557 ascribes
any of it to More. With the exception of "Lewis the Lost Lover" and
"Davy the Dicer," which were written in his last days in the Tower, all
More's poems were written by the end of the first decade of the six-
teenth century. The likelihood that they are the earliest of his writings
may have some bearing on both their subject matter and their generic
range. Perhaps his poems are best seen as a series of attempts to meet
occasional demands placed on a talented and ambitious young man,
rather than as evidence of a distinctive or powerful poetic talent. All
the early poems seem to have been commissioned for specific occasions
or as responses to particular events. This is certainly true of the Pag-
eant Verses and the "Rufull Lamentation." The Fortune Verses were
probably written as a prologue to a now lost translation. And *A Merry
Jest* may have been commissioned for some celebratory dinner or enter-
tainment, perhaps by the Mercers' Company of London. They all may
have been intended, in part at least, as demonstrations of youthful
virtuosity. More serious and substantial concerns led him away from
the writing of English verse and prompted him to devote his literary
energy to prose.

Pageant Verses

DATE AND OCCASION

T he only indication of the date and occasion of the Pageant Verses is
the rubric in the *English Works* of 1557: "Mayster Thomas More in his

xvii

youth deuysed in hys fathers house in London, a goodly hangyng of fyne paynted clothe, with nyne pageauntes, and verses ouer of euery of those pageauntes. . . ."[1] The crucial phrase is "in his youth." One might arbitrarily, but not unreasonably, gloss the phrase as indicating some point before More's first marriage (c. 1505) and not before his entry into the household of the Lord Chancellor, John Cardinal Morton (1491). One might further speculate that the verses were written when More was in reasonable proximity to his father's house, if not actually residing there. This assumption would lead one to discount the period 1491–92, when More was in Morton's household; his years at Oxford (1494–1496); and the years 1501–1504/5, when he was probably in residence at the London Charterhouse. Hence the most likely periods for composition are 1492–1494, the time between his residence in Morton's household and his stay at Oxford; and 1496–1501, when More was a member of Lincoln's Inn.[2] Either of these periods would place the Pageant Verses before the generally accepted date of 1503,[3] for which there is no supporting evidence, and would make them the earliest of More's poems.

It is possible to pronounce with slightly more confidence on the occasion of the poem, at least in general terms. John More's "hangyng of fyne paynted clothe" reflects an interest in tapestry and "counterfeit arras" (that is, painted rather than woven cloth), which was particularly widespread in England in the later Middle Ages.[4] Henry VII made extensive additions to the royal collection of tapestries, commissioning them from the most notable French tapestry weavers.[5] And there is

[1]Thomas More, *The Workes . . . in the Englyshe Tonge* (London, 1557; cited hereafter as *EW*), sig. 2v; no. 10876 in *A Short-Title Catalogue of Books Printed in England, Scotland, & Ireland . . . 1475–1640*, 2nd ed., rev. W. A. Jackson, F. S. Ferguson, and Katharine F. Pantzer, 3 vols. (London, 1976–91; cited hereafter as *STC²*).

[2]On this period of More's life see James McConica, "The Patrimony of Thomas More," in *History and Imagination: Essays in Honour of H. R. Trevor-Roper*, ed. Hugh Lloyd-Jones et al. (London, 1981), esp. pp. 58–61 on his connections with the London Charterhouse, connections that seem to militate against the composition of English verse.

[3]See, for example, R. W. Chambers, *Thomas More* (London, 1938; reprint, Ann Arbor, 1958), cited hereafter as "Chambers."

[4]On "counterfeit arras" see W. G. Thomson, *A History of Tapestry from the Earliest Times until the Present Day*, 3rd ed., rev. F. P. Thomson and E. S. Thomson (East Ardsley, 1973), pp. 239–41. See also the brief discussion of English tapestries of the late fourteenth and early fifteenth centuries in Joan Evans, *English Art, 1307–1461* (Oxford, 1949), pp. 92–95 and 138.

[5]See Thomson, *A History of Tapestry*, p. 148; and Gordon Kipling, "Henry VII and the Origins of Tudor Patronage," in *Patronage in the Renaissance*, ed. Guy Fitch Lytle and Stephen Orgel (Princeton, 1985), pp. 137–44.

testimony in early sixteenth-century English literature to an awareness of tapestries and hangings.[1] More particularly the *Trionfi* of Petrarch seem to have lent themselves to this form of visual representation. Such tapestries have been recorded in England from about 1507.[2] Cardinal Wolsey purchased a set in 1523, thereby exciting John Skelton's ire.[3] John More's choice of wall decoration was clearly a fashionable one.

THE LITERARY AND ICONOGRAPHIC TRADITIONS

THERE appears to be only one English precedent for appending a verse text to a tapestry: at least two poems by John Lydgate were explicitly designed to accompany tapestries. His antifeminist *Bycorne and Chychevache* is described as "þe deuise of a peynted or desteyned clothe for an halle a parlour or a chambre" made for "a werþy citeseyn of London"; and his *Legend of St. George* as "þe devyse of a steyned halle," made "at þe request of þarmonieres of London."[4] But there is no indication that More was aware of Lydgate as a model.

More's poem contains some remarkable innovations in the handling of iconographic and literary traditions. The first of these is his treatment of the iconographic tradition of Petrarch's *Trionfi*. More was not the first poet to embellish a visual representation of the *Trionfi* with verses of his own,[5] but he appears to have been the first to attempt to do so in English secular verse.[6]

---

[1]See, for example, the descriptions of "clothes and golde and arras" in Henry Bradshaw's *Life of St. Werburghe*, written in 1513 and printed in 1521 (*STC*[2] 3506), ed. Carl Horstmann, Early English Text Society, Original Series no. 88, cited hereafter as "EETS OS" (London, 1887), lines 1576–1666. See also *Lord Morley's Tryumphes of Fraunces Petrarcke*, ed. D. D. Carnicelli (Cambridge, Mass., 1971), pp. 52–53; and Thomson, *A History of Tapestry*, pp. 160–63.

[2]Thomson, p. 183. If my dating is correct, John More's "paynted clothe" would be earlier than these.

[3]See his comments on *Collyn Clout*, in *John Skelton: The Complete English Poems*, ed. John Scattergood (Harmondsworth, 1983), lines 940–68.

[4]I quote from the rubric of the scribe John Shirley from the edition of this poem in *The Minor Poems of John Lydgate (Part I: Secular Poems)*, ed. Henry Noble MacCracken, EETS OS no. 192 (London, 1934), p. 433; and from *The Minor Poems of John Lydgate (Part II: Religious Poems)*, ed. Henry Noble MacCracken, Early English Text Society, Extra Series no. 107, cited hereafter as "EETS ES" (London, 1911), p. 145 (the rubric is again Shirley's).

[5]Thomson, *A History of Tapestry*, p. 184, describes a set of French *Trionfi* tapestries containing verses from the late fifteenth century.

[6]See Robert Coogan, "Petrarch and Thomas More," *Moreana*, 21 (1969), 27: "In these stanzas More may be the first English poet to employ the *Trionfi*."

It seems unlikely, in spite of countervailing arguments,[1] that More had any direct knowledge of Petrarch's verses. That his response was engendered by iconographic representations rather than by circulation of some form of Petrarch's text is evident both from the lack of clear verbal parallels between the two works and also from the evidence of Stephen Hawes's *Pastime of Pleasure*. This work was composed around 1505/6 and first published by de Worde in 1509 (*STC*² 12948). It concludes with the four pageants that end More's poem: Death, Fame, Time, and Eternity;[2] these same four sections are accompanied by woodcuts specifically designed for Hawes's poem.[3] Two such responses to the *Trionfi* within such a short period, together with the existence of another *Trionfi* tapestry in England by 1507, seem to suggest a predominantly visual preoccupation with Petrarch's work.[4]

More's verses are also unusual in joining the iconographic tradition of Petrarch to a quite unrelated motif: the ages of man.[5] To the Petrarchan triumphs of Venus and Cupid, Death, Fame, Time, and Eternity, More adds stanzas on Childhood, Manhood, and Age, together with his final Latin summation, "The Poet." These stanzas seem to draw on an English iconographic tradition,[6] and the conjunction of the

---

[1]Coogan, "Petrarch and Thomas More," concludes: "In spite of the brevity of his verses, the order and subject matter selected by More evince a close relationship with Petrarch . . ." (p. 29). But he adduces no clear *verbal* parallels between Petrarch's poem and More's. And the parallels he does note are so general as to suggest the likelihood of visual rather than verbal transmission.

[2]See *The Pastime of Pleasure*, ed. William E. Mead, EETS OS no. 173 (London, 1928), lines 5383–5795.

[3]For discussion of these woodcuts see Anthony S. G. Edwards, "Poet and Printer in the Early Sixteenth Century: Stephen Hawes and Wynkyn de Worde," *Gutenberg Jahrbuch*, 1980, pp. 82–88; and Carnicelli, *Lord Morley's Tryumphes*, pp. 49–50.

[4]Carnicelli notes that Hawes's descriptions suggest "that he followed some fifteenth- or early sixteenth-century illustrator of the *Trionfi* rather than Petrarch's text" (p. 49).

[5]There is no comprehensive modern study of the ages of man in medieval literature; see, however, John A. Burrow, *The Ages of Man* (Oxford, 1986); Mary Dove, *The Perfect Age of Man's Life* (Cambridge, 1986); and Elizabeth Sears, *The Ages of Man* (Princeton, 1987), for discussion of the various iconographic and scholarly traditions.

[6]See, for example, a wall painting in Longthorpe Tower, near Peterborough, which portrays the seven ages of man and includes: "PUER, a boy holding a whip and top . . . the figure over the apex of the arch, presumably VIR . . . carried a hawk on his left wrist"; see E. Clive-Rouse and Audrey Baker, "The Wall-Paintings at Longthorpe Tower, near Peterborough, Northants.," *Archaeologia*, 96 (1955), 1–58 (quotation from p. 10). Thomas duke of Gloucester owned in 1397 a tapestry on the seven ages of man, as did John Baret of Bury St. Edmunds in 1463; see Evans, *English Art*, pp. 93, 138.

two motifs appears to be unique.[1] More may have been led to combine the motifs because both are concerned with the mutability of human affairs, all of which are subsumed finally by Eternity. The concluding stanza seems to stress this point:

Ergo homines, leuibus iamiam diffidite rebus,
    Nulla recessuro spes adhibenda bono.
Qui dabit eternam nobis pro munere vitam,
    In permansuro ponite vota deo. (116–119)[2]

The conjunction, though unusual, seems tonally and thematically apposite.[3]

"Rufull Lamentation"

DATE AND OCCASION

THE fullest account of the death of Elizabeth of York, queen of Henry VII, appears in the London chronicle contained in the British Library manuscript Cotton Vitellius A. xvi: "Upon Candylmesse day, In the nygth, The kyng & Quene beyng than at the Towyr, The Quene Travaylid of child sodenly, and was delyverd of a dowgthtir. . . . And upon the xi[th] daye of the said monyth beyng Satyrday In the mornyng dyed that most Gracious and vertuous pryncesse þe Quene. . . ."[4] Grief at her death appears to have been widespread and sincere. The accounts of her funeral procession and interment in Westminster Abbey

---

[1]This is a conclusion of Samuel C. Chew, *The Pilgrimage of Life* (New Haven and London, 1962), pp. 157–59 (cited hereafter as "Chew"), in a brief account of More's poem.

[2]The Latin lines are reprinted from Thomas More, *Latin Poems*, ed. Clarence H. Miller, Leicester Bradner, Charles A. Lynch, and Revilo P. Oliver, The Yale Edition of the Complete Works of St. Thomas More, vol. 3, part 2 (New Haven and London, 1965), 292/15–18. For volumes of the Yale Edition, which are cited hereafter as *CW* followed by the volume number, see the bibliography preceding the Commentary.

[3]For fuller discussion and analysis of More's pageant poems, see Sr. Mary Edith Willow, *An Analysis of the English Poems of St. Thomas More* (Nieuwkoop, 1974), pp. 73–138 (cited hereafter as "Willow"); and R. A. Duffy, "Thomas More's 'Nine Pageants,'" *Moreana, 50* (1976), 15–32.

[4]*Chronicles of London*, ed. C. L. Kingsford (Oxford, 1905), p. 258 (cited hereafter as "*Chronicles of London*"). Elizabeth died on February 11, 1502/3, her thirty-seventh birthday. For another account of her death see *The Great Chronicle of London*, ed. A. H. Thomas and I. D. Thornley (London, 1938), p. 321.

on February 25, 1502/3, stress the grand scale of the ceremonies.[1] Henry is reported to have spent £2,832 6s. 8d. on her funeral.[2]

More's poem must be considered against this background of contemporary lamentation,[3] which would have been given particular point for him by his personal acquaintance with Elizabeth's family. Erasmus recalls that while he was the guest of Lord Mountjoy in 1499 he visited in More's company several of the royal children mentioned in the "Rufull Lamentation":

> Pertraxerat me Thomas Morus, qui tum me in praedio Montioii agentem inuiserat, vt animi causa in proximum vicum expatiaremur. Nam illic educabantur omnes liberi regii, vno Arcturo excepto, qui tum erat natu maximus. Vbi ventum esset in aulam, conuenit tota pompa, non solum domus illius verum etiam Montioiicae. Stabat in medio Henricus annos natus nouem, iam tum indolem quandam regiam prae se ferens, hoc est animi celsitudinem cum singulari quadam humanitate coniunctam. A dextris erat Margareta, vndecim ferme annos nata, quae post nupsit Iacobo Scotorum regi. A sinistris Maria lusitans, annos nata quatuor. Nam Edmondus adhuc infans in vlnis gestabatur. Morus cum Arnoldo sodali salutato puero Henrico, quo rege nunc floret Britannia, nescio quid scriptorum obtulit.[4]

---

[1]See, for example, *Chronicles of London*, p. 259; *The Great Chronicle*, pp. 321–22; and T. Lott, "Directions for the Receiving of the Corpse of Elizabeth, Queen of Henry VII by the Lord Mayor and Commonality of London," *Archaeologia, 32* (1848), 126–29.

[2]See A. P. Stanley, *Historical Memorials of Westminster Abbey*, 5th ed. (London, 1882), p. 144.

[3]More's poem is followed in MS Balliol 354 by two other short poems on Elizabeth's death on fol. 176; these are printed in *Songs, Carols and Other Miscellaneous Poems from the Balliol MS. 354*, ed. Roman Dyboski, EETS ES no. 101 (London, 1908), pp. 99–100. John Weever, in his *Antient Funeral Monuments* (1631; reprint, London, 1767; *STC*² 25223), p. 254, prints a Latin epitaph on Elizabeth "transcribed out of a manuscript in sir ROBERT COTTON's library," which I have been unable to identify.

[4]*Opus epistolarum Des. Erasmi Roterodami*, ed. P. S. Allen et al., 11 vols. (Oxford, 1904–58; cited hereafter as "Allen"), *1*, 6. "I had been carried off by Thomas More, who had come to pay me a visit on an estate of Mountjoy's where I was then staying, to take a walk by way of diversion as far as the nearest town; for that was where all the royal children were being brought up, except only Arthur, who at that time was the eldest. When we reached the court, there was a solemn gathering not only of that household but of Mountjoy's as well. In the middle stood Henry, who was then nine years old and already looked somehow like a natural king, displaying a noble spirit combined with peculiar courtesy. On his right was Margaret, then perhaps eleven, who afterwards married James, king of Scots. On the left was Mary, a playful child of four; Edmund was still a babe in arms. More and his friend Arnold greeted the boy Henry, under whose rule England

It seems certain that the poem was composed as an immediate response to Elizabeth's death. Apart from the personal acquaintance that would have made such a response appropriate, if not expected, there is the evidence of lines 69–71:

> Adewe swet harte my lady dowghter Cate,
> Thou shalt good babe suche ys thi destenye,
> Thy moder never know . . .

The implication of these lines is that Elizabeth's infant daughter, Katherine, who appears to have died a few days after her mother, was still alive at the time the poem was written.[1]

Another reason for supposing the poem to have been written immediately after Elizabeth's death is the possibility that these verses were written as *tituli*, to be hung above Elizabeth's tomb after her interment. Such a practice was common in the later Middle Ages in England,[2] and features of the "Rufull Lamentation" lend support to a view that this was part of the original intention of the poem, particularly the refrain "lo here I lye," which seems to invite the reader to consider the poem in relation to a specific setting. Additional support comes from line 5, with its exhortation "loke here vpon me," and its variant in the British Library MS Sloane 1825, "loke vp here to me." Both suggest some connection between verse and funerary monument.

The possibility that the poem was composed for such an occasional purpose may help to clarify some of the problems of its transmission, especially as reflected in the two manuscript versions (Balliol 354 and Sloane 1825).[3]

Whatever the occasion of the poem, a *terminus ad quem* for its composition is provided by its appearance in a section of MS Balliol 354 that was transcribed by the beginning of 1505. The text of More's poem ends on the recto of folio 176 and is followed on the same page by two other sets of verses, one in Latin, one in English, both in the hand of

---

now flourishes, and gave him something he had written"; *The Correspondence of Erasmus, Letters 1252 to 1355, 1522 to 1523*, trans. R. A. B. Mynors, ann. James M. Estes (Toronto, 1989), 9, 299. More had other, posthumous connections with Elizabeth. On Henry VIII's accession he credited her son with her "matris dextra benigna" (*CW 3/2*, 19/153). And in 1513 More was one of the lawyers who participated in settling the estate of Elizabeth's sister, Katherine, mentioned in line 72 of the "Rufull Lamentation" (see *CW 2*, 159).

[1]See note on 12/69.

[2]For general discussion of *tituli* see Douglas Gray, *Themes and Images in the Medieval English Religious Lyric* (London, 1972), pp. 200–11.

[3]See pp. cxi–cxii.

Richard Hill. After the second set of verses Hill has written: "Iste liber pertineth Rycardo Hill seruant w^t Master Wynger alderman of London." John Wyngar was mayor of London for the year 1504/5, and his will was proved on January 7, 1505/6. Hence the appearance of the poem in Balliol 354 would seem to place it before the mayoral year 1504/5 began.[1]

FORM AND GENRE

MORE'S poem blends at least three significant, distinct components: the first-person lament by a historical figure, *de casibus* tragedy, and the verse epitaph. The integration of these components is possibly unique to More.

There are a few first-person laments by actual historical figures prior to the "Rufull Lamentation." The earliest of which I am aware is the "Lament of the Duchess of Gloucester" (c. 1447),[2] which appears in MS Balliol 354 just before the text of the "Rufull Lamentation."[3] Like More's poem it is a series of reflections on earthly mutability, stressing its exemplary nature in its refrain, "All women may beware by me." Another relevant poem, closer to More's time, is the poem on the death of Edward IV sometimes attributed to Skelton.[4] It stresses the funerary aspects of death through the monitory immediacy of its refrain: "Quia [or et] ecce, nunc in pulvere dormio." But other analogues to this feature of More's poem are hard to find, although some nearly contemporary historical laments do appear in MS Rawlinson C 813, particularly in the poems on the death of Sir Gruffydd ap Rhys and Edward Stafford.[5] The great popularity of this form of lament came later in

---

[1] See Arthur W. Reed in *Modern Language Review, 49* (1954), 490–91, in his review of *The Latin Epigrams of Thomas More*, ed. Leicester Bradner and Charles A. Lynch (Chicago, 1953); the information in this paragraph derives from Reed's review, correcting his earlier comments in *The English Works of Sir Thomas More*, ed. W. E. Campbell, A. W. Reed, R. W. Chambers, and W. A. G. Doyle-Davidson, 2 vols. (London, 1931), *1*, 224 (cited hereafter as "Campbell and Reed").

[2] *The Index of Middle English Verse*, ed. Carleton Brown and Rossell Hope Robbins (New York, 1943), no. 3720 (cited hereafter as *IMEV*); the poem is edited in *Historical Poems of the XIV and XV Centuries*, ed. Rossell H. Robbins (New York, 1959), pp. 176–80.

[3] It appears on fols. 169v–170v.

[4] The best edition of this poem is by Robert S. Kinsman, "A Lamentable of Kyng Edward the IIII," *Huntington Library Quarterly, 29* (1966), 95–108.

[5] See Sharon L. Jansen and Kathleen H. Jordan, *The Welles Anthology: MS Rawlinson C. 813, A Critical Edition*, Medieval and Renaissance Texts and Studies no. 75 (Binghamton, 1991), pp. 146–48, 198–201, for texts of these poems; see also Rosemary Woolf, *The English Religious Lyric in the Middle Ages* (Oxford, 1968), pp. 324–25 (cited hereafter as "Woolf").

the sixteenth century, with the publication of the *Mirror for Magistrates*.[1]

The *de casibus* tragedy also has relevance to the form of the "Rufull Lamentation." There was a continuing interest in *de casibus* tragedies in the English literature of the fifteenth and sixteenth centuries. The central document was John Lydgate's *Fall of Princes,* based indirectly on Boccaccio's *De casibus virorum illustrium.* Lydgate's poem, completed about 1438, was widely read and imitated until the end of the sixteenth century.[2] More would have known the work either in the numerous manuscript copies that were still circulating or in the printed edition by Pynson that had appeared in 1494 (*STC*[2] 3175). Thomas Warton went so far as to suggest that More's poem was "evidently formed on the tragic soliloquies which compose Lydgate's paraphrase of Boccaccio."[3] This connection seems unlikely, since there are very few soliloquies in the *Fall of Princes.* Indeed, parallels or correspondences are difficult to establish between Lydgate's work and More's poem beyond a common concern with mutability and the use of the rhyme royal form. It should be noted, however, that the influence of the *Fall of Princes* has been detected elsewhere in More's English verse, in his Fortune Verses.[4] And a servant of More's is known to have owned a copy.[5] A general debt to the form of Lydgate's work seems at least probable.

The poem also has obvious links to the medieval verse epitaph,[6] particularly since it was probably intended as a *titulus* over Elizabeth's tomb, a way of dramatizing "the corpse's traditional contrast between *quod eram* and *quod sum.*"[7] The contrast is strengthened by the use of the *ubi sunt* motif[8] and the farewell address from the dead to the living.[9] The best analogue for this developed, dramatic epitaph form spoken

---

[1] See Willard Farnham, *The Medieval Heritage of Elizabethan Tragedy* (Berkeley, 1936), pp. 271–339.

[2] See Anthony S. G. Edwards, "The Influence of Lydgate's *Fall of Princes,* c. 1440–1558: A Survey," *Medieval Studies, 39* (1977), 424–39.

[3] Thomas Warton, *History of English Poetry,* ed. W. C. Hazlitt, 4 vols. (London, 1871), *4,* 90.

[4] See Willow, pp. 200–01, and note on 38/187–93, below.

[5] Walter Smyth, who was More's personal servant from about 1520/1, bequeathed to John More, More's son, his "Chauscer of Talles and Boocas," that is, the *Canterbury Tales* and (most likely) the *Fall of Princes;* see Arthur W. Reed, *Early Tudor Drama: Medwall, the Rastells, Heywood, and the More Circle* (London, 1926), p. 154, cited hereafter as "Reed."

[6] On this form see Woolf, pp. 312–18, 320–26.

[7] Woolf, p. 312.

[8] See note on 11/37.

[9] See 11/44–13/85.

by a dead person is the poem beginning "Farewell, this world! I take my leue for evere," which also appears in MS Balliol 354.[1] This poem, like More's, stresses the untimely suddenness of the turn of Fortune's wheel:

> Today I sat full ryall in a cheyere,
>   Tyll sotell deth knokyd at my gate,
>   And onavysed he seyd to me, "Chek-mate!"
> Lo, how sotell he maketh a devors!
> And, wormys to fede, he hath here leyd my cors.[2]

More's merging of these generic components testifies to his knowledge of medieval vernacular poetic traditions and to his ability to employ them to create what has often been regarded as his most successful English poem.

A Merry Jest

DATE AND OCCASION

VARIOUS dates have been suggested for *A Merry Jest*. They all depend on linking the poem to a specific occasion. Arthur W. Reed suggested that it was written for the Feast of Sergeants at Law on November 13, 1503, when More's father, John, was elected a Sergeant,[3] a view that Raymond W. Chambers appears to endorse,[4] as does Richard Sylvester.[5] Sister Mary Edith Willow, however, has objected to this view on the grounds that the "dignity and solemnity" of such an occasion would be inappropriate for a comic poem. She suggests that *A Merry Jest* might well be associated with "the feast of the Lord Mayor's Pageant or with the feasts of the twelve livery companies of London."[6] As she notes, both More and his father were members of the Mercers' Company.[7]

---

[1]The best edition is in Douglas Gray, ed., *A Selection of Religious Lyrics* (Oxford, 1975), pp. 93–94.

[2]Lines 10–14 in Gray's edition.

[3]Campbell and Reed, *1*, 15.

[4]Chambers, p. 90.

[5]St. Thomas More, *The History of King Richard III and Selections from the English and Latin Poems*, ed. Richard S. Sylvester (New Haven and London, 1976), p. xix; cited hereafter as "Sylvester."

[6]Willow, p. 21. For an account of the Sergeants' Feast see A. Wigfall Green, *The Inns of Court and Early English Drama* (New Haven, 1931), pp. 48–52; there is no mention of poetic entertainments.

[7]Willow, p. 22.

Recently Willow's arguments have been developed by Alison Hanham, who has sought to establish the occasion of the poem as More's appointment as an honorary mercer of London in 1509.[1]

This identification has some merit. The concluding lines, "Now make good chere, / And welcome euery chone," clearly indicate that the poem was preliminary to some sort of festive occasion, most likely a banquet. And it is not unreasonable that More should have composed verses for a Mercers' Company feast, both in view of his own connections with the Company and also because the Mercers may have had a tradition of commissioning such forms of entertainment. In a mumming of Lydgate's surviving from the early fifteenth century, the players appeared "desguysed to fore þe Mayre of London, Eestfeld, vpon þe twelffeþe night of Cristmasse, ordeyned ryallych by þe worthy merciers, citeseyns of London."[2]

A   FORM AND GENRE

Merry Jest belongs within the form of the medieval comic poem,[3] a form quite distinct from the medieval fabliau.[4] The form obviously depends for its effects on comically appropriate reversals of expectation —in this case, the beating of the disguised sergeant for his deception. In its straightforward, unsubtle humor it belongs within a native tradition that was evidently extremely popular in the early sixteenth century.[5]

Although this is More's only verse "merry tale," it was evidently a

---

[1] See Alison Hanham, "Fact or Fantasy: Thomas More as Historian," in *Thomas More: The Rhetoric of Character,* ed. Alistair Fox and Peter Leech (Dunedin, 1979), p. 66.

[2] See MacCracken, *Minor Poems of Lydgate (Part I: Secular Poems),* pp. 695–98.

[3] There is no adequate study of the medieval comic poem; however, for helpful information and references see Frank P. Wilson, "The English Jest-books of the Sixteenth and Early Seventeenth Centuries," *Huntington Library Quarterly,* 2 (1939), 121–58, reprinted in his *Shakespearian and Other Studies,* ed. Helen Gardner (Oxford, 1969), pp. 285–324. The fullest collection of texts is William C. Hazlitt, ed., *Remains of the Early Popular Poetry of England,* 4 vols. (London, 1864–66); see also *Ten Fifteenth-Century Comic Poems,* ed. Melissa Furrow, Garland Medieval Texts no. 13 (New York, 1985).

[4] Alistair Fox characterizes the *Merry Jest* inexactly as "an imitation Chaucerian fabliau" (*Thomas More: History and Providence,* Oxford, 1982; New Haven and London, 1983, p. 23; cited hereafter as "Fox"); but there is virtually nothing Chaucerian about the poem, and it is doubtful whether it can be termed a fabliau, since it lacks any sexual element.

[5] Wynkyn de Worde, for example, printed a number of such verse tales: *The Mylner of Abyngton,* STC² 78 [1532–34?]; *Jack and his Stepdame,* STC² 14522 [1510–13?]; *XV Joys of Marriage,* STC² 15257.5 [c. 1507] and 15258 (1509); and *The Smith and his Dame,* STC² 22653.5 [c. 1505]. Curiously, More's poem seems to have been the only surviving merry tale in verse printed by Julian Notary.

form that he found very congenial. Evidence of his interest in such tales appears in his prose works.[1] It is entirely characteristic that his surviving verse compositions should include such a tale.

The device of the "fayned frere" (line 291) serves to link the poem to traditions of antimendicant satire. The existence of a specific tradition of poems using such a figure has been fully documented; it was a literary device whereby "the 'fenyeit freir' does no more than represent some of the qualities of the real one."[2] Elsewhere in More's works there is evidence of some interest in satire against friars, particularly in his earlier writings.[3]

Fortune Verses

DATE, OCCASION, AND GENRE

THE verses generally characterized as More's Fortune Verses are clearly an early work. Willow's efforts to date them as late as 1509[4] ignore the evidence of MS Balliol 354 (O), in which they appear before More's "Rufull Lamentation," which, as has been shown, must have been copied into the manuscript by the beginning of 1505.[5] Since the body of the manuscript was copied consecutively, the poem must date from before this *terminus ad quem*. And since this poem occurs some seventy leaves before the "Rufull Lamentation," it is quite possibly a much earlier work.

The only clue to the poem's occasion is provided by William Rastell's

---

[1]There are, for example, witty exempla in the *Confutation of Tyndale's Answer;* see, for example, *CW 8,* 604/16–605/37, 900/13–901/5. See also the exemplum explicitly characterized as a "mery tale" in *A Dialogue Concerning Heresies (CW 6,* 69/15–70/2), the "Festiuus dialogus fratris & morionis" in *Utopia (CW 4,* 80/23–84/20), and the five of "Syr Thomas Mores Jestes" printed by Samuel A. Tannenbaum, "Unpublished Harvey Marginalia," *Modern Language Review,* 25 (1930), 331.

[2]See Arthur G. Rigg, "William Dunbar: The 'Fenyeit Freir,'" *Review of English Studies,* New Series, *14* (1963), 269–73 (the quotation is from p. 273), who lists a number of fourteenth- and fifteenth-century poems employing the device. Dunbar wrote poems about the activities of John Damian, an Italian alchemist resident in Scotland, in one of which he is described as a "fenȝeit freir" (see *The Poems of William Dunbar,* ed. James Kinsley, Oxford, 1979, pp. 161–64; see also pp. 159–61). On the basis of the same phrase in More's poem, Willow (p. 25) has sought to find in the latter a reference to Damian's activities. But this wording seems more likely to have been merely coincidental.

[3]See, for example, the passage in *Utopia (CW 4,* 80/23–84/17) and the Latin poem on friars (*CW 3/2,* no. 277); see also *CW 14,* Commentary 1 at 471/9.

[4]Willow, pp. 174–76.

[5]See pp. xxiii–xxiv, above.

heading in the *English Works* (*1557*): "Certain meters in english written by master Thomas More in his youth for the boke of Fortune, and caused them to be printed in the begynnyng of that boke" (sig. ¶5). Neither of the other authorities, the Balliol manuscript and the edition printed by Wyer (*1556?*), contains any general heading. The heading in *1557* lets us know that all of More's Fortune Verses were a prologue to a whole book of fortune. More refers near the end of his poem to "the boke that ye shall rede" (line 307). *1557* has a note opposite this line: "He meaneth the booke of fortune." But the actual work has resisted identification. It was not included in any of the three extant texts. The title page of *1556* provides the fullest characterization:

> The Boke of the fayre Gentyl woman,
> that no man shulde put his truste, or confydence in:
> that is to say, Lady fortune: flaterynge euery man
> that coueyteth to haue all, and specyally, them
> that truste in her, she deceyueth them at laste.

But this is the only indication of the nature of the work the verses were designed to accompany. And it is obviously not very explicit. Efforts to identify "the booke of fortune" have proceeded speculatively and, at times, inaccurately.[1] It has been generally assumed that More's verses were intended as a prologue to some version of the *Libro della ventura, o vero Libro delle sorti,* by Lorenzo Spirito (1426–1496).[2] The authority for this view seems to have been George Lily, the son of More's friend and collaborator William Lily. He claimed that William Lily had translated Spirito's work from the Italian for More.[3] But evidence in support of this claim is lacking. The only extant translation into English of

---

[1] Willow, p. 176, asserts: "The first Italian copy of the *Boke of Fortune* was translated into French and edited in the year 1500 and shortly after translated into English by Caxton." I have been unable to identify the French incunabular edition to which she alludes. Caxton died in 1491. His successor, de Worde, did not print the work.

[2] There are several early editions of Spirito's work: Vicenza: Leonardus Achates de Basilea [1480–90]; Perugia: Stephanus Arndes, Gerardus Thomae, and Paulus Mechter, 1482; and Brescia: Boninus de Boninis, 1484. I am much indebted to Dr. Lotte Hellinga of the Incunable Short Title Catalogue at the British Library for details of these editions. J. B. Trapp and Hubertus Schulte Herbrüggen report that "more than fifty different editions are extant in Western European languages" (*"The King's Good Servant" Sir Thomas More 1477/8–1535,* London, 1977, p. 54, no. 82). The work was evidently of sufficiently enduring popularity for it to be copied in manuscript in the eighteenth century, possibly from a printed edition; see the manuscript of it sold at Sotheby's, December 8, 1981, lot 67.

[3] The claim is made in Paolo Giovio's *Descriptio Britanniae* (Venice, 1548), pp. 47–48.

Spirito's book survives in a unique copy of a 1618 edition in Sion College (*STC²* 3306), which cannot be identified as Lily's.[1] There are no specific parallels between More's verses and the 1618 edition. And the title "booke of fortune" is sufficiently common in the later Middle Ages to make it impossible to identify a particular work without more specific information. It could also be that More's verses were intended to preface some other English work, in verse or prose. For example, at least one extant Middle English prose prognosticatory work is entitled "the booke of fortune."[2] Middle English verses are extant that deal with the casting of dice to predict future events,[3] and there are other allusions to such poems in medieval English literature.[4]

What both Spirito's work and the extant Middle English verse have in common is the use of dice, evidently to answer various specific questions about the nature or course of life, in which the determinations are made on the basis of correspondences between particular combinations of numbers thrown and assigned fates in the "booke of fortune." More alludes to this procedure in lines 272–73: "The rollyng dise in whom your lukk doth stonde / With whose vnhappy chaunce ye be so wrothe . . . " Beyond this it does not seem possible to go. The identity of More's "booke of fortune," in the present state of our knowledge, cannot be more precisely established.

SOURCES

IT IS difficult, and perhaps fruitless, to seek to establish a general source or sources for More's poem. But we can point to a few likely sources for particular passages; for example, it seems clear that More drew on Aesop for one passage.[5] And he may have drawn on Petrarch

---

[1]The volume is briefly described by Elizabeth Edmondston, "Sion College: Unfamiliar Libraries IX," *Book Collector, 14* (1965), 177 and plates V and VI. It is now in the British Library. Hubertus Schulte Herbrüggen, "Sir Thomas More's Fortuna-Verse," in *Lebende Antike: Symposion für Rudolf Sühnel,* ed. Horst Meller and Hans-Joachim Zimmermann (Berlin, 1967), p. 162, points out the enormous popularity of Spirito's work, which survives in at least 33 Italian, 18 French, 3 Spanish, and one Dutch edition in addition to this English one.

[2]In Bodleian Library MS Ashmole 343 (fifteenth century); see Laurel Braswell, "Utilitarian and Scientific Prose," in *Middle English Prose: A Critical Guide to Major Authors and Genres,* ed. Anthony S. G. Edwards (New Brunswick, N.J., 1984), p. 347.

[3]See, for example, *A Common-place Book of the Fifteenth Century,* ed. Lucy Toulmin Smith (London, 1886), pp. 15–18; and Eleanor P. Hammond, "The Chance of the Dice," *Englische Studien, 59* (1925), 1–16. These items are *IMEV* nos. 3694.3 and 803, respectively.

[4]For details see Hammond, pp. 1–2.

[5]See note on 33/71–73.

at a couple of points, although this is by no means certain.[1] But the poem is generally organized around such a tissue of commonplaces that More quite probably had no specific source for much of it.[2]

Nevertheless, it may be worth pointing out that Lydgate's *Fall of Princes* was readily accessible to More in both printed and manuscript forms.[3] It is, moreover, a work whose influence has been detected in specific verbal parallels in this poem.[4] And Lydgate's poem is of more general thematic interest in that it both dramatizes the central conflict between Fortune and Poverty represented in More's verses[5] and also makes the metaphoric equation between the movement of Fortune's wheel and the chance of the dice.[6]

"Lewis the Lost Lover" and "Davy the Dicer"

DATE AND OCCASION

T HE two stanzas entitled "Lewis the Lost Lover" and "Davy the Dicer" appear consecutively in the *English Works* of 1557 (sigs. XX_8v–YY_1), preceded by the heading: "Here folow two short ballettes which sir Thomas More made for hys pastime while he was prisoner in the tower of London" (sig. XX_8v). Thus William Rastell placed their composition between the date of More's arrest and that of his execution, that is, between April 17, 1534, and July 6, 1535.

William Roper provides a fuller context for the first of these "ballettes." Immediately after describing More's reaction to the execution of Dr. Richard Reynolds, a priest of the Brigittine monastery of Sion,

---

[1]See the comments of Coogan cited in the note on 38/194.

[2]S. J. Kozikowski, "Lydgate, Machiavelli and More and Skelton's *Bouge of Court*," *American Notes & Queries*, *15* (1977), 66–67, notes some general parallels in the presentation of Fortune common to poems by all these writers; but the parallels are too general to justify any conclusions about influence.

[3]See p. xxv, above.

[4]See note on 38/187–93.

[5]See Lydgate, *Fall of Princes*, III, 204–707, for the debate between Fortune and Glad Poverty.

[6]Cf. the comments of Fortune in *Fall of Princes*, VI, 127–133:

Thus dyuersli my gifftes I departe,
Oon acceptid, a-nothir is refusid;
Lik hasardours my dees I do iuparte,
Oon weel foorthrid, anothir is accusid.
My play is double, my trust euer abusid,
Thouh oon to-day hath my fauour wonne,
To-morwe ageyn I can eclipse his sonne.

and three Charterhouse monks on May 4, 1535, he offers this occasion for the composition of "Lewis the Lost Lover":

> Within a while after, master Secretorye [Thomas Cromwell], cominge to him into the tower from the kinge, pretended much freindshipp towardes him, and for his comforte tolde him that the kings highnes was his good and gratious Lorde, and minded not with any matter wherein he should haue any cause of scruple, from henceforthe to trouble his consciens. As soone as master Secretory was gone, to expresse what comforte he conceaved of his wordes, he wrote with a cole, for Incke then had he none, thease verses folowinge.[1]

Nicolas Harpsfield gives the same account,[2] as does "Ro. Ba.," who, however, attributes the composition of both stanzas to this occasion.[3]

There appears to be no reason to doubt Roper's account. And although there is little to warrant Ro. Ba.'s addition of the "Davy the Dicer" stanza to it, the two stanzas do appear together in several early sources, and it is reasonable to suppose that one was written not long after the other. Thus, at the end of his life More returned to verse, the form of his earliest English compositions.

Critical Reaction to More's English Poems

DURING the first half of the sixteenth century there appears to have been a measure of consciousness among More's contemporaries of his identity as an English poet. His poems seem to have enjoyed a circulation that is consistent with a fair degree of popularity. *A Merry Jest* survives in both printed and (fragmentary) manuscript forms, as do the Fortune Verses. The "Rufull Lamentation" is extant in two manuscript copies that vary so extensively as to suggest the possibility that they reflect a fairly extensive manuscript tradition. The existence of these works in variant forms and traditions suggests an unusual interest in More's verse, given the small size of his oeuvre.

---

[1]William Roper, *The Lyfe of Sir Thomas More, Knighte,* ed. Elsie Vaughan Hitchcock, EETS OS no. 197 (London, 1935), 81/16–25 (cited hereafter as "Roper"). Roper placed these stanzas before the beginning of More's trial on July 1, 1535, as did Nicholas Harpsfield, *The Life and Death of Sr Thomas Moore, knight,* ed. Elsie Vaughan Hitchcock, EETS OS no. 186 (London, 1932; cited hereafter as "Harpsfield"); and "Ro. Ba.," *The Life of Syr Thomas More, Somtymes Lord Chancellour of England,* ed. Elsie Vaughan Hitchcock and P. E. Hallett, EETS OS no. 222 (London, 1950; cited hereafter as "Ro. Ba.").

[2]Harpsfield, 180/13–27.

[3]Ro. Ba., 224/18–226/4.

The most striking example of More's contemporary esteem as an English poet occurs about 1510 in a poem included in *The Great Chronicle of London* attacking the financial exactions of John Dudley:

O most cursid Caytyff, what shuld I of the wryte
Or telle the particulers, of thy cursid lyffe
I trow If Skelton, or Cornysh wold endyte
Or mastyr moor, they mygth not Inglysh Ryffe
Nor yit Chawcers, If he were now In lyffe
Cowde not In metyr, half thy shame spelle
Nor yit thy ffalshod, half declare or telle[1]

The casual, undeveloped comparison with such established contemporary poets as Skelton or William Cornish is a sufficient indication of More's status as poet in the mind of at least one contemporary.[2] Ironically, this acclaim coincides with the stage in his career at which More ceased to write English verse. From this point until the publication of the *English Works* in 1557 the only indicators of his popularity are those implied by the circulation of his poems in various forms. The *English Works* gave definition and focus to More's achievements in verse, which were admired in the later sixteenth century. *A Merry Jest* was reprinted about 1575 together with another comic verse tale.[3] At about the same time Robert Laneham in his famous *Letter . . . vntoo the Queens Maiesty* (1575) included in his account of Captain Cox's library both "The sergeaunt that became a Fryar" and "the booke of fortune."[4] Some, at least, of More's verse had become assimilated into contemporary popular poetry.

Other responses confirm an interest in the comic aspects of More's verse. The indefatigable annotator Gabriel Harvey has left some indication of this in a poem written about 1577 in which he links More's name with those of other notable English poets, including Chaucer, Gower, Lydgate, Skelton, and Surrey. After characterizing Skelton as "that same mad braynd knave," he goes on to compliment More:

---

[1]*The Great Chronicle of London*, ed. A. H. Thomas and I. D. Thornley (London, 1938), p. 361.

[2]For discussion of this passage see Robert S. Kinsman, "A Skelton Reference c. 1510," *Notes & Queries*, New Series 7 (1960), 210–11.

[3]*STC*² 79; R. W. Gibson and J. Max Patrick, *St. Thomas More: A Preliminary Bibliography of His Works and of Moreana to the Year 1750* (New Haven and London, 1961; cited hereafter as "Gibson"), no. 70.

[4]There are two editions of this work, both apparently in the same year, *STC*² 15190.5 and 15191; I quote from the latter, pp. 34, 35 (Gibson no. 376).

Perdy thou art much to reioice
  That good Syr Thomas More will deyne
His cuntryman at first insight
  So curteously to interteyne[1]

Elsewhere Harvey shows a more characteristic bibliographical concern with More's verse. In his annotations to his copy of Speght's 1598 edition of Chaucer he includes a list of "The fine poesies of Sir Thomas More" which includes all the English poems.[2]

References after Harvey become more meager and harder to assess. John Taylor invokes More's name in *The Praise of Hempseed* (1620) in a context that seems to indicate that he is thinking of him as an English poet:

In paper, many a Poet suruiues
Or else their lines had perish'd with their liues.
Old *Chaucer, Gower* and Sir *Thomas More,*
Sir *Philip Sidney* who the Lawrell wore,
Spencer, and *Shakespeare* did in Art excell,
Sir *Edward Dyer, Greene, Nash, Daniell,*
Siluester, Beumont, Sir *Iohn Harrington,*
Forgetfulnesse their workes would ouerrun,
But that in paper they immortally
Doe liue in spight of death, and cannot die.[3]

Some of these names recur with More's a little later, in John Webster's *Monuments of Honor* (1624), where he describes a celebration for the Lord Mayor of London. This includes "a beautiful spectacle, called the Temple of Honor . . . [in which] sit five famous scholars and poets of this our kingdom, as Sir Jeffrey Chaucer, the learned Gower, the excellent John Lidgate, the sharp-witted sir Thomas More, and last, as worthy both soldier and scholar, sir Philip Sidney." A speech then celebrates in verse these "five learn'd poets, worthy men."[4] Thomas

---

[1] *Letter Book of Gabriel Harvey,* ed. Edward J. L. Scott, Camden Society, New Series no. 33 (London, 1884), p. 57.

[2] Harvey's copy of Speght is now British Library Additional MS 42518; his list of More's English poems is printed in *Gabriel Harvey's Marginalia,* ed. Gregory C. Moore Smith (Stratford-upon-Avon, 1913), pp. 233–34. Harvey seems to have derived his information about More's poems from *EW,* a copy of which he probably owned; see David M. Rogers, "Edmund Spenser and Gabriel Harvey: A New Find," *Bodleian Library Record, 12* (1985–88), 334–37 (especially n. 8).

[3] *STC²* 23788; quoted in Caroline Spurgeon, *Five Hundred Years of Chaucer Criticism and Allusion, 1357–1900,* 3 vols. (Cambridge, 1925), *1,* 194.

[4] *STC²* 25175; quoted in Spurgeon, *1,* 198–99.

Farnaby in his *Index poeticum* (1634) includes More among seven English poets.[1] After this More's verse seems to have fallen into total eclipse. There are virtually no indications of any knowledge of his poems until Dr. Johnson's *Dictionary* (1755). Johnson quotes extensively from More's English poems in his "History of the English Language," printing complete texts of *A Merry Jest*, the "Rufull Lamentation," the Fortune Verses, "Lewis the Lost Lover," and "Davy the Dicer," as well as some prose passages, all taken from the *English Works* of 1557. He offers these justifications for so extensive a treatment:

> Of the works of Sir *Thomas More* it was necessary to give a larger specimen, both because our language was then in a great degree formed and settled, and because it appears from *Ben Johnson*, that his works were considered as models of pure and elegant style. The tale [*A Merry Jest*], which is placed first, because earliest written, will show what an attentive reader will, in perusing our old writers, often remark, that the familiar and colloquial parts of our language, being disused, among those classes who had no ambition of refinement, or affectation of novelty, has suffered very little change. There is another reason why the extracts from this author are more copious: his works are carefully and correctly printed, and may therefore be better trusted than any other edition of the *English* books of that, or the preceding ages.[2]

During the nineteenth century such meager attention as More's poems received was on generic or contextual grounds: Hazlitt included an edition of the *Merry Jest* in his collection of comic tales.[3] *Fugitive Tracts Written in Verse* (1875) reprinted Wyer's edition of the Fortune Verses.[4] Ewald Flügel included the Pageant Verses, "Lewis the Lost Lover," and "Davy the Dicer" in his *Neuenglisches Lesebuch* in 1895;[5] and Roman Dyboski transcribed both poems in MS Balliol 354 (the "Rufull Lamentation" and the Fortune Verses) as part of his work on that manuscript.[6] It was not until 1931, with the publication of the first

---

[1]*Review of English Studies, 12* (1936), 323.

[2]I quote from the first edition. On Johnson's use of More's poems see further W. B. C. Watkins, *Johnson and English Poetry before 1660* (Princeton, 1936), p. 50. Johnson owned a copy of *EW;* see J. D. Fleeman, ed., *The Sale Catalogue of Samuel Johnson's Library,* ELS Monograph Series no. 1 (Victoria, B.C., 1975), p. 51, no. 474.

[3]William C. Hazlitt, ed., *Remains of the Early Popular Poetry of England,* 4 vols. (London, 1864–66), *3,* 119–29.

[4]1st series, 1493–1600 (privately printed).

[5]Halle/Salle, pp. 40–42.

[6]*Songs, Carols and Other Miscellaneous Poems from the Balliol MS. 354,* ed. Roman Dyboski, EETS ES no. 101 (London, 1908), pp. 72–80, 97–99.

volumes of *The English Works of Sir Thomas More* by W. E. Campbell and
A. W. Reed, that the first attempt at a full critical edition was made. This
edition, like the subsequent ones by Richard Sylvester,[1] is in some
measure unsound in its choice of copy-texts. Sylvester relies on the
1557 edition throughout, even though he is aware of earlier, better
witnesses, such as MS Balliol 354. It has, however, led to a modest
flowering of critical interest.[2] The present edition, one which Sylvester
planned to undertake before death claimed him, seeks to provide the
firm basis he would have wanted for the understanding of More's En-
glish verse.

---

[1]He edited the *Merry Jest,* Pageant Verses, and "Rufull Lamentation" in *The Anchor
Anthology of Sixteenth-Century Verse* (Garden City, N.Y., 1974), pp. 105–28, and the same
texts, together with "Davy the Dicer" and "Lewis the Lost Lover"; Sylvester, pp. 97–124.

[2]The more important subsequent critical work is reprinted in Richard S. Sylvester and
Germain P. Marc'hadour, eds., *Essential Articles for the Study of Thomas More* (Hamden,
Conn., 1977).

LIFE OF PICO

THE title of More's *Lyfe of Johan Picus Erle of Myrandula* is somewhat misleading. More's translation of the *Vita* of Giovanni Pico della Mirandola, the famous Italian humanist philosopher, by Pico's nephew Gianfrancesco, amounts to no more than a third of the actual work More published under that title.[1] The bulk of the volume comprises More's translations of several of Pico's own works: three of his letters, his commentary on Psalm 15, his verse "Deprecatoria ad Deum," and More's own verse renderings of three of his prose duodecalogues: "The Twelve Rules of Spiritual Battle," "The Twelve Weapons of Spiritual Battle," and "The Twelve Properties or Conditions of a Lover." More's compilation is, then, both biography and anthology, supplementing the *Life* itself with a selection of Pico's works which he felt appropriate for the occasion that prompted his undertaking.

Date

THE *terminus ad quem* for the *Life* is provided by John Rastell's edition, which was published about 1510.[2] William Rastell claimed in the *English Works* of 1557 that the *Life* "was translated oute of latin, into Englishe by master Thomas More, about ye yeare of our Lorde .1510." (sig. a₁). This statement suggests that publication followed swiftly upon composition.

There is, however, a tradition that places More's translation earlier than 1510. It appears first in Thomas Stapleton's biography of More included in his *Tres Thomae* (1588). Stapleton dates the work to the time when More decided not to become a priest but rather to marry:

---

[1] In his preface addressed to Joyeuce Leigh, More speaks of "these warkis" (51/23, 52/4, 52/9) in contexts that make it clear he is referring to his actual translations of Pico's works. His rendering of Gianfrancesco's biography is mentioned only in passing ("as heraftir we peruse the course of his hole life," 52/2–3). Clearly, More felt his translations of Pico's own writings to be the more significant part of his undertaking.

[2] See pp. cxx–cxxi, below.

Statuit igitur aliquem sibi praeclarum virum ex ordine Laicorum
ante oculos ponere, ad cuius exemplum vitam suam conformaret.
Omnibus itaque qui tunc vel domi vel foris pietatis & eruditionis
nomine florebant, ad memoriam reuocatis, occurrit illi Ioannes
Picus Mirandula comes, de cuius sane multiplici & excellenti erudi-
tione per totam tunc Europam fama celeberrima peruolitabat, qui
etiam pietate & morum integritate non minus erat celebris. Huius
vitam Thomas Morus Latine conscriptam, epistolas quoque eius, &
duodecim bene viuendi praecepta in linguam Anglicam vertit: non
tam vt aliis ea communicaret, (quamquam & id quoque) quam vt
sibi ipsi magis familiaria illa omnia redderet.   (Sig. b₂r–v)[1]

Cresacre More, in his *Life* of More ([1631?]; *STC*² 18066), appears to
echo Stapleton's account: "he determined to marrie; and therefore he
propounded to himselfe, as a pattern of life, a singular lay-man *Iohn
Picus* Earle of *Mirandula,* who was a man famous for vertue, and most
eminent for learning; his life he translated, and sett out, as also manie
of his most worthie letters, and his twelue precepts of good life" (sig.
D₄r–v).

These accounts, which do not appear in the biographies of More by
Roper, Harpsfield, or Ro. Ba., would place the *Life* in the period 1504–
05, before More's marriage to Joan Colt. Scholars from Arthur W.
Reed[2] onward have tended to accept this as the date of composition,
although some have suggested an earlier date for part or all of the
work.[3] An early date has commended itself to scholars partly because

---

[1]"He determined, therefore, to put before his eyes the examples of some prominent
layman, on which he might model his life. He called to mind all who at that period, either
at home or abroad, enjoyed the reputation of learning and piety, and finally fixed on
John Pico, Earl of Mirandula, who was renowned in the highest degree throughout the
whole of Europe for his encyclopedic knowledge, and no less esteemed for his sanctity of
life. More translated into English a Latin Life of Pico, as well as his letters, and a set of
twelve counsels for leading a good life, which he had composed. His purpose was not so
much to bring these to the knowledge of others, though that, too, he had in view, as
thoroughly to familiarize himself with them"; Thomas Stapleton, *The Life and Illustrious
Martyrdom of Sir Thomas More,* trans. Philip E. Hallett, ed. E. E. Reynolds (London, 1966),
p. 9, cited hereafter as "Stapleton."

[2]Reed, p. 73: "I would suggest, therefore, that his New Year's gift was sent to Sister
Joyeuce Leigh at the beginning of the year 1505." Richard S. Sylvester also asserts that
"1505 . . . is, I think, the best date for More's translation" but cites no evidence for this
view; "*A Part of His Own:* Thomas More's Literary Personality in His Early Works,"
Moreana, 15–16 (1967), 35.

[3]E. E. Reynolds, *The Field Is Won* (Milwaukee, 1968), pp. 44–45, suggests a date before
1504. George B. Parks suggests that the verse portions of the text may have been trans-

of the pleasing congruence it establishes between More's biography and the time of translation. As Alistair Fox puts it: "If this date is accepted, the *Life of Picus* is surrounded by contextual ironies, being presented to a nun ostensibly in praise of the cloister by a man who had just decided to come out of it."[1]

But there is no real evidence to place the *Life* substantially earlier than the date of original publication, c. 1510. Since the Rastells were closely connected with the More family, their assertions must carry weight in the absence of earlier authoritative controverting evidence. James McConica observes of Cresacre More's dating: "This must carry authority, as a family tradition, but it is also suggestive of the hagiographic concerns of More's descendants. The *Life* cannot be taken in any obvious way as a pattern for More's since . . . Pico made the contrary decision to that made by More."[2] This very reasonable conclusion is supported by some internal evidence that seems to imply a date close to the actual time of publication. At a few points in the text More appears not to have finally revised his text or to have left it in so unclear a form that alternative renderings of the same Latin word remained.[3] The most obvious explanation for such a lack of final revision is that More was in some hurry to get the manuscript to his printer and failed to notice these oversights. If there was any extended period between composition and publication, it would be surprising if they had not been spotted.

In short, there is no solid evidence or logical necessity for a date of composition earlier than about 1510.

Occasion

THE occasion of the *Life* is clearly stated in More's prefatory address "Unto his right entirely beloued sister in crist Ioyeuce Leigh":

> Hit is and of longe time hath bene my well beloued sister a custome in the begynnyng of yᵉ new yere frendes to sende betwene presentis or yeftis as the witnesses of their loue and frendsship. . . . I

lated earlier than the prose works: "as early as 1497 or as late as 1504 . . . we might prefer dates closer to 1499"; "Pico della Mirandola in Tudor Translation," in *Philosophy and Humanism: Renaissance Essays in Honor of Paul Oskar Kristeller* (New York, 1976), p. 358.

[1]Fox, p. 28.

[2]"The Patrimony of Thomas More," in *History and Imagination: Essays in Honour of H. R. Trevor-Roper*, ed. Hugh Lloyd-Jones et al. (London, 1981), p. 65.

[3]See notes on 105/26, 113/16, and—though less certainly—63/10. See also note on 76/17, where the omission of a word may derive from More's draft.

therfore myne hartely beloued sister in good lukk of this new yere
haue sent you such a present as may bere witnes of my tendre loue
and zele to the happy continuannce and graciouse encreace of
vertue in your soule: and where as the giftis of other folk declare y^t
thei wissh their frendes to be worldeli fortunate myne testifieth
that I desire to haue you godly prosperous. (51/4-7, 17-23)

Although this explanation specifies the intention of the work with
sufficient clarity, the dedicatee remains a matter of some debate. Sev-
eral candidates have been advanced as the Joyeuce Leigh of More's
dedication. The most helpful discussion of the problem is that by
George Parks.[1] Parks notes that there are two contemporary Joyce
Leighs who have become confused by local historians,[2] and follows
Arthur W. Reed in identifying her as the daughter of Joyce Leigh
(whose will, drawn up and probated in April 1507, named the daughter
as "Dame Joisse").[3] The family had evident connections with Thomas
More. Among the other children named in the will is Edward Lee,
subsequently archbishop of York and, in his youth, a close friend of
More's.[4] The More and Lee families were fellow parishioners at St.
Stephen's, Walbrook.

This identification has been questioned by Daniel Kinney, who, ap-
parently unaware of Parks's study, also notes the confusion of the con-
temporary Joyce Leighs but goes on to suggest that More may have
dedicated his work to Edward Lee's mother, also, as we have seen, called
Joyce.[5] But she was dead by April 1507, probably before More began
his translations. More speaks of the dedicatee as alive.

In view of the evident connection between More and Joyce Leigh's
brother, Edward, she seems the most likely candidate as dedicatee of
More's work.

The Circulation of Pico della Mirandola's Works
after His Death

Pico della Mirandola died in 1494 at the age of thirty-one, leaving
behind a reputation as a philosopher which rested on works that were

---

[1]"Pico della Mirandola in Tudor Translation," pp. 352-69.

[2]See Parks, pp. 359-60, n. 18, for details.

[3]Campbell and Reed, *1*, 14. I am indebted to Anne Sutton of the Mercers' Company for
confirming this identification.

[4]See *St. Thomas More, Selected Letters*, ed. Elizabeth F. Rogers, trans. Marcus Haworth,
S. J., et al. (New Haven and London, 1961; cited hereafter as "Rogers"), nos. 48, 75, 84,
85, on the connections between them.

[5]See *CW 15*, xxxi–xxxii, esp. n. 6.

mainly unpublished. His nephew Gianfrancesco Pico della Mirandola compiled a posthumous *Opera omnia*, first published at Bologna in 1496 by Benedictus Hectoris,[1] prefaced by his own extremely laudatory life of his uncle.[2] This work provided the impetus to a wider dissemination of Pico's works in print.

How, and in what form, More became aware of Pico's works is unclear. A number of his friends had studied in Italy in the late fifteenth century at the time when editions of the *Opera omnia* had begun to appear. John Colet, who was a close friend of More's, may have provided the link.[3] He had studied in Italy, mainly in Florence and Rome, from 1492 to 1495 and certainly knew Pico's works well. His own writings include references to or quotations from *Heptaplus, Apologia, Hexaemeron,* and *Oratio.*[4] The range of his references suggests that he had access to an edition of the *Opera omnia,* but the only reference that clearly antedates More's translation is to the *Heptaplus,* one of the few works to appear in print during Pico's lifetime.[5] Another possible source for More's knowledge is Thomas Linacre, another close friend, who spent twelve years, from 1487 to 1499, in Rome, Florence, Padua, and Venice. No works of Pico's from Linacre's library survive, although he did own at least one early work of Gianfrancesco.[6] Yet a third possible source is Cuthbert Tunstall, More's contemporary at Oxford, who studied in Italy for about five years, beginning in 1499. Or, of course, the work could have been introduced to More by a visiting Italian.[7]

---

[1] This edition contains the misprint "Bononiae anno salutis Mcccclxxxv die uero xvi Iulii" on sig. L₃. On the misdating see *Catalogue of Books Printed in the XVᵗʰ Century Now in the British Museum* (London, 1930), 6, 843.

[2] Louis Valcke characterizes this life as "beaucoup plus proche de l'hagiographie que de la biographie"; "Jean Pic de la Mirandole lu par Thomas More," in *Miscellanea Moreana: Essays for Germain Marc'hadour,* ed. Clare M. Murphy, Henri Gibaud, and Mario A. di Cesare, Medieval & Renaissance Texts & Studies no. 61 (Binghamton, 1989), p. 78.

[3] See Roberto Weiss, "Pico e l'Inghilterra," in *L'opera e il pensiero di Giovanni Pico della Mirandola,* 2 vols. (Florence, 1965), *1,* 143–52, especially 144–45. This article provides a useful survey of English citations of Pico during the sixteenth and seventeenth centuries.

[4] For details of Colet's citations from Pico see John B. Gleason, *John Colet* (Berkeley, 1989), p. 338.

[5] An edition was printed in Florence c. 1490. On the chronology of Colet's works see Gleason, pp. 91–92. Colet had read the work by May 1498; Parks, "Pico della Mirandola in Tudor Translation," p. 353.

[6] *Liber de providentia dei contra philosophastros* (Modena, 1508), now Bodleian Library D 2 13 Art Seld; see Giles Barber, "Thomas Linacre: A Bibliographical Survey of his Works," in *Essays on the Life and Works of Thomas Linacre c. 1460–1524* (Oxford, 1977), p. 335.

[7] For an example of such an Italian at Henry VII's court during the mid-1490s, the poet Johannes Michael Nagonius, see Francis Wormald, "An Italian Poet at the Court of Henry VII," *Journal of the Warburg and Courtauld Institutes, 14* (1951), 118–19; and P. G.

But whatever the source of More's knowledge of Pico's works, it is clear that they quickly became popular after the publication of the 1496 *Opera omnia* in Bologna. The *Opera* was itself reprinted several times before the publication of the first edition of More's *Life:* in Lyons before 1498, in Venice in 1498, in Strassburg in 1504, and in Reggio in 1506. In addition, various selections from Pico's works were published in separate editions, including some portions translated by More in his *Life,* particularly editions of his *Epistolae,* which also include in most cases his verse "Deprecatoria ad Deum."[1]

None of these editions of Pico's Latin works was printed in England, although some were clearly circulating there by the beginning of the sixteenth century. An edition of the *Opera omnia* was in Canterbury College, Oxford, by 1508.[2] And there are additional indications of an interest in his works within court circles. Henry VII's Italian astrologer, William Parron, evidently had knowledge of at least one of Pico's works, *Disputationes adversus astrologiam divinitricem,* to which he refers in his own justification of astrology, completed in England on October 15, 1499.[3] In addition, and perhaps more significantly, three different translations of extracts from Pico into French were presented to Henry VII. One (British Library Royal 16 E XIV) was written for the king in 1509 and contains versions of Pico's three duodecalogues.[4] A second (British Library Royal 16 E XXIV) contains Pico's exposition of Psalm 15, while the third (British Library Royal 16 E XXV) also contains versions of Pico's three duodecalogues, in the same hand as that which copied Royal 16 E XXIV.[5] The second and third versions may antedate the first.

Gwynne, "The Frontispiece to an Illuminated Panegyric of Henry VII: A Note on the Sources," *Journal of the Warburg and Courtauld Institutes,* 55 (1992), 266–70.

[1] For details see Appendix A, pp. 281–90. We are greatly indebted to Dr. Lotte Hellinga of the British Library for kindly providing us with a printout of early printed editions of Pico's works from the Incunable Short Title Catalogue.

[2] Parks, "Pico della Mirandola in Tudor Translation," p. 353.

[3] But this work had also been separately printed; editions were published in Bologna by Benedictus Hectoris in 1495, by Bernardus Venetus in 1498, and again by R. Pafraet in Deventer in 1502. It clearly cannot, therefore, provide any evidence for the circulation of the *Opera omnia.* See John Armstrong, "An Italian Astrologer at the Court of Henry VII," in *Italian Renaissance Studies: A Tribute to the Late Cecilia M. Ady,* ed. E. F. Jacob (London, 1960), p. 437.

[4] For a description see George F. Warner and J. P. Gilson, *Catalogue of Western Manuscripts in the Old Royal and King's Collections,* 4 vols. (London, 1921), 2, 198–99; and Parks, "Pico della Mirandola in Tudor Translation," p. 355, who establishes the date of presentation.

[5] For descriptions see Warner and Gilson, 2, 200.

Whether or not More was aware of these translations, the circulation of selections from the *Opera* corresponding to some of those in his *Life* suggests that at least some of his choices may have been determined by antecedent traditions of selections from Pico's works. For these are not the only instances of selection that correspond to some of those included in More's *Life*. "Deprecatoria ad Deum," in addition to being found in most early editions of Pico's letters, is also found separately in manuscript.[1] The commentary on Psalm 15 can be found in at least one manuscript,[2] and "duodecim arma quibus homo uti debet" appears separately,[3] as does "duodecim condiciones amantis."[4] The latter also appears together with the "duodecim regulae" and "duodecim arma spiritualia,"[5] which also occurs separately.[6] The appearance elsewhere of extracts corresponding to More's own selections does seem to suggest that his collocation of texts may be, in part, at least, a reflection of contemporary "anthologizing" tendencies.[7] But no other surviving selection seems to contain all the texts More included. And none, to the best of my knowledge, excerpts Gianfrancesco's *Vita*. Nor do these selections reflect the same processes of careful editing (as in More's treatment of Gianfrancesco's biography) and expansion (as in his verse renderings of the prose duodecalogues).[8]

More as Translator

Mᴏʀᴇ's *Life* is one of his earliest works, quite probably his earliest prose work and his only extended translation of other writers' Latin into English. Whatever the exact source (or sources) of his translations, it is possible to reach some general conclusions about his treatment of his source texts and about his characteristics as a translator. It seems convenient to address these issues separately and in the following or-

---

[1]In Florence, Bibl. Nazionale Centrale, Fondo Palatino, cod. 52, and Bibl. Riccardianna, cod. 2726; British Library Add. 19050.

[2]Harvard University MS Typ. 78.

[3]Florence, Bibl. Nazionale Centrale, Fondo Principale II IV 192.

[4]Perugia, Bibl. Comunale Augusta, cod. J 52.

[5]Vatican Regin. lat. 853.

[6]Florence, Bibl. Nazionale Centrale, Fondo Principale II IV 192.

[7]The continuity of such traditions in England is confirmed by the appearance in 1589 of an independent translation of Pico's duodecalogues and psalm commentary; see pp. lvii–lviii, below.

[8]I derive the information about manuscript selections from Pico's works from the invaluable study by Paul Oskar Kristeller, "Giovanni Pico della Mirandola and His Sources," in *L'opera e il pensiero di Giovanni Pico della Mirandola, 1,* 35–123, esp. pp. 109, 112, 123, 121.

der: More's treatment of the Latin prose texts he translates, his handling of his verse translations, and finally, the distinctive features of More's translational technique. The first two sections that follow are concerned primarily with questions of More's relative fidelity to his putative original in terms of additions or deletions of material, the final one with his actual style as translator.

THE PROSE TRANSLATIONS

The *Life*

I T IS not possible to say with complete certainty which edition of Pico's works More used for his translation or, indeed, whether he used more than one. It is assumed for the present purposes that he did work directly from the Latin and that the most likely basis for his translations is the 1504 Strassburg edition of the *Opera omnia*.[1] The text of Pico's Latin, presented in the Appendix, is intended to provide a fixed point of comparison for More's translational practice. While this is perhaps not an exact version of the Latin text that More had before him, it is probably close enough to provide the basis for some generalizations about both the design of More's translations and his actual techniques.[2]

Such generalizations insofar as they concern design must take as their main focus More's translation of Gianfrancesco's life of Pico. It is only here that it is possible to discern any larger and relatively systematic shaping in More's treatment of his Latin source. The other prose translation, the three letters and the commentary on Psalm 15, are largely faithful versions which at times omit material irrelevant to More's purposes. And the remaining versifications are either More's invention or his expansion of the Latin. It is only in the *Life* itself that we see More making a sustained attempt to readjust Gianfrancesco's biographical concerns to meet new exemplary purposes.

These purposes are enunciated in More's preface (51/1–52/16), one of his longest additions to the *Life*. Here he enunciates the moral and exemplary purposes of his undertaking: "The warkes are such that

---

[1]See Appendix A, pp. 291–92.

[2]There have been earlier discussions of More as translator by Max Kullnick, "Thomas Morus *Picus Erle of Mirandula*," *Archiv für das Studium der neueren Sprachen und Literatur*, *121* (1908), 47–75, 316–40 and *122* (1909), 27–50; by Stanford E. Lehmberg, "Sir Thomas More's Life of Pico della Mirandola," *Studies in the Renaissance*, *3* (1956), 61–74; and by Margaret Esmonde, "'A Patterne of Life': A Critical Analysis of St Thomas More's *Life of Picus*" (Ph.D. Dissertation, University of Miami, 1971). The chief aim of all these studies is to indicate the additions or deletions More made to his source text, rather than to analyze More's techniques as translator.

trewly goode sister I suppose of yᵉ quantite ther commeth none in your
hande more profitable: neither to thachyuyng of temperaunce in pros-
perite nor to yᵉ purchasing of patience in aduersite nor to the dispising
of worldly vanite nor to the desiring of heuinly felicite" (52/4–9). Al-
though More here and elsewhere in the preface speaks of Pico's actual
"warkes," it is the *Life* itself that More singles out: "for asmuch as
heraftir we peruse the course of his hole life rather aftir our litle power
slenderly then aftir his merites sufficiently" (52/2–4). The "warkes," it
seems, acquire their importance in the context of the *Life* that precedes
them.[1]

More reshaped the *Vita* in a variety of ways. The most immediately
obvious of these is the division of the uninterrupted sequence of Gian-
francesco's work into a series of distinct sections or chapters. These
sections, which are unnumbered, create twenty-nine separate divisions
varying in length from a few lines to several pages.[2] Each of the sections
is given a heading, perhaps suggested in a few instances at least by the
sidenotes that appear in four of the early printed editions of the *Vita*.[3]

More does not state his purpose for this change, nor are there any
obvious models for it.[4] But it seems consistent with the design of the
work as a meditative or exemplary life appropriate for study by a
religious. The effect is to throw into sharp relief, through a more
episodic technique than Gianfrancesco employs, key facets of Pico's

---

[1]More never identifies the author of the *Vita*. In his preface he says: "These
warkis . . . were made in latyne by one Iohan picus erle of Mirandula" (51/23–52/1).

[2]The shortest is that titled "The burnyng of wanton bokes" (60/11–15); the longest are
"Of his mynde and vayngloriouse dispitions at Rome" (56/21–58/32) and "Of the state of
his sowle" (73/8–75/21).

[3]See Appendix A, p. 292.

[4]The closest I can find is John Blacman's *Collectarium Mansuetudinum et bonorum morum
regis Henrici. VI*, a work that Blacman apparently completed about 1480. It survives only
in a printed edition by Robert Copland [1523?] (*STC*² 3123); for a modern edition see
M. R. James, *Henry the Sixth* (Cambridge, 1919). Like More's *Lyfe*, Blacman's work is
organized topically under such sections as "Iuramenta eius" and "Pietas et patientia
eius." How, or indeed if, More could have known Blacman's work is unclear. The most
likely link is Carthusian: Blacman appears to have been for some period a member of the
London Carthusian house (where More was himself to reside) before repairing to the
Charterhouse at Witham in Somerset, where he died. (On Blacman's life see Roger
Lovatt, "John Blacman: Biographer of Henry VI," in *The Writing of History in the Middle
Ages: Essays Presented to Richard William Southern*, ed. R. H. C. Davis and J. M. Wallace-
Hadrill, Oxford, 1981, pp. 415–44). It seems possible that a manuscript of Blacman's
work circulated within Carthusian circles and thus came to More's notice; see further
A. S. G. Edwards, "More's *Lyfe of Pycus* and Blacman's *Collectarium*," *Notes & Queries*, New
Series, *40* (1993), 307–8.

personality and biography that More seemingly wished to stress so that they would make Joyeuce Leigh more "godly prosperous" (51/23).

More's attempts to present this exemplary *Life* caused him to make certain large excisions and additions to the Latin. The excisions are, at times, very substantial. The largest, which amounts to over a quarter of the entire Latin original,[1] removes Gianfrancesco's account of Pico's works and the extent of his library. The effect is clearly to reduce Gianfrancesco's emphasis on the range of Pico's intellectual interests, particularly those that concerned the occult and esoteric, which More seemingly saw as deflecting attention from the devotional focus he wished to impose on his work.

Other, smaller excisions seem to have been made with a similar intent. Thus More omits mention of Pico's interest in the Cabala and of his scientific and mathematical propositions[2] and a passage on his interest in the natural sciences, replacing it with his own dismissive comment.[3] He also removes, presumably on similar grounds, a passage in which Gianfrancesco compares Pico's achievements with those of other philosophers, including Albertus Magnus.[4] More reduces Gianfrancesco's emphasis on Pico's skill in disputations defending his propositions.[5] A similar concern with the perceived unsuitability of Pico's interest in such matters seems also to extend to those who sought to defend him. More omits, for example, the account of the defense of Pico by Bishop Buonfrancesco of Reggio against the charge of heresy.[6]

Some omissions sharpen the devotional focus on the figure of Pico himself. More seeks, for example, to impersonalize and objectify his account by removing all the authenticating touches in Gianfrancesco's narrative. Virtually all uses of the first person disappear, as do various personal reminiscences that reveal Pico's individual foibles.[7] Matters of direct personal concern to Gianfrancesco, such as the settling of the earldom of Mirandola, are also removed,[8] as are his account of his own relationship with Pico,[9] details about Pico's siblings,[10] and the attrac-

---

[1]See note on 60/17–18 and Appendix A, 304/12–314/34, for this long omission from the Latin text.

[2]See note on 57/7–8 and Appendix A, 298/23–30, for the omitted part of the text.

[3]See note on 61/28 and Appendix A, 318/15–20, for the omitted part of the text.

[4]See note on 61/4 and Appendix A, 316/26–31, for the omitted part of the text.

[5]See note on 61/12 and Appendix A, 318/1–3, for the omitted part of the text.

[6]See note on 58/9 and Appendix A, 300/15–20, for the omitted part of the text.

[7]See, for example, note on 68/9 and Appendix A, 326/25–30, for the omitted part of the text.

[8]See note on 64/3 and Appendix A, 320/23–27, for the omitted part of the text.

[9]See note on 53/20 and Appendix A, 294/6–20, for the omitted part of the text.

[10]See note on 54/1 and Appendix A, 294/32–296/2, for the omitted part of the text.

tions of Ferrara and Florence for Pico.[1] Also omitted, presumably on similar grounds, are the worldly esteem in which Pico was held, as evidenced by the offer of a cardinalate,[2] and his relationship with Charles VIII of France.[3] This concern with the shaping of Gianfrancesco's *Vita* into an acceptable contemplative and devotional form also leads More to his final radical treatment of the ending, in which Gianfrancesco's reflections on Christian prophecy and the authority of scripture are removed and More's own much more succinct account inserted, emphasizing the Christian significance of Pico's death.[4] In sum, the passages omitted by More from Gianfrancesco's *Vita* are primarily those that emphasize Pico's roles as scholar and controversial thinker or stress his relationship at various levels to the secular world. The overall effect of these changes is to reduce the length of the Latin *Vita* from about nine thousand words to about seventy-five hundred in More's English version, even allowing for More's additions.[5]

More's additions to his *Life* are few in both number and length, apart from the preface (51/4–52/16). The longest, near the beginning (52/25–53/28), treats the nature of honor in general and of Pico in particular, together with his own modesty topos. He also provides his own terse conclusion to the Latin (75/9–20) and adds short bridging passages made necessary by his omissions from the Latin.[6] Other additions consist of phrases, clauses, or brief sentences to emphasize the Christian focus of More's design. At one point More replaces the Latin "& veritatis amore" (320/2) with the phrase "and profit of his chirch" (00/0); at another he emphasizes that Pico changed his mind "by the especiall commaundement of god" (70/18–19); or again that he "cleued to god with very feruent loue and deuotion" (70/7–8). Apart from these generally small instances, More seems to have been content to translate faithfully those passages from the *Vita* that he chose to include.

The Other Prose Works

MORE's treatment of Pico's own Latin texts, varies chiefly according to the medium he chose for translation. He translates into prose three of the forty-seven letters of Pico that Gianfrancesco included in the

---

[1]See note on 69/25 and Appendix A, 328/24–37, for the omitted part of the text.
[2]See note on 66/10 and Appendix A, 324/4–21, for the omitted part of the text.
[3]See note on 73/7 and Appendix A, 332/36–334/2, for the omitted part of the text.
[4]See note on 75/9 and Appendix A, 338/14–340/10, for the omitted part of the text.
[5]I have followed the calculations of Myron E. Gilmore, "More's Translation of Gianfrancesco Pico's Biography," in *L'opera e il pensiero di Giovanni Pico della Mirandella nella storia dell'umanesimo*, 2, 301.
[6]See, for example, note on 72/21–22.

Opera omnia, two to Gianfrancesco himself and one to Andrea Corneo. To each of these letters More adds a brief preface or argument of his own. The most extensive of these (76/3–77/20) is to the first letter to Gianfrancesco and consists largely of an extended gloss on Pico's allusion to the Circe legend. In the actual letter itself, the longest of the three he translates, More makes virtually no changes beyond giving both Latin and English versions of scriptural citations, something he does elsewhere in the translation of the letters and also in the translation of Psalm 15. The third letter (88/24–93/29), also to Gianfrancesco, is, once again, essentially a faithful translation of Pico's Latin, with only minor additions.[1]

In the second letter, addressed to Andrea Corneo (85/15–88/10), More undertakes more radical surgery, eliminating material of a purely personal nature from both the beginning and the end.[2] And within the material he does translate he makes some small but significant additions to one passage. Where Pico rejects "these owtward thinges of yᵉ body or of fortune" (86/4), More adds the following qualification: "I am content ye study but I wolde haue you outwardli occupied also" (86/5–6), and he goes on to emphasize the point: "Loue them & vse them both as well study as worldly occupation" (86/8–9). He is concerned to emphasize the necessity of the active life rather than the reclusive life of the solitary scholar/divine.

Similar fidelity is shown in More's final prose translation, the commentary on Psalm 15 (94/3–103/16). He does, however, omit a sentence from the Latin[3] and elsewhere make a number of additions ranging from single words or brief phrases to full sentences.[4] It is difficult to discern any controlling purpose in these adjustments. They seem generally to add emphasis or clarification to the original.

If one is to generalize about More's treatment of his Latin texts, it must be to emphasize his fidelity to the Latin. Where More departed from the Latin he did so mainly by the omission of material that he seemingly felt to be irrelevant to the purposes for which he was translating. There are very few efforts to enlarge silently or otherwise significantly modify the text of his original.

---

[1] See, for example, notes on 89/16, 89/24, and 93/13.

[2] See notes on 85/15, and 88/9 for fuller details.

[3] See note on 98/18 for details.

[4] For details see notes on 95/14, 96/4, 97/30, 98/17–18, 98/20–21, 100/13–15, 101/17–18, 101/18–19, 101/20–21, 102/11, and 102/31.

THE VERSE TRANSLATIONS

Mofre's verse portions of the *Life* are his most radical treatments of the Latin. With the exception of the final "praiour of Picus Mirandula vnto god" (120/12–123/11), none of the Latin is in verse. And for most of the rest of More's verse there is no precedent in the Latin at all. The first of the duodecalogues, on the ".xii. rulys of . . . spirituall batail" (103/19–109/12), is an expansion of Pico's prose. But the second and third, on the ".xii. wepenis of spiritual bataile" (109/27–113/10) and the ".xii. propretees or conditions of a louer" (114/3–120/11), are entirely More's invention, based only on Pico's brief lists.

Where the Latin does provide a point of comparison it is clear that More's translations are much freer elaborations of the Latin than is the case in his prose translations. That this should be so is, of course, not surprising, given the entirely different constraints of verse translation. But the extent of his expansions is itself significant. Of the 161 lines of the ".xii. rulys . . . of spirituall batail" at least 17 are entirely More's invention,[1] while a number of others are substantial amplifications of the Latin. The final translation, of the "Deprecatoria ad Deum" (120/13–123/11), contains 62 lines in Pico's original and 84 in More's version; it is clear that More significantly amplified his Latin source.

It is obviously much more difficult to generalize about More's verse translations than about his prose ones. It seems clear that there is less inclination in them to excise materials than there is to enlarge them, as is almost inevitable with the demands of the rhyme royal form. But this tendency seems also to reflect a more general desire to sharpen the focus of his source materials by rendering the devotional implications of Pico's texts more explicit.

MORE'S TECHNIQUE AS TRANSLATOR

The most distinctive feature of More as translator is his fidelity to his original. This fidelity results at times in a literalness that extends considerably beyond simple accuracy of rendering. It can lead to such close syntactic replication of the original as to create structures that can be particularly cumbersome. Thus More offers such Latinate syntactic inversions as "Gret lybraries hit is incredible to considre with how meruelouse celerite he redd them ouer" (60/21–23) and "Picus all these thingis with equal study hath so receyued" (62/16–17), or such post-

---

[1]See, for example, notes on 103/21–22, 105/17–20, 107/4, 107/9, 107/16–19, 107/24, and 108/12–22.

positive adjectival constructions as "vice passed" (60/14), "vtensilis of howshold" (64/7), and "of wit connyng and conditions excellent" (71/26–27).

But it would be misleading to overemphasize such Latinate features of More's translations. In general his fidelity is to the actual sense of the Latin rather than to Latinate syntax or vocabulary. Indeed, one area in which he seems able to operate fairly independently is the coinage or adaptation of words. For a work of quite modest length, More introduced a surprisingly high number of neologisms. There are over eighty instances in which he either provides the earliest recorded occurrence of a form or usage in English or antedates the earliest recorded in *The Oxford English Dictionary*.[1] Fewer than half of those forms are derived from the Latin. The rest show More to be either creating or deriving his forms quite independently of his source.[2] It is striking that virtually all his neologisms (or apparent neologisms) appear in those portions of More's work where is he using a Latin source text, even

---

[1]The earliest recorded usages are: "alacrite" (70/9), "bedelem" (91/20), "culture" (85/26–27), "descanted" (88/16), "dispitions" (56/21), "dispiteouse" (110/18), "fast" (63/5), "fencyng" (70/16), "frekill" (68/1), "glideth" (110/11), "hawke" (87/24), "infatigable" (56/17), "insensibilite" (81/25), "laboriously" (91/13), "lightsomely" (67/16), "mediocrite" (87/18), "opprobriouse" (90/2), "persuasion" (85/22), "remitted" (88/3), "satisfie" (71/3), "serpentines" (57/30), "skittissh" (87/16), "stomak" (61/4). The antedatings of *OED* are: "abiecte" (68/9), "adeption" (91/17), "adnichilate" (97/8), "affectiones" (76/25), "allectiue" (80/23), "apply" (108/13), "attempt" (57/17), "brake" (70/13), "breuiary" (56/5), "brutissh" (76/28–29), "captions" (61/28), "castith" (106/22), "cauillations" (61/28), "ciuile" (85/15), "coeternalli" (71/15), "compaced" (75/7), "contract" (106/20), "contumeliouse" (81/7), "conuenient" (81/5), "deface" (57/24), "discomfortable" (101/19), "entreting" (85/18), "excercised" (62/13), "extremes" (71/4), "fence" (109/3), "garnisshe" (115/12), "gasing" (61/24), "glosse" (109/6), "integrite" (64/14), "inspecable" (75/19), "lukky" (51/8), "mercennari" (85/7), "mokking" (77/3), "ostentation" (61/21), "outward" (85/18), "passioned" (118/29), "persuaded" (66/10), "peruse" (105/16), "placabilite" (65/4), "populare" (90/18), "repaye" (71/3), "scrupulously" (56/15), "secundarily" (102/26), "sensuall" (104/24), "soteltes" (61/28), "sowre" (108/2), "stiked" (69/18), "trenches" (57/18), "trymme" (107/7), "twich" (79/23), "wageles" (119/28), "wanton" (112/9). Many of these are discussed in Susan Carole Weinberg, "A Study of the Vocabulary of Some of the English Works of Sir Thomas More, including *Richard III* and the *Life John Picus*" (M. Phil. Dissertation, University of London, 1973), pp. 89–138, a work that I have found very helpful on More's vocabulary.

[2]The ones that seem clearly suggested by the Latin are: "adnichilate" (97/8), "alacrite" (70/9), "allectiue" (80/23), "blandimentes" (59/16–17), "breuiary" (56/5), "captions" (61/28), "cauillations" (61/28), "contumeliouse" (81/7), "culture" (85/26–27), "descanted" (88/16), "dispitions" (57/14), "extremes" (71/4), "mediocrite" (87/18), "glosse" (109/6), "infatigable" (56/17), "mercennari" (85/7), "opprobriouse" (90/2), "ostentation" (61/21), "persuasione" (85/22), "placabilite" (65/4), "remitted" (88/3), "satisfie" (71/3), "secundarily" (102/29), "sensuall" (104/24).

when not derived from the Latin, rather than in those portions of his work, like the majority of his verse translations, where he is inventing.

Other superficial appearances of independence from the Latin are less easy to assess. This is particularly true of More's general tendency to translate single words from the *Vita* by English doublets. By doing so More aligns himself with Middle English traditions of prose translation from Latin into the vernacular[1] and also with some sixteenth-century translations,[2] in which such doublets are frequent. Examples recur throughout the *Life* for nouns, adjectives, adverbs, and verbs: "circle or garland" (54/10) translating "orbiculari" (296/5), "tendre and soft" (55/5), translating "molli (296/21), "more fast and suerely" (55/20–21) translating "tenaciores" (296/33), "fastened and set vp" (57/10) translating "affixit" (298/31). Such examples could be multiplied. But it is also true that in rendering doublets at a number of points More is doing no more than representing Gianfrancesco's own Latin.[3] Here More's use of doublets is perhaps less a characteristic of his own style and more of his fidelity as translator than it was in the later *History of King Richard III*.[4]

But it is not easy to discover features that are particularly distinctive.[5] It has been pointed out that the Latin prose rhythms are more pronounced in More's early translations, the *Life* and *Richard III*, than in his later prose works,[6] but this is hardly surprising given More's concern to represent the Latin carefully. The Latin works rarely require any very distinctive or sustained rhetorical effects, and More

---

[1] For discussion of More's use of doublets in general and the traditions from which it derives see *CW 2*, lvi–vii.

[2] For example, Mary Bassett's translation of More's *De Tristitia*, in *CW 14*, 1077–1165.

[3] See, for example, "breuiary or a summe" (56/5) translating "epitomen . . . seu breuiarium" (298/3–4), "craft and sleight" (57/17) translating "strophis . . . cuniculis" (298/36–37), "foly and rudenesse" (58/15–16) translating "insolentiae & ruditatis" (300/25–26), "glorye and profite" (59/19) translating "gloriam & . . . utilitatem" (302/31–32), "confusione & rebuke" (61/25) translating "infamiae confusionisque" (318/12–13), "besy & infatigable" (63/9) translating "iuge & infatigabile" (320/11).

[4] On More's use of doublets in this work see *CW 2*, lvii.

[5] One may note a tendency to eliminate Pico's superlatives; for example: "fewe" (82/8) translating "paucissimos" (346/12), "lightsomely" (67/16) translating "luculentissime" (326/9), "obscure" (91/8) translating "densissimis" (358/21), "swete" (91/10) translating "suauissima" (358/22), "laboriously" (91/13) translating "laboriosissime" (358/25). In addition, there is a less pronounced tendency to render Latin plurals as singulars; for example: "substance" (63/6) translating "facultates" (320/7), "banaire" (80/25) translating "uexillis" (344/14), "stipende" (80/26) translating "stipendiis" (344/14–15).

[6] See Sr. Mary Sullivan, *A Study of the Cursus in the Works of St. Thomas More* (Washington, D.C., 1943).

does not seem to have made any effort to improve rhetorically on his
original. Such few attempts at cadenced prose as appear are, at times,
effective representations of the Latin. For example, in the following
passage More succeeds in matching quite well the balanced cadences of
the Latin:

> O very happi mynde which none aduersite myght oppresse / which
> no prosperite might enhaunce: not the conning of all philosophie
> was able to make hym prowde / not the knowledge of the hebrewe /
> chaldey & arabie language beside greke and laten could make him
> waingloriouse / not his grete substance / not hys noble blode coude
> blow vp his hart / not yᵉ bewty of his body / not yᵉ grete occasion of
> sin were able to pull him bak in to yᵉ voluptuouse brode way yᵗ
> ledith to helle. (65/16–23)

> O felicem mentem, quae iam nullis posset adversis deprimi, nullis
> quoque commodis . . . extolli! Non illum certe universae philoso-
> phiae peritia, non Hebreae non Chaldeae Arabicaeque linguae
> (ultra Latinam & Graecam) cognitio tumidum reddiderant. Non
> amplae divitiae, non generis nobilitas inflaverant, non corporis
> pulchritudo & elegantia, non magna peccandi licentia in mollem
> illam & spatiosam multorum viam revocare poterant. (322/18–
> 25)

At other times he seeks with less than complete success to impose a
similar balanced rhythm by translation that is not confined to the
strictly literal. Thus where the Latin reads "Nihil enim illis est tutum,
nihil pacatum; omnia metum, omnia curas, intentant omnia mortem"
(342/36–37) More renders: "Ther is to him no thing sure no thing
peseable but al thing fereful al thing sorowfull al thing dedely" (80/6–
8). Although he preserves the parallelism of the second sentence of the
Latin ("omnia . . . omnia . . . omnia") he omits the verb "intentant,"
which varies the balance of the final clause in the Latin to avoid a
symmetrical replication of that of the first sentence ("Nihil . . . nihil").
At times, in shorter syntactic structures, he recognizes the verbal and
syntactic balance of the Latin but at the same time blurs its symmetries.
Thus, he renders "Aequa enim laus a laudatis laudari et improbari ab
improbis" (356/4) as: "Certainly as grete a prais as hit is to be comendet
of them yᵗ are commendable: as grete a commendation it is to be
reproued of them yᵗ are reprouable" (88/27–89/1). The insertion of
the phrase "grete a commendation" is unnecessary to sense and ob-
structive to rhythm.

Such clumsiness may reflect More's inexperience in translating into
English prose or the haste with which he undertook his translation. It is

also more generally reflective of the state of English prose, which had been rarely called upon in the later Middle Ages to imitate the rhetorical resources of Latin. More's lack of English stylistic precedents for this didactic and devotional compendium also imposed constraints on his translation to add to those imposed by his relative inexperience in translation.

It is only in his verse translations that More shows much inclination to extended elaboration of Pico's texts. In other respects he remains a conservative and literal translator.

Genre

ALTHOUGH it has some claims to be the first biography in English,[1] such a view of More's rendering of Pico's *Vita* is misleading. The *Life* is only one part of a larger entity whose affinities are more with hagiographic and devotional traditions. In the *Life* More deletes material that he apparently felt obscured this devotional focus, and he organizes the work episodically to emphasize the significant episodes of the exemplary life he translates. At times such an organization creates emphases that are typical of hagiography, as, for example, in the increased stress More gives to the portents surrounding Pico's birth (54/4–22) by omitting details of Pico's family and ancestry just before this. Or, again, the suppression of the very long passage in Gianfrancesco's *Vita* that emphasizes Pico's humanist achievements[2] serves to throw into relief those passages which emphasize his piety and generosity.[3] In such ways, together with the removal of the authenticating, autobiographical details of Gianfrancesco's own observations, Pico's work becomes less a biography and more an appropriate contemplative model for the rejection of the active life of the world.

But the devotional affinities with hagiography do not provide a completely satisfactory generic model for More's work, either for the *Life* itself or for the larger structure of which it is a part. For Pico was not, of course, a saint: he underwent no remarkable sufferings and did not reveal miraculous attributes as demonstrations of his sanctity. Although he is presented as rejecting the inducements of authority, wealth, and power, such inducements are not presented as occasions

---

[1]See, for example, Donald A. Stauffer, *English Biography before 1700* (Cambridge, Mass., 1930), pp. 35–37.

[2]See note on 60/17–18.

[3]For example, 64/25–65/3, 66/5–12, 67/5–25, 68/24–69/6.

for a distinctive testing leading in its turn to an affirmation of faith, as they would in hagiography.

Germain Marc'hadour has asserted that "clearly, from first page to last, the Pico volume is a spiritual nosegay, specifically Christian, resolutely geared toward the increase in 'godliness' of both compiler and reader."[1] Yet Pico himself does not emerge as a figure who affirms very heroic Christian values.[2] More follows Gianfrancesco in seeming as much concerned to·show what the secular and scholarly worlds lost through Pico's renunciation of them as to show what spiritual values he embodied. As we have seen, More does reduce the emphasis on the intellectual and scholarly Pico, also presenting him as swiftly reconciled with Christian orthodoxy after his early excesses in a way that is at odds with the facts.[3] But the actual narrative presents him (in More's phrase) as a man of "meruelouse cunnyng & excellent vertue" (53/20) or "an excellent cunnynge man (53/27). The terms suggest something of the divided emphasis of More's narrative. On the one hand, the narrative is conceived as one of spiritual edification; on the other, it is Pico's "cunnyng" as much as his "excellent vertue" that the narrative must stress, since that is the emphasis that inheres in More's source. More's own conclusion (75/9–20) emphasizes the equivocal nature of Pico's life as example: "eueri christen bodi" is asked to "shew theyr charite vppon him to helpe to spede him thedir [to heaven]" (75/12–13). The world is invoked to pray for him rather than he for the world.

What is unusual in this is not so much More's technique as its subject— a secular, not a religious figure. In his choice of subject More moves toward the form of secular, vernacular biography reflected in his later *Richard III* while also looking backward for a model for such biography in lives of exemplary religious, such as those found in Caxton's version of *The Golden Legend* or works derived from it.[4]

---

[1]"Thomas More's Spirituality," in *Saint Thomas More: Action and Contemplation*, ed. Richard S. Sylvester (New Haven and London, 1972), p. 130.

[2]Cf. the comment of J. H. Hexter: "[Pico] was also drawn to the ascetic renunciation required by the monastic life. Yet despite his own inclination, despite Savonarola's expostulations, despite even his threats, Pico held back. . . . He renounced the world only in extremis, when willy-nilly he was about to leave it forever"; *CW* 2, xcv.

[3]Thus More implies that Pico's pardon for his heretical propositions followed hard upon their condemnation in 1487, whereas in fact he was not pardoned until 1493. See note on 58/20–22.

[4]There were at least seven separate editions of *The Golden Legend* printed in England before 1510: see *STC*[2] 24873, 24874, 24875, 24876, 24877, 24878.3, 24878.5. Caxton, de Worde, Pynson, and other printers also produced before 1510 at least eighteen editions of Mirk's *Festial*, a work derived from *The Golden Legend;* see *STC*[2] 17957, 17958, 17959,

But there appear to be no precedents for the addition to the *Life* of selections from Pico's own works and for the translation of works in a variety of different forms—epistles, commentary, verse homilies, and a hymn—in both prose and verse,[1] some of which forms had not previously appeared in print in England—or in English.[2] The effect is to create a unique form of devotional compendium, one in which example and admonition are combined through the joining of Pico's biography to a variety of forms of spiritual instruction. This form reveals the rather uneasy relationship of some of its components to the ostensible contemplative design of the work. It is not easy to share Marc'hadour's view that the work has a systematically and specifically Christian texture throughout. Indeed, the most explicit and sustained Christian affirmations come in More's verse portions, largely his additions to Pico. But these affirmations come after he has recorded the ambivalences of Pico's own life and the letters which reveal his own sense of the conflicting claims of both the spiritual and material worlds. We see More ordering the components of the *Life* to move the reader steadily away from the pull of worldly affairs to a stable contemplation of Christian doctrine and exhortation. It is this contemplative movement that gives to the *Life* such coherence as it possesses.

Reception

THE *Life* belongs with a small group of More's English works of sufficient appeal to be reprinted during his lifetime. Only his *Dialogue Concerning Heresies* and *Supplication of Souls* also fall into this category. But both of these works were printed by the Rastells, and the reprints

---

17960, 17961, 17962, 17963, 17963.5, 17964, 17965, 17966, 17966.5, 17967, 17968, 17969, 17970, 17970.5, 17971. On the influence of *The Golden Legend* in the late fifteenth and early sixteenth centuries in England see Helen White, *Tudor Books of Saints and Martyrs* (Madison, 1963), esp. pp. 31–66.

[1]There are relatively few English works before More's that seek to combine both: Chaucer's *Canterbury Tales*, Thomas Hoccleve's *Series*, the *Speculum Christiani*, and the *Pilgrimage of the Soul* are the ones that seem to have circulated more extensively in manuscript. The latter two are religious works. Only the first and last of these were produced by early English printers: Chaucer, of course, frequently; and the *Pilgrimage* by Caxton in 1483. For the earlier history of the mixed form see Peter Dronke, *Verse with Prose from Petronius to Dante: The Art and Scope of the Mixed Form* (Cambridge, Mass., 1994).

[2]The *Life* may provide the first case of the printing in English of private correspondence and of commentary on the Psalms. More's verse translations of Pico's duodecalogues and his "Deprecatoria ad Deum" also provide the first English verse translations of contemporary Latin writings.

followed hard upon the original publication.[1] Moreover, these reprints date from late in More's career. The *Life* was the first of his works ever to be reprinted. It differs from these other works in the interval that separated Rastell's [1510?] edition from de Worde's [c. 1525]. The fact of such a reprint, one undertaken by such a prolific and commercial publisher as de Worde, suggests that More's *Life* had established itself as a work of some popularity during his lifetime. De Worde's main addition to Rastell's edition suggests why this should be so. He apparently designed specifically for this edition a woodcut depicting Christ crucified, surrounded by the instruments of the Passion.[2] Both the fact and the form of this woodcut are significant. It was relatively rare for de Worde to have woodcuts made specifically for works by contemporary writers. And the woodcut establishes the work as a devotional one, a market which de Worde seems to have been particularly eager to develop.[3]

But the demand seems to have faded quite rapidly without leaving many traces, even though there was evidently some continuing interest in having Pico's works available in English translation, including some of the works More himself had translated. This interest achieves its most sustained expression in Thomas Elyot's translation of "The rules of a Christian lyfe made by Picus Erle of Mirandula," first printed in 1534 as an addendum to *A Swete and devoute sermon of holy saynt Ciprian.*[4] These are prose translations of "The Twelve Rules of Spiritual Battle" (103/17–109/12 in More's text). They were reprinted in Thomas Lupset's *Workes* (1546)[5] and again in the 1585 reprint of Richard Whitford's translation of Thomas à Kempis' *De imitatione Christi*[6] and in the later translation of the same work by "B. F." (or "F. B.").[7] Although Elyot's translations make no reference to More's earlier ones and there

---

[1] The *Dialogue* (STC² 18084–5) was first printed by John Rastell in 1529 and reprinted by William Rastell in 1530; both editions of *The Supplication of Souls* (STC² 18091–2) were printed by William Rastell in 1529.

[2] See Edward Hodnett, *English Woodcuts, 1480–1535* (Oxford, 1935; reprint, 1973), no. 448.

[3] On de Worde's development of this market see A. S. G. Edwards and Carol Meale, "The Marketing of Printed Books in Late Medieval England," *The Library*, 6th series, *15* (1993), 95–124.

[4] STC² 6157, printed by Thomas Berthelet; the Picus translation appears on sigs. E₃–E₈.

[5] STC² 16932, printed by Thomas Berthelet; the Pico translation is on sigs. Bb₃–Bb₆.

[6] STC² 23968, printed by G. L'Oyselet of Rouen; the Pico translation is on sigs. P₁₀–P₁₂v.

[7] STC² 23988, printed by the English secret press in 1615; the Pico is on sigs. T₆–T₁₀.

are no clear parallels in phrasing, both are addressed to audiences of female religious.[1] And it has been argued, on rather tenuous evidence, that Elyot, a friend of More's, may have intended his work as some form of comfort to More in the Tower.[2] If this is so, it is somewhat ironic that Elyot's work seems to have enjoyed a sustained circulation that was denied to More's own translations. Perhaps the prosaic literalness of his translation made it more didactically attractive to posterity.

The period before the publication of the 1557 edition of the *English Works* seems to have produced only slight evidence of interest in More's translations of Pico. The inventory of John Rastell's printer's stock and private library in 1538 appears to have included a copy of his own or de Worde's edition.[3] And it was before the appearance of the 1557 edition that Robert Parkyn copied the text of the "Deprecatoria ad Deum" translation into his autograph manuscript (Bodleian MS Lat. th. d. 15), a transcription that must have been completed before April 1551.[4] The transcription seems derived, like others by Parkyn, from an independent source rather than from either *1510* or *1525* and appears to reflect some comparison with a Latin text of Pico.[5] But such interest seems to have no other parallels, although it does confirm other indications of Parkyn's evident Catholic sympathies in general and his pious enthusiasm for More's works in particular.[6]

Nor does the appearance of the 1557 *English Works* seem to have led to much specific interest in the Pico translations. *The Twelve Rvles, and Weapons Concerning the Spiritvall Battel, Together with a briefe exposition vpon the sixteene Psalme,* by "W. H.," was published in 1589.[7] It contains a prose translation of "The Twelve rules of Spiritual Battle," together with translations of "The Twelve Weapons" and "The Twelve Conditions of a Lover," the commentary on Psalm 15, and two of Pico's letters

---

[1]Elyot's translation is prefaced, like More's, by an epistle to "suster dame Susan Kyngestone" (A$_2$) and "our two susters religiouse Dorothe and Alianour" (A$_3$v), for whom he states his work was translated.

[2]On More's friendship with Elyot see John M. Major, *Sir Thomas Elyot and Renaissance Humanism* (Lincoln, Neb., 1964), pp. 89–108; the hypothesis that Elyot's work is a response to More's plight is advanced on pp. 105–7.

[3]See R. J. Roberts, "John Rastell's Inventory of 1538," *The Library,* 6th series, *1* (1979), 36:[55] "Picus Mirandula."

[4]See *CW 13,* cxli–ii for description of this manuscript and discussion of its date.

[5]For text and discussion of this transcript see A. S. G. Edwards, "Robert Parkyn's Transcript of More's 'Prayer of Picus Mirandola unto God,'" *Moreana,* 27 (1990), 133–38.

[6]On Parkyn's career and his interest in More's works see *CW 13,* cxxvii–ix and the references cited there.

[7]*STC*^{2} 19898a.3, printed by John Windet.

to Gianfrancesco, including the second translated by More (88/24–93/29). This collection reveals no acquaintance with More's translations and seems to draw independently upon the same sort of traditions of excerpting from Pico's works that may have influenced More.

One, apparently atypical, indication of such an interest appears in an early seventeenth-century manuscript (Sloane 848), which contains (fol. 12^{r-v}) a summary of More's translation of the actual Life and part of the first letter of Pico to Gianfrancesco. There are grounds for believing that this summary was made, like Parkyn's, by someone of recusant sympathies.[1]

Such sympathies are evidenced in the only significant seventeenth-century references to the *Life*. The first of these occurs in Robert Parsons, *A treatise of three conversions of England* (1603; STC^2 19416), a recusant work printed in St. Omer. This draws extensively upon More's works seemingly from the 1557 *English Works* and cites the *Life* at several points as evidence of Pico's Catholicism: "the life of the said Picus wrytten in English at large by Syr Thomas More, in the beginning of his works: which doth shew him in all things to have byn a Catholike.[2] The same point is made in *The converted Jew or certaine dialogues between Micheas a learned Jew, and others, touching divers points of religion* (1630), by "John Clare," a pseudonym for Roger Anderton.[3] This includes a summary of Pico's life as recounted by "Sir Thomas More of blessed memory" emphasizing his deathbed profession of "the Roman fayth."[4] But there is little subsequent indication of interest during the seventeenth century, apart from a brief allusion in Donne's *Essays in Divinity*.[5]

The early eighteenth century saw the first reprinting of More's *Life* since 1557. This was followed in 1723 by publication of *The lives of Picus and Pascal, faithfully collected from the most authentick accounts of them, to which is subjoined a parallel between these two Christian worthies*. This work,

---

[1]It is followed (fol. 14^{r-v}) by a series of extracts from a work of clear recusant interest, George Cavendish's *Life of Wolsey;* for a brief description of this manuscript see *Cavendish's Life of Wolsey*, ed. R. S. Sylvester, EETS OS no. 243 (London, 1959), pp. 282–83.

[2]This passage and the other references to the *Life* are printed in Jackson Campbell Boswell, *Sir Thomas More in the English Renaissance: An Annotated Catalogue*, Medieval & Renaissance Texts and Studies no. 83 (Binghamton, 1994), pp. 244–45. I owe my knowledge of this and the following citation to Professor Boswell's valuable catalogue.

[3]STC^2 5351, pp. 136–37; printed by the English secret press.

[4]Boswell, pp. 62–63.

[5]Gibson, no. 257. The reference appears in the essay "Of Genesis": "*Picus* Earl of *Mirandula* (happier in no one thing in this life, then in the Author which writ it to us)"; *Essays in Divinity*, ed. Evelyn M. Simpson (Oxford, 1952), p. 13.

which was several times reprinted, based the Pico biography on More's own. But for the rest of the eighteenth century More's work received virtually no attention. Even so sympathetic a student as Thomas Warton was moved simply to dismiss his verse translation as a "juvenile exercise . . . in the English stanza."[1]

There appears to have been no further documented interest in the *Life* until the latter part of the nineteenth century, when, in 1872, Wilfred Raynal reprinted the Whitford edition of Thomas à Kempis, including More's translation of Pico's duodecalogues. In 1890 J. M. Rigg produced the first modern edition of the whole *Life*, which was followed by the first serious modern scholarly study of it, by Max Kullnick in 1908–9.[2] The *XII Properties or Condicyons of a Lover* was reprinted in 1928 and again in 1933.[3] The appearance of the first volume of the *English Works* in 1931 has provided a secure reference point for all later scholarly study of More's *Life of Picus.*

---

[1]*History of English Poetry*, ed. William Carew Hazlitt (London, 1871), *4*, 92.

[2]Max Kullnick, "Thomas Morus' 'Picus Erle of Mirandula,'" *Archiv für das Studium der neueren Sprachen und Literaturen*, New Series, 22 (1908), 49–75, 316–40; 23 (1909), 27–50.

[3]By the St. Dominic's Press, Ditchling Common, Sussex; the first edition, in 1928, was limited to 250 copies.

THE LAST THINGS

Date and Circumstances of Composition

THERE is no contemporary testimony to the date of composition of More's treatise, and our most definite evidence remains William Rastell's assertion in the title of the *English Works* (1557) that *The Last Things* was "Made about the yere of oure lorde .1522." (sig. e₄v). Although Rastell's judgment in such matters occasionally needs refinement,[1] he was a careful editor and can be relied on to have supplied a fair notion of the date of composition of the English works when it was known to him.[2] Without external witnesses to confirm Rastell's date, we must be content to investigate the few clues provided by the text itself and by More's biographers, although none offers information that would discredit Rastell's claim or that helps us to fix the date with greater precision.

One clue offered by the work itself is the passage at the end of the section on envy describing the fate of "a great Duke" (160/33–34) who is executed "for secret treason lately detected to the king" (161/6). Arthur W. Reed identified this passage as a reference to the fall of Edward, third duke of Buckingham, tried and executed for treason (though not, as More's story has it, hanged, drawn, and quartered) in May 1521.[3] The additional detail in More's account of "the mariage of

---

[1]Rastell asserts, for example, that *A Treatise on the Passion* was written entirely during More's imprisonment in the Tower, whereas a letter to More's secretary, John Harris, suggests that part of the work had been written before More's arrest; see Rogers, pp. 185–86; and *A Treatise on the Passion, A Treatise on the Blessed Body,* and *Instructions and Prayers, CW 13,* xxxvii–xli. Even more to the point for our purposes is Rastell's dating of *Richard III,* which he assigns to "about the yeare of our Lorde .1513." Richard Sylvester concluded that the state of the text in the extant versions suggests revision over a number of years, while internal evidence reveals that composition could not have begun before early 1514; see *CW 2,* lxiii–lxv.

[2]For example, Rastell does not supply dates for either the Pageant Verses or the *Life of Pico;* this omission suggests that he assigned dates only when he knew them.

[3]Campbell and Reed, *1,* 21–22. For Buckingham's rise and fall, see *Letters and Papers, Foreign and Domestic, of the Reign of Henry VIII,* ed. J. S. Brewer, James Gairdner, and R. H. Brodie, 21 vols. (London, 1862–1932; reprint, Vaduz, 1965; cited hereafter as *LP*), *3/1,*

his chylde" (161/1) may lend further support to Reed's identification, since Buckingham's daughter Mary married George Neville, third baron of Bergavenny, about 1519.[1]

More was certainly acquainted with the Buckingham case. Aside from the notoriety of the duke's trial and execution, opportunity for firsthand knowledge of the affair was available to him through his father, who sat on the commission to indict Buckingham.[2] Indeed, More himself (ironically enough) profited from the duke's downfall, receiving the income from the confiscated south manor in Kent on May 8, 1522.[3]

To be sure, parts of More's description—the opulence of the duke's household, the details of his sentence, even the element of envy, which forms the basis of More's use of the episode—bear an outward resemblance to other sixteenth-century accounts of Buckingham's downfall.[4] Despite these similarities, however, and despite More's certain knowledge of the case, nothing in the passage permits us to do more than speculate about the people and events to which it alludes. At most, we can say that Rastell's date does not eliminate the possibility that Buckingham is the subject of More's cautionary tale. Certainly such an example of the ephemeral character of worldly success is not unlikely to have preoccupied More as he himself gained greater political power.

No less subject to speculation than the "great Duke" passage is More's reminiscence (also in the section on envy) of the pickpocket at Newgate "that cut a purse at the barre when he should be hanged on the morow" (172/18–19). Such an episode could have taken place during More's tenure as undersheriff of London from 1510 to 1518 and

---

490–513. Edward Hall, *Chronicle* (London, 1809), pp. 623–24; *The Anglica Historia of Polydore Vergil, 1485–1537*, ed. Denis Hay, Camden Society, 3rd series, no. 74 (London, 1950), pp. 262–64, 278–80; *Dictionary of National Biography*, 63 vols. (London, 1908–1950; cited hereafter as *DNB*), 53, 446–47; J. J. Scarisbrick, *Henry VIII* (London, 1968), pp. 120–23; and Mortimer Levine, "The Fall of Edward, Duke of Buckingham," in *Tudor Men and Institutions*, ed. Arthur J. Slavin (Baton Rouge, 1972), pp. 32–48.

[1] For the marriage, see *DNB* 50, 257.

[2] *LP 3/1*, 490, no. 1284.

[3] *LP 3/2*, no. 2239; and J. A. Guy, *The Public Career of Sir Thomas More* (New Haven and London, 1980), p. 25 (cited hereafter as "Guy"). The lease of this property was worth £20 a year.

[4] For Buckingham's original sentence (commuted before his execution) of hanging, drawing, and quartering, see Hall, *Chronicle*, p. 264. Polydore Vergil's account of Buckingham's downfall stresses Wolsey's connivance in the indictment and portrays the lord chancellor's duplicity as motivated by his envy of the duke's power; see *The Anglica Historia*, p. 262.

may represent some case over which he actually presided as judge.[1] On the other hand, the anecdote is not necessarily autobiographical and could have been reported to More by someone else, in which case it cannot stand as evidence for the date of the treatise.

Other possible internal testimony to the date of *The Last Things* is provided by the verbal and thematic parallels to More's other works, particularly *A Dialogue of Comfort*, where the similarities range from allusions and ideas to phrasing and diction. Twenty-four such parallels occur in the *Dialogue*,[2] more than in any other of More's works—indeed, more than twice the number found in the Latin epigrams (which has eleven) or in the *Utopia* (which has ten), the works in the canon containing the next largest number of parallels to *The Last Things*. The many parallels between *The Last Things* and *A Dialogue of Comfort*, coupled with Rastell's occasional imprecision in assigning dates, have led Friedrich-Karl Unterweg to speculate in his recent edition that *The Last Things* may have been written much later than Rastell claims, possibly as late as 1534–35, during More's imprisonment in the Tower.[3] Nevertheless, there is no positive external evidence to support this view, and although the significant number of parallel passages between the two works is undeniable, this congruence could as easily be the result of their similar subject matter as of contemporaneous composition.[4] If *The Last Things* were a Tower work, after all, we might reasonably expect it to share such parallel passages not just with the *Dialogue* but also with the other works written shortly before and during More's imprisonment: *A Treatise on the Passion, A Treatise on the Blessed Body, De Tristitia Christi,* and *Instructions and Prayers.* This is not the case.

The evidence provided by More's biographers, early and modern, is no more helpful than the textual clues. Roper, Harpsfield, and Stapleton give no indication of the date of the treatise (the first two do not

---

[1]For More's career as undersheriff, see Harpsfield, p. 20; Roper, p. 8; and Guy, pp. 5–6. An incident somewhat like that of the pickpocket is recounted in Stapleton, pp. 137–38, where More not only presides over the case but actually engineers the theft as a practical joke. Chambers has disputed the authenticity of the anecdote, quoting this passage from the treatise to illustrate More's distaste for the thief's conduct (p. 43).

[2]These parallels are noted in the Commentary.

[3]*Die Vier Letzten Dinge* (Koźle, 1984), pp. 28–39.

[4]Compare *CW 12*, Commentary at 4/12: "Possibly because of the subject matter, *The Last Things* contains a great many verbal parallels to *A Dialogue of Comfort* and similar references and allusions, more than in any of More's other works except those written in the Tower."

mention the work at all), while Ro. Ba. (perhaps taking his cue in part
from the sequence of the *English Works*) regards it as a youthful work
composed after the *Life of Pico* and about the same time as *Richard III*.[1]
The consensus among More's twentieth-century biographers is that
The Last Things was composed in the early 1520s.[2] I see nothing to stand
in the way of this view.

If we accept "about 1522" as the nearest we can come to the exact
date of composition, we can address the circumstances under which the
treatise was written. Again, Rastell's title in the *English Works* is our best
source of information. Recently knighted, More had added the office
of undertreasurer of the Exchequer to his duties as privy councillor.[3]
This information at least provides a *terminus ad quem* for the date of the
treatise, since More had to give up his post at the Exchequer in Septem-
ber 1525, when he was appointed to the chancellorship of the Duchy of
Lancaster.[4] This growing involvement in the government's business,
with its hectic, demanding schedule, perhaps accounts for the frag-
mentary state of *The Last Things*. Clearly, More's experience in the royal
service provided a wealth of examples for the analysis of pride, envy,
and greed in the treatise, and it has recently been suggested that the
work records More's private ambivalence, even repugnance, toward
the court at which he had become a regular attendant.[5]

Another intriguing piece of circumstantial information is Stapleton's
claim: "When More wrote his book on the Four Last Things, he gave
the same subject to Margaret to treat, and when she had completed her
task, he affirmed most solemnly that the treatise of his daughter was in
no way inferior to his own."[6] Since this assertion is our only witness, it is
impossible to verify the competition with Margaret. Regardless of the
authenticity of the anecdote, however, *The Last Things* does bear the
mark of a *declamatio*, putting its case by means of such oratorical devices

---

[1]*The Life of Syr Thomas More*, pp. 25 and 96.

[2]See Chambers, p. 43; E. E. Reynolds, *The Field Is Won* (Milwaukee, 1968), p. 175; and
Richard Marius, *Thomas More: A Biography* (New York, 1984), p. 293.

[3]For More's knighthood and appointment to the Exchequer, see Roper, pp. 11–12;
Harpsfield, p. 24; and Reynolds, pp. 145–51.

[4]More's enforced resignation from the Exchequer and appointment to the Duchy of
Lancaster are described by Guy, pp. 26–29.

[5]Alistair Fox regards the *contemptus mundi* of the work as the result of More's violent
reaction against his experience of political intrigue and comments: "one senses that
The Four Last Things may have been written out of remorse as a penitential exercise to
concoct a 'tryacle' capable of restoring him in his own mind to spiritual health"; see Fox,
pp. 103–4.

[6]Stapleton, p. 113.

as proving the unlikely, anticipating and overturning the objections of an implied audience, and appealing to authority.[1]

The Medieval Tradition

Fragmentary and unpolished as it is, *The Last Things* has long been regarded as marking a turning point in More's literary career from the humanistic interests of the early years (1500–1520) to the polemical and theological concerns of his later life (1520–1535).[2] The treatise does indeed measure the complex polyvalence of More's thought and registers a significant shift in tone from a work like *Utopia*. Yet *The Last Things* should not be seen merely as the first hint of a coming defensive, conservative posture. More's work belongs to but also recreates a tradition of devotional writing on the four last things—death, judgment, hell, and heaven—as objects of meditation conducive to the avoidance of sin. Although a certain *contemptus mundi* and such "gothic" elements as the *danse macabre*, the art of dying, and the seven deadly sins figure importantly in the treatise,[3] *The Last Things* is nevertheless humane and individual, a product of its sixteenth-century context. No one source determines the shape of the work; rather, a number of traditions are woven together to create what would have been, had More completed his project, a massive and impressive piece of devotional prose.

Two scriptural texts—Ecclesiasticus 7:40 and Deuteronomy 32:29—form the basis of the doctrine and literary tradition of the last things.[4] However, only the first of these texts concerns us, because it is the one that More, like many before him, chose as the *incipit* for his treatise: "In omnibus operibus tuis memorare novissima tua et in aeternum non peccabis." This injunction did not remain buried in scripture until the

---

[1]See pp. ciii–cv, below.

[2]See, for example, Louis A. Schuster in *CW* 8, 1145–46: "The unfinished *Quattuor Novissima* . . . stands at the end of one era and at the beginning of another. [It] is the peripety of More's literary career. It is the hinge on which the More canon swings from an outgoing attitude of affirmation and inclusiveness to one of negation and defense."

[3]See the discussion of these features by H. W. Donner, "St. Thomas More's Treatise on the Four Last Things and the Gothicism of the Transalpine Renaissance," in *Essential Articles for the Study of Thomas More*, ed. Richard S. Sylvester and Germain P. Marc'hadour (Hamden, Conn., 1977), pp. 343–55; cited hereafter as "*Essential Articles*." Cf. pp. c–ciii, below.

[4]For the scriptural sources of the theme, see *Dictionnaire de spiritualité*, ed. Marcel Viller et al., 17 vols. (Paris, 1932–1995), 5, 355–58. The literary tradition, with a short section on More's contribution to it, is outlined by Gunther Ott, *Die "Vier letzten Dinge" in der Lyrik des Andreas Gryphius* (Frankfurt am Main, 1985), pp. 47–118. Ott also discusses iconographic treatments of the theme on pp. 17–46.

late Middle Ages. Indeed, the church fathers often mention the value of meditation on the *novissima*. Tertullian, for one, recommends keeping the image of death continually in mind, while Augustine specifically and repeatedly identifies this exercise as a powerful tool against sin.[1]

These patristic comments are neither systematic nor thematically dominant, and they contain no definite doctrine of a series of four last things worthy of spiritual reflection. Before the eleventh century, extended treatments of the last things are scarce; one of the most notable is John Climacus' *Scala paradisi*, in which the sixth step concerns *memoria mortis* as a spiritual exercise.[2] Among the first writers to offer a clearly formulated treatment of the *novissima* as a series of four related topics is Peter Damien (1007–1072), a Benedictine monk and cardinal bishop of Ostia. Three chapters of his *Institutio monialis* deal with the efficacy of meditation on death and judgment as a shield (*clypeus*) against temptation; and a short work, *De novissimis et Antichristo*, further develops this theme with a strongly eschatological note.[3] Of greater interest here, however, is a set of four hymns by the same author, one for each of the last things, which in many ways anticipates the scope of later prose treatises on the subject.[4]

Since Peter Damien was a central figure in the pre-Gregorian reforms of the eleventh century,[5] it is not surprising to find that concern with amendment of life and the penitential value of meditation on the last things (themes which became increasingly important as the tradition developed) are vigorously enunciated in the hymns. Thus, the hymn on death presents the dying man tormented by his unrepented sins as an implicit warning to the reader, who still has time to repent:

---

[1]For Tertullian, see *Liber de anima* 43, in *Patrologiae Cursus Completus: Series Latina*, ed. J.-P. Migne, 221 vols. (Paris, 1884–1903; cited hereafter as *PL*), 2, 724b. For Augustine, see *Sermones* 220 and 257 (*PL 39*, 2153 and 2221), *De civitate Dei* 1.11 (*PL 41*, 25–26), and *In Joannis evangelium* 49.2 (*PL 35*, 1747).

[2]See *Patrologiae Cursus Completus: Series Graeca*, ed. J.-P. Migne, 161 vols. (Paris, 1857–66; cited hereafter as *PG*), 88, 794–99.

[3]*PL 145*, 737–41 and 837–42.

[4]*PL 145*, 977–83. I am grateful to Clarence H. Miller for bringing these hymns to my attention. For a more modern edition of the hymns and some commentary on their authenticity, see Guido Maria Drèves, ed., *Latinische Hymnendichter des Mittelalters* (Leipzig, 1905), pp. 62–67.

[5]See John Joseph Ryan, *Saint Peter Damiani and His Canonical Sources*, Pontifical Institute of Medieval Studies, Studies and Texts, no. 2 (Toronto, 1956). For general studies of Peter Damien's life and work, see Jean Leclercq, *Saint Pierre Damien: Ermite et homme d'église*, Uomini e Dottrine, no. 8 (Rome, 1960); and Vincenzo Poletti, *Pier Damiani e el secolo decimoprimo* (Faenza, 1972).

Praesto sunt et cogitatus,
  verba, cursus, opera,
Et prae oculis nolentis
  glomerantur omnia,
Illuc tendat, huc se vertat,
  coram videt posita.

Torquet ipsa reum suum
  mordax conscientia,
Plorat acta corrigendi
  defluxisse tempora,
Plena luctu caret fructu
  sera paenitentia.

Perhaps an even more authoritative formulation of the doctrine of the *novissima* occurs in the twelfth century in Peter Lombard's *Sententiae*, a vast synthesis of patristic thought and teaching which became the standard theological textbook in the Middle Ages.[1] The fourth book of the *Sententiae* concludes with a thorough discussion of eschatology, including such topics as the resurrection of the dead on the day of judgment (*De resurrectione et judicii conditione*), the fate of the soul after death (*De diversis animarum receptaculis post mortem*), and whether the condemned will continue to sin in hell (*Si mali in inferno peccabunt*).[2]

Although his analysis undoubtedly influenced the range of future discussion, Peter Lombard does not treat the *novissima* in either the sequence or the spirit that characterizes later works on the subject. In keeping with his eschatological concern, he does not address the *novissima* in relation to man's life and salvation before the last day; in effect, he has already discussed this topic in the first part of book IV, which is taken up with his treatment of the sacraments. As Denys the Carthusian, a fifteenth-century commentator on the *Sententiae* (who also wrote a treatise on the four last things), explains the relationship between the two parts of Lombard's work:

> Hucusque ab exordio hujus quarti libri tractavit Magister de ecclesiasticis sacramentis, quibus homines purgantur ac sanctificantur in vita praesenti. In sequentibus autem octo distinctionibus determinat de pertinentibus ad finem hujus mundi inferioris, de ultima omnium hominum resurrectione, de metuendissimo Dei judicio

---

[1] For the background to and importance of the *Sententiae* in medieval theology, see J. de Ghellinck, *Le mouvement théologique du douzième siècle* (Bruges, 1948), pp. 213–77.
[2] Distinctions 43–50 of *Sententiae* IV, *PL 192*, 943–62.

generali, de retributione extrema, et variis rebus ad ista spectan-
tibus.[1]

The use of the term *judicium generale* suggests the difference between
Lombard's scholastic, theoretical analysis and the moral, practical char-
acter of later treatises. Although fourteenth- and fifteenth-century
writers on the *novissima* relied on the doctrinal underpinnings of the
Sententiae, they emphasized the moral life of the individual and thus
interpreted the last things as much within the framework of the partic-
ular judgment of each soul at death as within the eschatological frame-
work of the general judgment of all souls at the last day.[2] The purpose
of later writers was practical and didactic, with the result that they
detached Lombard's doctrine of the *novissima* from its eschatological
context, creating the genre of the moral treatise on the four last things
and establishing the tradition into which More's work falls.[3] Because of
their wide availability in the sixteenth century, two such treatises in
particular deserve close attention: the *Cordiale de quattuor novissimis*, a
work written about 1380–1396; and Denys the Carthusian's *Liber util-
issimus de quattuor hominis novissimis*, written around 1455–1460.

The *Cordiale* has survived in Latin, French, and English versions, in
both manuscript and printed forms.[4] The original Latin treatise was
probably written by Gerard van der Vlyderhoven, a monk of the Ordo
Sanctae Mariae Theutonicorum in Utrecht. A French translation was
made around 1455 and printed by Colard Mansion and William Cax-
ton at Bruges c. 1475. The English version, translated by Earl Rivers
from the French edition of 1476, was printed in 1479 by Caxton and c.
1496 by Wynkyn de Worde.[5] There is no evidence that the *Cordiale* is a

---

[1]*In IV Libros Sententiarum, D. Dionysii Cartusiani Opera Omnia in unum corpus digesta ad
fidem editionum Coloniensum*, 44 vols. (Montreuil-sur-Mer, 1896–1935), 25, 243. The com-
plete commentary occupies vols. 25–28 of this edition.

[2]For the distinction between and the development of church teaching on general and
particular judgment, see *New Catholic Encyclopedia*, 16 vols. (New York, 1967–74), s.v.
"Judgment, divine," 8, 36–40.

[3]Ironically, Peter Lombard's discussion of the last things is itself based on an indepen-
dent work, the *Prognosticon futuri saeculi* (*PL 96*, 462–524), by Julian, seventh-century
bishop of Toledo; for Peter Lombard's dependence on this work, see Ghellinck, *Le
mouvement théologique*, pp. 34 and 239–40.

[4]For the manuscripts, translations, and printed editions of the *Cordiale*, see J. A. Mul-
ders, ed., *The Cordyal by Anthony Woodville, Earl Rivers* (Nijmegen, n.d.), pp. xi–xx. Rivers
figures in More's *Richard III*, where he is sympathetically portrayed as the would-be
protector of Prince Edward and one of Richard's undeserving victims; see *CW 2*, 14/6–
15/30. See also *DNB 62*, 410–13.

[5]*Cordyal*, pp. ix–xxi.

source for More's treatise, but since the English version could conceivably have been available in 1522, it is worth giving some attention to Caxton's English edition. Like More's *Last Things*, the English *Cordyal* begins with a discourse on Eccles. 7:40, although this prologue is far briefer than More's. The organization of the work is likewise less complicated than More's treatise, consisting of four parts, one for each of the *novissima*, with three chapters on relevant topics in each part. The title *Cordyal*, we are told in the prologue, marks out the work's goal for the reader: "to have an assured mynde and an hole Remembraunce of these four last thinges / and that they may cordyally be emprinted with in your hertes."[1]

The heart and the memory are the objects of the writer's appeal throughout as he compiles evidence from scripture, the church fathers, and occasionally Seneca and Aristotle to make his case for the efficacy of this spiritual exercise. Indeed, the *Cordyal* is really a *catena* of scripture passages and citations from various *auctores*, a kind of commonplace book on the amendment of life. Thus, latent in the meaning of "cordyal" is the notion that "an hole Remembraunce of these four last thinges" will act as a restorative (*OED*, s.v. *cordial* sb. 2) to the heart damaged by sin and, by extension, as a stimulus to penance. In this connection, the author offers his interpretation of Eccles. 6:20 ("In opere enim ipsius exiguum laborabis et cito edes de generationibus illius"): "Thou shalt a litle laboure and here in this world is the littlenesse of penaunce. and thou shalt soone ete and drinke the generacion thereof. that is to vnderstande / the fruites of the glorie / whiche be engendered with the labour of penaunce."[2] Penance is, as it turns out, a recurring theme in the work, most obviously in the third chapter of Part One, "Howe Remembraunce of dethe maketh a man to take vppon hym penaunce." The significance of this theme to the plan of the whole work is likewise apparent at the end of the *Cordyal*, where, having completed his encomium of the joys of heaven, the author reiterates the moral and penitential value of the *novissima* as a practical mnemonic device for avoiding sin:

> And whenne ony falle to synne / it is by cause they haue not the saide four thingis cordially enprinted in their myndes. . . . There be to fewe that considre and poise the sayd four last thingis. Many there be that thinke to lyue long and to repente them in their eage / and thereby appeyse the Iuge / and flee the daungier of helle. . . . O what presumptuouse folye is hit to beleue and truste

---

[1] *Cordyal*, p. 6.
[2] *Cordyal*, p. 146.

thereto. That argument concludeth not. but moketh and de-
ceiueth all suche / as haue hope or confidence therin. / Therfore
do penaunce to your saluacion / or ye shal perish and dye in your
sinnes to your dampnacion.[1]

As its title suggests, the *Liber utilissimus de quattuor hominis novissimis,*
by Denys the Carthusian, is similarly designed as a practical manual for
the amendment of life and the avoidance of sin. Sometimes printed
with an appendix containing prayers and litanies to assist those attend-
ing the dying, and including a "Colloquium de particulari iudicio ani-
marum," it is a substantial work of sixty-eight articles on topics pertain-
ing to the *quattuor novissima.* Although (as in the case of the *Cordyal*) we
have no evidence that More had this work in mind as he wrote, the
Carthusian associations of the *Liber utilissimus* make it at least worth
pondering as an analogue to *The Last Things,* since More spent four
years (1499–1503) living "without vowe" at the London Charter-
house.[2]

Denys van Leeuwen (1402/3–1471), called Denys (and sometimes
Dionysius) the Carthusian, entered the Charterhouse of Roermond in
1423 and there produced no less than 187 written works over the next
forty years.[3] These include theological and exegetical writings, as well
as ascetic and mystical ones, from a complete commentary on scripture
(1434–1440, 1452–1457) to an outline of mystical experience, *De con-
templatione* (1434). Although the place of the *Liber utilissimus* among
Denys's works is a relatively minor one, it enjoyed considerable popu-
larity after his death and, despite a period of disfavor during the Inqui-
sition, went through twenty-seven editions before the end of the six-
teenth century.[4]

---

[1]*Cordyal,* pp. 147–48.

[2]Roper, p. 6. For the Charterhouse, see E. Margaret Thompson, *The Carthusian Order
in England* (London, 1930), pp. 167–98.

[3]A modern edition of forty-four volumes has been issued by the Carthusians; see
p. lxvii, n. 1, above. References to Denys's writings are to this edition, cited hereafter as
"Opera omnia." Studies of Denys's life and thought include Martin Beer, *Dionysius' des
Kartäusers Lehre vom Desiderium Naturale des Menschen nach der Gottesschau* (Munich, 1963);
Norbert Maginot, *Der Actus Humanus Moralis unter dem Einfluss des Heilegen Geistes nach
Dionysius Carthusianus* (Munich, 1968); A. Mougel, *Dionysius der Karthäuser. Sein Leben, sein
Wirken, eine Neuausgabe seiner Werke* (Mülheim an der Ruhr, 1898); and Gerardus Ev-
erhardus Maria vos de Wael, *De Mystica Theologia van Dionysius Mysticus in de Werken van
Dionysius Carthusianus* (Utrecht, 1942).

[4]For the ecclesiastical objections to Denys's work, see *Dictionnaire de théologie catholique,*
ed. A. Vacant, E. Mangenot, and E. Amann, 15 vols. (Paris, 1908–50), *4/1,* 445. For its
printing history, see Anselm Stoelin, "Denys the Carthusian," *The Month,* New Series, *26*
(1961), 218–30.

The work is prefaced with an excursus on the text of Deut. 32:28–29 ("Gens absque consilio est et sine prudentia. Utinam saperent et intelligerent, ac novissima providerent"), but, like the *Cordyal* and More's treatise, its controlling scriptural text is Eccles. 7:40, with which the first article, "De connexione et ordine horum quattuor novissimorum," begins. The didactic purpose of the work quickly becomes clear: "In Ecclesiastico scripta sunt verba haec. In quibus admonemur ut novissima ista jugiter ac indelebiliter nostrae imprimamus memoriae, et in cunctis quae agimus, ea pensemus, ne Deum in aliquo offendamus."[1]

As in the *Cordyal*, the image of imprinting the scriptural imperative on the mind is here forcefully presented, and the link between thought and deed is underscored. Denys's primary rhetorical tool for reinforcing this link is an appeal to the reader's sense of fear: article after article, particularly those on death and judgment, emphasizes fear as the dominant emotion which should result from disciplined and serious meditation on the *novissima*, an emotion which has the obvious effect of providing compelling motivation for avoiding sin. The fruits of meditating on death, for example, spring from the sense of dread that it inspires:

> Primus ergo effectus ex consideratione mortis proveniens, est ipsam mortem timere. . . . Porro timor sollicitudinem ac diligentiam parit. Timor namque reddit hominem solicitum ac diligentem ad cavendum mala quae metuit, seu propter quae aliquid timet. Idcirco secundus effectus ex meditatione mortis consurgens, est sollicite ac diligenter mortem, hoc est mortem imparatam, cavere: quod nihil aliud est nisi de culpis praeteritis poenitere et a futuris vitiis abstinere. . . . Tertius . . . est consideratio et humiliatio propriae fragilitatis et mortalitatis. . . . Quartus . . . est depositio terrenarum curarum, turbationum et inquietudinum saeculi hujus. . . . Quintus . . . est totius inordinatae affectionis ad creaturas abjectio, et fervens integerque conatus placendi Deo. . . . Sextus . . . est consolatio et gaudium in Spiritu Sancto.[2]

Moral vigilance, penitence, awareness of one's mortality, abandonment of worldly inclinations, desire to please God, the comfort and joy of the Holy Spirit: all these are the result of *meditatio mortis* and the fear it evokes. Notably, the list achieves a kind of crescendo, moving from the negative to the positive effects of the spiritual exercise, and antici-

---

[1] *Opera omnia 41*, 495.
[2] *Opera omnia 41*, 501–2.

pating the movement of the entire work. Thus, after insisting relent-
lessly on the terrors of death, judgment, and hell for fifty-five articles,
Denys bursts into visionary eloquence on the joys of heaven:

> Possessio Beatorum paradisus vocatur, quorum tabernacula ex lu-
> mine sunt constructa, quorum vita Deus est, et conversatio immor-
> talis exsistit; in quorum capitibus sunt coronae ex auro purissimo
> ac variis gemmis; quorum imperator et rex est Deus deorum, cujus
> ministri sunt angeli lucis; et senatus Regis illius praeclarus est,
> cujus media pars sunt Prophetae, alia vero Apostoli. Porro nomen
> civitatis, Christopolis.[1]

In its emphasis on fear as the path to righteousness, the *Liber util-
issimus* is typical of its genre: works on the *novissima* do not seek to
propound Stoic acceptance of death as the inevitable end of human
experience on earth; rather, they attempt to instill in the reader, the
potential meditator and erstwhile sinner, an absolute fear of death,
which will issue, paradoxically, in beatific vision, not only in the course
of meditation and throughout his life, but also at the last day.

Thus the monitory note echoed throughout the *novissima* literature
is crucial to the objective of the spiritual exercise, and it does not
disappear as the genre approaches the sixteenth century. Although
Erasmus' short "Epigramma de quattuor novissimis" (c. 1489) displays
the theme in the less widely used form of poetry, it urges meditation on
the last things in the familiar warning tone of the treatises:

> Mortis amara dies, metuendi iudicis ira,
>   Et Phlegetontei stridula flamma lacus,
> Denique Iherusalem luctus ignara supernae
>   Gaudia, non finem, non habitura modum.
> Haec si sollicito semper sub pectore volvas
>   Non capient animum turpia quaeque tuum. . . .
> Ipsa sed et nebula citius fugientia mundi
>   Gaudia tristitiam duxeris esse gravem.[2]

We are, of course, severely handicapped in our effort to assess More's
contribution to this genre by the unfinished state of *The Last Things*.
Nevertheless, we can make several observations about More's method

---

[1]*Opera omnia 41*, 594.

[2]*The Poems of Desiderius Erasmus*, ed. Cornelis Reedijk (Leiden, 1956), pp. 173–74. See
also Erasmus, *Poems*, trans. Clarence H. Miller, ed. Harry Vredeveld, *Collected Works of
Erasmus*, vol. 85 (Toronto, 1993), pp. 272–3.

of handling the theme; and certainly enough of the work is complete to suggest that he adapts significantly what was by the sixteenth century a fixed, perhaps even a wooden format for writing about the *novissima*. Unlike Erasmus, More does not experiment with poetic expression of the theme. Rather, his foremost departure from the mainstream of the tradition arises from his choice of a more complicated scheme for organizing the topic, a scheme achieved by assimilating the seven deadly sins into the structural pattern of the four last things. Thus, the plan for the completed work was to write a four-part treatise with seven subdivisions showing the way in which each of the last things might assist the reader in avoiding a deadly sin. This was an ambitious project indeed, and it is easy to see why More might have had to abandon it. Not even the first part of the treatise is completed, and we begin to feel More straining at the format he has set himself as he moves into the fourth and fifth subsections, where the treatise ends.

The importance and limitations of this secondary tradition will be discussed more fully below,[1] but it is worth noting here that for all its structural weakness, there is a certain thematic felicity in the idea of joining the two topoi. The emphasis on the penitential importance of the *novissima* that runs throughout the medieval treatises follows naturally from the admonition of Eccles. 7:40, but it is developed only in general terms. More gives this emphasis further rhetorical amplification by illustrating the urgency of meditation on the last things as it applies to particular forms of sin. In the following passage, for example, the failure to contemplate death (the only one of the *novissima* that More addresses) is vividly indicted through this portrait of a miser:

> But loke if ye see not some wretches y^t scant can crepe for age, his hed hanging in his bosom, and his body croked, walk pit pat vpon a paire of patens wyth the staffe in the tone hand and the *pater noster* in the tother hande, the tone fote almost in the graue already, and yet neuer the more hast to part with any thynge, nor to restore that he hathe euyl gotten, but as gredy to geat a grote by the begiling of his neybour, as if he had of certaynty seuen score yere to liue. (172/30–173/2)

More's character sketch, with its lifelike, quotidian details, offers a different strategy from that of the *Liber utilissimus*, with its genealogy of fear as the parent of beatific vision. To be sure, More uses the argument from fear (with sensory elaboration) to full effect in *The Last Things;* commentators have frequently noted his "morbid" attention to the

[1]See pp. lxxxv–xci, below.

physical pain of the death throes and his "humorless" appeal to the
"depe conceiued fantasy of deathe in his nature."[1] But alongside such
emotive devices More places arguments based on a more reasoned
approach to the consideration of death. Thus, having urged the reader
to imagine his own literal death, More invites him more rationally,
indeed wittily, to envision the analogical death of daily life:

> What thing is dying? is it ani other thing, than yᵉ passage & going
> out of this present life?
>
> Now tel me than if thou wer going out of an howse whither arte
> thou goynge out onely whan thy fote is on yᵉ vttermost ynch of the
> threshold thy body halfe out of the doore, or els whan thou begin-
> nest to set the firste foote forward to goe out, in what place of the
> house so euer ye stand whan ye buskle forward? I wold say yᵗ ye be
> going out of the house, from the first fote ye set forwarde to go
> forth. . . . Now if one wer comming hither to this towne, he were
> not only comming hither while he wer entring in at yᵉ gate, but al yᵉ
> way also fro whence he came hitherward. Nor in lyke wyse in
> goyng hence fro this town, a man is not onely goyng fro this towne,
> whyle he hath his body in the gate goyng outwarde, but also whyle
> he setteth his fote out of his hostes house to go forwarde. And
> therfore if a man met him by yᵉ way, far yet within the town, and
> asked hym whither he wer going he should truelye answer, yᵗ he
> wer goyng out of yᵉ towne, al wer the towne so long that he had ten
> mile to go ere he came at the gate.   (148/31–149/13)[2]

This commonsense "proof" is more than a restatement of the old saw
that life is a journey toward death; it is infused with a Stoicism accom-
modated to a Christian text and molded by a wry humor that is dis-
tinctly Morean. In an early Latin epigram, "Vita Ipsa Cursus ad Mor-
tem Est," More had already reworked a passage from Seneca's *Epistulae
morales* as a straightforward humanist exercise in the fatalistic Stoic
theme *cotidie morimur*.[3] The witty play on this Stoic idea in *The Last*

---

[1] For these elements, see especially 139/24–30, and cf. the comments of Fox, pp. 101–2.

[2] For More's comparatively rational approach, see also *CW 13*, cii–cxiii, and *CW 14*, 760, 763, and Commentary.

[3] For this theme, see, for example, J. M. Rist, *Stoic Philosophy* (Cambridge, 1969), pp. 127–32; and H. B. Timothy, *The Tenets of Stoicism Assembled and Systemized from the Works of L. Annaeus Seneca* (Amsterdam, 1973), pp. 24, 57–58, 79, and 82–83. A brief but valuable exposition of the Stoic contribution to medieval and Renaissance thinking about death is offered in Arnold Stein, *The House of Death: Messages from the English Renaissance* (Baltimore and London, 1986), chap. 1. For More's Latin epigram, see *CW 3/2*, no. 75; also the Commentary on 148/21–31, below.

Things has quite another objective. For Seneca, the inevitability of death does not curtail man's freedom to choose the moment and manner in which he will die, but only reinforces the reasonableness of pursuing virtue for its own sake. In *The Last Things*, by contrast, the argument that death is inevitable is placed within an overtly Christian context: "our lord hath not endented wᵗ vs of yᵉ time. He hath appointed what we may not passe, but not how sone we shal go, nor where nor in what wise" (150/31–33). Moreover, the treatise sets a divinely ordained premium on virtue, which is pursued not for its own sake but for the sake of a heavenly reward.

Thus, for all his renunciation of secular literature at the beginning of the treatise, More's subtle adaptation of a Stoic idea to his purpose is a deftly artistic touch which somewhat undermines the claim that the treatise is essentially a derivative from its late medieval predecessors.[1] Certainly this level of subtlety is not sustained throughout the treatise, and much of the use of classical material is no more sophisticated than the allusion to Plato, the "best sorte" of philosopher, whose contribution to Western culture is summed up by the contention that the proper concern of philosophy is "the meditacion or exercise of death" (139/7). Nevertheless, the passage is wholly unlike anything we have encountered in medieval works on the *novissima*. Not only has More reorganized the traditional format of these works; he has also tried to discover richer, more artful ways of conveying the injunction set forth in Eccles. 7:40 while retaining the moral and practical thrust of his Christian models.

That *The Last Things* is intended as a practical treatise on Christian living is clear from the outset, when More identifies the value of his scriptural text as its efficacy in the "formyng and framing of mannes maners in vertue, and auoyding of sinne" (128/10–11). Indeed, More's translation of Eccles. 7:40, "Remember . . . thy last thinges, and thou shalte neuer sin in this world" (129/1–3), effectively locates the sweepingly general "in aeternum" of the original in the context of life on earth, a context reiterated in the discussion of how "penaunce and bodily paine" serve to secure joy "not onely in the worlde that is commyng, but also in this present life" (133/14–15).[2]

---

[1] See Nancy Lee Beaty, *The Craft of Dying: The Literary Tradition of the Ars Moriendi in England* (New Haven and London, 1970), p. 55.

[2] See also 177/20–22, where More again insists that his assertion that "vertue bringeth his plesure, and vice is not wᵗout pain" is not to be seen in an exclusively eschatological light: "And yet speake I not of the world to come, but of the life present."

Reflection on the last things thus entails benefits here as well as hereafter, and, taking this declaration a step further, More then pictures the text as a medicine or "receit" for spiritual health, an idea which, as we have seen, is suggested in the *Cordyal*, but which is here developed as a controlling metaphor throughout the treatise.[1] Indeed, More presses the metaphor to its limit in his zeal to show the universality of man's fallen condition:

> Now than I pray thee consider me, y^t all oure bodies be euer in suche case, so tender of themselfe, that excepte we lapped them continually w^t warme clothes, we were not hable to lyue one winter weke. Consider that our bodies haue so sore a sickenes and such a continual consumpcion in themselfe, that the strongest wer not hable to endure and continue .x daies together, wer it not y^t once or twise a day, we be fayne to take medicines inwarde to cloute them vp with al, & kepe them as longe as we can. For what is our meate and drinke, but medicines agaynst hunger and thyrst, that geue vs warnyng of that we daily lese by our inwarde consumpcion? And of that consumpcion shal we dye in conclusion, for al the medicines that we vse, though neuer other sickenes came at vs.   (146/10–22)

Yet this keen (some have said obsessive) awareness of our life as a long disease is coupled with an eye for the telling humble detail that imparts a wry, more humane tone to the treatise than this passage suggests in isolation. Thus, for example, More pleads for greater forbearance toward one another when, despite our common journey toward death, we argue maliciously over "very tryfles, as children shold fall at variaunce for cherystones" (166/5–6). Thus he pokes fun at the covetous man who reckons himself undone for the loss of eight out of ten thousand pounds when "if he had neuer hadde but one, hee woulde haue thoughte hym selfe a greate ryche manne, where now for the losse of eight, twain can do him no plesure" (170/12–15). And thus he debates the relative merits of silence and loquacity, advising that it is better to speak up if you have something worthwhile to say lest you be regarded as absentminded, your very face showing your mind "walking a pilgrimage" (136/6–137/21).

Such details add a new dimension to the practicality of the *novissima* tradition. Unlike the *Cordyal*, which habitually appeals to *auctoritas* for precepts of living, or the *Liber utilissimus*, which strives for an ultimate

---

[1] See notes on 128/18–129/27, below.

visionary experience overcoming the fear of death, judgment, and hell, More's treatise is rooted in ordinary, everyday life. Indeed, this rootedness in the quotidian may suggest yet another reason for More's inability, or disinclination, to finish *The Last Things*. Death is the only one of the *novissima* that is within reach of the reader's experience: "For what christen man is he yᵗ hath wit & discrecion, but he hath heard, and hauing any faith beleueth, these .iiii. last things: of which yᵉ first yᵗ is to say death, we nede no faith to beleue, we know it by dailye proofe & experience" (137/31–34).

More is quick to temper this remark with a reassertion of the value of continual, faithful meditation on death, for "though we dayly se men dye . . . yet our selfe neuer felte it" (138/9–10), and only obedience to the scriptural command to ponder our own death will permit us truly to bring our experience in line with our faith. Nevertheless, the world of *The Last Things* is the all-too-natural one that we know, not the supernatural one in which we believe. It is difficult to see how More could have suppressed this interest in the details of ordinary experience long enough to write about the visionary experience required to remember the other three *novissima*. *The Last Things* remains an experiment, at times a remarkable one, in redirecting its genre along a path it apparently could not take.

Ancillary Traditions

Two traditional themes combine with the four last things in the making of More's treatise: both the seven deadly sins (already discussed as a structural device) and the *ars moriendi* figure importantly in the work's call to godly living. Both traditions are too vast to attempt to survey them comprehensively here. Since More's use of these themes is eclectic, neither tradition provides a work or works which could rightly be called sources in the ordinary sense; rather, conventional material is recombined in ways that are often effective even if still conventional or (as in the case of the seven deadly sins) ultimately unworkable. More leaves neither tradition exactly as he found it, and he enlarges the literary possibilities of each.

The Ars Moriendi

DEATH had already been "tamed" (as one observer puts it) throughout the Middle Ages by customary attitudes and ceremonies surrounding the act of dying itself, but the fifteenth century gave these rituals extraordinarily influential form in the body of literature devoted to the art of dying.[1] For our purposes, the *ars moriendi* may be said to begin with the third part of Jean Gerson's *Opusculum tripartitum,* a work apparently composed around 1408 for consideration at the Council of Constance (1414–1418).[2] Jean Charlier de Gerson (1363–1429), chancellor of the University of Paris, was highly esteemed both during his lifetime and afterward for his efforts toward moderate reform within the church during a period of papal schism.[3] More had great admiration for Gerson's loyal opposition to ecclesiastical corruption, advocacy of improvements in clerical education, and emphasis on personal piety; this admiration is evident in the significant influence of Gerson's work on *A Treatise on the Passion* and *De Tristitia.*[4] Although the *Opusculum* does not seem to have had a similar influence on *The Last Things,* its importance to the development of the *ars moriendi* and the high regard in which More held its author make it worth noting here.

The "three parts" of Gerson's title are an exposition of the decalogue, a guide to hearing confession (which is, coincidentally, a discussion of the seven deadly sins); and *De scientia mortis,* a brief handbook on how to ease the passage of the dying into the next life. According to Gerson's introductory remarks, the *Opusculum* is meant to be read and

---

[1]The taming of death is described by Philippe Ariès in his brief but illuminating *Western Attitudes toward Death: From the Middle Ages to the Present,* trans. Patricia M. Ranum (Baltimore, 1974), pp. 1–26; see also Ariès' longer study, *The Hour of Our Death* (New York, 1981), pp. 5–296. For the history and development of the *ars moriendi,* see Sr. Mary Catherine O'Connor, *The Art of Dying Well: The Development of the Ars Moriendi* (New York, 1942); and Alberto Tenenti, *Il senso della morte e l'amore della vita nel rinascimento* (Turin, 1957), esp. pp. 80–138. Sociohistorical reasons for the appearance of the *ars moriendi* in the fifteenth century are suggested in Johan Huizinga's classic, *The Waning of the Middle Ages* (1924; reprint, London, 1976), pp. 124–59.

[2]For the date and circumstances of Gerson's composition of the *Opusculum,* see O'Connor, pp. 50–52.

[3]Gerson's life, university career, and efforts toward church reform have been studied by John Connally, *John Gerson, Reformer and Mystic* (Louvain, 1928); Christoph Burger, *Aedificatio, Fructus, Utilitas; Johannes Gerson als Professor der Theologie und Kanzler der Universität Paris* (Tübingen, 1986); John B. Morrall, *Gerson and the Great Schism* (Manchester, 1960); and Louis B. Pascoe, *Jean Gerson: Principles of Church Reform* (Leiden, 1973).

[4]More's reliance on Gerson's *Monotessaron* for *A Treatise on the Passion* is discussed by Garry Haupt in *CW 13,* xliv–xlviii. Numerous examples of the influence of Gerson's *De oratione et eius valore, De probatione spirituum,* and *Monotessaron* could be cited from *De Tristitia;* see esp. *CW 14,* 313–19, 789–91, 897–99, and 1033–35. More's admiration for Gerson is explicit in both works; see, for example, the passage in *A Treatise on the Passion* in which he invokes "that worshipful father maister Iohn Gerson" (*CW 13,* 50/8–9) and the reference in *De Tristitia* to Gerson as "vir eruditionis" (*CW 14,* 315/5), as he borrows a point from the latter's *De oratione.* See also *CW 7,* lxcvi, and *CW 12,* 98, 133, 153.

used both by clergy and by laity who may have been insufficiently
instructed in the faith, particularly the young and those who care for
the poor and the sick,[1] a slant which imparts a straightforwardly ped-
agogical drift to the work. The third part of the *Opusculum* bears out
this practical educational design, providing a sort of "layman's ritual"[2]
to be used at the deathbed of a friend or dependent:

> Si veraces fidelesque amici cuiuspiam aegroti curam diligentius
> agant pro ipsius vita corporali, fragili & defectibili conservanda;
> exigunt a nobis multo fortius Deus & Charitas pro salute sua spiri-
> tuali solicitudinem gerere specialem: in hac enim extrema mortis
> necessitate fidelis probatur amicus.[3]

Since true friendship is shown by caring for the soul as well as the
body, Gerson divides the work into four sections in which he envisions
the deathbed attendant exhorting the dying man to accept the inev-
itability of death ("Exhortationes"), asking him questions concerning
the state of his soul ("Interrogationes"), leading him in prayer ("Ora-
tiones"), and, finally, determining his preparedness to receive the last
rites ("Observationes"). Accordingly, *De scientia mortis* is really a kind of
formulary work written almost exclusively from the standpoint of the
deathbed attendant, rather than a devotional work intended for use by
the dying man himself. The urgency of Gerson's purpose—to ensure
that the patient dies well, that is, in the faith of the church—imposes an
urgency on his prose that leaves little room for elaboration of the dying
man's suffering or emotions. In the section titled "Interrogationes,"
for example, the interchange between attendant and patient is reduced
to a catechistic series of questions and answers:

> Vis tu mori & vivere in soliditate Fidei Christianae respectu Dei &
> Domini nostri Jesu Christi, tanquam verus fidelis & obediens sanc-

---

[1]"Salubre duxi sequens Opusculum tripertitum [*sic*], de Praeceptis, de Confessione, de
scientia mortis, brevitate qua potui tradere quatuor praesertim Christianorum generi-
bus profuturum. Primo, Sacerdotibus & Curatis illiteratis atque simplicibus qui Con-
fessiones audire debent. Secundo, indoctis quibuscunque personis saecularibus aut
Religiosis, quae Ecclesiae solitis Sermonibus aut Praedicationibus pro divinorum Prae-
ceptorum notitia interesse non possunt. Tertio, pueris & juvenibus qui a rudimentis
infantiae circa Fidei nostrae generalem tenorem & principalia puncta primitus debent
erudiri. Quarto, personis domos Dei vel Hospitalia loca frequentibus & infirmorum
solicitudinem gerentibus"; see *Joannis Gersonii opera omnia novo ordine digesta*, ed. M. L.
Ellies du Pin, 5 vols. (Antwerp, 1706), *1*, col. 427.

[2]The term is O'Connor's; see *The Art of Dying Well*, p. 23. Gerson's concern for the
spiritual development of the laity is discussed by Pascoe, *Jean Gerson*, pp. 165–74.

[3]*De scientia mortis*, col. 447.

tae Matris Ecclesiae filius? Respondeat, Volo. Petis a Deo veniam peccatorum tuorum commissorum & omissorum, quae contra ejusdem amorem, majestatem atque bonitatem fecisti, nec eum prout debebas honorasti? Respondeat, Peto.[1]

Despite this emphasis on the doctrinal rather than the devotional needs of the dying, it was nevertheless *De scientia mortis,* apparently approved by the Council of Constance, that inspired the devotional *Tractatus sive speculum artis bene moriendi,* the real fountainhead of the tradition.[2] This work by an anonymous author, perhaps written at the behest of the Council itself, was promptly copied, translated into several vernacular languages, and eventually printed in both Latin and vernacular forms.[3] The English version, *The Boke of the craft of dying,* may conveniently be studied as an exemplar of the tradition upon which More has drawn in *The Last Things.*

The Craft of dying was translated from the *Tractatus* in the early part of the fifteenth century.[4] Though longer than *De scientia mortis,* it is still a short work, consisting of six chapters generally following the progression from exhortation to final ministration recommended by Gerson as acts to be performed on behalf of those near death. In the *Craft,* however, the presentation of these rituals allows for a significant shift of viewpoint from the deathbed attendant to the dying man himself,[5] a shift that directs more attention to what might be called the psychology

---

[1]*De scientia mortis,* col. 448. Connally has with justification called the *Opusculum* "the first catechism of Christian doctrine"; see *John Gerson,* p. ix.

[2]For the actions of Constance regarding Gerson's *Opusculum* and for the relationship of the latter to the *Tractatus,* see O'Connor, *The Art of Dying Well,* pp. 50–55. Gerson's role at Constance is discussed (without reference to the *Opusculum*) by Connally, pp. 168–89.

[3]O'Connor gives an exhaustive list of both manuscript and printed editions of the *Tractatus* and its translations through the sixteenth century (pp. 61–171). In fact the term *ars moriendi* properly includes both the *Tractatus* and a series of woodcuts entitled *Ars moriendi,* which is based on the *Tractatus* and is accompanied by text describing the deathbed temptations. The woodcuts do not figure in this discussion; for a list of extant editions of it, see O'Connor, pp. 114–33.

[4]The work was attributed to Richard Rolle until found to be spurious by Carl Horstmann, the nineteenth-century editor of Rolle's works; see *Yorkshire Writers: Richard Rolle of Hampole and His Followers* (London and New York, 1896), 2, xxxix–xl. Horstmann printed the *Craft* as a spurious work, speculating that it was a translation of a Latin tract by Rolle. This Latin tract was in fact the *Tractatus* and bears no relation to Rolle; see O'Connor, p. 49. Quotations from the *Craft,* with modernized *eth, thorn,* and *yogh,* are taken from Horstmann's edition and cited by page number in the text.

[5]I owe this and most of the other insights about the *Craft* here articulated to the detailed literary and historical analysis in Nancy Lee Beaty, *The Craft of Dying: The Literary Tradition of the Ars Moriendi in England* (New Haven and London, 1970), pp. 7–53.

of dying. The author of the *Craft* thus accepts the general outlines of *De scientia mortis* while adapting, adding to, and departing from it at crucial points. The first chapter follows Gerson in urging the acceptance of death and asserting the importance of "cunnynge to dye well"; the second chapter departs from Gerson entirely by describing in detail "the temptaciouns of men that dyene" (p. 407). The third chapter returns to the pattern of *De scientia mortis,* providing alternative sets of questions to be put to the dying man concerning the state of his soul; one of these is explicitly drawn from Gerson himself.[1] Yet although this chapter clearly assumes the presence of attendants, it concludes by suggesting that the dying man may find it necessary to examine himself in the absence of competent assistants, a circumstance that Gerson does not entertain: "Who so euer is not askyd of a nother man of thes seven interrogacions when he is in such a perell of deth, for ther be ryght few that haue the kunnynge of this crafte of dyinge, he most remembre hym-selfe in his soule & aske hym-selfe & sotely fele & considre where he be so disposed as it is above seyde or no" (p. 414).

In the fourth chapter the dying man is enjoined to imitate the actions of Christ on the Cross, particularly by praying; and, like Gerson, the author of the *Craft* includes several prayers for the last moments of life. Both *De scientia mortis* and the *Craft* picture the dying man as able to pray for himself, although the *Craft* (rather inconsistently) emphasizes the potential role of attendants at this point: "And if he that is sike can not all this prayers . . . lett som man that is about hym sey hem be-fore hym" (p. 415). The final chapter of the *Craft* picks up this concern by offering nine more "praiers that shullen be seid vpon hem that bene a-dyinge of som man that is abowt him" (p. 418). This reorientation toward those assisting the dying man becomes, in the fifth chapter, an opportunity to widen the scope of the author's address so that the living are urged to prepare themselves for death. The *memento mori* thus sounded anticipates a major argument of *The Last Things:* "But it is gretly to be notid & to be take heed of, that right seld any man, amonge religiouse & deuote men, disposeth hym-selfe to dethe be tymes as he ought, ffor euery man wenneth hym-selfe to leve longe, & trowyth not that he schall dye in short tyme" (p. 416).

More clearly shares with the author of the *Craft* this concern that too many people lead heedless lives, never contemplating the eventuality

---

[1]"All crysten men bothe seculers and religiouse, after the doctour the noble clerk the chaunceller of Parise, in her laste end schuld be examyned, enquered and informed more certeynly & clerely of the state & the hele of hir soules"; Beaty, p. 413.

and significance of their own death. The contention that almost no one "disposeth hymselfe to dethe be tymes as he ought" is similarly put in *The Last Things* (although it is extended to include the other *novissima*) and affords More a platform from which to make the case for a work devoted to the consideration of death and the afterlife:

> For I lytle doubt, but that amonge foure thousande taken out at aduenture, we shal not find fourescore, but they shal boldly affirme it for a thyng to painefull, busilye to remember these fowre last thynges. And yet durst I lay a wageour, that of those foure thousande, ye shall not fynd fourtene, that hath depelye thought on them foure tymes in all theyr dayes.   (130/6–12)

The play on the word *four* underscores the point: no one thinks about death, but everyone ought to; hence, like the *Craft, The Last Things* is addressed not to the deathbed attendant, but to the potential patient, who, by preparing for death before its arrival, may obtain a better remedy for soul-sickness than any doctor could provide (128/28–34). As this orientation toward the patient suggests, *The Last Things,* again like the *Craft,* shows an interest in the psychological state of the dying man, a similarity apparent in More's adaptation of the deathbed temptations (139/30–144/4), although this episode reveals some significant departures from the *ars moriendi* as well.

According to the *Craft,* five temptations typically plague the dying man: unbelief, despair, impatience, complacency (that is, "the plesaunce of a man that he hath in hym-selfe," p. 411), and preoccupation with worldly matters (friends and relations, property and wealth). Description of these temptations, along with scriptural and patristic injunctions against them and comfort in the face of them, makes this the longest chapter in the *Craft,* the heart, as one critic has it, of the work.[1] The advice offered to the dying man who would avoid falling prey to these temptations is conventional and orthodox: salvation depends on adherence to the faith of the church, and the point of knowing the craft of dying is to strengthen that faith in the final moments of life. Comfortable words thus outnumber threats of damnation in the *Craft,* which, unlike the literature on the *novissima,* rarely evokes hellfire and purgatorial pains, seeking to reassure rather than to unsettle its readers. In the following passage, for instance, the author hastens to assuage any guilt caused by the dying man's unconfessed sins:

---

[1] Beaty, p. 5.

> But therfor ther schuld no man dispaire in no wyse; for though
> eny o[r] man or woman had do als many theftis or manslauters or
> as many other synnes as be droppis of water in the see & grauell-
> stones in the stronde, though he neuer had do pennaunce for hem
> afore ne neuer had bene shreuen of hem afore, neither than
> myght haue no tyme for syknesse or lacke of spech or schortnesse
> of tyme to be shreuen of hem, yette schuld he neuer despeire; ffor
> in such a cas verry contricion of herte with-in, and wyll to be
> schreuen if tyme sufficed, is sufficient & acceptable to god for to
> saue hym with euerlastingly.   (P. 409)

More's discussion of the deathbed proceedings is less rigidly sche-
matized than that in the *Craft,* and the temptations he mentions or
describes fall roughly into four categories, not five: complacency, impa-
tience, preoccupation with worldly concerns, and despair. Further-
more, the manner in which he presents these temptations follows no
clearly defined sequence of events corresponding to moments in a life
that is ebbing away. Two temptations, complacency and preoccupied
materialism, are conflated, for example, when More pictures Satan
(who is all but absent from the deathbed proceedings in the *Craft*)[1]
causing us at the last to dwell on our good deeds and on appointments
for an elaborate funeral:

> And if we be so farre gone, that we see we cannot recouer, than he
> casteth in our myndes, presumpcion and securitie of saluacion, as
> a thing well wonne by our owne workes: of whiche if we haue any
> done well, he casteth them into our mindes with ouer great liking
> and thereby withdraweth vs fro ye haste of doyng any more, as a
> thing that eyther nedeth not or may bee done by oure executours.
> And in steede of sorowe for our synnes and care of heauen, he
> putteth vs in minde of prouision for somme honorable burying, so
> many torches, so many tapers, so many black gownes, so many
> mery mourners laughyng vnder black hodes, and a gay hers, w^t the
> delite of goodly and honorable funeralles: in which the folish sicke
> man is sometyme occupied, as though he thought that he shovld
> stand in a window, and see how woorshipfullye he shall bee
> broughte to church.   (143/9–23)

Like both *De scientia mortis* and the *Craft, The Last Things* pictures the
dying person as surrounded by attendants of one sort or another. But
the deathbed entourage plays a different role in *The Last Things* than in

---

[1]For the inconspicuous role of Satan in the *Craft,* see Beaty, pp. 13–16.

either of the other works. In the *Craft,* anxiety ("ouer-much occupacion and besynesse") about one's family and property is presented as a temptation to cling to things that have been "loued inordinately before" (p. 412). In *The Last Things,* however, wives, children, and creditors are shown crowded around the deathbed, troubling the patient quite as much as Satan himself:

> wil it not be . . . a pleasant thing, to see before thine eyen, & heare at thine eare, a rable of fleshly frendes, or rather of flesh flies, skippyng about thy bed & thy sicke body, like rauens aboute thy corps now almost carreyn, cryinge to thee on euery side, what shall I haue what shall I haue? Than shal come thy children & crye for theyr partes. Than shal come thy swete wife, & where in thyne heale happelye shee spake thee not one swete worde in sixe wekes, now shal she call thee swete husband & wepe w^t much woorke and ask the what shal she haue. Than shall thyne executours aske for the kayes . . . and aske where thy money lyeth. And whyle thou lyest in y^t case, their wordes shalbe so tedious, that thou wilt wyshe all that they aske for, vpon a red fyre, so thou mightest lye one halfe howre in rest.   (141/23–142/3)

Not even the Passion offers the dying man any comfort from this relentless assault, although the *Craft* conveys a picture of Christ suffering as the patient himself is suffering, lovingly sacrificing himself for the salvation of the dying man's soul (p. 410). In *The Last Things,* by contrast, Christ's Passion is presented as an admonition to be braced for the painful business of dying: "Now if ye death was so painful and ragious to our sauiore Christ . . . what intollerable torment wil death bee than to vs miserable wretches" (141/1–8). Images of suffering, disease, and pain—though not as pervasive and unmitigated as some critics have suggested—are certainly much more numerous in *The Last Things* than they are in the *Craft.*[1]

---

[1] Beaty suggests that More's "emphasis on the physical loathsomeness of death" leaves him more indebted to the *danse macabre* than to the *ars moriendi* (p. 55, n. 3). As an iconographic and literary motif, however, the *danse macabre* seeks primarily to impress upon its audience the *fact* of death's universality. The *ars moriendi* literature and More use this fact to advocate different ends: holy dying, in the case of the *Craft;* holy living, in the case of *The Last Things.* In this regard, Tenenti's assertion that the macabre is associated with the love of life is perhaps relevant, although More's hapless, half-dead burgher appears only too ready to have done with living; see *Il senso della morte,* pp. 139–65. For More's use of the *danse macabre,* see text at 139/22, 156/8–12, and 160/28–33, and notes on 139/22, and 156/9–12.

The most significant difference between the *Craft* and *The Last Things,* however, is the time frame each work presumes, the period of life (or death) with which each is concerned. The *Craft,* like Gerson's *De scientia mortis,* focuses exclusively on the final moments of life, the passage from life to death.[1] Indeed, a kind of narrative chronology of the events of these final moments can be inferred from the sequence of actions and responses the author describes: the dying person experiences five temptations; he undergoes an examination (administered by himself or by an attendant) to ensure his spiritual preparedness for death; he imitates the actions of Christ on the Cross, especially by praying; he finally slips into unconsciousness as the attendants gathered about him pray for his soul.[2]

The Last Things, on the other hand, has the whole of life as its purview and ranges discursively from topic to topic, inserting the deathbed scene of the *ars moriendi* literature only as support for the argument that death is worth contemplating before its arrival because thinking about it will keep us out of trouble both here and hereafter. Indeed, of the three major themes More borrows from the tradition—the insistence that death should be the object of lifelong contemplation, the portrayal of the deathbed temptations, and the Passion seen in the light of the reader's own death—only the first is used without significant variation from its original context. In the end, More's use of the *ars moriendi* places him at the outer limits of the tradition: humanist versions of the art of dying are better represented by Erasmus' *De praeparatione ad mortem* (1533) and Thomas Lupset's *Waye of Dyenge Well* (1534).[3] For all More's concern to depict "the depe conceiued fantasy

---

[1]Richard Wunderli and Gerald Broce have recently drawn attention to the importance attached to the last moments of life in early modern England, and to the role played by the *ars moriendi* in popularizing the belief that these moments determined one's salvation or damnation; see "The Final Moments before Death in Early Modern England," *Sixteenth Century Journal,* 20 (1989), 259–75.

[2]Although she does not use the term, Beaty's chapter-by-chapter analysis of the *Craft* suggests this narrative element in the work; indeed, following O'Connor, she even assigns the protagonist a name—Moriens.

[3]Compare Tenenti's remark: "L'arte di ben morire infatti non interessava profondamente gli umanisti: essa costitui una di quelle svolte obbligatorie che conducono su una strada nuova e che si affrontano soltanto in vista di esso"; *Il senso della morte,* p. 81. Beaty (pp. 55–56) dismisses both Erasmus' and More's works as "derivative" and "medieval," perhaps as a result of a similar feeling that, without significant alteration, the art of dying is an "unhumanist" topic. (See, in contrast, her discussion of Lupset's work as a "humanistic" *Crafte,* pp. 54–107). For Erasmus' version of the art of dying, see Tenenti, pp. 123–29; and A. van Heck, "Introduction," in *Opera omnia Desiderii Erasmi Roterodami,* ed. J. H. Waszink et al., 11 vols. to date (Amsterdam, 1969–), 5/1, 326–33; cited hereafter as *ASD.*

of deathe in his nature" (139/28–9), the related matter of the nature of sin receives equal emphasis in *The Last Things*.

THE SEVEN DEADLY SINS

CATALOGUES, encyclopedic descriptions, and pageants of the seven deadly sins have been (as Morton W. Bloomfield's survey amply demonstrates) a recurrent feature of Western literature and theology since around 400, when the concept surfaced in the works of John Cassian in a form recognizably like its later, better-known manifestations in the works of Dante, Chaucer, and Gower.[1] More's treatment of the sins is a popular, not a theological, one, but this does not mean that what he has to say on the subject is shallow or hackneyed. Although the descriptions of each sin covered by *The Last Things* are full of commonplace material, they are frequently powerful and incisive, displaying a sophistication that is not always found in writing on the subject.

The order in which More discusses the sins (pride, envy, wrath, covetousness, gluttony, sloth, and, had he finished the treatise, lechery) follows, with some modification, a pattern established in the *Moralia* of Gregory the Great and widely used throughout the Middle Ages and Renaissance.[2] This traditional order, putting pride at the head of the list, is crucial to More, because the notion that pride is the source of all the other sins is a major tenet of his analysis.[3] The idea is scriptural (Eccles. 10:14–15) but also, by the late fifteenth century, proverbial; folklore mingles with biblical and patristic evidence in More's extensive discussion of it in the sections on envy and wrath, as well as in the section on pride itself. The description of the origins of envy, for example, is a constellation of images drawn from a wide variety of sources:

> And litle meruail it is though enuy be an vngracious grafe. For it commeth of an vngracious stocke. It is the first begotten doughter of pryde, gotten in baste & incest, by the deuil father of them bothe. For as soone as the deuil hadde brought out his doughter pryde, w^{t}oute wife of his owne bodye, like as the venemous spider bringeth forth her cobweb, whan this poysoned doughter of his had holpen him out of heuen, at the first sight of Adam and Eue in paradise sette in the way to such worship, ye deuil anon tooke his owne vnhappy doughter to wyfe, & vpon pride begat enuy. (158/28–159/5)

---

[1] See Morton W. Bloomfield, *The Seven Deadly Sins: An Introduction to the History of a Religious Concept* (Ann Arbor, 1952), esp. pp. 43–80.

[2] See notes on 153/1 and 181/31–182/7.

[3] See note on 153/12–14.

More's picture of envy as the offshoot of the "vngracious stocke" of pride is a variation on the medieval commonplace that the deadly sins are like the branches of a tree whose root is pride, while the image of the mother–daughter relationship of pride and envy is ultimately derived from Augustine.[1] Embellishing this genealogical allegory with the incestuous union of Satan and pride, More gives his own version of the more usual tradition (found in Gower's *Mirrour de l'omme* and later in *Paradise Lost*) that the triangle is Satan–Sin–Death.[2] The cluster of images is capped with a reference to the widespread notion that pride was the sin of the fallen angel Satan/Lucifer.[3] As a whole, the passage not only underscores the seminal role of pride in More's analysis but also reveals the highly pictorial nature of his theme; indeed, the seven deadly sins have a long history of iconographic representation, and *The Last Things* makes full use of this characteristic feature.[4]

Although it is less dominant in the succeeding sections, the theme of pride as the root of the other sins continues as a leitmotif in the discussions of covetousness and gluttony. Thus, the covetous are shown to be essentially proud, since in the end their desire for wealth can be traced to a desire for acclaim (170/21–28). Or again, pride is shown to have figured alongside gluttony in the original sin of Eve, "who besyde the proud appetite y^t she had to bee by knoweledge made in maner a goddes, yet toke she such delyte also in ye beholdyng of ye apple, y^t she longed to fele the tast" (174/30–32). Similarly, the relationship of pride to gluttony is demonstrated by the argument that more people "drink themself sow drunk of pride to be called good felowes, than for luste of the drink self" (153/20–21).

Although the idea that pride is the seminal sin is scarcely novel for a sixteenth-century treatise, and although, as we have seen, More presents it by means of traditional imagery, the consistency with which the theme recurs suggests that something more than pious repetition is intended whenever it appears. More's use of the notion might be contrasted, for example, with Chaucer's in "The Parson's Tale," where it is

---

[1] See notes on 154/33–34 and 158/31.

[2] See Bloomfield, p. 194.

[3] Thus Bloomfield, p. 382, n. 16: "It was generally agreed that Lucifer fell because of pride, i.e., insubordination and unwillingness to accept his proper place in the divine order." Hugh of St. Victor, for example, discussing concupiscence of the flesh, concupiscence of the eyes, and the pride of life, identifies the last as follows: "Hoc vitium primum est recedentibus: ultimum redeuntibus. Hoc est proprium diaboli; et ideo magis cavendum" (*Miscellanea, PL 177*, 791). See also note on 159/2.

[4] For the iconography of the seven deadly sins, see Chew, pp. 79–115.

billed with equal fanfare at the outset, only to disappear in the succeed-
ing discussion of the sins and their "remedies."[1] Indeed, these reme-
dies present yet another difference of emphasis, since More, proposing
that meditation on the last things is the best remedy for deadly sin,
omits the customary pairing of each vice with its opposing virtue—
pride with humility, envy with charity, and so forth[2]—with the result
that the sins themselves, their characteristics and the relationships
among them, become the focus of his analysis. The tree of vices is more
than a dead metaphor in *The Last Things* because More is able to make
connections among the sins in such a way as to produce an interesting
and cogent portrait of the sinner.

This interest in defining and understanding the nature of sinful man
is not, of course, original with More; the very identification of seven
sins leading to damnation is an effort to define sin and its effects on
human beings.[3] Aquinas, for one, discusses the deadly sins in terms of
different psychological motivations,[4] and (to cite a precedent from
popular rather than systematic theology) Walter Hilton's *Scala perfec-
tionis* includes several chapters on the deadly sins in which the "ymage
of sin" is carefully examined from the standpoint of its operation on
the human psyche.[5] More knew Hilton's work (his English prose style is
possibly indebted to it),[6] and his use of the seven deadly sins may
usefully be compared with that in the *Scala*.

It is worth noting, first of all, that for Hilton, as for many other
medieval thinkers, the soul is "made . . . to the ymage & the lyknes of
the blessyd trynyte"[7] but has been distorted by sin and so imprinted
with another "derke ymage" (I, 52, sig. g₂). Hilton's theological concep-

---

[1]See *Canterbury Tales*, in *The Works of Geoffrey Chaucer*, ed. Larry D. Benson et al., 3rd ed. (Boston, 1987), X, 387–88.

[2]For this traditional scheme, see Bloomfield, pp. 64–65.

[3]Compare Bloomfield, p. xiv.

[4]See *Summa theologica* I^a–II^{ae}, q. 84. Aquinas regards the deadly sins as final, not efficient, causes of other sins and would therefore have denied the validity of More's contention that pride gives rise to the other six sins.

[5]For Hilton's life and composition of the *Scala perfectionis*, see David Knowles, *The English Mystical Tradition* (New York, 1961), pp. 100–18; Joseph E. Milosh, *The Scale of Perfection and the English Mystical Tradition* (Madison, 1966); and Evelyn Underhill, "Introduction," in her edition of Walter Hilton, *The Scale of Perfection* (London, 1923), pp. v–liv.

[6]See pp. xciii–xciv, below.

[7]*Scala perfectionis*, I, 43, sig. e₄. This and subsequent quotations from Hilton's work are taken from the edition of Wynkyn de Worde printed in London in 1494 (*STC*^{2} 14042).

tion of the "imagery" of sin works itself out in his prose much as More's insistence on the generative nature of pride does in *The Last Things:* in pictures of the deadly sins. Speaking of sin as "a fals mysruled loue vnto thyself" (I, 54, sig. g$_3$), for example, Hilton explains; "Out from this comen al maner of synnes by seuen ryuers" (I, 55, sig. g$_4$); and later on, in his discussion of the distortions imposed by sin on the human soul, he ascribes different parts of the body to each of the sins, with scriptural justification for each correspondence: the head is pride, the heart is envy, the arms are wrath, and so forth (I, 85, sig. K$_3$).[1] Similarly, people who fall into deadly sin are identified with various animals, a feature of the tradition so common that it merits an appendix in Bloomfield's survey:[2]

> The proude man is torned into a lyon for pryde . . . for he wold be drade & worshypped of all men / and that noo man ayenstonde the fulfylling of hys fleshly wyll nother in worde ne in dede / . . . Enuyous & angry men arn formed in to houndes through wrath / and enuye that berkyth ayen her euen crysten and bityth hem by wycked & malicyous wordes . . . / Some men arne forshapen in to asses & arne slowe to the seruyce of god . . . and euyll wylled for to doo ony good dede to her euen crysten / They arn redy ynough for to renne for worldly profyte & for erthly worshypp or for pleisaunce of an erthly man / . . . Some are torned in to swyne for they are soo blynde in wytte & so bestly in manners that they haue noo drede of god: but folowen onnly the lustes & lyknges of her flessh / . . . Some men are torned in to wulfes that lyuen by raueyn as fals couetous men done that thrugh maystry & ouerledynge robben her euen cristen of her wordly goodes / Some men are torned in to foxes as fals men & deceywable men that lyuen in trecherye & gyle.   (II, 14, sig. O$_3$)

This analysis indicates that Hilton, like More, wishes to study in some detail the operation of sin on the mind and behavior of the sinner. His manner (and perhaps his objectives) in doing so, however, is different from More's. For one thing, Hilton's account of the deadly sins is less concentrated than More's, in the sense that, like Chaucer's Parson, he interpolates discussion of an appropriate virtue after each sin. In the case of pride, for instance, six chapters on the sin itself (I, 55–60, sig. g$_2$–g$_4$) are followed by two chapters on heavenly rewards and the vir-

---

[1]For other instances of this concept, see Bloomfield, pp. 221 and 433.
[2]Bloomfield, pp. 245–49.

tues of meekness and charity. Yet another chapter giving advice on discerning how much pride lies within one's soul intervenes before envy and wrath are finally discussed. The interpolation of spiritual guidance after a discussion of each sin was undoubtedly helpful to Hilton's audience, but it also has the effect of obscuring relationships among the sins, relationships that More, by contrast, is determined to emphasize.

Second, although both More and Hilton exploit the iconographic possibilities of the seven deadly sins, the images each one uses reveal the different audience and purposes for which he writes. Hilton, writing for an anchoress, chooses illustrations that will enhance his reader's ability to grow in her contemplative life and "yᵉ wayes whiche by grace leden therto" (I, 93, sig. l₄).[1] His images are more fantastic than mimetic, and he rarely attempts to evoke a lifelike portrait of the sinners he describes.[2] Not surprisingly for a mystical writer, his analogies tend to be drawn from the interior life of the soul rather than from the observable activities of noncontemplative people.[3]

More's audience is not as specifically defined as Hilton's, and his declared intention to frame men's manners in virtue has broader application than Hilton's desire to offer counsel to those called to a cloistered life. His portrayal of the deadly sins is as varied as the worldlings for whom he writes: by turns allegorical and naturalistic, his images are designed now to shock, now to revolt, now to amuse. Less interested than Hilton in the intangible "stirrings" of the soul, More demonstrates his ability to describe with some gusto the tangible manifestations of those stirrings in sinful people. Perhaps the best example of such portraiture in *The Last Things* is the devastating evocation of the glutton, whose sin is linked not only with pride but also with lechery.[4]

More's glutton is portrayed through a series of vignettes that show

---

[1]For the circumstances of Hilton's composition of the *Scala*, see Underhill, Introduction, in *The Scale of Perfection*, pp. x–xiv.

[2]A notable exception is the description of the hypocrite who is found guilty of pride in his own good deeds: "Thys rauyssyng in ghostly pryde is delectable / and therefore he kepeth it holdeth and norysseth it as moche as he may for this loue and vayne delyte he prayeth and waketh, he fasteth and wereth the hayre / and dooth other afflyccyons, and all this greueth hym but lityll / He loueth he thanketh god somtime with his mouthe / and somtyme wryngeth a tere oute of his eye: and thenne he thynketh all saaf ynough / But sothly all this is for loue of hymselfe which he cheseth and receyueth as it were loue and joye in god" (I, 59, sigs. f₂–f₃).

[3]The different methods Hilton and More use to handle the theme of the deadly sins are, of course, related to their stylistic differences; see pp. xciii–xcv, below.

[4]This too is a traditional linkage; see 176/14–15, 176/29–33, and notes.

him "scant able to bere yᵉ burden of his own bely, though it wer taken
fro yᵉ place, & layd vpon hys back" (176/1–2); falling into the gutter
and lying unconscious "tyll he be taken vp and born to bed as a corps
wer born in bere" (177/13–14); suffering a long list of physical ail-
ments from bad breath to apoplexy (179/3–13); "curing" his discom-
fort with "pilles, potions, plasters, glisters, and suppositaries" (179/29–
30); and, at last, unable to eat at all: "the mouth that was wont to powre
in by yᵉ pottell, & cram in the fleshe by the handfulles, shal scant be able
to take in three drips wᵗ a spone, & yet spew it out again" (181/11–14).

For all their vivid delineation and pithy articulation, even these vi-
gnettes might in themselves seem to border on caricature, were it not
for More's ability to combine the diagnostic observation of the doctor
with the passionate condemnation of the preacher. Harking back to the
pain/pleasure paradox which occupies so much of the work's introduc-
tion, for example,[1] he describes the vicious circle in which the glutton is
caught up in terms both analytic and emotive:

> The pleasure that the gloton hathe in his viand, can be no lenger
> any very plesure, than whyle it is ioyned with hunger, that is to say
> with payn. For yᵉ very pleasure of eatyng, is but the minishing of
> his payn in hungryng. Now all that euer is eaten after, in which
> glotony beginneth, is in effecte paine altogether. And than the
> head aketh, & the stomake knaweth, and the next meale is eaten
> wᵗout appetite, with gorge vppon gorge & grif vppon grief, til the
> gorbely be compelled to cast vp al again, and than falle to a rere
> supper.   (178/28–179/2)

In his description of the miser, More likewise muses philosophically
on the fact that avarice is harder to cure than other vices (gluttony and
lechery in particular) because "the couetous man . . . neuer ceaseth to
dote vpon his good" (172/12–13) and thus never feels remorse for his
sin. This desperate clinging to money when (the argument goes) we will
only lose it at death is likened to the incorrigibility of a courtroom
pickpocket, whose case More presents with rueful irony and brilliant
insight into the irrationality and addictiveness of sin: "I remember me
of a thefe once cast at Newgate, that cut a purse at the barre when he
shold be hanged on the morow. And when he was asked why he dyd so,
knowing that he shoold dye so shortelye, the desperate wretche sayd,

---

[1]See 130/13–136/14.

that it didde his heart good, to be lorde of that purse, one nyght yet" (172/18–22).

The considerable success of More's account of the afflictions and disturbances of the sinful raises again the question of why he failed to integrate this account into a completed work on the last things. The reasons for this failure, of course, may be circumstantial; or they may be (as already suggested) the result of the compositional difficulties inherent in the scheme More had imposed on the work. Significantly, at least two other means of organizing the deadly sins were available to him: the one mentioned above of pairing each sin with its opposing virtue, and the technique of grouping the sins according to the catego- ries provided by the "infernal triad" of the flesh (gluttony, sloth, lech- ery), the world (avarice), and the devil (envy, pride).[1] More, as we know, avoids the first of these schemes, emphasizing relationships among the sins, particularly the insidious importance of pride as the source of the other sins; and although he twice refers to the infernal triad,[2] he does not do so in the context of the deadly sins.

Perhaps it should not surprise us, however, that More adopted nei- ther of these traditional patterns: he set out, after all, to write a work on the last things, not on the deadly sins, and his organization of the latter is therefore generated by the former. But would More's problems of closure have been solved even if he had chosen another means of organizing the sins? In the end, his treatment of the sins turns out to be *too* compelling, and the conjugation of death by pride and the other sins begins to cut loose from the structure in which it is embedded and to assume a life of its own. More would later find a successful way to discuss the *novissima* by making the last things themselves a minor theme within *A Dialogue of Comfort*. *The Last Things* is, if not his final, at least his most thorough and incisive statement on the seven deadly sins.

The Style of More's Treatise

ALTHOUGH More's masterpiece is in Latin, the bulk of his prose is in English, and it is therefore surprising that no full-scale work on his English style has yet been written. The English works are frequently mentioned in histories of sixteenth-century literature and their style described in general terms, while individual works have been studied

---

[1]See Patrick Cullen, *The Infernal Triad: The Flesh, the World, and the Devil in Spenser and Milton* (Princeton, 1974), esp. pp. xxv–xxxvi.

[2]See 135/25–26, 138/33–34, and note on 135/25–26.

more closely from a stylistic standpoint.[1] However, the evolution of More's English style awaits detailed analysis. Moreover, critical assessment of the English works has been as various as it has (in some cases) been general, with the camps divided among those who find More's English prose retrogressive in its attempted Latinity, those who see his work as pioneering and central to later developments in sixteenth-century literature, and those who feel that his contribution to English literary prose is uneven. No stylistic account of *The Last Things,* which has come to us in incomplete and probably unrevised form, will settle the matter of More's place in the development of English style. But stylistic analysis should help to flesh out and modify some of the earlier generalizations made about More's English works as a whole.

At the very least, it is significant that *The Last Things* should have an English style at all: as we have seen, the subject of the *novissima* was typically treated in Latin, and its most widely available English exemplar was not really English at all, but a translation from the French version of a Latin original.[2] Indeed, the question of whether or not the vernacular was suitable for theological discourse was still an open one throughout the early Tudor period, and More's own defense of English in a well-known passage from *A Dialogue Concerning Heresies* testifies to the persistence of doubt, well into the sixteenth century, regarding the capabilities of the language as a literary medium.[3]

Furthermore, More's major compositions in English prose before

---

[1]For studies of More's place in the development of English prose, see R. W. Chambers, "The Continuity of English Prose Style," in Harpsfield, esp. pp. cxxi–cxxiv; John A. Gee, *The Life and Works of Thomas Lupset* (New Haven, 1928), pp. 194–97; George P. Krapp, *The Rise of English Literary Prose* (New York, 1915), pp. 100–1; C. S. Lewis, *English Literature in the Sixteenth Century, Excluding Drama* (Oxford, 1954), pp. 165–81; and Janel Mueller, *The Native Tongue and the Word: Developments in English Prose Style, 1380–1580* (Chicago, 1984), pp. 204–25. The most thorough study of More's style considered apart from English literary history is still Joseph Delcourt's *Essai sur la langue de Thomas More d'après ses oeuvres anglaises* (Paris, 1914), of which the last chapter is on style; see also his "Some Aspects of More's English," in *Essential Articles,* pp. 326–42. In addition, see W. A. G. Doyle-Davidson, "The Earlier English Works of Thomas More," *English Studies,* 17 (1935), 49–70, reprinted in *Essential Articles;* P. E. Hallett, "Blessed Thomas More as an English Prose Writer," *Dublin Review, 191* (1932), 117–28; Arthur I. Taft, Introduction, in *The Apologye of Thomas More, Knyght,* EETS OS no. 180 (London, 1930), esp. pp. lii–liii; and *de la Fédération Internationale des Langues et Littératures Modernes,* Bibliothèque de la Faculté de philosophie et lettres de l'Université de Liège, vol. 161 (Paris, 1961), pp. 165–85.

[2]See pp. lxvi–lxxi, above.

[3]The debate over use of the vernacular in theological works is discussed by Elizabeth J. Sweeting, *Early Tudor Criticism, Linguistic and Literary* (Oxford, 1940), p. xv. For More's defense of English, see *CW 6/1,* 337/21–16.

1522, the *Life of Pico* and *The History of Richard III*, were both written in close association with Latin texts: the one was a translation; the other, part of More's singular experiment in writing English and Latin versions of the same narrative.[1] *The Last Things* thus appears to be More's first extended piece of writing conceived solely in English, or at any rate without a Latin counterpart. It is arguable (and many have so argued) that More's English style was never wholly independent of Latin. Still, to write in English on the four last things was an innovation from the standpoint not only of past works in the genre but also of More's own habits of composition.

Stylistically, then, the treatise is heir not to the *novissima* tradition, but to native traditions, which Arthur W. Reed and Raymond W. Chambers identified some time ago as pulpit oratory and devotional prose of the fourteenth and early fifteenth centuries.[2] Reed stated the case concisely: "No one who has read . . . More's *Treatise of the Four Last Things* . . . and is familiar with our earlier prose writers, can fail to observe that More's prose style is like nothing that preceded it so much as the natural, lucid and easy prose of the school of Hilton."[3] To investigate the full extent of this inheritance is more than can be attempted here. Chambers, for example, traces such habits of More's style as his "trick of balanced sentences . . . many of which can be scanned as rough alliterative lines" to antecedents as farflung as the *Ancren Riwle* and the homilies of Aelfric.[4] Nevertheless, some brief remarks about the stylistic affinity of *The Last Things* with earlier devotional and homiletic works are certainly in order.

The ease and lucidity which Reed cites as the chief characteristics More's style shares with the school of Hilton are well displayed in Hilton's own *Scala perfectionis*, a work that More would later recom-

---

[1] For More as a translator from Latin to English, see Campbell and Reed, pp. 189–94. The composition of and relationship between the dual versions of *Richard III* are described by Richard Sylvester in *CW* 2, l–lix.

[2] See Chambers, "The Continuity of English Prose Style," pp. cxxi–cxxiv; and A. W. Reed, Introduction, in *The Works of Walter Hilton*, ed. Dorothy Jones (New York, 1929). Norman Davis has drawn attention to the shortcomings of Chambers' criterion of "a certain tone of self-possession" as a means of identifying stylistic advances and influence; however, he has not discredited the thesis that More's style is indebted to the devotional writers of the fourteenth and fifteenth centuries. See Davis, "Styles in English Prose of the Late Middle and Early Modern Period," in *Langue et Litterature; Actes du VIIIe Congrès de la Fédération Internationale des Langues et Littératures Modernes*, Bibliothèque de la Faculté de philosophie et lettres de l'Université de Liège, vol. 161 (Paris, 1961), pp. 165–85.

[3] "Introduction," in *Works of Hilton*, p. ix.

[4] "The Continuity of English Prose Style," p. cxxiv.

mend to lay and unlearned readers for its ability to "norysshe and encrease deuocyon."[1] The following passage illustrates the stylistic balance and rhythm that might have appealed to a budding English stylist:

> It is noo maystry to wake & faste tyl thyn hede ake ne for to renne to Rome & to Jerusalem vpon thy bare fete / ne for to sterte aboute & preche / as yf thou woldest turne al men by thy prechyng / Ne it is no maystry for to make chyrches and chapels: / for to fede poore men & make hospitals. But it is as maystry a man to loue his euenchrysten in charite / & wysely hate the synne of hym & loue the man.   (I, 65, sig. h₂)

Similarly, in this warning to the unscrupulous reader who has not really uprooted the greed still lurking in his heart, Hilton uses everyday examples which, though untypical of the *Scala* generally, are likely to have attracted More's notice: "Parauenture thou hast not forsaken thy couetyse / but thou hast chaunged it fro grete thynges in to smale / as fro a pownde unto a peny / and fro a syluer pece unto a dysshe of an halfpeny. This is a symple chaunge / thou art no good marchaunt" (I, 71, sig. i₃).

More's style certainly shares (and was perhaps schooled by) Hilton's unlabored syntax, his use of repetition and variation as devices of emphasis, his fine eye for vivid, well-realized illustration. In addition, the technique in the second passage of suddenly addressing the sinner (who may also be the reader) directly, so that the speaker assumes the role of accuser in a kind of imagined confrontation, brings to mind a passage in *The Last Things* which also occurs in the section on covetousness:

> But ye wyll saye that ye haue nowe loste of your worshippe, and shal not be sette by so muche as ye were, when ye were knowen for so riche. A well I say, nowe ye comme home loe. Me thoughte alway that ye couetous niggarde, how lowlye so euer ye loked, would if ye wer well serched, proue your selfe proud and highe harted. For surely make they neuer so meke and humble countenaunce, they haue muche pride in the mind, and putte their truste in theyr goodes, making theyr good their god.   (170/26–33)

In this passage, the second-person address is dropped as abruptly as it was taken up, creating the impression that we are listening to someone speaking, dramatizing his tale as he goes. The same device occurs

---

[1]See *The Confutation of Tyndale's Answer, CW 8,* 37/25–33.

earlier in the section on pride, capping an extended figure of the world as prison (157/24–158/4). Both examples are characterized by their caustic tone (a foretaste, perhaps, of the "snarling" that C. S. Lewis found so disagreeable in the polemical works),[1] distinguishing the object of the speaker's address from the more generalized, familiar "thou" elsewhere in the treatise. The lines from Hilton's work seem, by contrast, less full of gesture; certainly the diction and tone are less biting. Indeed, the style of the *Scala perfectionis* is generally higher than that of *The Last Things,* containing none of the earthy illustrations that pepper much of More's work, and maintaining a more evenly modulated tone.[2] Unlike More, Hilton tends to reach for the dehumanized, unemotional example that will make his point, as in this passage where he cautions the reader against demonic "illumynacyons" which can be mistaken for true spiritual insights:

> Sometyme the fyrmament shewyth a lyght fro the sonne / & semyth the sonne & is not / And sometyme shewyth the true sonne truly. The knowynge of that one from the other is this. The feyned sonne shewyth hym not but betwix two black reyny clowdes. Than bycause the sonne is nere there shyneth out fro the clowdes a lyghte as it were a sonne / & is none. But the true sonne shewith him when the frymament [sic] is clere or moche clered fro the black clowdes.   (II, 26, sig. r₃)

With this elegant, intangible celestial analogy we might compare More's discussion of the way in which pleasures of the flesh are so frequently preferred over those of the spirit:

> And truste it well, that in like wyse yf menne would well accustome themselfe in the taste of spyrytual pleasure, and of that sweete felyng that vertuous people haue of the good hope of heauen, they shoulde shortely sette at nought and at length abhorre, the foule delite and filthye lykinge that ryseth of sensuall and fleshly pleasure, whych is neuer so pleasantly spiced with delyte & lyking, but that it bringeth therewyth suche a grudge and grief of conscience, that it maketh the stomak wamble, and fare as it woould vomit.   (130/34–131/8)

The human and the palpable are intertwined with the impersonal and the abstract in More's lexicon: the association of "taste" with "spirytual

---

[1] See *English Literature in the Sixteenth Century,* p. 175.
[2] For a comparison of More and Hilton, see Garry E. Haupt in *CW 13,* xciii–xciv.

pleasure" and of "conscience" with "stomach" and "vomit" is typical of
The Last Things. Throughout, More's tone is at once admonitory, mor-
alistic, and familiar, his diction by turns exalted and salty; the speaker
of the treatise is at once spiritual guide and worldly-wise counselor
whose advice is based on observation of the humbler, even the seamier,
sides of life. Toward the middle of the treatise, the speaker points up
these variations of stylistic level by offering alternative categories of
illustration to show that "a man is alwaye dying from afore his birth"
(149/23–24). If the reader cannot accept this proposition argued ab-
stractly, he may do so if it is put to him in more homespun terms:

> Now if thou think this reson but a sophisticall sotiltie, & thinkest
> while thou art a yong man, thou maist for al this, think thy death far
> of, that is to wit as far as thou hast by likelihode of nature many yeres
> to liue, than wil I put thee an homely example, not very pleasant,
> but natheles very true, and very fit for the matter. (149/35–
> 150/4)

The "homely examples" of *The Last Things* are its hallmark, and
More's style is best in this work when it is lowest. In this vein, for
instance, he provides a wonderfully vivid picture of the "foule delite
and filthye lykinge" that result from drunkenness in what is surely one
of the most stylistically striking sentences in the whole treatise: "What
good can the great gloton do w^t his bely standing a strote, like a taber, &
his noll toty with drink, but balk vp his brewes in ye middes of his
matters, or lye down and slepe like a swine" (176/19–22). More's salty,
indeed scurrilous, language (he goes on in this passage to allude to an
obscene riddle showing that "slouth and lechery be the verye doughters
of glotony") mixed with the more dignified idiom we expect of a devo-
tional treatise sets *The Last Things* fundamentally apart from Hilton's
Scala perfectionis, however stylistically similar the works may be in other
respects. Perhaps the diction and street-life illustrations of More's work
violate decorum. If so, they also serve the purpose of portraying with
feeling and precision the various forms of human vice that are the
treatise's principal target.[1]

Diction is not the only means by which More creates his portraits of
human weakness. In the following passage, the additive technique of
piling clause on clause has the effect of mimicking the vertiginous

---

[1]Compare *The Apology*, where More quotes Horace to defend himself against the
charge that he introduces too many anecdotes into serious matters: "A man maye some-
tyme saye full soth in game" (*CW* 9, 170/31–36).

tedium felt by the dying man from whose perspective the scene is described:

> Thinke ye not now that it wilbe a gentle pleasure, whan we lye dying, al our body in pain, al our mind in trouble, our soul in sorow, our hearte al in drede, while our life walketh awaiward, while our death draweth toward, while yᵉ deuil is busy about vs, while we lack stomak & strength to beare any one of so manifold heynous troubles, wil it not be as I was about to say, a pleasant thing, to see before thine eyen, & heare at thine eare, a rable of fleshly frendes, or rather of flesh flies, skippyng about thy bed & thy sicke body, like rauens aboute thy corps now almost carreyn, cryinge to thee on euery side, what shall I haue, what shall I haue? (141/18–28)

The drama of the deathbed proceedings here imagined also hints at More's well-known gifts as a raconteur, and such naturalistic vignettes flavor the treatise here and there, contributing to the speaker's familiar tone. Some outstanding examples of this trait include the story of the "great Duke" hanged for treason (160/33–161/12), the incident of the Newgate pickpocket (172/18–22), and the portrayal of the old miser "as gredy to geat a grote by the begiling of his neybour, as if he had of certaynty seuen score yere to liue" (172/35–173/2). Portraits like these, along with occasional "moral essays" on topics of tangential importance to the argument, impart a conversational digressiveness to the style of *The Last Things* to which the author himself draws attention.[1] Thus, for example, More concludes an extended aside on the dangers of idle minds by declaring, "But now to retourne to my purpose" (137/22), and he apologizes for interjecting "a certayn fable of Esop" (159/18–160/6) into his discussion of envy.

More himself may be deliberate and self-conscious about appearing to stray from his topic, but it is digressiveness on the level of the individual sentence that has subjected his style to the disapproval of twentieth-century critics. The tendency of his prose to sprawl—as it does, for instance, in the passage describing the death throes (141/16–23)—so that the semantic nucleus is delayed or buried among subordinate clauses may leave the reader with the impression that the author is not

---

[1] For More's discursive habits of composition, particularly in *The Confutation of Tyndale's Answer*, see Louis L. Martz, "More as Author: The Virtues of Digression," *Moreana, 16* (1979), 105–19.

in command of his discourse; indeed, More also seems to be aware of this difficulty when he recapitulates his argument ("wil it not be as I was about to say") midway through the sentence.[1] The shift from the first person plural ("whan we lye dying") to the second person singular ("to see before thine eyen") further suggests a lack of syntactic control. It is true (as some critics have observed) that More's syntax is sometimes awkwardly handled in an apparent attempt to adapt Latin constructions to the English sentence.[2] An even more pronounced example of the sort of Latinate sprawl deplored by these critics occurs in the paragraph following the passage just quoted, where the description of satanic traps for mankind holds a few pitfalls for the reader:

> For sith that of his pestilente enuy conceiued fro the beginning of mans creacion, by which he lay in awayte to take our first mother Eue in a trayne, & therby drawing our former father Adam into the breache of gods beheste, founde the meanes not without the grieuous encrease of his owne damnacion, to depriue vs of paradise, & bereue vs our immortalitie, making vs into subieccion, not onely of temporal death but also of his eternal tormentry, wer we not by the great bounty of god and Christes painful passion, restored to the possibilitie of euerlasting life, he neuer ceased since, to run about like a ramping lion, lokyng whom he mought deuoure, it can be no dout, but he most busily trauaileth in that behalf, at the time y^t he parceiueth vs aboute to depart hence. (142/8–20)

More's Latinate suspensions are said to be failed attempts to create a learned, authoritative (perhaps even authoritarian) prose style.[3] In *The Last Things*, however, they could equally be seen as contributing to the conversational tone into which the work so often falls, conveying the sense of a speaker thinking aloud as he talks, digressing as one idea sparks another in his mind. In this regard, such aberrations as the pronoun shift noted earlier might be characterized as the natural slips

---

[1]Mueller has called this tendency "clausal spread"; see *The Native Tongue and the Word*, pp. 203–4. In her analysis of the polemical works (with which she is exclusively concerned), Mueller contends that More habitually attempts to Latinize English sentence form by "spreading" and suspending the main clause with the ultimate objective of bypassing native stylistic resources associated with heretical works.

[2]See Mueller, pp. 203–4; John A. Gee, *The Life and Works of Thomas Lupset* (New Haven, 1928), pp. 194–97; George P. Krapp, *The Rise of English Literary Prose* (New York, 1915), p. 101; and Taft, *Apologye*, pp. lii–liii, for negative judgments on More's "overly Latinate" English style.

[3]See Mueller, pp. 203–25; and Gee, pp. 194–97.

of a speaker uttering an involved sentence in which he wishes to appear both to share his listeners' frailties and to stand above his audience as moral guide.

If these effects are more accidents of More's uneasy command of the English sentence than results of his artistry, the same cannot be said of his management of another sort of sprawling construction, the list. Lists serve frequently in *The Last Things* to preserve the tension between the moralistic and the familiar aspects of the speaker's persona by overwhelming the reader with evidence for a point and, at the same time, providing a wealth of quotidian detail. Two such lists occur in the section on gluttony:

> If god would neuer punish glotony, yet bringeth it punishment ynoughe, w^t it self: it disfigureth the face, discoloreth the skin, & disfashioneth the body, it maketh the skin tawny, the body fat & fobby, the face drowsy, the nose droppyng, the mouth spetting, the eyen blered, the teth rotten, the breth stinkyng, the hands trimbling, the hed hanging, and the feete totterying, & finally no part left in right course and frame. And beside the daylye dulnes and grief y^t the vnwieldy body feleth, by the stuffing of his paunch so ful, it bringeth in by leysour, the dropsy, the colike, the stone, the strangury, ye gout, the cramp, the paulesy, the pocks, the pestilence, and the apoplexy, disseases and sicknes of such kinde, y^t either shortly destroy vs, or els y^t worse is, kepe vs in such pain and torment, that the lenger we liue the more wretched we be.   (179/3–16)

The recital of symptoms and diseases attendant upon gluttony becomes a kind of stylistic surfeit: the "stuffing of the paunch" is underscored by the stuffing of More's prose with accumulated detail.

Enough has been said about the conversational elements of *The Last Things* to suggest that the work contains its share of what Walter Ong has called "oral residue," vestiges of the spoken word in written composition.[1] Among the marks of More's oral style are his formulaic epithet phrases,[2] usually adjective-noun constructions such as "our ghostly

---

[1]See "Oral Residue in Tudor Prose Style," *PMLA, 80* (1965), 145–54. On the relationship between oral and written composition, see also Ong's *Orality and Literacy: The Technologizing of the Word* (London, 1982); and Eric A. Havelock, *The Literate Revolution and Its Cultural Consequences* (Princeton, 1982), pp. 3–38.

[2]For epithets as a feature of oral style, see Ong, "Oral Residue," p. 152. A habitual mannerism of euphuistic style, the device is not overused in More's prose; see Chambers, p. cxx.

enemy ye deuil" (142/6, 153/4, 155/5), "foule delite" (131/4, 132/13), and the various changes rung on the theme of pleasure in this passage in which the speaker exhorts "euery manne" to labor in penance:

> To thattaining of which mynde, by the putting away of the mali-
> cious pleasures of the deuil, the filthy pleasures of the fleshe, and
> the vain pleasures of the worlde, whiche once excluded, there is
> place made and cleane purged, to receiue the very swete and pure
> pleasure of the spirite, there is not anye one thyng lightly as I haue
> sayd, more accommodate nor more effectuall, than this thing that
> I haue begon with. . . .   (135/24–30)

Indeed, the very genre of the work, as given in the title of the 1557 edition, may have associations with oral expression, since treatises were sometimes regarded by sixteenth-century expositors as a species of homily.[1] While the word *Treatyce* in the title of Rastell's edition may or may not represent the author's own designation, it is clear that *The Last Things* is homiletic in the loosely applied sense of being an exposition of a scriptural text whose aim is both to explain the meaning of that text and to induce its audience to act in accordance with its message.[2] Sermons on the last things, especially death, were common in the six-teenth century; and it is not surprising that certain stylistic features of More's work should suggest a homiletic bent.[3] Some of these, such as the speaker's stance as moral guide and the use of naturalistic exempla in scriptural interpretation, have already been discussed.[4] Other fea-tures of *The Last Things* further demonstrate that pulpit oratory made its mark on More's English style.

The occasional digressions of More's work, which we have seen as contributing to its conversational style, are also characteristic of homi-

---

[1]The interchangeability of the terms *treatise* and *homily* are discussed by Haupt in *CW 13*, li–liv.

[2]For this definition of homily, formulated by Sixtus of Siena (*Bibliotheca sancta*, 1591), see Haupt, *CW 13*, liii–liv.

[3]For sixteenth-century sermons on the last things, see J. W. Blench, *Preaching in En-gland in the Late Fifteenth and Sixteenth Centuries: A Study of English Sermons, 1450–c. 1600* (Oxford, 1964), pp. 229–31, 234–36, and 321–24. An excellent example of medieval preaching on the last things is presented by "The Sermon of Dead Men," the work of an unknown Lollard preacher; see Gloria Cigman, ed., *Lollard Sermons*, EETS NS no. 294 (Oxford, 1989), pp. 207–40.

[4]For the use of naturalistic exempla in medieval preaching, see G. R. Owst, *Literature and Pulpit in Medieval England: A Neglected Chapter in the History of English Letters and of the English People* (Cambridge, 1933; reprint, New York, 1961), pp. 24–47.

letic procedure in the manner recommended by Gregory the Great, whose influence on early writers of English was considerable.[1] In the *Praefatio in Job* Gregory likens scriptural exposition to the meandering of a river and advises the homilist to take advantage of any "fitting instruction" (*congruens aedificatio*) he may find as he proceeds through his text.[2] An example of such serendipitous digression in *The Last Things* is the lengthy discussion of true and false pleasures into which More strays almost immediately after introducing his primary topic (130/13–135/33.) Conscious of the seeming absentmindedness, More defends this excursus on the grounds of moral utility and the great need of his audience: "I wold not so long tary in this point, nor make so many wordes, of the pleasure that men may finde by the receeyte of this medicine, were it not that I wel perceyue, the worlde so sette vppon the sekynge of pleasure, that they sette by pleasure much more than by profite" (133/6–10).

As for the frequently low style of the treatise, this too was sanctioned by the homiletic practice of More's day. J. W. Blench has identified three main styles in sermons of the period 1450–1600: a plain but uncolloquial style that makes sparing use of metaphor, narrative exempla, or fabliaux and only occasionally uses the rhetorical schemata; a colloquial style that uses a "racy and pungent speech idiom," favors "frequent homely exempla," but avoids the schemata; and an ornate style characterized by literary exempla and schemata clearly designed for "oratorical display."[3] The "mixed" style of *The Last Things* makes it a hybrid of the colloquial and ornate sermon styles outlined by Blench, since More uses both homely and (less frequently) literary illustrations and embellishes his colloquial idiom with generous use of rhetorical word patterns. Clearly, however, the lowly and sometimes slightly scurrilous elements of More's style were within the bounds of scriptural exposition as far as sixteenth-century homiletic propriety was concerned.

In this regard, one example of More's mixed style has particular significance because it contains a passage clearly modeled on lines from a sermon included in a late fifteenth-century revision of John Mirk's *Festial*. Extolling the efficacy of "the remembrance of death" for drawing the soul away "fro the wretched affeccions of the body" (139/15), More uses a familiar visual example in the colloquial style and drives

---

[1] See David C. Fowler, *The Bible in Early English Literature* (Seattle, 1976), pp. 40–78.
[2] *Praefatio in Job, PL* 75, 513; quoted by Haupt, *CW 13,* lvi.
[3] *Preaching in England,* p. 113.

home his point with the ornate devices of alliteration and assonance, reinforcing one of the work's characteristic lists:

> But if we not onely here this word death, but also let sink into our heartes, the very fantasye and depe imaginacion therof, we shall parceiue therby, that we wer neuer so gretly moued by the beholding of the daunce of death pictured in Poules, as we shal fele our self stered and altered, by the feling of that imaginacion in our hertes. And no maruell. For those pictures expresse only, ye lothely figure of our dead bony bodies biten away ye flesh. Which though it be ougly to behold, yet neither the sight therof, nor the sight of al ye dead heades in ye charnel house, nor the apparicion of a very ghost, is halfe so grisely as the depe conceiued fantasy of deathe in his nature, by the liuely imaginacyon grauen in thyne owne heart. For there seest thou, not one plain grieuous sight of the bare bones hanging by the sinewes, but thou seest (yf thou fantasye thyne own death, for so art thou by this counsell aduised) thou seeste I saye thy selfe yf thou dye no worse death, yet at the leastwise lying in thy bedde, thy hed shooting, thy backe akyng, thy vaynes beating, thine heart panting, thy throte ratelyng, thy fleshe trembling, thy mouth gaping, thy nose sharping, thy legges coling, thy fingers fimbling, thy breath shorting, all thy strength fainting, thy lyfe vanishing, and thy death drawyng on.   (139/18–140/7)

The oral qualities of this passage are suggested not only by the alliteration and assonance already noted (which gain their full effect only from being heard) but also by the repetitive "but thou seest . . . thou seeste I saye," which accommodates the speaker's parenthetical aside. That these oral/aural features have a specifically homiletic aspect is further suggested by the fact that More seems to have adapted his enumeration of the death throes with only slight variation from the following sermon excerpt:

> that thou maiste well know þat thou art at the pyttes brink: that is to say, whan thi hands quaketh; thi lippes blaketh, thyne hede rokkyth, thy nose droppith, thy shynnes sharpith, thi synewes starkith, thi brest pantith, thy breth wantyth, thy tethe rattlyth, thi throte rotelyth; anon thou thenkkest thyn hert wolde brast for the life may not laste.[1]

---

[1] Quoted by Blench, p. 117.

This echo of a prehumanist sermon raises an issue that has troubled critics of *The Last Things* for some time, the antihumanist stance More appears to adopt throughout. Although certain passages and features of *The Last Things* partake of a homiletic style, the work as a whole is certainly not expository in the sense in which More's later *Treatise on the Passion,* for example, is a homiletic exposition of scripture. The latter work more nearly conforms to humanistic exegesis *secundum ordinem textus,* with an emphasis on the literal/historical facets of the text, while *The Last Things* uses Eccles. 7:40 more or less as a springboard from which to launch a description and denunciation of various kinds of sin.[1] To some extent this springboard approach to exegesis derives from the text itself, since More is here dealing not with narrative (as he is in the case of the Passion), but with a sententious precept requiring moral rather than historical interpretation.[2]

More's interest in this kind of interpretation, combined with the "gothic" elements of the treatise, has, as we have seen, persuaded some commentators that *The Last Things* is somehow "unhumanist," a curiosity shop of medieval topoi and attitudes.[3] Indeed, my own discussion has thus far emphasized the indebtedness of More's style to native, medieval sources. I would not now wish to discount the importance of those sources to the work's general character, but we should also recognize an aspect of its style which is deeply humanistic, yet not at all at odds with its devotional and homiletic bent. There is some evidence to suggest that *The Last Things* incorporates certain rhetorical exercises recommended by humanist pedagogues for the perfection of eloquent composition, and since More's style is shaped by these structural, rhetorical elements, we need to examine them here.

The opening paragraphs of More's work, for example—the very

---

[1] For the *Treatise on the Passion* and humanist exegesis, see Haupt, *CW 13,* lxii–lxxxiii.

[2] These are the first and third of the traditional four senses of scripture understood by medieval exegetes to include literal/historical, allegorical, tropological/moral, and anagogical/eschatological interpretation. More does not address the last of these, although his text seems to demand an eschatological interpretation; see Clarence H. Miller in *CW 14,* 751. For the four senses of scripture in general, see Henri de Lubac, *Exégèse médiévale: Les quatre sens de l'écriture,* 3 vols. (Paris, 1959–64), esp. *1/1,* 23–42 and 119–70. For More's use of the senses in particular, see Germain Marc'hadour, *Thomas More et la Bible* (Paris, 1969), pp. 459–71.

[3] H. W. Donner finds *The Last Things* stylistically "medieval" but tempers this judgment by acknowledging analogues in the visual arts for the "Renaissance Gothic" style of More's imagery; see "St. Thomas More's Treatise on the Four Last Things," in *Essential Articles,* pp. 343–55.

passages in which he belittles "the doctryne of anye secular author" (128/2–3)—bear the mark of both the *chria,* or sentence, in which the student elaborates a well-known maxim, and the thesis, an exercise in which a question (philosophical, ethical, or practical) is debated.[1] In *The Foundation of Rhetoric* (1563), a formulary work that essentially Englishes a widely used Latin version of Aphthonius' *Progymnasmata,* Richard Rainolde advises the student to begin the *chria* by praising the maxim's author and extolling his virtuous life; if, however, the facts of his life are unknown, the maxim itself should furnish the author's commendation: "For godlie preceptes will minister matter of praise, as if these saiynges bee recited, thei are sufficient of them selues, to praise the authour."[2] Although Rainolde's work is not contemporary with More, it is among the first rhetoric books designed specifically to cultivate English style, and in so doing to provide English models for the student to imitate. In any case, something very like the principle just quoted appears to have guided More in his opening encomium of Eccles. 7:40:

> If ther were anye questyon amonge menne, whyther the woordes of holy scripture, or the doctryne of anye secular authour, were of greater force and effecte to the weale and profyte of mannes soule, (thoughe we shold let passe so many short & weighty wordes, spoken by the mouth of oure sauiour Christ himself, to whose heauenly wisedom, the wit of none earthly creature can be comparable) yet this onely text writen by the wise man in the seuenth chapiter of Ecclesiasticus is suche, that it conteineth more fruitfull aduise and counsayle, to the formyng and framing of mannes maners in vertue, and auoyding of sinne, then many whole & great volumes of the best of old philosophers, or anye other that euer wrote in secular litterature.   (128/1–12)

The thesis, a rhetorical form related to the *declamatio* (of which More was an experienced Latin practitioner),[3] provides the orator with a framework for advocating a specific viewpoint or action. The exercise always begins with a question (Is the soul immortal? Is it good to marry?

---

[1] For descriptions of these and other rhetorical exercises used in humanist classrooms, see Karl R. Wallace, "Rhetorical Exercises in Tudor Education," *Quarterly Journal of Speech,* 22 (1936), 28–51.

[2] *The Foundation of Rhetoric* (1563; facsimile ed., Menston, 1972), sig. D₂.

[3] For More's *declamatio* in reply to Lucian's *Tyrannicida,* see *CW* 3/1, xxxii–xxxviii. For the relationship of the declamatio to the thesis, see S. F. Bonner, *Roman Declamation in the Late Republic and Early Empire* (Liverpool, 1949), pp. 2–11.

Do old men or youths make better rulers?) and then proceeds through
the usual parts of the classical oration in defending an answer on one
side or the other. Along the way, as Rainolde has it, the orator may
strengthen his argument by anticipating the objections of his audience.
In defense of the proposition that it is good to marry, for example, a
speaker may wish to pause and address his audience thus: "But you will
saie parauenture, mariage is a greate bondage, alwaies to liue with one"
(sig. O₃). Conceivably, the first sentence of *The Last Things* is a subjunc-
tive modification of the thesis question; certainly the strategy of rhetor-
ical objection appears to be at work a few paragraphs later when More
breaks off a comparison of his scriptural text to a medicine "able to
kepe vs al our life fro sin" (129/6–7) and engages the reader directly:

> How happeth it than thou wilt happely say, that so few be pre-
> serued from sin, if euery man haue so sure a medicine, so ready at
> hand? For folk fare commonly as he doth that goeth forth fasting
> among sick folk for slouth, rather than he wyll take a litle tryacle
> before.
>
> Thou wilt saye paraduenture yᵗ some parte of thys medicine
> is verye bytter and paynfull to receyue. Surely there canne bee
> nothyng so bitter, but wysedome would brooke it for so gret a
> profyte.   (129/12–20)

Indeed, the practice of anticipating the objections of an implied
audience could be called a tic of More's style in *The Last Things,* occur-
ring throughout the treatise to advance the argument.[1] The device is
also a means of supplying *copia* to the composition, since (to use Rain-
olde's phrase) "The aunswere to [an] obiection will minister matter to
declaime vpon" (sig. O₂). Another rhetorical exercise, the retelling and
moral exposition of a fable, serves the same purpose, being essentially
amplification of the fable's didactic content.[2] The device occurs only
once in *The Last Things,* when More recounts Aesop's fable of the en-
vious man and the covetous man (159/17–160/6); but a similar effect is
achieved by the use of such *loci communes* as all the world's a stage
(156/15–22), the prison-house of life (157/11–24), and the dance of
death (156/23–158/13). Stylistically, the last passage serves as evidence
that these topoi are more than medieval bric-a-brac cluttering the trea-

---

[1]See 131/16–17, 135/33–136/1, 137/28–31, 145/29–30, 146/30, 148/20, 149/36–
150/2, 163/31–34, 165/30–31, 167/4–5, 168/15–17, 168/34–169/2, and 170/26–28.
[2]See Wallace, "Rhetorical Exercises in Tudor Education," p. 30. For More's use of
Aesop, see Nancy Cole Yee, "An Analysis of the Prose Style of Thomas More's *Dialogue of
Comfort*" (Ph.D. Dissertation, Boston University, 1975), pp. 413–19.

tise: More gives a skillful rehearsal of the commonplace material in a
series of parallel phrases whose rhythm is deftly varied and punctuated
by strategically placed alliteration. The didactic purpose of the com-
monplace thus elaborated is self-evident:

> There is no remedy therfore, but as condemned folk & remediles,
> in this prison of the yerth we driue forth a while, some bounden to
> a poste, some wandring abrode, some in the dungeon, some in the
> vpper ward, some bylding them bowers & making palaces in the
> prison, some weping, some laughing, some laboring, some play-
> ing, some singing, some chidinge, some fighting, no man almoste
> remembringe in what case he standeth, till that sodeynlye nothyng
> lesse loking for, yong, old, pore & rych, mery & sad, prince, page,
> pope and pore soul priest, now one, now other, some time a gret
> rable at once, w'out order, w'out respect of age or of estate, all
> striped stark naked & shifted out in a shete, bee put to deth in
> diuers wise in some corner of the same prison, & euen ther
> throwen in an hole, & ether wormes eat him vnder ground or
> crowes aboue.   (157/11–24)

The balanced phrases of the first half of this passage measure the
worldings' dance toward death, while the quickened, uneven pace of
the second half disturbs this stately rhythm, seeming (to shift the meta-
phor) to blur our focus and render the constituents of the *danse macabre*
indistinguishable, just as they are equalized by their common fate. The
grim irony of this "true fygure" (158/5) makes a mockery of worldly
values, "as if a gentleman thefe when he should goe to Tyburne, wold
leue for a memoriall, tharmes of his auncesters painted on a post in
Newgate" (158/2–4). It is a commonplace paradox that the powerful
are themselves powerless against death, and More exploits it here to
good effect. Paradox is, in fact, an important feature of *The Last Things*
and deserves mention as a rhetorical element of More's style.

The proof of the unlikely; the defense of the indefensible, the un-
worthy, or the unexpected subject; the encomium of a proposition that
cuts against the grain of received wisdom: these are the stuff of Renais-
sance paradox, of which Erasmus' paradoxical encomium, *The Praise of
Folly*, is surely the apex.[1] An idea of the classical works in the genre on
which the Renaissance versions were modeled is helpfully provided by

---

[1]The characteristics of Renaissance paradox are discussed at length by Rosalie L. Colie,
Paradoxia Epidemica: The Renaissance Tradition of Paradox (Princeton, 1966; reprint, Ham-
den, Conn., 1976), esp. pp. 3–40.

Folly herself when she speaks contemptuously of orators "who have spent sleepless nights burning the midnight oil to work out elaborate encomia of Bursiris, Phalaris, the quartan fever, flies, baldness, and other dangerous nuisances."[1] As Folly's mockery of the form she (paradoxically) revives would suggest, paradox is characterized by self-contradiction, equivocation, and involuted meanings. In *The Last Things*, however, these characteristics are never allowed (as they are in the *Folly*) to obscure or complicate a straightforward moral. More uses paradox at certain points in the argument to evoke apparently self-contradictory assertions and phenomena against which the speaker inveighs or which he presents as truths stranger than fiction. Thus the judgment rendered on the *avarus pauper* is unequivocal, although More's description conveys the paradoxical, self-contradictory delusions under which the covetous labor: "But these couetous folk that set theyr heartes on theyr hordes, and be proude when they loke on their heapes, thei recken themself rich, & be in dede very wreched beggers" (171/18–20). Similarly, when the speaker discusses the nature of gluttony, the value of temperance is not in question, and the paradox resides in gluttony itself:

> The pleasure that the gloton hathe in his viand, can be no lenger any very plesure, than whyle it is ioyned with hunger, that is to say with payn. For y[e] very pleasure of eatyng, is but the minishing of his payn in hungryng. Now all that euer is eaten after, in which glotony beginneth, is in effecte paine altogether.   (178/28–32)

This paradoxical metamorphosis of pleasure into pain harks back to the discussion of true and false pleasures at the beginning of the treatise, and (not surprisingly) paradoxes appear there too. Quoting not only Augustine but also scripture, the speaker proposes that a man "may be and hath cause to be glad because of hys sorowe" (133/25) and that mortification of the flesh has such great benefits to the soul that "it maketh the very labor easy, y[e] sowernes very swete, & the verye payne pleasant" (134/4–5). It is clear from these "sacred" paradoxes that More's use of the figure ties in with the stylistic heterogeneity of *The Last Things*. The near oxymorons ("easy labor," "sweet sourness," "pleasant pain") throw us off balance, just as the association of a griev-

---

[1] "Qui Busirides, Phalarides, febres quartanas, muscas, caluicia, atque id genus pestes accuratis magnaque et olei et somni iactura elucubratis laudibus vexerint"; *Moriae encomium, ASD 4/3*, 74/48–50. The English translation is that of Clarence H. Miller, *The Praise of Folly* (New Haven and London, 1979), p. 12.

ing conscience with the feeling of nausea (131/4–8) joins the spiritual with the physical in a jarring (and rhetorically effective) way. Likewise, a profound philosophical paradox that "we dye al the while we lyue" (148/30–31) is illustrated by some plainspoken calculations regarding the relative distance of the executioner's cart and the place of execution:

> If there wer two both condemned to deth, both caried out at ons toward execucion: of which two yᵉ tone wer sure yᵗ the place of his execucion were wᵗ in one mile, yᵉ tother .xx. mile of, ye an hundred & ye wil, he yᵗ were in the cart to be caried an .C. mile, wold not take much more plesure, than his felow in the length of his waye, notwithstanding yᵗ it were .C. times as long as his felowes, & that he had therby C. times as long to liue, beinge sure and out of al question to dye at the ende.
>
> Recken me now your self a yong man in your best luste .xx. yere of age if ye will. Let there be another .lxxxx. both must ye die, both be ye in yᵉ cart carying forward. His galowes & death standeth within .x. mile at yᵉ farthest, & yours wᵗin .lxxx. I se not why ye should recken muche lesse of your deth then he, though your waye bee lenger, synne ye bee sure ye shall neuer cease riding til ye come at it. (150/5–19)

A young man is not much farther from death than an old one: all paradoxes depend on such surprising or unexpected rhetorical twists, and in commending to his audience what is frequently regarded as the distasteful and even terrifying activity of contemplating death and the afterlife, More certainly follows the general outlines of paradoxy. But unlike the classical paradoxes in praise of baldness or flies, *The Last Things* criticizes the actual, not the official, conventions of human behavior. And unlike the Erasmian praise of folly, the treatise is unequivocal in this condemnation.[1] More's use of paradox rests on the assumption that "hauing our tast infected" (132/21), we mistakenly believe what is bitter to be sweet. The *real* paradox consists in the persistent human choice of pain when,

> If men would vouchesafe to putte in proofe and experience thoperacion and workyng of this medicine, the remembraunce of these foure last thinges, they should fynd therin, not the pleasure

---

[1] Compare Colie, p. 32: "Christian paradoxes are always orthodox, not only in the propriety of their doctrine but also in the fact that they appear to describe accurately feelings deeply rooted in human nature."

of their life loste, but so greate a pleasure grow therby, that they neuer felt ye lyke before, nor would haue supposed that euer they should haue felt any such.   (130/13–18)

On the whole, then, it seems fair to say that *The Last Things* succeeds much better as a stylistic experiment in English composition than it does as a formal treatment of the *novissima* theme. More's attempt to graft the tradition of the seven deadly sins onto that of the four last things may have exhausted his resources by pushing the treatise beyond manageable formal limits, but his style is, for the most part, able and expressive, giving the impression at once of conversational freedom and rhetorical control. If this were More's only work in English, we should still consider him a Latin, not an English, stylist. But nothing in *The Last Things* discredits the judgment of Ben Jonson that More should be counted among the founders of English eloquence.[1]

---

[1]"Cicero is said to bee the only wit, that the people of Rome had equall'd to their empire. Ingenium par imperio. We have had many, and in their severall Ages (to take in but the former seculum) Sir Thomas Moore, the elder Wiat; Henry, Earle of Surrey; Chaloner, Smith, Eliot, B. Gardiner, were for their times admirable: and the more, because they began Eloquence with us"; *Explorata: or Discoveries*, in *Ben Jonson*, ed. C. H. Herford and Percy Simpson, 11 vols. (Oxford, 1925–52), 9, 591.

THE TEXTS

English Poems

PAGEANT VERSES

THE only textual authority for More's Pageant Verses is the *English Works* of 1557 (sigs. 2v–4). The punctuation and capitalization of *1557* have been maintained, except in a few places where they are misleading; in these places I have emended the text and given the punctuation of *1557* in the variants. Rastell's font seems to have run short of uppercase forms of *W* and *Y*. I have silently capitalized lowercase forms of these letters at the beginning of lines.

"RUFULL LAMENTATION"

THERE are three substantive texts of More's "Rufull Lamentation":

   O   MS Balliol 354, fols. 175–76, Balliol College Library, Oxford

   L   MS Sloane 1825 fols. 88v–89v, British Library, London

 1557   William Rastell's edition of the *English Works* (*STC²* 18076), sigs. ¶4–5

O is clearly the earliest of these texts, since it must have been transcribed before 1504/5.[1] The authority of this manuscript is enhanced by the connection between Richard Hill, who copied the manuscript, and the More family. Hill was an apprentice to John Wyngar, grocer and mayor of London. Wyngar bought a house from More's father, John, before 1503; John More also served as an executor of Hill's father's will in 1500.[2] It may be that personal acquaintance with More prompted Hill to copy the poem into his manuscript. The poem is not, however, ascribed to More in *O*.

The other manuscript copy, *L*, was added in a mid-sixteenth-century hand at the end of the fifteenth-century manuscript of Thomas Hoc-

---

[1]For a full description of the contents of MS Balliol 354, see *Songs, Carols and Other Miscellaneous Poems from the Balliol MS. 354*, ed. Roman Dyboski, EETS ES no. 101 (London, 1908), pp. xxxiv–lix.

[2]See Campbell and Reed, *1*, 223–24, from which this information is derived.

cleve's *Regiment of Princes*.[1] Its provenance is unknown, and there are no clues to the identity of the copyist. Like *O*, it does not ascribe the poem to More.

The interrelations of these manuscripts and their relationships to the *1557* edition can be determined to some degree, although it is difficult to express these relationships in precise quantitative terms of agreements and variation because a number of the variants are indeterminate, such as the presence of final *e* of uncertain syllabic value and other spelling variations which offer syllabic additions that may not reflect actual syllabic value. My figures for numbers of variants are intended to be no more than approximations.

L contains about sixty unique variants. Some of them recast lines or groups of lines in a striking and almost certainly erroneous way.[2] The most notable instance occurs at lines 72–73, which in *O* read:

> O lady Cecill Anne and Kateryne,
> Farewell my wellbelouyd systers thre.

and in *1557:*

> Lady Cicyly Anne and Katheryne.
> Farewell my welbeloued sisters three,

but which in *L* become:

> O lady sessele O lady kateryne
> Farewell my lovying susteris bothe

Other variations in *L* prevent us from assuming any direct textual relationship between *L* and the other two witnesses.

It is not easy to advance reasons for *L*'s textual inferiority; it cannot be wholly the result of mere scribal ineptitude. One reading in *L* hints that it may derive from a version of the poem that was hung as a *titulus* over Elizabeth's tomb. Line 5 in *L*, "Remember deth and loke vp here to me," suggests an invitation to examine the nailed-up text. It seems reasonable that such a *titulus* might have been circulated in hastily printed or transcribed copies among those mourning Elizabeth's

---

[1] The manuscript is described in Michael C. Seymour, "The Manuscripts of Hoccleve's *Regiment of Princes," Transactions of the Edinburgh Bibliographical Society, 4,* part 7 (1974), 274–75.

[2] See, for example, the variants at lines 10 and 73, where the rewriting of the line destroys the rhyme scheme; or at line 22 where the nonsensical *L* reading, "so moved," js an obvious scribal corruption of the *O/1557* "somond"; or the syntactical confusion occasioned by the rewriting of lines 75–76.

death. *L* might therefore be the sole remaining vestige of an attenuated line of transmission that probably would not have extended beyond the immediate events surrounding Elizabeth's death and interment.[1]

L and *1557* agree against *O* in some thirty places. A number of these are of quite marginal significance,[2] and others can be reasonably explained as coincidental scribal error.[3] Still others reflect an attempt to adjust the refrain, to produce a smoother version.[4] These, in addition to a number of other agreements,[5] suggest that *1557*, despite its close textual relationship to *O*, had been contaminated to some degree by a source agreeing with *L* in some places. This circumstance does not lend credibility to the unique variants in *1557*, a number of which seem to continue the tendency in *L* to "tidy up" the text and to smooth the meter.[6]

Thus, *O* must be preferred as the copy-text for this edition. It is the earliest witness, it has some connection with More's own family, and it lacks both the contamination that makes *1557* suspect and the number of aberrant readings that disqualify *L*. This edition presents all substantive variant readings in *L* and *1557*, including final *-es* of potential syllabic value and other syllabic variations; mere spelling variations have been omitted.

The transcription of the copy of the "Rufull Lamentation" in *O* does not pose many problems. Capitalization at the beginning of lines and for proper names is generally consistent with modern practice, but not invariably so. And in some instances it is not possible to establish conclusively whether or not a form is a capital letter. Initial capitalization

---

[1]There is possibly an analogy with the anonymous elegy on Henry VII that survives in a manuscript copy in the muniments of Durham Cathedral and that appears to have been copied from a printed edition now surviving in fragmentary form; see G. V. Scammell and H. L. Rogers, "An Elegy on Henry VII," *Review of English Studies*, New Series, *8* (1957), 167–71. The practice of copying from printed books into manuscript was, of course, common in the fifteenth and early sixteenth centuries; see Curt. F. Bühler, *The Fifteenth Century Book* (Philadelphia, 1960), chap. 1.

[2]For example, "olde" for "old" in line 9 and "Rychesse" for "Ryches" in line 14.

[3]See, for example, line 31, where both witnesses omit "ay," presumably under the influence of the same word in the same position in line 30.

[4]See, for example, the variants at lines 8, 15, 36, and 43.

[5]For example, line 17, where *L* and *1557* read "witt" against "welth" in *O*; line 20, "is come" against "commyth"; line 33, "in sondry" against "Sondre"; line 52, "oft(e)" against "sore"; and line 56, "most" against "full."

[6]Some of these tinker with the refrain; see, for example, the variants at lines 22, 43, 57, 71, and 78; others like "vouchesafe" for "witsave" (line 41), are clearly modernizations, possibly made by Rastell himself.

has therefore been silently regularized, including the adjustment of initial *ff* to *F*.

All abbreviations except the ampersand have been silently expanded. Simple superscript letters have been lowered. There are occasional problems with final flourishes on some words. I have generally regarded these as otiose, but in some places it is difficult to make a confident discrimination. Thus, in line 37 I have expanded what may be a final flourish as "owr*e*," since it looks to me like an imperfectly formed *e*. Occasionally the superscript contraction for *a* or *au* is used for *u* (for example, lines 80 and 85, "serua*u*ntes, serua*u*nt"). And at one point the superscript contraction for *ri* is given the value of *rin* (line 62, "p*rin*ce").

The thorn, which has been retained here, occasions a few interpretive problems, since, as is often the case in late medieval manuscripts, it is indistinguishable in form from *y*. Thus the contracted forms þᵗ ("that") and yᵗ ("it") can be distinguished in the manuscript only by context. At only one point, line 56, does this form lead to any possible ambiguity: "þᵗ we lest fere, full oft yᵗ [*or* þᵗ] ys full nye." Other abbreviations are of a conventional kind and pose no difficulties.

O has no punctuation except a comma at line 8 and virgules at lines 15, 22, 29, 36, 42, 43, 50, 57, and 71, all of which are noted in the variants. The punctuation of this edition is generally in accord with that of *1557*, which is usually logical and correct. All departures from the punctuation of *1557* are noted in the variants.

A MERRY JEST

THIS edition is based on Julian Notary's (1516?) quarto edition, *A mery gest how a sergeaut woldel erne [sic] to be a frere.*[1] The copy-text has been collated with *1557* and with the quarto edition printed by R. Jhones, *A ryght pleasaunt and merye historie, of the mylner of Abyngton. Whereunto is adioyned another merye iest, of a sergeaunt that woulde haue learned to be a fryar* ([c. 1575], sigs. C₂–D₂).[2] Neither *1516* nor *1575* ascribes the poem to More.

---

[1]*STC*² 18091 (1516); Gibson, no. 69.

[2]*STC*² 79 (1579); Gibson, no. 70. A garbled version of the first twelve lines of the poem, possibly a memorial transcription, also appears in the Churchwarden's Accounts of Ashburton, Devon, fol. 240v, an otherwise blank page; these lines are printed in *The Churchwardens' Accounts of Ashburton, 1479–1580*, ed. Alison Hanham, Devon & Cornwall Record Society, New Series, *15* (Torquay, 1970), p. 194. The unattributed lines are of no textual value and cannot be confidently dated. They do testify, however, to the appeal of More's poem.

Notary's edition has been selected as copy-text because it is closest in time to More's putative original. It is, however, a carelessly printed text, with lines 2–10 misarranged and a number of obvious typographic errors.[1]

All three texts appear to be independently derived. *STC*[2] alleges that *1575* is reprinted from *1557*, but this does not appear to be the case. There are a number of points at which *1575* and *1557* do agree against *1516*.[2] But against these agreements must be set a number of places where all three texts vary in striking ways.[3] In addition, *1557* has a significant number of unique readings,[4] as does *1575*.[5]

Despite its typographic sloppiness, *1516* seems clearly superior at a number of crucial points.[6]

The capitalization of *1516* has generally been retained. But the text is set out according to *1557*. Both *1516* and *1575* print the poem in alternating long and short lines, in each case rather differently.[7] The long-short format has the effect of obscuring the quite intricate rhyme scheme, which is made manifest by the layout of the text in *1557*. The poem is conceived in a form of tail rhyme, *aabccb*.[8] There seem to have been few parallels to this scheme in the verse of the early sixteenth century, and this paucity may explain why it caused particular trouble for Notary.[9]

---

[1]See the variants at lines 18, 31, 39, 61, 62, 83, 113, 128, 183, 204, 242, 250, 255, 275, 283, 301, 320, 370, 371, 380, 381, 399, 428, and 433.

[2]For examples see the variants at lines 27, 28, 76, 109, 247, 270, 323, 343, 368, and 424.

[3]For examples see the variants at lines 65, 111, 112, 148, 310, 340, 373, and 423.

[4]For examples see the variants at lines 26, 35, 85, 87, 129, 178, 184, 219, 244, 245, 287, 290, 363, 366, 376, 382, 388, 406, and 430.

[5]For examples see the variants at lines 4, 16, 26, 40, 79, 90, 91, 120, 168, 169, 184, 198, 235, 243, 266, 268, 307, 309, 392, 403, 409, and 424.

[6]See, for example, notes on lines 65, and 111–12.

[7]The lineation of *1516* reflects neither rhyme nor sense; compare, for example, the lineation of lines 24–26: "Becum a cutler I wene shal proue a fole / In olde trot." *1575* organizes the text rather more logically, printing sequential rhymes as long lines: "Wise men alway, affirme and saye, / the best is for eche man. . . ."

[8]It has been characterized variously as "short-lined rhyming doggerel" (W. A. G. Doyle-Davidson, "The Earlier English Works of Sir Thomas More," *English Studies, 17* [1935], reprinted in *Essential Articles*, p. 363, as the form of a ballad (Willow, p. 46), and as "tail rhyme meter" (Richard S. Sylvester, "*A Part of His Own:* Thomas More's Literary Personality in His Early Works," *Moreana, 15–16* [1967], 32). This last is the best designation.

[9]The only parallels I have noted are in *The Notbrowne Mayde*, printed in *Arnold's Chronicle, STC*[2] 782 (Antwerp, [1503?]); and the parody of it, *yᵉ new notborune mayd vpon yᵉ passioun of cryste, STC*[2] 14553.7 (London, [1535?]). Both these poems are reprinted in William C. Hazlitt, ed., *Remains of the Early Popular Poetry of England*, 4 vols. (London, 1864–66), 2, 271–94 and 3, 1–22.

The punctuation of *1516*, which consists only of virgules used to mark the caesura in long lines, has not been retained. These virgules have not been recorded in the variants. Both *1557* and *1575* have quite rational systems of punctuation. I have generally followed *1557*; any departures from it are noted in the variants.

FORTUNE VERSES

THERE are three early texts of the Fortune Verses:

    O   MS Balliol 354, fols. 104–06

  1556? W. Wyer's edition of *The boke of . . . Fortune (STC²* 18078.5; Gibson, no. 47)[1]

  1557 Rastell's edition of the *English Works*, sigs. ❡ 5–8v

O gives no indication of authorship. *1556* has "quod T. M." (lines 24 and 51) and adds to line 52 "quod Tho. Mo." *1556* occupies an intermediate position, both chronologically and textually between *O* and *1557*. On the one hand, it has fewer than twenty unique readings,[2] most of which are quite minor, and some of which are readily explicable as errors.[3] But it also agrees with *1557* against *O* on at least twenty-six occasions.[4] A number of these agreements produce manifestly easier readings[5] and suggest that *1557* may have had access to *1556* and may have used it in pursuit of a general policy of producing a smoother, easier text. *1557* has nearly forty unique readings,[6] most of which seem consistent with this policy. Many of these are added words, usually

---

[1]The date given in *STC²* is [c. 1540]. Prudence B. Tracy, "Robert Wyer: A Brief Analysis of his Types and a Suggested Chronology for the Output of his Press," *The Library*, 6th series, 2 (1980), 302, no. 133, suggests 1552 as the date of publication, but she presents no evidence for this view. In a letter of August 20, 1986, Dr. Katharine F. Pantzer, editor of *STC²*, has informed me that Tracy's date of 1552 should be interpreted as "between 1552 and 1556, but much nearer 1556." Pantzer gives a revised date "[1556?]" in an addenda note in *STC²* 3, 293.

[2]See the variants at lines 54, 77, 117, 123, 133, 151, 173, 189, 191, 201, 203, 214, 219, 245, 263, 273, 275, 285, and 293.

[3]For example, the *1556* variant at 189, "how shulde go" for "howshold goth," is an obvious instance of misreading word divisions, while the variant at 191, "lyfe" for "lese," seems to derive from a misreading of long *s* as *f*.

[4]See the variants at lines 57, 67, 75, 79, 84, 98, 110, 115, 125, 128, 143, 150, 154, 158, 172, 179, 183, 185, 195, 199, 206, 215, 241, 265, 296, and 299.

[5]For example, line 128, where *1556* and *1557* agree in reading "drowsy" for "dowsy"; and line 158, where they read "curseth" for "cuseth."

[6]See the variants at lines 76 (twice), 80, 84, 87 (twice), 90, 105, 106 (twice), 120, 138, 145, 155, 160, 162 (twice), 164, 168, 175, 177, 186, 188 (twice), 204, 205, 208, 225, 232, 237, 253, 254, 260, 266, 268, 278, and 285.

qualifiers of various kinds[1] or added syllables[2] to clarify sense or give a more regular meter. There is no compelling evidence that *1557* had access to a source supplementary to *1556*.[3]

1556 is of particular importance because it is the only source for lines 1–51. Their appearance in a text of indeterminate authority, unsupported by witnesses that have greater credibility in different ways because of their links to More's circle, does inevitably render them open to suspicion.[4] Moreover, within this section objections have been raised to lines 26–51 on the grounds that "there is . . . no evidence that More ever knew French."[5] This assertion is not strictly correct, since More obviously had a knowledge of law French; and there are some grounds for believing that his knowledge of French was not merely rudimentary.[6] Nevertheless, these lines do provide the only indication that More wrote French verse. And although the authorship of the entire passage remains questionable, not least because metrically it is much less regular than the rest of the Fortune Verses, there are no conclusive reasons for rejecting the unique attribution of *1556* here. These lines have therefore been printed with square brackets as the opening of the poem. Otherwise, the copy-text for this edition is *O*. As in the case of the "Rufull Lamentation," *O* provides a very early text that can be linked to More's own circle.[7]

The orthographic forms of *O* have generally been preserved. All

---

[1]See, for example, line 175, where *1557* reads "full soft" for *O*'s "softe"; and line 117, where *1557* reads "most cruell" for *O*'s "cruell."

[2]See, for example, line 188, where *1557* reads "vppon" for *O*'s "on"; and line 204, where *1557* reads "blynded" for *O*'s "blynd."

[3]There are only a few points where *1556* and *1557* vary substantively from each other and from *O*; see the variants at lines 73, 97, 116, and the notes on these lines. Other points of variation, such as lines 180 and 304, also suggest independent editorial efforts to produce easier readings.

[4]It is, of course, possible that these lines were lost at an earlier stage through the excision of a leaf. But the earliest text, *O*, shows no evidence of such a loss before line 52. I am grateful to Dr. Carol Meale for information about the codicology of *O*.

[5]Fox, p. 19.

[6]In *A Dialogue Concerning Heresies*, More evidences a knowledge of French in his use of mocking phrases (see *CW 6*, 286/15–16, 290/7–8); and he probably makes a pun on the French and English meanings of a word in *A Dialogue of Comfort* (*CW 12*, 224/4 and Commentary). For other apparent indications of More's knowledge of French see also no. 95 of More's Latin poems, "In Anglvm Gallicae Lingvae Affectatorem" (*CW 3/2*, 152–55, esp. 154/25–39). More's claim in a Latin poem (no. 265; *CW 3/2*, 284/46–8) that "Nunc mihi sermonis quia non est copia Galli / . . . Omnibus absoluar" means no more than he was not very fluent in spoken French.

[7]See p. cx, above.

abbreviations except the ampersand have been silently expanded. The forms *y* and thorn (= *th*) are indistinguishable in the manuscript, but context invariably prevents ambiguity. The thorn has been retained. The first letter of each line is generally capitalized in the manuscript; where a form is ambiguous I have treated it as a capital without noting the ambiguity; lowercase letters at the beginning of lines have been silently capitalized. Initial *ff* has been rendered as *F* at the beginning of lines[1] but retained within the line.[2] The only significant problem about capitalization occurs in lines 124–30, where a number of concepts such as "labour," "ffere," and "hatred" are capitalized in *1557*, so that they seem more like personifications. Although this notion is attractive, it was not *O*'s intention; nor is there any ground for believing it to have been More's. I have retained *O*'s forms and recorded the capitalization of *1557* in the variants.

The punctuation of *O* consists solely of the virgule, which appears frequently, and the period, which appears less frequently. Since neither mark is employed with consistency, the same procedure has been adopted here as with the "Rufull Lamentation": the generally consistent and intelligible punctuation of *1557* has been adopted. All the punctuation of *O* is recorded in the variants, as are the few departures from the punctuation of *1557*. For the punctuation of lines 1–51, *1556* has generally been followed; otherwise the punctuation variants of *1556* have not been recorded unless they support a departure from *1557* that has been adopted.

The variants include all substantive or potentially substantive variants (such as those that affect syllabic value) from *1556* and *1557*, together with all rejected readings of *O*. Orthographic variants, such as variations between final *ith* and *eth*, between *i* and *y* forms, and between *v* and consonantal *u*, are not recorded.

LEWIS THE LOST LOVER

THE texts of this work fall into two groups, according to the context in which they appear. The first group comprises the versions in which "Lewis" is followed immediately by "Davy the Dicer":

    L   MS Royal 17 D XIV, fol. 453, British Library[3]

   Br The flyleaf transcription at the end of a copy of Juan Luis Vives' edition of Augustine's *De civitate Dei* (Basel, Johann

---

[1]Lines 75, 121, 124, 130, 139, 190, 200, 269, 286, and 291.

[2]For example, lines 125, 136, 201, 215, 216, 236, 270, 280, and 284.

[3]Described in *CW 13*, xx–xxvi.

Froben, 1522), in the sacristy library of the Catholic church in Lower Brailes, Warwickshire[1]

Cr The transcriptions in a copy of the third edition of More's *Utopia* and first edition of his *Epigrammata* (Froben, 1518), sold at Christie's, London, June 23, 1993, lot 170[2]

1557 Rastell's edition of the *English Works,* sig. XX$_8$v ("Davy the Dicer" follows on sig. YY$_1$)

In addition there are a number of copies in manuscripts of William Roper's *Lyfe of Sir Thomas Moore.* The following manuscripts containing copies were used by Elsie Vaughan Hitchcock in her edition; her sigla have been retained. I have been unable to examine the two Burns MSS (*B* and *J*) or the Brussels MS (*X*) and have relied on the variants in Hitchcock's edition.[3]

A   Additional MS 11388, fol. 60, British Library
A^2 Additional MS 4242, fol. 36v, British Library
B   Burns MS (not seen)
D   MS Dyce 46, p. 80, Victoria and Albert Museum, London
H^1 MS Harley 6166, fol. 16v, British Library
H^2 MS Harley 6254, fol. 36v, British Library
H^3 MS Harley 6362, fols. 38v–39, British Library
J   Burns MS (not seen)
M   MS Mm IV 21, fol. 22v, Cambridge University Library
S   MS Sloane 1705, fol. 25, British Library
T   MS Bodley 966, p. 214, Bodleian Library, Oxford
W   MS Willis 58, fol. 59v, Bodleian Library
X   MS 544, Bollandist Library, Brussels (not seen)

To these can be added:[4]

C   MS Additional 7958, fol. 44, Cambridge University Library
L^2 MS S L. V 21, fol. 53, Sterling Library, University of London
O   MS Osborn b 10, pp. 56–57, Beinecke Library, Yale University
O^2 MS Osborn a 25, p. 56, Beinecke Library

---

[1]See *CW 3/2,* 67; for a facsimile of *Br* see *CW 3/2,* 305.

[2]This copy was apparently owned by William Say (d. 1529), "a family friend of the Mores" (Chambers, p. 70). I have not been able to establish the present whereabouts of this book and have relied in my collations on the plate in Christie's sale catalogue.

[3]Roper, p. 82.

[4]I am indebted to Peter Beal, *Index of English Literary Manuscripts* (London, 1980), *1/2,* 348, for knowledge of these copies.

    R   MS 875, fol. 41, John Rylands Library, Manchester
    Y   MS 363, fols. 59v–60, Beinecke Library[1]

In such a short text it is not possible to arrive at very useful conclusions about the relationships among the various manuscripts and *1557*. There is little variation between what are probably the three earliest texts, *L*, *Br*, and *1557*. *L* and *Br* are identical; *1557* has two minor changes: "or" for "nor" in line 3 (a unique variant) and the omission of "euer" in line 7 (a variant shared with a number of the later witnesses).[2] Since *L* and *Br* are identical and slightly superior to *1557*—and probably earlier than it—the choice of copy-text clearly lies between these two. *L* has been selected because it occurs in a manuscript that seems to be connected to More's circle and is probably the earliest of the surviving witnesses. The punctuation of the text given here generally reflects *1557* where it accords with the editor's judgment. At two points (lines 6 and 7) *1557*'s punctuation has been rejected and recorded in the variants. Punctuation variation in the other texts has not been recorded. Occasionally capitalization at the beginning of lines has been silently regularized.

The later texts of this stanza in Harpsfield and Ro. Ba. have not been collated. Collations of them can be found in the Early English Text Society editions.

DAVY THE DICER

T HIS stanza appears in three early texts *L, Br,* and *1557,* as described above. The variations among these texts are very minor, as the variants show: *1557* adds punctuation and omits one word in line 2, while *BR* omits a word in line 6. Given such limited variation, the choice of copy-text is of no great moment. *L*, which lacks the omissions in the other two texts, seems the obvious choice. Since the manuscript as a whole may be linked to More's own circle,[3] it has seemed reasonable to use it as copy-text. The punctuation is that of *1557* because that punctuation best

---

[1]Not MS 367, as Beal has it. Beal also includes National Library of Scotland MS Adv. 337/6 and Corpus Christi College, Oxford, MS 318, among the manuscripts containing this stanza, but he appears to be incorrect. I am indebted to Professor George Keiser for information about the National Library of Scotland manuscript and for a transcription of *R*.

[2]Among the later witnesses there is significant agreement within the group *A*[2], *D, L, O*[2], *W.*

[3]See *CW 13*, xxv, where it is argued that *L* "was probably produced by some members of the More circle."

matches the sense. Capitalization at the beginning of lines has been silently regularized.

The later versions of this stanza in Ro. Ba.'s life of More have not been collated; collations from the manuscripts of this work are printed in the Early English Text Society edition.

Life of Pico

THE EDITIONS

John Rastell's Edition (c. 1510)

THE first edition (*STC*[2] 19897.7; Gibson, no. 67), which is undated, was printed in London by More's brother-in-law John Rastell, "dwellyng at y^e flete brydge at the abbot of wynchecombe his place" (sig. g$_4$v). It is the only printing of Rastell that bears the Fleet Bridge location, and Arthur W. Reed suggested it was the first book that Rastell printed.[1] Since John's son, William Rastell, in the table of contents of the 1557 *English Works,* said that More translated the *Life of Pico* "about y^e yeare of our Lorde .1510," the edition has been tentatively assigned to that year and is designed *1510* here and in the variants.[2] It is set entirely from Rastell's type font Textura 93a.[3] Rastell used the same font in his edition of *Linacri progymnasmata grammatices vulgaria,* which can be dated 1512 with a fair degree of certainty and which contains prefatory Latin verses by More.[4]

Rastell's edition is a quarto in sixes except for the first and last gatherings, which contain four leaves. The title page is unsigned and is followed by a single leaf signed "A" containing More's prefatory letter to Joyeuce Leigh. The text itself comprises gatherings a^{4}b–h^{6}g^4.[5] This makeup indicates that the preface was not available to Rastell when he began setting the book. He might have come across a manuscript lacking the preface, which thus would have had to be supplied later. But it is

---

[1]Reed, pp. 8, 12. Frank Isaac also noted that "from the state of the type it seems an early printed book" (*English & Scottish Printing Types 1501–35*1508–41,* Oxford, 1930, under "John Rastell").

[2]Reed (pp. 73–74) argued from very slender evidence that the *Life* was written in 1505 before More's marriage to Joan Colt, but he made it clear that it could not have been printed that early (p. 8). It might have been printed a few years after 1510.

[3]Isaac, fig. 36.

[4]See *CW* 3/2, 66, no. 275.

[5]The first leaf of gathering a is signed, as are the first three leaves of gatherings b–d and f, the first and third of e, and the first and second of g.

just as likely that More himself wrote the preface only after the printing had begun; he may well have given to Joyeuce Leigh as a New Year's gift not a manuscript copy (as one might expect) but a copy of the printed book. Since John Rastell, who came to London about 1508,[1] almost certainly did not print the *Life* before 1510, the setting of the preface after the text tends to confirm William Rastell's date of 1510 for More's translation.

Errors caused by misreading a series of minims or by confusing *f* and *s* show that *1510* was set from a manuscript rather than from a printed book.[2] At three places in his autograph manuscript More had apparently written two alternative words, intending to choose between them later. The manuscript used by the compositor of *1510* (which may or may not have been set from the autograph) contained the three pairs with no cancellations, so that the compositor simply set both alternatives.[3] At 76/17, where More mentions the dwelling place of Circe, Aeaea, the compositor could not make out the word and simply left a blank space. Hence it seems clear that More did not read proof: he might have overlooked some thirty obvious and easily corrected misprints (frequently *u* for *n*), but he would hardly have left the blank space or such an error as "barke" for "brake" (70/13). The punctuation of *1510* is also frequently defective or misleading. Nevertheless, it is closer to More's manuscript than the other two early editions, which derive from it, and hence it has been chosen as copy-text.

Wynkyn de Worde's Edition (c. 1525)

THE SECOND EDITION OF THE *Life* is a page-for-page and line-for-line reprint by Wynkyn de Worde (*STC²* 19898; Gibson, no. 68).[4] Unfortunately, this edition is also undated. But the format of de Worde's edition makes it clear that it is derived from Rastell's not the other way around: the title page is on A_1, the preface on A_2 and A_2v, and the whole book consists of the quarto gatherings A–H⁶G⁴.[5] Thus the title

---

[1]Reed, pp. 7–8.

[2]See the variants at 64/13, 70/13, 70/16, 72/9, 74/3, 74/10, 81/15, and 85/28.

[3]See the notes on 63/10, 105/26, and 113/16. More did the same thing in the Valencia autograph (*CW 14*, 759).

[4]As usual, the line-for-line correspondence is occasionally off by a few letters. The page-for-page correspondence is exact except for sigs B_4–B_4v, where three words that would normally have appeared at the end of B_4 are run over to the top of B_4v, perhaps to reduce the white space after the first unfilled line on B_4v. The compositor occasionally adjusted the lines to reduce white space in other places (for example, sigs. B_3 and D_2).

[5]In *1525* leaves 2 and 3 of gathering A are signed, as well as the first three leaves of the other gatherings. Neither *1510* nor *1525* has running heads or catchwords. In *1525* sigs.

page and preface have been incorporated into a regular sequence of gatherings.[1] The type font of de Worde's edition strongly suggests a date later than 1521: it is set in Textura 95 with the forms of lowercase *s* and *w* introduced in 1514 and 1519 and predominant after 1521.[2] Following *STC²*, we have tentatively designated it *1525* here and in the variants.[3]

In October 1525 de Worde was reprimanded by Bishop Tunstall of London for printing *The Ymage of Love*, a book that More went out of his way to censure at length in the second edition of his *Dialogue Concerning Heresies* (1531).[4] Perhaps de Worde printed the *Life*, an unexceptionable devotional work, to offset his reprehensible edition of such a suspect devotional work as *The Ymage of Love*.

By sixteenth-century standards de Worde's reprint is moderately competent. Apart from about a dozen easily corrected misprints, it introduces at least twenty-three substantive errors.[5] It corrects several obvious misprints in *1510* and attempts, sometimes successfully, to improve the punctuation. There is no evidence that it relies on any source other than *1510* or that More (or anyone else) read proof or corrected the copy from which it was set.[6]

J. M. Rigg's slightly modernized reprint of *1525* for the Tudor Li-

---

A_3, B_3, B_6v, C_1, D_1, D_3, E_1, F_1, F_3, and G_1 have "Pic⁹" or "Pyc⁹" immediately below the block of printed text. As Fred Bowers has shown, the pattern of these identifying words indicates that the inner half-sheets were printed by "twin" half-sheet imposition: see "Printing Evidence in Wynkyn de Worde's Edition of 'The Life of Picus' by St. Thomas More," *Papers of the Bibliographical Society of America, 43* (1949), 398–99.

[1]Campbell and Reed, *1*, 220, A. W. Reed correctly pointed out that de Worde reprinted from Rastell. But the only evidence he gives, "ugly crowding" at the bottom of de Worde's pages, simply does not exist; and if it did, it would argue for the priority of de Worde's edition, since a reprint usually has a superior distribution of type.

[2]Isaac, fig. 8.

[3]In his handlist of publications by Wynkyn de Worde, H. S. Bennett tentatively dated it 1520 (*English Books & Readers 1475 to 1557*, Cambridge, 1952, p. 262). Gibson, no. 68, wrongly dated it "1510?"

[4]*CW 6*, 734; Reed, pp. 165–69. De Worde was ordered to appear before Tunstall's consistory court on January 15, 1526, to clear himself of the suspicion of heresy, but we have no record of what happened on that occasion.

[5]See the variants at 56/3, 56/11, 56/21, 57/11, 60/14, 61/22, 62/21, 62/26, 63/17, 66/10, 67/28, 74/15, 74/21, 76/26, 77/3, 79/10, 80/27, 82/26, 111/24, 114/9, 115/2, and 123/1. The compositor simply closed the blank space for Circe's home, destroying the sense entirely.

[6]A. W. Reed disparaged de Worde's reprint as piratical (Reed, p. 8, n. 1; and Campbell and Reed, p. 220), but there was probably nothing furtive or underhanded about it. John Rastell (and perhaps More) must have known about it, and if Rastell objected he was sufficiently litigious to have taken action.

brary (London, 1890) is generally reliable and contains a useful introduction and commentary.[1]

William Rastell's Edition in *English Works* (1557)

THE third and last sixteenth-century edition was printed by William Rastell in the *English Works* of 1557; this edition of the *Life* is designated *1557* here and in the variants.[2] It is all but certain that *1557* was not set from *1525*, as shown by variants such as these:

folys *1510*, fooles *1525*, folies *1557* (61/22)
crist *1510*, chyrch *1525*, Christ *1557* (80/27)
byndyng *1510*, byndynges *1525*, bynding *1557* (89–24)[3]

But because *1557* was very carefully corrected, it is not easy to show that it was set from *1510* rather than from a manuscript. Nevertheless, William Rastell always set from earlier printed editions if there were any, and a few peculiar vestiges of *1510* in *1557* make it likely that William Rastell set the *Life* from a corrected copy of his father's edition:

abreuiary *1510*, a breuyary *1525*, abreuiary *1557* (56/5)
captiōs *1510*, capicions *1525*, captious *1557* (61/28)
he his called *1510*, he is called *1525*, he his called *1557* (78/12)
seuyngly *1510*, suyngly *1525*, semyngly *1557* (100/18)
sight *1510*, fight *1525*, sight *1557* (113/6)

The copy was corrected and the printing executed with extraordinary care. There are remarkably few of the ordinary typographical errors[4] and not very many substantive mistakes.[5] A number of changes are intentional but unnecessary (or even false) corrections,[6] and several are slight modernizations of syntax and diction such as are commonly found in the *English Works*.[7] As is also usual in *1557*, Latin passages from scripture are brought into closer conformity with the Vulgate,[8] usually unnecessarily and once wrongly (102/1); but in one place

---

[1]But it does contain an incorrect gloss, a misprint, and a false emendation (Rigg, pp. 93–94, n. 43; p. 95, nn. 51 and 52).

[2]*EW*, sigs. a₁–c₁v. The *Life* was the first part of the volume to be set; the title page, dedication, table of contents, and the English poems, which precede it in the bound book, are contained in two signatures signed ¶ and hence were set after the series of gatherings beginning with "a."

[3]See also the variants at 53/4–5, 91/3, 91/23–24, 92/13, 100/22, 102/30, 105/10, 111/15, 114/9, 115/2, 115/7, 120/20, and 121/2.

[4]See the variants at 57/14, 61/28, 79/18, 91/25, 96/5, and 99/3.

[5]See the variants at 54/18, 64/13, 67/17, 87/10, 89/21, 101/25, and 112/14.

[6]See the variants at 79/11, 79/23, 82/3, 88/8, 90/4, and 102/15.

[7]See the variants at 82/3, 82/14, 83/12, 96/21, 99/20, and 111/8.

[8]See the variants at 98/30, 101/1, 102/5, and Germain Marc'hadour, "Three Tudor Editors of Thomas More," in *Editing Sixteenth-Century Texts*, ed. R. J. Schoeck (Toronto, 1966), pp. 59–71.

(103/13) the correction is clearly needed. The capitalization and especially the punctuation have been thoroughly and intelligently corrected.[1] *1557* went beyond *1525* in correcting even easily recognizable misprints,[2] and it corrected several errors and omissions that are not easy to catch, although they would not necessarily have required recourse to a manuscript or to the Latin source.[3] But four corrections introduced by *1557* could hardly have been made without such a manuscript or a comparison with the Latin:

1. Ther holdith me some tyme by almighty god as hit were euin a swone and an insensibilite for wondre when I begin in my selfe: I wot neuer whethir I shall sey: to remembre or to sorrow / to meruaill or to bewaill the appetites of men / or yf I shall more plainli speke: ye very madnes not to beleue the gospell. . . . *1510* (81/24–29)

   There holdeth me sometyme by almighty god, as it wer euen a swone, and an insensibilitie for woonder, when I begin in my self, I wot neuer whether I shall say, to remember, or to sorowe, to meruayle or to bewayle the appetites of men: or if I shall more playnly speake: ye very madness. For it is verelye a great madnesse not to beleue the gospel. . . . *1557*

   Tenet me (Deum testor) aliquando extasis quasi & stupor quidam cum mecum incipio studia hominum aut (ut dixerim significantius) meras insanias nescio an cogitare potius quam dolere, mirari an deplorare. Magna enim profecto insania euangelio non credere. . . . (Appendix A, 344/32–35, below)

2. whan thou shalt in thi praier axe of god: both ye holy spyrit which praeth for vs and eke thin owne necessite shall eueri houre put in thi mynd. . . . *1510* (83/28–31)

   What thou shalt in thy praier axe of God: both the holy spirite whiche praieth for vs, & eke thyne owne necessitie shall euery houre put in thy mynd. . . . *1557*

   Suggeret tibi cum spiritus qui interpellat pro nobis tum ipsa necessitas singulis horis quid petas a deo tuo. . . . (Appendix A, 348/1–3, below)

---

[1]Only at 57/8 does *1557* falsify the sense by changing the punctuation. On the other hand, it restores the sense in an essential way by repunctuating at 85/17.

[2]See, for example, the variants at 63/2, 78/1, and 79/13.

[3]See the variants at 70/16, 85/11, 95/4, 107/13, and perhaps 112/18.

3. yf we obserue these two thingis in our requestis that is to wit y^t we require no thing but y^t which is good for vs. . . .   *1510* (95/13–15)

And yf we obserue these two thynges in oure requestes, that is to wytte, that wee require nothyng, but that whiche is good for vs. . . .   *1557*

Et si duas has conditiones observabimus, ut nunquam petamus a deo nisi ea quae nobis sunt salutaria. . . .   (Appendix A, 362/21–22, below)

4. who so to vertue estemith the waye. . . .   *1510* (103/19)

Whoso to vertue estemeth hard the way. . . .   *1557*

si homini videtur dura via virtutis. . . .   (Appendix A, 372/3, below)

The addition of "And" in the third item is such a small detail that even a comparison with the Latin might not catch it. Moreover, there is one place, 78/8–9, which tends to show that the corrections in *1557* (including the changes in Latin passages from scripture) derive not from the Latin but rather from a manuscript of the English:

Gaudete fratres qm̄ in temptationes varias incideritis.   *1510 1525*

Gaudete fratres quando in tentationes varias incideritis.   *1557*

gaudete, fratres, cum in tentationes varias incideritis.   (Appendix A, 340/29–30, below)

Omne gaudium existimate, fratres mei, cum in tentationes varias incideritis.   (Vulgate, James 1:2)

It may be that the compositor of *1557* mistook the "qm̄" (*quum*) of *1510* for "qn̄" (*quando*), but it is more likely that the corrector of the copy-text (perhaps William Rastell himself) found the error "quando" abbreviated or already written out in a manuscript he was using to correct his copy-text. Rastell pretty clearly used the Corpus Christi manuscript of *A Dialogue of Comfort* to correct Tottel's 1553 edition, which was the printer's copy.[1] and he did introduce corrections (some of them false) into the printer's copy for *The Supplication of Souls*.[2] If Rastell used such

---

[1]See *CW 12*, xliii–lv.

[2]This copy of the second 1529 edition of *The Supplication of Souls* is in the Beinecke Library at Yale University. See *CW 7*, Appendix F.

a manuscript to correct the printer's copy for *1557*, we have no way of knowing what it was like except that it was in some places superior, in others inferior, to *1510*. There is no reason to associate it with More himself. Corrections from *1557* can be accepted only when there is good reason (such as the Latin original or compelling evidence from the context) to believe that they are closer to what More intended.

A complete collation of the *Life* in three copies of the *English Works*[1] reveals what appear to be three genuine stop-press corrections on sig. a_6v and several puzzling discrepancies there and on sigs. a_5v and a_7. The three stop-press corrections in the first column of a_6v are:

> so-[new line]rowful, al thing deadly. Shall we then   *LR*(80/8)
>
> so-[new line]owful, all thing deadly. Shall we them   *K*

> bondemen *LR* (80/11)
>
> bondemeu *K*

> Dirūpamus vincula   *LR* (81/1)
>
> Disūqamus vencula   *K*

These three corrections extend from line 25 to line 57 of the first column. But it is surprising to find such slight corrections as from "what" (*K*) to "What" (*LR*) in line 11 of the same column (7/25) and from "contencion" (*K*) to "contenciō" at the end of line 5 of the second column (81/6), which contains no other changes. On sig. a_7 (at 84/18) the only difference (hardly a correction) is between "momētary life" (*K*) and "momentary lif" (*LR*). Moreover, sig. a_5v contains five changes that hardly seem to matter:

> especially,   *LR* (74/21)
>
> especially   *K*

> frustrate by his deth   *LR* (75/2)
>
> frustrat by his death   *K*

> her of the first death & temporal. And af-
> ter this, yᵉ same Hierome shewed to his   *LR* (75/5)

---

[1]The Larned Fund (*L*), Roper (*R*), and Klein (*K*) copies in the Beinecke Library at Yale. The Scolar Press facsimile (London, 1978) of the copy in the University Library at Cambridge agrees with *L* and *R* at all the places mentioned.

her of the first death and temporall. And
after this, yᵉ same hierome shewed to his   *K*

world, [line end]   *LR (75/14)*

world [line end]   *K*

affections   *LR (76/28)*

affettions   *K*

Only the last of these could be called a correction at all, and I can see no
satisfactory explanation for the differences. When whole pages of *En-
glish Works* were set twice (as sigs. v₄–v₅v were),[1] the differences in
spelling and accidentals are much greater than on these three pages of
the *Life*.

There is a version of More's translation of the "Deprecatoria ad
Deum" in Bodleian MS Lat. th. d. 15, ff. 119–20. This text has been
printed elsewhere[2] and has not been collated for this edition. Its read-
ings are occasionally noted in the Commentary.

Max Kullnick reprinted *1557*, together with the Latin from editions
of 1498 and 1601, in 1908–09.[3] It was also reprinted in facsimile and in
a modernized version in volume 1 of *The English Works of Sir Thomas
More*, ed. W. E. Campbell and A. W. Reed (London, 1931), with some
philological notes by A. W. Reed and collations with *1510* and *1525* by
W. A. G. Doyle-Davidson.[4]

A Note on the Text

THE copy-text of this edition (*1510*) is presented according to the
norms given in *CW 8*, 1447–50. John Rastell's font lacked uppercase W

---

[1] See *CW 7*, Appendix F, p. 466.

[2] A. S. G. Edwards, "Robert Parkyn's Transcript of More's 'Prayers of Picus Mirandola
unto God,'" *Moreana*, 27 (1990), 133–38.

[3] *Archiv für das Studium der neueren Sprachen und Literatur*, New Series, 22 (1908), 47–75,
316–40, and New Series, 23 (1909), 27–50. Kullnick (New Series, 22, p. 50) mentions a
1720 edition entitled *The life of the great Picus Prince of Mirandula. Taken from the workes of
Sir Thomas More Knight*, but he gives no place of publication or location; I have not been
able to find this edition.

[4] The printed catalogue of the British Library (*189*, cols. 613–14) mentions two edi-
tions of *The XII propertees or condicyons of a Lover*, by *Johan Picus, Erle of Miran-
dula . . . expressed in balade by Sir T. More* (1928 and 1933) (catalogue nos. 11631.i.17 and
11630.aa.23) and an edition of *The Rules of a Christian Life . . . translated into English by Sir
T. More* (1872) (catalogue no. IX.Eng.237).

and *Y*.[1] Lowercase *w* and *y* in the copy-text have been silently capitalized at the beginnings of sentences and lines of verse. In a few places the copy-text has 3 for *m* at the ends of Latin words; this character appears here as *m*. Pilcrows in the copy-text are represented by paragraph indentation. In the early editions the commentary on Psalm 15 is printed as an unbroken block, with commentary on verses beginning in midline. This procedure makes it difficult to find the commentary on particular verses, although *1557* makes it easier by printing the Latin in italic type. Here we have divided commentary on particular verses into separate blocks distinguished by line spaces. The first two editions have no sidenotes. The sidenotes in *1557* are given in the variants.

The Last Things

APART from the Pageant Verses, More's *Last Things* is the only one of his English works preserved in a single early source: William Rastell's *English Works* of 1557 (sigs. e₄v–fg₈; *STC*² 18076; Gibson, no. 73). The absence of manuscripts might suggest that Rastell printed directly from More's autograph;[2] on the other hand, if he had, we would expect him to have said so, as he did in the title of *King Richard III* in *1557*[3] and as John Fowler did on his title page when he printed More's *Letter to Bugenhagen* from More's own autograph.[4] Certainly Rastell sought out manuscripts and took uncommon care to produce reliable texts for *1557*.[5] When he set texts in *1557* from his own editions of the late 1520s and the 1530s, he made a few errors of commission or omission,[6] and he tended to modernize some forms (such as "much" for "myche," "altar" for "auter," and "brethren" for "brethern"). If we must rely on a single sixteenth-century editor-publisher of a work first issued after More's death, we could hardly do better than William Rastell. When Dr. Johnson remarked, in the history of the English language prefixed to his dictionary, that More's "works are carefully and correctly printed, and may therefore be better trusted than any other edition of the

---

[1] Isaac, *English & Scottish Printing Types*, under "John Rastell."

[2] In his *Il Moro* (Florence, 1556), Ellis Heywood makes it clear that he had read a manuscript of More's *Last Things*, but it might well have been the same manuscript his uncle William Rastell used to set *1557*. See the note on 150/5–31.

[3] *CW* 2, 2.

[4] See *CW* 7, clx and 2–3.

[5] See *CW* 2, xxix, and *CW* 12, xliii–lv.

[6] As he did in *The Last Things* (apart from a relatively small number of obvious and easily corrected misprints); see the variants at 138/6, 154/30, 159/3, 159/14, 159/25, 159/31, 175/14, 181/25, and 181/26.

English books of that or of the preceding ages," his words are essentially a tribute to William Rastell.[1]

An anomaly in the signature series of *The Last Things* probably has nothing to do with that work. The signatures of what should have been gathering f of *1557* (encompassing about the last two thirds of *The Last Things*) appear as "fg."[2] Apparently gathering h, which begins with *A Dialogue Concerning Heresies*, was already set (or being set) when it was decided to make a change in the order of the earlier gatherings. Since the first gathering of text, comprising *A Merry Jest*, the Pageant Verses, the "Rufull Lamentation," and the Fortune Verses ("foure thinges," Rastell says, which More "wrote in his youth for his pastime"),[3] is signed with a pilcrow, and since the second gathering begins with the undated *Life of Pico*, it seems likely that the youthful poems were originally intended to follow the *Life*, which itself ends with fourteen pages of translated poems. There would have been no reason to consider placing the gathering of youthful poems after either of the other two works that precede gathering h: *The History of King Richard III*, which Rastell dates about 1513; and *The Last Things*, which he dates about 1522. The gathering left vacant by the shift was then accounted for by merging gatherings f and g into one. At any rate, the anomalous signatures, though they occur in the last part of *The Last Things*, probably have no bearing on that work itself.

A modernized edition of *1557*, with a few omissions, was issued by Daniel O'Connor (London, 1903; reprint, London, 1935). P. S. Allen and H. M. Allen published modernized selections with a few notes in 1924.[4] A facsimile of *The Last Things* from *1557*, together with a modernized version and philological notes, was published by W. E. Campbell, A. W. Reed, and W. A. G. Doyle-Davidson in 1931.[5] A German translation, based on O'Connor's 1903 edition but loose and somewhat bowdlerized, was published by Alfred Tholen in 1936.[6] Marie Delcourt translated brief excerpts into French in 1936.[7] An Italian translation by Vittorio Gabrieli, with introduction and commentary, appeared in 1977.[8] Finally, a German translation by Friedrich-Karl

---

[1] *A Dictionary of the English Language*, 2 vols. (London, 1755), *1*, sig. G_2v.
[2] Except the first leaf, which is signed "f."
[3] Sig. ¶$_1$.
[4] *Sir Thomas More: Selections from His English Works* . . . (Oxford, 1924), pp. 79–89.
[5] Campbell and Reed *1*, 20–23, 211–18.
[6] *Die Kunst des gottseligen Sterbens* (Kevelaer, 1936).
[7] *Thomas More: Oeuvres choisies* (Paris, 1936).
[8] "Tommaso Moro, 'le quattro cose ultime,'" *La cultura: Revista di filosofia letteratura e storia*, *15*, 447–503.

Unterweg, also with introduction and commentary, was issued in 1984.[14]

The copy-text of this edition is *1557*, of which we have collated three copies[2] without discovering any press variants. The Textura 72 typeface of *1557*[3] appears here as roman; the single italic phrase at 172/33 remains italic;[4] and the Roman 96 typeface in the title[5] is given here in italic. Abbreviations have been expanded and certain adjustments have been made according to the norms given in *CW 8*, 1447–50. The printer's ornament before the title, the pilcrows before the subheadings, and the three dots within parentheses at the end have been omitted. The sidenotes in the margins of *1557* are recorded in the variants; abbreviations in them have been expanded, and the periods after most have been silently omitted.[6]

---

[1]*Die Vier Letzten Dinge* (Munich, 1984).

[2]The Klein, Roper, and Larned Fund copies in the Beinecke Library at Yale University. We have also collated the modern facsimile (ed. K. Jay Wilson, London: Scolar Press, 1978) of the copy of *1557* at the University Library at Cambridge.

[3]Isaac, *English and Scottish Printing*, fig. 142.

[4]Isaac, fig. 139.

[5]Isaac, figs. 139, 141a, 141b.

[6]In many places commas appear where periods were intended; they have silently been changed to periods. For example, "Psal, 138," appears as "Psal. 138."

ENGLISH POEMS

PAGEANT VERSES

Mayster Thomas More in his youth deuysed in hys fathers house
in London, a goodly hangying of fyne paynted clothe, with nyne
pageauntes, and verses ouer euery of those pageauntes: which
verses expressed and declared, what the ymages in those pag-
eauntes represented: and also in those pageauntes were payn-
ted, the thynges that the verses ouer them dyd (in effecte) de-
clare, whiche verses here folowe. [sig. ❡3]
In the first pageant was painted a boy playing at the top &
squyrge. And ouer this pageaunt was writen as foloweth.

Chyldhod

I am called Chyldhod, in play is all my mynde,
To cast a coyte, a cokstele, and a ball.
A toppe can I set, and dryue it in his kynde.
But would to god these hateful bookes all,
Were in a fyre brent to pouder small.
Than myght I lede my lyfe alwayes in play:
Whiche lyfe god sende me to myne endyng day.

In the second pageaunt was paynted a goodly freshe yonge man
rydyng vppon a goodly horse, hauynge an hawke on his fyste,
and a brase of grayhowndes folowyng hym. And vnder the horse
fete, was paynted the same boy, that in the fyrst pageaunte was
playinge at the top & squyrge. And ouer this second pageant the
wrytyng was thus.

Manhod

Manhod I am, therefore I me delyght,
To hunt and hawke, to nourishe vp and fede

---

4 ouer] ouer of *1557*   26 am,] am *1557*   27 fede] fede, *1557*

3

The grayhounde to the course, the hawke to the flyght,
And to bestryde a good and lusty stede.
30 These thynges become a very man in dede,
Yet thynketh this boy his peuishe game swetter,
But what, no force, his reason is no better.

In the thyrd pagiaunt, was paynted the goodly younge man, in
the seconde pagiaunt lyeng on the grounde. And vppon hym
35 stode ladye Venus goddes of loue, and by her vppon this man
stode the lytle god Cupyde. And ouer this thyrd pageaunt, this
was the wrytyng that foloweth.

Venus and Cupyde

Whoso ne knoweth the strength powre and myght,
40 Of Venus and me her lytle sonne Cupyde,
Thou Manhod shalt a myrrour bene a ryght,
By vs subdued for all thy great pryde.
My fyry dart perceth thy tender syde.
Now thou whiche erst despysedst children small,
45 Shall waxe a chylde agayne and be my thrall.

In the fourth pageaunt was paynted an olde sage father sittyng
in a chayre. And lyeng vnder his fete was painted the ymage of
Venus & Cupyde, that were in the third pageant. And ouer this
fourth pageant the scripture was thus.

50   ### Age

Olde Age am I, with lokkes thynne and hore,
Of our short lyfe, the last and best part. [sig. ¶3v]
Wyse and discrete: the publike wele therefore,
I help to rule to my labour and smart.
55 Therefore Cupyde withdrawe thy fyry dart,
Chargeable matters shall of loue oppresse
Thy childish game and ydle bysinesse.

---

32 what,] what *1557*   42 pryde.] pryde, *1557*   43 syde.] syde, *1557*   51 lokkes]
lokkes, *1557*   54 smart.] smart, *1557*   56 oppresse] oppresse, *1557*

In the fyfth pageaunt was paynted an ymage of Death: and
vnder hys fete lay the olde man in the fourth pageaunte. And
aboue this fift pageant, this was the saying. 60

DETH

Though I be foule vgly lene and mysshape,
Yet there is none in all this worlde wyde,
That may my power withstande or escape.
Therefore sage father greatly magnifyed, 65
Discende from your chayre, set a part your pryde,
Witsafe to lende (though it be to your payne)
To me a fole, some of your wise brayne.

In the sixt pageant was painted lady Fame. And vnder her fete
was the picture of Death that was in the fifth pageant. And ouer 70
this sixt pageaunt the writyng was as foloweth.

FAME

Fame I am called, maruayle you nothing,
Though with tonges am compassed all rounde
For in voyce of people is my chiefe liuyng. 75
O cruel death, thy power I confounde.
When thou a noble man hast brought to grounde
Maugry thy teeth to lyue cause hym shall I,
Of people in parpetuall memory.

In the seuenth pageant was painted the ymage of Tyme, and 80
vnder hys fete was lyeng the picture of Fame that was in the sixt
pageant. And this was the scripture ouer this seuenth pageaunt.

TYME

I whom thou seest with horyloge in hande,
Am named tyme, the lord of euery howre, 85
I shall in space destroy both see and lande.
O simple fame, how dareset thou man honowre,

---

64 escape.] escape, *1557*   65 magnifyed] magnifyed, *1557*

Promising of his name an endlesse flowre.
Who may in the world haue a name eternall,
90   When I shall in proces distroy the world and all?

In the eyght pageant was pictured the ymage of lady Eternitee,
sittyng in a chayre vnder a sumptious clothe of estate, crowned
with an [sig. ❡ 4] imperial crown. And vnder her fete lay the
picture of Time, that was in the seuenth pageant. And aboue this
95 eight pageaunt, was it writen as foloweth.

ETERNITEE

Me nedeth not to bost, I am Eternitee,
The very name signifyeth well,
That myne empyre infinite shalbe.
100   Thou mortall Tyme euery man can tell,
Art nothyng els but the mobilite
Of sonne and mone chaungyng in euery degre,
When they shall leue theyr course thou shalt be brought,
For all thy pride and bostyng into nought.

105 In the nynth pageant was painted a Poet sitting in a chayre. And
ouer this pageant were there written these verses in latin folow-
yng.

THE POET

Has fictas quemcunque iuuat spectare figuras,
110   Sed mira veros quas putat arte homines,
Ille potest veris, animum sic pascere rebus,
Vt pictis oculos pascit imaginibus.
Namque videbit vti fragilis bona lubrica mundi,
Tam cito non veniunt, quam cito pretereunt.
115   Gaudia laus & honor, celeri pede omnia cedunt,
Qui manet excepto semper amore dei.

---

88 name] name, *1557;* flowre.] flowre, *1557*   90 all?] all. *1557*   101 mobilite] mo-
bilite, *1557*

Ergo homines, leuibus iamiam diffidite rebus,
　　Nulla recessuro spes adhibenda bono.
Qui dabit eternam nobis pro munere vitam,
　　In permansuro ponite vota deo.   120

---

118 bono.] bono, *1557*

O you that putt youre trust & confydence

O ye that putt youre tryst and confidence

In worldely joye And frayle prosperyte
that leve here as you shuld never hence
Remember deth and loke up here to me
Ensample I thynke ther may no better be
Youre selffe wote well that in this reame was I
Youre quene but late and lo now here I ly

Was I
nott of olde worthy lynage
Was not my fader a kyng & my mader quene
Was I not a kyngs fere in maryage
Had I not plente of every plesaunt thyng
mersyfull god this is a strange rekenyng
Rychesse honoure welthe and auncestrye
Hath me forsake & lo now here I ly

Yff
worshyp myght have kept me I had not goone
yf witt myght have saved me I neded not to fere
yf money myght holpe me I lakked none
but o good god whate avaylyeth all this geer
whan deth is come that myghty messynger
Obey we must ther is no remedy
me hath he somoned that lo now here I ly

Yett
was I lately promysed otherwyse
this yere to leve in welthe and delyce
lo whereto cometh thy blandyshyng promyse
o false astrologe devynatryce
of goddes secrett makeng thy selfe so wyse
how trewe is for this yere thy prophecy
the yere yet lasteth and lo now here I ly

O Bryttell
welthe ay full of byttrnesse
thy syngley plesyr doblyd is with payne
Accounte my sorow first and my dystresse
In sondry wyse and rekon them agayne
the joye that I have had & I dare sayne
for all my plesure enduryd yet have I
 Never wo them welthe & lo now here I ly

THE LAMYTACYON OFF QUENE ELYZABETH

Ye þat put your trust & confydence,
In worldly riches & frayll prosperyte,
þat so leve here as ye shuld never hens,
Remember deth & loke here vpon me.   5
Insampull I thynk þer may no better be.
Your self wote well þat in þis realme was I
Your quene but late. Loo here I lye.

Was I not born of old worthy lynage?
Was not my moder quene & my fader kyng?   10
Was I not a kynges fere in maryage?
Hade I not plente of euery plesant thyng?
Marcyfull god þis ys a strange reconyng:
Ryches honor welth & auncetry
Hath me for sake. Loo here I lye.   15

1 The lamytacyon off quene Elyzabeth] O you that put youre trust & convydence L, A ruful lamentacion (written by master Thomas More in his youth) of the deth of quene Elisabeth mother to king Henry the eight, wife to king Henry the seuenth, & eldest daughter to king Edward the fourth, which quene Elisabeth dyed in childbed in February in the yere of our lord. 1503. & in the 18. yere of the raigne of king Henry the seuenth. / 1557   2 Ye] O you L, O ye 1557   3 riches] ioye L 1557   4 so] om. L; leve] lyue 1557; ye] you L   5 here vpon] vp here to L   7 I] I, 1557   8 Your] youe L, your 1557; late.] late, O, late and L, late, and 1557; loo] lo now L 1557   9 born] om. L 10 moder . . . kyng] my fader a kyng & my moder quene L; &] om. 1557   13 reconyng] resevyng L, reckenyng 1557   14 Ryches] Rychesse L 1557; honor welth] honoure welthe L, honour, welth, 1557; auncetry] auncetye L, auncestry? 1557   15 for sake.] for sake / / O, forsake & L, forsaken and 1557; loo] lo nowe L, lo now 1557

Yff worship myght haue kept me, I had not gon.
Yff welth myght me haue serued, I nedid not to fere.
Yff money myght haue hold, I laked non.
But o good god what avaylith all þis gere.
20 Whan deth commyth thy myghti mesanger,
Obey we must þer ys no remedye,
He hath me somond. Loo here I lye. [fol. 175v]

Yet was I latly promised oþerwyse,
This yere to leve in welth & delice.
25 Lo wher to cumyth thi blandyshyng promyse,
O false astrologye deuynatrice,
Of godes secrettes makying the so wyse.
How trew ys for this yere the prophesye.
The yere yet lastyth & lo now here I lye.

30 O brytill welth, ay full of bitternes,
Thy synglar plesure ay dowbled ys with payn.
Accompte my sorow fyrst & my distres,
Sondre wyse, & rekyn ther agayn
The yoy þat I haue had I dare not fayn.
35 For all my honour indured yet haue I
More wo than welth, & lo here I lye.

---

16 not gon] t *and* on *cropped in O*   17 welth] witt *L 1557;* me haue serued] haue saued
me *L,* haue me saued *1557;* nedid] nedet *L;* fere] *cropped in O*   18 haue] *om. L;* hold]
hold me *L,* holpe *1557*   19 avaylith] avaylys *L,* vayleth *1557*   20 commyth] is come
L 1557; thy] that *L*   21 Obey] Away *L;* þer] then *L;* no] no nother *L;* remedye] remedy,
L 1557   22 He hath me somond.] Me hath so moved that *L,* Me hath he sommoned,
and *1557;* somond.] somond / / *O;* Loo] lo nowe *L 1557*   23 latly] late
1557   24 leve] liue *1557;* welth] wethe *L*   26 astrologye deuynatrice] astrologye
dymynatrice *O*   27 makyng] maken *L;* the] thyselfe *L 1557*   28 the] thy *1557*
29 now] now / *O*   30 welth] wethe *L*   31 synglar] synguler *L,* single *1557;* ay] *om. L
1557*   32 Accompte] Acounte *L,* Account *1557*   33 Sondre] In sondry *L 1557;*
ther] them *L*   34 yoy] loye *L,* ioy *1557;* I dare] and I dare *1557;* not fayn.] sayne *L,*
sayne, *1557*   35 honour] sorowe *L*   36 welth] welth / *O;* lo] lo now *L 1557*

Wher ar owre castellis now & owr towers?
Goodly Richemond son art þou gon from me.
At Westmynster þat goodly werk of yours,
Myne owne dere lord, now shall I neuer se.   40
Almyghty god witsave to grante þat ye,
& your children well may edyfye.
My place bilded ys, for lo here I lye.

Adewe my trew spouse my worthi lord,
The feythfull love, þat dide vs to combyne,   45
In maryage & pesybull concorde,
Vnto your hondes here I clene resyne,
To be bestowed on your children & myne.
Erst were ye fader, now must ye supply
The moders parte also. Lo wher I lye.   50

Farewell my dowghter lady Margarete.
God wote full sore yt grevid hath my mynd,
þat ye shuld go wher we shuld seldom mete.
Now am I gon, & haue left you behynd.
O mortall folke what we very blynd.   55
þat we lest fere, full oft yt ys full nye.
Fro you departe I fyrst. Lo here I lye.

---

37 owre] youre L, our 1557; castellis] Castels, 1557; now & owr] Where are you L, now
where are our 1557; towers?] Towers, 1557   38 me.] me, 1557   39 Westmynster]
westmester L; goodly] costly 1557   40 Myne owne] My nowne L; lord,] lord O L 1557
41 god witsave] lord wytt saffe L, god vouchesafe 1557   42 &] For you and L 1557;
children] children / O; may] may you L   43 place] pales L, palyce 1557; ys, for lo] ys /
for lo O, so lowe now L, and low now 1557   44 my trew] myn owne treweL, myne owne
dere 1557   45 to combyne] two knytt L, both combyne 1557   46 pesybull] pos-
sybyll L, peasable 1557   47 Vnto] Into L 1557   48 on] betwene L, vppon 1557
49 Erst] ons [canc.] Erst O, fyrst L; now] & now 1557; ye] I you L; supply] supply,
1557   50 also.] also / O, also, 1557; Lo wher] for lo now here L 1557   51 lady] om.
L   52 sore] ofte L, oft 1557   53 ye] you L   54 am I] I am L   55 what we very]
whate we be euer L, that we be very 1557   56 yt] om. L; full] most L 1557; nye.] nye,
1557   57 Fro] frome L, From 1557; departe] now parte L, depart 1557; fyrst.] fyrst /
O, fyrst, 1557; Lo] and lo now 1557

Farewell madam my lordes worþi moder,
Comfort your son, & be ye of good chere.
60   Take all in worth, for yt will be non oþer.
Farwell my dowghter late the fere
To prince Arthur my own child so dere,
Yt botith not for me to wepe & crye,
Pray for my sowle, for now lo here I lye.

65   Adewe lord Harry my lovely son adewe.
Owr lord increase your honour & your estate.
Adewe my dowghter Mary bright of hewe.
God make you vertuous wyse & fortvnate.
Adewe swet harte my lady dowghter Cate,
70   Thou shalt good babe suche ys thi destenye,
Thy moder never know, for lo here I lye. [fol. 176]

O lady Cecill Anne and Kateryne,
Farewell my wellbelouyd systers thre.
O lady Brygyte dere syster myne,
75   Lo here the ende of worldly vanyte.
Lo well ar you þat erthly folye fle,
And hevynly thynges loue & magnyfye,
Farewell & pray for me, for lo here I lye.

---

59 ye] you *L;* good] god *L*   60 in worth] aworthe *L,* a worth *1557;* will be] wolbe *L;* non
oþer] no nother *1557*   61 dowghter] doughter kateryne *L,* doughter Katherine *1557;*
fere] fere, *1557*   62 my own] late my *L,* myne owne *1557*   63 &] or *1557*   64 my
sowle, for] *om. L;* now lo] lo now *L 1557*   65 lord] my lord *L;* Harry] Henry *1557;*
lovely] lovyng *L 1557*   66 your estate.] astate, *L 1557*   69 lady] lytyll *L,* litle
1557   70 good babe suche] good seche as *L,* swete babe suche *1557*   71 Thy moder
never know] thoughe I the neuer knewe *L;* know] know / *O;* lo] lo now *L 1557*   72 O
lady Cecill Anne and] O lady sessele O Lady *L,* Lady Cicyly Anne and *1557;* Kateryne,]
Katheryne. *1557*   73 wellbelouyd systers thre.] lovying susteris bothe *L*   74 Bry-
gyte] Bregytt *L,* Briget *1557;* dere] tho odere *L,* other *1557*   75 Lo . . . vanyte] here
may you see how this world gothe *L*   76 Lo . . . fle] Wele may ye be that doth foly lothe
L, Now well are ye that earthly foly flee *1557*   78 me] my sowle *L;* lo] now *L,* lo now
1557

Adewe my lordes & ladyes all,
Adewe my feythfull seruauntes euerychon, 80
Adewe my comyns whom I neuer shall
Se in þis world. Wherfor to the alone,
Immortall god very thre in on,
I me commend. Thy infenyte mercy,
Shew to thi seruaunt now for lo here I lye. 85

---

79 lordes] lordes, *1557;* &] adewe my *L 1557*   81 my] all my *L;* shall] ll *cropped in O,* shall, *1557*   82 the alone] you all *L*   83 very] verely *1557;* in] and *1557*   84 commend.] commend to *O L,* commende *1557* (to *inked out*)   85 seruaunt] seruauntes *O,* seruant, *L 1557;* now for lo] for lo nowe *L,* for lo now *1557*

⁋ A mery geſt how a ſergeaūt woldel erne to be a frere:

yſe men alwaye
Affecme t ſay / y beſt is
Foꝛ a dylygently (man
Foꝛ to apply / y beſynes
y he and in no wyſe (can
To enter pꝛyſe/ an other faculte
Foꝛ he that wyll
And can no ſkyll/is neuer lyke to the
He that hath laſte
The hoſiers crafte t falleth to makyge
The ſmythe that ſhall (ſhone
To pâtyge fall his thꝛyfte is wel nygh
A blacke dꝛaper (done
With wyte pap/ to go to wꝛytyge ſcole
An olde butler
Betū a cutler/J wene ſhal pꝛoue a fole
In olde trot
That good cā not/but euer kyſſe y cup
With her phyſyke
Wyll kepe one ſeke /tyll ſhe haue ſoued hym vp
A man of lawe
That neuer ſawe/the wayes to by and ſell
wenyn ge to aryſe
By marchaundyſe/J pꝛaye god ſpe de hym well
A marchaunt eke
That wyll good ſeke/by all the meanes he maye
To fall in ſute
Tyll he dyſpute/his monay clene awa ye
Pletynge the lawe
Foꝛ euery ſtrawe/ ſhall pꝛoue a thꝛyfty man
with bate and ſtryfe
But by my lyfe /J can not tell you whan
whan an hatter
wyll go ſmater In phylo ſophy
Oꝛ a pedlar
waye a medlar/in theolegy

A MERY GEST HOW A SERGEAUNT WOLDE LERNE TO BE A FRERE.

Wyse men alwaye,
Afferme & say,
   Y^t best is for a man: 5
Dylygently,
For to apply,
   Y^e besynes y^t he can,
And in no wyse,
To enterpryse   10
   An other faculte,
For he that wyll,
And can no skyll,
   Is neuer lyke to the.
He that hath lafte,   15
The hosiers crafte,
   & falleth to makynge shone,
The smythe that shall,
To payntyng fall,
   His thryfte is wel nygh done.   20

1–2 A MERY . . . FRERE.] *Preceding the title in 1557 is* These fowre thinges here folowyng Mayster Thomas More wrote in his youth for his pastime.; WOLDE LERNE] woldel erne *1516;* BE A] play the *1557*   3–11 Wyse . . . faculte] *1516 misarranges as follows:*

    Wyse men alwaye
    Afferme & say / y^t best is
    For a dylygently   (man
    For to apply / ye besynes
    y^t he and in no wyse (can
    To enterpryse / an other faculte

5 Y^t] the *1575;* a man] *1575* eche to man   8 Y^e] The *1557,* such *1575;* y^t] that *1557,* as *1575*   15 lafte] left *1575*   17 falleth] fall *1575*   19 payntyng] *1557,* pantynge *1516,* payntynge *1575*

A blacke draper,
With wyte paper,
   To go to wrytynge scole,
An olde butler,
Becum a cutler,
   I wene shal proue a fole.
An olde trot,
That good can not,
   But euer kysse ye cup,
With her physyke,
Wyll kepe one seke,
   tyll she haue soused hym vp.
A man of lawe,
That neuer sawe,
   The wayes to by and sell,
Wenynge to aryse,
By marchaundyse,
   I praye god spede hym well.
A marchaunt eke,
That wyll goo seke,
   By all the meanes he maye,
To fall in sute,
Tyll he dyspute,
   His monay clene awaye,
Pletynge the lawe,
For euery strawe,
   Shall proue a thryfty man,
With bate and stryfe,
But by my lyfe,
   I can not tell you whan.

---

24 butler] butteler *1575*   25 cutler] cutteler *1575*   27 An] *1575*, And an *1557*, In
1516   28 good can not] can (God wotte,) *1575*, can god wot *1557*   29 But euer]
nothinge but *1575 1557*   32 soused] *1575 1557*, soued *1516*   35 by] bye *1557*, buie
1575   36 aryse] ryse *1557*   40 goo] *1575 1557*, good *1516*   41 By] *om. 1575*
44 awaye,] away. *1557 1575*   45 Pletynge] Pleading *1575*

Whan an hatter
Wyll go smater,
   In phylosophy,
Or a pedlar,
Waxe a medlar, 55
   In theolegy, [fol. 1v]
All that ensewe,
Suche craftes newe,
   They dryue so fere a cast,
That euermore, 60
They do therfore,
   Beshrewe themselfe at laste.
This thynge was tryed
And verefyed,
   Here by a sergeaunt late, 65
That ryfely was,
Or he coude pas,
   Rapped aboute the pate,
Whyle that he wolde
Se how he coude, 70
   In goddes name play yᵉ frere:
Now yf you wyll,
Knowe how hyt fyll,
   Take hede & ye shall here.
It happed so, 75
Not longe ago,
   A thryfty man dyede.
An hondred pounde,
Of nobles rounde,
   That had he layde a syde: 80
His sone he wolde,
Sholde haue this golde,
   For to begyne with all:

---

59 fere] farre *1557*   62 Beshrewe] *1557 1575*, Boshrewe *1516*   63 tryed] *1557*
1575, cryed *1516*   66 ryfely] thriftly *1557*, rufully *1575*   77 man] man there *1557*
1575; dyede.] dyede, *1557*, dide. *1575*   80 That] than *1575*

But to suffyce
His chylde, well thryes
  Y^t monay were to small.
Yet or this daye
I haue herde saye,
  That many a man certesse,
Hath with good cast,
Be ryche at last,
  That hath begon with lesse.
But this yonge man,
So well beganne,
  His monaye to imploye,
That certenly,
His policy,
  To se hyt was a ioye.
For lest sum blaste,
Myght ouer caste,
  His shyp, or by myschaunce,
Men with some wyle,
Myght hym begyle,
  & mynysshe his substaunce,
For to put out,
All manere doubte,
  He made a good puruaye,
For euery whyt,
By his owne wyt,
  And toke another waye:
Fyrste fayre and wele, [fol. 2]
A grete dele,
  He dyght hyt in a pot,

85
90
95
100
105
110

---

84 suffyce] *1557 1575*, suffyte *1516*   85 thryes] thrise, *1557*, thryues *1575*
86 were] was *1557*   88 herde] hard *1557*   91 at] at the *1575*   92 hath] *om.*
1575   94 beganne] *1557*, he can *1516 1575*   97 policy] *1557*, po.cy *1516*, polecia
1575   99 lest] least *1575*   104 substaunce,] *1557*, substaunce. *1575*, substaunce
1516   107 puruaye] purauye *1516*   110 another] *1557 1575*, other *1516*   112
A grete] Therof much *1557*, A pretie *1575*   113 dyght hyt] dyghthyt *1516*, dygged it
1557, hyd it *1575*

But then hym thought,
That way was nought, 115
   And there he lefte hyt not.
So was he fayne,
Frome thens agayne,
   To put hyt in a cup,
And by and by, 120
Couetously,
   He supped hyt fayre vp.
In his owne brest,
He thought hyt best,
   His monaye to enclose. 125
Then wyst he well,
What euer fell,
   He coude hyt neuer lose.
He borowed than,
Of a nother man, 130
   Monaye and marchaundyse:
Neuer payde hyt,
Vp he layde hyt,
   In lyke maner wyse.
Yet on the gere,
That he wolde were, 135
   He rought not what he spente,
So hyt were nyce,
As for the pryce,
   Coude hym not myscontente. 140
With lusty sporte,
And with resorte,
   Of ioly company,
In myrthe and playe,
Full many a daye, 145
   He lyued merely.

---

114 then] *1557*, tehn *1516*, than *1575*   115 way] *1557 1575, om. 1516*   121 Coue-
tously] as couetouslie *1575*   122 vp.] vp, *1557*, vppe. *1575*   125 enclose.] enclose,
1557 1575   129 borowed] *1557 1575*, porowed *1516*   130 a nother man] other
men *1557*   137 spente,] *1557*, spent. *1516*, spent: *1575*

And men had sworne,
Some man is borne,
　　To haue a goodly floure,
150 And so was he,
For suche degre,
　　He gate and suche honoure,
That with out doubte,
Whan he went out,
155 　　A sergaunt well and fayre,
Was redy strayte,
On him to wayte,
　　As sowne as on the mayre.
But he doubtlesse,
160 Of his mekenes,
　　Hated suche pompe & pryde,
And wolde not go,
Compnyed so,
　　But drewe hym selfe a syde,
165 To saynt Katheryne, [fol. 2v]
Streyght as a lyne,
　　He gate hym at a tyde.
For deuocyon
Or promocyon,
170 　　There wolde he nedes abyde.
There spente he fast,
Tyll all was past,
　　And to hym came there many,
To aske theyr det,
175 But non coude get,
　　The valour of a peny.
With vysage stoute,

---

149 haue a goodly floure,] haue a lucky howre, *1557*, dignite and powre. *1575*
158 sowne] sone *1575 1557*   163 Compnyed] companied *1557*, accompanied *1575*
164 a syde,] aside. *1575*   167 tyde.] tyde, *1557*, tide *1575*   168 deuocyon] *1557*
promocyon *1516*, promotion, *1575*   169 promocyon] deuotion, *1575*   170 abyde]
bide *1575*

He bare hyt oute,
  Vnto the harde hedge,
A moneth or twayne,   180
Tyll he was fayne,
  To laye his gowne to pledge.
Than was he there,
In greter fere,
  Then or that he came thyder,   185
And wolde as fayne,
Departe agayne,
  But that he wyst not whyther.
Than after this,
To a frende of his,   190
  He went and there abode,
Where as he laye,
So syke al waye,
  He myght not come abrode.
Hyt happed than,   195
A marchaunt man,
  That he ought monaye to,
Of an offycere,
Than gan enquyre,
  What hym was best to do.   200
And he answerde,
Be not a ferde,
  Take an accyon therfore,
I you beheste,
I shall hym reste,   205
  And than care for no more.
I fere quod he,
Hyt wyll not be,
  For he wyll not com out.
The sergeaunt sayd,   210

---

179 Vnto] Euen vnto *1557*   184 greter] *1557 1575*, groter *1516*   185 Then] Than
1575; or] ere *1557*   199 Than] that *1575*   205 reste] *1557*, rrste *1516*, rest *1575*

Be not afrayde,
　　Hyt shall be brought aboute.
In many a game,
Lyke to the same,
215　　　　Haue I bene well in vre,
And for your sake,
Let me be bake,
　　But yf I do this cure.
Thus part they bothe, [fol. 3]
220　And forth hym goth,
　　　Apace this offycere,
And for a daye,
All his araye,
　　　He chaunged with a frere.
225　So was he dyght,
That no man myght,
　　　Hym for a frere deny,
He dopped and doked,
He spake and loked,
230　　　So relygyously.
Yet in a glasse,
Or he wolde passe,
　　　He toted and he pered:
His herte for pryde,
235　Lepte in his syde,
　　　To se how well he frered.
Than forth apace,
Vnto the place,
　　　He goeth in goddes name,
240　To do this dede,
But nowe take hede,
　　　For here begynneth yᵉ game.
He drewe hym nye,

220 forth hym] to hym *1516 1575*, foorth then *1557*   228 doked] douked *1575*,
dooked *1557*   233 pered:] peered, *1557*, pored, *1575*   236 frered] fryred *1575*
243 hym] *1557 1575*, hy *1516*

And softly,
　At the dore he knocked: 245
A damoysell,
That herde hym well,
　Came & it vnlocked.
The frere sayd,
God spede fayre mayde,   250
　Here lodgeth such a man,
It is tolde me:
Well syr quod she,
　And yf he do what than?
Quod he maystresse,   255
No harme doutlesse:
　Hyt longethe for our ordre,
To hurte no man,
But as we can,
　Euery wyght to fordre: 260
With hym truely,
Fayne speke wolde I.
　Syr quod she, by my faye,
He is so syke,
Ye be not lyke,   265
　To speke with hym to daye.
Quod he fayre maye,
Yet I you praye,
　This moche at my desyre,
Vouchesafe to do,   270
As to go hym to,
　And saye an austen frere,
Wolde with hym speke, [fol. 3v]
And maters breke,
　For his auayle certyne.   275

---

244 And] And then *1575;* softly] softely *1557,* softlie *1575*　　245 At] Streyght at
1557　　246 A] And a *1557;* damoysell] Damsell *1575,* damsell *1557*　　247 herde]
hard *1557,* heard *1575*　　248 Came] There came *1557 1575*　　251 lodgeth] *1575*
1557, lodget *1516*　　254 than?] than. *1557*　　256 doutlesse:] doublesse *1516,* doute-
lesse, *1557 1575*　　263 she,] she *1557*　　267 Quod] Quoth *1575*　　269 This] Thus
1575　　271 to go] go *1557,* goe *1575*

Quod she I wyll,
Stonde ye here styll,
   Tyll I come downe agayne.
Vp is she go,
280   And tolde hym so,
   As she was bode to saye.
He mystrystynge,
No maner thynge,
   Sayd mayden go thy waye,
285   And fetche hym hyder,
That we togyder,
   May talke. Adowne she goth,
And vp she brought.
No harme she thought,
290   But it made some folke wroth.
But this offycere,
This fayned frere,
   Whan he was come alofte,
He dopped than,
295   And grete this man,
   Relygyously and ofte.
And he agayne,
Ryght gladde & fayne,
   Toke hym there by ye honde.
300   The frere than sayd,
Ye be dysmayde,
   With trouble I vunderstonde.
In dede quod he,
Hyt hath with me,
305   Ben better than hyt is.
Syr quod the frere,

---

276 she] *1575 1557*, he *1516*   277 Stonde] Stande *1575*   279 go,] *1575*, go.
1557   281 was] *1557 1575*, wis *1516;* saye.] *1516 1575*, saye, *1557*   282 mys-
trystynge] mistrustinge *1575*, mistrustying *1557*   284 thy] *1557 1575*, they *1516*
288 And] *om. 1557;* she] him *1575*, she hym *1557;* brought.] brought, *1557*, brought
1575   291 But] *om. 1557*   299 honde.] honde *1516*, hande, *1557*, hande: *1575*
302 With] *1557*, hith *1516*, with *1575;* vnderstonde] vnderstande *1557*

Be of good chere,
   Yet shall hyt after this.
For crystes sake,
Loke that you take,   310
   No thought in your brest:
God may tourne all,
And so he shall,
   I truste vnto the best.
But I wolde now,   315
Com yn with you,
   In counsell yf you please,
Or elles nat
Of maters that,
   Shall set your herte at ease.   320
Downe went the mayde,
The marchaunt sayd,
   Now say on gentyll frere,
Of all this tydynge,
That ye me brynge,   325
   I longe full sore to here.
Whan there was none, [fol. 4]
But they alone,
   The frere with euyll grace,
Sayd I rest the,   330
Come on with me,
   And out he toke his mace:
Thou shalte obaye,
Come on thy waye,
   I haue the in my cloche.   335
Thou goest not hense,
For all the pense,
   The mayre hath in his pouche.
This marchaunt there,

---

308 Yet shall hyt] ye shall yet *1575;* this.] *1575,* this *1516,* this, *1557*   310 you]
ye *1575*   311 in] into *1575,* within *1557*   316 Com yn] Comyn *1516 1575,*
Comen *1557*   318 nat] not *1575*   321 went] *1557 1575,* weni *1516*   324 all] *om.*
1557 1575   335 cloche.] clouche, *1557 1575*

340   For wrathe and fere,
            Waxed welnyghe wode,
        Sayde horsone thefe,
        With a maschefe,
            Who hath taught the good?
345   And with his fyste,
        Vpon the lyste,
            He gaue hym suche a blowe,
        That bacwarde downe,
        Almoste in sowne,
350   The frere is ouerthrowe.
        Yet was this man,
        Well ferder than,
            Lest he the frere had slayne,
        Tyll with good rappes,
355   And heuy clappes,
            He dawde hym vp agayne.
        The frere toke herte,
        And vp he sterte,
            And well he layed aboute,
360   And so there goth,
        Betwene them bothe,
            Many a lusty cloute.
        They rente and tere,
        Eche other here,
365   And claue togyder fast,
        Tyll with luggynge,
        Halynge & tugynge,
            They fell doune both at last.
        Than on the grounde,
370   Togyder rounde,
            With many sadde stroke,

---

341 Waxed] He waxyng *1557*, waxinge *1575*   343 maschefe] mischefe *1557*, verie
mischefe *1575*   344 the] the thy *1557 1575; good?*] *1575*, good. *1557*   349 sowne]
1516 1557, swowne *1575*   364 other] others *1557*   367 Halynge &] And with
1557   369 Than] *1557 1575*, That *1516*   371 sadde] asdde *1516*, a heuy *1575*, a
sadde *1557*

They roll and rumble,
They tourne & tumble,
  Lyke pygges in a poke.
So longe aboue,   375
They heue and shoue,
  Togyder that at the last,
The mayde the wyfe,
To breke the stryfe,
  Hyed them vpwarde faste.   380
And whan they sye,
The captaynes lye,
  Waltrynge on the place, [fol. 4v]
The freres hode
They pulled agood,   385
  Adoune aboute his face.
Whyle he was blynde,
The wenche behynde,
  Lent hym on the flore,
Many a iolle   390
Aboute the nolle,
  With a grete batylldore.
The wyfe came yet,
And with her fete,
  She holpe to kepe hym downe,   395
And with her rocke,
Many a knocke,
  She gaue hym on the crowne.
They layde his mace,
Aboute his face,   400

---

372 They] *1575 1557*, The *1516*   374 Lyke pygges] lyke pygges do *1516*, As pygges
do *1557*   377 the] *om. 1557*   378 The] *1557 1575*, They *1516*; mayde the] mayd
and *1557*, maide and the *1575*   381 sye] se *1516*, spye *1557*, see *1575*   382 The]
1557, They *1516*, the *1575*   383 Waltrynge] Both waltring *1557*; on] in *1575*
384 The freres hode] The freres hood *1557*, The friers hood *1575* [frere *is missing in*
1516 because of a hole in the page]   389 hym] him leyd *1557*; flore,] *1516 1557*, flore.
1575   390 iolle] *1516*, ioule, *1557*, iole, *1575*   391 nolle] noule *1557*, nole *1575*
393 yet] to it *1575*   394 fete] feete *1575*   400 face] *1557 1575*, fuce *1516*

That he was wode for payne:
The frere frappe,
Gate many a swappe,
   Tyll he was full nyghe slayne.
405 Vp they hym lyfte,
And with euyll thryfte,
   Hedlynge all the stayre,
Downe they hym threwe,
And sayd adewe,
410   Commaunde vs to the mayre.
The frere arose,
But I suppose,
   Amased was his hede.
He shoke his eres,
415 And frome grete feres,
   He thought hym well a flede.
Quod he now lost
Is all this cost,
   We be neuer the nere.
420 Ill mote he the,
That caused me,
   To make my self a frere.
Now maysters all,
And now I shall,
425   Ende there I began.
In ony wyse,
I wolde auyse,
   And counseyll euery man,
His owne crafte vse,

402 frappe] frap *1575*   404 full] well *1575*   406 euyll] yll *1557*, euell *1575*
407 Hedlynge] Hedlyng *1557*, hedlong *1575;* all] a long *1557*   410 Commaunde]
recommaunde *1575*   413 hede.] hed, *1557*, heade: *1575*   414 eres]heres *1575*
417 lost] lost, *1557*   419 nere.] here: *1575*   424 And now] Here now *1557*, an
ende *1575*   425 Ende] make *1575;* there] there as *1557 1575;* began.] *1575*, began,
1557   429 crafte] *1575*, crafe *1516*, craft *1557*

All newe refuse,   430
   And vtterly let them gone:
Playe not the frere,
Now make good chere,
   And welcome euery chone.

Enprynted at London by me Iulyan Notary dwellyng   435
   in Powlys churche yarde at the weste dore
      at the sygne of saynt Marke

431 vtterly] lyghtly *1557*, vtterlye *1575*   434 euery] *1557 1575*, euey *1516*   435–
37 Enprynted . . . Marke] *Finis. 1557*, FINIS. *1575*

Fortune Verses, Balliol College, Oxford, MS 354, fol. 104 recto (detail, reduced)

[FORTUNE VERSES]

[A₁v]
The Prologue

[AS often as I consydre, these olde noble clerkes
Poetis, Oratours, & Phylosophers sectes thre,
Howe wonderfull they were, in all theyr werkes
Howe eloquent, howe inuentyue in euery degre   5
Halfe amased I am, and as a deed tre
Stonde styll, ouer rude for to brynge forth
Any fruyte or sentence, that is ought worth.

Neuertheles though rude I be, in all contryuying
Of matters, yet somwhat to make, I nede not to care.   10
I se many a one occupyed, in the same thynge.
Lo vnlerned men nowe a dayes, wyll not spare
To wryte, to bable, theyr myndes to declare
Trowynge them selfe, gay fantasyes to drawe
When all theyr cunnynge is not worth a strawe.   15

Some in french Cronycles, gladly doth presume.
Some in Englysshe, blyndly wade and wander.
Another in laten bloweth forth a darke fume
As wyse as a great hedded Asse of Alexandre.
Some in Phylosophye, lyke a gagelynge gandre   20
Begynneth lustely the browes to set vp,
And at the last concludeth in the good ale cup.

Finis Prologus.
quod T. M. [A₂]

Fortune peruerse   25
Qui le monde versse

1–51 THE . . . people] *om. O. 1557*

Toult a ton desyre
Iamais tu nas cesse
Plaine de finesse
30   Et y prens pleasire.

Par toy vennent maulx
Et guerres mortaulx
Touls inconueniens
Par mons et part vaulx
35   Et aulx hospitalx
Meurent tant de gens. [A₂v]

Fortune, O myghty & varyable
What rule thou claymest, with thy cruel power.
Good folke thou stroyest, and louest reprouable.
40   Thou mayst not waraunt thy gyftes for one houre.
Fortune vnworthy men setteth in honoure.
Thorowe fortune thinnocent in wo & sorow shricheth.
The iust man she spoyleth, & the vniust enrycheth.

Yonge men she kylleth, & letteth olde men lyue
45   Onryghtuously deuydynge tyme and season.
That good men leseth, to wycked doth she gyue.
She hath no difference, but iudgeth all good reason.
Inconstaunte, slypper, frayle, and full of treason
Neyther for euer cherysshynge, whom she taketh
50   Nor for euer oppressynge, whom she forsaketh.

Finish. quod T.M.] [fol. 104]

The wordes of / Fortune to þe people

Myne high estate power & auctoryte,
Yf ye ne know, enserche & ye shall spie,

---

45 deuydynge] deuydynge, *1556;* season.] season *1556*   46 gyue.] gyue *1556*
48 Inconstaunte] Inconstaunce *1556*   52 The wordes.] Certain meters in english
written by master Thomas More in hys youth for the boke of Fortune, and caused them to
be printed in the begynnyng of that boke. The wordes *1557;* people] O *1557,* people
quod Tho. Mo. *1556*   54 know] knewe *1556*

That riches, worshipe, welth, & dignite 55
Ioy, reste, & peace, & all thyng fynally,
That any pleasure or prophet may cum by,
To mannys comfort, aid, & sustynaunce,
Is all at my devise & ordeynance.

With owt my ffauour þer is no thyng wonne. 60
Many a mater haue I browght alaste
To good conclusion, þat fondely was begonne
& many a purpose, bownden sure & faste
With wyse provisioun, I have over caste.
With owt good happe þer may no wit suffise. 65
Better is to be ffortunate than wise.

And therfore hath som men bene or this
My dedly ffooys & wrytyn many a bok,
To my disprayse. And oþer cause ther nys,
But for me lyste not frendly on them loke. 70
Thus like the ffox thay fare þat ons forsok
þe plesant grapis, & gan for to defye them,
Because he lepte & cowld not cum by them.

But let them write, þe labowr is in vayn.
For well ye wote, myrth, honour, & riches 75
Better is than shame, penvry, & payn.
þe nedy wreche þat lyngereth in distresse,
Withowt myn helpe is euer comfortlesse,
A very bordon odyowse & lothe,
To all þe world, & to hym self bothe. 80

---

55 riches] richess *1557;* worshipe,] worshipe / *O;* welth] *om. O*　　56 reste, and peace]
reste / and / peace / *O*　　57 prophet] profyte *1556,* profit *1557*　　58 aid,] aid / *O*
61 alaste] at laste *1556,* at last, *1557*　　62 conclusion,] conclusion / *O*　　64 With] with
1556 1557; provisioun,] provisioun / *O*　　65 With owt] without *1556 1557*　　67 hath]
hath there *1556 1557;* this] this, *1557*　　69 disprayse] dispayre *O*　　70 loke.] loke *O*
1556 1557　　71 ons] ons / *O;* forsok] forsok, *1557*　　73 lepte &] lept & lept, & *1556,*
lept and yet *1557*　　74 write,] *1556,* write *O 1557*　　75 myrth, honour,] myrth hon-
our / *O;* riches] rychesse *1556 1557*　　76 Better] Much better *1557;* shame] *om.*
1557; shame, penvry,] shame / penvry / *O*　　77 wreche] wryteth *1556,* wretch *1557*
78 Withowt] without *1557*　　79 very] wery *1556 1557*　　80 &] and eke *1557*

But he þat by my ffavour may ascende,
To myghty power & excellent degre,
A common wele to govern & deffende,
O in how blessid condicoun stondith he:
85 Hym self in honour & ffelycyte,
And over þat, may forther & encrease
An hole regyon in ioy, reste & pease.

Now in this poynt þer is no more to say,
Eche man hathe of hym self þe gouernaunce.
90 Lett euery wight than take his own way.
& he þat owt of pouerte & myschaunce,
Lyste ffor to lyve & will hymself enhaunce,
In welthe & riches, cum forth & wayt on me.
And he þat will be a beggar, let hym be.

95   To them þat tristith in ffortune

Thow þat arte prowde of honour, shape or kynne,
þat hepeste vp this wrecchid worldes tresure,
Thy ffyngers shyned with gold, thy tawny skyn,
With freshe apparell garnysshed owt of mesure,
100 & weneste to haue fortune alway at þi plesure,
Cast vp thyn yee, & lok how slipper chaunce,
Illudethe her men with chaunge & variaunce. [fol. 104v]

Som tyme she loketh as lovely fayre & bryght,
As goodly Venus moder of Cupide.
105 She bekketh & smyleth vpon euery wight.

---

82 power] power / O   84 blessid] blessyd 1556, blist 1557; stondith] standeth 1556
1557   86 encrease] encrease, 1557   87 An hole regyon] 1556, An hole regyon / O,
A region hole 1557; ioy,] ioy / O, ioye 1556, joyfull 1557   90 take] folowe 1557
93 riches,] riches / O   94 beggar,] beggar / O   95 To them] Thomas More to
them 1557; tristith] trust 1557   96 honour,] honour O 1556 1557; kynne,] kynne.
1557   97 hepest] 1557, kepeste O, helpeste 1556   98 shyned] shryned 1556,
shrined 1557; gold,] gold / O   100 alway at] at 1557   101 yee] yee / O, eye 1556
1557   104 As] A O   105 smyleth vpon] she smileth on 1557

But þis ffayned chere may not abide.
þer commeth a clowde, & farewell all owr pride.
Lyk any serpent she begynneth to swell,
& loketh as ffers as any ffury of hell.

Yet ffor all þat we brytill men ar ffayn,   110
(So wrechid is owr nature & so blynde)
As sone as fortune list to lawgh agayn,
With fayre countenaunce & deceytffull mynde,
To crowche & knele & gape after þe wynde,
Not on or twayn but thowsandes on a rowt,   115
Lyke suarmyng bees cum flateryng her abowt.

Than as a bayte she bryngith forth her ware,
Syluer, gold, rich perle, & precyous stone:
On which þe mased peple gase & stare,
& gape þerfore, as dogges for the bone.   120
Fortune at them lawghith, & in her trone
Amyd her treasure & waveryng riches,
Prowdely she hoveth as lady & empres.

Faste by her side doth wery labowr stonde,
Thare ffere also, & sorow all bewepte,   125
Dysdeyn & hatred on þat oþer honde,
Eke restles wacche from slepe with travayle kept,
Hys eyes dowsy & lokying as he slepte.
Beffore her stondith danger & envye,
Flatery, disseit, myscheff & tyrannye.   130

---

106 ffayned chere] chere fayned *1557;* not] not long *1557*   108 Lyk] Lyk / *O*
110 Yet] yuet *1557;* brytill] brothle *1556,* brotle *1557*   113 With] with *1556 1557*
115 on a] in a *1556 1557*   116 flateryng] flakerynge *1556,* flickeryng *1557*   117 a]
om. *1556*   118 perle,] perle / *O*   120 dogges] dogges doe *1557*   122 riches]
rychesse *1556 1557*   123 hoveth] loueth *1556*   124 labowr] Labour *1557;* stonde]
stande *1556,* stand *1557*   125 Thare] pare *O,* Pale *1556 1557;* ffere] Fere *1557;* also,]
also / *O;* sorrow] Sorow *1557*   126 Dysdeyn] Dysdeyn / *O;* hatred] hatred / *O,* Hatred
1557; honde] hande *1556,* hand *1557*   128 dowsy] dowsy / *O,* drowsy *1556 1557*
129 stondith] standeth *1556 1557;* danger] Daunger *1557;* envye] Enuy *1557*   130 Flat-
ery,] fflatery / *O;* disseit] Dysceyt *1557;* myscheff] myscheff / *O,* Mischiefe *1557;* tyran-
nye.] Tiranny. *1557*

Abowt her commeth all þe world to begge.
He asketh londe, & he to passe wold brynge
This toye & þat, & all not worth an egge:
He wold in love prosper above all thynge:
135 He kneleth down & wold be made a kynge:
He fforseth not so he may money haue,
Thowgh all þe world accompt hym for a knave.

Lo thus dyueris heddes, dyueris wittes.
Fortune alone as dyueris as they all,
140 Vnstable here & þer amonge them fflittes:
& at aventure down her giftes fall,
Cacche who so may she throwith gret & small
Not to all men, as commeth sonne or dewe,
But for þe moste parte, all amonge a ffewe.

145 And yet her brotyll giftes may not laste.
He þat she gaue them, loketh prowde & hye.
She whirleth abowt & plukith away as fast,
& geveth them to an other by & by.
& thus from man to man contynvally,
150 She vsith to take & geve, & slyly tosse
On man to wynnyng of anothers losse.

& when she robbeth on, down goth his pride.
He wepith & wayleth & curseth her full sore.
But þat receyveth it, on þat other side,
155 Is glad, & blessith her a thousand tymes þerfore.

132 londe] lande *1557*; brynge] bryng, *1557*   133 toye] ioye *1556*; þat,] þat. *O*
137 knave] knee *O and superscript kc canc. before this word.*   138 thus] thus ye see
1557   142 may] may /*O*   143 men,] men / *O*; as] *1556 1557*, a *O*   145 giftes]
giftes long *1557*   147 whirleth] whirlth *1557*; plukith] plucketh *1556*, pluckth
1557   150 take & geve] gyue and take *1556*, geue and take *1557*   151 of] and of
1556   153 wayleth] wayleth / *O*   154 But] But he *1556 1557*   155 blessith]
blesseth *1556*, blesth *1557*; a thousand] a Mˡ *O*, a.M. *1556*, often *1557*

But in a whyle whan she loveth hym no more,
She glidith from hym, & her giftes to.
& he her cuseth as other foolis do. [fol. 105]

Alas þe ffolyshe people can not ceace,
Ne voyde her trayne, till they þe harme fele.   160
Abowt her alway, besyly they preace.
But lord what he thynkith hymself wele,
That may set onys his hond vpon her whele.
He holdeth ffaste: but vpward as he stithe,
She whippeth her whele abowt, & þer he lieth.   165

Thus ffell Iulius from his myghty power.
Thus ffel Darius þe worthy kyng of Perse.
Thus ffel Alysandre þe soverayn conquerowr.
Thus many mo than I may well reherce.
Thus dowble fortune, whan she liste reverce   170
Her slipper favour from them þat in her trust,
She ffleith away & layth them in þe dust.

She sodeynly enhaunceth them alofte.
& sodeynly myscheveth all þe floke.
The hede þat late lay easily & softe,   175
In stede of pilowse lith after on þe blokk.
& yet alas þe cruell prowd mokke:
The deynty mowth þat ladyes kissed haue,
She bryngith in case to kysse a knave.

Thus whan she chaungith her vncertayn coorse   180
Vp starteth a knave, & down þer fallith a knyght.

---

157 hym,] hym / O   158 cuseth] curseth *1556 1557*   160 trayne,] trayne / *O;*
harme] harme do *1557*   162 what he thynkith] how he doth thynk *1557;* wele,] full
wele. *1557*   163 hond] hande *1556 1557*   164 ffaste:] ffaste / *O;* stithe] styeth
1556, flieth *1557*   168 soverayn] great *1557*   171 slipper favour] slipper / fa-
vour / *O*   172 ffleith away] flyeth her waye *1556,* fleeth her wey *1557;* layth them]
lyeth hym *1556,* leyeth them *1557*   173 them] hym *1556*   175 softe] full soft
1557   176 lith] lyeth *1556 1557*   177 cruell] most cruell *1557*   179 case] the
case *1556 1557*   180 Thus . . . coorse] Thus when she chaunseth, her vncertayne
course *1556,* In chaungyng of her course, the chaunge shewth this, *1557*   181 start-
eth] startth *1557;* knave,] knave / *O;* fallith] falth *1557;* knyght.] knyght *1557*

The beggar riche, & þe riche man pore is.
Hatred totorned to love, love to dispight.
This is her sporte, thus proveth she her myght.
185 Gret bost she maketh yf on be by her power,
Welthy & wrechid both in an howre.

Pouerte þat of her giftes will no thyng take,
With mery chere, she loketh on þe prece,
& seth how fortunes howshold goth to wrak.
190 Fast by her stondith þe wise Socrates,
Aristippus, Pithagoras, & many a lese
Of old filosophers. & eke agaynst þe sonne
Bekith hym pore Diogenes in his tonne.

With her is Byas, whose contrey lakkid diffence,
195 & whilom of þer ffoes stode in dowt,
þat eche man hastyly gan to cary thens,
& asked hym why he nowght caried owt.
I bere, quod he, all myn with me abowt:
Wisedom he ment, no fortunes brotill ffees.
200 For nowght he countid his þat he myght lese.

Heracletus eke, liste ffeliship to kepe
With glad pouerte, Democretus also:
Of which þe ffirst can neuer cease but wepe,
To see howe thik þe blynd people go,
205 With gret labowr to purchase care & wo.
þat oþer laweth to se þe folishe apes,
How ernestly they walke abowt þer iapes.

182 riche,] riche. O   183 totorned] is turned 1556 1557; love,] love. O   184 sporte,]
sporte. O   185 maketh] maketh / O; be by] 1556 1557, by O   186 wrechid] wrechid
/ O; in] within 1557   188 she loketh] looketh 1557; on] vppon 1557   189 howshold
goth] how shulde go 1556, houshold goeth 1557   190 stondith] standeth 1556 1557;
Socrates] socrates O   191 Aristippus,] Aristippus / O; lese] lyfe 1556, lese. 1557
192 filosophers.] filosophers / O   194 Byas,] Byas. O   195 stode] stode so 1556
1557   198 bere, quod he,] bere quod he 1556 1557   199 no] not 1556 1557
201 eke,] eke. O, to 1556   203 cease] om. 1556   204 blynd] blynded 1557
205 gret labowr] great laboure 1556, labour great 1557   206 laweth] laugheth 1556
1557

Of this pore secte, it is the vsage,
Only to take þat nature may susteyn,
Banysshyng clen all oþer surplusage, 210
They be content, & of no thyng complayn.
No nygard eke ys of his good so ffayn,
But they more plasure haue a thousand ffold,
The secrete drawghtes of nature to behold. [fol. 105v]
Set ffortunes seruantes by them self & ye wull, 215
That on ys ffree, þat other ever thrall,
That on content, þat other never ffull,
That on in suerte, þat other lyke to ffall.
Who lyst to advise them both, perceyve he shall,
As gret differens betwen them as we see, 220
Betwyxt wrechidnesse & ffelicyte

Now haue I shewid you both: chese which ye liste,
Stately fortune, or humble poverte:
þat is to say, now lyeth it in your ffist,
To take you to bondage, or free lyberte. 225
But in this poynt & ye do after me,
Draw þe to fortune, & labowr her to please,
Yf that ye thynk your self to well at ease.

And ffirst, vpon þe lovely shall she smyle,
& frendly on þe cast her wanderyng eyes, 230
Enbrace þe in her armes, & for a while,
Put the into a ffoolis paradise:
& forthwith all, what so þou liste devise,
She will þe graunt it lyberally perhappes:
But for all þat beware of after clappes. 235

208 the] comen *1557*   213 a thousand] M¹ *O*   214 to] and to *1556*   215 them
self] them *1556 1557*   216 ffree,] ffree / *O*   217 content,] content / *O;* ffull,] full.
1557   218 suerte,] suerte / *O*   219 he] ye *1556*   223 fortune,] fortune / *O*
225 you to] here *1557*   226 ye] þ *O*   227 þe] you *1556 1557*   231 armes,] armes.
O   232 into] and kepe the in *1557*   233 all,] *1556*, all *O 1557*

Rekyn you neuer of her ffavour sure:
Ye may in þe clowdes as easily trace an hare,
Or in drye londe cause fishes to endure,
& make þe brennyng fyre his hete to spare,
240   & all this world encompace to forfare,
As her to make by craft of engyne stable,
That of her nature ys euer variable.

Serve her day & nyght as reverently,
Vpon thy knees as seruaunt may,
245   & in conclusion, þat þou shalt wynne þerbe
Shall not be worthe thy seruise I dare say.
& loke yet what she geveth þe today,
With labowr wonne she shall haply tomorow
Pluk it owt of thyn hond with sorowe.

250   Wherefor yf þou in suerte liste to stonde,
Take poverties parte & lat prowde fortune go,
Reseyue no thynge þat commeth from her honde:
Love maner & vertu: for they be only tho
Which dowble fortune may neuer tak þe fro.
255   Than mayst þou boldly defy her tornyng chance:
She can the noþer hyndre nor avaunce.

But & þou wilt nedes medill with her tresur,
Trust not þerin, & spend it lyberally.
Bere þe not prowde, nor tak not owt of mesur.
260   Byld not thyn hows high vp in þe skye.
Non ffallith ferre, but he þat clymeth hye,

---

237 þe] *om. 1557*   239 brennyng] burnynge *1556*, burnyng *1557*   240 &] As *1556;*
encompace] in compace *1557*   241 of] or any *1556 1557*   244 as] as any *1556*
1557   245 shalt] shall *1556;* þerbe] therby *1556*, thereby *1557*   247 loke yet] loke /
yet *O*, yet, loke *1556*, looke yet *1557*   249 owt of thyn hond] out of thy hande agayne
1556, agayne out of thyne hande *1557*   250 stonde] stande *1556 1557*   251 parte]
parte. *O;* lat] let *1556 1557*   252 Reseyue] Res *O;* honde] hande *1556 1557*   253 for]
om. 1557; tho] tho. *1557*   254 neuer] not *1557*   255 defy] *1556 1557,* desire
O   256 noþer] neyther *1556 1557*   258 þerin,] þerin / *O*   260 hows] hows. *O;*
high] hyghe *1556,* on heyth *1557*   261 clymeth] clynbeth *1556,* climbeth *1557*

Remembre nature sent þe hether bare,
þe gifts of fortune cownt them borrowed ware.

To them þat seketh ffortune

Who so deliteth to prove & assay,   265
Of waueryng fortune þe full vncertayn lot,
Yf þat þe answere plese þe not alway,
Blame not me: for I comande you not,
Fortune to trust, & eke full well ye wot,
I haue of her no brydyll in my ffiste,   270
She renneth lose, & torneth wher she lyste. [fol. 106]

The rollyng dise in whom your lukk doth stonde,
With whose vnhappy chaunce ye be so wrothe,
Ye know your self cam neuer in myn honde.
Lo in this pond be fishe & frogges bothe.   275
Cast in your nett: but be you leve or lothe,
Holde you content as fortune liste asigne:
Hit is your own fishyng & not myne.

And thowgh in on chaunce fortune you affende,
Grucche not þerat, but bere a mery fface.   280
In many anoþer she shall it amende.
Ther is no man so fer owt of her grace,
But he somtyme hath comfort & solace:
Ne non agayn so ferre forth in her ffavor,
þat ffully satysfied is with her behawor.   285

Fortune ys stately, solempne, prowde, & hye:
& riches geveth, to haue servise þerfore.

---

262 hether] hyther *1556 1557*   263 cownt them] compt them, as *1556*   264 To . . .
ffortune] *om. 1556*, Thomas More to them that seke fortune. *1557;* seketh] seketh.
O   265 prove] prouen *1556 1557*   266 full] *om. 1557*   267 þe not] you not
1557   268 Blame] Blame ye *1557;* you] ye *1556*   270 I] I. *O*   272 stonde] stand
1556, stande *1557*   273 wrothe] wrought *1556,* wroth *1557*   274 honde] hande
1556 1557   275 fishe] fysshes *1556*   276 nett:] nett / *O;* you leve] ye lyefe *1556,*
you liefe *1557*   278 Hit] For it *1557*   280 þerat,] þerat / *O*   282 fer] farre
1557   285 ffully satysfied is] full satyfyed is *1556,* is full satisfyed *1557*   286 stately,
solempne, prowde,] stately / solempne / prowde / *O*   287 riches] rychesse *1557;*
geveth,] geveth / *O*

The nedy beggar cacchith an half peny:
Som man a thousand pound, som lesse, some more.
290 But for all þat she kepeth euer in store
From euery man som parcell of his will,
That he may pray þerfore & serue her still.

Som man hath good, but children hath he non.
Som man hath both, but he can get non helthe.
295 Som hath all thre, but vp to honowrs trone
Can he not crepe, by no maner stelthe.
To som she sendith children, riches, welthe,
Honowr, worship, & reuerens all his lyff:
But yet she plucketh hym with a shrewed wyff.

300 Than for as mych as it is fortunes gyse
To graunt no man all thyng þat he will axe,
But as her self liste ordre & devise,
Doth euery man his parte devide & taxe,
I cownsell you eyther trusse vp your pakkes,
305 & take no thyng at all, or be content
With suche reward as fortune hath you sent.

All thynges in this boke þat ye shall rede,
Do as ye liste, þer shall no man you bynde,
Them to beleve, as surely as your crede.

---

289 a thousand pound] m¹ li O, a.M. pounde *1556*, a thousande pounde *1557*; lesse,]
lesse *1557*   290 store] O *1556*, store, *1557*   293 good,] good, O; he] *om. 1556*
294 both,] both / O   295 thre,] thre. O; trone] trone, *1557*   296 maner] maner of
1556 1557   297 sendith] sendith / O, sendeth, *1557*; children, riches,] children /
riches / O   298 Honowr, worship,] Honowr / worship / O   299 plucketh] pynch-
eth *1556 1557*   304 eyther] *om. 1556*, eche one *1557*   305 content] content,
1557   306 With] with *1556 1557*   307 *Sidenote 1557:* He meaneth the boke of for-
tune.   308 you] *1556 1557*, ye O   309 beleve] belene *1557*

But notwithstondyng certes in my mynde,   310
I durste well swere, as trew shall ye them fynd,
In euery poynt eche answere by & by,
As ar þe iugementes of astronomye.

Explicit

---

311 shall ye] ye shall *1556 1557*   314 Explicit] *O,* Here Fineth Lady Fortune. *1556,*
Thus endeth the preface to the booke of fortune. *1557 (see note)*

Lewes ye loste louer

Ey flatteringe fortune looke thow neuer so fayre
nor neuer so pleasauntely begynne to smile
As though thow wouldest my ruyne all repayre
Duringe my life thow shalt me not begile
Truste shall I god to enter in a whyle
hys hauen of heauen sure and vniforme
Euer after thy calme looke I for a storme.

Dauy the diser. &c.

Longe was I ladye lucke your seruynge man
and nowe haue I loste agayne all that I gate
Wherfore whan I thinke on you now and than
and in my mynde remember this and that
You may not blame me though I besshrew yor catte
but in fayethe I blysse you agayn a thousande tymes
for lendinge me nowe some laisour to make rymes.

Moraris si sit spes hic tibi longa morandi
Hoc te vel Morus More monere potest.
Desine morari et caelo meditare morari
Hoc te vel Morus &c.

Lewys the Lost Louer, British Library, MS Royal 17.D XIV, fol. 453 (reduced)

LEWES Yᵉ LOSTE LOVER

Ey flatteringe fortune, looke thow neuer so faire,
Nor neuer so plesauntely begynne to smile,
As though thow wouldest my ruyne all repaire,
Duringe my life thow shalte me not begile.   5
Truste shall I god, to enter in a while,
His hauen of heauen euer suer & vniforme:
Euer after thy caulme, looke I for a storme.

1 LEWES . . . LOUER] *Br, Cr, L, 1557*, Lewes . . . louer in fortunam, *CR; Sidenote CR:* T
M   2 Ey] Fye *C L² A² X, om. O T Ah X;* thow] you *J W;* neuer] nere *A² D L² O² W Y,* near
C; faire] fai *L² (MS cropped)*   3 Nor] or *1557;* neuer] nere *A² C D L² O²;* plesauntly]
lovingly *S*   4 though] *om. A H¹ H³ M O T;* wouldest] would'st *A² C D H¹ L² O² R Y 1557,*
would *X;* ruyne] ruins *A² B C D J L² O² R W X;* repaire] prepa *L² (MS cropped)*   5 life]
life, *Y;* thow] yow *H²;* me not] not me *A A² C D H¹ H² H³ L² M O R S T W;* begile] beguilde
A²   6 shall I] I ̇shall *A B C H¹ H² H³ J M O O² T W X Y;* in] within *R;* while,] while.
1557   7 His] The *A² B C D L¹ W X,* thy *A C H¹ H³ J M O O² T;* hauen] heauen *A² B D O²
T W X Y;* heauen] heauens *W X Y,* heauens, *O²;* euer] *om. A A² C D H¹ H² L² M O O² R S T W
Y 1557;* vniforme:] vniforme. *1557*   8 thy] the *M W X,* ye *A² W,* a *B C D L²;* a] noe *A H¹
H² H³ J M O;* storme] sto *L² (MS cropped)*

DAVY THE DISER

Longe was I ladye lucke your seruynge man,
And nowe haue I loste agayne all that I gate,
Wherefore whan I thinke on you now and than,
5 And in my mynde remember this and that,
You may not blame me though I beshrewe your catte,
But in faythe I blisse you agayn a thowsand tymes,
For lendinge me nowe some laisour to make rymes.

---

1 DAUY . . . DISER] Dauy . . . diser in fortunam *CR; Sidenote Br:* Thomae Mori; *Side-note Cr:* T M   2 I] *om. 1557*   3 gate] hast [*deleted before* gate] *BR*   6 me] *om. Br*

LIFE OF PICO

The life of John Picus Erle of Myrandula, a great Lorde of Italy, an excellent connyng man in all sciences, & vertuous of liuing: with diuers epistles & other workes of ye sayd John Picus, full of greate science, vertue, and wisedome: whose life and workes bene worthy and digne to be read, and often to be had in memory.

Translated out of latin into Englische by maister Thomas More.

(∴)

Unto his right entierly beloued sister in Christ, Joyeuce Leigh, Thomas More greting in our lorde.

The intēt or meanynge of new yeres gyftes.

IT is, and of lōge time hath bene (my well beloued sister) a custome in the beginnyng of the new yere, frendes to sende betwene, presentes or gyftes, as the witnesses of their loue and frendship, & also signifying, that thei desire eche to other that yere a good continuance and prosperous ende of that lucky beginnyng. But commonly all those presentes, that are vsed customably all in this maner betwene frendes to be sent: be such thinges as perteine only vnto the body, either to be fed, or to be clad, or some other wise delited: by whiche it semeth, that their frendship is but fleshly, and stretcheth in maner to the body only. But for asmuch as the loue & amitie of christen folke should be rather ghostly frēdship then bodily: sith that all faithfull people are rather spirituall then carnall. (For, as thapostle saith: we be not now in fleshe, but in spirit, if Christ abide in vs.) I therfore myne hertely beloued sister, in good lucke of this new yere, haue sent you suche a present, as maie beare witnesse of my tender loue and zele to the happy cōtinuaūce & gracious encrease of vertue in your soule. And whereas the giftes of other folke declare that thei wissh their frendes to be worldly fortunate: myne testifieth, that I desire to haue you godly prosperous. These workes more profitable thē

Presentes bodily.
Christē loue.
Rom.8.

large, were made in latine by one John Picus Erle of Mirandula, a lordship in Italye: of whose conyng and vertue we nede here nothing to speake: forasmuch as hereafter we peruse the course of his whole life, rather after our litle power slenderly, then after his merites sufficiently. The workes are suche, y trewly god sister, I suppose of the quātitie ther cometh none in your hande more profitable, neither to thatchieuyng of temperāce in prosperitie, nor to the dispising of worldly vanitie, nor to the desiring of heauēly felicitie: which workes I wolde require you gladly to receiue: ne were it, that thei be such, that for the gwdly mater (how so euer thei be translated) maie delite & please any person, that hath any meane desire and loue to God: and that your selfe is such one, as for your vertue and seruent zele to god, can not but ioyously receiue any thing, that meanely soundeth either to the reproch of vice, commendacion of vertue, or honoure and laude of God, who preserue you.

The profit of his workes.

The life of John Picus Erle of Mirandula.

JOhn Picus of the fathers side, descended of the worthy linage of themperoure Constantyne, by a neuewe of the sayde Emperour called Picus, by whō al the auncessors of this John Picus, vndoutedly beare that name. But we shall lette his auncessors passe, to whom (though thei were right excellent) he gaue agayn as much honour, as he receiued: & we shall speake of him self, rehearsing in part his learning, & his vertue. For these be the thinges, whiche we may accōpt for our owne: of which euery man is more properly to be cōmēded, thē of the noblenes of his aūcesters: whose honour maketh vs not honorable. For either they were themself vertouse or not: if not, thē had thei none honour thēself: had thei neuer so great possessiōs: for honour is the reward of vertue. And howe maie thei clayme the rewarde y properly longeth to vertue: if they lacke the vertue, that the rewarde longeth to? Then if thēselfe had

The linage of J. Picus.
Noblenesse of auncesters.
Honour.

a.j.

The workes of Sir Thomas More Knyght (London, 1557), sig. a₁ (reduced)

Here is conteyned the lyfe of
Iohan Picus Erle of Myrandula
a grete lord of Italy an excellent
conning man in all sciences.
& verteous of lyuing. with dyuers
epistles & other warkis of the
seyd Iohan Picus full of grete
science vertew and wysedome:
whos lyfe & warkys bene worthy
& digne to be redd & oftyn to
be had in memorye.

Unto his right entierly beloued sister
in crist Ioyeuce Leigh thomas more
greting in our lorde.

Hᴵᵀ is and of longe time hath bene my well beloued sister a
custome in the begynnyng of yᵉ new yere frendes to sende bet-   5
wene presentis or yeftis / as the witnesses of their loue and
frendsship and also signifyenge that they desyre eche to other
that yere a gode contynuance and prosperous ende of that lukky
bigynnyng. But communely all those presentes that are vsed
customably all in thys maner betwene frendis to be sent: be such   10
thyngis as pertayne only vnto the body eithir to be fed or to be
cledd or some othir wyse delyted: by which hit semyth that their
frendshyp is but flesshly and stretchith in maner to the body
only. But for asmoch as the loue and amyte of christen folke
shuld be rather gostly frendsshyp then bodili: sith that all feith-   15
ful peple are rather spirituall then carnall (for as thapostle seith
we be not now in flessh but in spiret if crist abide in vs) I therfore
myne hartely beloued sister in good lukk of this new yere haue
sent you such a present as may bere witnes of my tendre loue and
zele to the happy continuannce and graciouse encreace of vertue   20
in your soule: and where as the giftis of other folk declare yᵗ thei
wissh their frendes to be worldeli fortunate myne testifieth that I
desire to haue you godly prosperous. These warkis more profita-
ble then large were made in latyne by one Iohan picus erle of

---

3 *Sidenote 1557:* The intent or meanynge of new yeres gyftes   6 yeftis] *1510 1557,*
gyftes *1525*   8 prosperous] *1525 1557,* prosperons *1510*   10 *Sidenote 1557:* Pre-
sentes bodily   12 cledd] *1510,* cledde *1525,* clad *1557*   13 frendshyp] *1525,*
frendhyp *1510,* frendship *1557;* flesshly] flessly *1510,* flesshely *1525,* fleshly *1557*
14 *Sidenote 1557:* Christen loue   15 gostly] *1510,* goosty *1525,* ghostly *1557*   16 car-
nall (for] carnall. For *1510 1525,* carnall. (For *1557; Sidenote 1557:* Rom. 8   17 vs) I] vs.
I *1510 1525,* vs.) I *1557*   22 wissh] *1510 1557,* wyssheth *1525*   23 prosperous.]
1525 1557, prosperous *1510*   24 *Sidenote 1557:* Iohn Picus

Mirandula a lordshyp in Italy of whos connyng & vertue we nede here [A₁v] no thyng to speke for asmuch as heraftir we peruse the course of his hole life rather aftir our litle power slenderly then aftir his merites sufficiently. The warkes are such that

5 trewly goode sister I suppose of yᵉ quantite ther commeth none in your hande more profitable: neithir to thachyuyng of temperaunce in prosperite / nor to yᵉ purchasing of patience in aduersite / nor to the dispising of worldly vanite / nor to the desiring of heuinly felicite. Which warkis I wolde require you

10 glady to receiue: ne were hit that they be such that for the goodly mater (how so euir they be translated) may delite & please any person that hath any meane desire & loue to god: and that your self is such one as for your vertue & feruent zele to god can not but ioyously receiue any thing that meanely sownith eithir to the

15 reproch of vyce commendation of vertue or honoure and laude of god who preserue you. [a₁]

The life of Iohn Picus
Erle of mirandula.

IOHAN Picus of the faders side descendid of the worthy linage

20 of themperoure Constantine by a neuew of the seid emperoure called Picus by whom al the Auncestres of this Iohan Picus vndowtedly bere yᵗ name. But we shal let hys auncestres passe to whom (though they were right excellent) he gaue a gaine as much honoure as he receyued: and we shal speke of hym self

25 rehersing in part his lernynge and his vertue. For these be the thinges which we may accompt for our owne of which euery man is more proprely to be commended then of the noblenes of his auncestres: whose honoure makith vs nat honorable. For either they were them self vertuouse or not: if not then had they none

30 honoure themself: had they neuer so grete possessions: for hon-

---

4 Sidenote 1557: The profit of his workes   12 god: and] God: and 1557, god. And 1510 1525   17 Iohn] 1510 1557, Iohan 1525   19 faders] 1510 1525, fathers 1557; Sidenote 1557: The linage of I. Picus   24 receyued: and] receuyed. and 1510, receyued. And 1525, receiued: & 1557   26 which we] 1510 1557, which 1525   27 Sidenote 1557: Noblenesse of auncesters   28 For] 1525 1557, for 1510   30 Sidenote 1557: Honour

oure is the reward of vertue. And how may they clayme the
rewarde y^t propreli longith to vertue: if they lak the vertue y^t the
rewarde longith to. Then if them self had none honour how
myght they leue to theyr heyres y^t thing which they had not them
self? On the othir side if they be vertuouse and so consequently   5
honorable / yet may they not leue their honoure to vs as enhere-
taunce: no more then the vertue that them self were honorable
for. For neuer the more noble be we for theyr noblenes if oure
self lak those thyngis for which thei were noble. But rathir the
more worshipful y^t oure auncestres were the more vile and   10
shamfull be we: if we decline from the steppes of their worship-
ful liuinge: the clere beauty of whos vertue ma[a₁v]kith the
darke spot of oure vice the more euidently to apere & to be the
more marked. But Picus of whom we speke was him self so
honorable / for the gret plentuouse habundaunce of al such   15
vertues: the possession wherof very honoure folowith (as a
shadow folowith a bodi) y^t he was to al them y^t aspire to honowre
a very spectacle in whos conditions as in a clere pullished mir-
rour they myght behold in what pointes very honoure stondith:
whose meruelouse cunnyng & excellent vertue though my rude   20
lerning be ferr vnable sufficientli to expres: yet for as much as if
no man shuld do hit but he that might sufficiently do hit: no man
shuld do hit, and bettir it were to be vnsufficiently done then
vttirly vndone. I shal therfor as I can brefely reherce you his hole
lyfe: at the lest wyse to giue some other man here aftir (y^t can do   25
hit bettir) occasion to take hyt in hande when hyt shal happely
greue him to se the life of such an excellent cunnynge man so
ferr vnkunnyngly wrytin.

Of his parentis and tyme of his birth.

I N the yere of oure lord god .m.cccclxiii. Pius the seconde   30
beyng than the generall vicare of crist in his chirch: & Federik
the thryd of y^t name rulinge the empire this noble man was born
the last child of his moder Iulya, a woman commen of a noble

4–5 them self? On] them self. on *1510*, them selfe / on *1525*, themselues? On *1557*;
Sidenote 1557: Honour and vertue come not by inheritaunce   23 hit, and] hit. and
1510, hit / & *1525*, it: and *1557*   33 moder Iulya,] moder Iulya. *1510*, mother
Iulya / *1525*, mother Iulia, *1557*

stok. His fader hight Iohan frauncise a lord of grete honoure and auctorite.

Of the wondre that appered byfore his birth. [a₂]

A MERUELOUSE sight was there sene byfore his birth: there
5   appered a fyery garland standing ouer the chambre of his
moder whil she trauelled and sodenly vanished a way: which
apparence was peraduenture a tokene that he which shuld that
howre in the companye of mortall men be born: in the perfec-
tion of vndrestonding shuld be like the perfite figure of that
10   rounde circle or garland and that his excellent name shuld
round a bowt the circle of this hole world be magnified whose
mind shuld alwei as the fier aspire vpward to heuenly thing. And
whose fiery eloquence shuld with an ardent hart in tyme to come
worship and praise almyghti god with al his strenkyth. And as yᵗ
15   flame sodenly vanishid so shuld this fire sone from the yeen of
mortall peple be hidd. We haue oftyn tymes red that such
vnknowen and strange tokens hath gone by fore or folowith the
natiuitese of excellent wyse and vertuouse men departing (as hit
were and by goddis commaundement) seuerynge the cradils of
20   such speciall children fro the companye of other of the commyn
sorte. And shewing yᵗ they be born to the accheuing of some gret
thing. But to passe ouer other. The gret saynt ambrose: a
swarme of bees flew a bout his mouth in his cradle & som entred
in to hys mouth and aftir yᵗ issueyng out a gayne and fleyng
25   vppon high hiding them self amonge the clowdis eschaped both
the sight of hys fader and of all them that were present which
pronostication one Paulinus making much of: expowned yt to
signifie to vs the swete hony combis of his plesaunt wrytinge:

---

1 stok. His] stok. his *1510*, stok / his *1525*, stocke, hys *1557;* fader] *1510*, father *1525*
1557   4 birth: there] birth. there *1510*, byrthe / there *1525*, byrth: there *1557*
6 moder] *1510*, mother *1525 1557*   9 *Sidenote 1557:* The interpretacion of the won-
der   14 strenkyth] *1510*, strength *1525 1557*   15 yeen] *1510*, eyen *1525*, eyes
1557   16 hidd. We] hidd we *1510*, hydde we *1525*, hydde. We *1557*   18 natiuitese]
nanatiuitese *1510*, natyuytese *1525;* natiuitee *1557*   22 *Sidenote 1557:* S. Ambrose
25 eschaped] *1510*, escaped *1525 1557*   26 fader] *1510 1557*, father *1525*

which shuld shew out the cele[a₂v]stiall giftis of god & shuld lifte
vp the mynd of men from erth in to heuen.

Of his persone

HE was of feture & shappe semely & bewteouse / of stature
goodly and hygh: of flesh tendre and soft / his vysage louely and   5
fayre / hys coloure white entremengled with comely ruddis / his
yen gray and quike of loke / his teth white and euen / his here
yelow and not to pikede.

Of his setting forth to scole and study in humanite.

UNDER the rule and gouernaunce of hys moder he was set to   10
masters & to lerning: where with so ardent mynde he labored the
studies of humanite that with in short while he was (and not
without a cause) accompted amonge the chiefe oratours and
poetys of that tyme in lernynge meruellously swift and of so redy
a witt that the versis which he hard ones red: he wold agayne   15
bothe foreward and bak ward to the grete wonder of the herers
reherse / and ouer that wold holde hyt in sure remembraunce:
which in other folk is wont comenly to happen contrari. For they
yᵗ are swifte in takyng be oftin tymes slowe in remembring: and
they yᵗ with more laboure & difficulte resceiue hit: more fast &   20
suerely hold hit.

Of his study in Canone

IN the fouretene yere of his age by the commaundement of his
moder (which longed vere sore to haue him preest) he departed

---

6 *Sidenote 1557:* Vertue in a comely body is more estemed   7 yen] *1510,* eyen *1525,* eies
1557   9 humanite] humanitate *1510,* humanyte *1525,* humanitie *1557*   10 moder]
1510, mother *1525 1557*   15 *Sidenote 1557:* Witte receauethe   17 *Sidenote 1557:* Re-
membraunce holdeth   17 reherse / and] *1525,* reherse. and *1510,* reherse, and
1557; remembraunce: which] remembraunce which *1510,* remembraunce whiche*1525,*
remembrance which *1557*   18 folk is] folkis *1510,* folkes *1525 1557*; contrari. For]
contrari. for *1510,* contrary. For *1525 1557*   19 remembring: and] *1557,* re-
membring. and *1510,* remembrynge / and *1525*   21 suerely] *1525,* sue:rely *1510,*
surely *1557*   24 moder] *1510,* mother *1525 1557*

to Bononye to study in the lawes of the chirch: which when he
had two yere tasted parceyuing that the faculte leyned [a₃] to no
thing but onely mere traditions & ordinaunces: his mynde fill
from hit. Yet lost he not his tyme ther in for in that two yere yet
5   beyng a childe he compiled a breuiary or a summe vppon all the
decretallis in which as breifly as possible was he comprised
theffect of all yᵗ hole grete volume and made a boke no sclender
thing to right conning & parfite doctours.

10   Of his study in philosophie & diuinite.

A FTIR this as a desirous enserchour of the secretis of nature
he left these commyn troden pathis and gaue him self hole to
speculation & philosophy as well humane as dyuine. For the
purchasing wherof (aftir the maner of Plato and Apollonius) he
15 scrupulously sought out all the famous doctours of his tyme:
visiting studeously all the vniuersites and scolis not only through
Italy but also thorow fraunce. And so infatigable laboure gaue
he to those studies: that yet a child and berdles he was both
reputed: and was in dede both a parfit philosophre and a parfit
20 deuine.

Of his mynde and vaingloriouse dispitions at Rome.

N ow had he ben .vii. yere conuersaunte in these studies whan
ful of pride & desirous of glori and mannes praise (for yet was he
not kyndled in yᵉ loue of god) he went to rome & there (cou-
25 etinge to make a shew of his connyng & litil considering how
grete enuie he shuld reise a gainst him self) .ix.C. questions he

3 mere] *1510 1557*, mery *1525*   4 hit. Yet] hit. yet *1510*, hit / yet *1525*, it. Yet *1557*;
Sidenote 1557: The facultie canone   5 a breuiary] abreuiary *1510 1557*, a breuyary
1525   11 desirous] *1510 1557*, desyrours *1525*   12 self] *1510 1557*, sefe *1525*
14 aftir] *1510*, afte *1525*, after *1557*   15 out all] *1557*, out / all *1510 1525*; *Sidenote
1557:* Trauailyng from place to place wonderfully increaseth knowlage; tyme: visiting]
tyme. visiting *1510*, tyme. visytynge *1525*, time, visiting *1557*   19 philosophre] *1525
1557*, philosopre *1510*   21 dispitions] *1510*, dispicious *1525*, dispicions *1557*; at]
1510 1557, of *1525*

purposed / of diuerse and sondry maters / as well in logike and
philosophie as diuinite / with [a₃v] gret study piked and sought
owt as wel of the latin auctours as the grekis. And partly fet out of
the secret misteries of the hebrieus / Caldaies / & Arabies. and
many thingis drawen owt of yᵉ olde obscure philosophie of   5
Pithagoras / trimegistus / and orpheus / & many othir thyngis
strange: and to all folk (except right few speciall excellent
menne) byfore that day: not vnknowin onli: but also vnherd of /
all which questions in open places (that they myght be to all peple
yᵉ bettir knowen) he fastened and set vp, offering all so hym self   10
to bere the costis of all such as wold come thyther owt of ferre
contreis to dyspute / but thorough yᵉ enuie of his malitiouse
enemyes (which enuie lyke yᵉ fire euir drawith to yᵉ highest) he
coude neuir bring a bout to haue a daye to his dispitions ap-
poynted. For thys cause he taryed at Rome an hole yere in all   15
which time his enuiours neuir durst openly with open dispytions
attempt hym but rathir with craft and sleight and as it were with
pryuey trenches enforced to vndir myne hym for non other
cause but for malice and for they were (as many men thought)
corrupt with a pestylent enuie. This enuie as menne demed was   20
specially raised against hym for this cause that where there were
many which had many yeris: some for glory: some for couetyse:
giuen them self to lerninge: they thought that hyt shuld happely
deface their fame & minyssh thopinion of their connyng if so
yong a man plenteouse of substaunce and grete doctryne: durst   25
in the chife citie of the world make a profe of his wyt and [a₄] his
lerninge aswel in thinges naturall as in diuinite and in many such
thingis as men many yeris neuir attayned to. Now when they
parceyued that they coude not a gaynst his connyng any thyng
openly preuaile: they brought forth the serpentines of false   30

---

1 purposed / of] *1525*, purposed. of *1510*, purposed, of *1557; Sidenote 1557:* Iohn Picus
his disputacions at Rome; maters / as] maters. as *1510 1525*, maters, as *1557*   2 diui-
nite / with] diuinite. with *1510*, dyuynyte / with *1525*, diuinitee, with *1557*   4 he-
brieus] *1510*, hebrewes *1525*, Hebrewes *1557;* Caldaies] *1510*, caldeyes *1525*. Caldees
1557   6 trimegistus] *1510 1525*, Trismegistus *1557*   8 vnherd of /] vnherd.
of *1510*, vnherde / of *1525*, vnherd. Of *1557*   10 vp,] *1557*, vp / *1525*, vp. *1510*
11 thyther] *1510*, hyther *1525*, thither *1557*   13 *Sidenote 1557:* Enuie   14 dispi-
tions] *1510*, dyspicions *1525*, dispicious *1557*   20 This] *1510 1557*, ⁋ This *1525*
26 a profe] *1525 1557*, o profe *1510*

crime. And cried out that ther were .xiii. of his .ix.C. questions
suspect of heresye. Then ioyned they to them some goode
simple folk that shuld of zele to ye faith and pretence of relygion
impugne those questions as new thinges and with which their
5   eris had not be in vre. In which impugnation though some of
them happely lakked not good mynde: yet lakked they erudition
and lernynge: which questions: not with stonding by fore that
not a few famous doctours of diuinite had approued / as good
and clene and subscribed their names vndre them. But he not
10 bering the losse of his fame made a defence for those .xiii. ques-
tions. A warke of gret erudition and elegant and stuffed with the
cognition of many thingis worthy to be lerned. Which wark he
compiled in .xx. nyghtis. In which hit euedently aperith: not
only that those conclusions were goode and stondyng with the
15 faith: but also that they: which had barked at them: were of foly
and rudenesse to be reproued. Which defence and all othir
thyngis that he shulde write: he committed like a good christen
man to ye most holy iudgement of oure mother holy chirch.
Whych defence receiued: & the .xiii. questions duly by delibera-
20 tion examined: our holi fathir ye pope approued Picus and ten-
dirly fauored him / as by a bull of oure holy [a₄v] fathir pope
Alexandre the .vi. hit plainly apperith: but the boke in which the
hole .ix.C. questions with theyr conclusions were conteyned (for
as much as ther were in them many thyngis straunge and not
25 fully declared and were more mete for secrete communication
of lerned men then for open heryng of commune peple which
for lake of connynge might take hurt therby) Picus desired him
self y^t hit shuld not be redd. And so was the redynge therof
forboden. Lo this ende had Picus of his hye mynde and prowd
30 purpose / y^t where he thought to haue goten perpetuall prayse:
there had he much warke to kepe him self vpright: that he ranne
not in perpetuall infamye and sclaundre.

7 by fore that] *1510*, before that / *1525*, before that, *1557*   8 approued / as] *1525*,
approued. as *1510*, approued, as *1557*   21 him / as] him. as *1510*, hym / as *1525*,
him, as *1557*   30 purpose / y^t] purpose. y^t *1510*, purpose / that *1525*, purpose: y^t
1557

Of the chaunge of his life

Bᴜᴛ as him self told his neuiew he iudged that this cam thus to passe: by the especiall prouision and singuler goodnes of almigty god / that by this fals cryme vntrewly put vppon him by his euell willers he shuld correct his very errours / and that this shuld be to hym (wandering in darkenes) as a shyning light: in which he might behold & considre: how ferr he had gone owt of yᵉ waye of truth. For byfore this he had bene both desyrous of glory and kindled in vaine loue: and holden in volupteouse vse of women. The comelynes of hys body wyth the louely fauoure of hys vysage / and ther with all his meruelouse fame / his excellent lerninge / gret rychesse and noble kyndred set many women [b₁] a fier on him. From the desire of whom he not abhorring (the waye of lyfe set a side) was somwhat fallen in to wantonnesse. But aftyr that he was ones with this variaunce wakened he drew bak his mynd flowing in riot and turned hit to crist. Womennis blan-dimentes he chaunged in to the desire of heuenly ioyes & dispis-ing the blast of vayneglorie which he bifore desired / now with all his mynd he began to seke the glorye and profite of christis chirche and so bigan he to ordre his conditions that from thens forth he might haue ben approued & though his enemye were his iudge.

Of the fame of his vertue and the resort
vnto him therfore.

Hᴇʀᴇ vpon shortly the fame of his noble cunnyng and excel-lent vertue both ferre & nygh began gloriously to spring for which many worthi philosophres (& that were taken in nombre of the most cunning) resorted bisely vnto him as to a market of good doctrine: somme for to moue questions and dispute /

---

4 god / that] *1525*, god. that *1510*, god: that *1557*   12–14 *Sidenote 1557:* The best of vs all hathe had a maddyng tyme   13 him. From] *1557*, him. from *1510*, hym / frome *1525*   17 the] *1557*, te *1510*, yᵉ *1525*   25 *Sidenote 1557:* A right glorious fame   29 doctrine: somme] doctrine. somme *1510*, doctryne / some *1525*, doctrine. Some *1557*

somme (that were of more godly mynde) to here & to take the
holesome lessons & instruction of good lyuing: which lessons
were so much the more set by: in howe much thei cam from a
more noble man and a more wyse man and him also which had
5 him self some time followed yᵉ croked hilles of delitiouse plea-
sure. To the fasteninge of good discipline in the myndis of the
herers those thinges seme to be of grete effecte: which be both of
their owne nature good & also be spokin of such a master: as is
conuerted to the way of iustice from the croked & ragged path of
10 voluptuouse lyuing. [b₁v]

The burning of wanton bokis.

FIUE bokis that in his youth of wanton versis of loue with other
like fantasies he had made in his vulgare tonge: al to gither (in
detestation of his vice passed and lest these trifeles might be
15 some euil occasion aftirwarde) he burned.

Of his study and diligence in holy scripture.

FROM thensforth he gaue him selfe day & night most feruently
to the studies of scripture in which he wrot many noble bokes:
which welle testifie bothe his angelike wit / his ardent laboure /
20 and his profounde erudition of which bokes some we haue &
some as an inestymable tresure we haue lost. Gret lybraries hit is
incredible to considre with how meruelouse celerite he redd
them ouer / and wrot out what him liked. Of yᵉ olde fathirs of yᵉ
chirch: so gret knowlege he had as hit were harde for him to
25 haue yᵗ hath lyued longe & all his life hath don nothing ellis but
red them. Of these newer diuines so good iugement he had yᵗ yt
might apere there were no thyng in any of them that were
vnknowe to him / but al thing as rype as though he had al theyr

5–6 pleasure. To] *1557*, pleasure. to *1510*, pleasure / to *1525*   9 the croked] *1525*
1557, te croked *1510*; ragged] *1525 1557*, raaged *1510*   12–13 *Sidenote 1557:* De-
testacion of vicious life passed   14 passed] *1510*, passed) *1525*, passed, *1557*; might]
1510 1557, mygh *1525*   15 aftirwarde)] aftirwarde *1510*, afterwarde *1525*, after-
warde) *1557*; burned.] *1510 1557*, burned them. *1525*   23 liked. Of] liked. of *1510*,
liked: of *1525*, liked, of *1557*   24–26 *Sidenote 1557:* No diuine either olde or new, to I.
Picus vnknowen   28 him / but] *1525*, him. but *1510*, him: but *1557*

warkys euer byfore hys yen. But of all these new doctours he
specially commendith saint thomas as him y^t enforcith him self
in a sure pillar of treuth. He was veri quik / wise / and sobtle in
dispitions & had gret felicite therein while he had y^t hye stomak.
But now a grete while he had bode such conflictis farwell: and
euery day more and more hated them / and so gretly abhorred
them: that when hercules Estensis duke of ferrare: furst by
mes[b$_2$]sangers and aftir by him selfe: desired him to dispute at
ferrare: by cause y^e generall chaptre of freres prechours was
holden there / longe hit was or he coude be brought ther to: but
at the instant request of the duke which very singulerly loued
him he cam thyder wher he so behaued him selfe that was
wondre to be holde how all ye audience reioyced to here hym for
hit were not possible for a man to vttre neythir more connyng
nor more connyngly. But hit was a commune saying with him
that such altercations were for a logition and not metely for a
philosophre. He saide also that such disputations gretely prof-
ited as were exercised with a peasyble mynde to thenserching of
the treuth in secrete company with owt gret audience: but he
saide that those dispitions did gret hurt: that wer holden openly
to thostentation of lerning & to winne the fauoure of the com-
mune peple & the commendation of folys. He thought that vt-
tirly hit coude vnneth be but that with the desyre of worshippe
(which these gasing disputers gape aftir) there is with an insepar-
able bonde annexed ye appetite of his confusione & rebuke
whom they argue with. Which appetite ys a dedeli wounde to y^e
sowle & a mortall poyson to charite. There was nothing passed
him of those captions soteltes & cauillations of sophistrie / nor a

1 yen. But] yen. but *1510*, eyen / but *1525*, eies. But *1557*   3 treuth. He] treuth.
he *1510*, truth / he *1525*, trueth. He *1557*   6 them / and] *1525*, them. and *1510*,
them: and *1557; Sidenote 1557:* I. Picus loth to dispute   10 there / longe] *1525*,
there. longe *1510*, there: longe *1557*   15 saying] *1557*, saynig *1510*, sayenge *1525*
17 philosophre. He] philosophre. he *1510*, phylosophre / he *1525*, philosopher. He
1557   17 *Sidenote 1557:* Disputacions profitable   19 *Sidenote 1557:* Disputacions
hurtfull   22 folys] *1510*, fooles *1525*, folies *1557*   25 *Sidenote 1557:* To couet the
rebuke of other standeth not with charitie   26 dedeli wounde] dedeli. wounde *1510*,
dedly wounde *1525*, deadly wounde *1557*   27 charite. There] charite there *1510*
1525, charitie. There *1157*   28 captions] *1525*, captiõs *1510*, captious *1557*

gayn ther was no thinge y^t he more hated & abhorred consyder-
ing y^t they serued of nought but to y^e shaming of such other
folke as wer in very science much bettir lerned and in those trifles
ignorant. And y^t vnto thenserchinge of y^e treuth (to which he
5   gaue continuall laboure) they profited lytle or nought. [b$_2$v]

Of his lernying vniuersally.

B$_{UT}$ bi cause we will holde the reder no lenger in hand: we will
speke of hys lerninge but a worde or twayne generally. Sume
man hath shined in eloquence but ignorans of naturall thinges
10   hathe dishonested him / some man hath flowred in the knowl-
edge of diuers straunge langages but he hath wanted all the
cognition of philosophie. Sume man hath red the inuentions of
the olde philosophres but he hath not ben exercised in the new
scolis. Sume man hath sought connying as well philosophi as
15   diuinite for praise and vayneglory and not for any profet or
encreace of christis church. But Picus all these thingis with equal
study hath so receyued y^t thei might seme by hepis as a plen-
tuouse streme to haue flowen in to him. For he was not of the
condition of some folke (which to be excellent in one thinge set al
20   othir aside) but he in all sciencis profited so excellently: that
which of them so euer ye had considered in hym ye wolde haue
thought y^t he had taken that one for his onely studye. And al
these thyngis were in him so muche the more meruelouse in y^t he
cam therto by him selfe with the strength of his owne witte for y^e
25   loue of god and profit of his chirch with owt maisters so that we
maye sey of him that Epicure the philosophre said of him self
that he was his owne maister.

1–2 *Sidenote 1557:* Sophisticall cauillacions to what purpose thei serue   8 generally.
Sume] generally. sume *1510*, generally / some *1525*, generally. Some *1557*   10 man]
1557, men *1510 1525*   14 sought] *1510 1557*, sough *1525*   16 *Sidenote 1557*; Al
connyng & knowlage in learnyng, abounded in I. Picus   18 him. For] *1557*, him. for
1510, hym. For *1525*   21 ye] *1510 1557*, he *1525*; considered] *1557*, cousidered *1510*,
consydered *1525*   22 thought] *1525 1557*, though *1510*   24 *Sidenote 1557:* I. Picus
his own maister   25 of his] *1510 1557*, his *1525*   26 him self] *1510*, hym *1525*, him
selfe: *1557*

Fyue causes that in so short tyme brought him to so meruelouse connyng.

To the bryngyng forth of so wondreful effectes in so small time I considre fyue causes to haue come to gedir: first an incredible wit / secondly a mer[b₃]uelouse fast memory / thredly grete substance by the which to yᵉ bying of his bokes as well latin as greke & othir tongis he was especially holpen. vii.m. ducatis he had laide out in yᵉ gadering to gither of volumes of all maner of litterature. The fourth cause was his besy & infatigable study. The fyft was the dispising of al erthly thingis.

Of his conditions and his vertue.

But nowe let vs pass ouer those powars of his soule which appertaine to vndrestonding & knowledge & let vs speke of them yᵗ belonge to yᵉ acheiuing of noble actis / let vs as we can declare his excellent conditions yᵗ his mynde enflamed to godwarde may apere / and his riches giuen owt to pore folke may be vndrestonde / to thentent yᵗ they which shall here his vertue may haue occasion therbi to giue especial laude and thanke therfor to almighty god of whose infinite godenesse al grace and vertue commith.

Of yᵉ sale of his lordeshippis and almesse.

Thre yere before his deth (to thende that all yᵉ charge & besines of rule or lordship set a side he might lede his life in rest and peace wele considering to what ende this erthly honour & worldly dignite commith) all his patrimonye and dominions yᵗ is

---

2 so] *1557*, se *1510 1525*   4–5 *Sidenote 1557:* Witte. *Sidenote 1557:* Memórie.
5 memory / thredly] *1510*, memore. Thyrdely *1525*, memorie, thirdly *1557*   6 *Sidenote 1557:* Substuance   6–7 *Sidenote 1557:* Studie.   7 *Sidenote 1557:* Worldly contempte   8 gadering] *1510*, gaderynge *1525*, gathering *1557*   10 fyft] *1510*, fyfte *1525*, fyfth *1557*; dispising] contempt dispising *1510*, contempt dispysynge *1525*, contempt or dispising *1557 (see note)*   16 apere / and] apere. And *1510*, appere. And *1525*, appere: And *1557*   17 to thentent] *1510 1557*, thentent *1525*   18 *Sidenote 1557:* God is the geuer of all goodnes   23 *Sidenote 1557:* Quietnes of life to yᵉ godly is a most pleasaunt possession

to sey the thred parte of therldome of Mirandula and of concor-
dia: vnto Iohan franscis his neuieu he solde / & that so good
chepe that hyt semed rathir a gift then a sale. All that euer he
receyued of this bargaine partly he gaue owt to pore folk / partly
5   he bestowed in the bieng of a little londe to the finding of him &
his howsolde. And ouer y^t much siluer vessel & [b₃v] plate with
othir preciouse & costly vtensilis of howsold he deuided amonge
pore peple. He was content with meane fare at his table how be
hyt somwhat yet reteyning of the olde plenty in deynty viande &
10   siluer vessell. Euery day at certaine howris he gaue hem self to
praier. To pore men alway if eni cam he plentuosly gaue out his
money: and not content only to giue that he had him self redy:
he wrote ouer y^t / to one Hierom Beniuenius a florentin a wel
letred man (whom for his gret loue toward him and ye integrite
15   of his conditions he singulerly fauored) y^t he shold with his owen
money euer helpe pore folk: and giue maidens money to their
mariage: and alway send him worde what he had laide out that
he might paye hit him a geyn. This office he committed to hym
that he might ye more easeli by him as by a faithfull messanger
20   releue ye necessite & miseri of pore nedi peple such as him self
happely coude not cum by ye knowledge of.

❡ Of ye voluntari affliction & paining
of his own body.

O UER all this: many times (which ys not to be kept secret) he
25   gaue almes of hys own body: we knowe many men which (as seint
Hierom saith) put forth their hande to pore folke: but with the
plesure of ye flesh thei be ouer commen: but he: mani daies (and
namely those daies which represent vnto vs ye passion & deth y^t

---

1 thred] *1510*, thyrde *1525*, third *1557*   2 neuieu] neuien *1510*, neuewe *1525*, neuiew
1557; solde / &] solde. & *1510*, solde / and *1525*, solde: and *1557*   3 *Sidenote*
1557: Almesse   10 hem] *1510*, hym *1525*, him *1557*; *Sidenote 1557:* Praier   11 plen-
tuosly] *1510*, plentiously *1525*, plentuously *1557*   13 ouer y^t] *1510 1525*, ouer *1557*;
one] *1557*, one. *1525*, on *.1510*; Beniuenius] Benineuius *1510 1525 1557* (*see note*)
16 *Sidenote 1557:* O wonderful zeale to the relieuyng of the poore   28 *Sidenote 1557:*
The flesh voluntarely afflicted for goddes sake

Christ suffred for our sake) bet and scowrged hys own flessh in the remembraunce of that gret benefite and for clensing of his olde offencis.

Of his placabilite or beninge nature.

HE was of chere alwaye mery & of so beninge nature y^t he was 5
neuer trobled with Angre & [b₄] he said onis to hys neuieu that what so euir sholde happen (fell ther neuer so grete mysaduen-ture) he coud neuer as him thought be moued to wrath: but if his chestis perished in which his bokes lay: that he had with grete trauaile & watch compiled. But for as much as he considered y^t 10
he laboured only for ye loue of god & profit of his chirch: & y^t he had dedicate vnto him all his warkis / his studies & his doinges & sith he sawe y^t sith god is almighty they coulde not miscary but if hit were either by his commaundement or by his sufferaunce: he verily trusted: sith god is all good: y^t he wold not suffre him to 15
haue that occasion of heuines. O very happi mynde which none aduersite myght oppresse / which no prosperite might en-haunce: not the conning of all philosophie was able to make hym prowde / not the knowledge of the hebrewe / chaldey & arabie language beside greke and laten could make him wainglor- 20
iouse / not his grete substance / not hys noble blode coude blow vp his hart / not ye bewty of his body / not ye grete occasion of sin were able to pull him bak in to ye voluptuouse brode way y^t ledith to helle: what thing was ther of so meruelouse strenght y^t might ouertorne ye minde of him (which now as seneke sayth) was gotin 25
aboue fortune as he: which as well her fauoure as her malice hath set at nought / y^t he might be cowpled with a spirituall knot vnto crist and his heuinly citeseynes.

---

5 beninge] *1510*, benygne *1525*, benigne *1557*   6 *Sidenote 1557:* Angre or wrathe, can haue no place in a godly mind; neuieu] *1510*, neuew *1525*, neuiew *1557*   10 *Side-note 1557:* No misauenture coulde happen to I. Picus so greuous, as the losse of his bookes   17 oppresse / which] *1525*, oppresse which *1510*, opresse, whiche *1557* 20–21 waingloriouse] *1510*, vayngloryouse *1525*, vaingloriouse *1557*   24 strenght] *1510*, strength *1525 1557*

How he eschewed dignites.

W͟HAN he sawe mani men with gret labour & monei desire &
biseli purchace ye offices & dignites of ye chirch (which are now a
daies alas ye while communeli [b₄v] bought and solde) him self
refused to receyue them: whan two kingis offred them. Whan an
othir man offred him gret worldy promotion if he wolde go to
the kingis cowrte he gaue him such an Answer / that he sholde
well know that he neithir desired worship ne worldly richess but
rathir set them at nought y^t he might ye more quietly giue him
self to studie & ye seruice of god: this was he persuaded / y^t to a
philosophre and him that sekith for wisedome hit was no praise
to gader richesse but to refuse them.

Of the dispising of worldly glorie.

A͟LL praise of people and all erthli glory he reputed vttirly for
nothing but in ye renaying of this shadow of glory / he laboured
for very glory / which euer more folowith vertue as an vnsepa-
rable seruant. He saide that fame oftin tymes dyde hurt to men
whil they liue / & neuer good whan they be dede. So moche only
set he by his lerning in how moche he knewe that hit was profita-
ble to the chirch & to the extermination of errours. And ouer
that he was come to that prik of parfyt humilite that he lytle
forced whithir his workis went owt vndre his owne name or not
so that thei might as moche profite as if they were gyuen owt
vndre his name. And nowe set he litle by any othir bokes saue
onli the bible / in the only studi of which: he had appointed him
self to spende the residewe of his life / sauing that the commune
profit priked him when he considered so many and so gret

---

4 daies] daies) *1510*, dayes *1525*, daies, *1557*   6 *Sidenote 1557:* Ambicion subdued
8 richness] *1510*, ryches *1525*, richesse *1557*   10 was] weis *1510*, wyse *1525*, waies
1557   12 gader] *1510*, gather *1525 1557*   14–15 *Sidenote 1557:* Shadow of glo-
rie   17 seruant. He] seruant. he *1510*, seruaunt / he *1525*, seruaunt. He *1557; Side-
note 1557:* Fame   18 dede. So] dede. so *1510*, deed / so *1525*, dead. So *1557; Sidenote
1557:* Howe much lerning ought to be estemed   21 *Sidenote 1557:* The good man
trauaileth for the profit of other & not of himself, or ye auauncement of his owne
name   25 bible / in] *1525*, bible. in *1510*, bible: in *1557*   26 life / sauing] life. sau-
ing *1510*, lyfe / sauynge *1525*, life, sauing *1557*

warkis as he had conceyued and longe trauailed vppon how they
were of euery man by and by desired and loked aftir. [b₅]

How moche he set more by deuotion
then conning.

THE lytle affection of an olde man or an olde woman to god-   5
warde (wer hit neuer so small) he set more by: than by all his
owne knowledge aswell of natural thyngis as godly. And oftyn
times in communication he wold admonisshe his familiar
frendes how gretli these mortall thinges bowe and drawe to an
ende / how slyper and how falling hit is yᵗ we liue in nowe / how   10
ferme how stable yᵗ shalbe yᵗ we shall here aftir lyue in / whether
we be throwen down in to helle or lift vp in to heuyn. Wherfor he
exhorted them to turne vp their myndes to loue god which was a
thing farre excelling all the conning that is possible for vs in this
life to obtaine. The same thing also in his boke which he entitled   15
de ente et vno lightsomely he treteth where he interruptith yᵉ
course of his dispition and turnyng his wordis to Angelus Poli-
tianus (to whom he dedicatith that boke) he writeth in this wise.
But now behold o my welbeloued Angel what madnes holdith vs.
Loue god (whil we be in this body) we rathir maye, than either   20
know him or by spech vtter him. In louing him also we more
profit owre self / we laboure lesse & serue hym more. And yet
had we leuer alway by knowlege neuer finde yᵗ thing that we
seke: than by loue to possede yᵗ thing: which also with owt loue
were in vaine founde.   25

Of his liberalite & contempt of richesse.

LIBERALITE only in him passed mesure for so ferr was he from
the gyuyng of any diligence to erthely thingis that he semed

---

1 and] *1557*, an *1510 1525*   3 *Sidenote 1557:* Deuocion   10 ende /] ende *1510*
1525, ende, *1557*; nowe /] nowe *1510*, now: *1525*, nowe: *1557*   11 in / whether]
1525, in. whether *1510*, in, whether *1557*   13 *Sidenote 1557:* To loue god   17 dispi-
tion] *1510*, dispicion *1525*, disposicion *1557*   maye,] *1557*, maye: *1510 1525*
22 self /] sel / f *1510*, selfe / *1525*, self, *1557*; more. And] *1557*, more. and *1510*,
more / & *1525*   28 gyuyng] *1510* begynnyng *1525*, geuyng *1557*

somwhat besprent with the frekill of negligence. His frendes
often ti[b₅v]mes admonisshed him that he sholde not all vtterly
dispyce richesse / shewing him that hit was his dishoneste &
rebuke when hit was reported (were hit trew or false) that his
5   negligence & setting nought by money gaue his seruauntes occa-
sion of disceyt & robbry. Neuertheles that mynde of his: (which
euermor on high cleued fast in contemplation & in thenserching
of natures cownceill) cowde neuer let down hit selfe to yᵉ consid-
eration and ouerseing of these base abiecte and vile erthly trifles.
10   His high stiwarde came on a time to him & desired him to re-
sceiue his accompt of such money as he had in many yeris re-
sceyued of him: & brought forth his bokes of rekenyng. Picus
answered him in this wyse: My frende (sayth he) I know wele ye
haue mought oftyn tymes and yet may desceyue me & ye list:
15   werfore the examination of these expensis shal not nede. Ther is
no more to do. If I be ought in your dett I shall paie you by & bi.
If ye be in myn paye me: eythir now if ye haue hit: or here aftir if
ye be now not able.

Of his louing mynd & vertuouse behauour
20   to his frendis

H IS louers and frendes with gret benignite & curtesye he
entreted. Whom he vsid in all secrete communing vertuously
to exhorte to godward / whose godely wordes so effectually
wrought in the herers: yᵗ where a connyng man (but not so good
25   as connynge) cam to him on a daie for yᵉ grete fame of his
lerning to commune with hym as they fell in talkyng of vertue he

---

1 negligence. His] 1557, negligence. his 1510, negligence / his 1525   3 richesse /]
1525, richesse. 1510, richesse, 1557; dishoneste] 1510 1525, dishonestie 1557   6 rob-
bry.] robbry 1510 1525 robberie. 1557   10 His] 1525 1557, his 1510   12 him] his
1510 1525 1557   13 wyse: My] wise. my 1510, wyse / my 1525, wise: My 1557
14 Sidenote 1557: A shorte audite and a godly; list: werfore] list werfore 1510,
lyst / wherfore 1525, list: wherfore 1557   16 do. If] do. if 1510, do / yt 1525, doo, if
1557   16–17 bi. If] bi. if 1510, by / yf 1525, by. If 1557   17 me:] me. 1510,
me / 1525, me, 1557   19 behauour] 1510 1525, behaueour 1557   19 Sidenote
1557: Frendes   22 vertously] 1510, vertuously 1525 1557   23 godward /] god-
ward 1510 1525, godward, 1557   25–26 Sidenote 1557: Talke proceding of an earnest
zeale, worketh effectually

was wyth two wordes of Picus so thoroughly perced y^t forth with
all he forsoke hys accustomed vice and reformed his conditions.
The wordes y^t he saide [b$_6$] vnto him were these. If we hadd euer
more before oure yen y^e paynfull deth of crist which he suffred
for the loue of vs: & than if we wolde agayne think vppon oure   5
deth we sholde wele beware of synne. Meruelouse benignyte &
curtesy he shewed vnto them: not whom strengith of bodi or
goodes of fortune magnified but to them whom lernynge &
conditions bounde hym to fauour / for symilitude of maners ys a
cause of lou[e] & frendshippe. A lykenes of conditions is (as   10
Appollonius saith) an affinite.

What he hated & what he loued

THER was no thing more odiouse nor more intolerable to him
than (as horace saith) ye prowde palaces of stately lordes. Wed-
dyng / & worldy besynes / he fledd almost a like: notwithstond-   15
ing whan he was axed onys in sport whither of those two bur-
deyns semed lighter and which he wolde chese if he shuld of
necessite be dryuen to that one & at his election: which he stiked
thereat a while but at ye last he shoke his hede and a litle smylyng
he answered y^t he had leuer take him to mariage / as y^t thing in   20
which was less seruitude & not so moche ieopardie. Liberte a
boue all thing he loued to which both his owne naturall affection
& ye study of philosophy enclined him: & for y^t was he alway
wandering & flitting and wolde neuer take him selfe to any cer-
teyne dwelling.   25

---

1 two] *1557*, twe *1510*, the *1525;* thoroughly] *1510*, throughly *1525 1557*   1-2 forth
with all] *1510*, forthwithall *1525*, foorthwithall *1557*   4 yen] *1510*, eyen *1525*, eien
1557; paynfull] *1525*, payufull *1510*, painfull *1557*   7 strengith] *1510*, strength *1525*
1557   10 *Sidenote 1557:* Similitude of maners causeth loue   11 saith)] *1557*, saith
1510, sayth *1525*   14 (as horace] as (horace *1510 1525*, as (Horace *1557; Sidenote*
1557: Proude palace   17 chese] *1510 1525*, chose *1557*   20 mariage /] mariage.
1510, maryage / *1525*, mariage, *1557*   21 *Sidenote 1557:* Libertie; ieopardie. Liberte]
ieopardie. liberte *1510*, ieoperdy / lyberte *1525*, ieopardie. Libertie *1557*   22 affec-
tion] *1510*, affeccon *1525*, affeccion *1557*   24 selfe] *1510 1557*, sefe *1525*

Of his feruent loue to god.

O<small>F</small> outward obseruances he gaue no very grete force. We
speke not of those obseruances which the chirch commaundeth
to be obserued for in those he was diligent but we speke of those
5   cerimonies which folke bryng vp /setting ye very seruice of god a
syde [b₆v] whiche is (as christ saith) to be worshipped in spirite &
in treuth). But in the in ward affectes of the mynde he cleued to
god with very feruent loue and deuotion. Some tyme that mer-
uelouse alacrite langwished and almost fell: and eft ageyn with
10   grete strenght rose vp in to god. In the loue of whom he so
feruently burned that on a time as he walked with Iohn frauncis
his neuew in an orchard at farrare in ye talking of the loue of
christ he brake out in to these wordes: neuew sayde he this will I
shew the / I warne the kepe yt secret: the substaunce y^t I haue
15   left aftir certaine bokes of min fynisshed I entende to giue owt to
pore folke and fencyng my selfe with the crucifix bare fote walk-
inge a bowt the worlde in euery town and castel I purpose to
preche of crist. Aftirward I vndrestande by the especiall com-
maundement of god he chaunged that purpose and appointed
20   to professe him self in the ordre of freris prechours.

Of his deth.

I<small>N</small> the yere of oure redemption .m.cccc.iciiii. when hym self
had fulfilled y^e .xxxii. yere of his age & abode at florence he was
sodenly taken with a feruent axis whiche so fer forth crepte in to

---

2 *Sidenote 1557:* Obseruances; force. We] force we *1510 1525,* force, we *1557*   5 vp /]
vp *1510 1525 1557*   7 treuth).] *1525,* treuth) *1510,* truth: *1557*   8 deuotion. Some
tyme] deuotion. some tyme *1510,* deuocyon / some tyme *1525,* deuocion. Some-
time *1557*   11 Iohn] *1510 1557,* Iohan *1525*   13 brake] *1525 1557,* barke *1510;*
wordes:] *1557,* wordes. *1510,* wordes / *1525*   14 the /] the *1510 1525,* the, *1557;*·
Sidenote 1557: O exceding feruent loue to godwarde   15 fynisshed] fymsshed *1510,*
finysshed *1525,* finished *1557*   16 fencyng] *1557,* sencyng *1510,* sencynge *1525*
18 *Sidenote 1557:* I. Picus inclined to religion   22 .m.cccc.iciiii.] *1510,* .M.CCCC.iCiiii.
1525, .1494. *1557;* whan hym self] hym whan self *1510,* whan he *1525 1557*
24 sodenly] *1525,* sondenly *1510,* sodeinly *155;* axis] *1510 1557;* axes *1525.*

the interiore partis of his body y^t hit dispysed all medicynes &
ouercam all remedy and compelled him with in thre daies to
satisfie nature and repaye hir the life which he receiued of hir.

Of his behauour in the extremes of his life.

A FTIR that he had receyued the holy body of oure sauioure   5
whan they offred vnto him the crucifix (y^t in the ymage of cristis
ineffable passione [c$_1$] suffred for oure sake: he myght ere he
gaue vp the goste / receyue his full draught of loue and compas-
sion in the beholding of that pitefull figure as a stronge defence
ageinst all aduersite and a sure portculiouse ageinst wikked spir-   10
ites) the prest demaunded him whither he fermely beleued y^t
crucifix to be ye Image of hym that was very god & very man
which in his god hed was bifore all tyme bygoten of his fathir / to
whom he is also equall in all thing: and which of the holi gost god
also: of him & of the fathir coeternalli going forth (which .iii.   15
persones be one god) was in the chaste wombe of oure lady
a perpetuall virgine conceyued in tyme: which suffred hun-
gar thrust / hete / colde / laboure / trauaile / and watche: and
which at the last for washing of oure spotty synne contracted and
drawine vnto vs in the synne of adame for the soueraigne loue y^t 20
he had to mankinde: in the aulter of the crosse willingly and
gladli shede owt his most preciouse blode. When the prest en-
quired of him these thinges and such othir as thei be wont to
enqwere of folke in such case: Picus answered him y^t he not onli
beleued hit but also certanly knew it.   25
     Whan that one Albertus his sisters sonne a yong man both of
wit connyng / and conditions / excellent: began to comfort him
against deth: & by naturall reason to shew him why hit was not to
be fered but strongly to be taken: as y^t only thing which makith
an ende of all the labour / paine / trouble / & sorowe of this   30
short miserable dedly life: he answered y^t this was not the chiefe

---

1 interiore] *1510*, interiori *1525*, interior *1557*   4 behauour] *1510*, behaūyour
1525, behaueour *1557*   13 fathir / to] fathir. to *1510*, father / to *1525*, father, to
1557   15 forth (which] forth / which *1510*, forth (whiche *1525*, foorth, which *1557*
17 tyme:] tyme. *1510*, time / *1525*, tyme, *1557*   18 watche: and] *1557*, watche. and
1510, watche. And *1525*   24 case:] *1557*, case. *1510* *1525*   25 *Sidenote 1557:* A
constant faith

thing y^t shold make him content to dye: bi cause the deth de-
termineth the manyfolde incommoditees and paynfull [c₁v]
wretchednes of this life: but rathir this cause sholde make him
not content only: but also glade to die: for that deth makith an
5   ende of synne: in as much as he trusted: ye shortnes of his life
sholde leue him no space to synne & offende. He asked also all
his seruauntes foregiuenes / if he had euer before y^t daie of-
fended any of them / for whom he had prouided by his testa-
ment .viii. yeris before: for some of them mete and drink / for
10 some money iche of them aftir their deseruinge. He shewed also
to ye aboue named Albertus & many othir credible persones y^t y^e
qwene of heuin cam to hym y^t night with a meruelouse fragrant
odoure refreshing all his membres y^t were brosed & frushed
with that feuer & promised him that he shold not vttirly dye. He
15 lay alwaie with a plesaunt and a mery contenaunce and in the
very twitches and panges of deth he spake as though he behelde
ye heuines opene. And all y^t cam to him and saluted him offering
their seruice: with veri louing wordes he receiued / thanked /
& kissed. The executour of his moueable goodes he made one
20 Antony his brothir. The heyer of his landes he made ye pore
peple of the hospitall of florence: And in this wise in to ye handes
of oure sauioure he gaue vp his spirit.

How his deth was taken.

W HAT sorowe and heuines his departing owt of this worlde
25 was: both to ryche and pore high and lowe: well testifieth the
princes of Italie: well witnessith the citees and peple: wele re-
cordeth the grete benignite and singular curtesie of Charles king
of fraunce / which as he cam to floren[c₂]ce entending from

---

2 paynfull] *1525*, payufull *1510*, painfull *1557*   3 *Sidenote 1557:* What cause shoulde
make vs willyng & glad to dye   7 foregiuenes /] foregiuenes. *1510*, forgyuenes /
1525, forgeuenesse *1557*   8 them /] them. *1510 1525*, them, *1557*   9 .viij.] *1525
1557*, vni *1510;* before:] *1557*, before. *1510*, before / *1525*   11 *Sidenote 1557:* A vi-
sion   15 contenaunce] concontenaunce *1510*, countenaunce *1525*, countenance
1557   17 heuines] *1510*, heuens *1525*, heauens *1557;* opene.] *1525*, opene *1510*,
open. *1557*   19 one] *1525 1557*, on *1510*   26 Italie:] Italie. *1510*, Italye / *1525*,
Italie, *1557*   27 *Sidenote 1557:* Charles the frenche king   28 fraunce /] *1525*,
fraunce. *1510*, Fraunce: *1557*

thens to Rome and so forth in his viage against the Realme of
Naples hering of the sikenes of Picus in all conuenient hast he
sent him two of his owne phisicions as embassiatours both to visit
him and to do him all ye helpe they might. And ouer that sent
vnto him lettres subscribed with his owne hande full of such   5
humanite and courtese offres: as the benevolent mynde of such
a noble prince and the worthi vertues of Picus required.

Of the state of his sowle.

Aftir his deth (and not longe after) one hieronimus a frere
prechoure of ferrare a man as wel in connyng as holynes of   10
lyuing most famous / in a sermone which he reherced in the
cheyfe chirche of all florence saide vnto ye peple in this wise. O
thow Citee of florence I haue a secrete thing to shew the which is
as trew as ye gospell of seint Iohn: I wolde haue kept hyt secret
but I am compelled to shew hit. For he that hath auctoryte to   15
commande me hath byde me publisshe hit. I suppose verily that
ther be none of you but ye knew Iohan Picus erle of mirandula /
a man in whom god had heped mani gret giftis and singuler
graces. The chirch had of him an inestymable losse. For I sup-
pose if he might haue had the space of his life prorogyd: he shuld   20
haue excelled (bi such workes as he shold haue left behind him)
al them that died this .viii.C. yere be fore him. He was wont to be
conuersaunt with me and to breke to me the secretes of his hart
in which I parceyued that he was by priuey inspiration called of
god vnto religion. [c₂v] Wherfor he purposed oftin tymes to   25
obey this inspiration and folow hys calling. How be hit not being
kind ynowgh for so grete benefices of god: or called bak by the
tendrenes of hys flesh (as he was a man of delicate complexion)

---

3 embassiatours] *1510 1525*, embassadours *1557*   6 courtese] *1510*, courteyse *1525*,
courteous *1557*   10 holynes] *1525 1557*, holyues *1510*   11 famous / in] famous.
In *1510 1525 1557*   14 Iohn:] *1557*, Iohn *1510*, Iohan *1525*   17 mirandula /]
mirandula. *1510*, Mirandula / *1525*, Mirandula, *1557*   19 graces. The] graces. the
1510, graces / y^e *1525*, graces: the *1557;* losse. For] *1557*, losse. for *1510*, losse / for *1525*
22 him. He] *1557*, him. he *1510*, him / he *1525*   25 oftin tymes] oftim tymes *1510*,
oftentymes *1525 1557*   26 How be hit] how be hit *1510*, howbeit *1525*, How be it
1557   27 ynowgh] y nowgh *1510*, ynoughe *1525*, enough *1557*

he shrank from the labour / or thinking happely y^t the religion
had no nede of him differred hit for a time / how be hit this I
speke only by coniecture. But for this delaye I thretened hym
two yere togethir: y^t he wolde be punisshed yf he forslowthed y^t
5 purpose which our lorde had put in hys mynd / & certeinly I
prayed to god my selfe (I will not lye ther fore) that he might be
somwhat betin: to compell him to take that waye which god had
from aboue shewed him. But I desired not this scourge vppon
him y^t he was betyn with: I loked not for that: but oure lorde had
10 so decreed that he sholde forsake this present life and lese a part
of that noble crowne that he sholde haue had in heuyn. Not
withstonding ye most benigne iuge hath dalt mercifully with
him: and for his plentuouse almes giuen owt with a fre and
liberall hand vnto pore peple & for the deuout prayours which
15 he most instantly offred vnto god this fauoure he hath: though
his sowle be not yet in the bosome of oure lorde in the heuenly
ioye: yet ys hit not on y^t othir side deputed vnto perpetual
payne / but he is adiuged for a while to ye fire of purgatory there
to suffre payne for a season. Which I am ye gladder to shew you
20 in this bihalfe: to the entent that thei which knew him: & such in
especially as for his manyfolde benefices are singulerly beholden
vnto him: shold nowe with their prayers almes / & othir suf-
fra[c₃]ges helpe him. These thingis this holi man hierom this
seruaunt of god openly affermed / and also saide that he knew
25 well if he lied in that place: he wer worthy eternall dampnation.
And ouer y^t he said y^t he had knowen all those thingis within a
certain time / but ye wordes which Picus had saide in his sikenes
of ye apering of oure lady caused him to dowt & to fere lest Picus

3 coniecture] *1525 1557* comecture *1510*   5 mynd / &] mynd. & *1510*, mynde / &
1525, mind. And *1557*   6 selfe] *1510 1557*, sefe *1525*; *Sidenote 1557*: Punishement
desired for a godly intent   8 But] *1525 1557*, but *1510*   10 lese] lefe *1510*, leue
1525, leaue *1557*   12 dalt] *1510 1525*, dealt *1557*   13 plentuouse] *1510 1557*,
plentyouse *1525*   15 though] *1510 1557*, thought *1525*   18 payne /] payne. *1510*,
payne *1525*, paine: *1557*; *Sidenote 1557*: Purgatorie   20–21 in especially] *1510 1557*,
inspecially *1525*   22 *Sidenote 1557*: Prayer & almes auaylable for the dead   24 af-
fermed /]*1525*, affermed. *1510*, affirmed, *1557*   27 time / but] time. but *1510*,
tyme / but *1525*, time. But *1557*

had be deceyued by some illusion of ye deuill / in as much as the
promis of oure lady semed to haue ben frustrate by his deth. But
aftyrward he vndirstode y^t Picus was deceyued in the equiuoca-
tion of ye worde while she spake of ye seconde deth & euer
lasting: & he vndirtoke her of ye first deth & temporall. And aftir   5
this ye same hierom shewed to his acquaintance y^t Picus had aftir
his deth apered vnto him al compaced in fire & shewed vnto him
y^t he was suchwise in purgatorie punished for his negligence &
his vnkindnes. Now seth hit is so that he ys adiuged to y^t fire from
which he shal vndowtedly depart vnto glori & no man is sure how   10
longe hit shalbe furst: & mai be ye shorter time for oure interces-
siones: let eueri christen bodi shew theyr charite vppon him to
helpe to spede him thedir wher aftir ye longe habitation with y^e
inhabitauntes of this darke world (to whom his goodli conuersa-
tion gaue gret light) & aftir ye darke fire of purgatory (in which   15
veniall offences be clensed) he may shortly (if he be not all redy)
entre ye inaccessible & infinite light of heuyn where he may in y^e
presense of ye soueragne godhed so pray for vs y^t we may y^e
rathir bi his intercession be partiners of y^t inspecable Ioy which
we haue praid to bring him spedely to. Amen.   20
    Here endith the life of Iohan Picus erle of Mirandula.

                    Finis. [c₃v]

            Here folowith thre epistilles of ye saide
            Picus of which thre: two be wretin
            vnto Iohan fraunsces his neuieu / y^e   25
            thred vnto one Andrew Corneus
                a noble man of Italy.

---

1 deuill / in] deuill. in *1510*, deuyll: In *1525*, deuill, in *1557*   2 deth. But] *1557*, deth.
but *1510*, dethe / but *1525*   9 Now] *1510 1525*, ⁋ Now *1557*   11–12 interces-
siones: let] intercessiones. Let *1510*, intercessyons. Let *1525*, intercessions: Let *1557*
13 thedir] *1510*, thyder *1525*, thether *1557*   21 the life] *1557*, life *1510*, ye lyfe
1525   22 Finis] *om. 1525 1557*   25 neuieu /] neuien *1510*, neuew / *1525*, neuiew,
1557   26 thred] *1510*, thyrde *1525*, third *1557*

The argument & mater of the first epistle of Picus
vnto his neuieu Iohan fraunsces.

H<small>IT</small> aperith by this epistill y^t Iohan fraunsces the neuieu of
Picus had broken his mynde vnto Picus and had made him of
5 counceill in some secrete godly purpose which he entended to
take vppon him: but what this purpose sholde be: vppon this
letter can we not fully parceiue. Now aftir y^t he thus entended
there fill vnto him many impedimentes and diuers occasions
which withstode his entent and in maner letted him & pulled him
10 bak. Wherfor Picus comforteth him in this epistill and exhorteth
him to perseueraunce / by such meanys as are in the epistill
euident and plaine ynough. Notwithstonding in ye begynning of
this lettre where he saith that the flesh shall (but if we take goode
hede) make vs dronke in the cuppis of Circes and misshape vs in
15 to the likenes and figure of brute bestis: those wordes if ye par-
ceiue them not be in this wise vndrestonden. Ther was sumtyme
in.   A woman called Circes which by enchauntement as
vergill maketh mention vsed with a drink to turne as many men:
as receiued hit in to diuers likenes & figures of sondry bestis:
20 some in to lyones / some in to beris / some in to swyne / some in
to wolfes which aftir ward walked euer tame a bowt her hows and
wayted vpon her in [c₄] such vse or seruice as she list to put vnto
them. In like wise the flessh if hit make vs dronk in the wyne of
voluptuouse plesure or make the sowle leue ye noble vse of his
25 reason & enclyne vnto sensualite & affectiones of the body: then
ye flessh chaungeth vs from the figure of resonable men in to y^e
likenes of vnresonable bestis / and y^t diuersly: aftir the conuen-
ience & similitude betwen oure sensuall affectiones and the bru-
tissh propirtees of sondry bestis. As the prowde harted man in to

---

2 neuieu] neuien *1510*, neuew *1525*, neuiew *1557*   3 neuieu] neuien *1510*, neuew
1525, neuiew *1557*   6 him: but] *1557*, him. but *1510*, hym / but *1525*   11 per-
seueraunce /] *1525*, perseueraunce. *1510*, perseuerance, *1557*   12 ynough] *1525*,
yuough *1510*, enough *1557*   14 in] *1525 1557*, in in *1510*   17 in.   A]
1510, in a *1525*, in   A *1557* (*see note*)   17 *Sidenote 1557:* Circe   19 bestis:]
bestis. *1510*, beestes / *1525*, beastes: *1557*   20 beris] *1510*, beeres *1525*, beares
1557   23 *Sidenote 1557:* How reasonable men be chaunged into vnreasonable beas-
tes   26 in to] *1510 1557*, in *1525*   27 bestis /] bestis. *1510*, beestes / *1525*, bestes,
1557

a lyone / the irows in to a bere / the lecherouse in to a gote / The
dronken gloten in to a swyne / yᵉ rauenous extorcioner in to a
wolfe / yᵉ false deceiuoure in to a foxe / the mokking gester in
to an ape. From which bestly shapp may we neuer be restored to
oure owne likenes agayn: vnto the tyme we haue cast vp agayne   5
the drynk of the bodely affectiones bi which we were in to these
figures enchaunted. Whan there commith some tyme a mon-
strouse best to yᵉ town we runne & are glad to paie some money
to haue a sight therof / but I fere if menne wold loke vppon them
self aduisedly: thei shold se a more monstrouse best nerer home: 10
for thei sholde parceiue them self by yᵉ wreched inclination to
diuers bestly passiones chaunged in their sowle not in to the shap
of one but of many bestes / yᵗ is to sey of al them whos brutissh
appetites thei follow. Let vs then be ware as picus concellith vs yᵗ
we be not dronken in yᵉ cuppis of Circes / yᵗ is to sey in yᵉ sensual   15
affectiones of yᵉ flessh / lest we deforme yᵉ image of god in oure
sowles aftir whose image we be made & make oure self worse
then idolatres for if he be odiouse to god which turneth yᵉ image
of [c₄v] a best in to god: how much is he more odious which
turneth the ymage of god in to a best.   20

Iohan Picus erle of Mirandula to Iohan
fraunsces hys neuieu by his brothir
helth in him that is very helth.

THAT thou hast had many yuell occasions aftir thy departing
which trouble the & stonde against the vertuouse purpose that   25
thou hast takin ther is no cause mi son why thou sholdest eythir
meruail therof / be sory therfor / or drede hyt. But rathir how
gret a wondre were this if onli to yᵉ amonge mortal men the waye

---

1 lyone /] lyone. *1510*, lyon / *1525*, lione, *1557;* bere] *1510*, beere *1525*, beare *1557*
2 swyne /] *1525*, swyne *1510*, swyne, *1557*   3 wolfe /] wolfe *1510 1525*, wolfe,
1557   3 the mokking] *1510*, mokkynge *1525*, yᵉ mocking *1557*   4 ape.
From] *1525*, ape. from *1510*, ape: from *1557*   7 *Sidenote 1557:* Wittely
saide   9 therof /] *1525*, therof. *1510*, therof: *1557*   13 bestes /] bestes. *1510*, bee-
stes / *1525*, bestes, *1557*   14 be ware] *1510 1525*, beware *1557*   15 Circes /] Circes
1510, cerces *1525*, Circe, *1557*   16 flessh / lest we] flessh lest / we *1510 1525*, flesh, lest
we *1557*   22 neuieu] neuien *1510*, neuew *1525*, neuiew *1557*   26 thou] *1557*, thon
1510, yᵘ *1525*   27 hyt. But] hyt. but *1510*, hit / but *1525*, it. But *1557*

laye open to heuen with owt swet as though y^t now at erst / the
disceytfull world & the cursed deuill failed / & as though thou
were not yet in ye flesh: which couetith against the spiret: &
which fals flesh (but if we watch and loke well to oure self) shal
5 make vs dronk in the cuppes of circes & so deforme vs in to
monstrous shappis of brutissh & vnresonable bestis. Remembre
also that of this euell occasiones ye holi apostle saint Iames saith
thow hast cause to be glad writting in this wise. Gaudete fratres
quum in temptationes varias incideritis. Be glad saith he my
10 brethren whan ye fall in diuerse temptationes / and not causeles
for what hope is ther of glory if ther be none hope of victory: or
what place ys ther for victory wher ther is no bataill: he is called
to the crowne & triumphe which ys prouoked to the conflict &
namely to that conflict: in which no man may be ouercom against
15 his will / and in which we nede none othir strenght to vainqwissh
but y^t we list our selfe to vainquissh. Very happy is a christen man
sith y^t ye vi[c₅]ctori is bothe put in his owne frewill: & the rewarde
of the victory shalbe farr gretter than we can eithir hope or
wisshe. Tell me y pray the my most dere son if ther be ought in
20 this life of all those thingis: ye delite werof so vexith and tossith
these erthly myndes / Is ther I say ani of those trifles: in ye geting
of which a man must not suffre many labours many displeasurs
& many miseries or he get hit. The marchaunt thinkith him selfe
well serued if aftir .x. yeres sailing / aftir a .m. incommoditees /
25 aftir a .m. Ieopardyes of his life he may at last haue a litle the
more gadered to gither. Of the court & seruice of this worlde
ther is nothing y^t I nede to write vnto the / the wretchednes
wherof the experience hit self hath taught the & daily techith. In
obtayning the fauour of ye princes / in purchasing the frendship

---

1 though] *1557*, thought *1510 1525*   2 world] word *1510*, worlde *1525 1557;* failed /]
failed. *1510*, fayled / *1525*, failed: *1557*   3 *Sidenote 1557:* Galat. 5   8 *Sidenote*
1557: Iac. 1   9 quum] qm̃ *1510 1525*, quando *1557*   10 temptationes /] tempta-
tiones. *1510*, temptacions / *1525*, temptacions, *1557;* causeles] *1510 1525*, causels
1557   12 he is] *1525*, he his *1510 1557*   14 *Sidenote 1557:* In the conflict against
temptacion no man is ouercomen against his wil   15 will /] *1525*, will. *1510*, will:
1557; strenght] *1510*, strength *1525 1557*   17 sith] *1557*, sit *1510*, syth *1525*   19 y]
1510, I *1525 1557*   21 myndes /] myndes *1510 1525*, myndes. *1557*   22–
23 *Sidenote 1557:* No pleasure in this life is gotten without paine   26 gadered] *1510*
1525, gathered *1557*   27 the /] *1525*, the. *1510*, the: *1557*   28 taught] *1525 1557*,
tanght *1510 Sidenote 1557:* The wretchednesse of the court

of the company / in ambitiouse laboure for offices & honowres /
what an hepe of heuines ther is: how gret anguissh: how much
besynes and trouble I may rathir lerne of the then teche y^e /
which holding my self content with my bokes & rest / of a chylde
haue lerned to liue within my degree and as much as I may 5
dwelling with my self nothing owt of my selfe labour for / or
longe for. Now then these erthly thingis slypper / vncertaine /
vile & commune also to vs and brute bestis: sweting & panting we
shall vnneth obtayn: and loke we than to heuenly thingis and
godly (which neithir eye hath sene nor ere hath hard nor hert 10
hath thought) to be drawen slumbri & sleping magrey oure teth:
as though neythir god might reygne nor those heuenly citezens
lyue with out vs? Certeinly if this worldly felicite [c_5v] were goten
to vs with idelnes and ease than might some man that shrinketh
from labour: rather chese to serue y^e worlde then god. But now 15
if we be forlabored in the way of synne as much as in the wey of
god and much more (werof the dampned wretches crye out
lassati sumus in via iniquitatis we be weried in the way of wikk-
ednes) then must hyt nedis be a poynt of extreme madnes if we
had not leuer labour there where we go from laboure to rewarde 20
then wher we go fro laboure to paine. I passe ouer, how grete
peace & felicite hit is to the mynd whan a man hath nothing that
grudgith his conscience nor is not appaled with the secrete twich
of any preuy cryme. This pleasur vndowtedly farr excellith all y^e
plesurs y^t in this life may be obteined or desired. What thing is 25
ther to be desired a mong ye delites of this world? which in the

---

1 company /] company *1510 1525*, company, *1557*   1–2 honowres / what] hon-
owres. what *1510*, honoures. What *1525*, honours, what *1557*   3 trouble I]] *1510*,
trouble. I *1525*, trouble, I *1557*; y^e /] *1525*, y^e. *1510*, the: *1557*   7 *Sidenote
1557:* Paine ought to be take rather for heauenly then earthly things   8 commune]
1557, commune / *1510 1525*; bestis] *1510*, beest *1525*, bestes *1557*   10 godly] *1510
1557*, goodly *1525*; hath sene] *1557*, hath seen *1525*, hat sene *1510*; *Sidenote 1557:* 1.
Corin. 2   11 slumbri] *1510*, slumbry *1525*, slumbring *1557*   13 vs?] *1557*, vs. *1510
1525*; if] *1557*, of *1510 1525*   15 chese] *1510 1525*, chose *1557*   15–16 *Sidenote
1557:* The waie of synne more paynefull then the waie of vertue   18 lassati] *1510*,
Lassati *1525*, Lvssati *1557*; *Sidenote 1557:* Sap. 5   19 a poynt] apoynt*1510*, apoynte
1525, a point *1557*   23 twich] *1510*, twiche *1525*, touch *1557*   24 *Sidenote
1557:* Spirituall pleasure; This] *1557*, this *1510 1525*

seking wery vs / in the hauing blindeth vs / in the lesing payneth
vs. Dowtest thow my son whethir the myndes of wikked men be
vexed or not with continuall thought & torment: hit is the worde
of god which neithir may deceyue nor be deceyued. Cor impii
5   quasi mare feruens quod quiescere non potest. The wikked
mannes hart is like a stormy see y^t may not rest. Ther is to him no
thing sure / no thing peseable but al thing fereful / al thing
sorowfull / al thing dedely. Shall we then enuie these men: shall
we follow them: and forgeting our owne contre heuin / & oure
10 own heuinly fathir / wher we were fre born: shall we wilfully
make oure self their bondemen: & with them wretchedly liuing/
more wretchedli dye and at y^e last most wretchidly in euer lasting
fire be [c_6] punished? O the dark myndes of men. O the blinde
hartis. Who seyth not more clere than lyght that al these thingis
15 be (as they sey) trewer than treuth hit selfe / & yet do we not that
y^t we knowe is to be done. In vaine we wolde pluk oure fote out of
y^e clay but we stik styll. Ther shall come to the my sonne dowt hit
not (in these places namely where thou art conuersaunt) innu-
merable impedimentis euery howre: which might fere the from
20 the purpose of gode and vertuouse liuing (and but if thou be
ware) shall throw the down hedling. But amonge all thyngis the
very dedly pestilence ys this: to be conuersaunt day and night
amonge them whos life is not only on euery side an allectiue to
synne: but ouer that all set in the expugnation of vertue / vndre
25 their capitaine the deuill / vndre the banaire of deth / vndre the
stipende of hell / fighting a geinst heuen / a gainst oure lord god
and a gainst his christ. But crye thou therfore with the prophete

---

1 vs /] *1525*, vs. *1510*, vs, *1557*   2 *Sidenote 1557:* The minde of the wicked is neuer in
quiete; vs /] *1525*, vs. *1510*, vs, *1557*   4 *Sidenote 1557:* Esaie. 57   6 rest. Ther]
1557, rest. ther *1510*, rest / there *1525*   10 fathir / wher] fathir wher *1510*, father
where *1525*, father, where *1557;* were fre] *1557*, were / fre *1510*, were / free
1525   11 self their] *1557*, self their selfe their *1510*, selfe theyr *1525*   13 pun-
ished?] *1557*, punished. *1510*, punisshed. *1510*   14 seyth] *1510 1525*, seeth *1557*
15 selfe /]*1525*, selfe. *1510*, self? *1557*   21 *Sidenote 1557:* Euill company   24 ver-
tue /] *1525*, vertue. *1510*, vertue, *1557*   25 deuill /] deuill. *1510*, deuyll / *1525*,
deuill, *1557*   25 deth /] *1525*, deth. *1510*, death, *1557*   26 hell /] *1525*, hell.
1510, hell, *1557*   26 heuen /] *1525*, heuen. *1510*, heauen, *1557*   27 christ] *1510*,
chyrch *1525*, Christ *1557*

dirumpamus vincula eorum & proiiciamus a nobis iugum ip-
sorum. Let vs breke the bandes of them & let vs cast of the yook
of them. These be they whom (as yᵉ gloriouse apostill saint Paule
seith) our lord hath deliuered in to the passionis of rebuke and to
a reprouable sense to do those thingys that are not conuenient /
full of all iniquite / full of enuie / manslaughtir / contention /
gile / & malice / bakbiters odiouse to god / contumeliouse /
prowde / stateli / finders of euell thingis / folissh / dissolute /
with oute affection with out couenaunt with out mercy which
whan thei daily se the iustice of god yet vndrestonde they not
[c₆v] that such as these thingis committ: are worthy deth / not
only they yᵗ do such thingis: but also thei which consent to the
doing: wherfor my childe go thou neuer a bowt to plese them:
whom vertue displesith / but euer more lete these wordes of the
apostill be before thin yen. Oportet magis deo placere quam
hominibus we must rather please god then men. And remembre
these wordes of seint Paule also. Si hominibus placerem seruus
christi non essem If I shold plese men I were not christis ser-
uaunt. Let entre in to thin hert an holy pryde & haue disdaine to
take them for maistres of thi lyuing which haue more nede to
take the for a maister of theirs. Hit were farr more semyng yᵗ
they sholde with yᵉ by good lyuing begyn to be men then thou
shuldest with them by yᵉ leuing of thi good purpose shamfully
begyn to be a best. Ther holdith me some tyme by almighty god
as hit were euin a swone and an insensibilite for wondre when I
begin in my selfe: I wot neuer whethir I shall sey: to remembre
or to sorrow / to meruaill or to bewaill the appetites of men / or
yf I shall more plainli speke: yᵉ very madnesse. For it is verelye a
great madnesse not to beleue the gospell whos trouth the blode

1 iugum] *1525 1557*, ingum *1510*; *Sidenote 1557:* Psal. 2   3 *Sidenote 1557:* Rom.
1   6 manslaughtir /] manslaughtir. *1510*, manslaughter / *1525*, manslaughter, *1557*
7 god /] god *1510 1525*, god, *1557*   11 deth /] *1525*, deth. *1510*, death, *1557*
14 displesith /] displesith. *1510*, displeaseth / *1525*, displeseth, *1557*   15 thin] thim
1510, thyn *1525*, thine *1557*; yen] *1510*, eyen *1525*, eien *1557*; *Sidenote 1557:* Act.
5   16 men. And] *1557*, men. and *1510*, men / and *1525*   17–18 *Sidenote 1557:*
Gal. 1   19 *Sidenote 1557:* A holy pride   20 maistres] *1510*, maysters *1525*, maisters
1557   27 men /] *1525*, men. *1510*, men: *1557*   28–29 madnesse . . . madnesse]
1557, madnes *1510 1525*; *Sidenote 1557:* The trueth of the ghospell

of martirs crieth / yᵉ voice of apostles sowneth / miracles pro-
ueth / reason confermith / the worlde testifieth / yᵉ elementis
spekith / deuelis confessith. But a far gretter madnes ys hit if
thou dowt not but that the gospell ys trew: to lyue then as though
5 thou doutest not but that hit were fals. For if these wordes of the
gospell be trew / yᵗ hit ys very harde for a riche man to entre the
kingdome of heuen whi do we daily then gape aftir the heping
vp of riches? [d₁] And if this be trew that we shulde seke for the
glory and praise not that commith of men but that commeth of
10 god why do we then euer hange vppon the iugement & opinion
of men and no man rekkith whither god like him or not. And if
we surely beleue yᵗ ones the time shall come in which oure lorde
shall say go ye cursed peple in to euer lasting fire & againe come
ye my blessed childrin possede ye the kingdome that hath ben
15 prepared for you from the fourmyng of the worlde whi is ther no
thing then yᵗ we lesse fere then hell or yᵗ we lesse hope for / then
the kingdom of god. What shal we sey ellis but that ther be mani
christen men in name but fewe in dede. But thou my son enforce
thy selfe to entre by yᵉ streight gate yᵗ ledyth to heuin & take no
20 hede what thing many men do: but what thing yᵉ verey law of
nature / what thing very reason / what thing oure lorde him self
shewith yᵉ to be done for neithir thi glory shalbe les if thou be
happi with fewe nor thi pain more easy if thou be wretched with
many. Thou shalt haue .ii. specially effectuall remedies against
25 the world & the deuill with which two: as with .ii. whinges: thou
shalt out of this vale of miserie be lift vp in to heuin / that is to sey
almes dede and praier. What may we do with out yᵉ helpe of god
or how shal he helpe vs if he be not called vppon? But ouer that

---

1 crieth /]crieth *1510*, cryeth / *1525*, cryeth, *1557*   3 confessith] *1510*, confesseth *1525*,
confesse *1557*; *Sidenote 1557:* An extreme madnesse   5–6 of the gospell] *1557*, of the
wordes of the gospell *1510 1525*; *Sidenote 1557:* Marc. 10   8 riches?] *1557*, riches. *1510*
1525; *Sidenote 1557:* Io. 12   9–10 *Sidenote 1557:* Mat. 25;   14 *Sidenote 1557:* Mat. 25;
possede] *1510 1525*, possesse *1557*; kingdome] *1557*, kingdoine *1510*, kyngdome
1525   17 *Sidenote 1557:* Many christen men in name, & fewe in dede   19 streight]
1510, streygh *1525*, streyght *1557*; *Sidenote 1557:* Mat. 7   21 reason /] reason *1510*
1525, reason, *1557* 24 *Sidenote 1557:* Almes and praier .ii. speciall remedies against the
worlde & the deuill   26 in to] *1510*, in *1525*, into *1557*

certainly he shall not here the whan thou callest on him if thou
here not first ye pore man whan he callith vppon the & vereli hit
is according that god shuld despice the being a man whan thou
being a man despisest a man. For hit ys wryten in what mesure y^t
ye mete: hit shalbe mette you againe. [d₁v] And in an othir place
of ye gospell hit is seid blessed be mercifull men for they shall
gete mercy. Whan I stire the to praier I stire ye not to ye praier
which stondith in many wordes but to that praier which in y^e
secret chambre of the mynde / in the preuy closet of ye sowle
with very affect spekith to god and in ye most lightsome darkenes
of contemplation not only presentith the mynde to the father:
but also vnieth hit with him by inspekable waies which only thei
know that haue assaied. Nor I care not how longe or how short
thi praier be / but how effectual / how ardent / and rathir inter-
rupted & broken betwen with syghis then drawen on lenght with
a continuall rowe & nombre of wordis. If thou loue thin helth / if
thou desire to be sure from ye grennys of the deuill / from the
stormes of this worlde / from thawait of thin enemies if thou
longe to be acceptable to god if thou coueit to be happy at the
last: let no daie passe the but thou ones at ye lest wise present thi
self to god by praier and falling down by fore him flat to y^e
ground with an humble affecte of deuout mynde not from y^e
extremite of thi lippes but out of ye inwardnes of thin hart cry
thes wordes of the prophete. Delicta iuuentutis mee & ignoran-
tias meas ne memineris sed secundum misericordiam tuam
memento mei propter bonitatem tuam domine. The offencis of
my youth & myn ignorances remembre not good lorde / but
aftir thy mercy lorde for thy goodnes remembre me. What thou
shalt in thi praier axe of god: both ye holy spyrit which praeth
for vs and eke thin owne necessite shall eueri houre put in thi
mynd / & also what thou shalt praie for: thou shalt finde mater

5

10

15

20

25

30

4 *Sidenote 1557:* Matth. 7   5 againe.] againe *1510*, agayne *1525*, agayne. *1557*
6 blessed] *1510 1557*, blyssed *1525; Sidenote 1557:* Matth. 5   8 *Sidenote 1557:* Pray-
er   12 inspekable] *1510 1525*, vnspeakeable *1557*   14 effectual /] effectual *1510*,
effectuall *1525*, effectuall, *1557*   16 wordis. If] wordis if *1510*, wordes / yf *1525*,
woordes. If *1557*   17 be sure] *1525*, be-[*new line*]sure *1510*, bee sure *1557*   18 tha-
wait] tha wait *1510*, thawayte *1525*, thawayt *1557*   20 *Sidenote 1557:* No day without
praier   24 *Sidenote 1557:* Psal. 34   28 What] *1557*, whan *1510 1525*   31 mynd /
]mynd. *1510*, mynde / *1525*, mynd: *1557*

[d₂] ynough in the reding of holi scripture which yᵗ thou woldest
now (setting poetis fables & trifles a syde) take euir in thin hande
I hartely praie yᵉ. Thou mast do no thing more plesaunt to god
no thing more profitable to thi selfe: then if thyn hande cease not
5   day nor night to turne & rede the volumes of holy scripture.
Ther lyeth priuely in them a certein heuenly strenght quik and
effectual which with a meruelous powar transformeth & chaungith
yᵉ redars mynde in to the loue of god if they be clene & lowly
entreated. But I haue passed now yᵉ boundes of a lettre / yᵉ
10   mater drawing me forth & yᵉ gret loue that I haue had to the /
both euer before: & specially: syth yᵗ howre in which I haue had
first knowledge of thi most holy purpose. Now to make an ende
with this one thing I warne yᵉ (of which whan we were last
to gethir I often talked with yᵉ) yᵗ thou neuer forget these .ii.
15   thinges: yᵗ both yᵉ son of god died for the & yᵗ thou shalt also thi
self dye shortly liue thow neuer so longe. With these twayn as
with two spurrys yᵗ one of fere yᵗ othir of loue spurre forth thin
hors thorow the short waye of this momentary life to yᵉ reward of
eternall felicite sith we neither ought nor may prefix our selfe
20   any othir ende than yᵉ endles fruition of yᵉ infinite goodnes both
to sowle & body in euir lasting peace. Fare wel and fere god.

The mater or argument of the epistle
of Picus to Andrew Corneus.

THIS Andrew a worshipfull man and a especiall frende of
25   Picus had by his lettres geuin him cownceill to leue the study of
philosophi as [d₂v] a thing in which he thought Picus to haue
spent tyme Inough and which: but if hit were applied to yᵉ vse of
sum actuall besines: he iuged a thing vaine & vnprofitable.
Wherfor he counceiled Picus to surceace of study and put him

---

1 ynough] *1510 1525*, enough *1557*   3 mast] *1510*, mayst *1525*, maist *1557*   3–
4 *Sidenote 1557:* Readyng of holy scripture   9 lettre /] *1525*, lettre. *1510*, letter,
1557   12 purpose.] purpos *1510*, purpose *1525 1557*   15 thinges:] *1557*, thinges.
1510, thynges / *1525*   18 short waye] shortwaye *1510*, shorte way *1525*, short waie
1557   21 Fare wel] fare wel *1510*, Fare well *1525*, Farewel *1557*   24 a especiall]
1510 1525, an especiall *1557*

self with sume of ye grete princes of Italy. With whom (as this
Andrew saide) he sholde be moch more frutfully occupiede then
alway in the studi & lerninge of philosophe / to whom picus
answerid as in this present epistle apperith. Wher he saith these
wordes (By this hit sholde folow that hit were eithir seruile or at   5
ye lestwise not princely to mak the study of philosophy other
then mercennari) thus he meanith. Mercennary we call all those
thingys which we do for hire or rewarde. Then he makith philos-
ophi mercennary & vsith hit not as connyng but as marchaundise
which studieth hit not for pleasur of hit selfe: or for the instruc-   10
tion of his mynde in morall vertue: but to applie hit to such
thingis wher he may get sum lucre or worldly aduauntage.

Iohan Picus erle of mirandula
to andrew Corneus greting.

Y E exhort me by your lettres to the ciuile and actiue life saing   15
that in vaine: and in maner to my rebuke & shame haue I so
longe studied in philosophy / but if I wolde at the last exercise y^t
lerning in the entreting of sum profitable actis and outward
besines. Certainly my wel beloued andrew I had cast a way bothe
cost and labour of my study: if I were so minded that I coude   20
finde in my hert in this mater to assent vnto you and folow your
[d₃] counceill. This is a very dedly and monstrous persuasione
which hath entred the myndes of men: beleuing that the studies
of philosophie are of estates & princes: either vttirly not to be
touched: or at lest wise with extreme lippis to be sipped and   25
rather to ye pompe and ostentation of their wit then to the cul-
ture & proffit of their myndis to be litel & esely tasted. The
wordes of Neoptolemus they holde vttirly for a sure decree that

---

3 philosophe / to] philosophe to *1510*, philosophye / to *1525*, philosophie. To *1557;*
Sidenote 1557   7 Philosophie   4 apperith. Wher] apperith wher *1510*, appereth
where *1525*, appereth, where *1557*   6 philosophy] philosoply *1510*, phylosophy
1525, philosophie *1557*   7 *Sidenote 1557:* Mercennary   11 morall] *1557*, mortall
1510 1525   17 philosophy / but] philosophy. But *1510 1525*, philosophie, but
1557   22 *Sidenote 1557:* A monstrous persuasion touching the studie of philoso-
phy   25 sipped and] sipped (and *1510*, sypped (and *1525*, sipped, and
1557   28 Neoptolemus] Neoptolenius *1510 1525*, Neoptolomus *1557*

philosophy is to be studied eythir neuir or not longe / but the
saynges of wysemen they repute for Iapes & very fables: that
sure & stedfast felicite stondeth only in the goodnes of the
mynde & that these owtward thinges of yᵉ body or of fortune litle
5   or nought pertaine vnto vs. But here ye will sey to me thus. I am
content ye study / but I wolde haue you outwardli occupied also.
And I desire you not so to embrace martha that ye shulde vttirly
forsake Mari. Loue them & vse them both aswell study as worldly
occupation. Trewly my welbeloued frende in this point I gaine
10   sey you not: they that so do I finde no fault in nor I blame them
not / but certainly hit is not all one to sey we do well if we do so:
and to sey we do euell but if we do so. This is farr owt of the way:
to think that from contemplation to the actife liuing that is to sey
from the bettir to the worse is none errour to decline and to
15   thinke that it were shame to abyde styll in the bettir and not
decline. Shall a man then be rebuked by cause that he desirith
and ensueth vertue only for hit selfe: bi cause he studyeth yᵉ
mysteries of god: by cause he enserchith the counceill of nature:
bi cause he vsith continually [d₃v] this plesaunt ease & rest: sek-
20   ing none outward thing dispysing all othir thing: syth thos
thingis are able sufficiently to satisfie the desire of their folowers.
By this rekenyng hit is a thing eithir seruile or at yᵉ lest wise not
princely to make yᵉ study of wisedom other then mercennarye.
Who may well here this / who may suffre hyt? Certainly he
25   neuer studied for wisedome which so studied therfor that in
tyme to come eithir he might not or wold not studi therfor. This
man rathir exercised the study of merchaundise then of wise-
dom. Ye writ vnto me that hyt is tyme for me now to put my selfe

---

1 longe /] _1525_, longe. _1510_, longe: _1557_   3 _Sidenote 1557:_ Felicitie   6 study /
but] study. bnt _1510_, studye / but _1525_, studie, but _1557_   7 And] _1557_, Aud _1510_,
Ind _1525_   10 not:] _1557_, not. _1510_, not / _1525_; in] _1525_, in. _1510_, in: _1557_   11
not /] _1525_, not. _1510_, not: _1557_   12 so. This] _1557_, so. this _1510_, so / this
_1525_   13 _Sidenote 1557:_ Contemplacion   14 decline and] decline And _1510 1525_,
decline. And _1557_   18 nature:] nature _1510 1525_, nature, _1557_   24 this /] this
_1510 1525_, this, _1557_; hyt?] hyt. _1510_, hit. _1525_, it? _1557_; _Sidenote 1557:_ The studie of
wisedome neuer to be omitted   26 therfore. This] _1557_, therfore. this _1510_, ther-
fore / this _1525_   28 writ] _1510 1557_, wryte _1525_

in howsolde wyth some of the grete princes of Italy but I see well
y^t as yet ye haue not knowen the opinion that philosophres haue
of them selfe which (as horace seith) repute them self kingis of
kingis: they loue liberte: they can not bere ye prowde maners of
estates: they can not serue. They dwell with them selfe and be   5
content with the tranquillite of their owne mynde. Thei suffice
them selfe & more / they seke nothing owt of them selfe: the
thingis that are had in honoure amonge ye commune peple:
amonge them be not holden honorable. All that euir the volup-
tuouse desire of men thirsteth for: or ambition sigheth for: they   10
set at nought and despyce. Which while hit belongith to all men:
yet vndoutedly it pertaineth most propirly to them whom for-
tune hath so lyberally fauored that they may liue not only well
and plenteously but also nobly. These grete fortunes lift vp a
man hie and settith him owt to the shew: but oftyn times as a   15
fierce and a skittissh hors they cast of their maister. Certainly
alway they greue and vexe [d$_4$] him and rathir tere him then bere
him. The golden mediocrite the meanne estate is to be desired
which shall bere vs as hit were in handes more easili / which shall
obey vs & not maistre vs. I therfore abyding fermely in this   20
opinion: set more bi my little house / my study / the pleasure of
my bokes / ye rest and peace of my mynde: then by all your kingis
palacis / all your commune besines / all your glory / all the ad-
uauntage that ye hawke aftir / and all the fauoure of the court.
Nor I loke not for this frute of my study y^t I may therby herafter   25
be tossed in the flode and rombeling of your worldly besynesse:
but y^t I may ones bring forth the children that I trauaile on: y^t I
may giue owt some bokes of myn owne to the commune proffit

---

2 *Sidenote 1557:* philosophers   3 seith)] seith(*1510*, sayth) *1525*, saith) *1557*   6
mynde. Thei] mynde thei *1510*, mynde they *1525*, mynde, thei *1557*   10 sigheth]
1510, sygheth *1525*, seketh *1557*   11 while] *1525 1557*, whill *1510*   13 *Sidenote
1557:* Highe estate   16 Certainly] certainly *1510*, Certeynly *1525*, Certeinly *1557*
18 *Sidenote 1557:* Meane estate   19 easili / which] easili. which *1510 1525*, easely,
which *1557*   21 house /] house *1510 1525*, house, *1557*   23 palacis /] palacis
1510, palace *1525*, palacis, *1557;* glory /] *1525*, glory. *1510*, glorie, *1557*   24 aftir /]
aftir. *1510*, after *1525*, after, *1557;* court.] *1525 1557*, court *1510*   25 *Sidenote
1557:* The right fruite of studie

which may sumwhat sauour: if not of cunnyng yet at the lest wyse
of wit and diligence. And by cause ye shall not think that my
trauaile & diligence in studi is any thing remitted or slakked: I
giue you knowledge y^t after grete feruent labour with much
5 watch and infatigable trauaile I haue lerned both the hebrew
language and the chaldey and now haue I set hand to ouercome
the grete difficulte of the Araby tonge. These my dere frende be
thingis: which to apertaine to a noble prince I haue euir thought
and yet think. Fare ye well. Wretin at Paris the .xv. day of Octobre
10 the yere of grace .M. cccclxxxxii. [d$_4$v]

The argument of the epistill folowing.

A$_{FTIR}$ that Iohan Frauncise y^e nephiew of Picus had (as hit
aperith in y^e first epistle of Picus to him) bigon a chaunge in his
liuing: hit semith by this lettre y^t the company of the court wher
15 he was conuersaunt diuersly (as hit is their vnmanerly maner)
descanted therof to his rebuke as them thought: but as treuth
was vnto their owne. Sume of them iuged hit foly / sum called hit
ypocresy / sum scorned him / sum sclaundred him / of all
whych demeanour (as we may of this epistle coniecture) he wrote
20 vnto this erle Picus his vncle which in this lettre comforteth &
encoragith him as hit is in y^e course therof euident.

Iohan Picus erle of Mirandula to Franscis
his neuieu greting in oure lorde.

H$_{APPY}$ art thou my sonne whan that our lorde not only
25 giueth the grace well to liue but also that while thow liuest well he
giueth y^e grace to bere yuell wordes of euell peple for thy lyuing
well. Certainly as grete a prais as hit is to be commendet of them
y^t are commendable: as grete a commendation it is to be re-

---

8 to apertaine] *1510 1525*, do appertaine *1557*   17 foly /] *1525*, foly. *1510*, foly,
1557   18 ypocresy] *1510 1525*, hypocrisie *1557;* him /] *1525*, him. *1510*, him,
1557   20 comforteth] *1557*, comfortet *1510*, comforted *1525*   23 neuieu] neuien
1510, neuew *1525*, neuiew *1557*   25 but] *1525 1557*, bnt *1510;* while] *1557*, whill
1510; whyle *1525*   27 Certainly] *1557*, certainly *1510*, Certaynly *1525*   27 com-
mendet] *1510*, commended *1525 1557*

proued of them y^t are reprouable. Notwithstonding my sonne I
call the not therfor happy by cause this fals reprofe is worshipful
& glorious vnto ye but for by cause y^t oure lorde Iesu christ
(which is not only trew but also trewth hit selfe) affermith that
oure rewarde shalbe plentuous in heuyn when men speke euill
to vs and speke all euill against vs lying for hys name. This is an
Apostles dignite: to be reputed digne a fore god to be defamed
of wykked folk for his name. For we rede in the gospell of luke
that [d₅] the apostles went ioyfull and glad from ye counceill
hows of the iewes by cause god had acceptyd them as worthi to
suffre wronge and repriefe for his sake. Let vs therfore Ioye & be
glad if we be worthy so grete worship before god y^t his worshyp
be shewed in our rebuke. And if we suffre of ye world any thing
that is greuous or bittir: let this swete voice of our lorde be our
consolation. Si mundus vos odio habet scitote quia priorem me
vobis odio habuit. If the worlde (seith oure lorde) hate you: know
ye y^t hit hated me by fore you. If ye worlde then hated him by
whom ye worlde was made: we most vile and simple men and
worthi (if we considre our wretched liuing well) all shame &
reprofe: if folk bakbyte vs & sey iuell of vs: shal we so greuousli
take hit: that lest thei shulde sey yuel we shulde begin to do yuel?
Let vs rathir gladly receiue thes iuel wordis and if we be not so
happy to suffre for vertue & treuth as the olde seintis suffred
betingis / bynding / prison / swerdes / and deth: let vs think at
the lest wise we be wel serued if we haue the grace to suffre
chiding / detraction / & hatred of wikked men / lest y^t if all
occasion of deseruing be taken a way ther be left vs none hope of
rewarde. If men for thy good liuing praise the: thi vertu certainly
in that hit is vertue makith the like vnto christ: but in that hit is

2 *Sidenote 1557:* It is a commendacion to be reproued of the reprouable   6 lying]
1557, lyuing *1510,* lyuynge *1525; Sidenote 1557:* Mat. 5   7 *Sidenote 1557:* An apos-
tles dignitie   9 *Sidenote 1557:* Act. 5   11 sake. Let] *1525 1557,* sake Let *1510*
14 greuous] *1525 1557,* greuons *1510;* bittir] *1510,* bytter *1525,* better *1557*   15 *Side-
note 1557:* Iohn. 16   16 vobis odio] vobis *1510 1525 1557;* If] *1525 1557,* if *1510*
17 You. If] *1525 1557,* you If *1510*   21 sey yuel we shulde] *om. 1557*   24 be-
tinges /] betinges *1510,* betynges / *1525,* beatinges, *1557;* bynding] *1510 1557,* byn-
dynges *1525;* deth: let] deth. Let *1510 1525,* death. Let *1557*   26 men /] *1525,* men.
1510, men: *1557*

praised hit makith the vnlike him: which for the rewarde of his
vertue receiued ye opprobriouse deth of the crosse for which as
the Apostle seith god hath exalted him and giuen him a name y^t
is a boue all names. More desirefull is than to be condempned of
5 ye worlde and exalted of god then to be exalted of [d₅v] the
worlde and condemned of god. The worlde condemneth to life:
god exalteth to glori. The worlde exaltith to a fall: god condem-
nith to ye fire of hell. Finally if the worlde fawne vppon y^e:
vnneth hit may be but y^t thi vertue (which all lift vpward shulde
10 haue god alone to plese) shal sumwhat vnto ye blandisshing of y^e
worlde and fauoure of ye peple incline. And so though hit lese no
thing of the integrite of our perfection yet hit lesith of ye rewarde:
which rewarde whill hyt beginneth to be paide in ye worlde wher
all thing is litle hit shalbe lesse in heuin wher all thing is gret. O
15 happy rebukes which make vs sure: y^t neithir ye flowre of oure
vertue shall wither with the pestilent blast of vainglori: nor oure
eternall rewarde be minisshed for the vaine promotion of a litle
populare fame. Let vs my sonne loue these rebukes / & onli of y^e
ignominye and reprefe of oure lordes crosse let vs like feithful
20 seruauntes with an holy ambition be prowde. We (saith seint
Paule) preche crist crucified which is vnto the iewes dispite / vnto
ye gentiles foly / vnto vs the vertue & wisedom of god. The
wysedom of this worlde is folisshnes a fore god & the foly of crist
is y^t: by which he hath ouercome the wisedom of ye worlde bi
25 which hit hath plesed god to mak his beleuing peple safe. If that
thou doubt not but that thei be madd which bakbite thy vertue:
which the cristen liuing that is very wisedome reputith for
madnes: considre than how much were thi madnes: if thow
sholdest for the iugement of madd men swarue from the goode

---

3 Apostle] *1510 1557*, apopstle *1525; Sidenote 1557:* Phil. 2   4 is] *1510 1525*, is it
1557   6 god. The] *1557*, god. the *1510*, god / y^e *1525*   7 glori. The] glori the
1510, glorye / y^e *1525*, glory: the *1557;* fall:] *1557*, fall *1510*, fall / *1525*   8 Finally]
1557, finally *1510*, fynably *1525*   12 rewarde:] *1557*, rewarde *1510 1525*   13 be-
ginneth] *1557*, beginueth *1510*, begynneth *1525*   15 *Sidenote 1557:* Happie rebukes
16 wither] *1510*, wyther *1525*, wether *1557*   18 rebukes /] rebukes *1510 1525*, re-
bukes, *1557*   19 reprefe] *1510 1525*, reprofe *1557*   19 crosse let] crosse. Let *1510
1525 1557*   20 *Sidenote 1557:* 1. Cor. 1   21 dispite /] *1525*, dispite. *1510*, dispite,
1557   22 foly /] *1525*, foly. *1510*, foly, *1557*   27 which] which: *1510 1525*, whiche
1557

institution of thy life namely sith all erroure is with amendement
to be taken a waye & not with imitation & folowing [d$_6$] to be
encreaced. Let them therfore neghe let them bawll let them bark
go thou boldely forth thi iourney as thou hast bigone and of their
wikkednes & misery considre how much thi selfe art be holden to   5
god which hath illumined the sytting in the shadow of deth and
translating the owt of the company of them (which like dronken
men with out a guide wandre hythir and thither in obscure
darkenes) hath associate the to the children of light. Let that
same swete voice of oure lorde alwai sowne in thin eris. Sine   10
mortuos sepelire mortuos suos / tu me sequere. Let dede men a
lone wyth dede men / folow thow me. Dede be they that liue not
to god and in the space of this temporall deth laboriously pur-
chase them selfe eternall deth. Of whom if thou axe wherto they
draw wherto they referr their studies / their warkis and their   15
besines & finally what ende they haue appointed them selfe in
the adeption wherof they shuld be happy / eithir they shal haue
vttirly no thing to answer or thei shal bryng forth wordes repug-
naunt in them selfe and contrary eche to othir lyke the rauing of
bedelem peple. Nor they wot neuir them selfe what thei do but   20
like them that swyme in swifte flodes thei be born forth with y^e
violence of euel custom as hit were with ye boystious course of y^e
streme. And theyr wikkednes blinding them on this side: & the
deuyl prikking them forth warde on y^t syde: they rynne forth
hedling in to all mischiefe as blinde guides of blinde men / til y^t 25
deth set on them vnware and till that hyt be saide vnto them that
crist seyth in the gospell [d$_6$v] my frende this night y^e deuelis
shall take thy sowle from the: these goodis then that thou hast

---

3 neghe] *1510*, nyghe *1525*, nighe *1557;* bark] *1510*, karke *1525*, barke *1557*   4 their]
the *1510 1525 1557*   10–11 *Sidenote 1557:* Mat. 8   11 suos /] suos *1510 1525*,
suos, *1557* 12 me. Dede] me. dede *1510*, me / deed *1525*, me. Dead *1557; Sidenote
1557:* Deade be thei that lyue not to god   14 Of] *1525 1557*, of *1510;* axe] *1510 1525*,
aske *1557*   17 adeption] adoption *1510*, adopcyon *1525*, adopcion *1557*   20 be-
delem] *1510 1525*, bethlem *1557*   23 *Sidenote 1557:* Euil custome   24 forth
warde] *1510*, forwarde *1525*, forthwarde *1557;* rynne] *1510*, renne *1525*
1557   25 mischiefe as] mischiefe. as *1510 1525*, mischiefe, as *1557;* men / til] men.
Til *1510*, men / tyll *1525*, men, til *1557*   27 gospell] *1525*, gsopell *1510*, ghospell
1557; Sidenote 1557: Luke. 12

gedered whos shall thei be. Then shal thei enuie them whom thei
dispised. Then shal they commend them that thei mokked.
Then shal thei coueit to ensew them in liuing whan they may not
whom whan they might haue ensewed thei pursewed. Stop ther-
5 fore thin eris mi most dere son & what so euer men sey of the
what so euer men think on ye accompt hit for no thing / but
regarde only the iugement of god which shal yeld euery man
aftir his owne warkis when he shall shew him selfe from heuin
with ye aungellis of his vertue: in flame of fire doing vengeaunce
10 vpon them that haue not knowin god nor obeied his gospell
which (as the apostle seith) shal suffre in deth eternal peyn from
ye face of our lorde & from the glory of his vertue whan he shal
com to be glorified of his seintes & to be made meruelous in al
them that haue beleued. Hit is wrytin / nolite timere qui corpus
15 possunt occidere sed qui animam potest mittere in gehennam.
Fere not them (seith our lorde) that may sle the body but fere
him y^t may cast the sowl in to hell. How much lesse then be they to
be fered: y^t may neithyr hurt sowle nor body which if they now
bakbite the liuing vertuousely thei shal do the same neuer the
20 lesse if (vertue for saken) thou were ouerwhelmed with vice not
for y^t vice displeasith them but for y^t the vice of bakbiting alway
plesyth them. Flee if thou loue thin helth flee as ferre as thou
mast their company / and retourning to thy selfe often times
secretly pray vnto the most benigne fathir of heuin criyng with
25 the prophete. Ad te domine le[e₁]uaui animam meam deus
meus in te confido non erubescam etiam si irrideant me inimici
mei etenim vniuersi qui sperant in te non confundentur. Con-
fundantur iniqua agentes superuacue. vias tuas domine demon-
stra mihi et semitas tuas edoce me. dirige me in veritate tua et
30 doce me quia tu es deus saluator meus et in te sperabo tota die /

---

1 gedered] *1510 1525*, gathered *1557*   2–3 mokked. Then] mokked then *1510 1525*,
mocked, then *1557*   4 pursewed. Stop] persewed. stop *1510*, persewed / stop *1525*,
pursued. Stop *1557*   6 no thing /] no thing. *1510*, nothynge / *1525*, nothing:
1557   11 peyn from] peyn. From *1510 1525*, payne, from *1557*   13 glorified]
1510 1557, gloryed *1525*   14 *Sidenote 1557:* Mat. 10   15 *Sidenote 1557:* Luc. 12
16 sle] *1510 1525*, slay *1557*   22 them. Flee] them flee *1510 1525*, them: flee *1557*
23 mast] *1510*, mayst *1525*, mayest *1557*   25 te domine] *1525 1557*, the domine *1510*;
Sidenote 1557: Psal. 24; leuaui] *1525 1557*, leuani *1510*   27–28 Confundantur] *1525*
1557, Confundantnr *1510*

that is to sey. To ye lorde I lift vp my sowle in the I trust. I shal not
be shamed & though myn enemis mok me. Certainly al they that
trust in the shal not be ashamed. Let them be ashamed that
worke wikkednes in vaine. Thy weies good lorde shew me and
thy pathes teche me / directe me in thy treuth and teche me for   5
thow art god my sauiour / in the shal I trust al the day. Re-
membre also mi sonne y^t the deth lieth at hande. Remembre that
all the tyme of our life is but a moment & yet lesse than a mo-
ment. Remembre how cursed our olde enemy is: which offreth
vs ye kingdomes of this worlde that he might bereue vs ye king-   10
dome of heuen / how fals the flesshly plesures: which therfore
embrace vs y^t thei might strangle vs / how disceitfull these
worldly honores: which therfore lift vs vp: that thei might throw
vs downe / how dedly these richessis: which ye more they fede vs:
the more they poison vs / how short how vncertain how shadow   15
like fals ymaginary hit is that all thes thingis togethir may bring
vs: and though they flowe to vs as we wolde wissh them. Re-
membre again how grete thingis be promised and prepared for
them: which dispising these present thinges desire and longe for
that contre whos king is ye godhede / whos law is charite / whos   20
mesur is eternite. Occupie [e₁v] thy minde with these medita-
tiones and such othir y^t may waken ye when thou slepest / kindle
ye when thou waxest colde / conferme the when thou wauerest &
exhibit ye whinges of the loue of god whil thou laborest to heuin-
warde that whan thou commest home to vs (which with gret   25
desyre we loke for) we may se not only him that we coueyte but
also such a maner one as we coueyt. Farewell and loue god whom
of olde thow hast begonne to fere. At ferare y^e .ii. day of Iuly the
yere of our redemption .M.cccc.lxxxxii.

---

1 trust.] trust *1510 1525*, truste, *1557*   2 shamed] *1510 1525*, ashamed
1557   4 vaine.] vaine *1510*, vayne. *1525 1557*   5 me /] me *1510 1525*, me,
1557   6 sauiour /] sauiour *1510*, sauyoure *1525*, sauiour, *1557*   8–9 moment.]
1557, moment *1510 1525; Sidenote 1557:* Our lyfe is lesse then a moment   9–
10 *Sidenote 1557:* The deuil   10 worlde] *1557*, worde *1510*, world *1525; Sidenote
1557:* The worlde, *Sidenote 1557:* The flesh   12 vs / how] vs. how *1510 1525*, vs.
Howe *1557*   13 *Sidenote 1557:* Honour   14 downe / how] *1525*, downe. how *1510*,
downe. How *1557*   14 *Sidenote 1557:* Riches   15 vs / how] *1525*, vs. how *1510*, vs.
How *1557*   22 when] *1525 1557*, wene *1510;* slepest / kindle] slepest. kindle *1510*,
slepest / kyndle *1525*, slepest. Kindle *1557*   23 waxest] *1557*, waxis *1510*, waxes
1525   27 Farewell] farewell *1510*, Fare well *1525 1557*

The interpretation of Iohn Picus vpon this
psalme Conserua me domine.

Conserua me domine quoniam speraui in te. Dixi domino
deus meus es tu quoniam bonorum meorum non eges. Sanctis
5   qui sunt in terra mirificauit voluntates suas. Multiplicate sunt
infirmitates postea accelerauerunt. Non congregabo conuen-
ticula eorum de sanguinibus nec memor ero nominum eorum
per labia mea. Dominus pars hereditatis mee & calicis mei: tu es
qui restitues hereditatem meam michi. Funes ceciderunt mihi in
10   preclaris / etenim hereditas mea preclara est michi. Benedicam
dominum qui tribuit mihi intellectum insuper et vsque ad noc-
tem increpuerunt me renes mei. Prouidebam dominum in con-
spectu meo semper quoniam a dextris est michi ne commouear.
[e₂] Propter hoc letatum est cor meum et exultauit lingua mea
15   insuper et caro mea requiescet in spe. Quoniam non derelinques
animam meam in inferno nec dabis sanctum tuum videre cor-
ruptionem. Notas mihi fecisti vias vite / adimplebis me leticia
cum vultu tuo. Delectationes in dextera tua vsque in finem.

Conserua me domine.
20   Kepe me god lorde. If any parfit man loke vppon his owne
estate ther is one parel therin that is to wit lest he wax prowde of
his vertue & therfor Dauid spekyng in yᵉ parson of a righteous
man of his estate begynneth with these wordes. Conserua me
domine. That is to saye kepe me good lorde which worde kepe
25   me: if hit be well considered takith a way all occasion of pryde.
For he that is able of him self any thing to gete: is able of him self
that same thing to kepe. He that askith then of god to be kept in
the state of vertue signifieth in that askyng that from the begin-
nyng he gote not that vertu by him self. He then which re-
30   membrith that he attained his vertu: not by his owne powar but

---

3 *Sidenote 1557:* Psal. 16   4 eges.] *1557*, eges *1510 1525*   5 Multiplicate] *1525*
1557, Multiplicati *1510*   6 infirmitates] *1510 1525*, infirmitates eorum *1557*
8 mei:] *1525*, mei *1510 1557*   10 preclaris /] preclaris *1510 1525*, preclaris *1557;*
michi.] michi *1510*, mihi. *1525 1557*   13 commouear.] *1557*, commouear *1510*
1525   17 vite /] vite *1510 1525*, vite, *1557*   18 tuo. Delectationes] *1525*, tuo delec-
tationes *1510*, tuo, delectationes *1557*   19 domine. Kepe] *1525*, domine. kepe *1510*,
domine: kepe *1557*   22 righteous] *1510*, ryghteous *1525*, ryghtuous *1557*
26 able] *1510 1525*, hable *1557;* able] *1510 1525*, hable *1557*   27 He] *1525 1557*,
he *1510*

by the powar of god may not be prowed therof but rathir hum-
bled be fore god aftir those wordes of thapostell. Quid habes
quod non accepisti. What hast thou that thou hast not receiued
and if thou hast receiued hit: whi art thou prowde therof as
though thou haddest not receiued it. Two wordis then be there   5
which we sholde euer haue in oure mouth: y^t one / miserere mei
deus / haue mercy on me lorde whan we remembre oure vice:
that othir / Conserua me deus / kepe me good lorde when we
remembre oure vertue. [e$_2$v]

Quoniam speraui in te.   10
For I haue trusted in y^e. This one thing is hit y^t makyth vs
obtaine of god oure petition y^t is to wit whan we haue a full hope
& trust that we shall spede. And yf we obserue these two thingis
in our requestis that is to wit y^t we require no thing but y^t which is
good for vs and that we require hit ardently with a sure hope y^t 15
god shall here vs / oure praiours shal neuer be voide. Wherfor
whan we mys the effect of oure petition either hit is for y^t we aske
such thing as is noyous vnto vs (for as crist saith we wot neuer
what we aske & Iesus seyde what so euer ye shall aske in my name
hit shalbe giuen you. This name iesus signifieth a sauiour and   20
therfore ther is no thing asked in ye name of Iesus but that is
holsom and helping to the saluation of the asker) or ellis god
herith not oure praioure bycause that though ye thing that we
require be good yet we aske hit not well / for we aske hyt with litle
hope. And he that askith doubtingly askith coldly & therfor seint   25
Iames biddith vs aske in faith no thing doubting.

Dixi domino deus meus es tu.
I haue saide to oure lorde my god art thou. After that he hath
warded and fenced him self a gainst pride he describith in these

3 *Sidenote 1557:* 1. Cor. 4   4 hast receiued] hast not receiued *1510*, hast not receyued
1525, haste receiued *1557*   5 haddest] *1510 1525*, haddst *1557*; it.] *1525 1557*, it
1510   6 mouth:] mouth *1510*, mouthe: *1525*, mouthe *1557*; one /] one. *1510 1525*,
one, *1557*   7 deus /] deus. *1510 1525*, deus: *1557* vice:] vice. *1510*, vyce: *1525*, vice,
1557   8 othir /] othir. *1510*, other. *1525 1557*; deus /] deus. *1510 1525*, deus, *1557*
11 For] *1525 1557*, for *1510*   13 And yf] *1557*, yf *1510*, Yf *1525*; *Sidenote 1557:* Two
thinges to be obserued in prayer   16 voide. Wherfor] voide wherfor *1510*, voide
wherfore *1525*, voide, wherfore *1557*   18 saith] saith *1510*, sayth) *1525*, sayeth)
1557   19 *Sidenote 1557:* Iohn 14   20 you.] *1525 1557*, you *1510*   24 well /]
1525, well. *1510*, wel. *1557*   26–27 *Sidenote 1557;* Psalme. 117

wordes his estate. All ye estate of a righteous man standeth in
these wordis. Dixi domino deus meus es tu. I haue seide to oure
lorde my god art thow. Which wordes though thei seme com-
mune to all folk yet are ther very few that may sey them trewly.

5   That thing a man taketh for his god y^t he takyth for his chiefe
good. And that thing takith he for his chyefe good which onli
had though all other thinges lak he thin[e₃]keth him self happy
& whiche only lakking though he haue al other thinges he think-
eth him self vnhappy. The negard then seith to his money. Deus

10 meus es tu. My god art thou. For though honour faile & helth
and strenghte and frendes so he haue money he thinketh him
selfe well. And yf he haue al those thinges y^t we haue spoken of yf
money faile / he thinketh him selfe vnhappy. The gloton seith
vnto his flesshly lust / ye ambitiouse man seith to his vainglory /

15 my god art thou. Se than how few may trewly sey these wordes I
haue seyd to oure lord my god arte thou. For only he maye trewly
saye it which is content with god alone: so y^t if there were offred
him all the kingdomes of the worlde and all the good that is in
erth and all the good that is in heuen he wolde not ones offende

20 god to haue them all. In these wordes than / I haue seid to our
lord my god art thou / standith all the state of a rightwise man.

Quoniam bonorum meorum non eges.
For thou hast no nede of mi good. In these wordes he shewith
the cause whi he saith onli to our lorde. Deus meus es tu. My god

25 art thou: the cause is for that only oure lorde hath no nede of
oure good. There is no creature but that it nedith other crea-
tures and though thei be of lesse perfection than hit selfe as
philosophers and diuines prouen: for if thes more imperfite

---

1 righteous] *1510*, ryghteous *1525*, rightuous *1557*   4 trewly. That] trewly. that *1510*,
truely / that *1525*, truely. That *1557; Sidenote 1557:* God   6 chyefe] *1510 1525*, thief
1557   7 though] *1510 1557*, thought *1525*   9 *Sidenote 1557:* The niggards god,is
money   13 faile /] faile. *1510*, fayle. *1525*, fayle, *1557*   13–14 *Sidenote 1557:* The
gluttons god,is fleshlye lust; lust /] lust *1510 1525*, lust, *1557*; vainglory /] vainglory
1510, vaynglory *1525*, vainglory, *1557; Sidenote 1557:* The ambicious mans god is
vaineglory   16 For] *paragraph 1557*   21 rightwise] right wise *1510*, ryght wyse
1525, righteous *1557*   23 good. In] *1557*, good in *1510 1525*   24 tu. My] *1525*, tu.
my *1510*, tu, my *1557*   25 thou:] *1557*, thou *1510 1525*   28 imperfite] *1510*, im-
perfyte *1525*, imperfecte *1557*

creatures were not / ye other that are more parfite coude not be.
For yf ony parte of ye hole vniuersite of creatures were distroied
& fallen to nought all ye hole were subuerted. For certainly one
part of that vniuersite perisshing all parties perissh and all crea-
tures be partis of y^t vniuersite of which vniuer[e₃v]site god is no 5
part but he is the beginnyng nothing ther vppon depending. For
no thing trewly wanne he by ye creatione of this worlde nor no
thing shulde he lese if the worlde were adnichilate and turned to
nought a gayn. Than onli god is he which hath no nede of oure
good. Well ought we certainly to be ashamed to take such thing 10
for god as hath nede of vs / and such is euery creature. More-
ouer we shuld not accept for god y^t is to sey for the cheife good-
nes but only that thing which is the most soueraigne goodnes of
all thingis and that is not ye goodnes of any creature. Only ther-
for to oure lorde ought we to say my god art thow. 15

Sanctis qui sunt in terra eius mirificauit voluntates suas.

To his saintes that are in ye londe of him he hath made mer-
uelous his willes. Aftir god shulde we specially loue them which
are nerest ioyned vnto god as be the holy aungellis & blessed
saintes that are in theire contre of heuen. Therfor aftir that he 20
had seide to oure lord my god art thow he addeth ther vnto that
our lorde hath made meruelous his willis that is to sey he hath
made meruelous his loues and hys desyres toward his seintis that
are in the londe of him that is to wit in the contre of heuen which
is called ye lande of god and the lande of liuing peple. And verily 25
if we inwardeli considre how grete is the felicite of that contre
and how much is ye misery of this worlde / how gret is ye goodnes
and charite of those blessid citeseyns: we shall continually desire
to be hens that we were there. These thinges & such othir whan
we remembre we shuld euir more take hede y^t our meditations 30

---

1 parfite] *1510,* parfyte *1525,* perfecte *1557*   2 hole] *1510 1525,* whole *1557*
8 lese] *1510 1525,* lefe *1510*   11 vs / and] vs. and *1510,* vs / & *1525,* vs. And
1557   14 creature. Only] creature. only *1510,* creature / onely *1525,* creature. Onely
1557   17 To] *1525 1557,* to *1510;* saintes] *1510,* sayntes *1525,* sainctes *1557*   19
blessed] *1510 1557,* blyssed *1525*   20 saintes] *1510,* sayntes *1525,* sainctes *1557;* heuen.
Therfor] heuen therfor *1510,* heuen therfore *1525,* heanen. Therfore *1557*   25 *Side-
note 1557:* Heauen   27 worlde /] worlde *1510 1525,* worlde, *1557*   30 *Sidenote
1557:* Of euery meditacion to purchase a vertue

be not vnfruteful [e₄] but that of euery meditation we shulde all
waies purchace one vertue or othir / as for ensample by this
meditation of the goodenes of that heuenly contre we shulde
wynne this vertu that we shulde not only strongly suffre deth and
5   paciently whan oure time commeth or if hit were put vnto vs for
yᵉ faith of crist: but also we shulde willingly and gladly longe ther
fore desiring to be departed oute of this vale of wretchidnes that
we may raigne in yᵉ heuinly contre with god & his holy saintes.

Multiplicate sunt infirmitates eorum postea accelerauerunt.
10   Their infirmitees be multiplied and aftir they hasted. These
wordes the prophet spekith of wikked men. Bi infirmitees he
vndirstondeth Idoles & so hit is in the hebriew text. For as good
folk haue but one god whom thei worship so euill folk haue
many goddes and idoles for thei haue many voluptuouse plesurs
15   many vaine desyres many diuers passiones which they serue / &
wherfor seke thei many sondry pleasures? certainly for by cause
they can finde none yᵗ can set their hert at rest & for yᵗ (as yᵉ
prophet saith) wikked men walk a bout in a circuit or compace
wherof ther is none ende. Now aftir these wordes: their Idolles
20   be multiplied hit folowith. Aftir thei hasted yᵗ is to sei: aftir their
idolles aftir their passiones & bestly desires thei runne forth
hedling vnaduisedly with owt any consideration. And in this be
we taught that we shulde as spedely runne to vertu as thei run to
vice & yᵗ we sholde with no les diligence serue oure lord god than
25   they serue their lorde yᵉ deuill. The iuste man considering yᵉ
estate of iuell folke determineth fermely with him self [e₄v] (as
we shulde also) that vtterly he will in no wise follow them and
therfor he seith.

Non congregabo conuenticulam eorum de sanguinibus nec
30   memor nominum.
I shal not gather the congregation of them from the blode nor

_____

8 saintes] *1510*, sayntes *1525*, sainctes *1557*   11–12 *Sidenote 1557:* Wicked peple wor-
ship many gods   17 *Sidenote 1557:* Psalme. 11   19 ende. Now] *1557*, ende Now
1510 1525   21 forth] *1525*, fort *1510*, furth *1557*   30 memor nominum] *1510*
1525, memor ero nominum eorum *1557*   31 *Sidenote 1557:* Bloode

I shal not remembre their names. He sayth from the blode both
bi cause idolatres were wont to gather the blode of their sacrefice
to gither and ther a bout to do their serymonies / and also for
that all the life of yuell men forsaken reason which stondeth all in
the sowle and folowen sensualyte that stondeth all in the blode. 5
The prophet seith not only that he will not gathir their congrega-
tion to gethir from yᵉ blode that is to sey yᵗ he wolde do no
sacrifice to those idolles but also that he wolde not remembre
their names that is to sey that he wolde not talke nor speke of yᵉ
voluptuouse delytes whych are euyll peples goddes which we 10
myght yet lawfully do: shewing vs by yᵗ: that a parfit man sholde
abstaine not only from vnlawfull plesures but also from lawfull /
to thende yᵗ he may all to gither hole haue his mynde in to heuen
warde and the more purely entende vnto the contemplation of
heuenli thinges. And for as moch as some man wolde peraduen- 15
ture think that hit were foly for a man vttirly to depriue him self
from all pleasures therfor yᵉ prophet addith.

Dominus pars hereditatis mee.
Owre lord is yᵉ part of min enheretaunce / as though he wolde
saye meruaile yᵉ not though I forsake all thing to thentent yᵗ I 20
may haue yᵉ possession of god in whom al other thinges also be
possessid. This shuld be the voice of euery good christen man.
Dominus pars hereditatis mee. God ys the part of myn en-
here[e₅]taunce. For certainly we cristen peple to whom god is
promised for an enheretaunce ought to be ashamed to desire 25
any thing be syde him. But for yᵗ sum man might happeli repute
hit for a gret presumption that a man sholde promys him selfe
god for his enheretaunce therfor the prophet puteth therto.

---

1 names. He] names he *1510 1525*, names, he *1557*   2 sacrefice] *1510*, sacrefyce *1525*,
sasrifice *1557*   3 serymonies / and] serymonies. And *1510*, serymonyes. And *1525*,
ceremonyes. And *1557*   5 blode. The] blode the *1510*, blode / the *1525*, bloode. The
1557   9 to sey] sey *1510*, to say *1525 1557*   11–12 *Sidenote 1557;* A perfect man
should abstain not onely from vnlawfull pleasures, but also from lawfull   12 law-
full / to] *1525*, lawfull. to *1510*, lawful. To *1557*   13 his] *1525 1557*, is *1510*   18–
19 mee. Owre] mee. owre *1510*, mee. Our *1525 1557*   19 enheretaunce /] *1525*,
enheretaunce. *1510*, enheritance, *1557*   20 yᵉ not] *1510*, the not *1525*, not
1557   22 possessid.] possessid *1510*, possessed. *1525 1557*

Tu es qui restitues hereditatem meam michi.

Thow gode lorde art he that shal restore myn enheretaunce
vnto me. As though he wolde say. O good lorde my god i know
well that I am no thyng in respect of y^e. I wot well I am vnable to
5 ascende bi min own strength so high / to haue the in possession
but thow art he that shalt draw me to the by thy grace / thow art
he that shalt giue thi selfe in possession vnto me. Let a righteous
man then considre how grete a felicite hit is to haue god fall vnto
him as his enheritaunce. Hit folowith in the psalme.

10 Funes ceciderunt michi in preclaris.

The cordis haue fall to me nobly. The partes and lottys of
enheritaunces were of olde tyme met owt and diuided by cordis
or ropis. These wordes then the ropis or cordes haue fallen to me
nobly be asmuch to sey as the part or lot of myn enheretaunce is
15 noble. But for as much as ther be many menn which though thei
be called to this grete felicite (as in dede all christen peple are) yet
thei set litle ther by and oftin tymes chaunge hit for a small
simple delite / therfor ye prophet seith seuyngly.

Hereditas mea preclara est michi.

20 Min enheretaunce is noble to me. As though he wold sey that
as hit is noble in hit selfe so hit is noble to me / that is to sey I
reputen hit noble. And all othir thingis in respecte of hit I repute
(as [e₅v] seint Paule saith) for donge / but for as much as to haue
this lyght of vndrestanding where by a man may know this gyft
25 that is giuen him of god to be the gyft of god / therfor the
prophet suingly seith.

---

2 Thow] thow *1510*, Thou *1525 1557*   4 y^e.] y^e *1510 1525*, thee, *1557*   5 strength
so high /] strength. so high. *1510*, strength / so hyghe / *1525*, strength so high, *1557*
6 grace / thow] grace thow *1510*, grace thou *1525*, grace, thou *1557*   7 righteous]
1510, ryghteous *1525*, rightous *1557*   9 enheritaunce. Hit] enheritaunce hit *1510*,
enherytaunce hit *1525*, enheritance. It *1557*   11 fall] *1510 1525*, fallen *1557*; *Sidenote*
1557: Cordes or ropes   14 or] of *1510 1525 1557*   18 delite / therfor] delite ther-
for *1510*, delyte therfore *1525*, delyte. Therefore *1557*   18 seuyngly. Hereditas]
seuyngly. hereditas *1510*, suyngly. Hereditas *1525*, semyngly: hereditas
1557   19 michi. Min] Michi. min *1510*, michi. Myn *1525*, mihi. Myne *1557*   21 no-
ble to me /] noble. to me *1510*, noble to me *1525*, noble to me, *1557*   22 reputen]
1510, reputed *1525*, repute *1557;* noble.] *1525*, noble *1510*, noble,
1557   23 donge / but] *1525*, donge. but *1510*, dong, but *1557*

Benedicam dominum qui tribuit intellectum

that is to sey I shall blesse oure lorde which hath giuen me vndrestonding but in so much as a man often times entendith aftir reason to serue god and y^t notwitstonding yet sensualite and the flesh repugneth: than is a man perfit whan that not his 5 sowle onli but also his flessh draw forth to godward after those wordes of the prophet in an othir psalme. Cor meum & caro mea exultauerunt in deum viuum that is to sey my mynde & my flessh both haue ioyed in to liuing god & for this the prophet seith here suyngly. 10

Et vsque ad noctem increpuerunt me renes mei.

My reynis or kidney hath chiden me vnto the nyght / that is to sey my raynes in which is wont to be the gretest inclination to concupiscence not only now enclineth me not to syn but also chideth me / that is to sey with draw me fro synne vnto the 15 night / that is to sey they so ferforth withdraw me from synne that willingly they afflict and paine my body. Affliction is in scripture often tymes signified by the night by cause hit is the most discomfortable season. Then suyngly the prophet shewith what is the rote of this priuation or takyng a wey of flesshly 20 concupiscence in a man seying.

Prouidebam deum semper in conspectu meo.

I prouided god alway be fore my sight. For if a man had god alway bi fore his yen as a ruler of all his warkis & in all his warkis he shulde neithir seke his owne lucre his glory nor his owne [e$_6$] 25 plesure but only to y^e plesure of god he shuld shortly be parfit. And for as much as he that so doth prosperith in all thing therfor it folowith.

---

1 tribuit] *1510 1525*, tribuit mihi *1557*   2 blesse] *1510 1557*, blysse *1525*   7–
8 *Sidenote 1557:* Psalme. 83   12 kidney] *1510 1525*, kidneis *1557;* nyght /] nyght
1510, nyght: *1525*, night, *1557; Sidenote 1557:* Reynes   14 enclineth] *1510 1557*, en-
clyne *1525*   15 me /] me *1510 1525*, me, *1557*   16 night /] night *1510*, nyght
1525, night, *1557*   18 *Sidenote 1557:* The nyght   23 my] *1510 1557*, me *1525*
sight.] *1557*, sight *1510*, sight / *1525*   24 yen] *1510*, eyen *1525*, eies *1557; Sidenote
1557:* The meane how a manne maye sooneste come to perfeccion   25 he shulde]
1510 1525, shoulde *1557*   26 parfit.] parfit *1510*, perfyte. *1525*, perfect. *1557*

Ipse a dextris est michi ne commouear.

He is on my right hande that I be not moued or trobled. Then
the prophet declarith how grete is yᵉ felycite of a iuste man which
shalbe euir lastingly blessed both in body and in sowle and ther-
5   fore he seith.

Letatum est cor meum.

My sowle is glad knowyng yᵗ aftir deth heuin is made redy for
him.

Et caro mea requiescet in spe

10   & my flessh shall rest in hope that is to sey that though hit ioy
not by and by as in receyuing his glorious estate immediatly aftir
the deth yet hyt restith in the sepulcre wyth this hope that hyt
shall aryse in the day of Iudgement immortall and shynyng wyth
his sowle. And also the prophet more expressely declarith in the
15   verse folowing. For where he seide thus mi sowle is glad he ad-
dith the cause seying.

Quoniam non derelinques animam in inferno.

For thou shalt not leue my sowle in hell. Also wher the prophet
sayde that hys flessh shuld rest in hope he shewith the cause
20   seying.

Nec dabis sanctum tuum videre corruptionem.

Nor thou shalt not suffre thy saynt to se corruption / that is to
sey thou shalt not suffre yᵉ flessh of a good man to be corrupted.
For that that was corruptible shal arise incorruptible. And for as
25   much as crist was the first which entred paradise and opened the
lyfe vnto vs and was the first that rose a gaine and the cause of
oure resurrection: therfore thes wordes that we haue spoken of
the resurrection bene prin[e₆v]cipally vndrestondin of crist as
seint petir yᵉ apostle hath declared / & secundarily thei may be
30   vndrestondin of vs in yᵗ we be the membres of christ which only
neuer sawe corruption for his holy body was in his sepulcre
nothing putrified. For asmoch then as yᵉ wey of goude liuing

---

1 Ipse a] *1510 1525*, Ipse est a *1557*   2 He] *1525 1557*, he *1510*   4 blessed] *1510*
1557, blyssed *1525*   7 My] *1525 1557*, my *1510*   10 *Sidenote 1557:* The fleshe to
rest in hope what it is   11 immediatly] mediatly *1510 1557*, medyatly *1525 (see note)*
17 animam] *1510 1525*, animam meam *1557*   18 For] *1525 1557*, for *1510*   22 cor-
ruption /] *1510*, corrupcyon *1525*, corrupcion, *1557*   29 declared / &] *1525*, de-
clared. & *1510*, declared. And *1557*   32 putrified. For] *1557*, putrified. for *1510*,
putrified / for *1525*

bringeth vs to perpetuall life of sowle and body therfor y^e
prophet saith.

Notas michi fecisti vias vite

thou hast made the wayes of life knowen vnto me and by cause
that al the felicite of that stondeth in the clere be holding and   5
fruytion of god / ther for hit folowith.

Adimplebis me leticiis cum vultu tuo

thou shalt fill me full of gladnes with thi chere & for that our
felycite shalbe euir lasting therfor he saith.

Delectationes in dextra tua vsque in finem.   10

Delectation and ioy shalbe on thi right hand for euer: he seith
on thi right hande bi cause y^t our felicite is fulfilled in the visione
and fruition of the humanite of crist which sittith in heuen on
the right hande of his fathirs maieste aftir ye wordes of seint
Iohan. Hec est tota merces vt videamus deum et quem misisti   15
Iesum christum. This is all oure rewarde that we may be hold
god and Iesus christ whom thow has sent: to which rewarde he
bryng vs that syttith there and praith for vs. Amen. [f₁]

Here begin .xii. rulys of Iohan Picus erle of Mirandula partely
exciting partely directing a man in spirituall batail.   20

W_HO so to vertue estemith hard the waye /
Bi cause we must haue warre continuall
Against y^e worlde / y^e flessh / y^e deuill / that aye
Enforce them selfe to make vs bond & thrall
Let him remembre that chese what wey he shal   25
Euin aftir the worlde / yet must he nede susteyn
Sorow / aduersite / labour / greife / and payne.

The seconde rule

Think in this wretched worldes besy woo
The batail more sharpe & lenger is I wys: 30

---

1 to] *1510 1557*, to a *1525*   10 dextra] *1510 1525*, dextera *1557*   14 y^e] *1525*,
y^e / *1510*, the *1557*; Hec] *1525 1557*, hec *1510*   15 deum et] deum, & *1557*, deum
1510 1525; *Sidenote 1557*: Iohn 17   16 This] *1510 1557*, That *1525*   19 Here be-
gin] *om. 1557*   21 estemith hard] estemeth hard *1557*, estemith *1510*, estemeth *1525*;
Sidenote 1557: If we refuse the way of vertue for that it is painful for the like cause oughte
wee to refuse the way of sin   22 continuall] *1557*, coutinuall *1510*, contynuall *1525*

With more labour and lesse frute also.
In which the ende of labour: labour is.
And when the world hath left vs aftir this
Voide of all vertue: the reward when we dye:
5   Is nought but fire and peyne perpetually.

The thirde reule

Considre well that foly it is and vaine
To loke for heuin with plesure and delyght
Sith crist our lord and souereyne captaine
10   Ascended neuir but by manly fight
And bittir passion: then were hit no right
That any seruaunt / ye will your selfe recorde /
Shuld stonde in bettir condition then his lorde

The fourth rule

15   Think how that we not only shulde not grudge
But eke be gladd and ioyfull of this fight
And longe therfor al though we coud not Iudge [f₁v]
Howe that therby redounde vnto vs might
Any profite / but onely for delight
20   To be confourmed and like in some behauour
To Iesu Christ our blessed lorde & sauioure

As often as thou dost warre and striue /
By the resistence of any sinfull motion /
Against any of thi sensuall wittis fyue
25   Cast in thi mynde as oft with good deuotion
How thou resemblest christ / as with sowre potion
If thou payne thi tast: remember ther with all
How christ for the tasted eisell and gall

---

3 this] *1525 1557*, this. *1510*   10 fight] fight. *1510*, fyght *1525*, fight, *1557*   11 pas-
sion:] *1557*, passion. *1510*, passion / *1525*   12 recorde /] recorde *1510 1525*, re-
corde, *1557*; *Sidenote 1557:* Mathew. 10   14 fourth rule] *1525 1557*, fourth *1510*
19 profite / but] profite but *1510*, profyte but *1525*, profite, but *1557*; delight] de-
light. *1510*, delyght *1525*, delight, *1557*   20 behauour] *1510 1525*, behauiour *1557*
22 striue /] striue. *1510*, stryue. *1525*, striue, *1557*   23 motion /] motion *1510*,
mocyon *1525*, mocion, *1557*   26 christ /] christ. *1510*, chryst / *1525*, Christ, *1557*;
Sidenote 1557: Mat, 27   27 *Sidenote 1557:* Mark. 15   28 *Sidenote 1557:* Iohn. 19

Yf thou with drawe thin handes and forbere
The rauen of any thing: remembre than
How his innocent handes nailed were.
Yf thou be tempt with pride: think how that whan
He was in forme of god: yet of a bonde man 5
He toke the shapp and humbled him self for the
To the most odiouse and vile deth of a tree.

Considre when thou art moued to be wroth
He who that was god / and of all men the best
Seyng him selfe scorned and scorged both 10
And as a thefe betwene .ii. theuis threst
with al rebuke and shame: yet from his brest
Cam neuer signe of wrath or of disdayne
But patiently endured all the paine.

Thus euery snare and engine of the deuell 15
Yf thou this wise peruse them by and by [f₂]
There can be none so cursed or so euill
But to some vertu thow mast hit applie
For oft thou shalt: resistyng valianntly
The fendis might and sotle fiery darte: 20
Oure sauiour crist resemble in some parte.

The fyft rule

Remembre well that we in no wise must
Neither in the foresaide espirituall armour
Nor any othir remedy put oure trust: 25
But only in the strenght of our sauiour
For he it is by whos mighty powre
The worlde was veynquisshed & his prynce cast owt
Which reigned bifore in all the erthe abowt.

In him let vs trust to ouercome all euill 30
In him let vs put oure hope and confidence

---

5 *Sidenote 1557:* Phil. 2   10 scorned and] *1510 1557*, scorned *1525*   11 *Sidenote*
1557: Mark. 10   12 *Sidenote 1557:* Luke. 18   13 *Sidenote 1557:* Iohn. 19   14 pa-
tiently] *1557*, patienly *1510*, pacyently *1525*   18 mast] *1510*, mayst *1525 1557*
26 the strenght] the vertu strenght *1510*, the vertue strength *1525 1557* (*see note*)

To subdew the flessh and master ye deuill
To him be all honour and lowly reuerence.
Oft shuld we require with all our diligence
With praier / with teris / & lamentable plaintis
5   The aide of hys grace and his holy saintes

The sixt rule

One synne vainquisshed loke thou not tarye
But lye in await for an other euery howre
For as a wood lyon the fende oure aduersarye
10   Rynneth a bout seking whom he may deuoure.
Wherfore continually vppon thy towre
Lest he the vnpurueid and vnredy catche
Thou must with the prophite stonde & kepe wache

The .vii. rule

15   Enforce thi selfe not only for to stonde [f₂v]
Vnuainquisshed a gainst the deuilles might
But ouer that take valiauntly on hande
To vainquisshe him and put him vnto flight
And that is whan of ye same dede thought or sight
20   By which he wolde haue the with synne contract:
Thou takest occasion of some good vertuouse acte.

Some tyme he secretly castith in thi mynde
Some lawdable dede to stere the to pride
As vainglorie makith many a man blynde
25   But let humilite be thi sure guide
Thi good wark to god let hit be appliede
Think hit not thine but a gift of his
Of whose grace vndowtedly all goodnes is

The viii. rule

30   In tyme of bataile so put thi self in preace
As though thou shuldest aftir that victorie

---

2 reuerence.] reuerence *1510 1525*, reuerence: *1557*   9 *Sidenote 1557:*
1. Peter. 5   10 Rynneth] *1510 1525*, Runneth *1557;* deuoure.] deuoure *1510 1525,*
deuoure, *1557*   26 appliede] *1510*, applyede *1525,* applide *1557*   28 whose] *1525*
1557, wose *1510*

Enioye for euir a perpetuall peace
For god of his goodnes and liberall mercy
May graunt the gift / & eke thi prowd enemy
Confownded and rebuked by thi bataile
Shal the nomore happely for very shame assaile 5

But when thou mast onys the triumphe obtaine
Prepare thi selfe and trymme the in thy gere
As thow shuldest incontinent fight a gaine
For if thou be redy the deuill will the fere.
Wherfore in any wise so euin thou the bere 10
That thou remembre and haue euir in memory /
In victory bataile in bataile victory [f₃]

The .ix. rule

If thou think thy selfe wele fenced and sure
A gainst euery sotell suggestion of vice 15
Considre fraile glas may no dystres endure
And gret aduenturers oft curs the dice.
Ieopard not to ferr therfore and ye be wise
But euir more eschew the occasions of synne
For he that loueth parel shal perissh therin 20

The .x. rule

In all temptation with stonde the begynnyng.
The cursed infantes of wretchid Babilon
To suffre them wax / is a Ieopardous thing.
Bete out their braynes therfor at the stone. 25
Perilous is the canker that catchith the bone.
To late commyth the medicine if thou let the sore
By longe contynuance encreace more & more.

---

3 gift /] gift. *1510*, gyfte / *1525*, gift, *1557*   6 mast] *1510*, mayst *1525*, maist *1557*
7 selfe] *1525*, sefe *1510*, self *1557*   9 fere.] fere *1510 1525*, feare, *1557*   10 the]
1510 1525, thee *1557*   11 memory /] memory. *1510 1525*, memorie *1557*   13 the
.ix. rule] *1557*, *om. 1510 1525*   17 aduenturers] *1510 1525*, aduentures *1557;* dice.]
dice *1510*, dyce *1525*, dice: *1557*   22 begynnyng.] begynnyng *1510*, begynnynge
1525, beginning, *1557*   24 thing.] thing *1510*, thynge *1525*, thing, *1557*   25 stone.]
stone *1510 1525*, stone, *1557*   26 bone.] bone *1510 1525*, bone, *1557*

The .xi. rule

Though in the time of the bataile and warre
The conflict seme byttir sharpe and sowre
Yet considre hit is more pleasure farre
5   Ouer the deuill to be a conqueroure
Then is in the vse of thi bestly pleasoure.
Of vertue more ioy the conscience hath within
Then outward the body of al his filthy synne

In this poynt many men erre for necligence
10   For thei compare not the Ioy of the victory
To the sensuall pleasure of their concupiscence
But like rude bestis vnaduisedly
Lakking discretion thei compare & applye
Of their fowle synne the volupteouse delight
15   To the laberous trauaile of the conflict & fight [f₃v]

And yet alas he that ofte hath knowen
What griefe it is by longe experience
Of his cruell enemye to be ouer throwen
Shuld ones at the lest wise do his diligence
20   To proue and assay with manly defence
What plesure ther is / what honour peace & rest
In gloriouse victorie tryumphe and conquest

The .xii. rule

Though thou be tempted dispaire the no thing.
25   Remembre the gloriouse apostle seint Powle
Whan he had sene god in his parfite beyng
Lest such reuelation shulde his hert extolle
His flessh was suffred rebell a gainst the sowle.
This did almighty god of his goodnes prouide
30   To preserue his seruaunt fro yᵉ daunger of pryde

And here take hede that he whom god did loue
And for his most especiall vessell chose

---

6 pleasoure.] pleasoure *1510 1525*, pleasoure, *1557*   9 necligence] *1510 1525*, negli-
gence *1557*   16 knowen] *1510 1525*, knowne *1557*   18 ouer throwen] *1510 1525*,
ouerthrowne *1557*   21 is /] *1510 1525*, is, *1557*   24 the no thing.] the no thing
1510, the nothynge *1525*, thee nothing, *1557*   28 sowle.] sowle *1510*, soule *1525*,
soule, *1557*

Rauisshed in to the threde heuyn a boue
Yet stode in perel lest pride myght hym depose.
Well ought we then oure hertis fence & close
Against vainglorie the mother of reprefe
The very crop and rote of all mischefe 5

A gainst this pompe & wretched worldes glosse
Considre how crist the lorde souereyne powere
Humbled him selfe for vs vnto the crosse
And peraduenture deth with in one howre
Shal vs bereue welth riches and honowre 10
And bring vs down ful low both smal & grete
To vile carion and wretched wormes mete [f₄]

Here folow the .xii. wepenis of spiritual bataile which eueri
man shuld haue at hand when yᵉ plesure of a synful
temptation commyth to his mynde. 15

The plesur litle & short
The folowers grief &
  heuynes
The los of a bettir thing
This life a dreme and a
  shadowe
The deth at our hand &
  vnware

Yᵉ fere of impenitent
  departing
Eternal ioy eternal paine
Yᵉ natur & dignyte of man
Yᵉ peace of a good mynde 20
The gret benefites of god
The penyful cros of crist
The witnes of martyrs and
  example of seyntis.

The .xii. wepenis haue we more at lengh declared 25
as hit folowith.

The pleasur litle and short

Considre well the pleasure that thou hast:
Stande hit in towching or in wantone sight

---

1 threde] *1510*, thyrde *1525*, thirde *1557*   2 depose.] depose *1510 1525*, depose,
1557   6 glosse] *1510 1557*, glose *1525*   10 bereue] bereue: *1510 1525*, bereue,
1557   25 lengh] *1510 1525*, length *1557*   26 hit] *1510 1525*, om. *1557*
28 hast:] hast *1510 1525*, hast, *1557*

In vayne smell or in thy licorouse tast
Or fynally in what so euir delight
Occupyed is thi wretched appetight
Thou shalt hit fynde when thou hast al cast
5   Litle / simple / short / and sodenly past

The folowers griefe & heuynes

Any good wark if thou with labour do
The labour goth / the goodnes doth remayne.
If thou do yuel with pleasur ioyned therto
10   The pleasur which thyne yuell wark doth contayne
Glideth his wey / thou mast hym not restrane.
The yuel then in thy brest cleuith behynde
With grudge of hert & heuynes of mynde

The losse of a bettir thing.

15   When thou laborest thi plesure for to bye
Vppon the price loke thou the well ad vise [f₄v]
Thou sellest thi sowle therfore euyn by & by
To thi most vttre dispiteouse enemyes.
O mad merchaunt o folissh merchaundise
20   To by a trifle / o childissh rekenyng
And pay therefore so dere a precious thing

This life a dreme and a shadow

This wretched life (the trust & confidence
Of whos contynuaunce makith vs bolde to synne)
25   Thou perceiuest well by experience
Sith that howre in which hit did begynne
Hit holdeth on the course and will not lynne
But fast hit rynneth on and passen shall
As doth a dreme or shadowe on the wall

---

7 with] *1510 1557*, iwth *1525*   8 remayne.] remayne *1510 1525*, remayne, *1557*
11 wey /]wey *1510 1525*, way, *1557;* mast] *1510 1525*, maist *1557;* restrane.] restrane
1510, restrayne *1525*, restraine, *1557*   16 the well] *1510 1525*, thee well *1557*
18 enemyes.] enemyes *1510 1525*, enemies, *1557*   20 trifle /] trifle. *1510*, tryfle /
1525, tryfle, *1557*   24 bolde] *1525 1557*. blode *1510*   28 rynneth] *1510 1525*, run-
neth *1557*

Deth at our hand and vnware

Considre well that euir night and daye
While that we besily prouide and care
For oure disport reuell myrth and play
For plesaunt melody and deynty fare   5
Deth stelith on ful slily and vnware
He lieth at hand and shal vs entreprise
We not how sone nor in what maner wise

Fere of impenitent departinge

If thou shuldest god offende think how therfore   10
Thou were forthwith in very Ieopardous case
For happely thow shuldest not liue an houre more
Thi syn to clense / and though thou haddest space
Yet peraduenture shuldest thou lak the grace.
Well ought we then be ferde to done offence   15
Impenitent lest we departyn hens

Eternall rewarde eternall payne

Thou seest this worlde is but a thorow fare.
Se thou behaue the wisely with thin hoost. [f₅]
Hens must thou nedis departe naked & bare   20
And aftir thi desert loke to what coost
Thou art couuaied at such tyme as thy goost
From this wretched carkas shal disseuer
Be hit Ioy or paine / endure hit shal for euir.

The nature and dignite of man   25

Remembre how god hath made the resonable
Like vnto his Image and figure

---

8 not] *1510 1525*, wote not *1557 (see note)*   13 clense /] *1525*, clense. *1510*, clense,
1557; though] *1510 1557*, thought *1525;* space] space. *1510 1525*, space, *1557*   14 grace.]
grace *1510 1525*, grace, *1557*   15 ferde] *1510 1557*, a ferde *1525*   18 fare.] fare
1510 1525, fare, *1557*   19 the]*1510 1525*, thee *1557;* thin] *1510*, thy *1525*, thine *1557;*
hoost.] hoost *1510 1525*, hoost, *1557*   24 shal] *1510*, thou shall *1525*, shall *1557*
26 the] *1510, 1525*, thee *1557*

And for the suffred paines intollerable
That he for angell neuir wolde endure.
Regarde o man thyne excellent nature.
Thou that with angell art made to bene egall
5   For very shame be not the deuilles thrall.

The peace of a good mynde

Whi louest thou so this brotle worldes Ioy
Take all the mirth take all the fantasies
Take euery game take euery wanton toye
10   Take euery sport that men can the deuise
And amonge them all on warantise
Thou shalt no pleasure comparable finde
To thinward gladnes of a vertuouse mynde

The gret benefices of god.

15   By side that god the bought & fourmed both
Many a benefite hast thou receiued of his:
Though thou haue moued him often to be wroth
Yet he the kept hath and brought vs vp to this
And daily calleth vppon the to his blis.
20   How mast thou then to him vnlouing be
That euir hath bene so louing vnto the.

The paynefull crosse of christ.

Whan thou in flame of the temptation fryest [f₅v]
Think on the very lamentable payne
25   Think on the piteouse crosse of wofull christ
Think on his blode bet out at euery vayne
Think on his preciouse hert carued in twayne

---

1 the] *1510 1525*, thee *1557*   2 endure.] endure *1510 1525*, endure: *1557*   3 na-
ture.] nature *1510 1525*, nature, *1557*   10 the] *1510 1525*, thee *1557*   14 bene-
fices] *1510*, benefyces *1525*, benefites *1557*   15 the] *1510 1525*, thee *1557*   16 his:]
his *1510 1525*, his, *1557*   18 the] *1510 1525*, thee *1557;* vs] *1510 1525*, thee *1557*
19 the] *1510 1525*, thee *1557;* blis.] blis *1510*, blys *1525*, blisse, *1557*   20 mast] *1510*,
mayst *1525*, maist *1557*   24 payne] *1525*, payne. *1510*, paine, *1557*   26 Think]
think *1510*, thynke *1525*, Thinke *1557*

Think how for thi redemption all was wrought
Let him not lese that he so dere hath bought

The witnes of martirs & example of seyntes

Synne to with stonde say not thou lakkest might
Such allegations folye hit is to vse 5
The witnes of seyntes & martires constant fight
Shall the of slouthfull cowardise accuse
God will the help if thou do not refuse
If othir haue stande or this: thou mast eft sone
No thing impossible is that hath bene done 10

The .xii. propretees or conditions of a louer

To loue one a lone and contempne al othir for y^t one
To think him vnhappy that is not with his loue
To adourne him selfe for the plesure of his loue
To suffre all thyng though hit were deth to be with his loue 15
To desyre also to suffre harme for his loue & to think that
hurt swete.
To be wyth his loue euir as he may if not in dede yet in
thought.
To loue al thing y^t perteyneth vnto his loue
To coueyt ye praise of his loue and not to suffre ony dispraise 20
To beleue of his loue all thingis excellent & to desire that al
folke shulde think the same
To wepe often with his loue: in presence for Ioy / in [f₆]
absence for sorowe
To langwyssh euir and euir to burne in the desyre of his loue. 25
To serue his loue no thing thinkyng of any rewarde or profite.

---

6 fight] sight *1510 1557*, fyght *1525*   7 the] *1510 1525*, thee *1557*   8 the] *1510*
1525, thee *1557*   9 mast] *1510*, mayst *1525*, maist *1557*   11 a louer] *1525 1557*,
alouer *1510*   16 harme] shame harme *1510 1525 1557*   23 Ioy /] Ioy *1510*, Ioye
1525, ioy, *1557*

The .xii. propretees we haue at lengh more openly
expressed in balade as hit folowith.

THE first point is to loue but one a lone
And for that one all othir to forsake
5   For who so louith many loueth none:
The flode that is in many channelles take
In iche of them shall febill stremys make.
The loue that is deuided a monge many
Vnneth suffiseth that euery part haue any

10   So that thou hast thi loue set vnto god
In thi remembrance this enprynt & graue
As he in souerayne dignite is odd
So will he in loue no partyng fellows haue.
Loue him therfore with all that he the gaue
15   For body / sowle / witt / connyng / mynde & thought
Parte wil he none but eithir all or nought

The seconde proprete

Of his loue lo the sight and company
To the louer so gladd and pleasaunt is
20   That who so hath the grace to come therby
He iudgeth hym in parfite Ioy and blis
And whoso of that company doth mysse
Liue he in neuir so prosperous estate
He thinkith hym wretched and infortunate [f₆v]

25   So shulde the louer of god esteme that he
Which all the pleasure hath / mirth and disport
That in this worlde is possible to be
Yet til the time that he may onys resort
Vnto that blessed ioyfull heuinly port

---

1 lengh] *1510*, length *1525 1557*   5 none:] *1557*, none *1510 1525*   7 make.] make
1510 1525, make, *1557*   9 euery] *1510 1557* ony *1525*   13 haue.] haue *1510 1525*,
haue: *1557*   14 the] *1510 1525*, thee *1557*

Where he of god may haue the glorious sight
Is voide of parfite ioye and sure delight

The .iii. propirte

The third point of a parfit louer is
To make him fresshe / to see that al thing bene   5
Apointed wel and no thing set a mys
But all wel fasshoned / propre / goodly / clene
That in his parsone ther be no thing sene
In spech / apparaill / gesture / loke or pace
That may offend or mynyssh any grace.   10

So thou that wilt with god gete in to fauoure
Garnisshe thi self vp in as goodly wise:
As comely be as honest in behauoure
As hit is possible for the to deuise.
I meane not hereby that thou shuldest arise   15
And in the glasse vppon thi body prowle
But with faire vertue to adourne thi sowle

The fourth propirte

If loue be strong / hote / mighti / and feruent
Ther may no troble greife or sorrow fall   20
But that the louer wolde be well content
All to endure and think hit eke to small
Though hit were deth so he might there with all
The ioyfull presence of that person get
On whom he hath his hert and loue Iset [g₁]   25

Thus shulde of god the louer be content
Any distres or sorow to endure
Rather then to be from god absent
And glad to dye so that he may be sure
By his departing hens for to procure   30

---

2 sure delight] *1510 1557*, delyght *1525*   6 and] *1525 1557*, aud *1510*   7 clene]
1510 1557, & clene *1525*   12 wise:] wise *1510*, wyse *1525*, wise, *1557*   14 the] *1510
1525*, thee *1557;* deuise.] deuise *1510*, deuyse *1525*, deuise, *1557*   25 Iset] I set *1510
1525*, yset *1557*

Aftir this valey dark / the heuenly light
And of his loue the gloriouse blessed sight

The fyft proprete

Not only a louer content is in his hert
5   But couetith eke and longith to sustayne
Some labour incommodite or smart
Losse aduersite / trouble / griefe or payne
And of his sorow ioyfull is and fayne
And happy thinkith him self that he may take
10   Some misaduentur for his louers sake

Thus shuldest thou that louest god also
In thyne hert wisshe / coueyt and be glad
For him to suffre trouble paine and woo
For whom if thou be neuir so woo bestade
15   Yet thou ne shalt susteyne (be not adrad)
Halfe the dolour griefe and aduersite
That he al redy soffred hath for the

The .vi. proprete

The parfite louer longeth for to be
20   In presence of his loue both nyght & daye
And if hit happely so be fall that he
May not as he wolde: he wil yet as he may
Euir be with his loue / that is to sey
Where his heuy body nyl be brought
25   He will be conuersaunt in mynd and thought [g₁v]

Lo in like maner the louer of god shulde
At the lest in such wise as he may
If he may not in such wise as he wolde
Be present with god and conuersaunt alway
30   For certes who so list he may puruey
Though al yᵉ worlde wolde hym therfro bereuyn
To bere his body in erth his mynde in heuin

---

1 heuenly] heuenly / *1510 1525*, heauenly *1557*   15 (be not adrad)] *1510 1525*, be
not adrad, *1557*   23 loue /] loue *1510 1525*, loue, *1557*   25 conuersaunt] *1525*
1557, conuersauut *1510*

The .vii. proprete

There is no page or seruaunt most or lest
That doth vppon his loue attende & wayte
Ther is no litle worme no symple best
Ne none so small a trifle or conceyte
Lase / girdell / point / or propre gloue straite   5
But that if to his loue hit haue ben nere
The louer hath hit precious / leife / & dere

So euery relique Image or picture
That doth pertaine to goddis magnificence   10
The louer of god shulde with all besy cure
Haue hit in loue honowre and reuerence
And specially giue them preeminence
Which daily done his blessed body wirche
The quik reliques the ministres of his chirch   15

The .viii. proprete

A very louer aboue all erthly thyng
Coueytith and longeth euirmore to here
Thonoure lawde commendation and praising
And euery thing that may the fame clere   20
Of his loue / he may in no manere
Endure to here that therefro mighten vary
Or ony thing sowne in to the contrary [g₂]

The louer of god shulde coueit in like wise
To here his honour worship lawde and praise   25
Whos souerayne goodnes none hert may comprise
Whom hell / erth / and all the heuen obaise
Whos parfite louer ought by no maner wais
To suffre the cursed wordes of blasphemy
Or any thing spokyn of god vnreuerently   30

The .ix. proprete

A very louer beleuith in his mynde
On whom so euir he hath his hert Ibent

---

33 Ibent] I bent *1510 1525*, Ibente *1557*

That in that parsone men may no thing fynd
But honorable worthi and excellent
And eke surmownting farre in his entent
All other that he hath knowyn by sight or name
5   And wold that euery man shuld think the same

Of god like wise so wonderfull and hye
Al thing esteme & iudge his louer ought /
So reuerence worship honour & magnifie /
That al the creatures in this world Iwrought
10   In comparison shulde he set at nowght
And glad be if he might the meane deuise
That al the worlde wolde thinken in like wise

The .x. proprete

The louer is of coloure dede and pale
15   Ther wil no slepe in to his yen stalk
He sauorith neither mete / wyne / nor ale
He myndeth not what men about him talk
But ete he drink he / sit / lye down or walke
He burnith euir as hit were with a fire
20   In the feruent hete of his desire [g2v]

Here shulde the louer of god ensample take
To haue him contynually in remembrance
With hym in praier and meditation wake
Whyle othir play / reuell / syng / and dawnce.
25   None erthly Ioy / disport / or vaine plesaunce
Shulde hym delite or any thyng remoue
His ardent mynde from god his heuinly loue

The .xi. proprete

Diuersly passioned is the louers hert
30   Now plesaunt hope now drede and greuous fere

---

7 ought /] ought *1510 1525*, ought. *1557*   8 magnifie /] magnifie *1510*, magnyfye
1525, magnifie, *1557*   9 Iwrought *1510 1525*, I wrought *1557*   15 yen] *1510*, eyen
1525, eyes *1557*   16 nor ale] *1525 1557*, nor / ale *1510*   23 contynually] *1525*,
conty nually *1510*, continually *1557*   24 dawnce.] dawnce *1510*, daunce *1525*, daunce,
1557   26 Shulde] *1510*, Solde *1525*, Should *1557*

Now parfite blis now bittir sorow smart
And whither his loue be with hym or ellis where
Oft from his yen there fallith many a tere
For very Ioy / when they to gethir be /
When they be sondred: for aduersite.   5

Like affectiones felith eke the brest
Of goddis louer in praier and meditation:
Whan that his loue liketh in hym rest
With inward gladnes of pleasaunt contemplation
Owt breke the teris for Ioy and delectation   10
And whan his loue list eft to parte him fro
Owt breke the teris a gaine for paine & woo

The .xii. proprete

A very louer will his loue obaye
His Ioy hit is and all his appetight   15
To payne him self in all that euir he may
That parson in whom he set hath his delight
Diligently to serue bothe day and nyght
For very loue / with owt any regarde
To any profite gwerdon or rewarde [g₃]   20

So thow like wyse that hast thyne hart iset
Vpward to god so well thi selfe endeuere
So studiously that no thing may the let
Not fro his seruice any wise disseuere.
Frely loke eke thou serue that therto neuer   25
Trust of rewarde or profite do the binde
But only faithful hert & louing mynde

Wageles to serue .iii. thingis may vs moue:
First if the seruice selfe be desyrable
Second if they whom that we serue & loue   30

---

2 whither] *1510 1557*, whether *1525;* loue] *1525 1557*, lone *1510*   3 yen] *1510*, eyen
1525, eies *1557*   4 be /] be *1510 1525*, bee, *1557*   7 meditation:] meditation *1510*,
meditacyon *1525*, meditacion, *1557*   15 all his] *1525 1557*, all this *1510*   16 in]
1525 1557, iu *1510*   21 iset] I set *1510 1525*, I sette *1557*   24 fro] for *1510 1525*
1557; disseuere.] disseuere *1510 1525*, disseuere: *1557*   28 moue:] moue *1510 1525*,
moue, *1557*

Be very good and very amyable
Thredly of reason be we seruisable
With out the gaping aftir any more
To such as haue done much for vs bifore

5   Serue god for loue then / not for hope of mede.
What seruice may so desirable be
As where al turnith to thyne owne spede?
Who is so good so louely eke as he
Who hath all redy done so much for the

10   As he that first the made: and on the rode
Eft the redemed with his precious blode

A praiour of Picus Mirandula vnto god

O holy god of dredefull magestee
Verely one in .iii. and thre in one

15   Whom aungellis serue / whos wark al creaturis be
Which heuen and erth directest all alone
We the beseche good lorde with wofull mone
Spare vs wretchis & wassh away oure gilt
That we be not by thy iust angre spilt [g₃v]

20   In straite balance of rigorous iudgement
If thou shuldest oure synne pondre and wey:
Who able were to bere thy punisshment?
The hole engyne of all this world I say
The engyne that enduren shall for aye

25   With such examination might not stande
Space of a moment in thyne angry hande

---

2 Thredly] *1510*, Thyrdely *1525*, Thirdelye *1557*   5 mede.] mede *1510 1525*, meede,
1557   7 spede?] *1557*, spede: *1510*, spede *1525*   15 serue /] serue *1510 1525*
1557   19 iust] *1525*, inst *1510*, iuste *1557*   20 straite] *1510 1557*, straye *1525*
21 *Sidenote 1557:* Psal, 142   22 punisshment?] punisshment *1510*, punyssment *1525*,
punishement? *1557*   23 hole] *1510 1525*, whole *1557*   24 engyne] *1525*, engyue
1510, engine *1557*

Who is not borne in synne originall?
Who doth not actuall synne in sondry wise?
But thou good lorde art he that sparest all
With pyteouse mercy tempering iustice
For as thou dost rewardes vs deuice   5
Aboue oure merite / so dost thow dispence
Thi punishment far vndre oure offence

More is thy mercy ferr then all our synne.
To gife them also that vnworthi be
More godly is and more mercy ther in.   10
How be hit: worthi Inough ar they pardee
Be thei neuir so vnworthi: whom that he
List to accept which wher so euir he takith
Whom he vnworthi fyndeth worthi makith

Werfore good lorde that ay mercifull art   15
Vnto thi grace and souerayne dignite
We sely wretchis cry with humble hert.
Owre synne forget and oure malignite.
With piteous yes of thi benignite
Frendly loke on vs onys / thyne owne we be   20
Seruauntes or synnars whither hit likith the [g₄]

Synners if thou oure cryme beholde certaine
Oure cryme the wark of our vncorteyse mynde
But if thi giftis thou beholde a gaine
Thi giftis noble wondrefull and kinde   25
Thou shalt vs then the same persones finde
Which are to the and have be longe space
Seruauntes by nature children by thi grace

---

1 originall?] *1557* originall *1510 1525*   2 doth not] *1510,* doth *1525,* dothe not *1557;*
wise?] *1557,* wise *1510,* wyse *1525*   9 gife] *1510,* gyue *1525,* geue *1557*   10 ther
in.] ther in *1510,* therin *1525,* therein, *1557*   11 Inough] *1525,* I nough *1510,* ynough
1557   17 hert.] hert *1510,* herte *1525,* heart, *1557*   18 synne] *1510,* synnes *1525,*
sinne *1557;* malignite.] malignite *1510,* malygnite *1525,* malignitee, *1557*   19 yes]
1510, eyes *1525 1557*   20 vs onys /] vs onys *1510,* vs ones *1525,* vs once, *1557;* owne
we be] *1510,* owne *1525,* owne we bee *1557*   21 Seruauntes] *1525 1557,* Seruanntes
1510; whither] *1510 1557,* whether *1525*

But this thi goodnes wringeth vs alas
For we whom grace had made thi children dere
Are made thi gilty folk by oure trespace.
Synne hath vs gilty made this many a yere
5   But let thi grace / thi grace that hath no pere
Of our offence surmownten all the preace
That in our synne thyn honour may encreace

For though thi wisdom though thi souereyne powre
May other wise appere sufficiently
10   As thingis which thi creaturs euery howre
All with one voyce declare and testifie
Thi goodnes: yet thy singuler mercy
Thi piteous hert thi gracious indulgence
No thing so clerely shewith as oure offence

15   What but our synne hath shewed that mighti loue:
Which able was thy dredefull mageste
To draw downe in to erth fro heuen aboue
And crucifie god / that we pore wretchis we
Shulde from oure filthi synne Iclensed be
20   With blode and water of thyne owne syde
That stremed from thi blessed woundis wyde [g4v]

Thi loue and pite thus o heuenly king
Our euill makith mater of thi goodnes
O loue o pyte oure welth ay prouiding
25   O goodnes seruing thi seruauntes in distres
O loue o pite wel nigh now thankles
O goodnes mighti gracious and wyse
And yet almost now vainquisshed with oure vice

Graunt I the praie such hete in to myne hert
30   That to this loue of thyne may be egall
Graunt me fro sathanas seruice to astart

---

3 trespace.] trespace *1510 1525*, trespace, *1557*   12 thy] *1525 1557*, they *1510*
13 gracious] *1510 1557*, garcyous *1525*   18 god /] *1525*, god. *1510*, god, *1557*
19 Iclensed] I clensed *1510 1525*, yclensed *1557*   21 blessed] *1510 1557*, blyssed
1525   23 makith] makith: *1510*, maketh: *1525*, maketh, *1557*

With whom me rueth so longe to haue be thrall.
Graunt me gode lord and creatour of all
The flame to qwenche of all sinfull desire
And in thi loue set all myne hert a fire

That whan the iornay of this dedly life 5
My syly gost hath fynysshed and thense
Departen must: with owt his flesshly wife
Alone in to his lordis high presence
He may the finde / o well of indulgence /
In thi lordeship not as a lorde: but rathir 10
As a very tendre louing fathir

          Amen.

    Enprynted at london by Iohan Rastell
    dwellyng at yᵉ flete brydge at the abbot
      of wynchecombe his place. 15

---

1 to haue] *1510 1557*, to *1525;* thrall.] thrall *1510 1525 1557*   6 syly] *1510*, sely *1525*
1557   9 finde /] finde: *1510 1557*, fynde: *1525;* indulgence /] indulgence. *1510*, in-
dulgence *1525*, indulgence, *1557*   12 Amen.] *1510 1557*, Amen. Enprynted at Lon-
don in the Fletestrete at the sygne of the Sonne / by me Wynkyn de worde. *1525*   13–
15 Enprynted . . . place.] *1510, om. 1525 1557*

THE LAST THINGS

A Treatyce (vnfyny-shed) vppon these wordes of holye Scrypture,

Memorare nouissima, & in aeternum non peccabis. Remember the last thynges, and thou shalt neuer synne. Made about the yere of our lorde, 1522, by sir Thomas More than knyghte, and one of the pryue counsayle of kyng Henry theight, and also vnder treasorer of Englande.

IF there were anye quest̃on amonge menne, whyther the wordes of holy scripture, or the doctryne of anye seculer authour, were of greater force and effecte to the weale and profyte of mannes soule, (thoughe we shold let passe so many short & weigh ty wordes, spoken by the mouth of oure sauiour Christ himself, to whose heauenly wisedom, the wit of none earthly creature can be comparable) yet this onely text written by the wise man in the seuenth chapiter of Ecclesiasticus is suche, that it conteineth more fruitfull aduise and counsayle, to the forming and framing of mannes maners in vertue, and auoyding of sinne, then many whole & great volumes of the best of old philosophers, or anye other that euer wrote in seculer litterature.

Long would it be to take the beste of theyr wordes and compare it with these wordes of holy writ: Let vs consider the frute and profit of this in it selfe: which thyng wel aduised and pondered, shall wel declare, that of none whole volume of seculare litterature, shall aryse so very fruitful doctrine. For what would a man geue for a sure medicin, & wer of such strength, ŷ it should al his life kepe hym fro sicknes: namely if he mighte by tha noyding of sicknes be sure to contynue his life one hundred yere? So is it nowe ŷ these wordes geueth vs at a sure medicine (yf we forslouth not the receiuyng) by which we shal kepe from sicknes, not the body, which none health may longe kepe fro death (for dye we muste in fewe yeres liue we neuer so long) but ŷ soul, whiche here preserued fro the sicknes of sin, shal after this eternally liue in ioy, and be preserued from the deadly lyfe of euerlastyng payne.

The phisicion sendeth his bill to the poticary, & therin wryteth sommetime a costlye receite of many straunge herbes and rootes, fet out of far countreis, long & lten drugges, al the strength worn out, & some none such to be goten. But thys phisicion sendeth his bil to thy selfe, no straunge thing therin, nothing costly to bie, nothing farre to fet, but to be gathered al times of the yere in the gardein of thyne owne soule.

Let vs heare than what wholesom receit this is. Remember (saith this byll) thy last thinges, and thou shalte neuer sin in this world. Here is first a short medicine, conteinyng onely foure herbes, comen and well knowe, ŷ is to wit, deth dome, pain, and ioy.

This short medicine is of a maruey lous force, able to kepe vs al our life fro sin. The phisicion canne not geue no one medicine to euery man to kepe him from sicknes, but to diuers men diuers, by reson of the diuersity of diuers complexions. This medicine serueth euery man. The phisicion dothe but gesse & coniecture ŷ his receit shal do good: but thys medicine is vndoubtedly sure.

How happeth it than thou wilt happe ly say, that so few be preserued from sin. if euery man haue so sure a medicine, so ready at hande? For folk fare commonly as he doth that goeth forth fasting amõg sick folk for slouth, rather than he wyll take a litle tryacle before.

Thou wilt saye paraduenture ŷ some parte of thys medicine is verye bytter and paynfull to receyue. Surely there canne bee nothyng so bitter, but wysedome would brooke it for so gret a profyte. But yet this medicyne thoughe thou make a sowre face at it, is not so bytter as thou makesse for. For well thou wottest, he byddeth thee not take neyther deathe, nor dome, nor payne, but onelye to remember them, and yet the ioye of heauen therewith to temper them

A Treatyce (vnfynyshed) vppon
these wordes of holye Scrypture,
Memorare nouissima, & in eternum
non peccabis, Remember the last thynges,   5
and thou shalt neuer synne.
Made about the yere of our lorde .1522.
by sir Thomas More than knyghte,
and one of the priuye counsayle
of Kyng Henry theight,   10
and also vndertreasorer of Englande.

---

4 *in eternum*] *ineternum 1557*   4–5 *Sidenote 1557:* Ecclus. 7

If there were anye questyon amonge menne, whyther the
woordes of holy scripture, or the doctryne of anye secular au-
thour, were of greater force and effecte to the weale and profyte
of mannes soule, (thoughe we shold let passe so many short &
5 weighty wordes, spoken by the mouth of oure sauiour Christ
himself, to whose heauenly wisedom, the wit of none earthly
creature can be comparable) yet this onely text writen by the wise
man in the seuenth chapiter of Ecclesiasticus is suche, that it
conteineth more fruitfull aduise and counsayle, to the formyng
10 and framing of mannes maners in vertue, and auoyding of
sinne, then many whole & great volumes of the best of old philos-
ophers, or anye other that euer wrote in secular litterature.

Long would it be to take the beste of theyr woordes and com-
pare it with these wordes of holy writ: Let vs consider the frute
15 and profit of this in it selfe: which thyng wel aduised and pon-
dered, shall wel declare, that of none whole volume of seculare
litterature, shall aryse so very fruitful doctrine. For what would a
man geue for a sure medicin, y^t wer of such strength, y^t it should
al his life kepe hym fro sickness: namely if he mighte by thauoyd-
20 ing of sicknes be sure to contynue his life one hundred yere? So is
it nowe y^t these wordes geueth vs al a sure medicine (yf we for-
slouth not the receiuyng) by which we shal kepe from sicknes,
not the body, which none health may longe kepe fro death (for
dye we muste in fewe yeres liue we neuer so long) but ye soul,
25 whiche here preserued from the sicknes of sin, shal after this
eternally liue in ioy, and be preserued from the deadly lyfe of
euerlastyng payne.

The phisicion sendeth his bill to the poticary, & therin writeth
sommetime a costlye receite of many straunge herbes and
30 rootes, fet out of far countreis, long lien drugges, al the strength
worn out, & some none such to be goten. But thys phisicion
sendeth his bil to thy selfe, no strange thing therin, nothing
costly to bie, nothing farre to fet, but to be gathered al times of
the yere in the gardein of thyne owne soule.

---

12 litterature] litteratuce *1557*   23–24 *Sidenote 1557:* Dye we must

Let vs heare than what wholesom receit this is. Remember (saith this byll) thy last thinges, and thou shalte neuer sin in this world. Here is first a short medicine, conteinyng onely foure herbes, comen and well knowen, y^t is to wit, deth, dome, pain, and ioy.

This shorte medicine is of a marueylous force, able to kepe vs al our life fro sin. The phisicion canne not geue no one medicine to euery man to kepe him from sicknes, but to diuers men diuers, by reson of the diuersity of diuers complexions. This medicine serueth euery man. The phisicion dothe but gesse & coniecture y^t his receit shal do good: but thys medicine is vndoubtedly sure.

How happeth it than thou wilt happely say, that so few be preserued from sin, if euery man haue so sure a medicine, so ready at hand? For folk fare commonly as he doth that goeth forth fasting among sick folk for slouth, rather than he wyll take a little tryacle before.

Thou wilt saye paraduenture y^t some parte of thys medicine is verye bytter and paynfull to receyue. Surely there canne bee nothyng so bitter, but wysedome would brooke it for so gret a profyte. But yet this medicyne thoughe thou make a sowre face at it, is not so bytter as thou makeste for. For well thou wottest, he byddeth thee not take neyther deathe, nor dome, nor payne, but onelye to remember them, and yet the ioye of heauen therewith to temper [e$_5$] them with all. Nowe yf a manne bee so dayntye stomaked, that goyng where contagion is, he woulde grudge to take a lyttle tryacle, yet were he very nycely wanton, if he might not at the lestwise take a lyttle vynegre and rose water in his handkercher.

Yet wote I well that manye one wyll saye, that the bare remembrance of deth alone, yf a man consider it and aduise it wel, were able to bereue a man of al the pleasure of his lyfe. Howe muche more than should his lyfe be painful and greuous, yf to the remembrance and consideracion of death, a manne should adde and set to, the depe ymaginacion of the dredeful dome of

---

god, and bytter paines of purgatory or hell, of which euery one passeth & excedeth many deathes. Thys is the sage sawes of suche as make thys world their heauen, and theyr lust theyr God.

Now see the blindnes of vs worldlye folk, how precisely we
5 presume to shoote our folish bolte, in those matters most, in whiche we least can skill. For I lytle doubt, but that among foure thousande taken out at aduenture, we shal not find fourescore, but they shal boldly affirme it for a thyng to painefull, busilye to remember these fowre last thynges. And yet durst I lay a wa-
10 geour, that of those foure thousande, ye shall not fynd fourtene, that hath depelye thought on them foure tymes in all theyr dayes.

If men would vouchesafe to putte in proofe and experience thoperacion and workyng of this medicine, the remembraunce
15 of these foure last thinges, they should fynd therin, not the pleasure of their life loste, but so greate a pleasure grow therby, that they neuer felt yᵉ lyke before, nor would haue supposed that euer they should haue felt any such. For it is to be knowen, yᵗ like as we be made of two far diuers and vnlike substances, the body
20 and the soule, so we be apt and hable to receiue two diuers and vnlike pleasures, the one carnall and fleshly, yᵉ tother ghostly and spirituall. And like as the soule excelleth the bodye, so dothe the swetnes of spiritual pleasure, farre passe & excel yᵉ grosse and filthy pleasure of al fleshly delyte: whiche is of trouth no very
25 true pleasure, but a false counterfayte ymage of pleasure. And the cause why menne bee so madde theron, is onelye for ygnoraunce and lacke of knowledge of the tother. As those that lacke insyght of precious stones, holde themselfe as well contente and satisfyed, with a byrall or Christall wel counterfayted, as with
30 a ryght natural Dyamonte. But he that by good vse and experyence, hathe in his eye the ryghte marke and very trewe lustre of the Dyamonte, reiecteth anone, and lysteth not to looke vpon the counterfayte, be it neuer so well handeled, neuer so craftely polyshed. And truste it well, that in like wyse yf menne

---

1 *Sidenote 1557:* Purgatory   19 *Sidenote 1557:* Of two substances   23 *Sidenote 1557:* Spiritual pleasure   24 *Sidenote 1557:* Fleshly delite

would well accustome themselfe in the taste of spirytual plea-
sure, and of that sweete felyng that vertuous people haue of the
good hope of heauen, they shoulde shortelye sette at nought and
at length abhorre, the foule delite and filthye lykinge that ryseth
of sensuall and fleshly pleasure, whych is neuer so pleasantly 5
spiced with delyte & lyking, but that it bringeth therewyth suche
a grudge and grief of conscience, that it maketh the stomak
wamble, and fare as it woould vomit. And y^t notwithstanding
such is our blynd custom, that we perseuer therin without care or
cure of the better: as a sow contente w^t draffe, durt and mire, 10
careth neither for better meate nor better bedde.

Think not that euery thing is plesant, y^t men for madnes
laughe at. For thou shalt in Bedleem se one laugh at ye knocking
of his own hed against a post, & yet there is litle pleasure therein.
But ye think paraduenture this ensample as mad as the mad 15
man, & as litle to ye purpose. I am content ye so think. But what
wil ye say if ye see men that are taken and reputed wise, laugh
much more maddelye than he? Shal ye not see suche laughe at
their own craft, whan thei haue as they think, wilily done their
neybour wrong? Now whoso seeth not, that his laughter is more 20
madde than the laughter of the mad man, I hold him madder
than they both. For the mad man laughed whan he had done
himselfe but little hurte, by a knocke of his head to the poste.
Thys other sage foole laugheth at the castyng of his own soule
into the fire of hel. For whych he hath cause to wepe al his life. 25
And it canne not be but the grudge and feare therof foloweth his
laughter, and secrete sorowe marreth all suche owtewarde
myrth. For the heart of a wicked wretch is like a stormy sea y^t
cannot rest: except a manne be fallen down into the dongeon of
wretchednes, and the doore shit over his hed. For whan a synner 30
is once fallen down into the depth, he waxeth a desperate
wretche and setteth al at [e$_5$v] nought, and he is in the worste
kynd of all, and farthest from all recouery. For like as in the body
his sicknes is moste vncurable, that is sick and feleth it not, but
weneth hymself whole, (for he that is in that case is commonly 35

---

7 *Sidenote 1557:* Grudge of conscience   10 draffe,] draffe *1557*   20 wrong?]
wrong. *1557*   28–29 *Sidenote 1557:* Esay. 57. A wicked hert

madde) so he that by a mischieuous custome of sinne parceiueth
no fault in his euill dede, nor hath no remorse therof, hath lost
the natural light of reason, and the spirituall light of faith: which
.ii. lightes of knowledge and vnderstanding quenched, what re-
mayneth in him more, than the bodily senses and sensuall wittes
commune to man and brute beastes.

Nowe albeit so that the fleshelye and worldly pleasure is of
truth not pleasant but bitter, and the spirituall pleasure is of
trouth so swete, that ye swetenes therof many times darketh and
minisheth ye felyng of bodily payne, by reason wherof good
vertuous folk fele more plesure in the sorow of their synnes &
affliccion of their penaunce, than wretches fele in the fulfyllyng
of their foule delite, and credible is it that thinwarde spirituall
pleasure and coumfort whiche many of thold holy martirs had in
the hope of heuen, derked and in maner ouerwhelmed the
bodily paines of their tormente, yet this notwithstanding, like as
a sick man feleth no swetenes in suger, & some women with child
haue such fond lust that thei had leuer eate terre than tryacle &
rather pitch than marmelade, and some whole people loue talow
better than butter, & Iseland loueth no butter till it bee long
barrelled, so we grosse carnal people hauing our tast infected, by
the sicknes of sin & filthy custom of fleshly lust, fynd so gret
liking in the vile & stinking delectacion of fleshly delite, that we
list not once proue, what maner of swetenes good and vertuous
folke fele & parceiue in spiritual pleasure. And ye cause is why,
because we can not perceiue the tone, but if we forbeare the
tother. For lyke as the ground that is al foregrowen with nettels,
breers, and other euil weedes, canne bring foorth no corne til
they be weded out, so can oure soule haue no place for the good
corne of spiritual plesure, as long as it is ouergrowen with the
barreyn weedes of carnall delectacion. For the pullyng owte of
whych weedes by the roote, there is not a more mete instrument,
than the remembrance of the fowre last thinges, which as they
shall pull owte these weedes of fleshelye voluptuousnes, so shal

---

7 *Sidenote 1557:* Worldly and spiritual pleasure   21 *Sidenote 1557:* An infected tast
27 nettels,] nettels *1557*   31–33 *Sidenote 1557:* An instrument to pul out the wedes of
the soule

they not fayle to plant in their places, not onely wholesom ver-
tues, but also marueilous ghostelye pleasure and spiritual
gladnes, whiche in euery good soule riseth of the loue of god,
and hope of heauen, and inward liking that the godly spirit
taketh in ye diligent labor of good and vertuous busines. 5

I wold not so long tary in this point, nor make so many wordes,
of the pleasure that men may finde by the receeyte of this medi-
cine, were it not that I wel parceyue, the worlde so sette vppon
the sekynge of pleasure, that they sette by pleasure much more
than by profite. And therefore to thentente that ye maye par- 10
ceyue, that it is not a fantasye fownden of myne own head, that
the abandoning and refusyng of carnall pleasure, and then-
suyng of laboure, trauaile, penaunce and bodily paine, shall
bryng therwith to a christen man, not onely in the worlde that is
commyng, but also in this present life, very swetenes, comfort, 15
pleasure, and gladnes, I shal proue it to be true by theyr testi-
mony and witnes, whose authoritie speaking of theyr own expe-
rience, there wyl I wene none honest man mistrust.

Lo the holy doctor sainct Austine, exhortying penitentes and
repentant synners to sorow for theyr offences, sayeth vnto them. 20
Sorowe (saith this holy man) and be glad of thy sorow. In vain
shold he bid him be glad of his sorow, yf man in sorow could not
be glad. But this holy father sheweth by this counsel, not only
that a man may be ioyfull and glad for al his sorow, but also that
he may be and hath cause to be glad because of hys sorowe. 25

Long wer it to reherse the places that proue this point among
the holy doctors of Christes church. But we wil in stede of them
al, allege you the wordes of him y^t is doctor of them al, our sauior
Jesu christ. He saith that the way to heauen is straite & aspre or
painful. And therfore he sayth that few folk find it out or walke 30
therin. And yet sayth he for al that, my yoke is easy & my burden
light. Howe coulde these .ii. sayinges stand together, wer it not y^t
as the labor, trauel & affliccion of the body, is painful & sharp to

4 heauen] heanen *1557; Sidenote 1557:* Wherof godly plesure riseth   19 *Sidenote*
1557: S. Austyne   22 *Sidenote 1557:* Gladnes in sorow   29 christ.] christ *1557;*
Sidenote 1557: Mat. 7   30 *Sidenote 1557:* Mat. 11   33 labor,] labor *1557*

the flesh, so the comfort & gladnes y^t the soule conceiueth
therof, rising into the loue of oure lord & hope of his glory to
come, so tempereth & ouermastreth the bitternes of the grief, y^t
it maketh the very labor easy, ye sowernes very swete, & the verye
5   payne pleasant. [e₆]

Wyll ye see the sample? Looke vppon his holy apostles, whan
thei were taken and scourged with whippes for christes sake, did
it grieue them thinke ye? Imagine your self in the same case, & I
think ye wil think yea. Now see than for all ye paine of their
10   fleshe, what ioy and pleasure they conceiued in their soule. The
holy scripture saith, that they reioysed & ioyed that god had
accounted them worthy for Christes sake, not onely to be
scourged, but also which wold be far greater grief to an honest
man than the payne it selfe, to bee scourged with dispite and
15   shame, so that the more theyr payn was, the more was their ioy.
For as the holy doctor saint Chrisostome saith, thoughe pain be
grieuous for the nature of ye affliccion, yet is it pleasaunte by the
alacritie and quick mind of them that willyngly suffer it. And
therefore though ye nature of the tormentes make gret grief and
20   payne, yet the prompt and willyng mynde of them that were
scourged, passed and ouercame the nature of ye thing, that is to
wit, mastryng the outewarde fleshlye payne with inwarde spiritu-
all pleasure. And surely this is so trewe, y^t it may stande for a very
certaine token, that a penitent beginneth to profite and grow in
25   grace and fauour of god, whan he feleth a pleasure and quicknes
in his labor and pain, taken in prayer, almes dede, pilgrimage,
fasting, discipline, tribulacion, affliccion, and such other spiri-
tual exercise, by which the soule wyllingly worketh with the
bodye by theyr own punishment, to purge and rub out the rusty
30   cankerd spots, that sinne hath defiled them with, in the sight of
God, and to leaue the fewer to be burned out in the fire of
purgatory. And when so euer as I say y^t a man feleth in this pain a
pleasure, he hath a token of gret grace and that his penance is

---

10 *Sidenote 1557:* Actes. 5   16 *Sidenote 1557:* S. Chrisostom   17 *Sidenote 1557:*
Pleasant pain   24 *Sidenote 1557:* A token of gods fauor   26 *Sidenote 1557:* Pilgrim-
age   32 *Sidenote 1557:* Purgatory

pleasant to god. For as the holy scripture saith, our lord loueth a
glad geuer. And on the tother syde wher as one doth such spiri-
tual busines with a dulnes of spirite & werines of minde, he doth
twyse as much & therby taketh fouretimes as muche payne, sith
his bodily paine is releued with no spiritual reioyce nor comfort. 5
I wil not say that his labour is lost, but I dare be bold to say, that he
profiteth much lesse with much more payne. For certaine it is, y^t
the best soules, and they that haue best trauailed in spiritual
busines, find most coumfort therein. And therfore yf thei most
pleased god, that in the bodily pain of their penance toke lesse 10
spirytuall pleasure, it should therof folow, that the farther a
manne proceded in the parfeccion of spiritual exercise, in y^e
worsse case he were. Which can in no wise bee so, sythe that wee
see the holye apostles & other holy men and women, the better y^t
they were, the more pleasure thei parceiued in their fleshly af- 15
fliccions, eyther put vnto them by god, or taken by them selfe for
goddes sake.

   Therfore let euery manne by ye labour of his minde and helpe
of praier, enforce himself in all tribulacion and affliccion, labour,
paine and trauaile, without spot of pride or ascribing any praise 20
to himself, to conceiue a delite and pleasure in such spiritual
exercise, and thereby to ryse in the loue of our lord, with an hope
of heauen, contempt of the world, and longing to be with god.
To thattaining of which mynde, by the putting away of the
malicious pleasures of the deuil, the filthy pleasures of the fleshe, 25
and the vain pleasures of the worlde, whiche once excluded,
there is place made and cleane purged, to receiue the very swete
and pure pleasure of the spirite, there is not anye one thyng
lightly as I haue sayd, more accommodate nor more effectuall,
than this thing that I haue begon with, and taken in hand to 30
entreate, that is to wit the remembrance of the foure last thinges,
which is as the scripture saythe so effectual, that yf a man re-
member it wel, he shall neuer synne.

   Thou wilt happely say, that it is not ynough that a man do none

1–2 *Sidenote 1557:* 2. Cor. 9   9 *Sidenote 1557:* Comfort   19 affliccion, labour,] af-
fliccion labour *1557*   21 himself,] himself *1557; Sidenote 1557:* Pleasure in spiritual
exercise

euyl, but he must also do good. This is verye truth that ye say. But
first if ther be but these two steppes to heauen, he y^t getteth hym
on the tone is halfe vp. And ouer y^t, who so doth none euil, it wil
be very hard but he must nedes do good, syth mans mind is
5   neuer ydle, but occupyed commonly either with good or euil.

And therefore whan folke haue fewe wordes & vse much mus-
yng, likewise as among many wordes al be not alwaye well and
wisely set, so whan the tounge lyeth still, if the mynde be not
occupyed well, it were lesse euil saue for worldlye rebuke, to
10 blabber on trifles somewhat sottishlye, than whyle they seeme
sage, in kepyng silence, secretely paraduenture the meane whyle
to fantasye wyth them self, fylthy sinful deuises, whereof theyr
tonges if they wer set on babling, could not for shame vtter and
speake the lyke. [e$_6$v]
15 I say not this, for that I woulde haue folk fal to babling, well
woting that as the scripture saith, in many wordes lacketh not
sinne, but that I woulde haue folke in their sylence take good
heede, y^t their mindes be occupied w^t good thoughts: for vnoc-
cupyed be they neuer. For yf euer the mind wer emptye, it
20 woulde bee empty whan the bodye slepeth. But yf it wer than al
empty, we shoulde haue no dreames. Than if the fantasies leue
vs not sleping, it is not likely that euer thei leaue vs waking.
Wherfore as I saye, let vs kepe oure mindes occupyed wyth good
thoughtes, or els the deuil will fill them with euill.
25 And surely euery thing hath his mene. Ther is as scripture
saith, time to speke & time to kepe thy tong. Whansoeuer y^e
communicacion is nought and vngodly, it is better to holde thy
tong & thinke on some better thing the while, than to geue eare
therto & vnder pinne the tale. And yet better were it then hold-
30 ynge of thy tong, properly to speake, & with som good grace and
pleasant fashion, to break into some better matter: by whiche thy
speache and talking, thou shalt not onely profite thy selfe as thou
sholdest haue done by thy well minded sylence, but also amende
the whole audience, which is a thyng farre better and of muche

---

2 *Sidenote 1557:* Two steppes to heauen   4–5 *Sidenote 1557:* The mynd neuer ydle
6–7 *Sidenote 1557:* Musing   15 *Sidenote 1557:* Bablyng. Prou. 10   17 *Sidenote
1557:* Silence   26 *Sidenote 1557:* Eccle. 3

more merite. Howbeit if thou can find no proper meane to breake the tale, than excepte thy bare authoritie suffice to commaunde silence, it were paraduenture good, rather to keepe a good silence thy self, than blunt forth rudely, and yrryte them to anger, which shal happely therfore not let to talke on, but speake much the more, lest thei should seme to leue at thy commaundement. And better were it for ye while to let one wanton woorde passe vncontrolled, than geue occasyon of twain. But if the communicacion be good, than is it better, not onely to geue eare therto, but also firste well and prudently to deuise w^t thy self vpon ye same: & than moderatelye & in good maner yf thou find oughte to the purpose, speake therto & say thy minde therin. So shal it appere to the presence, y^t your mynd was wel occupied the while, & your thought not wandring forty mile thence whyle your body was ther. As it often happeth, y^t the very face sheweth ye mind walking a pilgrimage, in such wise y^t not w^toute som note & reproch of suche vagaraunte mind, other folk sodainly say to them: a peny for your thought. Whiche maner of wandring mind in company, may parcase be ye more excusable somtime by some chargeable busines of ye party: but surelye it is neuer taken for wisedome nor good maner.

But now to retourne to my purpose sith ye remembrance of these .iiii. last thinges is of such force & efficacy, y^t it is able alway to kepe vs fro sin, & sith we canne neuer be long void of both, it must thereof, ensue, y^t we shal consequently do good: & therof must it nedes folow, y^t this only lesson wel learned & busily putte in vre, must nedes leade vs to heauen.

Yet wil ye paraduenture saye, that ye know these .iiii. thinges wel inough: & if ye knowlege therof had so gret effect as ye scripture speaketh of: there should not be so mani nought as ther be. For what christen man is he y^t hath wit & discrecion, but he hath heard, and hauing any faith beleueth, these .iiii. last things: of which ye first y^t is to say death, we nede no faith to beleue, we know it by dailye proofe & experience.

1–2 *Sidenote 1557:* When to kepe silence   17 *Sidenote 1557:* A vagaraunt mynde

I say not nay, but that we know them either by faith or experi-
ence. And yet not so very thorowly as we might peraduenture, &
herafter vndoutedli shal. Which if we knewe once thorowlye,
and so feelyngly perceyued as we myght percase and nameli as
5   we sureli shal, ther wold be litle dout, but the least of al the foure,
woulde well keepe vs fro synne. For as for y^t though we haue
heard of ye dome yet were we neuer at it. Thoughe we haue
heard of hel, yet came we neuer in it. Though we haue hearde of
heauen, yet came we neuer to it. And though we dayly se men
10 dye, and therby knowe the death, yet our selfe neuer felte it. For
yf we knewe these thinges thorowlye, the least of al foure, were as
I sayd inough to keepe vs from synne.
How be it the foresaid words of scripture, byddeth thee not
knowe the foure last thinges, but remember thy .iiii. last thinges,
15 and then he saythe thou shalte neuer synne.
Many thynges knowe we that we seldome think on. And in the
things of the soule, the knowledge without the remembraunce
lytle profiteth. What auaileth it to knowe that there is a God,
whiche thou not only beleuest by faith, but also knowest by rea-
20 son, what auaileth y^t thou knowest him if thou think litle of him?
The busi minding of thy .iiii. last things, & y^e depe consideracion
therof, is y^e thing y^t shall kepe thee fro synne. And yf thou putte
it [e$_7$] in a saie and make a proofe, thou shalte well fynde, by that
thou shalte haue no luste to sinne, for the tyme that thou depelye
25 thinkest on them, that yf oure frailtye coulde endure neuer to
remitte or slake in the depe deuising of them, we shoulde neuer
haue delite or pleasure in any sinful thing.
For the proofe whereof, let vs firste begynne at the remem-
braunce of ye first of these fowre last, whiche is vndoutedly farre
30 the least of the fower, and thereby shall we make a profe, what
marueilous effect may grow by the diligent remembraunce of all
fower, towarde thauoiding of all ye traines, dartes, sleightes, en-
tisinges, and assaultes, of the three mortall enemies, the deuil,
the worlde, and our owne fleshe.

---

6 y^t] yet *1557*   17 *Sidenote 1557:* Knowledge without remembraunce litle prof-
iteth   32 sleightes,] sleightes *1557*   33 *Sidenote 1557:* Thre enemies

The remembrance of death.

WHAT profite and commoditye commeth vnto mans soule by the meditacion of death, is not onelye marked of the chosen people of god, but also of such as wer the best sorte among gentiles & painims. For some of the olde famous philosophers, whan thei wer demaunded what facultie philosophy was, answerd y^t it was the meditacion or exercise of death. For like as death maketh a seuerance of the body & the soul, whan thei by course of nature must nedes depart a sonder, so (said thei) dothe the study of philosophy, labor to seuer the soule fro ye loue & affeccions of the body while thei be to gether. Now if this be the whole study & labour of philosophy, as the beste philosopher said that it is, than may we with in shorte time be well learned in phylosophy. For nothyng is there that maye more effectuallye withdrawe the soule fro the wretched affeccions of the body, than may the remembrance of death, yf we do not remember it hourely, as one heareth a worde, and let it passe by hys eare, without any receiuing of the sentence into his heart. But if we not onely here this word death, but also let sink into our heartes, the very fantasye and depe imaginacion therof, we shall parceiue therby, that we wer neuer so gretly moued by the beholding of the daunce of death pictured in Poules, as we shal fele our self stered and altered, by the feling of that imaginacion in our hertes. And no maruell. For those pictures expresse only, ye lothely figure of our dead bony bodies biten away ye flesh. Which though it be ougly to behold, yet neither the sight therof, nor the sight of al ye dead heades in ye charnel house, nor the apparicion of a very ghost, is halfe so grisely as the depe conceiued fantasy of deathe in his nature, by the liuely imaginacyon grauen in thyne owne heart. For there seest thou, not one plain grieuous sight of the bare bones hanging by the sinewes, but thou seest (yf thou fantasye thyne own death, for so art thou by this counsell

5

10

15

20

25

30

---

2 *Sidenote 1557:* Death; What] *the first letter is a blockletter* V   6 *Sidenote 1557:* Phy-losophye   16 *Sidenote 1557:* The remembrance of deth   22 *Sidenote 1557:* The daunce of Poules   27 charnel] charuel *1557*

aduised) thou seest I saye thy selfe yf thou dye no worse death,
yet at the leastwise lying in thy bedde, thy hed shooting, thy
backe akyng, thy vaynes beating, thine heart panting, thy throte
ratelyng, thy fleshe trembling, thy mouth gaping, thy nose
5 sharping, thy legges coling, thy fingers fimbling, thy breath
shorting, all thy strength fainting, thy lyfe vanishing, and thy
death drawyng on.

    If thou couldeste nowe call to thy remembraunce, some of
those sicknes that haue most grieued thee & tormented thee in
10 thy dayes, as eueri man hath felt some, & than findest thou that
some one disease in some one part of thy body, as parcase y^e
stone or the strangurye, haue put thee to thine own minde to no
lesse torment, than thou shouldest haue felt if one had put vp a
knife into the same place, and wouldest as thee than semed, haue
15 bene content with such a chaunge think what it wil be than, whan
thou shalt fele so many such paines in euery part of thy bodi
breaking thy vaines & thy life stringes, w^t like pain & grief, as
though as manye kniues as thy body might receiue, shold eu-
eriwhere enter & mete in the middes.

20   A stroke of a staffe, a cut of a knife, the fleshe senged with fire,
the pain of sundry sicknes, many men haue assaid in them self.
And thei that haue not yet, somewhat haue heard by them that
felte it. But what maner dolor & payne, what maner of grieuous
panges, what intollerable torment, the sely creature feeleth in
25 the disolucion and seueraunce of the soule fro the body, neuer
was there body, that yet could tel the tale.

    Some coniecture and token of thys poynt we haue, of the bitter
passion and piteous departyng of our sauiour Iesu Christ, of
whom we nothyng rede, that euer he cryed for any payne, eyther
30 for the whyppes and roddes beatyng hys blessed bodye, or the
sharp thornes pricking his holy head, or the greate longe [e₇v]
nailes percyng his precious handes and fete. But whan the poynt
approched in which his sacred soule shold depart out of his
blessed bodye, at y^t pointe he cryed loude once or twise to his
35 father in heuen into whose mighty & mercifull handes, at y^e

---

2 *Sidenote 1557:* The paines of death   34–35 *Sidenote 1557:* Christ cryed. Mat. 27.
Mar. 15. Luke. 23

extreme point, w^t a gret lowde crye he gaue vp the gost. Now if ye death was so painful and ragious to our sauioure Christ, whose ioy, & comfort of his godhed if he would haue suffered it, moughte in such wise haue redounded into his soul, & so furth into his body, y^t it should not onely haue supped vp al his pain, but also haue transformed his holy body into a glorious forme and made it impassyble, what intollerable torment wil death bee than to vs miserable wretches, of which ye more part among ye panges of our passage, shal haue yet so painful twiches of our owne conscience, y^t the feare of hell, the dread of the deuil, and sorow at our heart at the sighte of our synnes, shal passe and excede the deadly paynes of our body.

Other thinges are there, whiche wyll paraduenture seme no greate matter to them y^t fele them not. But vnto hym y^t shall lye in that case, they shalbe tedious oute of al measure.

Haue ye not ere this in a sore sicknes felt it very grieuous to haue folk babble to you, and namely suche thynges as ye shold make aunswere to, whan it was a pain to speake? Thinke ye not now that it wilbe a gentle pleasure, whan we lye dying, al our body in pain, al our mind in trouble, our soul in sorow, our hearte al in drede, while our life walketh awaiward, while our death draweth toward, while ye deuil is busy about vs, while we lack stomak & strength to beare any one of so manifold heynous troubles, wil it not be as I was about to say, a pleasant thing, to see before thine eyen, & heare at thine eare, a rable of fleshly frendes, or rather of flesh flies, skippyng about thy bed & thy sicke body, like rauens aboute thy corps now almost carreyn, cryinge to thee on euery side, what shall I haue, what shall I haue? Than shal come thy children & crye for theyr partes. Than shal come thy swete wife, & where in thyne heale happelye shee spake thee not one swete worde in sixe wekes, now shal she call thee swete husband & wepe w^t much woorke and ask the what shal she haue. Than shall thyne executours aske for the kayes, and aske what money is owyng thee, aske what substance thou hast and aske where thy

5

10

15

20

25

30

16 *Sidenote 1557:* Troubles in death   22 toward,] toward *1557*   26 *Sidenote 1557:*
Fleshe flyes   28 haue,] haue *1557; Sidenote 1557:* Children   29 *Sidenote 1557:*
Wyfe   33 and] (and *1557; Sidenote 1557:* Executours   34 thou] thon *1557*

money lyeth. And whyle thou lyest in y^t case, their wordes shalbe
so tedious, that thou wilt wyshe all that they aske for, vpon a red
fyre, so thou mightest lye one halfe howre in rest.

Nowe is there one thyng which a lytle I touched before, I wote
5 not whither more paineful or more perilous, ye merueilous in-
tentife busines and solicitacion of our ghostly enemy ye deuil, not
only in one fashion present, but surely neuer absent from him y^t
draweth toward death. For sith that of his pestilente enuy con-
ceiued fro the beginning of mans creacion, by which he lay in
10 awayte to take our first mother Eue in a trayne, & therby drawing
our former father Adam into the breache of gods beheste,
founde the meanes not without the grieuous encrease of his
owne damnacion, to depriue vs of paradise, & bereue vs our
immortalitie, making vs into subieccion, not onely of temporal
15 death but also of his eternal tormentry, wer we not by the great
bounty of god and Christes painful passion, restored to the pos-
sibilitie of euerlasting life, he neuer ceased since, to run about
like a ramping lion, lokyng whom he mought deuoure, it can be
no dout, but he most busily trauaileth in that behalf, at the time y^t
20 he parceiueth vs aboute to depart hence. For wel he knoweth y^t
than he either winneth a man for euer, or for euer leseth him.
For haue he him neuer so fast afore, yet if he breake from him
than, he can after his death neuer geat hym again. Wel he maye
paraduenture haue him as his gailour in his prison of purgatory,
25 for the time of his punicion temporal. But as he wold haue him
for his parpetual slaue, shal he neuer haue him after, how sure so
euer he hadde hym afore, yf he geate from him at the tyme of his
death. For so lost he sodaynelye the thefe, that honge on the
ryghte hande of Christe.

30   And on the tother syde yf he catche a manne faste at the tyme
of hys death, he is sure to keepe hym for euer. For as the Scryp-
ture sayeth, wheresoeuer the stone falleth there shall it abyde.
And sythe he knoweth thys for very suretye, and is of malyce so
venemous and enuious, that he had leuer double his own payn,

---

6 *Sidenote 1557:* The deuil   16–17 *Sidenote 1557:* Psal.21   18 *Sidenote 1557:* 1. Pe-
ter. 5   24 *Sidenote 1557:* Purgotorye   32 *Sidenote 1557:* Eccle. 11

than suffer vs to scape from pain, hee whan wee drawe to deathe, dooeth hys vttermoste deuoyre to brynge vs to damnacion: neuer ceasynge to mynyster by subtylle and incogytable [e$_8$] meanes, firste vnlawefull longyng to lyue, horrour to goe gladly to god at his callyng.

Than geueth he some false glade of escapyng that sickenes, and thereby putteth in our minde, a loue yet & cleauyng to the world, keping of our goodes, lothsomnes of shrifte, slouth to-warde good workes. And if we be so farre gone, that we see we cannot recouer, than he casteth in our myndes, presumpcion and securitie of saluacion, as a thing well wonne by our owne workes: of whiche if we haue any done well, he casteth them into our mindes with ouer great liking and thereby withdraweth vs fro ye haste of doyng any more, as a thing that eyther nedeth not or may bee done by oure executours. And in steede of sorowe for our synnes and care of heauen, he putteth vs in minde of prouision for somme honorable burying, so many torches, so many tapers, so many black gownes, so many mery mourners laughyng vnder black hodes, and a gay hers, w^t the delight of goodly and honorable funeralles: in which the folish sicke man is sometyme occupied, as though he thought that he should stand in a window, and see how woorshipfullye he shall bee broughte to church.

And thus enueigleth he them that either be good, or but metely badde.

But as for those that he hath knowen for special wretches, whose whole lyfe hath in effect bene al bestowed in his seruice, whom he hath brought into gret & horrible sinnes, by the horrour wherof he hath kept them fro confession, these folke at their end he handleth on a nother fashion. For into their mindes he bringeth their shameful sinnes by hepe, & by the abominable sight therof, draweth them into desperacion. For thagreuing wherof, oure lord after their deseruing, suffreth hym to shew himself to them for their more discomfort, in some feareful figure & terrible likenes: by the beholding wherof thei conceiue

---

4–6 *Sidenote 1557:* The deuils temptacions at the tyme of death   17 *Sidenote 1557:* Burying   21 should] shovld *1557*   28 *Sidenote 1557:* Wicked sinners

somtime dispaire of saluacion, & yeld themself as captiues quick,
beginning their hel in this world, as hath appeared by ye wordes
& wretched behaueor of many, y^t of a shameful sinful life, haue
died & departed w^t heuy desperate death. Nowe death being
5   such as I haue described, or rather much more horrible then any
man can describe, it is not to be doubted, but if we besily re-
membred ye terror & grief therof, it must nedes be so bitter to y^e
fleshlye mind, y^t it could not faile to take away ye vain delite of al
worldly vanities. But ye thing y^t letteth vs to consider deth in his
10 kind, & to take great profit y^t wold arise of the remembrance
thereof, is that for by the hope of long life, we looke vppon
death, either so far of that we se him not at al, or but a sleight &
vncertain sight, as a man maye see a thing so far of, that he
woteth not whither it be a bushe or a beast. And surely so fare we
15 by death, lokyng there at a far of, through a gret long space of as
manye yeares as we hope to liue. And those we imagine manye,
and perilously and folily beguile oure selfe. For likewise as wiues
would their husbandes shoulde wene by thexaumple of Sara,
that there wer no woman so olde but she might haue a childe, so
20 is there none olde man so olde, but that as Tully saith he trusteth
to liue one yere yet. And as for yong folk, they loke not how many
be dead in theyr owne dayes yonger than themselfe, but who is y^e
oldest manne in the towne, & vpon his yeares thei make their
reckening. Where the wiser way wer to recken, that a yonge man
25 may die soone, and an olde manne cannot liue long, but within a
litle while die the tone may, the tother muste. And with this
reckening shal thei loke vpon death muche nerer hande, & bet-
ter parceiue him in his owne likenes, & therby take the more fruit
of the remembrance and make themself the more ready therto.
30   Thou wouldest somewhat remember death ye more effec-
tually, and loke vpon him somwhat the more nerely, yf thou
knewest thy self sick, & specially of anye perilous sicknes y^t wold
make an end of thee, though thou feltest yet little payne. For
comonly when we be sick, then begin we to know our self, than
35 paine bringeth vs home, than we think how meri a thing it wer to

---

9–10 *Sidenote 1557:* Let from the consederacion of death   18 *Sidenote 1557:* Sara
20 *Sidenote 1557:* Tully   25 *Sidenote 1557:* An olde man cannot liue long   28 fruit]
fruit, *1557*   32 *Sidenote 1557:* Remembraunce of death by sicknes

be praying in health, which we cannot now do for grief. Than
care we litle for our gay gere, than desire we no delicate deinties.
And as for lady Lechery than abhorre we to think on. And than
we think in our self, that if euer we recouer & mend in body, we
wil amend in soul, leaue al vices & be vertuouslye occupied the   5
remenaunt of our life. In so much y^t very true we fynde the
wordes of the pistle, that the wel learned man Plinius Secundus
after his sicknes wrote vnto his frende, wherin after the descrip-
cion of mens fantasies in their disease, he closeth vp his letter in
this wyse, loke (saith he) all the good counsell and preceptes y^t 10
[e$_8$v] al the phylosophers and wise men in this world geue vs for
instruccion of vertuous liuing, al that can I compendiously geue
to my self and thee in few woordes. No more lo, but let vs bee
such whan we be whole, as we thinke we will bee whan we be
sicke.   15

Nowe than if thou be euer sicke, and euer sicke of a perilous
sickenes, wouldest thou not if thou knewest thy self in suche case,
haue better remembraunce of death than thou haste? It woulde
bee hard paraduenture to make thee beleue thy self sick whyle
thou felest no harme, and yet is that no sure knoweledge of   20
health. Trowe ye not that many a man is infect with the great
sicknes, a good while ere he perceyue it, and the bodye sore
corrupt within ere he fele the grief? How many men haue there
bene, that haue gone aboute with goddes markes on their body,
neuer perceiuing themselfe to be sicke, but as mery as euer thei   25
wer in their liues, till other men gaue them warning how nere
thei wer their dethes? And therfore neuer recken thy self hole
though thou fele no grief.

But thou wilt happely saie, be it that I cannot surely recken my
self whole, yet ye shew me not why I should recken my self sicke.   30
Thou sayest right wel, & that shall I shewe thee now. Tell me yf
one were in case that he muste bee fayne once or twise a day to
swaddle and plaster his legge, and els he could not kepe his life,
wouldest thou recken his legge sicke or whole? I wene ye will
agre that his legge is not well at ease, nor the owner neither. Now   35
if ye felt your belly in suche case, that ye must be fayne al daye to

---

7 *Sidenote 1557:* Plinius secundus   16 *Sidenote 1557:* Euer sick

tende it with warme clothes, or els ye were not able to abide the
payne, would ye recken your belly sicke or whole? I wene ye
would recken your belly not in good quart. If thou shouldest see
one in suche case, that he could not hold vp his head, that he
5   coulde not stande on hys fete, that he should be fayne to lye
down a long, and there lye specheles as a dead stock an houre or
two euery day, wouldest thou not say that he wer perilously sicke,
and had good cause to remember death, whan he lyeth euery
daye in such case as though he were dead already?

10   Now than I pray thee consider me, y^t all oure bodies be euer in
suche case, so tender of themselfe, that excepte we lapped them
continually w^t warme clothes, we were not hable to lyue one
winter weke. Consider that our bodies haue so sore a sickenes
and such a continual consumpcion in themselfe, that the strong-
15   est wer not hable to endure and continue .x daies together, wer it
not y^t once or twise a day, we be fayne to take medicines inwarde
to cloute them vp with al, & kepe them as longe as we can. For
what is our meate and drinke, but medicines agaynst hunger and
thyrst, that geue vs warnyng of that we daily lese by our inwarde
20   consumpcion? And of that consumpcion shal we dye in conclu-
sion, for al the medicines that we vse, though neuer other sicke-
nes came at vs.

Consider also that al our swadlynge and tending with warme
clothes, and dayly medicines, yet can our bodyes not beare them-
25   self, but that almost half our tyme euer in .xxiiii. houres we be
fayne to fal in a swowne whiche we cal slepe, and there lye like
dead stockes by a long space or we come to our selfe again: in so
much that among al wise men of old, it is agreed that slepe is the
very ymage of death.

30   Nowe thou wilt paraduenture saie, that this is but a fantasie.
For thoughe we call this hunger sickenes, and meat a medicine,
yet men knowe wel inough what very sickenes is, and what verye
medicines be, and therby we know wel inough that they be none.

If thou thinke this, than wold I wit of thee what thou callest a

---

sickenes. Is not that a sickenes that will make an end of thee if it be not holpen? If that be so, than I suppose thou bearest euer thy sickenes with thee. For very sure arte thou, that it wil make an ende of thee yf thou be not holpen.

What callest thou than a medicine? is it not suche a thing, as 5 either applied outwardely to thy body, or receiued inwarde, shall preserue thee against that sore or sickenes that els would put thee or some part of thee in peril? What can be than more properly and more verely a medicine, than is our meat and drink, by which is resisted the peril & vndoubted death, that els should in 10 so few daies folow, by the inward sicknes of our own nature, continually consuming vs w^{t}in? For as for that ye recken that we know which be sicknesses, that is but a custom of calling, by which we call no sicknes by that name, but such as be casual and come and goe. For that that is comen to al men, and neuer from 15 any manne, because we recken it naturall, we geue it not the name of sickenes, but we name [fg$_1$] sickenes, a passion y^t commeth seldomer, & as we recken against nature, where as the conflict of the diuers qualifyed elementes tempered in our body, continually laboring ech to vanquish other, & thereby to dissolue 20 the whole, though it be as sore against the continuance of our nature, & as sore laboreth to the dissolucion of ye whole body as other sicknes do, yet we neither cal it sicknes, nor the meat y^t resisteth it we cal no medicin, & that for none other cause, but for the continuall familiaritie that we haue therewith. 25

But now consider if it wer so, that one whole country wer born al lepers, which is a sicknes rather foule & perilous than painful, or al an whole country borne w^t ye falling sickness, so y^t neuer any of them had euer in their liues knowen or herd, either themself or any other voyd of those disseases, trow ye y^t than that they 30 wolde euer have reckened them for sicknes? Nay surely, but thei would haue counted for sicknes, ye colike & the stone, & such other like as come and go. But as for their lepry & falling euill, thei would neuer account it, other than we account hunger or slepe. For as for y^t that thy hunger doth thee pleasure whan it is 35

---

1 *Sidenote 1557:* Sickenes   5 *Sidenote 1557:* Medicine   12 w^{t}in?] w^{t}in. *1557*

fed, so dothe somtime the ytch of a sore leg, whan thou clawest
about the brinkes.

And thus maist thou surely se, that al our whole life is but a
sicknes neuer curable, but as one vncurable canker, w^t continual
5 swadeling & plastring, botched vp to liue as long as we may, & in
conclusion vndoutedly to dye of ye same sicknes, & thoughe
there neuer came other.

So that if thou consider this well, thou maist loke vpon deth,
not as a stranger, but as a nigh neibour. For as the flame is next
10 the smoke, so is deth nexte an vncurable sicknes, and such is al
our lyfe.

And yet if this moue you litle, but y^t ye think for al this y^t deth is
far from you, I wil go somwhat nere you. Thou recknest euery
man nere his death whan he is dying. Than if thy self be now
15 alredy dying, how canst thou recken thy self far fro deth?

Some man saith merely to his felow, be mery manne, thou shalt
neuer dye as long as thou liuest. And albeit he seme to say true,
yet saith he more than he can make good. For if y^t wer true, I
could make him much merier, for than he shold neuer die.

20 Ye wil paraduenture meruel of thys, but it is ethe to proffe. For
I thinke ye wil grant me, y^t there is no time after y^t a man hath
once life, but he is eyther alyue or dead. Than wil there no man
say y^t one can dye, either before he geat lyfe, or after y^t he hath
loste it, & so hath hee no time left to die in, but while he hath life.
25 Wherfore if we neither dye before oure life, nor whan we be
dead alredy, nedes muste it folowe, that we neuer dye but while
we liue.

It is not all one to dye, and to be dead. Trouth it is y^t we be
neuer dead, whyle we liue. And it is me seemeth as trewe, not
30 only y^t we dye while we liue, but also y^t we dye al the while we
lyue. What thing is dying? is it ani other thing, than ye passage &
going out of this present life?

Now tel me than if thou wer going out of an howse whither arte
thou goynge out onely whan thy fote is on ye vttermost ynch of
35 the threshold thy body halfe out of the doore, or else whan thou

---

4 *Sidenote 1557:* Our lyfe a continual sicknes   9 *Sidenote 1557:* Death, a nigh neybour
30 *Sidenote 1557:* We dye al the while we liue   32 life?] life. *1557*

beginnest to set the firste foote forward to goe out, in what place
of the house so euer ye stand whan ye buskle forward? I wold say
y^t ye be going out of the house, from the first fote ye set forwarde
to go forth. No man will think other as I suppose, but al is one
reason in going hence and comming hither. Now if one wer   5
comming hither to this towne, he were not only comming hither
while he wer entring in at ye gate, but al ye way also fro whence he
came hitherward. Nor in lyke wyse in goyng hence fro this town,
a man is not onely goyng fro this towne, whyle he hath his body in
the gate goyng outwarde, but also whyle he setteth his fote out of   10
his hostes house to go forwarde. And therfore if a man met him
by ye way, far yet within the town, and asked hym whither he wer
going he should truelye answer, y^t he wer goying out of ye towne,
al wer the towne so long that he had ten mile to go ere he came at
the gate.   15

And surely me thinketh y^t in likewise, a man is not only dying,
that is to say going in his way oute of this life, while he lyeth
drawyng on, but also al the while that he is going toward his
ende: which is by al the whole time of his life, since ye first
momente til the laste finished, that is to wit sithe the first moment   20
in which he began to lyue, vntill the last moment of his life, or
rather the first in which he is ful dead.

Nowe if this be thus, as me semeth y^t reason proueth: a man is
alwaye dying from afore his birth: and euery houre of our age as
it passeth by, cutteth his own length out of our life, & maketh it   25
shorter by so muche, and our death so much the nerer. Whiche
measuryng of time and [fg$_1$v] minishing of life, with approchyng
toward deth, is nothing els but from our beginning to our end-
ing, one contynual dying: so that wake we, slepe we, eate we,
drink wee, morne wee, syng wee, in what wise so euer liue we, all   30
the same while die we.

So that we neuer ought to loke toward deth, as a thing farre of,
considring y^t although he made no hast toward vs, yet we neuer
cease our self to make hast toward him.

Now if thou think this reson but a sophisticall sotiltie, & think-   35
est while thou art a yong man, thou maist for al this, think thy

---

8 lyke wyse] lykewyse

death far of, that is to wit as far as thou hast by likelihode of nature many yeres to liue, than wil I put thee an homely example, not very pleasant, but nathles very true, and very fit for the matter.

5   If there wer two both condemned to deth, both caried out at ons toward execucion: of which two ye tone wer sure y^t the place of his execucion were w^tin one mile, ye tother .xx. mile of, ye an hundred & ye wil, he y^t were in the cart to be caried an .C. mile, wold not take much more plesure, than his felow in the length of
10 his waye, notwithstanding y^t it were .C. times as long as his felowes, & that he had therby C. times as long to liue, beinge sure and out of al question to dye at the ende.

Recken me now your self a yong man in your best luste .xx. yere of age if ye will. Let there be another .lxxxx. both must ye
15 die, both be ye in ye cart carying forward. His galowes & death standeth within .x. mile at ye farthest, & yours w^tin .lxxx. I se not why ye should recken muche lesse of your deth then he, though your waye bee lenger, synne ye bee sure ye shall neuer cease riding til ye come at it.

20 And this is true, although ye wer sure that the place of your execucion stode so farre beyond his.

But what if there were to the place of your execucion two waies, of which the tone were fourescore mile farther about than your felowes, the tother nerre by v. mile than his: & whan ye wer
25 put in ye cart had warning of both: and thoughe ye wer shewed y^t it wer likely y^t ye shold be caried the lenger way, yet it might hap ye shold go the shorter, & whether ye wer caried the tone or the tother, ye shold neuer know, til ye com to the place: I trow ye could not in this case make much lenger of your life than of your
30 felowes.

Now in this case are we all. For our lord hath not endented w^t vs of ye time. He hath appointed what we may not passe, but not how sone we shal go, nor where nor in what wise. And therfore if y^u wylt consider how litle cause thou hast to recken thy deth so far of, by reson of thi youth, recken how many as yong as thou
35 haue bene slain in ye self same waies in which thou ridest. How

31–32 Sidenote 1557: Iob. 14

many haue bene drouned in ye selfsame waters in which thou
rowest. And thus shalt y^u well see, that y^u haste no cause to looke
vppon thy deth as a thing far of, but a thing vndoubtedlye nigh
thee, & euerwalking with thee. By which not a false imaginacion,
but a veri true contemplacion, thou shalt behold him, & aduise   5
him such as he is, & thereby take occasion to flee vain plesures of
the flesh, that kepe out y^e very plesures of y^e soule.

"Temptacio dyaboli de vana gloria." *Ars Moriendi,* block-book (region of Upper Rhine, c. 1465?)

Of pride

Now sith I haue somewhat layd afore thy face the bodily paines of deth, y^e troubles & vexacions spiritual, that come therewith by thy gostly enemy ye deuil, ye vnrestfull cumbrance of thy fleshly frendes, ye vncertentie of thy self, howe soone this dreadfull time shal come, y^t thou art euer sick of that incurable sicknes, by whiche if none other come, thou shalt yet in fewe yeres vndoutedly die, & yet moreouer y^t thou art alredy dying, & euer hast bene since thou first begannest to liue, let vs now make some profe of this one part of our medicin, how ye remembrance of deth in this fashion considred in his kind, wil work with vs to ye preseruacion of our soules from euery kind of sin: beginning at ye sin y^t is the very hed and rote of al sinnes, that is to wit pride, the mischieuous mother of al maner vice.

I haue sene many vices ere this, y^t at ye first semed far fro pride, & yet wel considred to ye vttermost, it wold wel appere, y^t of y^t rote thei sprang. As for wrathe and enuy, be the knowen children of pride, as rising of an hie estimacion of our self. But what shold seme farther fro pryde than dronken glotonye. And yet shal ye find mo y^t drink themself sow drunk of pride to be called good felowes, than for luste of the drink self. So spredeth this cursed roote of pride his braunches into all other kindes, beside his proper malyce for his own part, not onely in hye mind of fortune, rule, and authoritie, bewtye, wit, strength, lerning, or such other gifts of god, but also ye fals pride of Ipocrites that faine to haue the vertues that they lack: and the perilous pride of them, that [fg₂] for theyr few spotted vertues, not w^tout the mixture of other mortall vices: take themself for quick saintes on earth: proudly iudging ye liues of their euen christen, disdaining other mens vertue, enuying other mens praise, bering implacable anger where they perceue themself not accepted & set by, after the worthines of theyr own estimacion. Which kind of spiritual pride, & therupon folowing enuy & wrath, is so much ye more pestilent, in y^t it carieth w^t it a blindnes almost incurable

---

12 beginning] beginniug *1557*   13–14 *Sidenote 1557:* Pride the mother of al vice
18 *Sidenote 1557:* The children of pride   25 *Sidenote 1557:* Ipocrites   26 *Sidenote
1557:* Spirituall pryde

saue gods gret mercye. For the lechor knoweth he doth nought,
& hath remorse therof. The gloten perceiueth his own faut, &
somtyme thinketh it bestly. The slouthful body misliketh his dul-
nes, & thereby is moued to mend. But this kind of pride, y^t in his
5 own opinion taketh himself for holy, is farthest from al recouery.
For how can he mend his faut y^t taketh it for none, y^t weneth all is
wel y^t he doth himself, & nothing y^t anye man doth els, y^t cou-
ereth his purpose w^t ye pretext of some holy purpose, y^t he wil
neuer begin while he liueth, taketh his enuy for an holy desire, to
10 get before his neybour in vertue, & taketh his wrath & anger for
an holy zele of iustice. And thus whyle he proudly liketh his
vices, he is out all ye way to mend them. In so far forth y^t I surely
think there be some, who had in good faith made the best
marchandise y^t euer they made in theyr liues for theyr owne
15 soules, if they had changed those spiritual vices, of pride,
wrathe, & enuy, for the beastly carnal sinnes of glotony, slouth, &
lechery. Not that these thre wer good, which be vndoutedly dam-
nable, but for y^t like as god said in thapocalips vnto ye churche of
Laodice. Thou arte neyther hote nor cold but luke warme, I
20 would thou were colde y^t thou mighteste waxe warme, signifying
y^t if he wer in open & manifest sinnes, he wold haue more occa-
sion to cal feruently for grace & help, so if these folk had these
carnall sinnes, they could not be ignorant of theyr own fauts. For
as saint Poule saith ye fleshly sinnes be eth to perceiue: & so shold
25 they haue occasion to cal for grace & wax good. Wher now by
theyr pride taking themselfe for good where they be nought,
they bee far from al occasion of amendment, sauing the knock-
yng of our lord, which alway standeth at the dore of mans hert
and knocketh, whome I praye god we maye geue eare vnto and
30 let him in. And one of his good & gracious knockings is, y^e
putting vs in remembrance of deth, which remembrance as I
haue said, let vs se what stede it may stand vs in against this
cursed synne of pride. And surely against this last braunch of
pride, of such as repute themself for holy w^t the disdayn of
35 other, & an inwarde liking of al their spiritual vices, which they

---

18 *Sidenote 1557:* Apoc. 3   23 fauts.] fauts *1557*   24 *Sidenote 1557:* Gala. 5; y^e] (y^e
1557   27–28 *Sidenote 1557:* Apoca. 3. Godde alway knocknnge [*sic*]   30 knock-
ings] knocking *1557*

commend vnto themself, vnder ye cloke & shadow of some kind of vertue, moste hard it is to take remedy by the remembrance of deth, forasmuch as they recken themself therby redy to go strayt to heuen. But yet yf they consider the labor & solicitacion of our gostly enemy the deuill, y^t shal at the time of their death, be busye to destroy the merites & good workes of all theyr life before, & y^t his suttillest crafte, & most venemous dart, & the most for them tauoyd, shalbe vnder ye colour of a faithful hope of heuen, as a thing more than dew to their own holines, to send them wrechedly to ye fire of hel for their sinful & wilful blind presumpcion, I say ye remembrance and consideracion of this perilous point & fereful ieopardy, likely to falle on them at the time of their death, is a right effectuall ointment long before in theyr life to were away the web y^t couereth ye eyen of theyr soules, in suche wise as they cannot w^t a sure sight loke vpon theyr own conscience.

As for al other kindes of pride, risyng of bewty, strength, wit, or cunning, me thinketh y^t the remembrance of deth, may right easily mend it, sithe y^t they bee suche thinges as shal shortly by deth leese al theyr glosse, thowners wote nere how soone.

And as lightly maye there by the same consideracion be cured, the pride of these foolish proude ypocrites, whiche are yet more fooles than they y^t plainly folow the wayes of the worlde & pleasure of theyr body. For they though they go to the deuil therfore, yet somwhat they take therfore. These mad ypocrites bee so mad, y^t where they sink in hel as depe as the tother, yet in reward of al theyr pain taken in this world, they bee content to take ye vain praise of the people, a blast of wind of theyr mouthes, which yet percase praise them not but cal them as they be. And if they do, yet themself here it not often. And sure they be that within short time deth shall stop theyr eares, and the cloddes keuer all the mouthes y^t praise them. Whiche if they wel and aduisedly considered, they would I wene turne theyr appetites fro the laud of sely mortall men, and desyre to deserue their thanke and commendacion of god onely, whose prayse can neuer dye.

Now the hye minde of proud fortune, rule, & authoritye, lord

---

22 *Sidenote 1557:* Ipocrites   28 *Sidenote 1557:* Vain glorye   36 fortune,] fortune *1557; Sidenote 1557:* Ambicion

god how sleight [fg₂v] a thing it wold seme to him, that wolde often & depely remember, yᵗ deth shal shortly take away al this ryalty, & his glorye shal as scripture saith neuer walk with him into his graue: but he yᵗ ouerloketh euery man & no man may be
5   so homelye to come to nere him, but thinketh yᵗ he dothe much for them whom he vouchsafeth to take by the hand or beck vpon, whom so many men drede & fere, so many wait vpon, he shal wᵗin a few yeres, & only god knoweth wᵗin how few dayes, whan deth arresteth him, haue his deinty body turned into stinking
10 carien, be born out of his princely paleys, layd in the ground & there lefte alone, wher euery leud lad wilbe bolde to tread on his hed. Wold not wene ye yᵉ depe consideracion of this sodein chaunge so surely to come, & so shortly to come, withdraw yᵉ wind yᵗ puffeth vs vp in pride, vpon yᵉ solemne sight of worldly
15 worship? If yᵘ sholdest perceue yᵗ one wer ernestly proud of the wering of a gay golden gown, while the lorel playth the lord in a stage playe, woldest yᵘ not laugh at his foly, considering that yᵘ art very sure, yᵗ whan yᵉ play is done, he shal go walke a knaue in his old cote? Now yᵘ thinkest thy selfe wyse ynough whyle yᵘ art
20 proude in thy players garment, & forgettest that whan thy play is done, yᵘ shalt go forth as pore as he. Nor yᵘ remembrest not that thy pageant may happen to be done as sone as hys.

We shal leue thexample of plaies & plaiers, which be to mery for this matter. I shal put the a more ernest ymage of our condi-
25 cion, & that not a fained similitude, but a very true fassion & fygure of oure worshipful estate. Mark this well, for of this thing we be very sure, that olde & yong, man & woman, rich & pore, prince and page, al the while we liue in this world, we be but prisoners, & be wᵗin a sure prison, out of which ther can no man
30 escape. And in worse case be we, than those yᵗ be taken & imprisoned for theft. For thei, albeit their hert heuily harkeneth after yᵉ sessions, yet haue they some hope eyther to breke prison yᵉ while, or to escape there by fauor, or after condemnacion some hope of pardon. But we stand al in other plight, we bee

---

3–4 *Sidenote 1557:* Psal. 4.8 [*sic*]   17 *Sidenote 1557:* A stage playe   29 *Sidenote 1557:* All prisoners   31 harkeneth] harkeneth, *1557*   34 pardon.] pardon *1557*

very sure that we be alredy condemned to deth som one, som
other, none of vs can tel what deth we be demed to, but surely can
we al tel that die we shal. And clerely know we y^t of this deth we
get no maner pardon. For the king by whose hyghe sentence we
be condemned to dye, wold not of this deth pardon his own   5
sonne. As for escaping no man can looke for. The prison is large
and many prisoners in it, but the gailor can lese none, he is so
present in euery place, that we can crepe into no corner out of his
sight. For as holy Dauid saith to this gailor whither shal I go fro
thy spirit, & whither shal I fle fro thy face: as who saith no-   10
whither. There is no remedy therfore, but as condemned folk &
remediles, in this prison of the yerth we driue forth a while, some
bounden to a poste, some wandring abrode, some in the dun-
geon, some in the vpper ward, some bylding them bowers &
making palaces in the prison, some weping, some laughing, some   15
laboring, some playing, some singing, some chidinge, some
fighting, no man almoste remembringe in what case he standeth,
till that sodeynlye nothyng lesse loking for, yong, old, pore &
rych, mery & sad, prince, page, pope and pore soul priest, now
one, now other, some time a gret rable at once, w^tout order,   20
w^tout respect of age or of estate, all striped stark naked & shifted
out in a shete, bee put to deth in diuers wise in some corner of the
same prison, & euen ther throwen in an hole, & ether wormes eat
him vnder ground or crowes aboue. Nowe come foorth ye
proude prisoner, for ywis ye be no better, loke ye neuer so hie,   25
when ye build in y^t prison a palais for your blode, is it not a gret
rialty if it be wel considred? Ye build the tower of Babilon in a
corner of the prison, & be very proud therof: & somtime the
gailor beteth it down again w^t shame. Ye leue your lodging for
your owne blode: & the gailor when ye be dede, setteth a strange   30
prisoner in your building, & thrusteth your blode into some
other caban. Ye be proud of the armes of your auncesters set vp
in the prison: and al your pride is because ye forget that it is a
prison. For if ye toke the mater a right, the place a prison, your

---

1 *Sidenote 1557:* Al condemned to death   9 *Sidenote 1557:* Psal. 138   26 *Sidenote
1557:* Builders   32 *Sidenote 1557:* Armes of ancestrye

self a prisoner condemned to deth, fro which ye cannot escape,
ye wold recken this gere as worshipful, as if a gentleman thefe
when he should goe to Tyburne, wold leue for a memoriall,
tharmes of his auncesters painted on a post in Newgate. Surely I
5   suppose, that if we toke not true fygure for a fantasye, but reck-
ened it as it is in dede, the verye expresse fassion and maner of al
our estate, men wold beare themself not much higher in theyr
hertes, for any rule or authority that they bere in this world,
which they may wel parceyue to bee in deede no better, but one
10 prisoner beryng a rule amonge the remenaunte, as the tapster
dothe in the marshalsye: or at the vttermoste, one so put in trust
w^t the gaylor, that he is half [fg$_3$] an vnder gailor ouer his fel-
owes, till y^e shyryfe and the cart come for him.

Of enuy.

15 $\mathbf{N}$ow let vs se what help we may haue of this medicin against
the sicknes of enuy, which is vndoutedly both a sore torment & a
very consumpcion. For surely enuy is suche a torment, as al the
tyrants in Sicil neuer deuised a sorer. And it so drynketh vp the
moysture of the body, and consumeth the good bloode, so dis-
20 coloreth the face, so defaceth ye bewty, so dysfigureth ye visage
leuing it al bony, leane, pale, & wan, y^t a parson wel set awork w^t
enuy, nedeth none other image of deth, than his own face in a
glasse. This vyce is not onely deuilish, but also very folysh. For
albeit y^t enuy where it may ouer, doth al ye hurt it can, yet sith y^e
25 worse most commonly enuieth ye better, & the febler the strong-
er, it happeth for the more parte, y^t as the fire of the burnyng hyl
of Ethna burneth only it self, so doth the enuious parson, fret,
fume, & burne in his owne hert, w^{t}out ability or power to do the
tother hurt. And litle meruail it is though enuy be an vngracious
30 grafe. For it commeth of an vngracious stocke. It is the first
begotten doughter of pryde, gotten in baste & incest, by the deuil
father of them bothe. For as soone as the deuil hadde brought
out his doughter pryde, w^{t}oute wife of his owne bodye, like as the

---

7 much] mnch *1557*   22 *Sidenote 1557:* The image of deth   31 *Sidenote 1557:* En-
uye the doughter of pryde

venemous spider bringeth forth her cobweb, whan this
poysoned doughter of his had holpen him out of heuen, at the
first sight of Adam and Eue in paradise sette in the way to such
worship, ye deuil anon tooke his owne vnhappy doughter to
wyfe, & vpon pride begat enuy. By whose enticement, he set   5
vpon our fyrst parentes in paradyse, and by pride supplanted
them, and there gaue them so great a fal by theyr owne foly, that
vnto thys daye all their posteritye goe crooked thereof. And
therfore euer since enuy goth forth mournyng at euerye mannes
welfare; more sory of another mannes wealthe, than glad of her   10
owne, of which she taketh no pleasure if other folke fare well
with her. In so farforth that one Publius a Romaine, whan he
sawe one Publius Mutius sad and heauye, whome he knew for an
enuious person, surely (quod he) ether Mutius hath a shrewd
turn himself, or some man els a good turne, notyng that his   15
enuyous nature was as sory of another mannes weale, as of his
owne hurt.

I cannot here, albeit I nothing lesse entende then to meddle
muche with seculare authours in this matter, yet can I not here
holde my hande, fro the puttyng in remembraunce of a certayn   20
fable of Esop, it expresseth so properly ye nature, thaffeccion,
and the rewarde of .ii. capitall vyces, that is to wit enuye and
couityce. Esop therefore as I thynke ye haue heard, fayneth that
one of the paynym goddes came down into earth, and fyndyng
together in a place two men, ye tone enuious, the tother couetise,   25
shewed hymselfe wyllynge to geue eche of them a gyft, but there
should but one of them aske for them both, but loke whatsoeuer
that one that should ask would aske for hymself, the tother
should haue the selfe same thyng doubled. Whan this condicion
was offered, than began there som courtesye betwene the en-   30
uyous and the couetyse, whether of them shoulde aske: for that
wold not ye couetous be brought vnto for nothing, because hym-
self wold haue his felowes request doubled. And whan the en-
uious man saw y^t, he wolde prouide that his felowe should haue

---

1 cobweb,] cobweb *1557*   2 his] his, *1557*   3 sight of] sight *1557*   14 ether Mu-
tius] ether *followed by a one-word gap 1557 (see note)*   21 *Sidenote 1557:* A fable of Esop
of enuye

lytle good of the doublyng of his peticion. And forthwith he
required for his part, that he might haue one of his eyen putte
out. By reson of which requeste, the enuious man lost one eye,
and the couetouse man lost both. Lo such is the wretched appe-
tite of this cursed enuy, redy to run into the fyre, so he may draw
his neybor with him. Which enuy is as I haue said and as saint
Austine sayth, ye doughter of pryde in so farreforth that as this
holy doctor sayeth, strangle the mother & thou destroyest the
doughter. And therfore loke what maner consideracion in the
remembrance of deth, shal bee medicynable against the pesti-
lent swelling sore of pride, the self same consideracions be the
next remedies, against the venemous vice of enuy. For whoso-
euer enuye another it is for some thyng, wherof him self wold be
proude if he had it. Than if such consideracions of deth as we
haue before spoken of in the repressing of pride shold make the
set neither much by those thinges, nor much the more by thy
selfe for them if thy self haddest them, it muste nedes folow, y^t
the self same consideracions shal leue the litle cause to enuye the
selfe same thinges in any other man. For thou woldest not for
shame, that men should think thee so mad to enuy a poore soule,
for playing the lord one night in an en[fg$_3$v]terlude. And also
couldest y^u enuy a perpetual sick man, a man y^t carieth his dethes
wound w^t him, a man that is but a prysoner damned to deth, a
man that is in y^e cart alredy carying forward? For all these
thinges are as I think, made metely probable to the before. It is
also to be considered, y^t syth it is so, y^t men commonly enuy their
betters, the remembraunce of deth shold of reson be a great
remedy ther of. For I suppose yf there wer one right farre aboue
thee, yet thou wouldest not greatly enuy his estate, if y^u
thoughteste that thou myghteste bee his matche the next weke.
And why shouldest thou than enuy him now, whyle thou seest y^t
deth may make you bothe matches the nexte night, & shal
vndoubtedlye within fewe yeres? If it so were that thou knewest a
great Duke, kepyng so great estate and princely port in his
howse, that y^u being a ryght meane manne, haddest in thyne
heart great enuy thereat, and specially at some special daye, in

33–34 *Sidenote 1557:* A similitude

which he kepeth for the mariage of his chylde, a gret honorable
court aboue other times, if thou beyng thereat and, at the syght
of the rialty and honoure shewed hym of all the country about
resorting to hym, whyle they knele & crouche to hym, & at
euerye word barehed bigrace him, if thou sholdest sodeinly be   5
surely advertised, y^t for secret treason lately detected to the king
he shold vndoutedly be taken the morow, his courte al broken vp,
his goodes ceased, his wife put out, his children dysherited, him-
selfe caste in prison, broughte furth & arrayned, the matter out
of question, & he should be condemned, his cote armour re-   10
uersed, his gilt spurres hewen of his heles, himself hanged
drawen and quartered, howe thinkeste thou by thy fayth amyd
thyne enuy, shouldeste thou not sodaynly chaunge into pity?

Surelye so is it, that if we consydered euerye thyng a ryght, and
estemed it after the very nature, not after mennes false oppin-   15
ion, syth we be certayne that deth shal take away all that we enuy
any manne for, and we be vncertain how sone, and yet verye sure
that it shall not be long, we should neuer see cause to enuy anye
manne, but rather to pitye euerye manne: and those moste, that
moste hathe to bee enuyed for, sythe they be those that shortly   20
shall most leese.

Of wrathe.

Let vs now somewhat see, howe this parte of our medycine,   25
that is to wit the remembrance of deth, may cure vs of ye fierce
ragious feuer of wrathe. For wrathe is vndoutedly another
doughter of pryde. For albeit that wrathe sometyme ryseth vpon
a wrong done vs, as harme to oure parson, or losse in our goodes,
which is an occasion geuen vs and often sodein, by reason wher
of the sinne is somwhat lesse grieuous, the rule of reson being
letted for the while by the sodaine brunte of the iniurye not   30
forethought vpon, but commyng vpon vs vnprouided, yet shall
ye fynd that in them whiche haue so turned an euyl custome into
nature, that they seme nowe naturally disposed to wrathe and

---

7 morrow,] morrow *1557*   13 enuy] enny *1557*

waywardnes, the very roote of that vyce is pride, althoughe theyr
maner and behauiour be suche besyde, that folke would lytle
wene it. For goe they neuer so simplye, looke they neuer so lowe-
lye, yet shall ye see them at euerye lyghte occasyon testye. They

5 canne not abyde one merye woorde that towcheth them, thei
canne not beare in reasonynge to bee contraryed, but they frette
and fume yf theyr oppynyon bee not accepted, and theyre in-
uencyon bee not magnyfyed.

Wherof riseth thys waywardnesse? but of a secret rote of set-

10 tyng muche by themselfe, by whyche it goeth to theyre hearte,
whan they see any manne lesse esteme them then they seme
woorthye to themselfe.

Wylt thou also well parceyue that the settynge by oure selfe is
more than halfe the weighte by oure wrathe? Wee shall proue it

15 by them that woulde happelye saye nay. Take me one that reck-
eneth hymselfe for woorshypfull, and looke whether hee shall
not bee muche more wrothe wyth one opprobryouse and re-
bukefull woorde, as knaue parcase or beggar (in whyche is no
greate sclaunder) spoken to hys face by one that hee reckeneth

20 but hys matche or farre vnder hym, than wyth the selfe same
woorde spoke to hym by one that he knoweth and knowlegeth
for a great dele his better.

We see thys poynte confyrmed by al the lawes made among
menne, whiche lawes forasmuch as thaccions of trespas be geuen

25 to reuenge men, not of the wronges only done vnto them in
theyr bodies or theyr goodes, but also of theyre contumelies,
griefes & dispites, wherby they conceyue anye displeasure at
hart, lest in lacke of lawe to doo it for them, they shold in
folowyng theyr yrous affeccion, [fg₄] reuenge themself immod-

30 erately wᵗ theyr own handes, the lawes I saye consydereth, pon-
dereth, and punisheth, the trespasses done to euery manne, not
onelye after the hurte that is done or losse that is taken: but and
if it be such as the party grieued is like to be wrothe with all, the
punyshement is aggreued or mynyshed, made lesse or more,

35 after the difference in degre of woorshippe and reputacion be-

---

1 *Sidenote 1557:* Pride the rote of wrathe   24 *Sidenote 1557:* Accions of trespas
26 contumelies] contnmelies *1557*

twene the parties. And this is the prouision of the lawes almost in euery countrey, and hath bene afore christe was borne. By which it appeareth by a common consent, that a mannes owne estimacion settyng by himself, dysdaynynge to take rebuke of one worse than himself, maketh his wrathe the sorer.   5

For thaswaginge whereof, the lawe contenteth hym with the larger punishment of his offender.

And this so farfoorth, that in Spayn, it is sorer taken, and sorer punished, yf one geue another a drye blowe with his fyst, than yf he draw bloode vppon him with a sweord. The cause is none   10 other but thappeasyng of his minde that is so stricken, for as much as commonly they take themselfe for so very manly men, y^t three strokes with a sweorde coulde not anger one of them so muche, as that it should appere that by a blowe geuen him with a bare hande, anye manne shoulde so recken him for a boy, that he   15 wold not vouchsafe to draw any weapon at him.

So that as I said it wel appeareth by the common confession of the world, expressed and declared by theyr lawes, y^t the pointe and redines that men haue to wax angry, groweth of the secret pryde by which we set ouermuche by our self. And lyke as that   20 kinde of good anger y^t wee cal a good zeale, ryseth of that wee sette as we should do, so muche by oure lord god, that we cannot be but wrothe with them whom we see set so litle by him, that they let not to breake his high commaundementes, so riseth of muche settyng by our self that affeccion of anger, by which we be   25 moued agaynst them w^t yre and disdayne that displease vs, and shew by theyr behauiour, that they sette lesse by vs than our proude heart loketh for. By which though we marke it not, yet in dede we recken our selfe worthye more reuerence than we do god himself only.   30

I doute not but men wyll say nay: & I verely beleue that they thynke nay: and the cause is, for that we parceiue not of what rote the braunches of oure sinnes spryng. But wyl ye see it proued that it is so? Loke whether we be not more angry with our seruantes for the brech of one commaundement of our own,   35

---

8 *Sidenote 1557:* In spayne a drye blowe   21 *Sidenote 1557:* Good anger

than for the breche of gods al tenne: and whither we be not more
wroth with one contumelious or dispiteful worde spoken against
ourself, than with many blasphemous wordes vnreuerentely
spoken of god. And could we trow ye be more moued with yͤ
5 minishyng of our own worship than gods, or loke to haue our
own commaundementes better obeyed than gods, if we dyd not
in dede sette more by our self than him?

And therefore this deadly sore of wrath of which so much
harme groweth, that maketh men vnlike themselfe, yͭ maketh vs
10 lyke woode wulfes or furyes of hell, that driueth vs furth head-
longe vppon sweord poyntes, that maketh vs blindlye run furth
vpon other mens destruccion with our owne ruine, is but a
cursed braunche rising and springyng out of the secrete roote of
pride.

15 And like as it is in phisicke a special thyng necessary, to know
where and in what place of the body lyeth the begynnyng, and as
it wer the fountayn of the sore, fro which the matter is alway
ministred vnto the place where it appereth (for the fountayne
once stopped, yͤ sor shal sone heale of it self, the matter faylyng
20 that fed it, which continuallye resorting fro the fountain to the
place, men may wel daily purge and clense the sore, but they shal
hardely hele it:) lykewise I say fareth it by the sore of the soule, if
we perceue once the rote and digge vp that, we be very sure the
branches be surelye gone. But while the rote remayneth, while
25 we cut of the braunches, we lette wel the growyng and kepe it
somwhat vnder: but fayle they may not alway to spring agayne.

And therefore, sithe this vngracious braunche of wrath,
springeth out of the cursed rote of pryde and settyng muche by
our selfe, so secretly lurkyng in oure hearte, that vnnethe we can
30 parceyue it our selfe, lette vs pull vppe well yͤ roote, and surely
the braunche of wrathe shall soone wither awaye. For taken once
awaye the settyng by oure selfe, wee shall not gretly dote vppon yͭ
we set lyttle by.

So shall there of suche humility contempt and abieccion of our
35 self shortely folow in vs, hye estimacion, honor, and loue of god,

---

8–9 Sidenote 1557: The harmes of wrathe   25 wel the] welt he 1557   29 secretly]
secrtely 1557

and euery other creature in order for his sake, as they shall
appeare [fg₄v] more or lesse liefe vnto him.

And sith yᵗ by the destruccion of pryde, foloweth as I haue said
yᵉ destruccion of wrath, we shal apply to the repression of wrath,
yᵉ selfsame consideracions in yᵉ remembrance of death, yᵗ we   5
before haue shewed to serue to the repression of pryde.

For who coulde be angry for yᵉ losse of goodes, if he well
remembred howe litle while he should kepe them, how sone deth
might take them from him? Who could set so much by himself, to
take to heart a leude rebukeful word spoken to his face, if he   10
remembred himself to be as he is, a pore prisoner damned to
deth: or so very wroth as we be now wᵗ som bodily hurt done vs
vpon some one part of yᵉ body, if we depely remembred that we
be as we bee in dede, already laid in the cart carying toward
execucion.   15

And if the wrechednes of our owne estate nothing moued vs,
whiche beyng such as it is, shold if it wer well pondred, make vs
lytle regard the causes of oure wrath, considring yᵗ all yᵉ whyle
we liue we be but in dying, yet might thestate of him yᵗ we be
wrothe wᵗal, make vs ashamed to be wroth. For who wold not   20
disdain to be wroth wᵗ a wretched prisoner, wᵗ him yᵗ is in the cart
& in yᵉ way to hanging, wᵗ him yᵗ wer a dying. And of thys wold a
man be the more ashamed, yf hee considred in how much peril &
ieopardy of hymself, his own life & his own soule is, while he
striueth chideth and fighteth wᵗ another, & yᵗ oftimes for how   25
very trifles. First shame were it for men to bee wroth like women,
for fantasies & thinges of nought, if ther wer no worse ther in.
And now shal ye se men fall at varyance for kissyng of the pax, or
goyng before in procession, or setting of their wiues pewes in the
church. Doubt ye whether this wrath be pride? I dout not but   30
wise men wil agree, that it is eyther foolyshe pride or proud foly.

How much is it now yᵉ more foly, if we consider yᵗ we be but
going in pilgrimage, & haue here no dwellyng place, than to
chide & fight for such folyes by the way.

How much more shame and folye is it yet, when we be goyng   35
together to oure deth, as we be in dede.

If we should see two men fighting together for very great
thinges, yet wold we recken them both mad, if they lefte not of,
whan they should see a ramping Lyon commyng on them bothe,

redy to deuoure them bothe. Nowe when wee see surely that the
death is comming on vs all, and shall vndoutedly within shorte
space deuoure vs all, and howe soone we know not all, is it not
nowe more than madnes to be wrothe and beare malyce one to
5 another, and for the more part for as very tryfles, as children
shold fall at variaunce for cherystones, death commyng as I say
vpon vs to deuoure vs all?

   If these thinges and such other as thei be very true, so they wer
wel and depely remembred, I litle doubt but they wold both
10 abate the croked branch of wrathe, and pul vp fro the botom of
the hert, the cancred rote of pride.

Of couetise.

L ET vs now somwhat see, what this part of this medicin maye
do to the cure of couetise, which is a sicknes wherein men be very
15 sore deceued. For it maketh folk to seme farre of another sort
than they be in dede. For couetous men seme humble, and yet be
they very proude. They seme wyse, and yet be they very folish.
They seme chrysten, and yet haue no trust in Christ. And which
most marueil is of all, they seme rich, and yet be very beggers,
20 and haue nought of their own.

   As for pride of the possession of theyr goodes, whoso be wel
acquainted wyth them, shal wel parceiue it, how hartelye they
reioyce, where they dare speak and call their betters beggers, if
money bee not so rife w^t them, because they regarde it lesse and
25 spende it more liberally.

   Men wene them wise also, & so thei do them self, because thei
seme to haue prouidence & be folk of foresight, & not to regard
only the time present, but make prouision for time to come. But
than proue thei more foles, than they y^t liue fro hande to
30 mouthe. For they take at the lest wyse some tyme of pleasure w^t
their owne, thoughe they fare harde at another. But these cou-
etous nigardes, while they passe on with pain alway ye time pre-
sent, & alway spare al for their time to come, thus driue thei forth

---

7 all?] all. *1557*   20 their] fheir *1557*   30 some tyme] sometyme *1557*

wrechedly, til al their time be past & none to come. And than whan they lest loke therfore, leue al y^t they haue heaped, to strangers y^t shall neuer can them thanke.

If ye wil say there be no such fooles, I might say y^t I haue sene som such in my time. And if ye beleue not me, I coulde fynd ye record. But to thentent ye shal not denie me, but that there haue bene suche foles of old, ye shal here what Salomon said seuen yere ere I was borne. I haue sene (saith he) another plague vnder the [fg$_5$] sunne, & it is comon among men. A man vnto whom god hath geuen riches, substaunce & honor, so y^t he wanteth nothing y^t hys hert can desire, yet god hath not geuen him leue to eat of it or to enioy it, but a stranger deuoureth. Of suche sort of foles also speaketh y^e psalmist, thus a man disquieteth himself in vayn, & hepeth vp riches, & cannot tel for whom he gathereth them. And in the .xlviii. psalme the prophete expresseth plainely the foly of such foles, for (sayth he) both ye riche & the pore shal dye, & leaue their riches vnto straungers. And surely wher they seme christen, thei haue none earthly trust in Christ. For they be euer afrayd of lack in tyme to come, haue they alredye neuer so much. And me thinketh vtterly on ye tother side, y^t albeit euery man y^t hath children, is bounden by the law of God & of nature to prouide for them, til thei be able at ye lest by ye labor of their handes, to prouide for their belies (for god & nature loketh not as me thinketh muche farther, nor thrust vs not out of ye para-dise of plesure, to make vs loke & long to be lordes in this wreched erth) yet I say me semeth verely, y^t haue we neuer so litle, yf we be not in spirit mery therewith, but liue in puling & whimpering & heuines of hert, to ye discomfort of our self & them y^t are about vs, for feare and drede of lack in tyme to come, it appereth I say playnly, y^t speak we neuer so muche of faith & of truste in Christ, we haue in our heartes neyther more belief in his holy wordes nor trust in his faithful promise, than hath a Iew or a Turke.

Doth not holy scripture say, caste thy thought into god & he shall norishe thee? Why takest y^u thought now in thy self, and fearest to fayle for foode?

Saith not our sauior himself, haue no care for to morowe? And than furnisheth & enforceth his commaundement by ensample, saying, loke vpon the byrdes in ye ayre, they neither sow nor repe, nor gather to no barns, & your heauenly father feedeth them. Are not ye far more excellent then thei? Your father in heuen knoweth y^t ye haue nede of al these thinges. Seke ye fyrste for ye kingdom of heuen & ye iustice of hym, & al these thinges shal be cast vnto you beside. Whosoeuer he be y^t hereth this, and yet puleth & whimpereth for dout & fere of lack in time comming, either he beleueth not y^t Christ spake these wordes (and than beleueth he not ye gospel) or els yf hee beleue y^t Christ spake them, & yet feareth lest he will not kepe them, howe beleueth he Christ or trusteth in his promyse? Thou wilt happely say, that Christ wold not for any trust of him, y^t thou sholdest not prouide for to morow, but loke to be fed by miracle. In this thou sayest true: & therefore he sayd not, prouide not for to morow, nor labor not for to morow. In token wheof he sent the Iewes double Manna, wekely the daye before the sabbaot day, to be prouided for before ye hand. But he said vnto vs, haue none anxietie nor care of mind for to morow. For the mind wold christ haue clene discharged of al earthly care, to thende y^t we should in hert, only care & long for heuen. And therefore he sayde: long for first & chiefly the kingdom of heuen, & al these earthly thinges god shall cast vnto vs beside: shewyng therby y^t by ye herty longyng for heuen, we shal haue both twayne.

And surely the thynges comming of ye earth for ye necessary sustenance of man, requireth rather ye labor of ye body than the care of ye mind. But the gettynge of heuen, requireth care, cure, & ardent desire of ye mind, much more than ye laboure of the body, sauing y^t the busy desyre of the mind, can neuer suffer the body to be idle.

Thou wilt happely say, what yf I can not labor, or haue mo small children to find, than my labor of thre dayes, wyll suffice to

---

fede for one day, shal I not than care & take thought how they
shall lyue to morow? or tell what other shift I shal find. First shall
I tel thee what shyfte y^u shalt make in suche case: and after shal I
shew thee, y^t if all shifte fayle thee, yet if thou be a faithfull man,
thou shalt take no thought. I saye if thou lacke, y^u shalte labour to   5
thy power by iuste and trewe busynesse, to geate that thee and
thyne behoueth. If thy laboure suffice not, thou shalte shew thy
state that thou hast lytle money & much charge, to som such men
as haue much money & litle charge: & thei be then bounden of
duety, to supply of theirs y^t the lacketh of thine. What yf they wil   10
not? Than I say y^t yet oughtest thou not to take thought & care in
herte, or dispayre of gods promyse for thy lyuing: but to make
thy self very sure, y^t either god wil prouide thee & thyne meate
by puttyng other menne in the mynde to releue thee, or send
thee meate by miracle (as he hathe in deserte wildernesse sente   15
some menne their meat by a crow) or else his pleasure is that thou
and thine shal liue no lenger but die and depart by famine, as he
wyll that some other dye by sickenes. In whiche case y^u must
willingly w^{t}out grudge or care (which care [fg$_5$v] thou neuer so
sore cannot geat thee a penny the more) conforme thy self to his   20
ordinaunce. For though he hath promised to prouide vs meat,
yet hath he not promysed it for longer tyme than hym lyketh to
let vs liue, to whom we be al dettours of death. And therfore
though he sente Danyell meate ynoughe by Abacuk the proph-
ete into the lake among lions: yet sente he none at al to Lazarus,   25
but let hym dye for famyne at ye rich glotons gate. There dyed he
w^{t}out grudge, without anxietie, with good wyll and glad hope,
whereby he went into Abrahams bosom. Nowe if thou do the
lyke, thou shalt go into a better bosome, into heuen into ye bosom
of our sauior Christ.   30

Nowe if the pore manne that nought hathe, shewe himselfe to
lacke fayth and to haue no trust in Christes wordes, yf he fere
lack of findyng: what faith hath than the couetous wretch, that
hathe ynough for this daye, for to morowe, for this weke, for the
next, for this monethe, for the next, for this yere, for the next, ye   35

---

15 meate] meare *1557*   16 *Sidenote 1557:* 3. Regum. 17   21 ordinaunce] ordi-
nannce *1557*   24 *Sidenote 1557:* Dan. 14   25-26 *Sidenote 1557:* Luk. 16   35
monethe,] monethe *1557*

and paraduenture for many yeres, yerely comming in, of landes,
offices, or merchandise, or other waies, and yet is euer whining,
plaining, morning, for care & feare of lacke many yeres hereaf-
ter for him or his children, as thoughe god eyther would not, or
5   wer not able to kepe his promise with vs. And (whiche is the more
madnes) his care is all for the lyuing of hymself and his children,
for some such time as neither himself nor his children shal hap-
pely liue therto. And so leseth he ye commodity of al his whole
life, w^t the fere of lack of liuing when he is dead.
10 Now if he hap to haue a great losse, in what heuines falleth he
than? For if he had tenne thousand pounde, and therof had
eight thousande taken from him, he would wepe and wene he
wer vndone. And yet if he had neuer hadde but one, hee woulde
haue thoughte hym selfe a greate ryche manne, where now for
15 the losse of eight, twain can do him no plesure.
Whereof riseth thys hygh follye, but of the blynde couetous
affeccion that he had to that he lost. If he had had it styll, yet he
wold paraduenture not haue occupied it: for this y^t is left, is
more than he wil spend, or happely shal nede to spende.
20 If ye would haue spent it wel, ye haue no cause to be sory of the
losse, for godde accepteth your good will. If ye woulde haue
kepte it couetouslye or spente it noughtely, ye haue a cause to be
gladde, and recken that ye haue wonne by the losse, in that the
matter and occasion of youre synne, is by goddes goodnes gra-
25 ciously taken from you.
But ye wyll saye that ye haue nowe loste of your worshippe,
and shal not be sette by so muche as ye were, when ye were
knowen for so riche. A well I say, nowe ye comme home loe. Me
thoughte alway that ye couetous niggarde, how lowlye so euer ye
30 loked, would if ye wer well serched, proue your selfe proud and
highe harted. For surely make they neuer so meke and humble
countenaunce, they haue muche pride in the mind, and putte
their truste in theyr goodes, making theyr good their god. Which
thing is the cause that our sauiour Christ said it were as harde for
35 the riche manne to come into heauen, as a great cable or a Camel

---

14 haue] hane *1557*   32 *Sidenote 1557:* Couetous men be proude   34 *Sidenote*
1557: Mathewe. 19 Mar. 10 Luk. 18

to go through a nedles eye. For it is not sinne to haue riches, but to loue riches.

If riches come to you, set not your hert theron saith holy scripture. He that setteth not his hearte thereon, nor casteth not his loue theron, reckeneth as it is in dede, himself not the richer by them, nor those goodes not his owne, but delyuered hym by god to be faythfully disposed vpon himselfe and other: and that of the disposicion he must geue the reckening. And therefore as he reckeneth hymselfe neuer ye richer, so is he neuer ye prouder.

But he y^t forgetteth his goodes to be ye goodes of god, & of a disposer, reckeneth himself an owner, he taketh himself for rich. And because he reckeneth the riches his own, he casteth a loue therto, & so muche is his loue the lesse set vnto god. For as holy scripture saith, wher thy tresure is ther is thyne heart: where if y^u dydst recken ye tresure not thine, but the tresure of god de-liuered the to dispose & bestow, thy tresure shold be in erth & thy hert in heuen.

But these couetous folk that set theyr heartes on theyr hordes, and be proude when they loke on their heapes, thei recken themself rich, & be in dede very wreched beggers: those I mene y^t be ful christened in couetise, y^t haue al ye properties belonging to y^t name, y^t is to wit, y^t be as loth to spend ought, as thei be glad to get al. For thei not only part nothing liberally w^t other folk, but also liue wrechedly by sparing from themself. And so thei recken themselfe owners, & be in dede but ye bare kepers of other mens goodes. For sith they find in their hert to spend nothing vpon themself, but kepe al for their executors, they make it euen now not their own while they vse it [fg6] not, but other mens for whose vse and behoofe thei kepe it. But now let vs see as I said before, how the remembrance of deth may quicken mens eyen, againste this blind foly of couetice. For surely it is an hard sore to cure: it is so mad, y^t it is much work to make any good counsell sink into the hert. Wilt y^u see it proued? loke vpon the yong man whom Christ him self councelled, to sel y^t he had & geue it to pore folk, & come & folow him. He clawed his hed & went his way heuily,

5

10

15

20

25

30

35

---

4 *Sidenote 1557:* Psal. 61   14 *Sidenote 1557:* Math. 6   16 bestow,] bestow *1557*
33 *Sidenote 1557:* Mathewe. 19 Mar. 10 Luk. 18

because he was riche: whereas saint Peter & other holy apostles, at the first call left theyre nets, which was in effect al y^t they had, & folowed him. Thei had no gret things wherupon they had set theyr heartes to holde them backe. But and if theyr hertes had

5   bene sore set vppon righte small thinges, it wold haue bene a great let.

And no maruaile thoughe couetous be hard to hele. For it is not ethe to find a good tyme to geue them counsel. As for ye gloten is redy to here of temperance, ye & to preach also of

10   fasting himself, when his bely is wel filled. The lecherous, after his foule plesure past, may suffer to here of contynence, and abhorreth almost ye tother by himself. But the couetous man because he neuer ceaseth to dote vpon his good, and is euer alyke gredy therupon, who so geueth him aduise to be liberall, semeth

15   to preach to a gloton for fasting, when his bely is empty & gapeth for good meat: or to a lusty lechour, when his leman is lately light in his lap. Scantly can deth cure them when he commeth.

I remember me of a thefe once cast at Newgate, that cut a purse at the barre when he shold be hanged on the morow. And

20   when he was asked why he dyd so, knowing that he shoold dye so shortelye, the desperate wretche sayd, that it didde his heart good, to be lorde of that purse, one nyght yet. And in good faythe me thynketh as muche as wee wonder at hym, yet se we many that do much like, of whom we nothynge wonder at all. I

25   let passe olde priestes that sewe for vowsons of yonger priestes benefices. I let passe olde men that houe and gape to be execu- tours to some that be yonger than themself: whose goodes if thei wold fal, they recken wold do them good to haue in their keping yet one yere ere they dye.

30   But loke if ye see not some wretches y^t scant can crepe for age, his hed hanging in his bosom, and his body croked, walk pit pat vpon a paire of patens wyth the staffe in the tone hande and the *pater noster* in the tother hande, the tone fote almost in the graue already, and yet neuer the more hast to part with any thynge, nor

35   to restore that he hathe euyl gotten, but as gredy to geat a grote

---

33 *noster*] *noste* 1557

by the begiling of his neybour, as if he had of certaynty seuen
score yere to liue.

The man that is pore blinde, cannot see far from hym. And as
to loke on deth we be for the most part pore blinde all ye mayny:
for we cannot see hym til he come very nere vs. But these folk   5
be not pore blynde but starke blynde: for they cannot see him
when he commeth so nere, y^t hee putteth almoste his finger in
theyr eye.

Sure the cause is, for that thei willingly wink, & liste not to loke
at him. They be loth to remember deth, loth to put thys oynt-   10
ment on theyr eyen. Thys water is somewhat pricking, and
woulde make theyr eyen water, and therefore they refuse it. But
surely if they would vse it, if they woulde as aduisedlye remem-
ber deth, as they vnaduisedly forgeat hym, thei should sone see
theyr foly, & shake of theyr couetise. For vndoutedly, if they wold   15
consider depely how sone thei may, ye and how sone they must,
lese all that they labor for, they would shortly cease theyr
busines, & would neuer be so mad, gredily to gather together
that other men shal merely sone after scatter abrode.

If they thought howe soone in what painefull plight they shall   20
lye a dying, while theyr executours afore their face ransake vp
theyr sackes, they woulde I wene shortly empty theyr sackes
themselues. And if they doute how farre that deth is from them,
let them here what Christ saith in the ghospell to the ryche
couetous gatherer, y^t thoughte to make his barnes and his ware-   25
houses larger to laye in the more, because he reckened in himself
to lyue and make mery many yeres: and it was sayde vnto hym:
thou foole this nyghte shall they take thy soule fro thee: and than
these thynges that thou haste gathered, whose shall they bee.
And holye Sayncte Barnarde sayth, that it may be sayd vnto hym   30
farther, thou that hast gathered them, whose shalt thou be?

If wee woulde well aduyse vs vppon this poynte, and remem-
ber the paynefull peryll of deathe, that we shal so sone come to,
and that of all that we gather, we shall cary nothing with vs, it
would cause vs to consider, y^t this couetous gathering & nigar-   35

27–28 *Sidenote 1557:* Luk. 12

dous keping, with al the delyte y^t we take in the behol[fg$_6$v]dyng
of our substance, is in al oure lyfe but a very gay golden dreame,
in which we dreame that we haue great riches, & in y^e slepe of
this life we be glad & proude therof. But whan death shal once

5   waken vs, our gay golden dreame shal vanish, & of al the tresure
y^t we so merely dremed of, we shal not (as the holy prophet saith)
find one peny left in our handes. Which if we forgate not, but wel
and effectually remembred, we woulde in tyme caste couetise
out of our hedes, & leauyng lytle busines for our executours

10 after our deth, not fayle to dispose and distrybute our substance
with our owne handes.

If thou knewest very certaynlye, that after all thy good gath-
ered together, y^u shouldest be sodainly robbed of al together,
thou woldest I wene haue litle ioy to labor and toyle for so

15 muche, but rather as y^u sholdest happen to get it, so woldest thou
wysely bestow it there as nede wer, & where thou mightest haue
thank therfore: & on them specially y^t wer likely to help the w^t
theirs when thyne wer al gone. But it is so, that thou art of
nothing so sure, as y^t deth shall bereue thee of al y^t euer thou

20 hepest, & leue the scante a shete. Which thyng if we dyd as well
remember, as we wel know, we shold not faile to labor lesse for y^t
we shal so lese, & wold put into pore mens purses our money to
kepe, y^t deth the cruell thefe, shold not finde it about vs, but they
should releue vs therwith when the remenaunte wer bereft vs.

Of glotony.

25 N ow haue we to consider, howe this part of our medicyn, that
is to wit the remembrance of deth, may bee applied to the cure
and helpe of glotony, which is a beastly sicknes & an old sore. For
this was in the beginning ioyned with pride in oure mother Eue:

30 who besyde the proud appetite y^t she had to bee by knoweledge
made in maner a goddes, yet toke she such delyte also in y^e
beholdyng of ye apple, y^t she longed to fele the tast. And so
entred death at the wyndowes of our own eyen into the house of

---

2 *Sidenote 1557:* A golden dreme   6–7 *Sidenote 1557:* Psal. 48   13 al together] al-
together *1557*

our hert, & there burned vp al the goodly building, that god had
wrought therin. And surely so falleth it daylye, y^t the eye is not
only ye coke & the tapster, to bring the rauenous appetite of
dilicate meate & drink into the bellye (so farforth y^t men com-
monly say, it wer better fil his bely than his eye, & many men   5
mind it not at al til thei se ye meat on ye bord) but ye eye is also the
baud, to bring the hert to ye desyre of the foule bestly pleasure
benethe the bely. For when the eye immoderatelye deliteth in
long loking of the beutuous face, w^t the white neck & round
pappes, & so forth as far as it findeth no let, the deuil helpeth the   10
herte to frame and forme, in the fantasye by foule imaginacions,
all that euer the clothes couer. And y^t in such excellente fashion,
as the mynde is more kindled in the fained figure of his own de-
uyse, than it shold happely bee, if the eye saw the body belly
naked such as it is in dede. And therfore saith ye holy prophet.   15
Turn away thine eyen fro ye beholding of vanities. Now as I
began to say, sith it is so that this olde sore of glotony, was the vice
& sin by whiche our forefathers eating ye forbidden fruit, fel
from the felicitie of paradise, & from their immortality into
deth, & into ye misery of this wretched worlde, well ought we to   20
hate & abhorre it, although there sholde now no new harme
grow therof. But so is it now, that so muche harme dayly groweth
therof new, not to ye soul only, but to the body also, y^t if we loue
ether other, we se gret cause to haue it in hatred & abominacion,
though it had neuer done vs hurt of old. For hard it is to say   25
whither this vice be more pestilent to ye body or to ye soul: surely
very pestilent to both. And as to the soul no man douteth howe
deadly it is. For sithe the body rebelleth alway against the spirite,
what can bee more venomous & mortal to the soul, than gor-
belyed glotony, which so pampereth ye body, y^t the soul can haue   30
no rule thereof, but carieth it furth like an headstronge hors, til
he haue caste his mayster in the mire. And if the corruptible
body be (as the wiseman saith) burdenous to ye soule: w^t what a
burden chargeth he the soule, y^t so pampereth his paunch, y^t he

---

2–3 *Sidenote 1557:* The wyckednes of the eye   14 it] if it *1557*   15–16 *Sidenote*
1557: Psal. 118   28–29 *Sidenote 1557:* Gala. 5   29–30 *Sidenote 1557:* Gorbelied
glotonye   33–34 *Sidenote 1557:* Sapi, 9

is scant able to bere yᵉ burden of his own bely, though it wer taken
fro yᵉ place, & layd vpon hys back. If the body be to the soule a
prison, how strayt a prison maketh he the body, yᵗ stuffeth it so
full of rif raf, yᵗ the soule can haue no rome to stirre it self, but as
5 one wer so set hand & fote in a strayte stockes, yᵗ he can neither
stand vp nor lye down, so the soule is so stifled in suche a stuffed
body, that it can nothyng wield it self, in doyng of any good
spirituall thynge that appertayneth vnto his part, but is as it were
enclosed, not in a prison but in a graue, dead in maner all redy,
10 for anye good operacion that thunwieldye body can suffer it to
do. And yet is glotony to the soule, not so pernicious and [fg₇]
pestilent for the hurt it doth it self, as for the harme and destruc-
cion that is done by such other vyces as commonly come theron.
For no man douteth, but slouth and lechery be the verye dough-
15 ters of glotony. And then nedes must it be a deadlye enemy to yᵉ
soule, yᵗ bringeth foorth two such doughters, of which eyther
one killeth the soule eternally, I meane not the substaunce of the
soule, but the wealth & felicitie of the soule, wᵗout which it wer
better neuer to haue bene borne. What good can the great gloton
20 do wᵗ his bely standing a strote, like a taber, & his noll toty with
drink, but balk vp his brewes in yᵉ middes of his matters, or lye
down and slepe like a swine. And who douteth but yᵗ the body
dilicately fed, maketh as yᵉ rumour saith an vnchast bed. Men
are wont to write a short rydle on yᵉ wal yᵗ, D. C. hath no .P. Rede
25 ye this rydle I cannot: but I haue hard say, yᵗ it toucheth yᵉ
redines yᵗ woman hath to fleshly filth, if she fal in dronkenes.
And if ye fynde one that can declare it, thoughe it be no greate
authoritie, yet haue I heard saye that it is very true.

Of our gloton festes, foloweth not only slouth & lechery, but
30 often times leud and perilous talking, fole hardines, backbiting,
debate, variance, chiding, wrath, & fighting, wᵗ redines to al
maner myschief running to ruine for lack of circumspeccion,
which can neuer bee wᵗout sobernes. The holy scripture rehear-
seth, yᵗ in desert yᵉ children of Israel when they had sitten down

---

2–3 *Sidenote 1557:* The body, a prison to the soul   14 *Sidenote 1557:* Slouth & lech-
erye the doughters of glotony   25 toucheth] toucheh *1557*   29 *Sidenote 1557:* In-
conueniences folowing gloton festes   33–34 *Sidenote 1557:* Exod. 32

& wel eaten & dronken, then roose they vp & playd yᵉ ydolaters, whereof by thoccasion of glotony, yᵉ wrath of god fell vpon them. Holy Job, when his children fel to feasting, fered so gretlye yᵗ thoccasion of glotony shold in theyr festes make them fal into folish talking, and blasphemy, that while they wer about theyr festes, he fel to praier & sacrifice, yᵗ god mygnte at his praier send them grace so to make good chere, yᵗ they fell not in yᵉ vices vsually commyng of glotony. Now to yᵉ body what sin is so noyous? what sin so shameful? Is it not a bestly thing to se a man yᵗ hath reson, so to rule himselfe that his fete may not beare him? but when he commeth out he weneth yᵗ the skie wold fall on his hed? & there royleth & releth till he fal downe yᵉ canel, & there lye down tyll he be taken vp and born to bed as a corps wer born in bere? And in good fayth in my minde much wrong is there done him yᵗ any man presumeth to take him vp, and that he is not suffred to take his ease all night at his pleasure in the kynges hye way that is free for euerye man.

Wonder it is yᵗ the worlde is so mad, that we had leuer take sinne with pain, than vertue with pleasure. For as I said in yᵉ beginning and often shal I say, vertue bringeth his plesure, and vice is not wᵗout pain. And yet speake I not of the world to come, but of the life present. If vertue wer al painfull, and vice al pleasant, yet sith deth shal shortly finish both yᵉ pain of the tone and the pleasure of the tother, gret madnes wer it, if we would not rather take a short pain for the winning of euerlasting plea- sure, than a short plesure for the winning of euerlastyng pain. But now if it be true as it is in dede, that our sin is painful and our vertue pleasant, how much is it than a more madnes, to take sinnefull paine in thys world, that shal win vs eternal pain in hell, rather than pleasant vertue in this world, that shal win vs eternall plesure in heauen?

If thou wene that I teach thee wrong, when I say that in vertue is plesure and in sin is pain, I might preue it by many plain textes of holy scripture, as by the wordes of the psalmist where he saith, I haue had as gret plesure in yᵉ way of thy testimonies, as in all

---

2–3 *Sidenote 1557:* Iob. 1   20 *Sidenote 1557:* Vertue is plesant, Synne is paineful
34 scripture] scripiure *1557*   35 *Sidenote 1557:* Psal. 118

maner of riches. And Salomon saith of vertue thus: her wayes
are al ful of plesure, & her pathes are pesable. And further he
saieth, The way of the wicked, is as it were hedged w^t thornes:
but the way of the righteous is without stumbling. And we be
5 weried (shal the wretches say) in the waye of wickednes, we haue
walked in hard and comberous waies: and the wise man saith,
The way of the sinners is set or layd w^t stones, but in the end is hel
darknes and paynes. But to tell vs worldly wretches the wordes of
holy wrytte, is but a dul profe. For our bestly taste sauoreth not
10 the swetenes of heauenly thynges. And as for experience, we can
none geat of the tone parte, that is to wit the pleasure that is in
vertue. The tother parte we cannot perceue for bitter, for the
corrupcion of our custome, wherby sowre semeth vs swete. But
yet if we woold consider our sinne wel, with the dependants
15 therupon, we shold not faile to perceiue the painful bitternes of
our walue swete sin. For no man is so mad y^t will recken that
thing for pleasant, y^t hath with litle plesure much pain. For so
might we call a man of Inde white, because of his whit teeth.
[fg$_7$v] Now if thou shouldest for a litle ytche, claw thy self sod-
20 einly depe into y^e flesh, y^u wouldest not cal thy clawing pleasant,
though it liked thee a litle in y^e beginning. But so is it, y^t for y^e litle
ytching pleasure of sin, we claw our self sodenly to y^e hard bones,
& win therby not a litle pain, but an intollerable torment. Which
thyng I might proue beginning at pride in euery kinde of sin,
25 sauing that the degression would be ouer long. For thabridgynge
wherof, let vs consider it but in the selfe same sinne that we haue
in hand.

    The pleasure that the gloton hathe in his viand, can be no
lenger any very plesure, than whyle it is ioyned with hunger, that
30 is to say with payn. For ye very pleasure of eatyng, is but the
minishing of his payn in hungryng. Now all that euer is eaten
after, in which glotony beginneth, is in effecte paine altogether.
And than the head aketh, & the stomake knaweth, and the next
meale is eaten w^{t}out appetite, with gorge vppon gorge & grif

---

1–2 *Sidenote 1557:* Prou. 3   2–3 *Sidenote 1557:* Prou. 15   4–5 *Sidenote 1557:*
Sapi, 5   6–7 *Sidenote 1557:* Eccl. 21   21 beginning.] beginning *1557*   28–
29 *Sidenote 1557:* That glotony is paynefull

vppon grief, til the gorbely be compelled to cast vp al again, and than falle to a rere supper.

If god would neuer punish glotony, yet bringeth it punishment ynoughe, w^t it self: it disfigureth the face, discoloreth the skin, & disfashioneth the body, it maketh the skin tawny, the body fat & fobby, the face drowsy, the nose droppyng, the mouth spetting, the eyen blered, the teth rotten, the breth stinkyng, the hands trimbling, the hed hanging, and the feete totteryng, & finally no part left in right course and frame. And beside the daylye dulnes and grief y^t the vnwieldy body feleth, by the stuffing of his paunch so ful, it bringeth in by leysour, the dropsy, the colike, the stone, the strangury, ye gout, the cramp, the paulesy, the pocks, the pestilence, and the apoplexy, disseases and sicknes of such kinde, y^t either shortly destroy vs, or els y^t worse is, kepe vs in such pain and torment, that the lenger we liue the more wretched we be.

Howbeit very long lasteth no man with the surfets of glotony. For vndoutedly, nature which is sustained with right litle (as wel appered by the olde fathers y^t so many yeres liued in deserte with herbes only & rotes) is very sore oppressed, & in maner ouerwhelmed, with the great weight and burdein of much and diuers viande, and so much laboreth to master the meat, and to deuide and sonderly to sende it into al parties of the bodye, and there to turn it into the like, and retaine it, that she is by the force and great resistence of so muche meate as she hathe to work vpon (of which euery part laboreth to conserue and kepe his owne nature & kind such as it is) foreweried & ouercom & geueth it ouer, except it be holpen by some outward aide. And this driueth vs of necessitie to haue so much recourse to medicins, to pilles, potions, plasters, glisters, and suppositaries: and yet al to lytle, our glotony is so greate & therewith so diuers, y^t while one meat digesteth, another lieth & putrifieth. And euer we desire to haue some help to kepe the bodye in helth. But whan we be counsailled to liue temperately, & forbear our delicates & our

5

10

15

20

25

30

4–5 *Sidenote 1557:* Glotony dysfygureth the body   11–13 *Sidenote 1557:* Disseases commyng of glotony   20–21 *Sidenote 1557:* Glotonye oppresseth nature   29–30 potions] potious *1557*

glotonye, y^t will we not here of: but fain wold we haue some
medicins, as purgacions & vomites, to pul down & auoid y^t we
cram in to much. And in this we fare (as the gret moral philoso-
pher Plutarch saith) like a leude master of a ship, y^t goth not
5 about to see the ship tight and sure, but letteth by his leudnes his
shyp fal on a leke, and than careth not yet to stop the chines, but
set mo men to ye pump rather with much trauel and gret peryl to
draw it drye, than with litle labor and gret surety to kepe it drie.
Thus fare we saith Plutarch, y^t through intemperate liuing driue
10 our self in sicknes, & botch vs vp with phisik: wher we might wyth
sober diet & temperance, haue lesse nede of and kepe our self in
helth.
    If we se men die some dere yere by famin, we therof make a
gret mater, we fall to procession, we pray for plenty, and recken
15 the world at an end. But wheras yerely there dyeth in good yeres
gret people of glotony, thereof we take none hede at al, but
rather impute the blame to the sicknes wherof they dye, than to
the glotony wherof the sicknes commeth.
    And if there be a man slain of a stroke, there is as reson is
20 muche speache made thereof, the coroner sitteth, the queste is
charged, the verdit geuen, the felony founden, the doer endited,
the proces sued, the felon arrained, & dyeth for the dead. And
yet if men wold enserche how many be slain with weapen, and
how many eate & drink themself to death, there should be found
25 (as Salomon saith) mo dead of the cup and the kechen, than of
the dente of sworde: and thereof is no wordes made at all.
    Nowe if a manne willyngly kil hym selfe with a knife, the world
wondereth therupon, & as wel worthy is, he is endited of his own
deth, his goodes forfeted [fg$_8$] and his corse cast out on a dong-
30 hyll, hys bodye neuer buried in christen buryall. These glotons
daily kil themself their own handes, & no man findeth fault, but
carieth his carien corse into y^e quere, and w^t much solemne
seruice, burieth y^e body boldly at the hie alter, when thei haue al
their life (as thapostle saith) made theyr belly their god, & liked
35 to know none other: abusing not only ye name of chrysten men,

preferring their belly ioy before all the ioyes of heauen, but also abusing yᵉ part & office of a natural man and resonable creature. For where as nature & reason sheweth vs, yᵗ we shoulde eate but for to liue, these glotons are so glutted in the bestly pleasure of their tast, yᵗ they wold not wish to liue & it were not for to eate. 5

But surely wisedome were it for these glotons, wel & effectually to consider, yᵗ as saint Paul saith, yᵉ meat for the belly and the belly to the meat: but God shall destroy both the meate and the belly.

Now shold they remember & think vpon yᵉ painful time of 10 deth, in which yᵉ handes shal not be able to fede yᵉ mouth, and the mouth that was wont to powre in by yᵉ pottell, & cram in the fleshe by the handfulles, shal scant be able to take in three drips wᵗ a spone, & yet spew it out again.

Oft haue thei had a sick dronken hed, & slept theemself sober. 15 But than shal they fele a swimming & aking in theyr dronken hed, when the dasyng of death, shall kepe all swete slepe oute of their waterye eyes. Oft haue they fallen in the myre, & thence born to bed. But now shall they fal in the bed, & fro thence laid and lefte in the mire, til Gabriell blowe them vp. 20

Where as these consideracions much ought to moue anye man, yet speciallye shoulde it so muche the more moue those glotons, in how much yᵗ they maye well wit, yᵗ their maner of liuing must nedes accelerate this dredfull day, & drawe it shortly to them, albeit that by course of nature, it might seme many yeres 25 of. Which thing if these intemperate would wel and aduisedly remember, I would wene verely, it wold not fayle to make them more moderate in their liuyng, and vtterly flee suche outragious ryot and pestilent excesse.

Of slouth. 30

Oᶠ yᵉ mortal sinne of slouth, men make a smal matter. Slouthe is a sinne so comon, and no notable act therin, that is

---

3–4 *Sidenote 1557:* Eate for to lyue   5 *Sidenote 1557:* Glotons lyue to eate   7–8 *Sidenote 1557:* 1. Cor. 6   25 nature] nature intemperate dyet *1557* (*see note*) 26 if] of *1557*

accounted for heynous and abhomynable in thestimacion of the worlde, as is in theft, manslaughter, fals forswering, or treason, with any of which, euery man wold be loth to be defamed, for yᵉ worldly perils that do depend therupon, that therfore of slouth,

5   there is no man ashamed, but we take it as for a laughynge matter and a sporte.

But surely sith it is a great capytall sin in dede, the lesse that we set thereby, the more perilous it is: for the lesse wee go about to amende it.

10   Now to thentent that we do not deadly deceiue our selfe, it is necessarye that we consider wel the weight. Whiche yf we doo, we shal fynd it farre greater than we would before haue went.

There are ye wote well two poyntes requisite vnto saluacion, that is to wit, the declinyng or goyng aside from euil, and the

15   dooyng of good. Nowe where as in the first part, ther are al the tother six to be eschewed, yᵗ is to wit, pride, enuy, wrath, glotony, couetise, & lechery, the tother part, yᵗ is yᵉ one half of our way to heauen, euen slouth alone is hable to destroye.

Sir Thomas More wrote no farther of thys woorke.

13–15 *Sidenote 1557:* Psal. 33. 1. Peter 3. Two pointes requisite to saluacion
18 destroye.] destroye *1557*

COMMENTARY

COMMENTARY

The following bibliography includes works and abbreviations cited frequently in the Introduction and the Commentary. The titles of works referred to only once or occurring only in a brief cluster of references are given in full as they occur. Unless otherwise noted, references to the Bible and Latin quotations from it are from the Clementine Vulgate. For quotations from the Latin text of the Life of Pico della Mirandola by Gianfrancesco Pico della Mirandola and from the Latin texts of Pico's own works translated by More, the reader is referred to Appendix A, where these works are reprinted and translated.

BIBLIOGRAPHY AND SHORT TITLES

Allen. *See* Erasmus, Desiderius.

ASD. See Erasmus, Desiderius.

Beaty, Nancy Lee. *The Craft of Dying: The Literary Tradition of the Ars Moriendi in England,* New Haven and London, 1970.

Bloomfield, Morton W. *The Seven Deadly Sins: An Introduction to the History of a Religious Concept,* Ann Arbor, 1952. Cited as "Bloomfield."

Campbell and Reed. *See* More, Thomas.

Chambers, R. W. *Thomas More,* London, 1938; reprint Ann Arbor, 1958. Cited as "Chambers."

Chew, Samuel C. *The Pilgrimage of Life,* New Haven and London, 1962. Cited as "Chew."

Chronicles of London, ed. C. L. Kingsford, Oxford, 1905. Cited as "Chronicles of London."

Curtius, Ernst R. *European Literature and the Latin Middle Ages,* trans. W. R. Trask, New York, 1953. Cited as "Curtius."

CW. See More, Thomas.

Delcourt, Joseph, *Essai sur la langue de Thomas More d'après ses oeuvres anglaises,* Paris, 1914. Cited as "Delcourt."

Dictionary of National Biography, ed. Leslie Stephen et al., 63 vols. London, 1885–1900. Cited as *DNB.*

Dionysius the Carthusian. *In IV Libros Sententiarum, D. Dionysii Cartusiani Opera Omnia in unum corpus digesta ad fidem editionum Coloniensium,* 44 vols., Montreuil-sur-Mer, 1896–1935. Cited as *"Opera omnia."*

DNB. See Dictionary of National Biography.

EETS ES. Early English Text Society, Extra Series.

EETS OS. Early English Text Society, Original Series.

Erasmus, Desiderius. *Opera omnia,* ed. J. Clericus (Jean LeClerc), 10 vols., Leiden, 1703–6. Cited as *"Opera Omnia."*

———. *Opera omnia Desiderii Erasmi Roterodami,* ed. J. H. Waszink et al., 20 vols. to date, Amsterdam, 1969–. Cited as *ASD.*

———. *Opus epistolarum Des. Erasmi Roterodami,* ed. P. S. Allen et al., 12 vols., Oxford, 1906–58. Cited as "Allen."

Essential Articles. See Sylvester, Richard S., and Germain P. Marc'hadour.

EW. See More, Thomas.

1557. See More, Thomas.

Fox, Alistair. *Thomas More: History and Providence,* Oxford, 1982; New Haven and London, 1983. Cited as "Fox."

Gibson, R. W., and J. Max Patrick. *St. Thomas More: A Preliminary Bibliography of His Works and of Moreana to the Year 1750,* New Haven and London, 1961. Cited as "Gibson."

Guy, John A. *The Public Career of Sir Thomas More,* New Haven and London, 1980. Cited as "Guy."

Harpsfield, Nicholas. *The Life and Death of Sr Thomas Moore, knight, sometymes Lord high Chancellor of England,* ed. Elsie Vaughan Hitchcock and R. W. Chambers, Early English Text Society, Original Series no. 186. London, 1932. Cited as "Harpsfield."

IMEV. The Index of Middle English Verse, ed. Carleton Brown and Rossell Hope Robbins, New York, 1943; *The Supplement to the Index of Middle English Verse,* ed. Rossell Hope Robbins and John L. Cutler, Lexington, Kentucky, 1965.

Lehmberg, Stanford E. "Sir Thomas More's Life of Pico della Mirandola," *Studies in the Renaissance, 3* (1956), 61–74. Cited as "Lehmberg."

LP. Letters and Papers, Foreign and Domestic, of the Reign of Henry VIII, ed. J. S. Brewer, James Gairdner, and R. H. Brodie, 21 vols., London, 1862–1932; reprint Vaduz, 1965.

MED. Middle English Dictionary, ed. Hans Kurath, Sherman M. Kuhn, and Robert F. Lewis, 15 vols. to date, Ann Arbor, 1952–.

More, Thomas. *The English Works of Thomas More,* ed. W. E. Campbell, A. W. Reed, R. W. Chambers, and W. A. G. Doyle-Davidson, 2 vols., London, 1931. Cited as "Campbell and Reed."

———. *The History of King Richard III and Selections from the English and Latin Poems,* ed. Richard S. Sylvester, New Haven and London, 1976. Cited as "Sylvester."

———. *St. Thomas More, Selected Letters,* ed. Elizabeth F. Rogers, trans. Marcus Haworth, S. J., et al., New Haven and London, 1961. Cited as "Rogers."

———. *The Workes . . . in the Englyshe tonge,* London, 1557; *STC²* 18076. Cited as *EW* or *1557.*

———. *The Yale Edition of the Complete Works of St. Thomas More:* Vol. 2, *The History of King Richard III,* ed. R. S. Sylvester; Vol. 3, Part 1, *Translations of Lucian,* ed. C. R. Thompson; Vol. 3, Part 2, *Latin Poems,* ed. C. H. Miller, Leicester Bradner, C. A. Lynch, and R. P. Oliver; Vol. 4, *Utopia,* ed. Edward L. Surtz, S. J., and J. H. Hexter; Vol. 5, *Responsio ad Lutherum,* ed. J. M. Headley, trans. Sister Scholastica Mandeville; Vol. 6, *A Dialogue Concerning Heresies,* ed. T. M. C. Lawler, Germain Marc'hadour, R. C. Marius; Vol. 7, *Letter to Bugenhagen, Supplication of Souls, Letter against Frith,* ed. Frank Manley, Germain Marc'hadour, Richard Marius, and C. H. Miller; Vol. 8, *The Confutation of Tyndale's Answer,* ed. L. A. Schuster, R. C. Marius, J. P. Lusardi, and R. J. Schoeck; Vol. 9, *The Apology,* ed. J. B. Trapp; Vol. 10, *The*

Debellation of Salem and Bizance, ed. John Guy, Ralph Keen, C. H. Miller, and Ruth McGugan; Vol. 11, *The Answer to a Poisoned Book,* ed. S. M. Foley and C. H. Miller; Vol. 12, *A Dialogue of Comfort against Tribulation,* ed. L. L. Martz and Frank Manley; Vol. 13; *Treatise on the Passion, Treatise on the Blessed Body, Instructions and Prayers,* ed. G. E. Haupt; Vol. 14, *De Tristitia Christi,* ed. C. H. Miller; Vol. 15, *In Defense of Humanism: Letter to Martin Dorp, Letter to the University of Oxford, Letter to Edward Lee, Letter to a Monk, with a New Text and Translation of Historia Richardi Tertii,* ed. Daniel Kinney; New Haven and London, 1963–90; cited as *CW* followed by volume number.

Mustanoja, Tauno F. *A Middle English Syntax,* Helsinki, 1960. Cited as "Mustanoja."

O'Connor, Sr. Mary Catherine. *The Art of Dying Well: The Development of the Ars Moriendi,* New York, 1942.

OED. The Oxford English Dictionary, 2nd ed., ed. R. W. Burchfield et al., 13 vols., Oxford, 1989.

Otto, August, *Die Sprichwörter und sprichwörtlichen Redensarten der Römer,* Leipzig, 1890. Cited as "Otto."

PG. Patrologiae Cursus Completus: Series Graeca, ed. J.-P. Migne, 161 vols., Paris, 1857–66.

Pico della Mirandola, Giovanni. *L'opera e il pensiero di Giovanni Pico della Mirandola nella storia dell'umanesimo: Convegno Internationale (Mirandola, 15–18 Settembre, 1963),* Instituto Nationale di Studi sul Renascimento, 2 vols., Florence, 1965.

PL. Patrologiae Cursus Completus: Series Latina, ed. J.-P. Migne, 221 vols, Paris, 1884–1903.

Reed, Arthur W. *Early Tudor Drama: Medwall, the Rastells, Heywood, and the More Circle,* London, 1926. Cited as "Reed."

Rigg, J. M., ed. *Giovanni Pico della Mirandola . . . Translated from the Latin by Sir Thomas More,* London, 1890. Cited as "Rigg."

Ro. Ba. *The Life of Syr Thomas More, Sometymes Lord Chancellour of England,* ed. Elsie Vaughan Hitchcock and P. E. Hallett, Early English Text Society, Original Series no. 222, London, 1950.

Rogers. See More, Thomas.

Roper, William, *The Lyfe of Sir Thomas Moore, knyght,* ed. Elsie Vaughan Hitchcock, EETS OS no. 197, London, 1935. Cited as "Roper."

Stapleton, Thomas. *The Life and Illustrious Martyrdom of Sir Thomas More,* trans. Philip E. Hallett, ed. E. E. Reynolds, London, 1966. Cited as "Stapleton."

STC2. A Short-Title Catalogue of Books Printed in England, Scotland, & Ireland and of English Books Printed Abroad 1475–1640, 2nd ed., rev. W. A. Jackson, F. S. Ferguson, and Katharine F. Pantzer, 3 vols., London, 1976–91.

Stow, John. *A Survey of London,* ed. Charles Lethbridge Kingsford, 2 vols., Oxford, 1908. Cited as "Stow."

Sylvester. See More, Thomas.

Sylvester, Richard S., and Germain P. Marc'hadour, eds. *Essential Articles for the Study of Thomas More*, Hamden, Conn., 1977. Cited as "*Essential Articles.*"

Tilley, Morris P. *A Dictionary of the Proverbs in England in the Sixteenth and Seventeenth Centuries*, Ann Arbor, 1950. Cited as "Tilley."

Visser, F. T. *A Syntax of the English Language of St. Thomas More*, 3 vols., Materials for the Study of the Old English Drama, New Series, nos. 19, 24, 26, Louvain, 1946–56. Cited as "Visser."

Whiting, Bartlett J., and Helen W. Whiting. *Proverbs, Sentences, and Proverbial Phrases from English Writings Mainly before 1500*, Cambridge, Mass., 1968. Cited as "Whiting."

Willow, Sr. Mary Edith. *An Analysis of the English Poems of St. Thomas More*, Nieuwkoop, 1974. Cited as "Willow."

Woolf, Rosemary. *The English Religious Lyric in the Middle Ages*, Oxford, 1968. Cited as "Woolf."

3/2 **deuysed.** For some discussion of the implications of this term see Geoffrey Webb, "The Office of Devisor," in *Fritz Saxl, 1890–1948: A Volume of Memorial Essays from His Friends in England*, ed. D. J. Gordon (London, 1957), pp. 297–308.

3/4 **pageauntes.** This is the first recorded use of the word in the sense of a scene represented in painted cloth (*OED*, s.v. *pageant* sb. 1d—citing this passage from *1557*). On the likelihood that More is using the word simply in the sense of "picture" see A. S. G. Edwards, "ME pageant = picture?" *Notes & Queries*, New Series, *39* (1992), 25–26.

3/10 **squyrge.** That is, "scourge," a whip to drive the top.

3/13 **coyte.** That is, "quoit," a flattish iron ring used in the game of quoits.

3/13 **cokstele.** A stick to throw at a cock at Shrovetide (*OED*, s.v. *cock* sb.¹ 33); cf. the variant or misprinted form in *CW* 11, 198/24–27: "And whan so euer his new sling & his new stone . . . come onys into my handes, I shall turne his slynge into a cokstewe, & his stone into a fether." For an account of the practice of cock-throwing on Shrove Tuesday see Joseph Strutt, *The Sports and Pastimes of the People of England* (London, 1876), pp. 378–79.

3/14 **in his kynde.** That is, "in its way" (*OED*, s.v. *kind* sb. 8)

3/21–22 **horse fete.** That is, "the horse's feet"; genitives without final *s* are common in Middle English and in sixteenth-century English: see Mustanoja, pp. 71–73; and *Merry Jest*, 26/364.

4/28 **course.** "The action or practice of coursing, or pursuing game with houndes (*esp.* hares with greyhounds)" (*OED*, s.v. *course* sb. 7).

4/28 **flyght.** More's usage, in the sense of pursuit of game by a hawk, antedates the earliest recorded in *OED* (s.v. *flight* sb.¹ 1c).

4/31 **peuishe.** That is, "foolish" (*OED*, s.v. *peevish* a. 1); cf. *CW 12*, 15/17: "these pevesh worldly thynges."

4/32 **no force.** That is, "no matter" (*OED*, s.v. *force* sb¹ 20). More uses the phrase elsewhere; see *CW 6*, 79/18; *CW 12*, 116/17.

4/43 **fyry dart.** From classical times Cupid was frequently portrayed holding a flaming brand or dart; cf. Chaucer, "The Knight's Tale" "Love hath his firy dart so brenningly / Y stiked thurgh my . . . herte" (I, 1568–69); and *Mirror for Magistrates*, ed. Lily B. Campbell (Cambridge, 1938): "the shot of Cupids firy shaftes" (p. 444, line 38).

4/56 **oppresse.** That is, "put an end to" (*OED*, s.v. *oppress* v. 3).

4/56–57 **Chargeable . . . bysinesse.** These lines are syntactically awkward; presumably the phrase "of loue" (56) is to be read as if it appeared at the end of line 57.

5/58 ymage of Death. A skeleton, such as is frequently found in wood-cuts like Holbein's Dance of Death. More mentions "the daunce of death pictured in Poules [St. Paul's Cathedral]," which "expresse only, yᵉ lothely figure of our dead bony bodies biten away yᵉ flesh" (*The Last Things*, 139/22–25); see Stow, *1*, 327.

5/65 magnifyed. More's usage in the sense of "lauded" significantly antedates the earliest recorded in *OED* (s.v. *magnified* ppl.a. 1).

5/74 with tonges I am compassed all rounde. Compare Stephen Hawes's *Pastime of Pleasure*, ed. W. E. Mead (EETS OS no. 173, London, 1928), where Fame appears "with brennyng tongues," lines 54–97; see also lines 176, 196, and de Worde's woodcut of Fame (sig. S₁v), no. 1016 in Edward Hodnett, *English Woodcuts, 1480–1535*, rev. ed. (Oxford, 1973). The tradition of this aspect of Fame derives ultimately from the representation of Fama in Virgil, *Aeneid* 4.183: "tot linguae, totidem ora sonant."

5/78 Maugry thy teeth. That is, "in spite of you" (*OED*, s.v. *tooth* sb. 5); the phrase is proverbial; Whiting T406, Tilley S764.

5/84 with horyloge in hande. Compare Hawes's *Pastime of Pleasure*, where Time appears with "an horology" (5614); see also de Worde's accompanying woodcut of Time (sig. S₄), Hodnett, *English Woodcuts*, no. 1017.

6/97–104 Me nedeth . . . nought. Elizabeth McCutcheon, *Moreana*, 70 (1981), 29–31, has suggested that the change here from a seven-line to an eight-line stanza has some numerological significance: "eight was the number of eternity and with it renewal and regeneration" (p. 29). The change in stanza form "underscores major shifts in feeling and perspective from the temporal world to the eternal one, and prepares the way for the Poet's meditative intervention [in the final stanza]" (p. 30).

6/109–7/20 Has . . . deo. This poem is reprinted here as it appears (with an English translation) in *CW 3/2*, no. 272.

9/5 loke here vpon me. This exhortation, coupled with the refrain "Loo here I lye," suggests that these verses may originally have been written as a *titulus* to be hung over Elizabeth's tomb. See the Introduction, p. xxiii.

9/8 here I lye. Elizabeth was the first person to be buried in Henry VII's new chapel in Westminster Abbey, on which work had begun only in January 1503. She was interred on February 25 of that year; see Arthur P. Stanley, *Historical Monuments of Westminster Abbey*, 5th ed. (London, 1882), p. 144; and Stow, 2, 107.

9/9 old worthy lynage. Elizabeth was the daughter of Elizabeth Woodville and Edward IV, and hence a descendant of the royal Plantaganet line.

9/11 **a kynges fere in maryage.** Elizabeth had married Henry VII on January 18, 1486.

9/13 **reconyng.** The context suggests some sense like "outcome" or "end of life," but *OED* does not record such a usage (s.v. *reckoning* sb.).

10/18 **Yff money . . . non.** The insistence here and in line 17 on such affluence, while dramatically apposite, is much less than historically exact. In fact Elizabeth seems to have been often in considerable debt. The editor of her Privy Purse expenses observes: "Her Majesty's revenue was inadequate to [the] demands [placed on it], and she was not unfrequently obliged to borrow money, pledging her plate as security for its repayment. The King sometimes relieved her necessities, but the same security was given; and her pecuniary difficulties are apparent from her being obliged, in most cases, to pay her tradesmen part of their bills only, instead of discharging the whole amount" (*Privy Purse Expenses of Elizabeth of York*, ed. N. H. Nicolas, London, 1830, p. ciii). In 1497 she borrowed £2,000 from Henry to pay her creditors, and there are records of other, smaller sums; see further Agnes Strickland, *Lives of the Queens of England* (London, 1842), *4*, 51.

10/21 **Obey . . . remedye.** An unrecorded variant of Whiting D78.

10/23 **Yet . . . oþerwyse.** An allusion to the astrological prognostications of Gulielmus Parronus Placentinus, otherwise William Parron, who appears to have been Henry VII's court astrologer in the period c. 1496–1503. He published various prognostics (*STC²* 385.3, 494.8, 494.9, 494.10) printed by Pynson and de Worde. He also presented several sets of manuscript prognostications to Henry, including *Liber de optimo fato Henrici Eboraci ducis ac optimorum ipsius parentum*, which survives in British Library MS Royal 12 B vi and Bibliothèque Nationale MS Lat. 6276. This work, composed sometime between April 1502 and February 1503, contains the following prediction: "De optima itidem ac omni genere virtutum ornatissima regina coniuge tua dico quod ex significationibus astrorum sue geniture debet diu viuere per unam regulam circa octuaginta annos. Et per aliam regulam circa xc" (British Library MS Royal 12 B vi, fol. 34). Parron's printed *Prognostica anni M.d.iii. ab vndecima die martii* (*STC²* 494.10, printed December 24, 1502) is more general: "De optima domina Elizabet regina anglie. Optima et omni genere virtutum ornatissima domina Elizabet regina anglie se bene habebit" (sig. b₂v). For discussion of Parron and his prophecies see C. A. J. Armstrong, "An Italian Astrologer at the Court of Henry VII," in *Italian Renaissance Studies*, ed. E. F. Jacob (London, 1960), pp. 433–54, esp. 452–54. More's scorn for astrological predictions is reflected in a number of his Latin poems; see *CW 3/2*, nos. 60–65, 67, 101, 118,

169, 182, some of which may have been prompted by Parron's activities (see *CW 3/2*, Commentary at 60/1–5). See also his dismissive comments in *Utopia* (*CW 4*, 160/5 and 438–39).

10/26 **astrologye deuynatrice.** *O* reads "dymynatrice," while both *L* and *1557* read "deuynatrice." But the only citation for this latter word in *OED* is here (s.v. *divinatrice* a: "That divines, divining"); it does not appear in *MED*. The form *diminatrice* does not appear in either *OED* or *MED*. The expression is presumably an anglicization of the Latin *astrologia divinatrix;* cf. Pico's *Disputationes adversus astrologiam divinatricem* (Bologna, 1495/6). It is perhaps significant that Parron (see note on 10/23) had attacked this work; see further *CW 3/2*, 349.

10/27 **the.** That is, "thee"; see also 13/82.

10/30 **brytill.** More's usage in the figurative sense of "frail" or "transitory" (see also Fortune Verses, above, 35/110, 36/145, 38/199) antedates the earliest recorded usage in *OED* (s.v. *brittle* a. 3).

10/33 **Sondre wyse.** The omission of the preposition "in" in *O* gives a harder reading, but one for which there is warrant (*OED*, s.v. *sundry* a. 6c), albeit from the later sixteenth century.

10/33–34 **rekyn . . . fayn.** That is, "dare not willingly to reckon."

11/37 **Wher . . . towers.** The *ubi sunt* motif was a commonplace in medieval literature; for examples of the formula in Middle English shorter poems, see the thirteenth-century *Sayings of Saint Bernard* (*IMEV* 3310) and the fourteenth-century *Cur mundus militat* (*IMEV* 4160); there are fifteenth-century examples in the works of James Ryman (*IMEV* 2807) and John Lydgate (*IMEV* 1865); for discussion of the use of the formula see Woolf, pp. 94–97, 108–10.

11/38 **Goodly Richemond.** Henry VII's palace at Sheen burned down at Christmas 1497; he had a new palace rebuilt on the site and renamed it Richmond (Henry's title was Earl of Richmond before he became king). The new palace was completed by 1500; see *Chronicles of London*, pp. 222, 232.

11/38 **son.** That is, "soon."

11/39–40 **At Westmynster . . . se.** See note on 9/8. The Chapel of Henry VII in Westminster Abbey was not completed until the reign of Henry VIII.

11/43 **My place bilded ys.** That is, her tomb, in contrast to the "castellis" and "towers" like Richmond and Westminster, her former "places."

11/45–10/85 **The feythfull . . . I lie.** The farewell address from the dead to the living is a common feature of the medieval verse epitaph; see the Introduction, pp. xxv–xxvi.

11/45 **to.** That is, "two."

11/45–46 **The feythfull . . . concorde.** In fact the marriage between Henry and Elizabeth appears to have been an unusually happy one; see S. B. Chrimes, *Henry VII* (London, 1972), pp. 302–04.

11/51 **lady Margarete.** Margaret (b. November 29, 1489), eldest daughter of Elizabeth and Henry.

11/53 **ye shuld . . . mete.** Negotiations for Margaret's marriage to James IV of Scotland had been concluded on January 25, 1503—just before her mother's death. The marriage took place on August 8, 1503.

11/55 **what we very blynd.** The construction, though elliptical, seems defensible. *What* is seemingly used here as an exclamation to denote surprise, indignation, or both (cf. *OED*, s.v. *what* int. B2); a verb has also been omitted. Mustanoja (p. 510) notes that the verb is frequently omitted in exclamatory phrases in Middle English. But the sense is clear: "how very blind we are."

11/56 **þat . . . nye.** The line has a proverbial ring but does not appear in Whiting or Tilley. Cf. *CW* 2, 52/11–16.

12/58 **madam . . . moder.** Margaret Beaufort, countess of Richmond (1443–1509), mother of Henry VII. More praises her elsewhere, in his poem celebrating Henry VIII's accession, where he attributes to Henry "mens aviae, mens relligiosa paternae" (*CW 3/2*, 19/154).

12/61–62 **my dowghter . . . Arthur.** Catherine of Aragon (1485–1536) had married Elizabeth's eldest son, Prince Arthur, on November 14, 1501. He died on April 2, 1502.

12/65 **lord Harry.** The future Henry VIII (b. June 28, 1491) was eleven at the time of his mother's death. On his good looks, see *CW 3/2*, Commentary at 19/67.

12/67 **my dowghter Mary.** Elizabeth's second surviving daughter was born in March 1496. She married Louis XII of France in 1514 and, after his death, Charles Brandon, duke of Suffolk, in 1515. She died on June 24, 1533.

12/69 **my lady dowghter Cate.** Elizabeth's last child was born on February 2, 1503. The *Chronicles of London* reports that "vpon the Saterday folowyng was the said doughter Cristened w^tin the parisshe chirch of the Towre, and named Kateryn" (p. 258). The date of her death appears to be unrecorded, but there seems no reason to doubt the assertion of N. H. Nicolas that "the child . . . quickly followed its mother to her grave" (*Privy Purse Expenses of Elizabeth of York*, ed. N. H. Nicolas, London, 1830, p. xciii). Elizabeth's apostrophe, which implies that the child was still alive when More's poem was written, strengthens the assumption that its composition followed swiftly upon Elizabeth's death. *OED* notes that "in the fifteenth and sixteenth centuries *The* (or *My*) *Lady* was prefixed to the Christian name of a female member of the Royal Family, as 'Princess' is now" (*OED*, s.v. *lady* sb. I6).

12/72 **Cecill Anne and Kateryne.** See *CW 2*, Commentary at 3/9–14. Cecily, the third daughter of Edward IV, was born in 1469 and died August 24, 1507. She is described in *Richard III* as "not so fortunate as fayre" (*CW 2*, 3/9). Anne, Edward's fifth daughter, was born on November 2, 1475, and died on November 23, 1511. Katherine, the sixth daughter, was born in 1479. More speaks of her in *Richard III* (written c. 1514–1518): "Katheryne whiche longe tyme tossed in either fortune sommetime in wealth, ofte in aduersitye, at the laste, if this bee the laste, for yet she lyueth, is by the benignitye of her Nephewe, King Henrye the eighte, in verye prosperous estate, and woorthye her birth and vertue" (*CW 2*, 3/13–17 and Commentary). She died on November 15, 1527. *L* omits the reference to Anne and changes the reference in line 73 to "susteris bothe." The death of Anne was not the reason for the omission, since Cecily, who is mentioned, died before Anne. The efforts to excise any reference to Anne in this manuscript are puzzling. Perhaps it is connected with her husband, Thomas Howard, third duke of Norfolk (1473–1554), a much unloved man, best known as the ruthless suppressor of the Pilgrimage of Grace. He was indicted for treason in 1546 and spent all of Edward VI's reign in the Tower. (For a recent biography see J. M. Robinson, *The Dukes of Norfolk: A Quincentennial History*, Oxford, 1982, pp. 23–40.) Possibly the copyist of *L* wished to excise any link between Elizabeth and so unpopular a figure. If so, the transcription of *L* may well have occurred in the period 1447–1553.

12/74 **lady Brygyte.** Bridget, the youngest of Edward's seven daughters, was born in 1480 and died in 1513. She became a Dominican nun at Dartford Abbey. The reference in lines 76–77 to "you þat erthly folye fle, / And hevynly thynges loue and magnyfe" is apparently directed to her. She is described in More's *Richard III* as one who "representynge the vertue of her, whose name she bare, professed and obserued a religious lyfe at Dertforde, an house of close Nunnes" (*CW 2*, 3/10–12 and Commentary).

12/75 **Lo here . . . vanyte.** An exclamation based on a proverbial commonplace found elsewhere in late Middle English literature; see Whiting W664.

13/81 **comyns.** That is, "common people," neither nobles nor clergy.

13/82 **the.** That is, "thee."

13/84 **commend.** Both *O* and *1557* fall into some syntactic confusion here, adding "to" after "commend." Lines 82–84 ("Wherfor . . . commend") clearly form a single sentence, as do lines 84–85 ("Thy . . .

lye"). The "to" has been canceled by hand in all copies of *1557* I have examined.

13/85 **seruaunt.** *O* has a flourish after the final *t* that elsewhere seems to signify a contraction for final *es*. But the reading of *L* and *1557* seems superior, even if *O* offers a genuine variant here rather than an otiose scribal flourish, in view of the singular form "me" in line 84.

15/3–14 **Wyse men . . . lyke to the.** Whiting M47.

15/13 **can no.** That is, "knows no."

15/15–17/62 **He that . . . at laste.** These lines draw on the tradition of medieval *impossibilia* verses, in which the established order of events or activities is imagined as cast into confusion. It was a device often used for satirical purposes in the Middle Ages; see Curtius, pp. 94–98; and Sarah M. Horrall, "A Poem of Impossibilities from Westminster Abbey MS 34/3," *Notes & Queries,* New Series, *32* (1985), 453–55. Some Middle English *impossibilia* poems survive: for example, *IMEV* 3941.5 and 3999 (the latter occurs in MS Balliol 354, a manuscript that also contains More's English verses).

15/20 **His thryfte . . . done.** That is, "his prosperity is nearly gone."

16/27–29 **An olde trot . . . cup.** Whiting C629. The expression "kiss the cup" means "to drink" (*OED,* s.v. *kiss* v. 6b).

16/32 **soused hym vp.** The expression appears in *CW 12,* Commentary at 63/10, but there the editors prefer the reading "sower hym vpp," without noting the occurrence of the phrase here or the entry in *OED* (s.v. *souse,* v.[1] 4: "to bring to extremity"). This usage antedates the earliest recorded in *OED.*

16/36 **aryse.** The *1557* emendation to "ryse" presumably reflects editorial notions of metrical regularity; but the emendation ignores the likelihood of elision in "to aryse."

16/45 **Pletynge.** That is, "pleading (in court)."

17/62 **Beshrewe themselfe.** *OED* does not give a reflexive usage of the verb *beshrew.*

17/66 **ryfely.** That is, "frequently." Both *1575* and *1557* substitute easier readings, "rufully" and "thriftly," respectively. The *1575* reading is a creditable stab at a hard word; but the nonsensical *1557* reading suggests some of the limitations of this text.

17/79 **nobles rounde.** The gold coin, the noble, could mean one of two coins in More's time: the angel noble, worth 6s. 8d; or the royal, or rose, noble, worth 10s. See John H. Munro, "Money and Coinage of the Age of Erasmus," in *The Correspondence of Erasmus,* trans. R. A. B. Mynors and D. F. S. Thomson (Toronto, 1974), *1,* 312, 325, and 329.

18/97 **policy.** *1516* has "po.cy"; *OED* does not sanction either "polcy" or "poicy" as variant spellings for "policy" (*OED*, s.v. *policy* sb¹).

18/107 **made a good puruaye.** *OED* cites only this example for the use of "purvey" meaning "arrangement" (*OED*, s.v. *purvey* sb. 2).

18/110 **another.** *1516* reads "other"; since this edition is poorly printed, the reading of *1557* and *1575* has been adopted because it creates a syllabically regular line.

18/112–19/116 **Fyrste . . . not.** For a tenuous parallel to this passage see *CW 12*, 210/25–29.

18/112–13 **A grete . . . pot.** Here both the construction and sense seem to have bothered *1575* and *1557*. *1575* reads, for these lines: "a pretie deale, / he hyd it in a potte"; *1557* reads: "Therof much dele, / He dygged it in a pot," a reading that is unintelligible. Hazlitt retains the *1575* reading while Sylvester reads: "Thereof grete dele, / He dighth yt in a pot." (102).
The main problem in line 113 seems to be "hyt," which is syntactically otiose. The pleonastic use of the personal pronoun is not uncommon in Middle English (see Mustanoja, pp. 121, 138–39), and its retention is metrically necessary here. The lines mean: "He put a great part of the money into a pot."

19/119 **put hyt in a cup.** That is, "he drank it."

19/134 **In lyke maner wyse.** "In the same way"; that is, on drink. See line 118.

19/142 **resorte.** That is, "assistance."

20/149 **To haue a goodly floure.** That is, "to have preeminence"; for examples of the phrase see *OED*, s.v. *flower* sb 6b; the variant in *1557*, "to haue a lucky howre," is proverbial; Whiting A53.

20/155–58 **A sergaunt . . . mayre.** The reference to the eagerness of the sergeant to wait upon the man is, of course, ironic. He wishes to seize him for debt. There is doubtless a play here on the different meanings of "sergeant" reflecting his legal and ceremonial function (*OED*, s.v. *sergeant* sb. 8b). See the next note.

20/157–58 **On him . . . mayre.** The mayor was accompanied on ceremonial occasions by the mayor's sergeants, who were entitled to bear "mases of siluer and guilt with the kings armes" (Stow, 2, 165).

20/161–70 **pryde . . . abyde.** This is the only place where two stanzas are joined by tail rhyme.

20/165 **to saynt Katheryne.** The allusion is apparently to the Hospital of St. Katherine by the Tower, founded by Queen Matilda, wife to King Stephen. Stow reports that "it was of late time called a free chappell, a colledge, and an Hospitall for poore sisters. . . . this house was valued at 315. pound, foureteene shillings, two pence, being now of late yeres inclosed about, or pestered with small tenements, and homely cottages, hauing inhabitants, English and strangers, more in number then in some cities in England" (Stow, *1*, 124). I have not been able to confirm Sylvester's assertion that it was "a well-known sanctuary for thieves and debtors" (p. 104). But W. H. Godfrey points out that Henry VI presented the hospital with a new charter in 1442 "which converted the whole precinct into a liberty, free from the jurisdiction of the City and of the Bishop of London" (*The English Almshouse*, London, 1955, p. 27); so the size and relative autonomy of the area make the conclusion reasonable. This is perhaps the same "Saynt Catheryns" mentioned in *The Confutation, CW 8*, 815/16, 24.

20/166 Streyght as a lyne. Whiting L301, Tilley L303.

20/167 at a tyde. That is, "for a period of time" (*OED*, s.v. *tide* sb. I1).

20/169 promocyon. More's usage here, in the sense of "laying of information against him because of his debts" antedates the earliest recorded in *OED* (s.v. *promotion* sb. 3).

20/174 to aske theyr det. That is, "to ask payment for his debt to them."

20/176 the valour of a peny. Proverbial; cf. Whiting P118 (where this version is unrecorded).

21/179 Vnto the harde hedge. Whiting H321; it means "to the very end."

21/182 To laye his gowne to pledge. That is, "to put his gown in pawn."

21/205 reste. An aphetic form of "arrest"; see also 25/330.

22/215 Haue I bene well in vre. That is, "I have been used to practice expertly" (*OED*, s.v. *vre* sb.¹ I 1a); and see the use of the phrase in *CW 8*, 60/7.

22/220 forth hym goth. *1516, 1575*, and Sylvester all read "to hym goth," a reading that does not make sense since there is no referent for "hym." *1557* and William C. Hazlitt (*Remains of the Early Popular Poetry of England*, 4 vols., London, 1864–66) recognize the problem and read "foorth then" for "to hym," a defensible reading since it is syntactically possible; *him* can be used for the nominative in ME (see Mustanoja, pp. 129–30). I have adopted *1557*s reading "forth" but retained "hym" as a nominative; thus "hym goth" = "he goes."

22/228 dopped and doked. That is, "bobbed and ducked his head." *OED* gives 00/293 as the first instance of this meaning for "dop" (*OED*, s.v. *dop* v. Obs. 2).

22/233 toted and he pered. That is, "peered and examined"; cf. *CW 6*,

296/3: "therein he toteth and poreth often." *Peer* in the sense of "look closely at" antedates the earliest recorded usage in *OED* (s.v. *peer* v.² 1).

22/236 **frered.** That is, "act the part of a friar." More's usage here is the first cited in *OED* (s.v. *friar* v. Obs.).

22/242 **here . . . game.** Possibly an echo of Chaucer's *Troilus & Criseyde*, 1.868: "here bygynneth game."

23/246 **damoysell.** Used here in the sense of "a young, unmarried woman" without any connotations of rank or respect (*OED*, s.v. *damsel* I2).

23/266–68 **daye . . . praye.** This is the only place where the last rhyme of one stanza is carried over as the first rhyme of the next.

23/272 **an austen frere.** St. Katherine's, where the young man had gone, was an Augustinian hospital (see D. Knowles and R. N. Hadcock, *Medieval Religious Houses in England and Wales*, London, 1971, p. 373); so the disguise is appropriate if the "frende" (line 189) with whom he subsequently stayed also resided within the precinct of St. Katherine.

23/274 **maters breke.** That is, "disclose certain matters;" cf. the use of the phrase in *CW 8*, 537/12. The usage does not seem to be recorded in *OED*.

24/288 **vp she brought.** That is, "she brought him up." On the non-expression of the object pronoun see Mustanoja, pp. 144–45.

25/308 **shall hyt.** That is, "it shall be better" (line 305).

25/318 **Or elles nat.** That is, "unless you would prefer not to."

25/330 **rest.** See note on 21/205.

25/332 **out he toke his mace.** The sergeant's mace was the symbol of his office; see the reference to "sergeant of the mace" in *OED* (s.v. *sergeant* sb. 8b).

26/343 **With a maschefe.** Used here in an expletive or imprecatory sense, "bad luck to you!" see *OED*, s.v. *mischief* sb. 9, citing among other examples this from *1565:* "What, with a mischiefe, haste thou to doe with it?" More's usage here antedates any of the examples cited in *OED*.

26/344 **the.** That is, "thee."

26/346 **Vpon the lyste.** Campbell and Reed (p. 195) note the parallel with Chaucer, "The Wife of Bath's Prologue." "he smoot me ones on the lyst" (III, 634).

26/352 **Well ferder.** That is, "more afraid."

26/364 **Eche other here.** That is, "each other's hair"; genitives without final *s* are very common in Middle English and in sixteenth-century English; see Pageant Verses, 3/21.

27/372–74 **They roll . . . poke.** The use of alliterative phrasing here is clearly parodic; it was often a feature of battle descriptions in Middle English verse, even in nonalliterative poems; cf., for example, Chaucer, "The Knight's Tale" I, 2605–16.

27/374 **pygges in a poke.** Whiting P190.

27/385 **agood.** More's usage antedates the earliest recorded citation in *OED* (s.v. *agood* adv.).

27/390 **iolle.** That is, "blow"; *OED* (s.v. *jowl* sb.⁴) cites this as the first occurrence of this meaning.

28/402 **frere frappe.** Sylvester (p. 112) suggests that this expression means "friar manqué, fake friar," but there seems no etymological warrant for such a gloss. *OED* (s.v. *frapart*) cites More's phrase and connects it with the French *frère frapart*, which is glossed there as "d'un moine libertin et debauché." But a more likely derivation here is an adjectival form from ME *frapen*, "beaten" (cf. *MED*, s.v., v. a, "to beat"). The proper name Frere Frappe also appears in *CW 8*, 42/14–16: "frere Frappe, that fyrste gapeth and then blessyth, and loketh holyly and precheth rybaudye to the peopell that stande aboute."

28/410 **Commaunde.** That is, "commend."

28/419 **neuer the nere.** That is, "no nearer to recovering the money."

31/6 **a deed tre.** Whiting T455 (not citing this occurrence).

31/15 **not worth a strawe.** Whiting S815, Tilley S918, neither, however, citing this occurrence, but noting its appearance in More's *Debellation of Salem and Bizance* (*CW 10*, 134/33).

31/18 **darke fume.** "Fume" appears to be used here in the sense of "something which . . . clouds the faculties or the reason" (*OED*, s.v. *fume* sb. 6). *OED* does not record this meaning before 1574.

31/19 **Asse of Alexandre.** The allusion is a puzzling one, and made more so because "Alexandre" could mean either "Alexander" or "Alexandria"; but I have been unable to clarify its meaning. It may be that this is another of More's contemptuous references to Alexander the Great's excess and drunkenness; see *CW 14*, 147/3–5; and *CW 7*, 211/6–7, a passage that is cited as proverbial: Whiting A85.

31/20 **gagelynge gandre.** Cf. *CW 8*, 1013/7–8 ("except these geese go from theyr olde flock and giue ouer all theyr olde gagelynge"); and *CW 7*, 144/12–13 ("some other Iohan Goose bygan to bere that byll abrode agayn & made some gagling a whyle"). More's usages (in the sense of "cackling") antedate the earliest recorded in *OED* (s.v. *gaggling* ppl.a. 1).

32/39 **reprouable.** The adjectival form is used here as a substantive ("those deserving reproof").

32/42 **shricheth.** That is "shriek," "cry in pain." More's usage antedates the earliest recorded in *OED*, which is for 1577 (s.v. *shriek* v.).

32/46 **That.** Used here in the sense of "those things which"; on the nonexpression of the antecedent for *that* in Middle English see Mustanoja, p. 190. Cf. 39/209, below.

32/47 **good reason.** That is, "rational conduct"; cf. *OED*, s.v. *reason* sb. 10b.

32/48 **Inconstaunte.** The sense requires an adjectival form, but 1556 reads "Inconstaunce." A confusion between *c* and *t* is an obvious form of compositional or scribal error.

33/57 **prophet.** That is, "profit."

33/65 **With owt . . . suffise.** Whiting H104.

33/66 **Better . . . wise.** Seemingly proverbial, but not in Whiting or Tilley.

33/67–70 **And . . . loke.** The assertions here are too general for very certain identification. But More likely would have had in mind such works as Boethius' *Consolation of Philosophy* (printed by Caxton from Chaucer's translation in [1478?]) and Lydgate's *Fall of Princes* (printed by Pynson in 1494), both influential works that "disprayse" Fortune.

33/69 **disprayse.** The *O* reading "dispayre" has been rejected. 1556 and 1557 agree in reading "disprayse," which is obviously superior. It is, moreover, easy to postulate forms of homoeographic error that could have produced the *O* reading.

33/71–73 **like the ffox . . . by them.** Whiting F597. The source of the proverb is Aesop's fable of the fox and the grapes. There were numerous incunable editions of Aesop printed in England, beginning with Caxton's in 1484; see *STC²* 175–177.3 and also several printed in the early 1500s; see *STC²* 168–69. For other evidence of More's knowledge of the fables see *CW 2*, 93/1–10; *CW 3/2*, nos. 42, 61, 134, 135, 180, 198, 222; *CW 6*, 296/1–6, 313/33–34, 369/20–22; *CW 9*, 3/8–11, 83/11–21; and *The Last Things* (159/20–160/5), above. See also the index entry "Aesop" in *CW 12*.

33/74 **But . . . in vayn.** Whiting L11.

34/96 **shape.** Probably used here in the sense of "beauty" (*OED*, s.v. *shape* sb. 4a–b).

34/97 **hepeste.** 1516 reads "kepeste," while 1556 has the nonsensical reading "helpeste." There is an obvious possibility of scribal confusion between *h* and *k*, a possibility that could have been influenced in favor of reading *k* for *h* by the form "kynne" at the end of the preceding line. It is hard to find a defensible reading for the expression "kepeste vp." I have therefore adopted 1557's reading here.

34/98 **shyned.** Both *1556* and *1557* read "shrined" ("shryned"); such a form must presumably be understood in the rare sense recorded in *OED* (s.v. *shrine* v.: "? to cover with rich ornament"), for which the only citation is from *1582*. The usage seems insufficiently attested to justify emendation, though the variant is attractive. "Shyned" seems to have the rare meaning "illuminated" (*OED*, s.v. *shine* v. 8). Cf. *CW 6*, 88/27.

34/99 **garnysshed.** Used here in the sense of "dressed elegantly." More's usage here antedates the earliest recorded in *OED* (s.v. *garnish* v. I3), which is in *A Dialogue of Comfort* (*CW 12*, 210/7).

35/109 **as ffers . . . hell.** Whiting F705, citing this as the only occurrence.

35/110 **brytill.** See note on "Rufull Lamentation," above, 10/30.

35/114 **gape after þe wynde.** That is, "to desire something insubstantial"; Whiting W322.

35/116 **suarmyng bees.** Whiting B177, not, however, noting this occurrence.

35/116 **flateryng.** *1556* reads "flakerynge" and *1557* "flickering." The *1556* reading seems unattested in *OED* and only rarely in *MED* in the sense of "fluttering," and the *1557* reading presumably takes "swarmyng bees" as the referent here. But *O*'s reading is clearly superior, since it is the "thowsandes in a rowt" (line 115) who are coming "To crowche & knele & gape" (line 114); hence the *O* reading continues the metaphor.

35/120 **as dogges . . . bone.** Whiting D325.

35/123 **hoveth.** An elided form of "hovereth"; cf. *CW 12*, 268/8–9: "the griesly cruell hang man deth . . . hath ever hovid a lofe."

35/128 **dowsy.** *1556* and *1557* read "drowsy," producing an obviously easier reading. *O*'s form (meaning "stupid") is attested in More's *Supplication of Souls:* "howe be it sone after beeing so dowsie drunke . . ." (*CW 7*, 212/11). More's usage probably antedates the earliest recorded in *OED*, which is for 1508 (s.v. *dowsy* a). *OED* characterizes this as an exclusively Scottish form.

36/132–36 **He . . . He.** That is, "one person . . . another."

36/132 **asketh.** That is, "asks for."

36/132 **to passe wold brynge.** More's use of the construction "to bring to pass" antedates the earliest recorded in *OED* (s.v. *pass* v. 6b).

36/133 **toye.** More's usage here, in the sense of "foolish trifle," antedates the earliest recorded in *OED* (s.v. *toy* sb. 4).

36/133 **not worth an egge.** Whiting A259, Tilley E95.

36/138 **dyueris . . . wittes.** Whiting H230, Tilley H279.

36/141 **at aventure.** That is, "at random" (*OED*, s.v. *adventure* sb. 3b); used in this sense in *CW 9*, 10/13–14; *CW 12*, 117/1.

36/142 **Cacche who so may.** Whiting C112.

36/143 **as.** *O*'s form, "a," lacks any lexical warrant as a variant form of "as."

36/150–51 **tosse . . . losse.** That is, "to throw to one man as his winnings what another has lost."

36/154 **But.** *1556* and *1557* add "he," clarifying the syntax; but nonexpression of a subject pronoun is quite common in Middle English; see Mustanoja, pp. 138–45.

37/158 **cuseth.** *1556* and *1557* read "curseth"; either reading is acceptable sense, but *O*'s appears the harder and has therefore been retained. It is presumably an aphetic form of "*accuse*," but it is not recorded in *OED*.

37/162–65 **But lord . . . lieth.** Whiting F506; Tilley F617, S768.

37/164 **stithe.** *O*'s reading is a form of the verb *sty*, "rise up" (*OED*, s.v. *sty* v.¹ B1), a form also reflected in *1556*'s "styeth"; the *1557* reading, "flieth," is obviously easier and probably derives from a confusion between long *s* and *f*.

37/166 **Iulius.** The fate of Julius Caesar is described in Lydgate's *Fall of Princes*, VI, 2759–2870.

37/167–68 **Darius . . . Alysandre.** Alexander and Darius seem to have been proverbially linked in the later Middle Ages; see Whiting A82 (citing an anonymous translation of the *Polychronicon*): "Whereof a proverbe was spronge, that kynge Alexander myghte putte rather kynge Darius from his realme then Diogenes from vertu." Brixius in his *Antimorus* links Alexander and Darius in one of his Latin poems (*CW 3/2*, 506/446).

37/167 **Darius.** Possibly Darius III, who was defeated by Alexander the Great; see *Fall of Princes*, IV, 1604–1967.

37/168 **Alysandre.** The death of Alexander the Great by poison is recounted in *Fall of Princes*, IV, 2143–70.

37/179 **in case.** *1556* and *1557* read "in the case," a variant that does create a decasyllabic line. But the phrase "in case" (meaning here "in the event") is sanctioned by *OED* (s.v. *case* sb.¹ 10a). More uses the phrase in a similar sense in *CW 8*, 406/14.

37/179 **kysse a knave.** The collocation here is possibly proverbial or formulaic rather than specific; otherwise it would require the assump-

tion of a change of gender for lines 178–79 from masculine to femi-
nine, since it seems unlikely that the same mouth in the line 178—if it
were masculine—could be kissing a knave (always masculine) in line
179. However, Tilley K121 records: "Better it is to kisse a knave than be
troubled" (first recorded in 1611). Possibly the phrase means "to be
humbled."

38/183 **totorned.** That is, "violently changed" (*OED*, s.v. *to* prefix[2] 2).
1556 and *1557* produce an easier reading, "is turned"; the use of *to* as
intensive is common in Middle English (see *OED*, s.v. *to* prefix[2]).

38/187–93 **Pouerte . . . tonne.** Willow (p. 200) detects the influence of
Lydgate's *Fall of Princes*, which reports that Diogenes "His duellyng
made withynne a litil tunne, / Which turned a-boute with concours off
the sunne"; I, 6229–30.

38/189 **goth to wrak.** That is, "falls into ruin." The same phrase ap-
pears in *CW 8*, 59/37.

38/190–91 **Socrates, Aristippus, Pithagoras.** Of these three Aris-
tippus is the most puzzling because of his association with the Hedonist
philosophers. He was, however, attestedly a close friend of Socrates. He
is alluded to in *CW 8*, 455/1–2, as an "olde fylosopher." But none of the
three is elsewhere, to the best of my knowledge, identified with poverty.

38/192–93 **agaynst . . . Bekith hym.** That is, "warms himself by expo-
sure to the sun" (*OED*, s.v. *beek* v[1] 1).

38/194 **Byas.** One of the seven sages of Greece. Campbell and Reed
(p. 197) note that More's anecdote seems to come from Cicero's *Paradoxa
Stoicorum* (1.1.8): "cuius cum patriam Prienea cepisset hostis, ceterique
ita fugerent ut multa de suis rebus secum asportarent; quum esset
admonitus a quodam ut idem ipse faceret: Ego, vero, inquit, facio: nam
omnia mecum porto mea. Ille haec ludibria fortunae ne sua quidem
putavit, quae nos appellamus etiam bona." Robert M. Coogan, "Pe-
trarch and More's Concept of Fortune," *Italica*, 46 (1969), 170, suggests
that the delineation of Byas may derive from Petrarch's *Rerum me-
morandarum libri;* he argues that More's representation "amounts to a
translation of Petrarch's characterization of Byas" and quotes the fol-
lowing passage from that work: "Cum enim patria eius expugnata et
incensa omnes cives quos cladi publice fortuna subduxerat, variorum
rerum sarcinulas efferent atque ipsum vacuum abeuntem ut idem fac-
eret monerent: 'Ita' inquit Bias, 'facio: omnia mea mecum porto,' que-
cunque extra animum sunt, nec sua bona iudicans, sed fortune."
Coogan points out (p. 171) that More would have had access to Gro-
cyn's copy of *Rerum memorandarum libri.* Either source is plausible.

38/195 **stode.** *1556* and *1557* add "so," creating a decasyllabic line; but
the addition is not necessary to the sense, and the meter is not suffi-
ciently regular to warrant an emendation solely on metrical grounds.

38/197 **why he nowght caried owt.** That is, "why he did not carry away any of his possessions."

38/201 **Heracletus.** Heraclitus, the Greek philosopher (c. 535–c. 475 B.C.E.).

38/202 **Democretus.** Democritus, the Greek philosopher (c. 460–c. 370 B.C.E.). The conjunction of Heraclitus, who "can neuer cease but wepe" (line 203), and Democritus, who "laweth" (line 206), is a commonplace of Renaissance literature.

38/204 **thik.** That is, "numerous" (*OED*, s.v. *thick* a. 5).

38/206 **laweth.** *1556* and *1557* read "laugheth"; but *O*'s form is a genuine variant sanctioned by *OED* (s.v. *laugh* v.).

39/209 **þat.** That is, "that which."

39/214 **drawghtes.** Seemingly used here in the sense of "plans." Such a usage antedates the earliest recorded in *OED* (s.v. *draught* sb. 33).

39/215 **them self.** *1556* and *1557* omit "self," presumably seeing "them" as a personal pronoun referring back to "they" (line 213). But *O*'s reading is acceptable in that the phrase "by themself" can mean simply "apart"—that is, distinct from the "pore secte." The lack of a final *s* on "themself" is not unusual at this date, since its appearance was a late fifteenth-century development (see Mustanoja, p. 147).

39/215 **&.** That is, "and" meaning "if."

39/226 **&.** That is, "and" meaning "if."

39/232 **ffoolis paradise.** Whiting F411, Tilley F523.

39/235 **beware of after clappes.** "After clappes" is used here in the figurative sense of "unexpected (unfavorable) further consequences"; Whiting A67, Tilley A57.

40/237–40 **Ye . . . forfare.** These lines are examples of the *impossibilia* motif, which More employs elsewhere (see note on 15/15–17/62).

40/239 **brennyng.** *1556* and *1557* read "burnyng(e)," a clear instance of modernization.

40/240 **this world . . . forfare.** That is, "encircle the world so as to destroy it" (*OED*, s.v. *forfare* v.¹ 2).

40/244 **as.** *1556* and *1557* add "any"; the sense seems to invite an indefinite article or a possessive pronoun, but there is warrant for the omission in Middle English (see Mustanoja, pp. 266–72), and in such an instance *O* provides a harder reading.

40/249 **owt of thyn hond.** *1556* and *1557* add "agayne," albeit at different points in the line: *1556* after "hond," and *1557* before "owt." The reading is unnecessary to sense and merely tends to regularize the line.

40/252 **Reseyue.** *O* reads "Res." Presumably after writing the contraction for *–es* he omitted the rest of the word through eyeskip.

40/253 **maner.** The usage here in the sense of "virtuous way of living" antedates the earliest recorded in *OED* (s.v. *maner* sb.¹ 4d); the earliest recorded usage, in Lyly's *Euphues* (1579), similarly collocates "maner and vertu."

40/254 **dowble fortune.** A quasi-proverbial formulation (cf. Whiting F516).

40/255 **defy.** *O* reads "desire," an error presumably occasioned by an initial confusion between long *s* and *f* (for a comparable error see note on 113/6).

40/257 **&.** That is, "and" meaning "if."

40/261 **None ffallith . . . hye.** Whiting C296; Tilley C414, F131.

41/262 **Remembre . . . bare.** Whiting N167.

41/263 **Þe giftes . . . ware.** Whiting G71.

41/263 **giftes of fortune.** As distinct from the other two traditional classes of gifts, those of body and of soul, which belong to nature.

41/272–78 **The rollyng . . . myne.** On this allusion to playing the game of fortune see the Introduction, p. xxx.

41/275–78 **Lo . . . myne.** Whiting F675, Tilley F767.

41/285 **behawor.** *O*'s form is unusual, but there are instances of interchange of *v* and *w* in sixteenth-century orthography; it has been allowed to stand.

42/299 **she pluckerh . . . wyff.** Possibly intended as a proverbial phrase; cf. also Whiting W246, citing More, *A Dialogue Concerning Heresies:* "There is but one shrewde wyfe in the worlde but . . . every man weneth he hath her" (*CW* 6, 313/26–28). Coogan, *Italica, 46* (1969), 170, suggests that the reference to the shrewish wife could be based on More's reading of Petrarch's *De remediis*, book 2, dialogue 19. Both *1556* and *1557* read "pyncheth" for "pluckerh," thus giving an easier reading. "Pluck" is sanctioned in the sense of "humble" or "humiliate" (*OED*, s.v. *pluck* v. 3a).

42/309 **Them . . . crede.** Whiting C541, Tilley C819.

43/311–13 **I durste . . . astronomye.** A similar parallel between astronomy and the "book of Fortune" game is made in the 1618 translation of Spirito's *Book of Fortune*. The preface to this work explains: "It is named the Booke of Fortune, as comprehending things that lye vnder chance, destiny, or lot, answering and declaring twenty questions following after the manner of Astronomie. Neuertheless I will that euery man know that it is no Astronomie, Necromancy nor Witch-craft, but

rather a Conceipt scorning priuily them that follow such false illusions:
And as I said before, made for recreation of the mind. Wherfore it is
not required that credence and faith bee giuen to euery figure and
Claus as it sheweth. Beleeue stedfastly in God alone, for hee alone
knoweth the mind and thought of man and disposeth all things as it
pleaseth him." A little later the preface asserts that "this Boke was made
for them that would faine bee merry and can take sport."

43/314 **Explicit.** After this, *1556* adds:

> Fortune speketh.
> Fortune ou est Dauid, et Salmon
> Mathusale, Iosue, Machabee
> Olofernes, Alexandre, et Sampson
> Iulles Cesar, Hector, Ausy, Pompee
> Ou est Vlyxes, et sa grant remommce
> Artur le roy, Godefroy, Charlemaine
> Daires le grant, Hercules Tholomee
> Ils sont tous mors, ce, monde est chose vaine
>
> Quest deuenu Phaton, le roy Felon
> Iob le couitois, Thobie, et leur lignce
> Aristote, Ypocras, et Platon
> Iudith, Hester, Boece, Peneloppee
> Royne dido, Palas, Iuno, Medee
> Geneiure, ausse la tresnoble Helaine
> Palamidee, Tristan, auec son espee
> Ilz sont tous mors, ce, monde est chose vaine
> Imprynte by me Robert Wyer dwelling/ge, in Saynt
> Martyns parysshe, in / The Duke of Suffolkes rentes, /
> besyde Charynge / Crosse. / Ad imprimendum / Solum.

45/2–5 **fortune . . . begile.** Possibly a reminiscence of Chaucer, *Troilus
& Criseyde*, 4. 2–3: "ythonked be Fortune, / That semest trewest whan
she wol bygyle."

45/7 **hauen of heauen.** R. G. Howarth, "Hopkins and Sir Thomas
More," *Notes & Queries*, *192* (1947), 389, argues that this is an echo of Ps.
107:28–30 in its play on "haven"/"heaven." Cf. Rogers, p. 233.

45/8 **Euer . . . storme.** Whiting C12, Tilley C24.

46/2 **ladye lucke.** *OED* records this as the earliest instance of personi-
fication of luck (s.v. *luck* sb. Ic).

46/6 **beshrewe your catte.** Sylvester notes: "'To turn the cat' was a
dicing term which meant 'to reverse the order of things so dexterously
as to make them appear the opposite of what they really were'"; he
glosses the phrase as "to 'curse whatever deceptive plans you may have
made for me'" (p. 123). See *OED*, s.v. *cat* sb.[1] 12.

51/1–2 **entierly beloued sister . . . Ioyeuce Leigh.** On Joyeuce Leigh see above, Introduction, p. xxxix–xl.

51/4–52/16 **Hit is . . . preserue you.** The preface is More's addition to the Latin.

51/5 **a custome in the begynnyng of yᵉ new yere.** The tradition of presenting works at the beginning of the new year is attested in England from the twelfth century; see the *Chronica* of Jocelyn of Brakelond, ed. H. E. Butler (London, 1949), p. 62. Earlier examples in English during the Middle Ages include a number of fairly brief verse texts; see, for example, Lydgate's "A Lover's New Year's Gift" and "Ballade on a New Year's Gift of an Eagle, Presented to Henry VI," both in *The Minor Poems of John Lydgate*, ed. H. N. MacCracken (EETS OS no. 192, London, 1934), pp. 427–29 and 649–51. See also Dunbar's "To the King," in *The Poems of William Dunbar*, ed. James Kinsley (Oxford, 1979), no. 18; Kinsley cites a number of French parallels (p. 278). See also the carol "Lerges of this New Yeirday," in *The Early English Carols*, ed. R. L. Greene, 2nd ed. (Oxford, 1977), no. 121.2, and his commentary on p. 375 for further discussion of the tradition. More's work is the earliest extended prose work of which I am aware within the medieval English tradition. There is a parallel between More's work and a work that More attacked in the second edition of *A Dialogue Concerning Heresies,* the prose *Ymage of Loue* (1525), which was also written as a New Year's gift for female religious; see *CW 6/2*, 729.

51/5–6 **sende betwene.** The context clearly indicates that the term means "exchange," but no such usage is recorded in *OED.*

51/8 **lukky.** More's usage antedates any of those recorded in *OED*, s.v. *lucky* a.

51/13 **stretchith.** That is, "extends to." It appears in this sense also in *CW 6*, 218/8.

51/16–17 **for as thapostle . . . vs.** Rom. 8:10–11.

51/23 **warkis.** The use of the plural here and again at 52/4 and 52/9 makes clear that More sees his translations of Pico's works, as well as of Gianfrancesco's *Vita,* as important aspects of his undertaking.

52/1 **Mirandula a lordshyp in Italy.** Mirandola is north of Modena, in central Italy.

52/5 **of yᵉ quantite.** That is, "in relation to their size."

52/14 **ioyously.** Perhaps a pun on "loyeuse" is intended here.

52/16 **who preserue you.** That is, "may he preserue you."

52/19–20 **descendid . . . Constantine.** Rigg notes (p. 82) that "the descent from the nephew of Constantine is mythical."

52/12 **vndowtedly.** Not in the Latin.

52/22 **name.** After this More omits a clause from the Latin: "ab ipso . . . initium" (294/22–24).

52/23 **though . . . excellent.** Not in the Latin.

52/24 **receyued.** After this More omits a passage from the Latin (294/25–27).

52/24–25 **and . . . vertue.** Not in the Latin.

52/25–53/28 **For . . . wrytin.** This passage is More's addition to the Latin. The distinction between the nobility of self and the nobility of ancestry was a common one from the Middle Ages; a number of references are conveniently assembled in *The Riverside Chaucer*, ed. L. D. Benson et al. (Boston, 1986), p. 874, note on "The Wife of Bath's Tale," III, 1109. For a general survey of the tradition see George M. Vogt, "Gleanings for the History of a Sentiment: *Generositas Virtus, non Sanguis*," *Journal of English & Germanic Philology*, 24 (1925), 101–24. Cf. also *CW 3/2*, 642/12–18.

52/30–53/1 **honoure . . . vertue.** Proverbial; Tilley H571. For a similar sentiment elsewhere in More see *CW 4*, 192/23–29.

53/29 **Of his parentis . . . birth.** The division of the text into sections with headings has no parallel in the Latin. Some of the headings may have been suggested by sidenotes in five early editions of the *Vita* in the *Opera omnia*. See Appendix A, p. 292.

53/30 **In the yere.** Before this point More omits most of the first page of the Latin (294/6–20), in which Gianfrancesco describes his relationship to Pico and asserts the objectivity of his narrative.

53/30 **Pius the seconde.** Aeneas Sylvius Piccolomini (1405–1464) became pope in 1458.

53/31–32 **Federik the thryd.** Frederick III (1415–1493) became Holy Roman Emperor in 1452.

53/32 **was born.** Pico was born on February 24, 1463.

53/33 **the last child.** Pico was the youngest of six children. He had three sisters, Caterina, Giulia, and Lucrezia, and two brothers, Galeotto and Antonio Maria; see further Rigg, pp. 81–82.

53/33–54/1 **Iulya . . . noble stok.** His mother was Giulia Boiardo, from the family of the poet. The Latin specifies this: "ex nobili Boiardorum familia" (294/31–32). For Giulia's biography see F. Ceretti, *Giulia Boiardo* (Modena, 1881).

54/1–2 **Iohan frauncise . . . auctorite.** His father (also Gianfrancesco) was count of Mirandola and Concordia. The phrase "a lorde . . . auctorite" does not appear in the Latin.

54/1 **frauncise.** After this More omits details of Pico's siblings that appear in the Latin (294/32–296/2).

54/3 **Of the wondre . . . birth.** The Latin sidenote is "Prodigium."

54/9–10 **the perfite . . . garland.** Translating "orbiculari figurae" (296/5). The use of doublets is a recurrent feature of More's translation; see the Introduction, p. li.

54/14 **god.** More omits a clause from the Latin: "qui ignis comburens est" (296/9–10).

54/17 **tokens . . . folowith.** On the treatment of plurals as singular in Middle English see Mustanoja, pp. 64–65.

54/22–55/2 **The gret . . . heuen.** The source is the *Vita sancti Ambrosii Mediolanensis episcopi,* by Paulinus of Milan; see M. Pellegrino, ed., *Paolino di Milan* (Rome, 1961).

54/28 **swete . . . wrytinge.** The Latin is "scriptorum eius favos" (296/19).

55/6 **entremengled . . . ruddis.** Translating "rubore interspersa" (296/22–23). More uses the singular form "comly rud" in *CW* 2, 54/32. *OED* does not record the use of plural for singular with this form (s.v. *rud* sb.1).

55/7–8 **his teth . . . to pikede.** More reverses the order of the Latin here (see 296/23–24).

55/8 **to pikede.** Translating "inaffectato." Literally, "not picked to pieces" (see *OED,* s.v. *to* prefix²)—that is, "carefully dressed."

55/9 **Of his setting . . . humanite.** The Latin sidenote is "Profectus in studiis humanitatis aetate tenella."

55/9 **humanite.** *1510* has "humanitate," a form not sanctioned in English. The phrase "in humanitate" could be Latin; but *1525* and *1557* read "humanyte" and "humanitie" respectively at this point.

55/10 **rule and gouernaunce.** Translating "imperio" (296/25).

55/12 **studies of humanite.** That is, "classical studies" (translating "studia humanitatis," 296/26).

55/17 **sure   remembraunce.**   The   Latin   is   "tenacissima-que . . . memoria" (296/30). Here, as elsewhere, More omits or modifies the superlative.

56/1 **Bononye.** Bologna was one of the great centers for the study of canon law in the Middle Ages. Pico went there in 1477.

56/2 **had . . . tasted.** Translating "degustasset" (296/36).

56/3–4 **his mynde fill from hit.** Translating "alio deflexit" (298/1).

56/4 **Yet . . . therin.** The Latin is "non tamen absque bonae frugis foetura" (298/1–2).

56/4–5 **yet beyng a childe.** The Latin is "quando iam puer & quidem tenellus" (298/2). Cf. 56/18.

56/5 **breuiary.** More's usage in the sense of "summary" or "epitome" antedates the earliest recorded in *OED* (s.v. *breviary* 1).

56/5–6 **breuiary . . . decretallis.** This work has not survived. Gratian's *Decretum* and the subsequent papal decretals were the principal texts of canon law.

56/8 **right conning & parfite doctours.** Translating "consummatis professoribus" (298/5).

56/12 **hole.** Translating "penitus" (298/9).

56/14 **Plato.** On Plato's travels to study with various philosophers and wise men see Diogenes Laertius, *Vitae philosophorum* 3.6.

56/14 **Apollonius.** According to Philostratus' *Life of Apollonius of Tyana*, Apollonius traveled to learn from sages in India, Babylonia, and Egypt (1.18; 3.16–20, 34; 6.6, 19). Pico owned a manuscript of Philostratus' *Life* (see Pearl Kibre, *The Library of Pico della Pirandola*, New York, 1936, p. 124, no. 43); see also 69/17. More cites "Appolonius Thianeus" in *CW 6*, 241/27–29.

56/15–17 **all the famous . . . fraunce.** Pico left Bologna in 1478 and visited Florence and Ferrara before studying at the University of Padua from 1480 to 1482. From 1484 to early 1485 he was in Florence. He visited the Sorbonne from July 1485 to March 1486 before returning to Florence, after which he went to Rome, in November, seeking to present his nine hundred theses (see below, note on 57/15). In November 1487 he returned to France, where in 1488 he was arrested at Lyons on the orders of Innocent VIII. On his time in France see L. Dorez and L. Thuasne, *Pic de la Mirandole en France (1485–88)* (Paris, 1897).

56/17 **infatigable.** *OED* gives the earliest occurrence of this form at 88/5 (s.v. *infatigable* a. Obs.).

56/18 **yet a child and berdles.** Cf. 56/5. Pico was about sixteen when he left Bologna to pursue philosophical studies.

56/21 **dispitions.** *OED* gives this form at 57/16 as the earliest recorded usage in the sense of "disputation" (s.v. *dispicion*).

56/22 **Now . . . .vii. yere.** That is, about 1486.

56/24 **kyndled in.** Translating "caluerat" (298/16).

56/24 **loue of god.** More omits a clause after this: "ut palam fiet" (298/16–17).

56/25–26 **litil . . . self.** The Latin says that he wished to show how much envy he could arouse.

56/26 **ix.C. questions.** Pico's *Conclusiones DCCCC publice disputandae* were published in Rome by Eucharius Silber on December 7, 1486; they were reprinted in 1487 at Ingolstadt. There is a modern edition by Bohdan Kieszkowski, Travaux d'Humanisme et Renaissance 131 (Geneva, 1973).

57/1–2 **of diuerse . . . diuinite.** The Latin reads "de dialecticis & mathematicis, de naturalibus divinisque rebus" (298/18–19). Pico's theses draw on an astonishingly wide range of materials. According to Ernst Cassirer, "metaphysics and theological dogmatics, mathematics and astrology, magic and cabbalistic speculation, the history of philosophy, church history, natural history—we encounter them all in motley array. It is as though Pico's ambition was to assemble the positions he desired to treat and defend from every region of the *'globus intellectualis.'*" ("Giovanni Pico della Mirandola," in *Renaissance Essays*, ed. Paul Oskar Kristeller and Philip P. Wiener, New York, 1968, pp. 12–13).

57/4 **hebrieus Caldaies & Arabies.** See also the references to his study of these languages at 65/19 and at 88/5–7.

57/4 **Caldaies.** The Chaldeans were a Semitic race who established a Babylonian empire in the sixth and seventh centuries B.C.E. They became particularly identified with the study of astrology.

57/5–7 **olde . . . strange.** A reference to the corpus of Hermetic writings that appeared in Greek in the third century C.E. Many were ascribed to Hermes Trismegistus; the earlier figure of Pythagoras (c. 580 B.C.E.) and the legendary Orpheus became associated with this corpus during the Renaissance.

57/6–8 **thyngis strange . . . vnherd of.** More omits references to the Cabala, Origen, and Hilary and to "multa etiam de naturali magia" (298/23–26) as well as fuller details of Pico's propositions, replacing them with this brief summary.

57/14 **dispitions.** See note on 56/21.

57/15 **an hole yere.** Pico arrived in Rome toward the end of November 1486 and remained there until November 1487.

57/17 **attempt.** Used here in the sense of "attack," translating "aggredi" (298/36).

57/18 **pryuey trenches.** Translating "cuniculis" (298/37). *OED* does not record "trenches" in the sense of tunnels.

57/24 **deface.** More's usage antedates the earliest recorded in *OED* in the sense of "discredit" (s.v. *deface* v. 4).

57/25 **doctryne.** After this More omits a phrase in the Latin: "quasi fertilis ager luxurians" (300/5).

57/27 **thinges naturall.** That is, "natural philosophy," as opposed to theology; the Latin is "naturalibus diuinisque rebus" (300/6). Cf. 62/9.

57/28–30 **Now . . . preuaile.** Translating "et cum nihil adversus doctrinam veris machinis moliri posse animadverterent" (300/8–9). The association with siege warfare ("machinis moliri") is lost in More's translation.

57/30–58/1 **serpentines . . . crime.** Although *OED* gives this as the first usage in the sense of "malicious actions" (s.v. *serpentine* sb. 9), the Latin "tormenta calumniae" (300/9) makes it clear that More is referring to a kind of cannon, the sixteenth-century equivalent of the Roman catapult.

58/1 **.xiii. of his .ix.C. questions.** Seven of Pico's theses were explicitly condemned by an examining commission on March 5, 1487, and the orthodoxy of six others held questionable.

58/4–5 **with which their eris had not be in vre.** Translating "utpote insuetas eorum auribus" (300/11–12). The phrase "in vre" seems to be used here in the sense of "used to" or "accustomed"; cf. the usage in *CW* 2, 20/8–9: "But himself had bene al his dayes in vre therwᵗ."

58/9 **vndre them.** After this More omits a passage in the Latin (300/15–20) describing Buonfrancesco, bishop of Reggio, who sought to defend Pico; see Lehmberg, p. 63.

58/10 **a defence.** That is, the *Apologia conclusionum suarum*, according to its imprint published on May 31, 1487, in Naples but alleged by contemporary opponents of Pico to have been written later and backdated. Dr. Lotte Hellinga, of the Incunable Short Title Catalogue at the British Library, advises me that the date appears to be that of writing rather than that of printing.

58/14–15 **conclusions . . . faith.** Translating "conclusiones catholicos potuisse sensus recipere" (300/24–25).

58/18 **holy chirch.** After this the Latin adds "eiusque praesidis," (300/27), that is, the pope. After this More also omits a passage (300/28–31) in which Pico's reasons for this course of action are elaborated; see Lehmberg, pp. 62–63.

58/19 **questions.** After this More omits a clause, "quae prius calumniis infestatae fuerant" (300/32–33).

58/20 **examined.** More omits a phrase, "per editionem Apologiae" (300/32).

58/20 yᵉ **pope.** The Latin specifies that this is Innocent VIII, not, as More's syntax seems to imply, Alexander VI.

58/21–22 **our holi fathir . . . apperith.** In fact the bull for Pico's absolution was not promulgated until June 18, 1493, by Pope Alexander VI.

58/22 **apperith.** After this More omits a passage from the Latin (302/3–5) in which Gianfrancesco explains that the text of this bull is printed in *Opera omnia* with the text of Pico's *Apology*.

58/23–28 **for . . . redd.** More conveys a general sense of the Latin (300/34–302/2) here, but he omits the fact that Pope Innocent VIII specifically forbade the reading of the *DCCCC Conclusiones*.

58/27–29 **Picus . . . forboden.** Pico retracted his *900 Conclusions* before a papal commission in July 1487. Pope Innocent VIII ordered their suppression.

58/29–32 **Lo . . . sclaundre.** This passage is More's addition. He omits a passage from the Latin (302/4–18) that elaborates Pico's arguments against reading his conclusions.

59/1 **as him self . . . neuiew.** Here, as almost invariably elsewhere, More changes Gianfrancesco's use of the first person singular. The Latin is "quemadmodum mihi rettulit" (302/20).

59/11 **his meruelouse fame.** More's addition to the Latin.

59/16 **in riot.** Translating "diffluentem" (302/29); More's usage, in the figurative sense "wildly," antedates the earliest usage recorded in *OED* (s.v. *riot* sb. 3b).

59/21 **& though.** That is, "even if."

59/25–26 **noble cunnyng and excellent vertue.** Translating "gloriosa . . . fama" (302/34).

59/28–29 **market of good doctrine.** Translating "mercaturam bonarum artium" (302/36). More omits the clause "ut inquit Cicero" (302/36–37). The reference is to Cicero, *De officiis* 3.6: "tamquam ad mercaturam bonarum artium sis profectus."

60/4 **more noble . . . more wyse.** More reverses the order of the Latin and renders the superlatives as comparatives: "doctissimo . . . nobilissimo" (304/3).

60/5–6 yᵉ **croked hilles of delitiouse pleasure.** Translating "devios mollitudinis voluptariae anfractus" (304/4).

60/9 **ragged.** Translating "distorto" (304/7).

60/12 **Fiue bokis . . . loue.** These books are lost, although more than fifty love sonnets do survive. For discussion and bibliography see Paul

Oskar Kristeller, "Giovanni Pico della Mirandola and His Sources," in *L'opera e il pensiero di Giovanni Pico della Mirandola, 1,* 43, 48–50, 85–88.

60/13–15 **in detestation . . . aftirwarde.** More's addition.

60/17–18 **From . . . scripture.** Translating "Sacras deinde litteras ardentissimo studio complexus" (304/12). After this More omits a very long section of the Latin, amounting to between a quarter and a third of the whole work (304/12–316/31). The omitted passage is largely an account of Pico's writings and his library. It is summarized in 60/18–21. See Lehmberg, pp. 71–72, for an account of this omission.

61/1–3 **But . . . treuth.** A rendering of an isolated passage in the Latin: "Thomam vero Aquinatem . . . nitentem" (316/14–17). As Gilmore notes, Aquinas is the only authority cited by Gianfrancesco to be specifically mentioned by More; see Myron Gilmore, "More's Translation of Gianfrancesco Pico's Biography," in *L'opera e il pensiero di Giovanni Pico della Mirandola, 2,* 303.

61/2 **saint thomas.** Pico's library included nearly thirty separate works or editions of Aquinas; see Pearl Kibre, *The Library of Pico della Mirandola* (New York, 1936), nos. 30, 50, 94, 95, 99, 100, 101, 160, 187, 193, 348, 363, 378, 417, 472, 474, 537, 555, 619, 644, 651, 654, 683, 765, 931, 986, 1118.

61/3–4 **He . . . stomak.** Translating an isolated sentence in the Latin: "Disceptandi porro peritissimus fuit frequentemque & impensissimam operam literariis agonibus, dum ferueret animus, impendit" (316/25–26).

61/4 **hye stomak.** Translating "dum ferveret animus" (316/26). Cf. *CW 13,* 14/7: "proud enuious stomake." *OED* cites this phrase as the first combined usage in the sense of "elevated state of feeling," s.v. *stomach* sb. 8. After this point More omits a passage from the Latin (316/26–31) comparing Pico's intellectual powers with those of a number of scholastic philosophers, including Duns Scotus, Aquinas, and Albertus Magnus.

61/7 **hercules Estensis.** Ercole d'Este (1431?–1505), who had become duke of Ferrara in 1471.

61/9 **freres prechours.** That is, the Dominican order. On Pico's plan to join this order see 70/18–20.

61/12 **thyder.** At this point More omits most of a passage from the Latin (318/1–3) describing Pico's demeanor in debate.

61/14–15 **neythir more connyng nor more connyngly.** Rendering "solertiorne an eloquentior, doctior an humanior" (318/1).

61/24 **gasing.** Translating "frontiuagi" (318/11), a nonclassical adjective that seems to mean "boldly turning their heads in various directions." More settles on the reason the head is turned, that is, in order to stare. More's usage antedates the earliest recorded in *OED* (s.v. *gazing* ppl. a.).

61/27–28 **nothing passed him.** That is, "nothing which escaped him."

61/28 **captions soteltes & cauillations of sophistrie.** Translating "captiunculas cavillasque sophistarum" (318/14–15). After this More omits a passage from the Latin (318/15–20) in which Gianfrancesco inveighs against trifling dialectical and scientific speculation.

61/28 **captions.** More's usage antedates the earliest recorded in *OED* in the sense of "sophisms" (s.v. *caption* sb. 2).

61/28 **soteltes.** More's usage antedates the earliest recorded in *OED* in the sense of "niceties of thought" (s.v. *subtlety* sb. 7).

61/1–2 **consydering.** More omits "meo iudicio" (318/21).

62/9 **naturall thinges.** See 57/27 and note.

61/10 **man.** The Latin "alius" and the parallelism with the preceding and following sentences show that "man" (*1557*) is the correct reading, not "men" (*1510, 1525*).

62/11 **wanted.** The Latin is "non calluit" (318/28), "was not expert in": More's rendering means simply "lacked."

62/13 **hath not been excercised.** The Latin is "non . . . concinnavit" (318/28–29). More's usage in the sense of "accustomed" antedates the earliest recorded in *OED* (s.v. *exercise* v. 3c).

62/13–14 **new scolis.** Translating "nova dogmata" (318/28–29).

62/17 **by hepis.** Translating "turmatim & coacervatim" (318/32).

62/19–20 **which . . . aside.** Not an accurate translation of the Latin (318/33–34), which means "who excel in no one branch of learning but know something of all of them."

62/24–25 **for yᵉ loue . . . chirch.** The phrase is More's substitution for the Latin "& ueritatis amore" (320/2); for discussion see Lehmberg, p. 73.

62/26 **Epicure . . . maister.** The Greek philosopher (341–270 B. C. E.). Rigg (p. 83) cites Diogenes Laertius, *Vitae philosophorum* 10.13, where Epicurus claims to have taught himself.

63/5 **fast.** *OED* cites this as the earliest recorded usage in the sense of "gripping," "tenacious" (s.v. *fast* a. 6). More is translating "tenacissimam" (320/6–7).

63/6–9 yᵉ bying . . . litterature. It is unclear at what period of Pico's life this great expenditure took place. Kibre observes: "Of the gradual building up of the library there is little information to be gathered" (*Library of Pico della Mirandola*, New York, 1936, p. 12).

63/7 holpen. After this More omits Gianfrancesco's "rettulisse mihi memoria repeto" (320/9).

63/9 his besy . . . study. On the importance of study elsewhere in More's works see *CW 4*, Commentary on 180/2.

63/10 dispising. Both *1510* and *1525* read "contempt dispising," while *1557* has "contempt or dispisinge." The Latin is "contemptionem" (320/11). In view of More's tendency to translate the Latin nouns in doublets it may be that an ampersand has simply dropped out. It seems also possible, however, that More was uncertain, at a number of points, as to what form he wanted to use and failed to cancel the rejected form (for evidence of this tendency elsewhere see *CW 14*, 759, n. 4), as seems to have happened twice in his verse renderings of Pico; see notes on 105/26 and 113/16.

63/10 thingis. After this More omits two sentences of the Latin: "Hunc igitur si prisca illa aetas Laconum tempore protulisset, si Aristoteli credimus, divinum illum virum appellavisset" (320/12–13).

63/12 pass ouer. More omits Gianfrancesco's parenthetical "ut arbitror" (320/14).

63/17 which . . . vertue. More's substitution for "qui tandem divinae legi sunt addicti" (320/18).

63/18 laude and thanke. Translating "gratias" (320/18).

63/23–24 rest and peace. Translating "in alta pace" (320/21).

63/24–25 wele . . . commith. Translating "securus quo sceptra caderent" (320/21).

64/3 sale. After this More omits a passage in the Latin (320/23–27) in praise of the emperor Maximilian, "qui nobis est rex & dominus" (320/24), who confirmed the sale. For an account of the division of the earldom and the ceding of Pico's share to his nephew see Rigg, p. 83, n. 11, who summarizes the conflict between Pico's brothers that led to this division.

64/6 howsolde. After this More omits a passage from the Latin: "nominatimque Corbulas in agro Ferrariensi multis aureorum milibus nummum" (320/30–31).

64/11 plentuosly. More's addition to the Latin.

64/13 Hierom Beniuenius. On Girolamo Benivieni (1453–1498) see Cesare Vasoli's entry in *Dizionario biografico degli Italiani* (Rome, 1966),

5, 550–55. The Latin shows that "Beniuenius" is the correct form of the name. The error in the early editions was caused by misreading the two series of minims. Pico wrote, probably c. 1486, a commentary on Benivieni's *Canzone d'amore* that was published posthumously in Benivieni's *Opere* (Florence, 1519). For a modern critical edition of Pico's commentary see Eugenio Garin, ed., *De hominis dignitate, Heptaplus, De Ente et uno e scritti vari* (Florence, 1942), pp. 443–581.

64/14 **integrite.** More's usage in the sense of "freedom from sin" antedates the earliest recorded in *OED* (s.v. *integrity* 3a).

64/25–26 **seint Hierom.** Jerome's "Epistola ad Eustochium Virginem," quoted in Rigg, p. 84, n. 13; see the edition in *Sancti Eusebii Hieronymi Epistulae*, ed. Isidor Hilberg, Corpus Scriptorum Ecclesiasticorum Latinorum 55/2 (Vienna, 1912), p. 328.

64/26–65/3 **but he . . . offencis.** More omits Gianfrancesco's autobiographical authentication concluding this passage: "meisque oculis saepius (cuncta in dei gloriam redeant) flagellum vidi" (322/9–10).

65/4 **placabilite.** Meaning "mildness of disposition." More's usage antedates the earliest recorded in *OED* (s.v. *placability*).

65/6 **Angre.** After this More omits "multis etiam audientibus testatus sit" (322/12).

65/6 **he said . . . neuieu.** Translating "Recolo mihi inter loquendum dixisse" (322/12–13).

65/13–16 **sith . . . heuines.** More added the clauses "sith god is almighty" and "sith god is all good" to the Latin, which says only that Pico trusted he would not be grieved if his papers were lost, not that he believed God would not permit them to be destroyed.

65/15–16 **he . . . heuines.** The Latin says "he [Pico] trusted that he would not be saddened [by the case]" (322/18).

65/16 **very.** More's addition.

65/17–18 **enhaunce.** More omits a clause after this ("ut palam fiet," 322/20).

65/19–20 **the hebrewe chaldey and arabie language.** See above, 57/4, and note on 88/5–6. "Chaldey" means "Aramaic," not the actual Chaldean language, which was recovered in the nineteenth century.

65/20–21 **waingloriouse.** For another instance of the interchangeability of *w* and *v* see 41/285, above.

65/22 **ye bewty of his body.** Translating "corporis pulchritudo & elegantia" (322/23).

65/22 **occasion.** Translating "licentia" (322/24). "Occasion of sin" was a set phrase. Confessors admonished penitents to avoid the occasions of sin, as Chaucer's Parson insists that the truly repentant must "fle the occasiouns of synne" (*Canterbury Tales*, X [I], 1005). More uses "occasiouns" in the same sense at 77/24 and 78/7, and "occasions of synne" at 107/19.

65/23 y^e **voluptuouse brode way.** Translating "in mollem illam & spatiosam multorum viam" (322/24–25).

65/23–24 y^t **ledith to helle.** More's addition. Cf. Matt. 7:13.

65/24 **ther.** More omits "inquam" (322/26).

65/25 **as seneke sayth.** Seneca, *De brevitate vitae* 5.3.

65/26–27 **which . . . he.** A compression of the Latin: "cum illam, sive secundis flatibus tumidam sive adversis reflatibus humilem, aliquando contempserit" (322/27–29).

65/27 **he.** Translating "eius mens" (322/29).

66/2 **Whan.** Before this More omits a clause: "Quod vel hoc argumento liquido percipitur" (322/31).

66/5 **to receyue them.** More omits "per internuntios oblatas (testes adsunt gravissimi, testis ego) se sacris initiari nolle respondens" (322/33–34).

66/5 **two kingis.** These kings cannot be identified.

66/5–6 **an othir man.** The Latin is simply "alter" (322/35), and the figure cannot be identified.

66/6 **promotion.** Translating "reditus" (322/36, "income"), although *OED* does not give that meaning.

66/6 **worldy.** Although this form does not seem to appear in any of More's other works, it also appears later, at 69/15. The form is attested elsewhere: *OED*, s.v. *worldy* a. Obs. rare.

66/7 **cowrte.** After this More omits "conspicatus angulum non relinqui in quem se conderet ademptaque esse cuncta suffugia" (324/1–2).

66/10 **god.** After this More omits a lengthy passage from the Latin describing how Pico declined the office of cardinal (324/4–21). The passage is discussed in Lehmberg, pp. 64–65.

66/10 **this was he persuaded.** The sense here is somewhat awkward: "this weis," the reading of *1510*, could perhaps be seen as an adverb ("thus"; *OED*, s.v. *thiswise* adv.). But such a construction with "he persuaded" and followed by a substantive clause seems very unusual. It is better to take "this" as an adverbial form ("thus"). It seems clear that the form "weis" gave problems to the early printers. In *1525* it seems to have been seen as a form of "wise," the sense seeming to be "this way he (was) persuaded"; but the compositor of *1510* may have intended it to be a form of "was." Alternatively "was" may have been omitted through eyeskip after "weis." Since it appears necessary to emend for sense we have understood "this" as a form of "thus" and emended "weis" to "was."

66/10 **persuaded.** More's usage here in the sense of "came to believe" antedates the earliest recorded in *OED* (s.v. *persuade* v. 1b).

66/12 **richesse.** After this More omits "non quaesisse honores" (324/22–23).

66/12 **refuse them.** After this More omits a passage from the Latin here (324/23–25) and places it after the next sentence.

66/17 **dyde hurt.** The Latin (324/25–26) says that fame often does some good for men while they are alive. More may have read "nihil" for "non nihil."

66/18 **neuer good.** That is, "never did good."

66/18 **So moche.** More omits "agnovimus" (324/27).

66/20 **extermination.** Translating "eliminandis explodendisque" (324/27–28).

66/20–21 **over that.** More omits "percepimus" (324/29).

66/26–27 **commune profit.** Translating "publica . . . utilitas" (324/34–35). More uses the same phrase at 87/28.

67/2 **by and by.** Substituted for "passim" (324/35).

67/2 **aftir.** More omits "sed & immatura exigi" (324/36).

67/9 **bowe.** All the early Latin editions have "laborant" (326/3), which is incorrect because a subjunctive form is required. More (or the text he used) emended to "labant," "to fall." It would also be possible to read "laborent."

67/10 **falling.** Translating "fluxum" (326/4) and used here apparently in the sense of "transitory."

67/16 **de ente et vno.** The full title is *De ente et uno ad Angelum Politianum.* This treatise on the problems of being and unity was composed by Pico in 1491 but was not published until after his death.

67/16 **lightsomely.** *OED* cites this as the earliest recorded usage in the sense of "clearly, lucidly" (s.v. *lightsomely* adv.²). More is translating "luculentissime" (326/9).

67/17–18 **Angelus Politianus.** Angelo Poliziano (1454–1494), poet and humanist, a close friend of Pico's.

67/19–25 **But now . . . founde.** This passage is a quotation from chapter 5 of Pico's work.

67/25 **founde.** After this More omits a sentence from the Latin in which Pico quotes St. Francis (326/16–17).

68/1 **besprent with the frekill of negligence.** Translating "incuriositatis naeuo macularetur" (326/19–20). More's use of "frekill" in a figurative sense is the earliest recorded in *OED* (s.v. *freckle* sb. 1).

68/4–5 **that . . . money.** This passage has no parallel in the Latin.

68/8–9 **consideration and ouerseing.** Translating "pensiculanda" (326/25).

68/9 **these base . . . trifles.** Translating "haec infima abiectaque" (326/25). More's use of "abiecte" in the sense of "degraded" antedates the earliest recorded in *OED* (s.v. *abject* 3).

68/9 **trifles.** After this More omits a reminiscence of Gianfrancesco's about observing Pico's attention to his accounts, which Pico claimed resulted from the request of his "familiares" (326/25–30).

68/12 **him.** All the early editions read "his," which the Latin and the syntax show to be a misprint for "him." After this More omits six words from the Latin (326/33) concerning the steward's motive and Gianfrancesco's presence at this incident.

68/15–16 **Ther is no more to do.** This sentence is More's addition.

68/21 **gret benignite & curtesye.** The Latin has "multa indulgentia" (328/1).

68/22 **secrete communing.** Translating "hortatoriis . . . locutionibus" (328/1–2).

68/23 **to godward.** The Latin has "ad benevivendum" (328/2).

68/23–24 **so . . . herers.** More's addition.

68/24 **yᵗ where.** More's substitution for Gianfrancesco's "novi" (328/2).

68/24 **a connyng man.** The Latin is "hominem" (328/2).

68/24–25 **but . . . daie.** This passage is More's addition.

69/4 **paynfull.** The adjective is More's addition.

69/10 **frendshippe.** After this More omits a sentence about Pico's support of young scholars (328/9–11).

69/10–11 **A lykenes . . . affinite.** More omits "erga sapientem virum" and "teste" (328/12).

69/11 **Appollonius.** See 56/14 and note. In Philostratus' *Life of Apollonius* (6.40) Apollonius reprimands a young man who had fallen in love with a statue of Aphrodite: "but I know this much about loving and being loved: gods fall in love with gods, and human beings with human beings, and animals with animals, and in a word, like with like" (trans. F. C. Conybeare, London, 1912, 2, 137).

69/11 **affinite.** After this More omits a passage, a syllogistic sentence showing that knowledge makes a man more nearly perfect and therefore good and worthy of love (328/13–14).

69/14 **as horace saith.** *Epodes* 2.7–8. Horace is referring to the palaces of powerful men, but the basic meaning of "limina" (328/16, "thresholds") also suggests suitors waiting at the doorway.

69/14–15 **Weddyng & worldy besynes.** Translating "Militiam quoque saeculi & coniugale vinculum" (328/16–17). Reed's note on this passage (p. 199) is in error in translating "militia" as "military service"—see the note on 78/26 for the same usage. On "worldy" see note on 66/6.

69/18–19 **he stiked thereat.** Translating "haesitabundus" (328/19). More's usage in the sense of "hesitate" antedates the earliest recorded in *OED* (s.v. *stick* v.¹ 24).

69/21–22 **Liberte a boue all thing he loued.** For More's own sympathy with this sentiment see *CW 4*, Commentary at 56/1. See also Pico's letter to Corneo, 87/2–4.

69/23 **him.** After this More omits Gianfrancesco's "autumo" (328/24).

69/23–24 **alway wandering & flitting.** On Pico's travels see Rigg, pp. 84–86, and notes on 56/15–17 and 57/15.

69/25 **dwelling.** After this More omits a passage from the Latin (328/24–37), which describes the attraction of Ferrara and Florence to Pico: the former because of its proximity to Mirandola and its associations with his youth; the latter because of his friendship with Angelo Poliziano and Ficino and the presence of the Platonic Academy. See Lehmberg (p. 72) for discussion of this omission.

70/4 **diligent.** After this More omits four words in the Latin: "prae oculis eum vidimus" (330/2).

70/5 **bryng vp.** Translating "prosequuntur & provehunt" (330/4).

70/6 **as christ saith.** This clause is More's addition. The reference is to John 4:24.

70/8 **and deuotion.** This phrase is More's addition.

70/9 **alacrite.** *OED* cites this occurrence as the earliest in the sense of "cheerfulness" (s.v. *alacrity*).

70/9 **langwished and almost fell.** Translating "elanguescebat & decidebat" (330/6).

70/10 **grete.** The Latin is "maiori" (330/6).

70/11 **walked.** More omits Gianfrancesco's "memini" (330/7) and all other first person details in this passage.

70/13 **brake out.** Translating "proruperit" (330/9). In medieval Latin the verb meant "to break into speech." More's usage here antedates the earliest recorded in *OED* (s.v. *break* v. 54e).

70/15 **fynisshed.** Translating "absolutis consummatisque" (330/10–11).

70/16 **fencyng.** More's usage here in the sense of "protecting" is the earliest recorded in *OED* (s.v. *fence* v. 2c). See also note on 109/3.

70/18 **I vndrestande.** One of the few places where More preserves Gianfrancesco's first person.

70/18–19 **by the especiall . . . god.** The phrase is More's addition, as was noted by Lehmberg (p. 62).

70/19 **appointed to professe himself.** Translating "se addicere statuisse" (330/14). Cf. More's reflexive use of "appoint" ("to resolve") in *CW* 2, 35/22: "But yf you appoint your selfe to tary here."

70/20 **the ordre of freris prechours.** That is, the Dominican order.

70/20 **prechours.** After this More omits a sentence: "Interim eorum quae conceperat operum quaeque inchoaverat maturabat editionem" (330/14–15).

70/24 **feruent.** Translating "insidiosissima" (330/18).

71/1 **interiore partis.** Translating "in humores & viscera" (330/19).

71/2 **thre daies.** Either an error in the Latin before More or his own mistranslation of "tertium decimum" (330/21).

71/3 **satisfie.** *OED* cites this as the first usage in the figurative sense of "pay one's debt to" (s.v. *satisfy* v. 1d).

71/3 **and . . . of hir.** This passage is More's addition to the Latin. At this point he omits a passage from the Latin (330/22–24) in which Gianfrancesco claims to have received his accounts of Pico's death from "gravissimis testibus qui aderant."

71/3 **repaye.** More's usage antedates the earliest recorded in *OED* (s.v. *repay* v.).

71/4 **extremes.** More's usage in the sense of "last moments of life" antedates the earliest recorded in *OED* (s.v. *extreme* sb. 2b).

71/10 **portculiouse.** Used here in a figurative sense ("protection") to translate "propugnaculum" (330/29). *OED* does not record such a figurative usage (s.v. *portcullis* sb.).

71/11 **prest.** Translating "seniori" (330/29). More elsewhere objects to the translation of "senior" as "priest": "And yf he mene to take yᵉ latyn worde senior that worde in yᵉ latyn tonge neuer sygnyfyed a prest but onely an elder man" (*CW 6*, 286/17–19).

71/12 **Image.** The Latin is "veram . . . imaginem" (330/30). Possibly More felt the repetition of "veram . . . dei veri verique hominis imaginem" (330/30) to be excessive.

71/15 **coeternalli.** More's usage antedates the earliest recorded in *OED* in the sense of "with equal eternity" (s.v. *coeternally* adv.).

71/17–18 **hungar . . . watche.** The order of the Latin is different: "famem . . . sitim . . . labores, aestus, vigilias" (330/34–35); an equivalent of "colde" does not appear in the Latin. Since "labores" is translated twice ("laboure," "trauaile"), More may have intended to choose between them later.

71/19 **washing . . . synne.** Translating "sordibus nostris abluendis" (330/36).

71/20 **synne.** After this More omits "proque reseranda ianua coeli" (330/36).

71/22 **shede owt.** Translating "effudisset" (330/38). For other instances of "shed" with the preposition see *OED*, s.v. *shed* v.¹ 7b.

71/25 **knew it.** After this More omits a phrase: "Et item illud" (332/2).

71/26 **Albertus his sisters sonne.** Alberto was the son of Pico's eldest sister, Caterina. More omits "quem nominavimus inter huius vitae initia" (332/2–3).

71/27–31 **began . . . life.** More specifies the argument in the Latin (332/4–7), omitting the references to "Alexander ex Aphrodisiade" (332/5–6), Themistius (332/6), and Averroes (332/6–7), as well as Gianfrancesco's "inquam" (332/7).

71/31 **dedly.** Not in the Latin.

72/6 **to synne & offende.** Translating "crebriores . . . offensas" (332/11). After this phrase More omits "Et illud praeterea" (332/12).

72/7–10 **He asked . . . deseruinge.** This passage does not appear at this point in the Latin, but later (332/20–24).

72/9 **.viii. yeris.** A mistranslation of the Latin "ante acto anno" (332/22), presumably either because More misread "acto" as "octo" or because there was such an error in More's Latin text. Pico's will was actually dated September 1, 1493.

72/9 **mete and drink.** After this More omits "& tegumentum" (332/23).

72/10 **He shewed.** More returns here to the sequential translation of the Latin at 73/10. Before doing so he omits a phrase, "Et illud praeterea" (332/12).

72/11 **Albertus.** See note on 71/26.

72/11 **persones.** More omits "ex Praedicatorum collegio" (332/12–13).

72/13 **frushed.** Translating "confracta" (332/15). More uses the form elsewhere; see, for example, *CW 8*, 215/6; and *CW 13*, 18/24, 54/29.

72/16 **twitches and panges.** Translating "aculeos" (332/18). More's use of "twitch" in the sense of "pains" antedates the earliest recorded in *OED* (s.v. *twitch* sb.[1] 2), which is for *CW 8*, 215/1.

72/16–17 **as though . . . opene.** Cf. Acts 7:56. The Latin "coelos . . . patefactos" (332/18) shows that "opene" was an adjective, not a verb.

72/19 **kissed.** More omits "ut moris est" (332/19).

72/19–21 **The executour . . . florence.** More reverses the order of these statements as they appear in the Latin (332/24–25).

72/20 **Antony his brothir.** See note on 53/33.

72/20 **landes.** A concise translation of "eorum dumtaxat quae moveri non poterant" (332/24–25).

72/21 **the hospitall of florence.** That is, San Marco.

72/22 **And . . . spirit.** The sentence is More's addition; cf. Luke 23:46.

72/22 **he gaue vp his spirit.** Cf. Matt. 27:50. Pico died on November 17, 1494.

72/26 **peple.** After this More omits a sentence from the Latin: "testes hi reges quos supra citavimus" (332/27–28).

72/22–23 **Charles king of fraunce.** Charles VIII (1470–1498).

73/1–2 **the Realme of Naples.** Charles took Naples in February 1495.

73/5 **hande.** After this More omits Gianfrancesco's "quas & vidimus & legimus" (332/33).

73/7 **required.** After this More omits a passage in the Latin (332/36–334/4) in which Gianfrancesco elaborates on Pico's relationship with Charles.

73/9 **Aftir . . . not longe after.** Savonarola preached his sermon on November 23, 1494, six days after Pico's death. The phrase is More's addition.

73/9 **Aftir his deth.** Before this More omits a passage from the Latin in which Gianfrancesco announces he will give the accounts he heard of Pico's death (334/3–4).

73/9 **hieronimus.** Girolamo Savonarola (1452–1498).

73/11–12 **the cheyfe chirche.** The Latin is "in aede sacra quae Sanctae Reparatae dicitur" (334/5); that is, the Duomo.

73/12 **wise.** After this More omits a passage in which Gianfrancesco says that he himself heard the sermon and insists that whatever seems strange in his account would be easily credible if it were probed more deeply (334/8–12).

73/13 **the.** That is, "thee."

73/14 **as trew . . . Iohn.** On the proverbial authority of John's gospel see *CW* 7, lxxx, n. 2, and the references cited there. Here, however, More omits "proverbium illud apud te frequens" (334/15) before "Ioannis evangelium."

73/19 **graces.** After this More omits "multifariaque preditus disciplina fuerat. Nulli forte mortalium tam celebre obtigit ingenium" (334/19–20).

73/22 **this .viii. C. yere be fore.** Used in the sense of "a very long time"; see More's usage at *CW* 9, 44/2–3 and Commentary.

74/1–2 **thinking . . . him.** More mistranslated "arbitratus eius opera religionem indigere" (334/28–29) ("thinking that the religious life needed his [literary] endeavors") by inserting a negative ("had *no* nede of him). Gianfrancesco presumably implied by his phrasing that entry into the religious life would interrupt or preclude Pico's scholarly endeavor ("opera").

74/3 **coniecture.** Translating "coniectatum & presumptum" (334/30).

74/11 **in heuyn.** After this More omits "famamque & nominis celebritatem, quae ad summum cumulum si vixisset fuerat habiturus, ad plenum non assequeretur" (334/36–336/2).

74/14–15 **deuout . . . god.** The Latin ("orationes quae ad deum instantissime effusae sunt," 336/4) is ambiguous: it might refer to Pico's prayers, as More takes it, or to the prayers of others for him.

74/16 **oure lorde.** The Latin has "patris" (336/5).

74/19 **for a season.** That is, "for a while" (*OED*, s.v. *season* sb. 12b). The Latin is "temporarias paenas" (336/7).

74/22 **prayers . . . suffrages.** The Latin has only "suffragiis" (336/9).

74/23 **These thingis.** More omits after this "& plura alia" (336/9).

74/24 **openly.** Translating "clara voce" (336/10).

74/24 **he.** More, in this clause, changes plural to singular and the original plural subject, "verbi dei precones" (336/11), to the third person singular pronoun.

74/25 **in that place.** That is, the pulpit.

74/25 **worthy eternall dampnation.** The omission of "of" is common in late Middle English; see also 81/11 and 89/19.

74/27 **Picus.** The Latin is "aegrotus" (336/14).

75/1 **illusion of yᵉ deuill.** On diabolic illusions see *CW 12*, 133/9–23 and Commentary.

75/4 **worde.** The Latin adds "mortis" (336/17).

75/5–9 **And aftir . . . vnkindnes.** The Latin (336/32–36) here is ambiguous: either a man who had been present at the sermon approached Savonarola and told him of the vision (the more likely meaning), or Savonarola told the man of his own vision (as More takes it).

75/6–7 **aftir his deth apered vnto him.** On visions of souls in purgatory both traditionally and elsewhere in More's works, see *CW 7*, Commentary at 196/15–17.

75/7 **compaced in fire.** Translating "vallatum igne" (336/34–35). More's use of "compassed" in the sense of "surrounded" antedates the earliest recorded in *OED* (s.v. *compassed* ppl.a. 2).

75/9 **vnkindnes.** After this point until the conclusion of the Latin Life (338/1–340/13) More largely replaces the Latin with his own summary. In this passage Gianfrancesco defends Savonarola, affirming the truth of his vision. More emphasizes prayer for Pico in purgatory.

75/14 **darke world.** More's translation of "cedar" (340/13). In *Tractatus in Psalmos*, commenting on Ps. 119:5, Jerome notes that "cedar" is Hebrew for "darkness" ("tenebrae"); see *Corpus Christianorum: Series Latina*, Vol. 78, 2nd ed. rev., ed. Germanus Morin (Turnholt, 1958), p. 256.

75/13–20 **aftir . . . to.** More's rendering of "quippe mortalis vitae munere perfunctus, diuque cum habitantibus cedar, quos luce non pauca perfuderat, conversatus, inaccessible & infinitum supernae patriae lumen iamiam ingrediens, ineffabili divinitate, nobis etiam in dies laturus opem, sine fine fruetur" (340/13–16).

75/15 **yᵉ darke fire of purgatory.** More also mentions purgatory's "dark fyre" in *CW 7*, 225/18–19; for discussion of the tradition of the dark fire of hell see *CW 7*, Commentary at 225/18–19.

75/15–16 **in which . . . clensed.** More's addition.

75/19 **inspecable.** More's usage, in the sense of "unspeakable," antedates the earliest recorded in *OED* (s.v. *inspeakable* a.).

75/23 **thre epistilles.** Gianfrancesco included forty-seven of Pico's letters in the *Opera omnia*. More translated three of them, two (340/18–348/21, 356/1–362/3) to Gianfrancesco himself (the first and last letters in the *Opera omnia*), and the third to Andrea Corneo (348/22–354/28).

76/1–77/20 **The argument . . . a best.** This passage is More's addition to the Latin.

76/4 **had broken his mynde vnto.** More uses this construction elsewhere; for example, *CW 6*, 352/16; *CW 8*, 884/15.

76/13–15 **the flesh . . . bestis.** A quotation from Pico's letter; see 78/4–6.

76/17 **in.** The compositor of *1510* left a blank space, presumably either because he could not read his copy (which was perhaps in Greek letters) or because More failed to include the word. The missing word is "Aeaea" (Homer, *Odyssey* 10.135), the island where Circe resided.

76/17–23 **A woman called Circes . . . vnto them.** Cf. *Aeneid* 7.15–20.

76/25 **affectiones of the body.** Here and elsewhere in this passage (for example, 76/25, 76/28, 76/6), "affectiones" is used in the sense of "desires" or "appetites."

76/27–28 **conuenience.** More's usage antedates the earliest recorded in *OED* in the sense of "correspondence," which is for *CW 13*, 12/12 (s.v. *convenience* sb. 1b).

76/28–29 **brutissh.** More's usage antedates the earliest recorded in *OED* in the sense of "pertaining to animals" (s.v. *brutish* a. 1).

77/17 **aftir . . . made.** Gen. 1:26–27.

77/18–20 **idolatres . . . best.** Possibly a reminiscence of Rom. 1:23.

77/21–84/21 **Iohan Picus . . . god.** The Latin text of this letter is in Appendix A, 340/18–348/21.

77/23 **helth . . . helth.** The Latin ("salutem in eo qui est vera salus," 340/18–19) puns on the meanings of "salutem": "greetings" and "salvation."

78/2 **& as though.** The Latin is "aut quasi" (340/25).

78/3 **flesh . . . spiret.** Gal. 5:17.

78/4 **oure self.** The Latin is "saluti nostrae" (340/26); the error is possibly the result of the compositor's misreading of "helth" as "self" in More's copy.

78/5 **so.** More omits "illecebrosa" (340/27–28) from the Latin here.

78/6–7 **Remembre . . . occasiones.** More's addition to the Latin.

78/8 **Gaudete fratres.** James 1:2.

78/20 **vexith and tossith.** Translating "agitat" (342/7).

78/26 **Of the court & seruice of this worlde.** Translating "militia saeculi" (342/11); cf. 69/14–15, where "Militiam quoque saeculi & coniugale vinculum" (328/16–17) is translated as "Weddyng & worldy besynes."

78/28 **daily techith.** Translating "docet" (342/12).

79/1 **of the company.** Translating "in aequalium" (342/13).

79/4 **of a chylde.** Translating "a pueris" (342/16).

79/5 **within my degree.** Translating "usque intra fortunam" (342/16).

79/10–11 **which . . . thought.** 1 Corinthians 2:9.

79/11 **magrey oure teth.** Translating "propemodum inviti" (342/21–22). More uses the same phrase in Pageant Verses, above, 5/78. It is proverbial: Whiting T406, Tilley S764.

79/11 **teth.** More omits after this "a diis" (342/22).

79/14 **idelnes and ease.** Translating "otiosis" (342/23).

79/18 **lassati . . . iniquitatis.** Wisdom 5:7.

79/21–25 **I passe . . . desired.** Cf. *CW 4,* 174/29–32.

79/23–24 **the secrete . . . cryme.** The Latin is simply "culpa" (342/30).

80/4 **which.** The Latin shows that the antecedent is "god," not "words."

80/4 **neithir . . . deceyued.** The Latin "qui nec falli potest nec fallere" (342/35) derives from St. Augustine's *Enarrationes in Psalmos,* 88.2.6.45.

80/4–5 **Cor . . . potest.** Isa. 57:20.

80/14 **them.** More omits after this "obliti proprie dignitatis" (344/1). The omission may well have been caused by eyeskip to the following "obliti."

80/15 **as they . . . selfe.** Translating "ipsa veritate veriora" (344/6), a Latin proverb; see Erasmus, *Adagia* no. 3802, *Opera omnia,* 2, 1145AB; Otto, no. 1878.

80/18 **where thou art conuersaunt.** Translating "in quibus habitas" (344/9–10).

80/19 **fere the.** Translating "deterreant" (344/11).

80/23 **allectiue.** Translating "illecebra" (344/13). More's usage, in the sense of "that which has the power to allure," antedates the earliest recorded in *OED* (s.v. *allective* a. & sb. B).

80/24 **the expugnation of vertue.** Translating "in expugnanda virtute" (344/13–14). *OED* does not record a figurative sense for *expugnation*.

80/25 **banaire.** Translating "vexillis" (344/14).

80/26 **stipende.** Translating "stipendiis" (344/14–15). As the context makes clear, the word is used in the sense of "soldier's pay" (*OED*, s.v. *stipend* sb. 1).

80/27 **his christ.** That is, "his Messiah, his anointed one." Cf. Ps. 2:2.

81/1–2 **dirumpamus . . . ipsorum.** Ps. 2:3.

81/2 **cast of.** That is, "cast off."

81/3–4 **as . . . seith.** More's addition.

81/4–11 **our lord . . . deth.** Rom. 1:26, 28–32.

81/5 **not conuenient.** Translating "non conveniunt" (344/19). More's usage in the sense of "appropriate," "fitting," antedates the earliest recorded in *OED* (s.v. *convenient* a. & sb. 2).

81/7 **contumeliouse.** More's usage, in the sense of "supercilious" as applied to persons, antedates the earliest recorded in *OED* (s.v. *contumelious* a. 1b).

81/11 **worthy deth.** On the omission of "of" see note on 74/25.

81/15–16 **Oportet . . . hominibus.** Acts 5:29.

81/16–17 **And . . . also.** The Latin is simply "& illud" (344/27).

81/17–18 **Si . . . essem.** Gal. 1:10.

81/20 **maistres.** That is, "masters," not "mistress" (translating "magistros," 344/29).

81/25 **insensibilite.** *OED* cites this as the earliest usage in the sense of "unconsciousness" (s.v. *insensibility* 2).

82/1 **voice.** Translating "voces" (344/36).

82/6–7 **y^t . . . heuen.** Matt. 19:23, Mark 10:23–24.

82/7 **gape aftir.** Translating "inhiamus" (346/4); but More's construction means not literally "gape" but "long for." Cf. above, Fortune Verses, 35/114 and note.

82/8–10 **we shulde . . . god.** John 12:43.

82/10 **why . . . iugement.** The sidenote in *1557* refers to Matt. 25, but this may be simply compositorial error, duplicating the next gloss. There is no clear reference here to Matthew.

82/10 **iugement and opinion.** Translating "iudiciis" (346/6).

82/13 **go ye . . . fire.** Matt. 25:41.

82/13–14 **come ye . . . world.** Matt. 25:34.

82/14 **kingdome.** *1510* alone has "kingdoine," a form that lacks warrant elsewhere and could obviously have been caused by compositorial minim error.

82/18 **fewe.** Translating "paucissimos" (346/12).

82/19 **entre . . . heuin.** Matt. 7:13.

82/19 **yᵗ ledyth to heuin.** More's addition. See note on 65/23–24, above.

82/21 **oure lorde.** Translating "deus" (346/15).

82/26 **vale of miserie.** Translating "lacrimarum valle" (346/18). The expression, found in the *Salve Regina*, comes from Ps. 83:7. More used it in 1534 in the Tower (as reported by Margaret Roper); see Rogers, 519/202–3.

83/4–5 **in what mesure . . . againe.** Matt. 7:2.

83/6–7 **blessed . . . mercy.** Matt. 5:7.

83/10 **affect.** Translating "affectu" (346/28). In this context it appears to mean "feeling" or "desire." If so, it antedates the earliest usage in this sense recorded in *OED* (s.v. *affect* sb. Obs. 1c).

83/13 **or how short.** More's addition.

83/16 **helth.** Translating "salus" (346/32).

83/17 **yᵉ grennys of the deuill.** That is, "the snares of the devil." The word "grinnes" is used in a figurative sense in *CW 11*, 175/26. Here it translates "laqueis" (346/33).

83/22–23 **yᵉ extremite of thi lippes.** Translating "summis labris" (346/36); "extremite" in opposition to "inwardnes" (83/23) means "outer point"—not from the outer point ("extremite") of your lips, but out of the inner part ("inwardnes") of your heart. Cf. "extreme lippis" (85/25). *OED* does not record such a sense (s.v. *extremity*). See also Erasmus, *Adagia* no. 893, *Opera omnia*, 2, 363C–364A; Otto, no. 894.

83/24–26 **Delicta . . . domine.** Ps. 24:7. The *1557* sidenote, "Psal. 34.," is a compositorial error.

84/5 **turne & rede.** Translating "versare . . . versare" (348/6).

84/13 **last.** Translating "hic" (348/13).

84/21 **god.** After this word More omits the date and place of writing: May 15, 1492, from Ferrara.

84/23 **Andrew Corneus.** Andrea Corneo, a humanist friend of Pico's and translator of Lucian's *Paraste*, lived in Urbino in the service of

Ludovico, duke of Milan. He dedicated his translation to Guidobaldo, duke of Urbino. Two other letters to Corneo were included in the 1496 *Opera omnia:* one (undated) on sigs. VV₂r–v, the other (dated "1489") on sigs. VV₃r–v. From these letters we learn that Corneo was of frail health from childhood; that at Corneo's request Pico sent him some of his own early compositions; that Corneo suffered some misfortune in 1489; that Pico urged Corneo to publish his own *Laura* without waiting for the publication of Pico's poems, because Lorenzo de Medici had instructed Pico to write a commentary on the Psalms and a defense of the Septuagint translation against the criticism of the Jews; and finally, that Pico sent his regards to Hermolaus Barbarus and Jacobo Volterrano, from whom he would like to borrow the epistles of Symmachus so as to have them copied. For a brief biography see Carlo Grossi, *Degli uomini illustri di Urbino, Comentario* (Urbino, 1819), p. 124. The Latin text of Pico's Letter appears in Appendix A, 348/22–356/28.

84/22–85/12 **The mater . . . aduauntage.** This passage is More's addition to the Latin.

85/5–7 **By this . . . mercennari.** This is a quotation from Pico's letter (86/22–23).

85/7 **mercennari.** More's own definition of the word at 85/7–8 confirms that this usage antedates the earliest recorded use of "mercenary" as applied to conduct (*OED*, s.v. *mercenary* adj. AIb).

85/10 **which.** That is, "who."

85/15 **Ye exhort.** Before these words More omits several sentences from the Latin (348/23–30) in which Pico apologizes for his delay in responding to Corneo's letter and affirms his perpetual friendship.

85/15 **ciuile.** Translating "civilem" (348/31), which seems used in the sense of "public." Such a usage antedates the earliest recorded in *OED* (s.v. *civil* a. 1).

85/17–19 **exercise . . . besines.** Translating "in agendarum tractandarumque rerum palaestra desudem" (348/32–33).

85/18 **entreting.** More's usage in the sense of "undertaking" antedates the earliest recorded in *OED* (s.v. *entreat* v. 2).

85/18 **outward.** Used here in the sense of "external" in opposition to the inner working of the mind, More's usage antedates the earliest recorded in *OED* (s.v. *outward* a. 5).

85/19 **I had cast a way.** Translating "perdidissem" (348/34); cf. the same construction, meaning "to waste," in *CW 11*, 48/28. The Latin construction "oleum operamque . . . perdidissem" ("I had lost both time and trouble") is proverbial in both classical and medieval Latin; see Otto, p. 253 (s.v. *oleum* 3); and Hans Walther, *Lateinische Sprichwörter und Sentenzen des Mitttelalters* (Göttingen, 1965), *3*, 574, no. 68.

85/22–27 **This . . . tasted.** Margaret Powell Esmonde, "'A Patterne of Life:' A Critical Analysis of St. Thomas More's Life of John Picus" (Ph.D. Dissertation, University of Miami, 1971), p. 131, points out that this passage has clear parallels with Pico's *Oration on the Dignity of Man.*

85/22 **persuasione.** *OED* cites this as the first usage in the sense of "belief" (s.v. *persuasion* sb. 2b).

85/25 **extreme lippis.** Translating "summis labiis" (350/1); see note on 94/17.

85/26–27 **culture.** *OED* cites this as the first usage in the figurative sense of "the development of the mind" (s.v. *culture* sb. 4).

85/28 **wordes of Neoptolemus . . . longe.** Among the surviving fragments of Ennius are two lines assigned to a character named Neptolemus in one of his plays: "Philosophari est mihi necesse, paucis: nam omnino haud placet / Degustandum ex philosophia, non in eam ingurgitandum"; See *Ennianae poesis reliquiae,* ed. Johann Vahlen (Leipzig, 1928; reprint, Amsterdam, 1976), p. 191. The lines have survived because they are quoted by Cicero (*Tusculan Disputations* 2.1.1; *De oratore* 2.37, 156; *De republica* 1.18.30) and Aulus Gellius 5.15.9, who mentions that they are spoken by Neoptolemus.

86/5–6 **I am . . . also.** This passage is More's addition.

86/7–8 **martha . . . Mari.** The allusion is to Luke 10:38–42.

86/8–9 **Loue . . . occupation.** This passage is More's addition.

86/9 **my welbeloued frende.** More's addition.

86/11 **but . . . do so.** This passage is More's addition.

86/13–14 **that is . . . worse.** More's addition.

86/19–20 **seking . . . othir thing.** Translating "caeterarum rerum despector & negligens" (350/14), More's two phrases may have been alternative translations between which he did not choose. The English form "thing" is plural.

86/20–21 **thos thingis.** Both this phrase and the Latin it translates ("illa," 350/14) refer to the pursuits of the philosophers, not to the other things which they despise but which are sought by worldlings.

86/26 **he might not.** The Latin has merely "possit" (350/18), without "non," but the sense seems to require "non" here, and More may simply have supplied it. On the other hand, "possit" alone might mean "merely be able to philosophize—without actually doing it."

87/1 **in howsolde wyth.** More's addition to the Latin, which reads: "alicui ex summis Italiae principibus dedam" (350/20).

87/2–4 **philosophres . . . loue liberte.** For similar expressions by both Pico and More see note on 69/21–22.

87/3 **which.** That is, "who."

87/3 **as horace seith.** Horace, *Epistles* 1.1.106–7.

87/4 **they loue liberte.** More's addition.

87/4 **they can not . . . serue.** More's expansion of the Latin: "mores pati & servire nesciunt" (350/22).

87/10 **sigheth.** The Latin "suspirat" (350/26) shows that this reading is correct. *1557* reads "seketh," which is probably a misprint or false correction.

87/15 **settith him owt to the shew.** Cf. *CW 13*, 10/10–11: "they wil set it oute goodly to the shewe." The expression means "to display ostentatiously."

87/16 **skittissh.** *OED* cites this as the first usage in the sense of "unduly lively" (s.v. *skittish* adj. 2).

87/16 **of.** That is, "off."

87/18 **golden mediocrite.** Translating "aurea . . . mediocritas" (350/31); cf. Horace, *Odes* 2.10.5. *OED* cites this as the earliest usage in the sense of "golden mean" (s.v. *mediocrity* 1b).

87/18 **the meanne estate.** Not in the Latin.

87/19 **which shall bear . . . handes more easili.** More's Latin had (or he misread) "manus" ("hand") for "mannus" (350/32, "cart horse"), a confusion first noted by Rigg (p. 88, n. 34). See Appendix A, p. 291.

87/22 **then.** That is, "than."

87/23 **commune besines.** Translating "publicis negotiis" (350/35–36).

87/23 **all your glory.** Not in the Latin.

87/23–24 **the aduauntage that ye hawke aftir.** Translating "vestris aucupiis" (350/36).

87/24 **hawke.** *OED* cites this as the first occurrence of the verb in the sense of "attempt to catch" (s.v. *hawk* v. 4).

87/26 **be tossed.** Translating "iacter & fluctuem" (352/2).

87/26 **of . . . besynesse.** Translating "rerum publicarum" (350/1).

87/27–28 **children . . . bokes.** More spells out the pun on the single Latin word "liberos" (352/2).

87/28 **commune proffit.** The same phrase occurs at 66/26–27.

88/3 remitted. *OED* cites this as the first occurrence of the verb in the sense of "slackened" (s.v. *remit* v. 6).

88/3 remitted or slakked. Cf. *The Last Things*, above, 138/26, where the same collocation occurs.

88/5 infatigable. See note on 56/17.

88/5–6 the hebrew language . . . the Araby tonge. On Pico's study of these languages see 65/19, above.

88/9 Fare ye well. This sentence is More's addition.

88/9 well. More omits the rest of this letter (352/10–354/28), in which Pico discusses his plans to visit Rome, Corneo's marital affairs, Pico's Italian verses, a wayward servant of Pico, and mitigates the amorous escapades of an unnamed lover, evidently Pico himself, who had abducted Margherita, the wife of Giuliano Mariotto dei Medici, on May 10, 1486. She was pursued by her husband, restored to him, and Pico was wounded and imprisoned. For an account of this episode see Eugenio Garin, *Giovanni Pico della Mirandola: Vita e dottrina*, Pubblicazioni della Università degli Studi di Firenze, Facoltà di Lettere e Filosofia, 3 serie, 5 (Florence, 1937), p. 25. More could have learned of this abduction from Colet or Linacre, both of whom were in Italy not long after this well-known scandal.

88/9 Paris. This is a mistranslation of "Perusiae" (354/28)—Perugia.

88/10 .M. cccclxxxxii. The Latin is actually dated 1486 (354/28). For the argument that the change of date and place was deliberate on More's part to make Pico into a more appropriate spiritual hero by passing over the time when "Pic avait l'intention d'affronter les plus éminents docteurs de la chrétienté" in his confrontation with papal authority, see Louis Valcke, "Jean Pic de la Mirandole lu par Thomas More," in *Miscellanea Moreana: Essays for Germain Marc'hadour*, ed. Clare M. Murphy, Henri Gibaud, and Mario A. di Cesare, Medieval & Renaissance Texts & Studies, no. 61 (Binghamton, 1989), pp. 86–87. It seems as probable that More (or his source text) could have been concerned to disassociate Pico from the other controversial event of 1486, his kidnapping of Margherita dei Medici; see note on 88/9.

88/11–21 The argument . . . euident. This passage is More's addition.

88/16 descanted. *OED* cites this as the earliest usage in the sense of "made comment on" (s.v. *descant* v. 2).

88/22 Franscis. More omits "Ioanni" before this word.

88/22–93/29 Iohan . . . .M. cccclxxxxii. For the text of the Latin see Appendix A, 356/1–362/3. There is an independent translation of this letter in "W. H.," *Twelve Rvles and Weapons Concerning the Spiritval Battel* (1589, *STC*² 19898a.3), pp. 35–39.

88/23 in oure lorde. Not in the Latin.

88/25–26 the . . . yᵉ. That is, "thee" (translating "tibi," 356/2).

88/26 of euell peple. Not in the Latin.

89/1 my sonne. Not in the Latin.

89/4 trewth hit selfe. See John 14:6.

89/4–6 affermith . . . name. See Matt. 5:11–12.

89/6 lying. Translating "mentientes" (356/8).

89/7 dignite. After this More omits "si nescis" (356/9).

89/7 a fore god. Not in the Latin.

89/8 of. That is, "by."

89/8 for his name. Translating "pro evangelico nomine" (356/9–10).

89/8 the gospell of luke. The reference is in fact not to Luke's gospel but, as the sidenote in *1557* indicates, to Acts 5:27–42, which was also written by Luke. Acts 5:41 has "pro nomine Iesu."

89/9–10 yᵉ counceill hows. Translating "a conspectu . . . concilii" (356/11).

89/12 worthy. See note on 74/25.

89/14 voice. Here and at 91/10 and 99/22 this word, like the Latin "vox," means "saying."

89/15–16 Si . . . habuit. John 15:18.

89/16 seith oure lorde. More's addition.

89/19 worthi . . . all shame. See note on 74/25.

89/19 if . . . well. That is, "if we consider well our wretched living."

89/23 to suffre. That is, "as to suffer."

89/23 olde seintis. Translating "heroes nostri" (356/22).

89/24 and deth. More's addition.

90/2 opprobriouse. More's addition. *OED* cites this as the earliest usage in the sense of "shameful" (s.v. *opprobrious* a. 2).

90/2–3 as the Apostle seith. Phil. 2:9.

90/6 condemneth. Translating "crucifigit" (356/32).

90/8 **yᵉ fire of hell.** Translating "Gehennam" (356/33).

90/8 **all lift vpward.** The Latin "tota sursum erecta" (356/34) makes this awkward construction clear: "totally directed on high."

90/12 **of our perfection.** More's addition.

90/15–16 **yᵉ flowre of oure vertue.** Translating "iustitiae flos" (358/5).

90/18 **populare.** Translating "popularis" (358/6). More's usage here in the sense of "common" or "vulgar" antedates the earliest recorded in *OED* (s.v. *popular* a. 2c).

90/20–21 **saith seint Paule.** 1 Cor. 1:23–24.

90/22 **vertue.** Here and at 92/9 and 92/12 the word, like the Latin forms of *virtus*, means "power."

90/23–24 **The wysedom . . . god.** 1 Cor. 3:19.

90/24 **hath ouercome.** The Latin has the present tense, "vincit" (358/13).

90/27 **which . . . reputith.** That is, "who . . . consider."

91/4 **forth thi.** "On" must be understood after "forth."

91/6 **the sytting.** That is, "thee sitting."

91/8–9 **obscure darkenes.** Translating "densissimis tenebris" (358/21). More's translation, unlike the Latin, seems tautological.

91/10 **voice.** See note on 89/14.

91/10–11 **Sine . . . sequere.** Matt. 8:22.

91/13 **laboriously.** *OED* cites this as the earliest usage in an adverbial sense (s.v. *laboriously*).

91/17 **adeption.** That is, "obtaining." The Latin "adeptione" (358/27) makes it clear that the reading in all the early editions, "adoption," which does not make good sense, is an error. More's use of the word antedates the earliest recorded usage in *OED* (s.v. *adeption*).

91/19–20 **lyke the rauing of bedelem peple.** Translating "verba velut fanaticorum deliramenta" (358/29). More alludes to "Bedleem," the Bethlehem Hospital for the insane, in *The Last Things*, above, 131/13, and in *CW 8*, 555/28 and 584/7.

91/20 **bedelem.** *OED* cites this as the earliest usage in an attributive sense meaning "mad" (s.v. *Bedlam* 6).

91/25 **blinde . . . men.** Matt. 15:14.

91/26–27 **that . . . gospell.** More's addition.

91/27 **yᵉ deuelis.** Not in the Latin.

91/27–92/1 **this night . . . thei be.** Luke 12:20.

92/5 **eris.** After this More omits "ceras" (360/4).

92/11 **as the apostle seith.** 2 Thess. 1:7–10.

92/14–15 **nolite . . . gehennam.** Matt. 10:28, Luke 12:4.

92/18 **which.** That is, "who."

92/19 **the.** That is, "thee."

92/19 **vertuousely.** Translating "ex ratione" (360/14).

92/24 **of heuin.** More's addition.

92/25–30 **Ad te . . . die.** Ps. 24:1–5.

93/13 **worldly.** This is More's addition.

93/15–16 **shadow like.** Translating "umbratile" (360/31).

93/26–27 **him . . . one.** The Latin uses the second person singular ("te" 362/2) where More has the third.

93/28 **fere.** After this More omits "Bigus te salutat" (362/3).

93/28–29 **the yere . . . redemption.** More's addition.

94/1–103/16 **The interpretation . . . Amen.** This commentary on Psalm 15 (as it is in the Vulgate) is the only part of Pico's commentary on the Psalms to be printed in his *Opera omnia*. Other fragments, on Ps. 11, 17, 47, and 50, survive in manuscript; for details see Paul Oskar Kristeller, "Giovanni Pico della Mirandola and His Sources," in *L'opera e il pensiero di Pico della Mirandola*, pp. 109–10, 115. Psalm 15 is one to which More was drawn: he quotes from it in *CW 12*, 48/19–21, and annotated part of it in his *Prayer Book; see Thomas More's Prayer Book*, ed. Louis L. Martz and Richard S. Sylvester (New Haven and London, 1969), pp. 42, 191. More's translation is also the first printing in English of a psalm commentary. Indeed, such commentaries in Middle English are relatively rare; for a survey of translations and commentaries on the Psalms see Lawrence Muir, "Translations and Paraphrases of the Bible and Commentaries," in *A Manual of the Writings in Middle English*, ed. J. B. Severs (Hamden, Conn., 1970), 2, 385–90. For the text of Pico's Latin see Appendix A, 362/4–370/40.

94/23 **these wordes.** Translating "hoc verbo" (362/8).

94/24 **domine.** Not in the Latin.

95/2–5 **Quid . . . it.** 1 Cor. 4:7. More retains the opening words of the Vulgate and translates both them and the rest of the passage.

95/6–7 **miserere mei deus.** Ps. 50:1.

95/14 **in our requestis.** More's addition.

95/15 **require.** After this word More omits "a deo" (362/22).

95/18–19 **we wot . . . aske.** Matt. 20:22.

95/19–20 **what so . . . you.** Cf. John 14:12.

95/22 **holsom . . . saluation.** Translating "ad salutem" (362/28).

95/26 **aske . . . doubting.** James 1:6. The *1557* sidenote in this line to Psalm 117 is incorrect.

95/29–96/1 **he . . . wordes.** The Latin is "incipit describere" (364/1).

96/4 **all.** The Latin is "fere omnibus" (364/3).

96/4 **very.** More's addition.

96/5–9 **That thing . . . vnhappy.** In this sentence More renders Pico's first person plural forms as third person singular.

96/18–19 **The gloton . . . lust.** More's rendering of "Gulosus item crapulae, et incontinens libidini" (364/11–12).

96/19 **vainglory.** More omits before this "imperio sive" (364/12).

96/18 **good.** The use of the singular "good" for the plural is sanctioned in English usage (*OED*, s.v. *good* II 7a); see also 96/23, 96/26, 97/10.

96/19 **erth . . . heuen.** More reverses the order of the Latin (364/15).

96/27 **and though.** That is, "even if."

96/28–97/1 **more imperfite creatures.** More's addition.

97/1 **that are more parfite.** More's addition.

97/2 **vniuersite of creatures.** Translating "universi" (364/23); the use of *university* to mean "universe" is sanctioned in English from the late fifteenth century (*OED*, s.v. *university* sb. 2c); see also 97/4–5.

97/3–4 **one part of.** More's addition.

97/8 **adnichilate.** An obsolete form of *annihilate;* More's usage in the sense of "reduce to nonexistence" antedates the earliest recorded in *OED* (s.v. *annihilate* v. 1a).

97/16 **mirificauit voluntates suas.** These words do not appear in the Latin at this point (364/38), but after "lorde" (97/22).

97/20 **in theire contre of heuen.** Translating "in caelesti patria" (366/2).

97/22 **our lorde . . . willis.** The translation of the rest of the lemma for the third verse. The English of the first part appears above at 97/17. In the Latin the text of this part of the lemma immediately precedes this point.

97/22 **our lorde.** Translating "dei" (366/2).

97/28 **blessid.** More's addition.

97/30 **euir more.** More's addition.

98/1–2 **all waies.** Translating "semper" (366/6).

98/6–7 **we shulde . . . desiring.** Translating "ultro etiam eam appetamus" (366/11).

98/8 **heuinly contre.** Translating "patria" (366/12); cf. 97/20.

98/8 **saintes.** After this More omits a sentence in the Latin: "Cum ergo iustus descripsit statum suum, qui totus est in affectu erga deum & diuina, despicitque ex alto statum hominum malorum & dicit" (366/13–15). But he seems to translate the last four words at 98/10–11.

98/9 **postea accelerauerunt.** These words are omitted here in the Latin (see 366/16) and appear at 366/22; see 98/20 for their occurrence in More's translation.

98/17–18 **as . . . saith.** More's addition; the reference is to Ps. 11:9.

98/18–19 **circuit . . . ende.** Translating "circuitu" (366/21).

98/19–20 **their . . . multiplied.** More's addition.

98/20 **Aftir thei hasted.** More's translation of the remainder of the Latin lemma; see note on 97/22, above.

98/20–21 **aftir their idolles.** More's addition.

98/21 **passiones & bestly desires.** Translating "sua desideria" (366/22–23).

98/21 **forth.** *1510* has "fort," not an attested form for *forth;* the introduction of such an erroneous form is clearly explicable by eyeskip to the initial *h* of the next word.

98/22 **vnaduisedly with owt any consideration.** Translating "inconsiderate" (366/23).

98/23 **vertu.** Translating "virtutes" (366/24).

98/29 **conventiculam.** This is the reading of all the early Latin and English editions, though the Vulgate has "conventicula."

98/30 **memor nominum.** The Latin is "memor ero nominum" (366–29–30). More gives all three Latin words at 94/7.

99/2 **sacrefice.** Translating "victimarum" (366/32).

99/4–5 **forsaken . . . folowen.** The subject of these verbs is singular ("life"), but they have become plural by attraction to "men."

99/4–5 **which stondeth all in the sowle.** More's addition.

99/6–10 **The prophet . . . goddes.** More's addition.

99/15–17 **And . . . pleasures.** Cf. *CW 4*, 226/12–15.

99/20 **yᵉ.** That is, "thee."

99/21 **whom.** After this word More omits "denique" (368/5).

99/22 **voice.** That is, "saying."

99/24 **certainly.** More's addition.

100/9 **in the psalme.** More's addition.

100/11 **nobly.** Translating "in praeclaris" (368/16). Most sixteenth-century and modern translations have "in pleasant places."

100/11–12 **of enheritaunces.** More's addition.

100/12–13 **by cordis or ropis.** Translating "funes" (368/17).

100/13–15 **These wordes . . . noble.** More's addition.

100/21–22 **that is . . . noble.** More's addition.

100/23 **seint Paul . . . donge.** Phil. 3:8.

101/7 **of . . . psalme.** More's addition.

101/7–8 **Cor meum . . . viuum.** Ps. 83:3.

101/9 **in to liuing god.** In the absence of "liuing," "in to" could easily and idiomatically be taken to mean "unto," but "liuing" seems to require a definite article, so that "to" may be a misprint for "the."

101/12 **reynis or kidney.** Translating "renes" (368/32).

101/7–8 **in scripture.** More's addition.

101/18–19 **by cause . . . season.** More's addition. Cf. *CW 12*, 107/9–10: "night is of the nature selfe discumfortable & full of fere."

101/19 **discomfortable.** *OED* gives the earliest usage in the sense of "comfortless" in *CW 12*, 107/9–10 (see previous note).

101/20–21 **or takying . . . man.** More's addition.

101/23 **prouided.** The closest meaning to More's in the *OED* is "foresaw" (*provide* v. 1).

101/25 **his owne lucre.** Translating "propriam utilitatem" (370/2–3).

102/11 **glorious.** More's addition.

102/11 **immediatly.** The Latin "statim" (370/13) shows that the "mediatly" of the early editions is an error. *Mediately* is not sanctioned as a form in this sense by *OED*.

102/13 **shynyng.** Translating "splendidissima" (370/15).

102/14 **declarith.** After this word More omits "hoc totum" (370/15).

102/17 **Quoniam.** The Latin has "quia" (370/18).

102/23 **that is . . . corrupted.** More's addition.

102/29 **seint petir . . . declared.** Acts 2:26–31.

102/29 **secundarily.** More's usage antedates the earliest recorded in *OED* in the sense of "secondly" (s.v. *secondarily* adv. 2).

102/31 **holy.** More's addition.

103/3 **of that.** The Latin has "huius vitae" (370/32).

103/11–12 **his fathirs.** More's addition.

103/12–13 **seint Iohan . . . christum.** John 17:3.

103/15 **to . . . vs.** More's addition.

103/15 **he bryng.** That is, "may he bryng."

103/17–109/12 **Here begin .xii. rulys . . . mete.** These "Rules" are written in prose by Pico. For the text of the Latin see Appendix A, 372/1–376/5.

103/21–22 **that . . . thrall.** More's addition.

103/27 **this . . . woo.** The Latin is "rebus mundi" (372/7).

104/3–5 **And . . . perpetually.** These lines are More's expansion of the Latin, which reads simply "& tandem paena eterna" (372/8–9).

104/7 **foly . . . vaine.** Translating "stultum" (372/10).

104/8 **with plesure and delyght.** Translating "nisi per huiusmodi pugnam" (372/11).

104/9 **our . . . captaine.** Translating "caput nostrum" (372/11).

104/11–13 **then were . . . lorde.** Matt. 10:24.

104/12 **ye . . . recorde.** More's addition.

104/17–19 **And . . . delight.** More's expansion of the Latin: "etiam si nullum inde nobis praemium perueniret" (372/15–16).

104/24 **sensuall.** *OED* cites the earliest recorded usage in the sense of "perceptible to the senses" as *A Dialogue Concerning Heresies:* "his sensual partyes of his owne body" (*CW 6*, 336/24–25).

104/25 **with good deuotion.** More's addition.

104/27 **tast.** More omits after this "gulae resistens" (372/18).

104/28 **eisell and gall.** Mentioned in Matt. 27:34, Mark 15:36, and John 19:29. Translating "illum felle potatum & aceto" (372/19). For examples of this collocation in Middle English, see *MED*, s.v. *aisel* n. 3.

105/3 **innocent.** More's addition.

105/4 **tempt with.** That is, "tempted by."

105/5 **He . . . bonde man.** Phil. 2:6–7.

105/6 **the shapp.** After this word More omits "pro te" (372/21).

105/7 **most odiouse and vile.** More's addition.

105/7 **tree.** That is, "cross."

105/9 **the best.** The Latin is "iustissimus" (372/24).

105/10 **scorned and scorged.** The Latin is "illudi & conspui & flagellari" (372/25).

105/11 **.ii. theuis.** Cf. Mark 15:27, Luke 23:33. (The *1557* sidenotes, referring to Mark 10 and Luke 18, are erroneous.) The Latin is simply "latronibus" (372/26).

105/13 **Cam . . . disdayne.** John 19:1–11.

105/15–16 **Thus . . . by.** More's addition.

105/16 **peruse.** Seemingly used in the sense "recount in order"; if so, it antedates the earliest usage in this sense, which *OED* gives as More's *Dialogue of Comfort* (*CW 12*, 40/22).

105/17–20 **There . . . darte.** More's expansion of the Latin "& sic discurrendo per singula inuenias nullam esse passionem" (372/28–29).

105/24 **the foresaide espirituall armour.** Translating "in illis duodecim armis" (372/30).

105/25 **remedy.** Translating "humano remedio" (372/31).

105/26 **strenght.** Apparently More left both "vertu" and "strenght" standing as alternative translations of "virtute" (372/31), intending to decide between them later, as he did elsewhere (see notes on 63/10 and 113/16). The monosyllabic "strenght" is metrically superior to "vertu."

105/27–28 **For . . . veynquisshed.** More here paraphrases the Latin quotations of John 12:31 and Rev. 12:9 (69/16–17).

105/28 **his.** That is, "its."

106/4 **with teris & lamentable plaintis.** More's addition.

106/5 **The aide of hys grace.** The Latin is "auxilium" (372/35).

106/9 **as a wood lyon the fende oure aduersarye.** The phrase has no parallel in the Latin, but the collocation is a commonplace, deriving from 1 Peter 5.8. The phrase "as wood as a lion" was also proverbial (Whiting L327).

106/11–12 **vppon . . . catche.** The Latin is simply "servire in timore" (374/3).

106/13 **stonde & kepe wache.** Hab. 2:1. The Latin is only "Super custodiam meam stabo" (374/3–4), but the rest of the verse justifies More's addition of "towre": "et figam gradum super munitionem."

106/16 **might.** After this word More omits "quum te tentat" (374/5).

106/19 **dede thought or sight.** Translating "ex ea re" (374/6–7). The line is hypermetrical, and More may have intended to cancel either "dede" or "thought" (see notes on 63/10, 105/26, and 113/16).

106/20 **with synne contract.** Translating "non peccas" (374/6). More seems to be using "contract" in the sense of "become infected with"; if so, his usage antedates the earliest recorded in *OED* (s.v. *contract* v. 5).

106/21 **some good vertuouse acte.** Translating "alicuius boni" (374/7).

106/22 **secretly castith in thi mynde.** The Latin is "tibi offert" (374/8). More's use of *cast* in a transitive sense antedates the earliest recorded in *OED* (s.v. *cast* v. 42b).

107/2 **his goodnes and liberall mercy.** Translating "ex gratia sua" (374/12–13).

107/4 **Confownded and rebuked.** Translating "confusus" (374/13).

107/5 **Shal . . . assaile.** More's addition.

107/7 **trymme the.** That is, "dress yourself"; translating "geras" (374/14). *OED* does not record a reflexive sense of the verb, and More's usage in the sense of "dress" antedates the earliest recorded there (s.v. *trim* v. 7).

107/9 **For . . . fere.** More's addition.

107/17–19 **Considre . . . synne.** More's addition; see the second note on 65/22.

107/18 **and.** That is, "if."

107/20 **For he . . . therin.** Ecclus. 3:27; the saying had become proverbial in Middle English; Whiting P143.

107/23 **The cursed . . . Babilon.** Ps. 136:9.

107/24 **To . . . thing.** More's addition.

107/25 **stone.** After this word More omits "petra autem est Christus" (374/20).

107/26 **Perilous . . . bone.** This sounds like a proverbial dictum, but it is not recorded in Whiting.

107/27–28 **To late . . . more.** An expansion of the Latin "quia sero medicina paratur" (374/20–21). More completes the quotation from Ovid, *Remedia amoris* 91–92; see Latin variants at 95/16–18. The saying was also proverbial in English; Whiting M484.

108/3 **sowre.** Translating "amara" (374/23). *OED* does not record *sour* in a figurative sense of "bitter" as applied to actions (s.v. *sour* a.).

108/5 **the deuill.** Translating "tentationem" (374/23).

108/6 **bestly pleasoure.** Translating "peccatum" (374/24).

108/7–8 **Of vertue . . . synne.** More's addition.

108/12–22 **But like . . . conquest.** These lines are a considerable expansion and modification of the Latin (374/25–28).

108/13 **applye.** That is, "liken." More's usage antedates the earliest recorded in *OED* (s.v. *apply* v. 12).

108/24 **dispaire . . . no thing.** More's compression of the Latin: "aut deo . . . perfectum" (374/30).

108/25 **the gloriouse apostle seint Powle.** The Latin is "Paulus" (374/31).

108/31–109/2 **And here . . . depose.** 2 Cor. 12:1–10, a passage More cites elsewhere; for example, *CW 8*, 454/1–14; *CW 12*, 29/21–30.

108/31 **he whom god did loue.** The Latin is "Paulus" (374/33).

108/32 **most especiall vessell.** The Latin is "vas electionis" (374/34). See Acts 9:15.

109/2 **hym.** The Latin is "suis virtutibus" (374/35).

109/2 **depose.** After this More omits a passage from the Latin ("sicut ipse . . . collaphizet," 374/35–36).

109/3 **fence.** More's usage here, in the sense of "protect," antedates the earliest recorded in *OED* (s.v. *fence* v. 2); see also note on 70/16.

109/4 **the mother of reprefe.** More's addition.

109/5 **crop and rote.** Translating "radix" (376/2). That is, "totality"; the phrase is used in this sense in Chaucer, *Troilus & Criseyde*, 2.348.

109/6 **glosse.** That is, "superficial luster." More's usage in this sense antedates the earliest recorded in *OED* (s.v. *gloss* sb.² 1).

109/7 **the lorde souereyne powere.** More's addition.

109/9 **with in one howre.** More adds this and omits "invitos" (376/4).

109/10 **Shal . . . honowre.** More's addition.

109/10 **bereue welth.** That is, "deprive of." On the omission of "of" see note on 74/25.

109/11 **both smal & grete.** More's addition. It means "whether of high or low station."

109/12 **vile carion.** More's addition.

109/12 **wormes mete.** Translating "esca vermium" (375/5). A stock locution of proverbial force in Middle English; see Whiting W675 and, for some discussion A. S. G. Edwards, "A Fifteenth-Century Didactic Poem in British Museum Add. Ms. 29729," *Neuphilologische Mitteilungen,* 70 (1969), 702–6.

109/13–24 **Here folow . . . seyntis.** More translates the title and list of headings (376/6–19 of the Latin), which are all that Pico gives. The verse paraphrases are entirely More's.

110/11 **Glideth.** *OED* cites this as the earliest usage in the sense of "slip away" (s.v. *glide* v. 5b).

110/18 **dispiteouse.** *OED* cites this as the earliest usage in the sense of "evil" (s.v. *despiteous* a. 2).

110/23–111/8 **This wretched life . . . wise.** Cf. Latin poem no. 75, *CW 3/2,* 142.

110/29 **shadowe on the wall.** The phrase is biblical in origin (cf. Ps. 143:4; Eccles. 7:1, 8:13, 9:8; Wis. 2:5) and had become proverbial in Middle English; see Whiting S185 (not, however, citing this occurrence). On "dreme" see Job 20:8 and Ps. 72:20.

111/8 **not.** This is a contracted form of "ne wot." *1557* has "wote not," most probably because the obsolete form was modernized.

111/18 **this worlde is but a thorow fare.** Whiting W663, Tilley W883. Cf. Chaucer: "This world nys but a thurghfare ful of wo" ("The Knight's Tale," I, 2847).

111/20 **Hens . . . bare.** Cf. Latin poem no. 7, *CW 3/2,* 85 and Commentary.

111/21 **loke to what coost.** That is, "to whatever region" (*OED,* s.v. *look* v. 4b).

112/2 **for angell . . . endure.** Christ did not redeem the fallen angels.

112/7 **brotle worldes Ioy.** Cf. Chaucer, *Troilus & Criseyde:* "O brotel wele of mannes joie unstable" (3.820) and "The Merchant's Tale," in *The Canterbury Tales,* IV, 2061.

112/9 **wanton.** More's usage in the sense of "frivolous" antedates the earliest recorded in *OED* (s.v. *wanton,* a. 3c).

112/11 **on warantise.** That is, "it can be guaranteed that" (*OED,* s.v. *warrantise* sb. Obs. 2). More uses the word (but not the phrase) elsewhere; for example, *CW 6,* 27/16; *CW 12,* 245/2, 247/5.

112/13 **thinward . . . mynde.** See note on 79/21–25.

112/18 **vs.** It is tempting to make the pronouns consistent by adopting "thee" from *1557,* but "vs" also makes sense, and More may not have intended to be consistent.

113/6 **fight.** In this context "fight" makes better sense than "sight," since "constant fight" seems to stand in opposition to "slothful cowardice" (113/7). It is a rare instance where *1525* made a correction missed by *1557.* See the variant at 70/16.

113/11–120/11 **The .xii. . . . blode.** With the exception of the list of headings (113/12–26) and a passage at the end of More's poem (119/28–120/11) these lines have no parallel in Pico's Latin.

113/11 **propretees or conditions.** The Latin is "conditiones" (376/20).

113/13–25 **his loue . . . his loue.** The pronouns in Pico's Latin show that the beloved is a man. By translating "his love" More makes the object of the love ambiguous; the reader of the English would assume "his love" is a woman.

113/14–15 **To adourne . . . loue.** These lines reverse the order of the Latin (376/24–25).

113/16–17 **To desyre . . . swete.** These lines appear later in the sequence of the Latin headings, at 376/30–31.

113/16 **harme.** More apparently wrote "shame harmes" without choosing between them. The Latin is "aliquod incommodum" (376/30). See notes on 63/10, 105/26, and 106/19.

113/19 **loue.** After this word More omits a portion of the Latin: "amicos omnes, domus, vestes, imagines" (376/26–27).

113/20 **dispraise.** That is, "dispraise of his love."

114/29 **heuinly port.** On the figurative use of *port* to mean "heaven" in Middle English see Douglas Gray, ed., *A Selection of Religious Lyrics* (Oxford, 1975), pp. 155–56. See note on 45/7, above.

115/12 **Garnisshe.** More's usage in the sense of "dress elegantly" antedates the earliest recorded in *OED,* which is for *CW 12,* 210/7 (s.v. *garnish* v. 3).

115/16 **prowle.** Although *prowl* can mean "to search, seek for something (without moving about)" (*OED*, s.v. *prowl* v. 1b), More seems to use the word in the strained sense "gaze," perhaps for the sake of rhyme.

116/31 **al yᵉ worlde . . . bereuyn.** That is, "though all the world wished to tear him away from it [heaven]." One might wonder if More wrote "wolde hym therfor be reuyn" ("would therefore be seized from him"), but the present reading, which is present in all three editions, is intelligible and acceptable. Cf. Chaucer, "The Summoner's Tale," III, 2111–13: "For whoso wolde us fro this world bireve . . . / He wolde bireve out of this world the sonne."

117/9–15 **So . . . chirch.** For a similar defense of images see *CW 6*, 47/19–31.

117/11 **besy cure.** A Chaucerian phrase: "The Knight's Tale (I, 2853), "The Man of Law's Tale" (II, 188), *The Parliament of Fowls* (line 369), *Troilus & Criseyde* (3.1042). It means "anxious concern."

117/13–15 **And . . . chirch.** For parallel arguments for respect for the clergy see *CW 6*, 53/20–30.

117/14 **wirche.** Rigg wrongly wished to emend "wirche" to "nyrche" ("nourish"). "Wirche" is a verb ("Those who daily cause his body to be made"—that is, consecrate the host).

117/15 **quik reliques.** Priests are left behind by Christ, but unlike the ordinary relics they are alive.

118/18 **ete . . . walke.** That is, "whether he eat or drink . . . or walk."

118/29 **passioned.** More's usage, in the sense "affected by passion," antedates the earliest recorded in *OED* (s.v. *passioned* ppl.a. 1).

119/24 **Not fro.** All early editions read "Not for," which does not make sense here; the error *for* for *fro* is commonplace. Possibly "Not" is an error for "Nor," which would make the syntax clearer.

119/28 **Wageles . . . blode.** These stanzas are based on 378/10–14 of the Latin, although the parallels are selective and not very close.

119/28 **Wageles.** More's usage antedates the earliest recorded in *OED* (s.v. *wageless* a.).

120/2 **of reason.** That is, "as is reasonable."

120/13–123/11 **O holy god . . . fathir.** This is More's rendering of Pico's verse "Deprecatoria ad Deum," which appears on 378/15–380/77 of Appendix A. This is the only part of More's Pico translations that survives in manuscript; see above, Textual Introduction, p. cxxvii.

120/13–19 **O holy god . . . spilt.** More's omissions are given in italics in Appendix A.

120/13 **dredefull magestee.** More uses the same expression at 122/16.

120/14 **one . . . one.** Cf. Chaucer, *Troilus & Criseyde*, 5.1863–65.

120/20–21 **If . . . wey.** The gloss is to Ps. 142:2.

120/23 **the hole engyne of all this world.** Translating "machina" (378/31); cf. *CW 6*, 73/5–6: "all this hole engyne of the worlde." Cf. Lucretius, *De rerum natura:* "machina mundi" (5.96).

121/2 **actuall synne.** A theological term denoting sins committed as distinct from inherited original sin.

121/5 **deuice.** That is, devise."

121/13 **which.** That is, "who," referring back to "he" (line 12).

122/20–21 **With blode . . . wyde.** John 19:34.

122/24 **ay.** The reading of manuscript *O*, "ay well," is the only instance where one of its unique variants has the support of the Latin; cf. "bene" (Appendix A, 380/64).

123/7 **with owt . . . wife.** The phrase, a metaphor for the body, has no parallel in the Latin.

127/2 **Treatyce.** For *The Last Things* contrasted with *A Treatise on the Passion*, see the Introduction, p. ciii.

127/2–6 **wordes . . . synne.** Ecclus. 7:40: "In omnibus operibus tuis memorare novissima tua et in aeternum non peccabis." Nicholas de Lyra's commentary on this verse in the Froben Bible of 1498 identifies *novissima* as *mortem*, but More, following a medieval tradition engendered by the *Sententiae* of Peter Lombard, adds "dome, pain, and joy," although he completes only his analysis of death. See 129/3–5 and note. See also the Introduction, pp. lxvi–lxviii. Hans Walther records four medieval Latin proverbs on the importance of meditating on the last things; see nos. 15205–11 in *Proverbia sententiaeque Latinitatis medii aevi*, 6 vols. (Göttingen, 1963–), 1924.

127/7 **1522.** Concerning this date, assigned to More's treatise by William Rastell in the *English Works* of 1557, see the Introduction, pp. lx–lxiii.

127/9–11 **counsayle . . . vndertreasorer.** More was both knighted and appointed as undertreasurer of the Exchequer (a highly lucrative office) in 1521, three years after his entry into the Privy Council. He was replaced as undertreasurer by Sir William Compton in 1525, a move engineered by Wolsey and designed to undermine the influence of Henry's Privy Chamber; Guy, pp. 6–11, 24, 26–27.

128/18–129/28 **medicin . . . handkercher.** For theme of *scriptura medica*, see the Introduction, pp. lxxv. The healthful properties of this text are also described at 133/7–8, 153/10–12, 155/11–16, 158/15–17, 161/25–27, 166/13–15, 173/10–15, and 174/26–28. See also *CW 14*, 505/9–507/5; and *CW 6*, 294/24–26 and 343/11–25.

128/21 **wordes geueth.** The ending of a third person plural verb could be either *s* or *th* in sixteenth-century English; both forms often occur side by side in More. See Visser, *1*, 43.

128/8 **bill.** That is, "prescription."

129/3–5 **Here . . . ioy.** Cf. *CW 12*, 4/10–14, where Antony denounces those who offer "such a customable maner of uncristen comfortyng / which albeit that in any sik man yt doth more harm than good / with drawyng hym in time of sikenes with the lokyng & longyng for lyfe, fro the meditacion of deth, iugement, heven, & hell, whereof he shuld beset much part of his tyme /even all his whole lyfe in his best helth." Cf. above, 145/6–15.

129/16 **tryacle.** A medicinal compound, usually an antidote against snakebite or poisons, but here a preventive medicine against infectious diseases. It is frequently mentioned by More (*CW 8*, 37/34; *CW 12*, 9/12). See also above, 180/34.

130/3 **world . . . God.** Cf. Phil. 3:18–19: "Multi enim ambulant, quos saepe dicabam vobis, nunc autem et flens dico, inimicos crucis Christi, quorum finis interitus, quorum deus venter est, et gloria in confusione ipsorum, qui terrena sapiunt." See also *CW 6*, 73/13; and above, 180/34.

130/5 **shoote . . . bolte.** Whiting F408; Tilley F515.

130/19–131/8 **diuers . . . vomit.** While acknowledging the value of bodily pleasure, the Utopians likewise draw a distinction between carnal and spiritual, false and true pleasures, prizing the latter above the former. See *CW 4*, 162/4–178/12; and compare 178/9–16, above.

130/28–34 **lacke . . . polyshed.** Cf. *CW 2*, 82/25–30, where More, describing the imposture of Perkin Warbeck as the younger of the princes in the Tower, laments that "all thynges wer in late daies so couertly demeaned . . . but that yet for the comen custome of close & couert dealing, men had it euer inwardely suspect, as many well counterfaited iewels make yᵉ true suspected." For the comparison of real and counterfeit jewels to true and false pleasure, see *CW 4*, 168/12–23.

131/10–11 **sow . . . bedde.** Tilley S681.

131/13 **Bedleem.** The Hospital of Saint Mary of Bethlehem, or "Bedleem," located in Bishopsgate, London, until 1676, received and maintained the mentally ill. See note on 91/19–20, above; Stow, *1*, 164–65; and *CW 8*, Commentary at 555/28.

131/24 **sage foole.** For More's coinage "folosophers" see *CW 11*, Commentary at 179/31.

131/28–29 **heart . . . rest.** Isa. 57:20: "Impii autem quasi mare fervens, quod quiescere non potest, et redundant fluctus eius in conculcationem et lutum."

132/5 **senses . . . wittes.** The "bodily senses" are the external senses: sight, hearing, smell, taste, and touch. The "sensuall wittes" are the internal senses shared by animals and men: the common sense, which coordinates and unifies pieces of information from the individual external senses; the imagination, which retains information from the external senses and the common sense; the estimative power, which provides instinctive knowledge (such as natural enemies or nest-building); and sense memory, which retains information from the estimative power. See Thomas Aquinas, *Summa theologica*, I, q.78, aa.3–4. Cf. 104/24, above, where "sensuall wittis" seems to refer to external rather than interior senses.

132/8–9 **spirituall . . . swete.** More uses this figure for the spiritual sense of scriptural truth in *CW 8*, 45/2–4, 26–29, and 33. The figure is derived from scripture itself, as at Ps. 33:9: "Gustate et videte quoniam suavis est Dominus." See also Tilley T75.

132/13–16 **thinwarde . . . tormente.** More discusses the experience of martyrdom and the compensations of spiritual pleasure in *CW 14*, esp. 243/3–245/6.

132/17–19 **sick . . . marmelade.** For the "infected taste" of the sick and pregnant, see *CW 4*, 172/3–5. More's marmalade could have been any fruit (not just citrus) boiled with sugar to make a preserve or confection (*OED* 1).

132/20–21 **Iseland . . . barrelled.** A. W. Reed (Campbell and Reed, p. 212) quotes a nineteenth-century account, *Iceland, Greenland, and the Faroe Islands* (Edinburgh, 1840), p. 199: "They use butter in immense quantities and prefer it unsalted and very old, when it has a sour taste and will keep for any length of time without becoming worse." Sabine Baring-Gould, in *Iceland: Its Scenes and Sagas* (London, 1843), points out that salted butter cannot be preserved "beyond a year, whereas sour butter can be kept for ten or twelve without losing either its goodness or its first acidity. In the old Catholic times, there were large magazines attached to each bishopric, serving as storehouses for sour butter . . . but these magazines fell into disuse after the Reformation. This kind of butter is prepared by freeing it from all its milk by repeated churning and washing. . . . It first becomes mouldy and unsavoury, then loses its yellow colour and becomes white; in six months the butter is sour, and fit for consumption, whereas ordinary butter would become completely rancid. If the sour butter be too old, it loses its acidity and weight, turns rancid, and dries up" (p. 74). While trade between England and Iceland (a Danish possession) had been brisk since the fifteenth century (see Eleanora Carus-Wilson, "The Iceland Trade," in *Studies in English Trade in the Fifteenth Century,* ed. Eileen Power and Michael M. Postan, London, 1933, pp. 155–82), we have not been able to locate a contemporary reference that might account for More's knowledge of Icelandic habits of butter consumption.

132/27–31 **For lyke . . . delectacion.** Although the imagery recalls the parable of the wheat and tares (Matt. 13;24–30, 36–43), the moral here is less apocalyptic than the scriptural one. See also Tilley B595.

133/19–22 **sainct Austine . . . sorow.** The quotation is actually based on a passage from the pseudonymous twelfth-century *Liber de vera et falsa poenitentia,* XIII, 28 (*PL 40,* 1124): "Hinc semper doleat, et de dolore gaudeat, et de doloris poenitentia, si contigerit, semper doleat." This tractate had been widely attributed to Augustine in the Middle Ages, although Erasmus and others correctly rejected its authenticity; see Allen, 5, 120. In *CW 8,* 867/30–34, More again attributes this saying to Augustine, while twice in *CW 12* (90/13–15 and Commentary, 97/27–98/1) he identifies the source as Jerome.

133/29–31 **He . . . therein.** More paraphrases Matt. 7:14 ("Quam angusta porta et arta via est quae ducit ad vitam, et pauci sunt qui inveniunt eam!") and Luke 13:24 ("Contendite intrare per angustam portam; quia multi, dico vobis, quaerent intrare et non poterunt").

133/31–32 **And . . . light.** Matt. 11:30: "Iugum enim meum suave est, et onus meum leve."

133/32–134/5 **Howe . . . pleasant.** Cf. Chrysostom, quoted in the *Catena aurea* on Matt. 7:14: "Sed postea dicat, infra 11, *jugum meum suave est, et onus meum leve:* qualiter hic angustam esse viam ait et arctam? Sed et hic monstrat eam levem esse et suavem: quoniam via est et porta est; sicut et altera, quae lata et spatiosa dicitur, ipsa via et porta est. Horum autem nihil mansurum est, sed omnia pertranseunt. Transire autem labores et sudores, et in bonam finem devenire, scilicet in vitam, sufficiens est mitigare eos qui agones patiuntur." See Chrysostom, *In Matthaeum homilia, PG 57,* 314.

134/6–15 **Looke . . . ioy.** More refers to the apostles' chastisement by the council of the Jews in Acts 5:27–41 and quotes the last verse: "Et illi quidem ibant gaudentes a conspectu concilii, quoniam digni habiti sunt pro nomine Iesu contumeliam pati." De Lyra's comment on this passage reads: "Ita quae adversa non solum sustinebant patienter: sed etiam gaudenter in quo consistit excellentissimus gradus" (*Biblia sacra,* 6 vols. (Basel, Johan Froben, 1498).

134/9 **yea.** See *CW 8,* Commentary at 231/18–232/12; and *CW 11,* 158/35–159/7.

134/16–18 **For . . . it.** Cf. Chrysostom's Homily 24 on Matthew (*PG* 57, 314): "Quapropter Paulus levem tribulationem vocavit, non ob naturam accidentium rerum, sed ob promptam voluntatem certantium, et spem futurorum."

135/1–2 **For . . . geuer.** 2 Cor. 9:7: "Hilarem enim datorem diligit Deus."

135/6 **labour is lost.** Cf. Tilley L9: "You lose your labor." See also Whiting L11.

135/19–21 **enforce . . . to conceiue.** The infinitive is far separated from its controlling verb.

135/25–6 **malicious . . . worlde.** For the three traditional sources of temptation, see 1 John 2:15–16: "Nolite diligere mundum neque ea quae in mundo sunt. Si quis diligit mundum, non est caritas Patris in eo; quoniam omne quod est in mundo concupiscentia carnis est et concupiscentia oculorum et superbia vitae; quae non est ex Patre, sed ex mundo est." The "infernal triad" of *caro–mundus–diabolus* was associated in patristic and medieval literature with the temptations of Adam in Eden (Gen. 3) and of Christ in the wilderness (Matt. 4:1–11; Luke 4:1–13); see Donald R. Howard, *The Three Temptations: Medieval Man in Search of the World* (Princeton, 1966), pp. 43–75; Chew, pp. 70–78; and Patrick Cullen, *The Infernal Triad: The Flesh, the World, and the Devil in Spenser and Milton* (Princeton, 1974), pp. xxv–xxxvi. See also *CW 6*, 110/2–3.

135/34–136/1 **not . . . good.** Cf. Ps. 33:15: "Diverte a malo et fac bonum, inquire pacem et persequere eam." See also 1 Pet. 3:10–11 and 182/13–15, above.

136/11–14 **secretly . . . lyke.** Cf. *CW 14*, 117/4–123/3.

136/16–17 **in . . . sinne.** Proverbs 10:19: "In multiloquio non deerit peccatum, qui autem moderatur labia sua prudentissimus est."

136/19–22 **For . . . waking.** In *A Dialogue of Comfort*, More associates dreams and dreaming with the discernment of spirits, false versus true revelation (*CW 12*, 137/16–140/24). The word *fantasies*, which More here uses interchangeably with "dreames," often had negative connotations in the sixteenth century, referring to "illusory appearance" (*OED* 2), "delusive imagination" (*OED* 3), "caprice, changeful mood" (*OED* 6), or "inclination, liking, desire" (*OED* 7). Ultimately, More's understanding of fantasy is derived from scholastic psychology; see *Aristotle's De Anima and the Commentary of Thomas Aquinas*, trans. K. Foster and F. Humphries (London, 1951), III, iii, 696, p. 390. In *De Tristitia*, More compares the person incapable of concentrating on his prayers with a sleeping man whose mind is full of frenzied dreams; see *CW 14*, 119/8–123/3 and 307/6–7. Cf. 139/19–20, 165/26–27, and note on 175/8–15.

136/25 **And . . . mene.** See Tilley M806; Whiting M438, M444.

136/26 **time . . . tong.** Eccles. 3:7: "Tempus scindendi et tempus con-suendi, tempus tacendi et tempus loquendi."

136/12–21 **So . . . maner.** More similarly castigates those whose minds wander while praying in *CW 14*, 123/4–129/4.

137/18 **a . . . thought.** See Tilley P203.

137/6 **y^t.** As Reed points out, "yet" in *1557* must be a misprint for "y^t"; Campbell and Reed, p. 213.

138/23 **a saie** That is, "assay."

138/33–34 **three . . . fleshe.** See 135/25–26 and note.

139/5–14 **some . . . phylosophy.** More is thinking of Plato's Socrates, "the beste philosopher" (139/12), who asserts and demonstrates that philosophers study nothing but death and dying; see *Phaedo* 63e–67e and 81e. In *A Dialogue of Comfort,* More likewise mentions the efforts of "the old morall philosophers" to find "strength and comfort agaynst tribulacion / exirtyng men to the full contempt of all worldly losse, & dispisyng of syknes, & all bodely grefe, paynfull deth and all" (*CW 12*, 9/22–10/15). This view of philosophy was given much attention in humanist literature; see, for example, Erasmus' scholia to Jerome's *Epitaphium Nepotiani* in *Omnium operum diui Eusebii Hieronymi Stridonensis,* 9 vols. (Basel, 1516), *1*, 14C, sig. b₄: Marsilio Ficino, "Theologica Platonica" 16.8, in *Opera omnia,* 2 vols. (Turin, 1959–62) *1*, 383; and Mantuan, *De patientia . . . de vita beata* (Strasbourg, 1510), fol. 88.

139/17 **hovrely.** That is, "hoverly," meaning "transiently."

139/17–18 **as . . . heart.** Cf. the Parable of the Sower, Matt. 13:19: "Omnis qui audit verbum regni et non intelligit, venit malus et rapit quod seminatum est in corde eius."

139/22 **daunce . . . Poules.** The mural, now destroyed, depicting the *danse macabre* in the north cloister of St. Paul's, is described by Stow, *1*, 327: "About this Cloyster, was artificially and richly painted the dance of Machabray, or dance of death, commonly called the dance of *Paul's:* the like whereof was painted about S. Innocents cloyster at Paris in France: the meters or poesie of this dance was translated out of French into English by Iohn Lidgate, Monke of Bury, the picture of death leading all estates, at the dispence of Ienken Carpenter in the raigne of Henry the sixt." For the text of Lydgate's poem, see Florence Warren and Beatrice White, eds., *The Dance of Death,* EETS OS no. 181 (London, 1931); and Eleanor Hammond, ed., *English Verse between Chaucer and Surrey* (London and Durham, N.C., 1927), pp. 124–42, 418–35.

139/25 **bodies . . . fleshe.** That is, "bodies with the flesh bitten away." For this unusual construction, see Visser, *1*, 322.

140/2–7 **lying . . . on.** Such enumeration of the death throes was a common device of medieval preaching, as in the sermon for the first Sunday in Lent in John Mirk's *Festial:* "Thenkythe how a man ys borne febull, and seke, and naked, and pore; and how he gothe yche day a journay toward his deth, woll he, nyll he; and how that, at the last, dethe comythe and castythe hym down seke yn hys bed, gronyng and sykyng, and sone castythe up hys mete and hys drynke, and turnet hyde and hew; and how his brethe stinkyth hys lyppys wexyn blew, hys face pale, hys een yolow, hys mowthe frothys: and so, at the last, wyth depe yoskyng yeldyth vp the gost." See *Mirk's Festial,* ed. Theodor Erbe, EETS ES no. 96 (London, 1905), p. 84; and G. R. Owst, *Preaching in Medieval England: An Introduction to Sermon Manuscripts of the Period c. 1350–1450* (Cambridge, 1926), p. 342. See also the Introduction, p. xcvii.

140/4–5 **thy nose . . . fimbling.** Reed (Campbell and Reed, p. 214) points out the parallel with the hostess description of Falstaff's death in *Henry V,* II, iii 9–25. Perhaps More is thinking of the Hippocratic prognosis that fatal diseases frequently cause the patient's nose to sharpen, as if tapering to a point (*Prognosticon,* II).

140/8–19 **If thou . . . middes.** Cf. *CW 12,* 302/9–18.

140/9 **sicknes.** Seemingly a plural without the usual added –*es.* See Delcourt, pp. 87–90, 138–41.

140/28–141/12 **passion . . . body.** Cf. Matt. 27:50, Mark 15:37, and Luke 23:46. In *De Tristitia,* More similarly denies that even martyrs feel pain as excruciating as that felt by Christ; see *CW 14,* 231/6–235/2. The use of Christ's passion here differs from its appearance in the *ars moriendi* literature, where meditation on the crucified Christ is offered as solace to the dying man: "his heed enclyned to salve the, his mouth to kysse the, his armes I-spred to be-clyp the, his hondis I-thrilled to yeve the, his syde opened to love the, hys bodye alonge straught to yeve all hym-selfe to thee." See *The Boke of the craft of dyinge* in *Yorkshire Writers: Richard Rolle of Hampole and his Followers,* ed. Carl Horstmann, 2 vols. (London, 1896), 2, 410; cf. the Introduction above, p. lxxxiii.

141/3 **if he . . . it.** Cf. *CW 14,* 87/4–89/1.

141/7 **impassyble.** An unusual technical word often applied to glorified bodies, meaning "incapable of suffering or pain" (*OED,* s.v. *impassible* 1).

141/24–142/3 **see . . . rest.** By contrast with More's deathbed scene, the corresponding episode in the *ars moriendi* depicts the presence of wife, children, and friends as troublesome because they tempt "most carnall & seculer men [to] ouer-much occupacion & besynesse a-bought outward temporall thingis that thei haue loved inordinately before." See *The Boke of the craft of dyinge*, 2, 412, and the Introduction above, pp. lxxxii–lxxxiii.

141/26 **flesh flies.** According to *OED* (s.v. *flesh-fly* 1), "A fly which deposits its eggs in dead flesh." More here uses the term figuratively to describe persons who hover about a dying man in the hope of inheriting property; elsewhere, he uses it to denote a person of worldly inclinations (*CW 8*, 179/3).

142/8–15 **For sith . . . tormentry.** Cf. *A Treatise on the Passion* on the events in Gen. 3:1: "But oh wo worth wicked envy yᵉ doughter of pestilent pryde. For the proud hateful enemy of God, and traiterous wretch yᵉ dyuel, beholdyng this newe creature of mankynd, set in so welthy state, & either coniecturing by hys natural vnderstanding, or to thencrease of his grief for his proud enuious stomake, hauing it reueled unto him, that of thys kinde should be restored the ruine that was happed in heauen, by the fal of himselfe and hys felowes, conceiued so great hart burning againe the kynde of man therefore, that he rather wold wish his own dampnacion doubled, so that he might destroy them, then suffer God honoured in them, and them so to proceede and prosper, that their grose myngled nature so base in respect of his, should ascend vp to that height of heauen that himself was fallen fro" (*CW 13*, 14/2–14). Cf. also *CW 6*, 48/10–14; and 158/31 and note, 158/32–159/8 and note, and 174/29–31.

142/17–18 **he . . . deuoure.** Cf. 1 Pet. 5:8: "Sobrii estote et vigilate, quia adversarius vester diabolus tanquam leo rugiens circuit quaerens quem devoret." In *A Dialogue of Comfort*, More uses this passage as a monitory text against undue fears of oppression by men, which can distract us from guarding against Satanic attack. See *CW 12*, 317/12–318/12; and cf. above, 165/39–166/1, where the lion is a figure of death.

142/20–23 **For . . . again.** The deathbed temptations enumerated in *The Boke of the craft of dyinge* depend on the conviction that men are most vulnerable to temptation at the point of death. See the Introduction above, lxxxii–lxxxiii.

142/24–25 **gailour . . . temporal.** In *The Supplication of Souls*, More pictures the souls in purgatory "emprysoned by . . . the damned spyrytys the very gaolers of god"; see *CW 7*, 178/34–179/1 and Commentary.

142/28–29 **For . . . Christe.** See Luke 23:40–43.

142/31–32 **For . . . abyde.** More seems to be thinking of Ecclesiastes 11:3: "Si ceciderit lignum ad austrum aut aquilonem, in quocumque loco ceciderit, ibi erit." See Whiting T477.

143/4–144/4 **unlawefull . . . death.** The satanic traps into which the soul may fall at the point of death are similar to some of the deathbed temptations enumerated in the *The Boke of the craft of dyinge,* specifically: "complacens, or plesaunce of a man that he hath in hym-selfe," "ouer-much occupacion & besynesse abought outwarde temporall thingis," and "dispercion" (2, 409, 411–12).

143/4 **lyue, horrour.** As Reed suggests, the compositor may have omitted "and" after this word (Campbell and Reed, p. 215).

143/6 **glade.** For this place in More, *OED* suggests tentatively the meaning "a gleam of hope," a figurative use based on the established meaning, "a flash of light or lightning" (*OED,* s.v. *glade* sb.² 3b), but Reed (Campbell and Reed, p. 215) suggests the meaning "an open track in a wood particularly made for placing traps for woodcocks" (*OED* 1b).

143/17–23 **honorable . . . church.** Cf. the warning against ostentatious funerals made by the souls in purgatory in More's *Supplication of Souls:* "Much haue many of us bestowed upon rich men in golde ringes & black gownes, much in many tapers & torches: much in worldly pompe and high solemne ceremonies aboute our funeralles: whereof the brotle glory standeth us here god wot in very little stede, but hath on the tother side done us greate displeasure" (*CW* 7, 219/29–34). Cf. also Erasmus, *Moriae encomium, ASD 4/3,* 126/23–28.

144/13–14 **man . . . beast.** Cf. *CW 12,* 109/27–28: "For in the nyght euery bush to hym that waxeth ones a ferd seemeth a thefe."

144/17–19 **wiues . . . childe.** Sarah's conception of a child in her old age is recounted in Gen. 20–21.

144/20–21 **none . . . yet.** In *De senectute* 7.24, Cicero speaks of Sabine farmers who never leave their fields during planting and harvest: "Quamquam in aliis minus hoc mirum est, nemo est tam senex qui se annum non putet posse vivere; sed idem in eis elaborant, quae sciunt nihil ad se omnino pertinere: 'serit arbores, quae alteri saeculo prosint.'" Cf. *CW 12,* 4/17–19.

144/24–26 **Where . . . muste.** The idea and phrasing are perhaps based on a passage in Cicero's *De senectute* 9.68: "Sed redeo ad mortem impendentem. Quod est istud crimen senectutis, cum id ei videatis cum adulescentia esse commune? . . . At sperat adulescens diu se victurum, quod sperare idem senex non potest. Insipienter sperat; quid enim stultius quam incerta pro certis habere, falsa pro veris? At senex ne quod speret quidem habet. At est eo meliore condicione quam adulescens, quoniam id quod ille sperat hic consecutus est: ille volt diu vivere, hic diu vixit." See also 144/20–21 and note, where More quotes directly from Cicero's work, and cf. *CW 12,* 4/15–17 and 86/7–10 and Commentary, where the saying is used to make the same point.

145/1–3 **Than . . . on.** Cf. *CW 12*, 307/22–28: "But when the tyme shall come, that these fowle filthy pleasures shalbe so taken from hym, that yt shall abhore his hart ones to thinke on them / whereof euery man hath a mong a certayne shadow of experience in a fervent griefe of a sore paynfull siknes, while the stomake can scant abide to loke uppon any meate / and as for actes of the tother fowle filthy lust / ys redy to vomyt yf yt hap hym to thynke thereon." See also Pliny's letter to Maximus (*Epistolae* 7.26) about the sickness of a friend: "Quem enim infirmum aut avaritia aut libido sollicitat?" For the omission of the expected pronoun (here "it") in the main clause of sentences beginning with an "As for" construction, see Visser, *1*, 33–34.

145/3–6 **And . . . life.** Cf. Pliny's letter to Maximus (*Epistolae* 7.26), from which More quotes directly in the next sentence: "Haec summa curarum, summa votorum, mollemque in posterum et pinguem, si contingat evadere, hac est innoxiam beatamque, destinat vitam."

145/7–15 **wordes . . . sicke.** Pliny's letter to Maximus (*Epistolae* 7.26) concludes: "Possum ergo, quod plurimis verbis, plurimis etiam voluminibus philosophi docere conantur, ipse breviter tibi mihique praecipere, ut tales esse sani perseveremus, quales nos futuros profitemur infirmi." Cf. note on 145/3–6 and *CW 12*, 4/10–14.

145/21–22 **great sicknes.** In the summer of 1517 England was ravaged by plague: "Sodeinly there came a plague of sickenes, called the Swetyng sickenes. . . . This malady was so cruell that it killed some within three hours, some within twoo houres, some mery at diner and dedde at supper. Many died in the kynges Courte. . . . In some one toune halfe the people died, and in some other toune the thirde parte, the Sweate was so feruent and infeccious"; Edward Halle, *The Vnion of the Two Noble and Illustre Famelies of Lancastre & Yorke* (London, 1809), p. 592.

145/24 **goddes markes.** The physical signs of the plague (*OED*, s.v. *God* 16c). Margaret Roper had "gods markes" (Roper, 29/11).

146/3 **in good quart.** That is, "in good health" (*OED*, s.v. *quart* adj. and sb.¹ B).

146/18–20 **For what . . . consumpcion?** Cf. Augustine, *Confessiones* 10.31.43–44: "Nam fames et sitis quidam dolores sunt, urunt et sicut febris necant, nisi alimentorum medicina succurrat. . . . Hoc me docuisti, ut quemadmodum medicamenta sic alimenta sumpturus accedam" (*CCSL* 27, 178). This passage is paraphrased by Nicholas Love in *The Mirrour of the Blessed Lyf of Jesu Christ*, a translation and adaptation of Pseudo-Bonaventure's *Meditationes vitae Christi:* "as saint Augustyn saith in his booke of Confessions that a man take of mete & drynk to sustenaunce of the body only as he wold take of medecyn for to hele his Infirmyte . . . soo for as mykel as honger and thurst ben Infirmyte of mankynde thorugh the firste synne of man mete & drynke that ben as medecyn to this Infirmyte should be take only as for hele therof / as saint Augustyn seith" (William Caxton, 1486; *STC*[2] 3259; sig. h₆v). More himself recommended *The Mirrour* (*CW 8*, 37/25–33), which was issued in ten editions between 1486 and 1530. See *CW 13*, lxxxvi–lxxxvii.

146/27 **or.** That is, "ere."

146/28–29 **slepe . . . death.** The sentiment is at least as old as Homer and can be found in Plato's *Phaedo* (71c–d) and Cicero's *De senectute* (22.81). Cf. Tilley S527, where the first English use is cited from an early seventeenth-century work by Walkington.

147/19–25 **conflict . . . therewith.** In sixteenth-century physiology, the "diuers qualified elementes tempered in our body" were the four humors: blood, phlegm, choler, and bile. Differences of personality and temperament were ascribed to varying proportions of these humors in the body, and (as More here suggests) health was seen as a reasonable balance among them. Cf. *CW 4*, 172/23–174/3; and *CW 12*, 150/2–7 and Commentary.

147/30 **yᵗ than that.** The second "that" seems superfluous and may have been wrongly repeated by the compositor. But Delcourt (pp. 221–26) gives many similar pleonasms from More's writings, although some of those may have resulted from the setting of two alternatives in a manuscript between which More had not yet chosen by canceling one of them.

148/2 **brinkes.** That is, the edges of the sore.

148/3–4 **our whole life . . . curable.** See note on 145/7–15.

148/9–10 **the flame . . . smoke.** Tilley S569: "No smoke without some fire." See also Otto, no. 666.

148/16 **merely.** That is, "merrily."

148/16–17 **thou . . . liuest.** Tilley L385: "We shall live till we die."

148/18–27 **For . . . lyue.** Cf. *CW 3/2*, no. 75, "Vita Ipsa Cursus ad Mortem Est," and Wisdom 5:13: "Sic et nos nati continuo desivimus esse, et virtutis quidem nullum signum valuimus ostendere, in malignitate autem nostra consumpti sumus." Cf. Seneca, *Epistulae morales* 24.20: "Non repente nos in mortem incidere, sed minutatim procedere; cotidie morimur. Cotidie enim demitur aliqua pars vitae, et tunc quoque, cum crescimus, vita decrescit." See the Introduction, pp. lxxiii–lxxiv. Whiting L411: "We no sooner begin to live than we begin to die."

148/28 **It is not . . . to be dead.** In Old and Middle English, and as late as Moore's time, "to be dead" was used to mean "to die" (*OED*, s.v. *dead* a. A1d).

148/33 **whither.** That is, "whether."

149/23–26 **man . . . nerer.** Cf. *CW 3/2*, no. 75, lines 4–7: "Scilicet ex illa, qua primum nascimur hora, / Prorepunt iuncto uitaque morsque pede. / Partem aliquam furtim qua se metitur, et ipsam / Surripit e uita quaelibet hora tua." It is presumably this passage and its content that Vittorio Gabrieli ("Tommaso Moro: 'Le quattro cose ultime,'" *La cultura: Rivista di filosofia letteratura e storia, 15* [1977], 449) thinks is clearly echoed by Thomas Lupset in his *Compendious and a Very Fruteful treatyse, teachynge the waye of Dyenge well . . .* (London, 1534; *STC²* 16934): "dailye sithen our fyrste byrthe we haue died, in as moche that dayly some parte of our life, hath ben diminished, & euer as we haue growen, so euer life hath decresed. . . . This same selfe day that we nowe lyue, is deuyded and parted with death. Styll without ceasing we approche to death by thexpence & wast of lyfe. Thus dyinge we always be, though death be not alway vpon us" (sig. E₆). But this passage hardly shows that Lupset must have seen More's *Last Things* in manuscript. If Lupset had a source here, it is more likely to have been one of More's Latin poems or Seneca (see note on 148/18–27).

149/35–150/30 **Now . . . felowes.** In *A Dialogue of Comfort*, Antony and Vincent similarly debate the "sophisticall fantasies" or "substanciall trewth" of the assertion that all men are prisoners of the flesh, condemned to death by the penalty of original sin. See *CW 12*, 262–70.

150/5–31 **If there . . . we all.** As Roger L. Deakins points out in his fascimile edition and translation of Ellis Heywood's *Il Moro* (Cambridge, Mass., 1972; first printed in Florence in 1556), Heywood must have seen a manuscript of More's *Last Things*. One of the characters in Heywood's dialogue addresses More, who is also a participant, as follows: "Let me give you an exposition more to the point than Laurence's, using the vivid metaphor that you, Mr. More, used in one of your books, which I hope it may please God to see translated into a more universal language as it is well written in the native language of this island. You compare our condition with that of those who, all guilty of the same crime, are condemned to death by the same judgment, loaded together into one cart, and sent off to execution. They are sent to various regions instead of all to the same place, so that their exemplary punishment will be more vividly known, one to the closest city, another to a more remote place, and another to the very borders of the country. We humans, equally guilty of that first sin of Adam, are all condemned to death by the Supreme Judge, sent off together in the same chariot, that most rapid chariot of time that rushes us over a street hard and rough toward death, and, as it pleases Fate or Fortune (who execute the sentence very day) we all die—this one in his early years, this one in middle age, and some, but not many at the extremity of life" (pp. 62–63; the Italian of the 1556 edition is given on p. 112). Heywood (1530–1578), who was William Rastell's nephew, went to Italy in 1552 to become a servant of Cardinal Pole; he may have returned to England around 1554 (see Deakins' introduction to *Il Moro*, p. x).

It is presumably this same passage in *The Last Things* that Vittorio Gabrieli ("Tommaso Moro," pp. 449–50) thinks is clearly echoed in Lupset's *Compendious and a Very Fruteful treatyse:* "If you sawe one stande in the numbre of many that shoulde be hedded, makynge most instant suit to the hangman, that he might be yᵉ last that shulde put his head to the blocke, wolde you not say, fye vpon such a wretched knaue, that so moche feareth deathe, beynge nowe at the poynt to dye, whether he wylle or no? and yet this maner nowe is with vs all" (sigs. D₃–D₃v). But the similarity is not close enough to make it clear that Lupset saw a manuscript of More's *Last Things*.

150/31 **endented.** that is, "entered into agreement by indentures" (*OED,* s.v. *indent* v.¹ 3). *1557* has the sidenote "Job. 14" (Job 14:5).

153/1 **pryde.** By beginning his analysis of the capital sins with pride, More follows the order established by Gregory in *Moralia* 31.45: *superbia, ira, invidia, avaritia, acedia, gula, luxuria;* see *PL* 76, 620–23. Like many others, however, More does not adhere rigidly to this "normative" order: he reverses envy and wrath, as well as gluttony and sloth. For the prevalence of and variations upon the Gregorian order in the Middle Ages, see Bloomfield, pp. 69–104. See also Introduction, p. lxxxv; and below, note on 181/31–182/7.

153/12–14 **beginning . . . vice.** The commonplace notion that pride is the source of all other forms of sin is articulated in scripture at Ecclus. 10:14–15: "Initium superbiae hominis apostatare a Deo; quoniam ab eo qui fecit illum, recessit cor eius, quoniam initium omnis peccati est superbia." In *De civitate Dei,* Augustine twice refers to this text (at 12.6 and 14.3), and it was proverbial by the late fifteenth century (see Tilley P578). In *Utopia,* More describes pride as "una tantum belua, omnium princeps parensque pestium" (*CW 4,* 242/24–25), while in *A Treatise on the Passion,* he comments: "For surely thys synne of pride, as it is the first of all synnes, begon among the angels in heauen, so it is the heade and roote of all other sinnes, and of them al most pestilent" (*CW 13,* 9/20–23).

153/17–18 **As for wrathe . . . self.** Cf. 158/26–159/5, 161/7–8, 162/9–12, and the preceding note.

153/20 **sow drunk.** That is "extremely drunk"; Whiting S534. Cf. *CW* 7, 212/12 and 212/25.

153/27 **quick.** That is, "alive."

153/32–33 **spiritual pride.** In *De coenobiorum institutis*, Cassian identifies two kinds of pride: "Unum hoc quo diximus spiritales viros summosque pulsari, aliud quod etiam incipientes carnalesque complectitur. Et licet utrumque superbiae genus tam in Deum, quam in homines noxia inflet elatio; tamen illud primum specialiter refertur ad Deum, secundum ad homines proprie pertinet" (12.2, *PL 49*, 423–24). What More calls "spiritual pride" seems closer to Cassianus' carnal pride, to which novice monks are particularly susceptible, and which manifests itself in an air of self-righteous superiority toward others (12.25; *PL 49*, 462–67). Spiritual pride, in Cassianus' sense, is the belief that one can attain perfection without the grace of God (12.15–17; *PL 49*, 449–54).

154/1 **doth nought.** That is, "does evil" (*OED*, s.v. *nought* sb., a., & adv., 8c).

154/6–11 **For . . . iustice.** In a similar spirit, Richard, in More's *History of King Richard III*, feigns righteousness by commanding the bishop of London to put Shore's wife to public penance; see *CW 2*, 54/24–26. Cf. also the hypocritical zeal of the friar in *CW 4*, 82/23–84/7.

154/18–20 **thapocalips . . . warme.** See Rev. 3:14–15: "Et angelo Laodiciae ecclesiae scribe: Haec dicit amen, testis fidelis et verus, qui est principium creaturae Dei: Scio opera tua, quia neque frigidus es neque calidus: utinam frigidus esses aut calidus!"

154/24 **saint Poule . . . perceiue.** See Gal. 5:19: "Manifesta sunt autem opera carnis." Cf. *CW 8*, 757/12–14; and *CW 9*, 170/6–7.

154/27–29 **sauing . . . knocketh.** See Rev. 3:20: "Ecce sto ad ostium et pulso: si quis audierit vocem meam et aperuerit mihi ianuam, intrabo ad illum et cenabo cum illo et ipse mecum."

154/33–34 **braunch of pride.** The image of the sins as the branches of a tree whose root is pride was a medieval commonplace. Cassianus was among the first to use it, around 425 (*Collationes* 5.10; *PL 49*, 622); and the immensely influential twelfth-century work by pseudo-Hugh of St. Victor, *De fructibus carnis et spiritus* (*PL 174*, 997–1006) popularized the image in the later Middle Ages. Cf. Chaucer, "The Parson's Tale," X(I), 387–88.

155/3–4 **strayt to heuen.** The same phrase occurs in a similar context in *A Dialogue of Comfort* when Antony recounts the story from Cassianus' *Collationes* (2.5; *PL 49*, 529–30) about "a very specall holy man" who is brought by the devil "into such an high spiritall pride" that he commits suicide believing "that it was godes will he shuld do so / & that therby shuld he go strayt to hevyn" (*CW 12*, 129/9–25). See also 153/32–33 and note, above.

155/14 **web.** That is, "film, cataract" (*OED*, s.v. *web* sb. 7).

155/25 **therfore.** That is, "in return for it [their punishment in hell]."

155/28 **blast . . . mouthes.** An image More frequently uses to convey the idea of empty praise, as in the beginning of the prayer in his *Book of Hours (Prayer Book,* pp. 3–4 and 185): "Gyve me thy grace good lord . . . not to hange vppon the blaste of mennys mowthis." See also *CW 9,* 69/5–6; and *CW 12,* 212/4–5.

156/3–4 **glorye . . . graue.** See Ps. 48:18: "Quoniam, cum interierit, non sumet omnia, neque descendet cum eo gloria eius."

156/9–12 **deinty . . . hed.** Death as the leveler of rich and poor alike is a central theme of the *danse macabre* tradition. Cf., for example, the remarks of John Bromyard, chancellor of Cambridge in the late fourteenth century: "If we would but consider well how quickly we shall be placed beneath the feet not only of men, friend and foe alike, but of dogs, and the beasts of the field . . . we should find little reason for pride. . . . *Sic transit gloria mundi!*"; quoted in G. R. Owst, *Preaching in Medieval England* (Cambridge, 1926), p. 343. See also *CW 3/2,* 80/8–13; and above, 160/28–33.

156/14 **wind . . . pride.** Cf. Col. 2:18–19: "Nemo vos seducat volens in humilitate et religione angelorum, quae non vidit, ambulans, frustra inflatus sensu carnis suae."

156/16–22 **wering . . . hys.** This use of the "all the world's a stage" metaphor probably owes something to the passage in Lucian's *Menippus,* which More had translated in 1505–6, where Menippus reflects during a trip to Hades on the leveling effects of death: "Haec igitur spectanti mihi, persimilis hominum uita pompae cuipiam longae widebatur, cui praesit ac disponat quaeque fortuna, ex his qui pompam agunt, diuersos uariosque cuique habitus accommodans. . . . Et aliquantisper quidem eo cultu permittit uti, uerum ubi iam pompae tempus praeterijt, apparatum quisque restituens, & cum corpore simul exutus amictu, qualis ante fuit efficitur, nihilo a uicino differens" (*CW 3/1,* 37/20–35). Cf. also *CW 4,* 98/10–14; and *CW 2,* 81/1 and Commentary. About 1530 John Rastell published *Necromantia, A dialog of the Poete Lucyan (STC² 16895),* an English verse translation, together with More's Latin translation (see *CW 3/1,* 142–43). For the history of the metaphor in classical and medieval literature, see Curtius, pp. 138–44; E. R. Dodds, *Pagan and Christian in an Age of Anxiety* (Cambridge, 1965), pp. 8–12; and Minos Kokolakis, *The Dramatic Simile of Life* (Athens, 1960). Erasmus uses the metaphor in *Moriae encomium (ASD 4/3,* 104/593–602) and at the end of his colloquy *Abbatis et eruditae (ASD 1/3,* 407/163–64).

156/26–158/13 **Mark . . . for him.** For the idea of the world as a prison (current at least by the time of Plato's *Phaedo* 62b and the allegory of the cave in his *Republic* 514a–517b), cf. *CW 3/2,* no. 119; *CW 2,* 81/1–8, 258; and *CW 12,* 258–78.

156/32 **sessions.** The periodic sittings of the justices of the peace.

156/33 **there.** That is, at the sessions of the peace.

157/6–9 **prison . . . sight.** Cf. *CW 12*, 271/21–22: "Yet the chiefe gay-lour ouer this whole brode prison / the world is (as I take it) god." The devil, by contrast, presides over purgatorial imprisonment; see above, 142/24–25 and note.

157/9–10 **David . . . face.** Ps. 138:7: "Quo ibo a spiritu tuo? et quo a facie tua fugiam?"

157/11 **therfore.** That is, "for it."

157/15–17 **some wepyng . . . fighting.** In *Moriae encomium,* Erasmus, imitating Lucian's *Icaromenippus* 15, made the gods look down on swarms of men, "inter se rixantium, bellantium, insidiantium, rapientium, ludentium, lascivientium, nascentium, cadentium, morientium" (*ASD 4/3*, 138/458–59).

157/27 **tower of Babilon.** The use of "Babylon" as a synonym for "Babel" is a common medieval conflation derived not from the Vulgate translation of Gen. 11:8–9 but from patristic reliance on the readings for this text in the Septuagint and Vetus Latina; for the former, see Alan E. Brooke and Norman McLean, *The Old Testament in Greek,* 3 vols. (Cambridge, 1906), *1/1*, 26–27; for the latter, see Bonifatius Fischer, *Genesis, Vetus Latina, Die Reste der altlateinischen Bibel,* 2 (Freiburg, 1951–54), pp. 144–45. The tower is here the symbol of pride; More uses it in the *Apology* to symbolize the discordancy of heretical opinion: "For lyke wyse as they that wolde haue byelded vppe the toure of Babylon for them self agaynste god, hadde suche a stoppe throwen vppon them, that sodaynely none vnderstode what another sayed / surely so god . . . hath rered vp and sent amonge these heretykes the spyryte of errour and lyenge, of dyscorde and of dyuysyon, the dampned deuyll of hell, whyche so entangleth theyre tunges and so dystempereth theyr braynes, that they neyther vnderstande well one of them another, nor any of them well hym selfe." See *CW 9*, 41/10–11 and Commentary. Cf. also *CW 6*, 6/24–25.

158/2–4 **gentleman . . . Newgate.** The inmates of Newgate prison in the northwest entrance to London were taken for public execution to Tyburn outside the city; see Stow, *1*, 36 and 2, 91; and cf. above, 172/18–29.

158/10–11 **tapster . . . marshalsye.** Marshalsea was a prison in the borough of Southwark; see Stow, 2, 53.

158/12–13 **half . . . felowes.** In *A Dialogue of Comfort,* More identifies the underjailers as angels and devils; see *CW 12*, 271/21 and 273/21–22. Cf. also above, 142/24–25, 157/6–9, and notes.

158/13 **shyryfe . . . him.** Compare Thomas Smith, *De Republica Anglorum. The maner of Government or policie of the Realme of England* (1583): "[the sheriff] hath also the charge of all the prisoners committed to the prison which we call the gaole, and when any is condemned to die, it is his charge to see the sentence executed" (II, 14).

158/18 **tyrants in Sicil.** Dionysius and Phalaris were the most notorious of the ancient tyrants of Sicily. Phalaris ordered the construction of a brazen bull that, when heated, caused its enclosed victim to bellow; the tyrant made the maker of the bull its first victim. See Otto, no. 1405; and Erasmus, *Adagia*, no. 886 (*Opera omnia*, 2, 392DE).

158/18–23 **it so drynketh . . . glasse.** The pale, bloodless, emaciated appearance of envy was traditional (for example, Ovid, *Metamorphoses* 2.760–82), but the comparison with a death's head (which adapts the description to More's subject) apparently was not.

158/24 **ouer.** P. S. Allen and H. M. Allen emend to "ever" and note: "The original has *ouer*, which has been interpreted *hover;* but the correction to *ever* seems easier" (*Sir Thomas More: Selections from His English Works and from the Lives by Erasmus & Roper*, Oxford, 1924, p. 177). But it seems better to identify "ouer" here with an obsolete Scottish verb meaning "to overcome, master" (*OED*, s.v. *over* v. 3), even though More's use, unlike any of the examples given by *OED*, is intransitive.

158/26–28 **as the fire . . . hert.** As one explanation of the decreasing height of Aetna, Seneca advances the hypothesis that the mountain is being consumed by its own fires (*Epistulae morales* 79.2). He also contrasts the mountain wasted by flames with imperishable virtue (79.10), and he goes on to assert at length that fame will come to virtue, however delayed, once envy has withdrawn (79.14).

158/31 **doughter of pryde.** Augustine frequently discusses the mother/daughter relationship between pride and envy. See *Sermones* 303.2, 304.5 (*PL 39*, 1561, 1565): "Invidia filia est superbiae." See also *Enarrationes in Psalmos* 100.9 (*Corpus Christianorum: Series Latina*, vol. 39, 2nd ed. rev., ed. Germanus Morin, Turnholt, 1958, p. 1414); *De genesi ad litteram*, 11.14 (*PL 34*, 436); *De catechizandis rudibus* 4 (*PL 40*, 315); *Epistolae*, 140.54 (*PL 33*, 561). Cf. *CW 13*, 14/3 and Commentary.

158/31 **baste.** That is, "bastardy" (see *CW 2*, 66/33).

158/32–159/8 **deuil . . . thereof.** Cf. *CW 6*, 48/10–14: "And this must nedes be an enuy comynge of an hye deuelysshe pryde / and farre passynge the enuuye of the deuyll hym selfe / for he neuer enuyed / but suche as he sawe / and was conuersaunt with / as when he sawe man and the glory of god." See also 142/8–15 and note.

159/1–2 **this . . . heuen.** The tradition that pride was the sin of the fallen angel Satan/Lucifer was almost universally acknowledged by medieval commentators. See, for example, Hugh of St. Victor, *PL 177*, 791. See also Bloomfield, p. 382, n. 16, and above, note on 153/12–14.

159/3 **sight of Adam and Eve.** The omission of "of" in *1557* was almost certainly merely a misprint.

159/12–17 **In so farforth . . . hurt.** Macrobius, *Saturnalia* 2.8: "Publius Mucium in primis maliuolum cum uidisset solito tristiorem aut Mucio inquit nescio quid incommodi accessit aut nescio cui aliquid boni." Erasmus quotes the passage in *Apophthegmata*, 6, Varie mixta 12 (*Opera omnia, 4,* 288c).

159/14 **quod.** The abbreviation ꝙ in *1557* may stand for either of the equivalent forms "quoth" or "quod." Both the abbreviation and the full form *quod* appear frequently in the early editions of *A Dialogue Concerning Heresies*.

159/14 **Mutius.** The compositor of *1557* left a blank space for this word, probably because he could not decipher it in his copy.

159/21 **fable of Esop.** More here retells what is actually the twenty-second fable of Avianus, "De cupido et invido" (*The Fables of Avianus,* ed. Robinson Ellis, Oxford, 1887, pp. 22–26). Caxton includes it in his *Historyes and Fables of Esop* (1484) as "The xvij fable . . . of Phebus . . . the Avarycious and . . . the envious"; see *Caxton's Aesop,* ed. R. T. Lenaghan (Cambridge, Mass., 1967), pp. 185–86. Cf. also *CW 8,* 182/32–34: "For thys is a lyke amendynge, as yf he wolde where a man were blynde of the tone eye / amende hys syghte by puttynge out the tother." Unlike More, neither Caxton's translation nor Avianus' original specifies that Apollo actually granted the envious man's request.

159/25 **couetise.** The form "couetise" in *1557* is a less common, Middle English spelling of the adjectival ending.

160/6–9 **saint Austine . . . doughter.** We have not been able to find this exact formula in Augustine, but perhaps More is encapsulating the obvious conclusion from Augustine's frequent insistence that pride precedes and causes envy. See note on 158/31 and cf. Augustine's *De sancta virginitate,* 31 (*PL 40,* 413): "Hanc [superbiam] sequitur invidentia tanquam filia pedissequa: eam quippe superbia continuo parit, nec unquam est sine tali prole atque comite. . . . Itaque contra superbiam matrem invidentiae maxime militat universa disciplina christiana."

160/15 **the.** That is, "thee."

160/18 **the litle.** That is, "thee little."

160/22–25 **perpetual . . . before.** See 144/30–148/11, 149/35–151/7, and 156/30–158/13.

160/28–33 **one . . . yeres?** See 156/9–12.

160/34–161/13 **Duke . . . pity?** A. W. Reed identified More's "great Duke" as Edward Stafford, third duke of Buckingham, who was tried and executed for treason in May 1521; see Campbell and Reed, pp. 21–22 and 216. Although Buckingham's seizure and trial bear an outward resemblance to More's description, the identification is speculative; see the Introduction above, pp. lx–lxi. For Buckingham's trial, see *LP 3/1*, 1283–84; J. J. Scarisbrick, *Henry VIII* (London, 1968), pp. 120–23.

161/10–11 **cote armour reuersed.** The reversal of the coat of arms was heraldic convention for treason; see Thomas Woodcock and John Martin Robinson, *The Oxford Guide to Heraldry* (Oxford and New York, 1988), p. 68.

161/20 **hathe.** See note on 128/21.

161/32–33 **turned . . . nature.** Whiting C646, Tilley C932: Custom is a second nature.

162/1 **roote . . . pride.** See 153/12–14 and note.

162/23-163/2 **al . . . borne.** More's large claim that "this is the prouision of the lawes almost in euery countrey, and hath bene afore christe was borne" (163/1–2) is difficult to confirm but at least gains credibility from the widely influential witness of Justinian's *Corpus iuris civilis* (c. 529–34), a four-part work that assimilated and superseded Roman law (including the Twelve Tables). In this code, a wrong, or *iniuria*, done to a person was not restricted to assault or property damage, but encompassed any unlawful act ("omne quod non iure sit") that damaged a person's reputation or otherwise offended his honor: "Iniuria autem committitur non solum, cum quis pugno puta aut fustibus caesus vel etiam verberatus erit, sed etiam si cui convicium factum erit" (*Institutiones*, 4.4). Injury thus included *contumeliae* (More's "contumelies," 162/26) of various kinds, and penalties took into account the social rank and community standing of the plaintiff; see *Corpus iuris civilis*, ed. Paul Krueger et al., 3 vols. (Berlin, 1912–28), *1*, 46.

162/24 **thaccions of trespas.** In early Tudor law, actions of trespass were taken for assault upon or damage done to persons or property when such damage had immediate results; see David M. Walker, *The Oxford Companion to Law* (Oxford, 1980), p. 1237.

162/30–31 **lawes . . . punisheth.** See note on 128/21.

163/8–10 **And . . . sweord.** We have not been able to identify a source for More's statement about Spanish law. Indeed, the thirteenth-century *Fuero real* suggests that penalties for wounds that actually pierced the body were more severe than for those that drew no blood; see *Fuero real de España*, libro 4, titulo 5, in *Los codigos españoles*, 12 vols. (Madrid, 1847), *1*, 406.

163/18 **pointe.** Reed suggests that the notion of "a point of honor" (*OED*, s.v. *point*, sb. b9) may be relevant here, but the conjunction with "readiness" makes his reading of "suddenness" (in the sense of precipitate action) more plausible, although the *OED* does not record this meaning for *point;* see Campbell and Reed, p. 216.

163/21–24 **anger . . . commaundmentes.** A fourteenth(?)-century sermon for the seventh Sunday after Trinity concludes: "Bot ther be two ires, on gode, a-nother euell. The tone comyth of the flessh, that other of the spryte"; see Woodburn O. Ross, ed., *Middle English Sermons*, EETS OS no. 209 (London, 1940), p. 306. Erasmus, however, warns in the *Enchiridion* against falsely attributing impulses of anger to zeal on God's behalf (*Opera omnia*, 5, 14–15). Cf. also *Utopia*, where the friar at Cardinal Morton's dinner table is unwittingly made a laughing-stock for claiming that his anger is "bonus zelus" (*CW 4*, 84/2–3).

165/14–15 **laid . . . execucion.** Cf. 158/13 and note.

165/28–29 **And now . . . procession.** Cf. Chaucer, "The Parson's Tale," X (I), 406–7: "And yet is ther a privee spece of Pride, that waiteth first to be salewed er he wole salewe, al be he lasse worth than that oother is, peraventure; and eek he waiteth or desireth to sitte, or elles to goon above hym in the wey, or kisse pax, or been encensed, or goon to offryng beforn his neighebor, and swiche semblable thynges, agayns his duetee, peraventure, but that he hath his herte and his entente in swich a proud desir to be magnified and honoured beforn the peple." Also we are told of the Wife of Bath in the General Prologue: "In al the parisshe wif ne was ther noon / That to the offrynge before hire sholde goon; / And if ther dide, certeyn so wrooth was she, / That she was out of alle charitee" (I[A], 449–52). A regular feature of the mass was the kiss of peace, given first by the celebrant to the deacon, by the deacon to the subdeacon, and so on in a descending order of status (*Missale ad usum insignis et praeclarae ecclesiae Sarum,* ed. Francis H. Dickinson, 2 vols., Burntisland, 1861–83, *1*, 624–25). Beginning in the thirteenth century, the "pax" was a tablet bearing a picture of the crucifixion "which was kissed by the celebrating priest at Mass, and passed to the other officiating clergy and then to the congregation to be kissed" (*OED*, s.v. *pax* 3).

165/33 **pilgrimage . . . place.** Heb. 13:14: "Non enim habemus hic manentem civitatem, sed futuram inquirimus." Beryl Smalley notes that medieval exegetes "often quoted this text whenever they came to the word *city* or *kingdom* in their explanation of Scripture"; see *The Study of the Bible in the Middle Ages,* 2nd ed. (Oxford, 1964), p. 328. More quotes the text twice in *A Dialogue of Comfort* (*CW 12*, 41/6–14 and 251/16–19) and once in *A Treatise on the Passion* (*CW 13*, 3/16–17). See also Erasmus, *Adagia* no. 3974 (*Opera omnia*, 2, 1177a); Tilley L249.

165/39 **ramping . . . bothe.** Cf. 1 Pet. 5:8.

166/5–6 **children . . . cherystones.** According to *OED* (s.v. *cherry-pit* 1), "A children's game which consists in throwing cherry-stones into a small pit or hole;" see also *OED*, s.v. *cherry-stone*. Cf. *CW 8*, 492/19; and *CW 12*, 285/15–18 and Commentary. In the *Supplication*, the souls in purgatory see "baggys stuffed with gold" as having no more worth than "a bag of chery stonys" (*CW 7*, 221/27–29).

166/15–20 **folk . . . own.** In Homily 47 on Acts 22:17–20, Chrysostom emphasizes the danger of mistaking vices for virtues: "Discamus ergo et mansuetudinem, ut in utrisque simus perfecti. Multa enim accuratione opus est, ut discatur quid hoc, quid illud sit: accuratione autem opus est quia vicina sunt virtutibus vitia, dicendi libertati audacia, mansuetudini ignavia. Cavendum autem est, ne quis vitium tenens virtutem se putet habere; ut si quis opinetur se jungi dominae, dum jungitur ancillae" (*PG 60*, 336).

166/19–20 **they . . . beggers.** Cf. *CW 3/2*, nos. 41 and 76.

166/27–28 **prouidence . . . come.** Cf. the fourteenth-century *Speculum Christiani*, where, in a passage on mistaking vice for virtue, the author gives the example of covetousness construed as "true puruyance of purchacynge"; EETS OS no. 182 (London, 1933), p. 232. Bloomfield (p. 418n.) notes that in the *Sacrum commercium beati patris nostri Francisci cum Domina Paupertate* (MS. Biblioteca Communale, Siena F IV 11, fols. 79r–85r), Avarice bears the pseudonyms Discretion and Foresight (Providentia).

166/29–30 **liue . . . mouthe.** Tilley H97. Cf. Erasmus, *Adagia* (*Opera omnia*, 2, 322D): "In diem vivere. Ex tempore vivere."

166/30–33 **pleasure . . . come.** Cf. the advice given in Latin poem no. 5: "Tanquam iam moriturus partis utere rebus, / Tanquam uicturus denuo parce tuis. / Ille sapit, qui perpensis hijs rite duobus, / Parcus erit certo munificusque modo" (*CW 3/2*, 5/12–15). See also *CW 3/2*, nos. 41 and 76, lines 5–10; and 171/18–20, above, and note.

166/31 **at another.** That is, "at another time."

167/7–8 **Salomon . . . borne.** John M. Headley suggests that More, on the model of Jesus' reply to Peter in Matt. 18:21–22, uses the expression "seuen yere" to signify many years; see *CW 5*, Commentary at 396/22–25. For other instances, see *CW 15*, 104/23; and above, 173/1–2.

167/8–12 **I . . . deuoureth.** Eccles. 6:1–2: "Est et aliud malum quod vidi sub sole, et quidem frequens apud homines: vir, cui dedit Deus divitias et substantiam et honorem, et nihil deest animae suae, ex omnibus quae desiderat; nec tribuit ei potestatem Deus ut comedat ex eo, sed homo extraneus vorabit illud: hoc vanitas et miseria magna est."

167/13–15 **psalmist . . . them.** Ps. 38:7: "Veruntamen in imagine pertransit homo; sed et frustra conturbatur, thesaurizat et ignorat cui congregabit ea."

167/15–17 **.xlviii. psalme . . . straungers.** Ps. 48:11: "Simul insipiens et stultus peribunt et relinquent alienis divitias suas."

167/34–168/1 **caste . . . thee?** Ps. 54:23: "Iacta super Dominum curam tuam, et ipse te enutriet."

168/3–10 **sauior . . . beside.** Matt. 6:25–26, 32–33: "Ideo, dico vobis, ne solliciti sitis animae vestrae, quid manducetis, neque corpori vestro quid induamini. . . . Respicite volatilia caeli, quoniam non serunt neque metunt neque congregant in horrea; et Pater vester caelestis pascit illa. Nonne vos magis pluris estis illis? scit enim Pater vester quia his omnibus indigetis. Quaerite ergo primum regnum Dei et iustitiam eius, et haec omnia adicientur vobis." See also Luke 12:24, 31–32.

168/19–21 **Iewes . . . hand.** Exod. 16:4–5.

168/22 **anxietie.** That "anxitie" in *1557* is a misprint is shown by "anxietie" at 169/27.

168/34–169/17 **Thou . . . famine.** By contrast with this advice, Hythlodaeus' condemnation of enclosures in *Utopia* lays the blame for the plight of the unemployed more squarely on rich landholders, and he suggests action on the part of the government, rather than passive suffering on the part of the poor; see *CW 4*, 66/11–70/12.

169/16 **meate . . . crow.** More refers to Elijah's sustenance by a raven in 1 Kings 17:6.

169/20 **geat . . . more.** For the expression "geat thee a penny the more," compare Whiting P119: "Not to win one Penny."

169/24–25 **Danyell . . . lions.** Dan. 14:32–38.

169/25–28 **Lazarus . . . bosom.** Luke 16:19–22.

169/28–30 **Nowe . . . Christ.** The distinction between "Abraham's bosom" and "ye bosom of our sauior Christ" draws on the notion of a *limbus patrum*, where the souls of the faithful departed were believed to repose before Christ's harrowing of hell; see *CW 7*, 179/21 and Commentary, and 186/16–187/1; and *CW 8*, 366/9, 407/19, 881/21. In *De anima et ejus origine* 4.16 (*PL 44*, 538) Augustine glosses "Abraham's bosom" as "Remotam sedem quietis atque secretam ubi est Abraham. Et ideo Abrahae dictum, non quod ipsius tantum sit sed quod ipse pater multarum gentium sit positus, quibus est ad imitandum fidei principatu propositus," a description that More appears to follow; cf. *CW 12*, 47/16–20.

170/9 **liuing when he is dead.** Reed points out the pun: "life" and "livelihood" (Campbell and Reed, p. 217).

170/29 **ye couetous niggarde.** Reed (p. 217) says that this should be corrected to "niggardes," presumably because he considers "ye" to be plural. But *ye* could be singular in More's time; it was usually addressed to a person worthy of respect or honor ("your worshippe," line 26), but here these overtones are ironic. In this passage More is inconsistent in his use of pronouns, switching from "he" (170/10–19) to "ye" (170/20–21) to "they" (170/31–33) and then back to "he"(171/4–13). See the Introduction, p. xciv–xcv.

170/33 **makyng . . . god.** Cf. Phil. 3:19: "quorum deus venter est."

170/34–171/1 **harde . . . eye.** Mark 10: 25; see also Luke 18:25 and Matt. 19:24. The variant χάμιλος ("cable") is found in a few Greek witnesses of the eleventh century (see *Novum Testamentum Graece*, ed. Eberhard Nestle et al., 26th ed., Stuttgart, 1979, p. 123) and has Old Latin and Syriac support (see H. B. Swete, *The Gospel according to St. Mark*, London, 1909, p. 228). Although Origen and Cyril of Alexandria mention the interpretation "cable" for χάμηλος at Matt. 19:24 (see *A Patristic Greek Lexicon*, ed. G. W. H. Lampe, 5th ed., Oxford, 1978, p. 700), More might have known of the reading from Theophylactus' remark in the *Catena aurea in quatuor evangelia* of Thomas Aquinas (*Opera omnia*, Parma, 1861–62; reprint, New York, 1949), *11*, 398: "Camelum siquidem oportet intelligere aut ipsum animal, aut funem illum crassum, quo naves magnae utuntur." In his *Annotationes in Novum Testamentum* (1516, sig. aa₂, with a few embellishments in later editions) Erasmus discusses the cable/camel crux at length, agreeing with Jerome that "camel" is the correct meaning (*Opera omnia*, 6, 102). Unlike Erasmus, More is not certain which reading to take, and habitually offers both alternatives when quoting this text; see *CW 12*, 171/1–2, 18–19; *CW 7*, 247/16–18.

171/3–4 **riches . . . scripture.** Ps. 61:11: "Divitiae si adfluant, nolite cor apponere." Cf. *CW 12*, 171/16.

171/13–14 **holy . . . heart.** Matt. 6:21.

171/18–20 **couetous . . . beggers.** The well-known paradox of the *avarus pauper* occurs frequently in More's Latin epigrams; see *CW 3/2*, no. 41: "Te ditem appellant omnes, ego plane inopem te. / Nam facit usus opes, testis Apollophanes. / Si tu utare tuis, tua fiunt. Sin tua serues, / Haeredi, tua iam nunc aliena facis." Cf. Ovid, *Metamorphoses* 3.466 ("Inopem me copia fecit"); and Tilley P427 ("Plenty makes poor"). Cf. also *CW 3/2*, no. 76; and 166/30–33 and note, above.

171/24–29 **And so . . . kepe it.** Cf. *CW 3/2*, no. 2; and Tilley M1044: "He that hoards money takes pains for other men."

171/33–172/1 **yong . . . riche.** Matt. 19:21–22; Mark 10:21–22; Luke 18:22–23.

172/1–3 **saint Peter . . . him.** Matt. 4:18–22; Mark 1:16–20; Luke 5:9–11.

172/4–6 **and if . . . let.** Cf. *CW 14*, 601/1–603/8.

172/7 **couetous.** It is not necessary to emend this to "couetise," as Reed claims (Campbell and Reed, p. 217). More sometimes uses adjectives as plural substantives (Delcourt, pp. 190–91), and "them" in the next sentence (171/8) confirms that "couetous" means "covetous persons." But see 159/31 and note on 159/25.

172/8–9 **As for . . . redy.** For the omission of the expected "he" before "is redy," see Visser, *1*, 33–34.

172/16–17 **leman . . . lap.** The sexual innuendo of the tableau in which a man places his head in the lap of a seductive woman is ultimately derived from Judg. 16:19, where Delilah forces Samson to "sleep upon her knees" (Authorised Version) before cutting off his hair. Marie Collins has traced the use of this scene through the morality plays and interludes to *Hamlet*, III, ii, 125 ("Lady, shall I lie in your lap?"); see *Notes and Queries*, 226 (1981), 130–32; and cf. the episode in the anonymous *The Marriage of Wit and Science* (ed. A. Brown, Malone Society Reprints, Oxford, 1960), in which Wit is invited by Dame Idleness to sleep in her lap: "Come come and ease thee in my lappe" (IV, iv, 1126). Cf. also *CW 12*, 29/18.

172/18–22 **thefe . . . yet.** A somewhat similar incident is related in Stapleton, pp. 137–38. In Stapleton's account, More engineers the theft of a self-righteous magistrate's purse when the latter chides the plaintiffs in a suit against a gang of pickpockets for their lack of vigilance. More persuades one of the accused thieves to pick the magistrate's pocket in the courtroom. For Newgate, see note on 158/2–4.

172/33 **pater noster.** That is, his rosary; see *OED*, s.v. *paternoster* 3b.

172/33 **the tone . . . graue.** Tilley M346.

173/3 **pore blinde.** That is, "purblind, near-sighted" (*OED*, s.v. *purblind* 2b).

173/9 **wink.** That is, "close their eyes" (*OED*, s.v. *wink* 1).

173/19 **merely.** That is, "merrily." Cf. 174/6.

173/24–29 **Christ . . . bee.** Luke 12:16–20. See also *CW 12*, 168/16–23. Cf. 91/27, above; *CW 13*, 209; and *CW 14*, 643/7.

173/30–31 **Barnarde . . . thou be?** We have not been able to find this idea in St. Bernard in the form of a question, but in *Sermo de conversione* *ad clericos* 8.16–17 (*PL 182, 843*) Bernard quotes Luke 12:19–20, adding: "Atque utinam tantum congregata perirent, et non deterius ipse quoque periret congregator eorum."

174/2–4 **gay . . . thereof.** In Lucian's *Gallus* (a dialogue in praise of poverty included in Erasmus' translation of 1506), Pythagoras, in the reincarnated form of a cock, awakens the cobbler Micyllus from a "golden dream" ("somnium aureum") in which he is fabulously wealthy. See Erasmus, *Opera omnia, 1,* 247C–D. See *CW 3/2,* nos. 79 and 139, and the Commentary on both.

174/4–7 **death . . . handes.** Although the marginal note in *1557* cites Ps. 48, the reference is actually to Ps. 75:6: "Dormierunt somnum suum et nihil invenerunt omnes viri divitiarum in manibus suis." Cf. also *CW 13,* 64/33–65/4; *CW 3/2,* 79.

174/8–11 **couetise . . . handes.** Cf. the advice offered to the living by the purgatorial souls in *The Supplication:* "And god gyue you ye grace whych many of vs refused / to make better prouysyon whyle ye lyue than many of vs haue done. For mich haue we left in our executours handes / whych wold god we had bestowed vppon pore folk for our owne soulys & our frendys wyth our own handys" (*CW 7,* 219/25–29).

174/20 **shete.** That is, a winding-sheet, shroud.

174/31 **goddes.** That is, "goddess."

174/31–32 **toke she . . . tast.** Cf. Gen. 3:6: "Vidit igitur mulier quod bonum esset lignum ad vescendum, et pulchrum oculis, aspectuque delectabile." Cf. *CW 6,* 139/22 and 394/14; *CW 8,* 50/18; and *CW 13,* 16/9.

175/4–5 **men . . . eye.** Whiting B238, Tilley G146: "Better fill a Glutton's belly than his eye."

175/8–15 **eye . . . dede.** See 132/3–6 and 136/19–22 and note. Scholastic psychology conceived of man as endowed with both a rational and a sensible soul. The latter (which was common to men and beasts) received sense impressions from the body and combined them by means of the phantasy into an image of the thing perceived; see Aquinas, *Summa theologica,* I, q. 76, a.3; and compare *CW 12,* 281/25–282/8 and Commentary. The expression "belly naked" is proverbial (Whiting B246).

175/14 **it.** When he set "if it" the compositor of *1557* was wrongly anticipating the following "if."

175/16 **Turn . . . vanities.** Paraphrasing Ps. 118:37 ("Averte oculos meos, ne videant vanitatem"), More turns the righteous man's supplication to God into a command to the sinner.

175/28–32 **body . . . mire.** Gal. 5:18. The image of the horse and rider to portray the body's rebellion against the soul is derived from Plato's metaphor of the charioteer in *Phaedrus* 246a and 253d–254a. Cf. also *CW 12*, 282/22–25.

175/32 **in the mire.** Whiting M573, Tilley M989. See *CW 8*, 560/36, 573/35–36; *CW 11*, 180/34.

175/32–33 **corruptible . . . soule.** Sap. 9:15: "Corpus enim quod corrumpitur adgravat animam." Cf. *CW 13*, 33/25.

176/1–2 **bely . . . back.** Tilley B288: "The Belly robs the back."

176/2–3 **body . . . prison.** More refers to Plato's well-known teaching of the soul's enslavement by the body; see *Phaedo* 66b–67b. Cf. Whiting B497 and above, 130/18–25.

176/4 **rif raf.** Whiting R126.

176/14–15 **lechery . . . glotony.** Whiting B168: "Gluttony wakens lechery."

176/19 **better . . . borne.** Of Judas, Christ said: "vae autem homini illi per quem Filius hominis tradetur! bonum erat ei, si non esset natus homo ille" (Mark 14:21).

176/20 **bely . . . taber.** That is, "his belly projecting out in front of him like a drum."

176/21 **balk vp his brewes.** A. W. Reed glosses this phrase: "to belch up his broth," quoting from Nashe's *Pierce Penilesse*, "the broth of theyr folly made a dish of divinitie Brewesse." *Balk* is a variant form of *belch* (see *OED*, s.vv. *belch* and *belk*). *Brewis* meant "broth, a thick beef and vegetable soup," but its form was also influenced by the verb *to brew* (*OED*, s.v. *brewis*).

176/22 **slepe . . . swine.** Cf. Whiting S970 and *CW 10*, 322/26.

176/22–23 **the body . . . bed.** Whiting B426 gives only this citation from More.

176/23–24 **Men. . . . P.** Tilley C901 and Whiting C619 supply the riddle's answer thus: "A drunken cunt hath no porter." Whiting gives only More as his source. One of the two examples given by Tilley ("Ane drunken cunt had neuer ane good dore bar") makes it clear that "porter" refers to the custodian of a house door: anyone can get in.

176/24–25 **Rede . . . rydle.** Cf. *CW 6*, 285/31; *CW 7*, 160/16–17.

176/29–33 **gloton . . . soberness.** A late fourteenth- or early fifteenth-century sermon in MS. Royal 18 B XIII similarly warns the glutton against "rybald words and songes of lecherie, blasfemynge God with many grett othes, backe-bytynge, slaunder, and envie, and being ilke besy to begyle othur with many qweynte sleygthes"; see Ross, *Middle English Sermons*, p. 101.

176/34–177/2 **desert . . . them.** Exod. 32:6: "Surgentesque mane obtulerunt holocausta et hostias pacificas; et sedit populus manducare et bibere et surrexerunt ludere."

177/3–8 **Job . . . glotony.** Job 1:4–5.

177/11–12 **weneth . . . hed?** Tilley W516: "What if the sky fall?"

177/18–31 **Wonder . . . heauen?** For a similar idea, see 79/15–21 and 108/2–22, above; see also *CW 12*, 169/11–19.

177/20–21 **beginning . . . pain.** See 130/21–132/27, above.

177/34–178/1 **psalmist . . . riches.** Ps. 118:14: "In via testimoniorum tuorum delectatus sum, sicut in omnibus divitiis."

178/1–2 **Salomon . . . pesable.** Prov. 3:17 says of the wise man: "Viae eius viae pluchrae, et omnes semitae illius pacificae."

178/3–4 **way . . . stumbling.** Prov. 15:19: "Iter pigrorum quasi saepes spinarum, via iustorum absque offendiculo."

178/4–6 **we . . . waies.** Wis. 5:7: "Lassati sumus in via iniquitatis et perditionis et ambulavimus vias difficiles, viam autem Domini ignoravimus." Cf. 79/18–19, above; and *CW 12*, 169/10–16.

178/6–8 **wise . . . paynes.** Eccles. 21:11: "Via peccantium complanata lapidibus, et in fine illorum inferi et tenebrae et poenae."

178/9–16 **bestly . . . sin.** For the inability to distinguish pleasure from pain, compare 130/19–131/8 and note. The metaphor of infected taste is developed at 132/7–27; see also 132/18–19 and notes on 132/8–9 and 132/17–19. For the expression "walue swete sin" (that is, "cloyingly sweet sin"), see Campbell and Reed, p. 218; and *OED*, s.v. *walue*. Cf. also the expression "walow swete" used to describe heretical works in *CW 8*, 39/13.

178/16–17 **man . . . teeth.** One of the fallacies given by Aristotle in *De sophisticis elenchis* 5.35.167a: "Thus, for example, 'Suppose an Indian to be black all over, but white in respect of his teeth; then is he both white and not white.'" Cf. also Tilley E186 ("To wash an Ethiop white"); Erasmus, *Adagia* no. 350 (*Opera omnia*, 2, 169F); and *CW 8*, 907/31–34.

178/19–21 **ytche . . . beginning.** More similarly uses scratching an itch as an example of false pleasure in *CW 4*, 176/9–11. Cf. also *CW 11*, 32/10–19: "And surely besyd the punyshement of god in another world, & besyde all the paynes that euyn in this worlde thorough sykenesse & sorys aryse and sprynge of such glotonye / they that gladly wold endure a gryefe perpetually, to haue the pleasure of the continuall swagyng, haue in theyr beste welth but a dyspleasaunt pleasure / except men be so mad as to thynke that he were well at ease that myghte be euer a hungred & euer eatyng, euer a thurst & euer drynkyng, euer lowsy & euer clawing, euer skoruy & euer scratchyng."

178/21 **it liked thee.** For this construction, see Visser, *1*, 17–22.

178/25–27 **degression . . . hand.** For More's concern not to prolong his discussion, see the Introduction, pp. xcvii and c–ci.

178/28–32 **pleasure . . . altogether.** Hythlodaeus uses this point to explain why the Utopians value mental pleasures more highly than carnal ones: "Nempe cum edendi voluptate copulatur esuries, idque non satis aequa lege. Nam ut vehementior, ita longior quoque dolor est" (*CW 4*, 176/14–16).

179/2 **rere supper.** According to *OED*, s.v. *rere-supper*: "A supper (usually of a sumptuous nature) following upon the usual evening meal, and thus coming very late at night."

179/18 **nature . . . little.** Tilley N45: "Nature is content with little."

179/25–27 **of which . . . it is.** That is, all the different kinds of food strive to remain as they are, without being transformed into the materials of the body.

180/3–12 **And in this . . . helth.** Plutarch, *De tuenda bona sanitate, Moralia* 127cd. Erasmus translated the passage as follows: "Proinde cauendum est, ne, sicuti ⟨mali⟩ naucleri, posteaquam ob auiditatem multum oneris in nauem coniecerint, deinde perpetuo labore sentinam exhauriunt aquamque marinam eiiciunt, ita nos quoque, simulatque corpus expleuerimus onerauerimusque, tum rursum repurgemus et clysteribus exoneremus. Sed leue et expeditum seruare conueniet, quo, si quando etiam continget premi, suberis in morem ob leuitatem sursum emicet" (*ASD 4/2*, 197/263–198/269). Erasmus' translation of this tract was first published in London by Richard Pynson in 1513; it was dedicated to John Yonge (1467–1516) as a New Year's gift (*ASD 4/2*, 187–88; Allen, *1*, no. 268). Yonge was a fellow of New College, Oxford, from 1485 to 1500 and became Master of the Rolls in 1508. He held several lucrative ecclesiastical preferments and undertook diplomatic missions for Henry VII and Henry VIII. In 1502 he become rector of St. Stephens Walbrook, where, as More says, he lived before he moved to Chelsea (*DNB, 63*, 327; *CW 6*, 79/1–2).

180/25–26 **Salomon . . . sworde.** Seemingly a pithy reworking, unusually free for More, of Eccles. 37:33–34: "Propter crapulam multi obierunt; qui autem abstinens est adiiciet vitam." Cf. Eccles. 28:22.

180/27–30 **manne . . . buryall.** The church's first interdict against Christian burial of suicides was issued by the Second Council of Braga in 563; see *Dictionnaire de théologie catholique*, ed. A. Vacant, E. Mangenot, and E. Amann, 15 vols. (Paris, 1908–50), *14/2*, 2743. Temptations to suicide are a major topic in *CW 12*, 122/1–157/5.

180/31 **their own handes.** For the omission of a preposition such as *with*, see Visser, *1*, 121.

180/34 **thapostle . . . god.** Phil. 3:18–19. Cf. 130/3, above.

181/3–5 **eate . . . eate.** Whiting E37, Tilley E50: "Eat to live, not live to eat." This saying of Socrates became proverbial in ancient times (Otto, no. 588).

181/7–9 **saint Paul . . . belly.** 1 Cor. 6:13: "Esca ventri, et venter escis; Deus autem et hunc et has destruet."

181/18–20 **myre . . . mire.** See note on 175/32.

181/20 **til Gabriell blowe them vp.** Tilley G1, Whiting G2: "Till Gabriel blow his horn."

181/25 **nature, it.** The context makes it clear that the words "intemperate dyet" after "nature" in *1557* are a sidenote wrongly included in the text.

181/31–182/7 **mortal . . . sin.** Although More uses the terms interchangeably, systematic theology preserved a distinction between "mortal" sins (which result in damnation, the death of the soul) and "capital" sins (which give rise to other forms of sin; see *Dictionnaire de théologie catholique*, *12/1*, 225–38). The notion of mortal as opposed to non-deadly sin is derived from 1 John 5:16 ("Qui scit fratrem suum peccare peccatum non ad mortem petat, et dabitur ei vita peccanti non ad mortem. Est peccatum ad mortem: non pro illo dico ut roget quis") and was repeatedly and authoritatively discussed by Augustine, who gave currency to the words *mortal (mortifera, letalia)* and *venial (venialia, levia, quotidiana)*; see, for example, *Speculum de scriptura sacra, PL 34*, 994; *De symbolo ad catechumenos, PL 40*, 635–36; and *De civitate Dei*, 21, xxvi–xxvii (*PL 41*, 743–52). In *Summa theologica*, IIa–IIae, q. 84, a. 3, Aquinas defines a capital sin as one "ex quo alia vitia oriuntur, et praecipue secundum originem causae finalis, quae est finalis origo, ut supra dictum est." By this definition, a capital sin need not be a mortal one as well, but after the fourteenth century this subtlety went unobserved by most laymen and some theologians. Instead, the seven sins (including sloth) enumerated in Gregory's *Moralia* (see note on 153/1) were thought of as both mortal and capital; for this conflation, see Bloomfield, pp. 43, 69–99; and the Introduction above, pp. lxxxv.

182/14–15 **declinyng . . . good.** See note on 135/34–136/1.

APPENDIX A

More's Latin Sources for the Life of Pico

Giovanni Francesco Pico's Life of His Uncle Giovanni Pico della Mirandola and the Following Short Works by Giovanni Pico della Mirandola:

Three Letters
A Commentary on Psalm 15
The Twelve Rules for Spiritual Warfare
The Twelve Weapons of Spiritual Warfare
The Twelve Qualities of a Lover
A Prayer to God for Mercy

BY CLARENCE H. MILLER

APPENDIX A

More's Latin Sources for the Life of Pico

Presented here are texts of the Latin works that More translated, adapted, and paraphrased in his *Life of Pico*. They are based on a complete collation of the following printed Latin editions available before 1510, the *terminus ad quem* for More's *Life*.

OPERA OMNIA[1]

1. Bologna   1496 (= 96)[2]

Title: Commentationes Ioannis Pici Mirandulae in hoc uolumine contentae: quibus anteponitur uita per Ioannem franciscum illustris principis Galeotti Pici filium conscripta. . . .

Colophon (sig. yy₉): Opuscula haec Ioannis Pici Mirandulae Concordiae Comitis. Diligenter impressit Benedictus Hectoris Bononien. adhibita pro uiribus solertia & diligentia ne ab archetypo aberraret: Bononiae Anno Salutis.Mcccclxxxxvi.die uero.xx.Martii.

---

[1]These five are the only known editions of Pico's *Opera omnia* printed before 1510. In his edition of Giovanni Pico's *De hominis dignitate, Heptaplus, De ente et uno, e scritti vari* (Florence, 1942), p. 90, Eugenio Garin lists the following edition: "*Opera omnia.* Parisiis impensa Joannis Parvi, anno MDV, die nona mensis iunii. [Panzer, VIII, 39]." This edition is a "ghost," since the Paris edition of Jehan Petit listed by Georg Wolfgang Panzer, *Annales typographici*, 11 vols. (Nürnberg, 1793–1803), *8*, 39, no. 942, is dated "anno milesimo quingentesimo decimo septimo die nona mensis Junii," that is, 1517, not 1505. I have examined a copy of this edition, dated 1517, in the Beinecke Library at Yale University. The error is repeated by Giovanni di Napoli, *Giovanni Pico della Mirandola e la problematica dottrinale del suo tempo* (Rome, Paris, Tournai, New York, 1965), p. 521.

[2]Ludwig Hain, *Repertorium Bibliographicum*, 4 vols. (Stuttgart and Paris, 1826–38), *12992; M.-Louis Polain, *Catalogue des livres imprimés au quinzième siècle des bibliothèques de Belgique*, 4 vols. (Brussels, 1932), 3144; Frederick R. Goff, *Incunabula in American Libraries: A Third Census of Fifteenth-Century Books Recorded in North American Libraries* (New York, 1964; reprint, Kraus, 1973), P-632; Alodia Kawecka-Gryczowa, Maria Bohonos, and Elisa Szandorowska, *Incunabula quae in bibliothecis Poloniae asservantur*, 2 vols. (Wratislawa, Warsaw, Krakow, 1970), 4431; *Bibliothèque nationale: Catalogue des incunables*, 2 vols. (Paris, 1985), P-344.

The life of Giovanni Pico: sigs. a_4–a_{11}v.
First letter (Discedenti): sigs. RR_3v–RR_4v
Second letter (Quas proxime): sigs. TT_5–TT_6
Third letter (Felix es): sigs. VV_5–VV_6
Psalm commentary: sigs. YY_5–YY_6
12 rules: sigs. YY_4v–YY_5v
12 weapons: sig. YY_5v
12 conditions of a lover: sigs. YY_5v–YY_6
Prayer to God: sigs. VV_6–VV_6v

Copy used: British Library

This is the *editio princeps,* overseen by Giovanni Francesco, who prefaced to it his life of his uncle. It is the source, direct or indirect, of all other editions of Pico's *Opera omnia* published before 1510, none of which gives any evidence of independent authority. As one might expect from the confused and difficult manuscripts left behind by Giovanni Pico,[1] the *editio princeps* is marred by frequent misprints and errors, many of which are corrected in an extensive errata list, probably provided by Giovanni Francesco.

At 340/18 this edition omits "ex fratre," which More translated. Hence it is quite unlikely that it was the source of More's translation.

2. Lyons   before 1498 (= 96+)[2]

Title (sig. A_1): Conmentationes [*sic*] Ioannis Pici Mirandulae in hoc uolumine contentae: quibus anteponitur uita per Ioannem franciscum illustris principis Galeotti Pici filium conscripta . . .

Colophon (sig. BB_4): Opuscula haec Ioannis Pici Mirandulae Concordiae Comitis. Diligenter impraessit Benedictus Hectoris Bononien. adhibita pro uiribus solertia & diligentia ne ab archetypo aberraret: Bononiae Anno Salutis.Mcccclxxxxvi.die uero.xx.Martii.

The life of Giovanni Pico: sigs. A_2–B_3v
First letter (Discedenti): sigs. V_5v–V_6v
Second letter (Quas proxime): sigs. Y_6v–Z_1v
Third letter (Felix es): sigs. Z_4v–Z_5v
Psalm commentary: sigs. BB_4–BB_5v

---

[1] See below, 312/11–21.

[2] W. A. Copinger, *Supplement to Hain's Repertorium Bibliographicum,* 2 vols. (Berlin, 1926), 4745; Polain 3145; Goff P-633; *Bibliothèque nationale: Catalogue des incunables* P-346. For the date before 1498 see P. Aquilon, "Sur quelques incunables de la Bibliothèque municipale de Bourges," in *L'humanisme français au début de la Renaissance* (Paris, 1973), p. 113.

12 rules: sigs. BB_2v–BB_3v
12 weapons: sig. BB_3v
12 conditions of a lover: sigs. BB_3v–BB_4
Prayer to God: sigs. Z_5v–Z_6

Copy used: Universiteitsbibliotheek, Ghent

This edition, printed by Jacobino Suigo and Nicolas Benedetti, is a close imitation of *96*. At least six readings found only in *96* and *96+* show that *96* was the copy-text for *96+*, as one would expect from the close correspondence in print and format. The errata list of *96* was omitted in *96+* because it had been incorporated into the text.

3. Venice   1498 (= *98*)[2]

Title: IOANNIS PICI MIRANDVLAE OMNIA OPERA Opuscula haec Ioannis Pici Mirandulae Concordiae Comitis diligenter impressit Bernardus Venetus . . . Venetiis Anno Salutis. Mcccclxxxxviii.die.ix.Octobris

The life of Giovanni Pico: sigs. $1A_2$–$1A_{10}$
First letter (Discedenti): sigs. T_6v–V_2
Second letter (Quas proxime): sigs. X_6v–Y_1v
Third letter (Felix es): sigs. Y_4–Z_1
Psalm commentary: sigs. $\&_4$–$\&_5v$
12 rules: sigs. $\&_2v$–$\&_3v$
12 weapons: sig. $\&_3v$
12 conditions of a lover: sig. $\&_3v$
Prayer to God: sigs. E_4–E_4v

Copy used: British Library

That *98* was set from *96*, not *96+*, is shown by a place where *98* incorrectly incorporates a correction in the errata of *96*.[3] *98* also introduces a considerable number of new errors into the text.

4. Strassburg   1504 (= *04*)[4]

Title: Opera Ioannis Pici:Mirandule Comitis Concordie:litterarum principis:nouissime accurate reuisa (addito generali super omnibus

---

[1]See, for example, the variants at 332/15.
[2]Hain *12993, Polain 3144–44A, Kawecka-Gryczowa 4432, Goff P-634, *Bibliothèque nationale: Catalogue des incunables* P-345.
[3]See the variants at 338/18–19.
[4]Panzer 6, 31.

memoratu dignis regesto) quarumcunque facultatum professoribus tam iucunda quam proficua.

Colophon (sig. n_6 of second part, aduersus astrologos): Disputationes has Ioannis Pici Mirandulae / concordiae Comitis / litterarum principis / aduersus Astrologos: diligenter impressit Industrius Ioannes Prüs Ciuis Argentinus. Anno salutis.M.-CCCCCIIII.Die vero.XV Marcij.

> The life of Giovanni Pico: sigs. []5v–aa$_6$
> First letter (Discedenti): sigs. P_6v–Q_1v
> Second letter (Quas proxime): sigs. R_5–R_5v
> Third letter (Felix es): sigs. S_2–S_3
> Psalm commentary: sigs. T_4v–T_5v
> 12 rules: sigs. T_3v–T_4
> 12 weapons: sig. T_4
> 12 conditions of a lover: sig. T_4
> Prayer to God: sig. D_2v

Copy used: British Library

On the verso of the title page is a prefatory letter from Jerome Emser to the printer John Prüs, saying that he agreed to the printer's request to draw up the register or index and that Prüs is to be congratulated for using as his copy-text the Bologna edition, which was printed from Pico's own originals. In fact, it is clear from numerous errors found only in *98* and *04* that this edition was set from *98*, not from *96*.

On the page after the index (sig. []5) is a letter from Jacob Wimpfeling dated from Strassburg on March 20, 1504, praising the book, especially *Adversus astrologos*.

5. Reggio   1506 (= *06*)

Title: IOANNIS PICI MIRANDVLAE OMNIA OPERA . . .

Colophon (sig. t_4v): Disputationes has Ioannis Pici Mirandulae concordiae ue Comitis / litterarum uerarum principis / aduersus astrologos diligenter Impressit dominus Ludouicus de Mazalis Ciuis regiensis Anno salutis.M.D.VI. xv.Nouembris.

> The life of Giovanni Pico: sigs. A_2–A_{10} (falsely imposed:
> A_4v–A_8)
> First letter (Discedenti): sigs. T_6v–V_2
> Second letter (Quas proxime): sigs. X_6v–Y_1v (British Library
>   copy falsely bound: Y gathering precedes X gathering)

Third letter (Felix es): sigs. Y_6–Z_1

Psalm commentary: sigs. $\&_4$–$\&_5$v (& gathering comes after Z gathering)

12 rules: sigs. $\&_2$v–$\&_3$v

12 weapons: sig. $\&_3$v

12 conditions of a lover: sig. $\&_3$v

Prayer to God: sigs. E_4–E_4v

Copy used: British Library

The text of this edition agrees in many places only with *98* and *04*, but in at least two places errors found only in *04* and *06* show that *04* was the copy-text for *06*, which introduces many new misprints and errors.

At 320/33 this edition has the plausible error "laetitiae" where More translated from the correct reading "lautitiae." Hence it is unlikely that he used this edition.

A SEPARATE EDITION OF THE *VITA* (= *V-06/7*)

Title: Ioannis Francisci Pici Mirandulae . . . De rerum praenotione libri nouem. Pro Veritate religionis contra superstitiosas vanitates editi. De fide theoremata. De morte Christi & propria cogitanda: Libri tres. De studio diuinae & humanae philosophiae: Duo. De diuini amoris imaginatione: Vnus. Vita patrui & defensio de uno & ente & alia quaepiam. Expositio tex. Decreti de con. dis. ij. Hilarij. Epistolarum libri Quattuor. Iustini tralatio. Staurostichon de mysterijs Germaniae Heroico carmine.

Colophon (sig. o_7): Ioan.Fran.Pici . . . opera . . . finiunt: Argentoraci Pridiae Kalen.Februarias Ann. M.D.VII. . . . Ioannes Knoblochus Imprimebat: Recognouit Mathias Schürerius.

Colophon (sig. u_8): Finiunt Theoremata Ioan.Francisci Pici . . . Argentoraci . . . formis excusa die.xxij.Decemb.Ann.M.D.vi.

The life of Giovanni Pico: sigs. i_2–k_3v. It has no sidenotes.

Copy used: The British Library. The gatherings of this copy are bound in the wrong order.

At least eight variants found only in *04* and *V-06/7* show that the copy-text for *V-06/7* was *04*. *V-06/7* is especially important for the text of the life because Gianfrancesco himself provided for this edition sixteen pages of errata ($[]_1$–$[]_8$v), which for the life correct not only errors that had crept into *04* but also readings that had been present in the *editio princeps* and succeeding editions of the *opera omnia*.[1] In a note at the beginning of the errata, Giovanni Francesco also remarks that he has not corrected many errors in spelling (especially diphthongs), punctuation (both medial and final), capitalization, and Greek diacriticals; he trusts that the judgment of the reader will enable him to correct such matters for himself.

Separate Editions of the Letters of Giovanni Pico[2]

1. Aureae epistolae, Speyer, after January 3, 1495 (= *E-95* +)[3]

Title: Epistole. Auree Epistole Ioannis Pici Mirandule viri omnium mortalium doctissimi eloquentissimique ab Ascensio recognite

Colophon (sig. E_4v): Impressum. S[peyer]. per. C[onrad]. H[ist].

Copy used: Beinecke Library at Yale University

The edition is dated by the date of the last letter in the collection (sig. E_4v): die. iij. Ia. M ccccxcv.

In this edition the third letter is wrongly dated 1482, where More

---

[1]See the variants at 308/28, 310/36, 318/20, 320/25, 326/5–6, 326/29, 328/34, and 336/14.

[2]I have examined the British Library copy of *Francisci Philelfi breuiores elegantioresque Epistolae . . . Angeli Politiani viri & Eruditissimi aeque illustris ad numerum vsque quintum & decimum perbreves . . . Auree epistole Ioannis Pici Mirandule viri omnium mortalium doctissimi eloquentissimique;* [colophon on sig. L_7v] Finiunt Epistole breuiores elegantioresque Francisci Philelfi cum quibusdam viri illustris epistolis. Impresse Antwerpie per me Henricum eckert de homberch. Anno domini Milesimo.CCCC.viij. (Wouter Nijhoff and M. E. Kronenberg, *Nederlandsche Bibliographie van 1500 tot 1540*, The Hague, 1923–58, no. 3722). Sigs. L_2v–L_7v contain twenty-three of the shorter letters of Pico, but none of the three that More translated.

I have also examined a microfilm of the Folger Library copy of *Illustrium virorum Epistole . . .* [with an introductory epistle by Jodocus Badius Ascensius; printed at Lyons; colophon on sig. o_6] Hoc opus diligenter impressum est Anno a natali christiano .M.ccccxcix. ad Idus Februarias. In officina Nicolai Vvolf: Lutriensis . . . (Goff E-98, Kawecka-Gryczowa 2094). This book consists primarily of letters from and to Angelo Poliziano. It also contains six letters by Giovanni Pico, but none of the three translated by More.

[3]Hain 12995, Polain 3147, Goff, P-636. Panzer 9, 111 (no. 44), gives "Epistole auree, *ab Ascensio recognite. Impress. 1509.* 4" (simply repeated by Garin, p. 95, no. 47). Panzer gives as his source Rasmus Nyerup, *Catalogi bibliothecae Thottianae*, vol. 7 (Copenhagen, 1795), p. 214. But in fact Nyerup gives "Ep. aureae, ab Ascensio recognitae, impress. S. per C. H." What the Thott library contained was clearly the Speyer edition of Conrad Hister, and Panzer's 1509 Ascensian edition is a ghost.

has the correct 1492.[1] Hence it seems unlikely that More's translation is directly or indirectly based on this edition.

2. Aureae epistolae [Paris], Michel le Noir   1499 (=E-99)[2]

Title: Auree Epistole Ioannis pici Mirandulae viri omnium mortalium doctissimi eloquentissimique.

Colophon (sig. E_5v): Impressum. per Michaelem le noir. Anno.-D.Mcccclxxxxix.

This edition contains not only the tree letters (sigs. A_2–A_3v, D_2v–D_4, E_2–E_3v) but also the prayer to God for mercy (sigs. E_3v–E_4).

Copy used: microfilm of the copy at the Bridwell Library, Southern Methodist University, Dallas, Texas

At 78/22–23 this edition omits "ex fratre," which More translated.

3. Aureae epistolae, Paris   1500 (= E-00)[3]

Title: Auree epistole ioannis Pici Mirandule viri omnium mortalium doctissimi eloquentissimique. [Woodcut identifying printer as Alexander Aliate de Mediolano] Peritissimi viri Iohannis pici mirandule opus epistolarum accusatissime [*sic*] nuper recognitum sedulaque opera impressum a quo omnia menda que in prima imprssione [*sic*] comperiebantur omnino abstersa sunt.

Colophon (sig. d_5v): Impressum parisius [*sic*].Anno domini M.quingentesimo die mensis augusti.

This edition contains not only the three letters (sigs. a_2–a_3, c_4–c_5v, d_2v–d_3v) but also the prayer to God for mercy (sigs. d_3v–d_4v).

Copy used: British Library

At 340/18 this edition omits "ex fratre," which More translated. In two places it has plausible readings that More would have found no reason to correct (see variants at 342/16 and 344/3–4); but in these places More's translation follows the readings of the other editions. Moreover, at 350/32 this edition has the correct reading "mannus," whereas More's translation shows that he had the erro-

---

[1]See the variant at 364/3.
[2]Hain *12996, Goff P-636.
[3]Hain *12997, *Bibliothèque nationale: Catalogue des incunables,* P-347, Goff P-638.

neous reading "manus." Hence it is quite unlikely that this edition is the direct or indirect source of More's translation.

4. Aureae epistolae [Antwerp, Thierry Martin]   1502 (=E-02)[1]

Title: Auree epistole Iohannis Pici Mirandule viri omnium mortalium doctissimi eloquentissimique. [Woodcut: two men under a tree, one sleeping, the other writing] Peritissimi viri Iohannis Pici Mirandule opus epistolarum accuratissime nuper recognitum sedulaque opera impressum a quo omnia menda que in prima impressione comperiebantur omnino abstersa sunt.

Colophon (sig. f_3v): Impressum Auno [sic] domini.M.quingentesimo.-Secundo.Octauo kalendas Octobris.

This edition contains not only the three letters (sigs. a_2–a_4, e_1–e_2v, e_7v–f_1 [missigned e_1]) but also the prayer to God for mercy (sigs. f_1v–f_2).

Copy used: microfilm of the copy in the Houghton Library at Harvard University

Omissions and errors in this edition[2] show that it was not More's source. Errors found only in *E-oo* and *E-02* show that *E-oo* was the copy-text for *E-02*.

5. Aureae epistolae [Paris], Robert Gourmont   1504 (= E-04)[3]

Title: Auree Epistole Iohannis Pici Mirandule viri omnium mortalium doctissimi eloquentissimique [printer's mark with the name Robert Gourmont]

Colophon (sig. E_5v): Impressum per Robertum gourmont Anno .D. M v cccc.iiii [sic]

This edition contains not only the three letters (sigs. A_2r–A_3v, D_2v–D_4r, E_2r–E_3v) but also the prayer to God for mercy (sig. f_1v–f_2r).

---

[1]Nijhoff-Kronenberg 3729; British Library 1087.e.31; Panzer 9, 107. The British Library could not locate its copy of this book in June 1992. This is presumably no. 43 in Garin, wrongly assigned to Badius Ascensius at Paris. It is the same as the book assigned tentatively but wrongly to Paris, J. B. Ascensius, by *The National Union Catalogue: Pre-1956 Imprints*, 718 vols. (London: Mansell, 1968–80) *457*, 333.

[2]See the variants at 340/18, 346/22, 346/29, 350/24–25, and 358/8–9.

[3]*Catalogue général des livres imprimés de la bibliothèque nationale*, 231 vols. (Paris, 1924–81), *136*, 754 (Rés. Z790).

Copy used: microfilm of the copy in the Bibliothèque Nationale, Paris

At 340/18 this edition omits "ex fratre," which More translated. At least four errors found only in *E-99* and *E-04* make it very likely that *E-99* was the copy-text for *E-04*.

6. Auree Epistole [Paris, for John Gourmont,   after 1507][1] (= *E-07*+)

Title: Auree Epistole Ioannis Pici Mirandulae viri omnium mortalium doctissimi eloquentissimique. [Woodcut of two angels holding a crowned shield with three fleurs-de-lis] Vaenit in aedibus Ioannis Gormontij ad insigne Geminarum Cipparum

No colophon.

This edition contains not only the three letters (sigs. A_1v–A_2v, D_4–E_1v, E_4v–F_2) but also the prayer to God for mercy (sigs. F_2–F_2v).

Copy used: Microfilm of the copy at the Huntington Library, San Marino, California

At 340/18 this edition omits "ex fratre," which More translated.

7. Epistolae   [Paris? 1508?] (= *E-08*)[2]

Title: page lacking in the British Library copy

Running heading: Ioannis Pici Mirandulae Epistolae

There is no colophon, but at the end is a poem by N. Bonaspes in praise of this book, which he sends to his former students and which concludes: "Ex panhisiens [*sic*] achademia.MiD.viij."

The first two letters are complete (sigs. a_2–a_3v and c_8v–d_2), but the third (sigs. e_3–e_3v) is incomplete (ending with "quo sua studia," 358/26) because one or two leaves are lacking in the e gathering.

Copy used: British Library

At 340/18 this edition omits "ex fratre," which More translated. At 342/32 it has the error "uoluntatibus" for "uoluptatibus." Since

---

[1]According to the catalogue card in *The National Union Catalogue, 457*, 333.

[2]*A Short-Title Catalogue of Books Printed in France and of French Books Printed in Other Countries from 1470 to 1600 Now in the British Museum* (London, 1924), p. 351, tentatively assigns this book to Paris, 1508, and to the printer Nicolas Du Pré.

More translated "delites" and it would probably not have been easy for him to correct the error himself, it is unlikely that this edition is the source of his translation.

8. Aureae epistolae [Antwerp, Thierry Martin],   1509 (= E-09)[1]

Title: Auree epistole Iohannis Pici Mirandule viri omnium mortalium doctissimi eloquentissimique. [Woodcut: two men under a tree, one sleeping, the other writing] Peritissimi viri Iohannis Pici Mirandule opus epistolarum accuratissime nuper recognitum sedulaque opera impressum a quo omnia menda que in prima impressione comperiebantur omnino abstersa sunt.

Colophon (sig. f_3v): Impressum Anno domini .M. quingentesimo. Nono.xxviii.Nouembris.

This edition contains not only the three letters (sigs. a_2–a_4, e_1–e_2v, e_7v–f_1) but also the prayer to God for mercy (sigs. f_1v–f_2).

Copy used: microfilm of the copy in the Folger Shakespeare Library, Washington, D.C.

Omissions and errors in this edition[2] show that it was not More's source. Many errors found only in E-02 and E-09 make it clear that E-02 was the copy-text for E-09. E-09 is in fact a page-for-page (and usually line-for-line) reprint of E-02.

A Separate Edition of Giovanni Pico's Letter That Could Not Be Consulted

Gravissime et copiosissime . . . epistole XXXXVI, Leipzig, per Baccalaureum Wolfgangum Monacensem [Wolfgang Stöckel of Munich], 1504. *Verzeichnis der im deutschen Sprachbereich erschienenen Drucke: VD 16*, I Abteilung, 18 vols. to date (Stuttgart, 1983–), *16*, 80, P2625. Panzer, *9, 483*. On November 2, 1992, Dr. Junginger of the Bayerische Staatsbibliothek in Munich wrote me that he knows no more than the reference in Panzer, *9, 483*, which places the edition in the Bibliotheca Joschiana, apparently a private library that can no longer be located. On November 23, 1992, Christian Hogrefe of the Herzog August Bibliothek in Wolfenbüttel wrote me that he knows of no location for this edition.

---

[1]Nijhoff-Kronenberg, no. 1723.
[2]See the variants at 340/18, 346/22, 346/29, 350/24–25, and 358/8–9.

Lemmata

96 = Opera omnia, Bologna, 1496
96+ = Opera omnia, Lyons, before 1498
98 = Opera omnia, Venice, 1498
04 = Opera omnia, Strassburg, 1504
06 = Opera omnia, Reggio, 1506
V-06/7 = Gianfrancesco's *Vita*, Strassburg, 1506–7
E-95+ = Aureae epistolae, Speyer, after January 3, 1495
E-99 = Aureae epistolae, Paris, 1499
E-00 = Aureae epistolae, Paris, 1500
E-02 = Aureae epistolae, Antwerp, 1502
E-04 = Aureae epistolae, Paris, 1504
E-07+ = Aureae epistolae, Paris, after 1507
E-08 = Epistolae [Paris? 1508?]
E-09 = Aureae epistolae, Antwerp, 1509

More's Latin Text

The evidence does not allow us to say with full certitude which edition More used, but among the editions available to him one reading suggests that the most probable source is the Strassburg *Opera omnia* of 1504 (*04*).[1]

At 350/32 More translated the incorrect reading "manus" (hand) instead of "mannus" (pony). Two editions have "mannus" and six have the correct abbreviation "mañus." Since "mannus" (unlike "manus") fits the context well and is not a rare or obscure word,[2] it seems unlikely that More would have translated wrongly unless his text actually had "manus," a reading found only in *04*, *E-95+*, *E-02*, *E-07+*, and *E-09*. *E-95+* seems to be ruled out because it misdates the second letter to Gianfrancesco 1482, whereas More has the correct 1492.[3] *E-07+* is ruled out because of errors and omissions,[4] as are *E-02* and *E-09*.[5] It is true that in some places *04* does have incorrect readings where More's translation is correct, but More could easily have seen and corrected

---

[1] Errors or omissions make it highly unlikely that More used *96*, *06*, *E-95*, *E-99*, *E-00*, *E-02*, *E-04*, *E-07+*, *E-08*, or *E-09*.

[2] It occurs three times in Horace and at least once in Lucretius, Ovid, Propertius, Seneca, and Jerome.

[3] See the variant at 362/3.

[4] See the variants at 340/8, 348/35, 356/21, 358/21, 358/32, and 358/34.

[5] See the variants at 340/18, 346/22, 346/29, 350/24–25, and 358/8–9.

the errors.[1] Naturally, More could have translated from a manuscript, but if he used a printed book, it was almost surely the Strassburg edition of 1504.[2]

THE HANDLING OF THE TEXT

Spelling, punctuation, capitalization, and indentation have been modernized, in accordance with Gianfrancesco's own recommendations.[3] I have presented a correct reading text,[4] not a fully definitive edition, but the apparatus at the bottom of the pages indicates emendations and gives substantive variants from the editions printed before 1510, including the Strassburg edition of 1504 (*04*). The running heads above the Latin text indicate the pages of More's translations in this edition. Passages italicized in this appendix were omitted by More in his translations.

The editions of the *Life of Pico* printed during More's lifetime (*1510* and *1525*) contain no sidenotes, but they do have twenty-seven headings (presumably More's) to break up the Life into major sections.[5] The *Vita* in the early *Opera omnia*[6] has no headings, but it has fifty-six sidenotes in the parts that More translated. Of these only four are fairly close to More's headings (55/9, 65/4, 70/1, 73/8), and for the first three of these More could have got the correspondences from the Latin text itself. At 73/8 the correspondence is close ("Of the state of his sowle," "Status animae") and has no exact correspondence in the Latin text itself; but this single instance is not enough to show that More made use of the Latin sidenotes, and I have omitted them here.

---

[1]See the variants at 330/33, 350/11, 358/1, 358/2, 358/32, 366/22, 366/24, 366/35, 370/18, and 374/7.

[2]We should not rely very much on the correspondence between More and *04* at 340/30: like More, only *04* omits "quidem" (or the erroneous "quod").

[3]See above, p. 286.

[4]The Latin text and Italian translation of Gianfranceso's *Vita* by Tomasso Sorbelli (Modena, 1963) should be used with great caution. He says "collazionavo le varie edizioni tenendo a baso la Bolognese de 1496" (p. 14), and he lists the editions of 1498, 1504, and 1506 (p. 102). But apart from ten typographic errors, he gives at least forty-two readings not found in any of the editions he mentions, and of these twenty-two are omissions or errors. In one place (see the variants at 338/18–19) he gives an error which is not present in *96* and which appears for the first time in *98*. In at least fifteen places the translation is erroneous or seriously misleading.

[5]The selections after the Life proper have no headings.

[6]*96, 96+, 98, 04, 06*. The *Vita* in the collection of Gianfrancesco's works (V-*06*/7) has neither sidenotes nor headings.

A NOTE ON "SUISETICAS" (318/15)[1]

This adjectival form refers to Richard Swineshead (Latinized as Sui-seth), a philosopher at Merton College, Oxford (fl. c. 1344–1354), who wrote *Liber calculationum* and was known as *Calculator*.[2] Swineshead, together with Thomas Bradwardine and William of Heytesbury at Oxford and John Buridan and Nicolas Oresme at the University of Paris, contributed to the mathematical quantification of Aristotelian physics that provided the groundwork for Galileo's laws of motion. Pico had Swineshead's book and those of other *calculatores* in his library. Although he opposed them strenuously in his early career, in his last work, *Adversus astrologos*, he had come to admire and accept much of their work.[3]

---

[1]For the information in this note I am grateful to Professor Louis Valcke of the University of Sherbrooke.

[2]See Alistair C. Crombie, *Augustine to Galileo: Science in the Middle Ages; Science in the Later Middle Ages and Early Modern Times*, 2 vols. in one, 2nd ed. (Cambridge, Mass., 1961), 2, 71, 101, 105, 108, 122, 154, 162. On the reputation of the *calculatores* in Italy and the editions of Swineshead's book in Padua, Pavia, and Venice, see Carlo Dionisotti, "Ermolao Barbaro e la Fortuna di Suiseth," in *Medioevo e Rinascimento: Studi in onore di Bruno Nardi*, 2 vols. (Florence, 1955), *1*, 219–53.

[3]See Louis Valcke, "Des *Conclusiones* aux *Disputationes*: Numérologie et mathématiques chez Jean Pic de la Mirandole," *Laval théologique et philosophique, 41* (1985), 43–56; and idem, "'Calculatores', Ermolao Barbaro e Giovanni Pico della Mirandola," in *Mentis itinerarium: L'educazione e la formazione intellettuale nell' età dell' umanesimo*, Istituto di Studi Umanistici F. Petrarca, Atti del II convegno internazionale—1990, ed. Luisa Rotondi Secchi Tarugi (Milan, 1992), 275–84.

IOANNIS PICI MIRANDVLAE,
VIRI OMNI DISCIPLINARVM GENERE
CONSVMATISSIMI, VITA PER IOANNEM
FRANCISCVM, ILLVSTRIS PRINCIPIS
GALEOTTI PICI FILIVM, EDITA

Ioannis Pici patrui mei vitam scribere orsus, praefandum lectoribus imprimis duco (ne aut quod fratris filius aut quod discipulus fuerim, me aliquid in gratiam, blandientium more, dicturum suspicarentur) nihil hic amicitiae datum, nihil familiae nihilque beneficiis, quae maxima profecto in me exs-
10 *titerunt, ficticia laude repensum. Tantum quippe ab adulatione seiuncta est narratio mea, quantum abfuit adulandi necessitas, tantumque cavi ne me vel mentitum vel vehementem in laudibus legentes arbitrarentur, si quicquid de ipso conceperam litteris tradidissem, ut illud fuerit fortasse periculum ne parcum potuerint vel ipsaemet virtutes excelsae vel earum assertores coarguere. Quod vel*
15 *hoc argumento videre licet: cum plurimae doctorum nostrae aetatis hominum, & ex primoribus quidem, elucubratissimae scriptiones non modo his quae sumus dicturi locupletissimum reddiderint testimonium, sed dum uteretur hac luce, & postquam eam cum potiore commutavit, in eius me & morum & doctrinae praeconiis praecelluerint. Quarum nonnullas in huius libri calce post commen-*
20 *tationes ipsius adscribi iussi, ut firmior testibus non gentiliciis fides adhiberetur.*

Paternum genus (licet ab Constantino caesare per Picum pronepotem a quo totius familiae cognomentum memoriae proditum sit traxisse primordia) missum facientes, *ab ipso tempore nativitatis sumemus initium,* tum quod familiae forsan non minus honoris ille contulerit
25 quam acceperit, *tum quod proprias animi dotes reliquaque totius vitae & obitus seriem prae se ferentia, quae vel propriis aut auribus aut oculis hausi, vel ab gravissimis excepi testibus, aperienda duxerim,* posthabitisque & stemmate & praeclaris avorum facinoribus recensenda. Anno a partu virginis tertio & sexagesimo supra millesimum & quadringentesimum,
30 Pio Secundo pontifice maximo ecclesiae praeside & Federico Tertio habenas Imperii Romani moderante, mater Iulia ex nobili Boiardorum familia Ioanni Francisco patri ultimo eum partu peperit. *Iam enim Galeottum maiorem natu, ex quo sum genitus, et Antonium Mariam, sororesque duas enixa fuerat. Quarum altera Leonello iam coniugi Albertum Pium ex Carpi*
35 *Principibus unum edidit, nunc Rodulphi Principis Gonzagae consors; altera*

THE LIFE OF GIOVANNI PICO DELLA MIRANDOLA, A MAN OF THE MOST CONSUMMATE EXCELLENCE IN ALL BRANCHES OF LEARNING, ISSUED BY GIANFRANCESCO, THE SON OF THE FAMOUS PRINCE GALEOTTO PICO

Having undertaken to write the life of my uncle Giovanni Pico, I think it especially important to inform my readers at the outset (lest they should suspect, because I am the son of his brother and was once his pupil, that what I am about to say is prejudiced by favor or flattery) that I have made no allowance here for friendship or family and that I am in no way repaying with fictitious praise the benefits he bestowed on me, though they were very great indeed. In fact, my narrative is as far removed from flattery as it is from the need for it, and I have taken so much care lest my readers should think that I have been inaccurate or excessive in praising him by putting down in writing what I actually think of him, that there is perhaps some danger that either his lofty virtues themselves or their champions might tax me for praising too grudgingly. That becomes quite clear when one considers that many of the most thoughtful and well-considered writings by the learned men of our time (and those, indeed, of the first rank) have not only given very ample testimony to what I am about to say but have also gone far beyond me in proclaiming his character and learning, both while he was alive and after he had exchanged this life for a better one. And I have seen to it that some of those are included at the end of this book, after his own works, in order to gain firmer credence from the testimony of those who have no familial relation to him.

Leaving aside his paternal ancestry although according to tradition it goes back to the Emperor Constantine through his great-grandson Picus, from whom the whole family derives its name), *I shall begin with the time of his own birth*, both because he perhaps bestowed as much honor on the family as he acquired from it *and because, in recounting the special gifts of his mind and the other circumstances which make up the history of his whole life and death, I thought it proper to disclose what I learned with my own eyes and ears or what I heard from very reliable witnesses*, prescinding from any account of his family tree and the famous deeds of his ancestors. In the fourteen hundred and sixty-third year after the Virgin gave birth, while Pope Pius II presided over the church and Frederick III held the reins of the Roman Empire, his mother, Giulia, of the noble Boiardo family, gave birth to him as the last child she presented to his father, Giovanni Francesco. *For she had already given birth to the elder son, Galeotto, who is my father, and Antonio Maria, as well as two sisters. One of them bore for Leonello, her husband at that time, an only son, Alberto Pio di Carpi; she is presently the spouse of Rodolpho, prince of Gonzaga. The other,*

Pino Ordelapho Forolivensi Principe, cui iampridem nupserat, vita functo,
Montis Agani Comiti secundas nuptias concessit.

Prodigium haud paruum ante ipsius ortum apparuit. Visa enim cir-
cularis flamma est supra parientis matris astare cubiculum moxque
5 evanescere, fortasse nobis insinuans orbiculari figurae intellectus per-
fectione simillimum eum futurum qui inter mortales eadem hora pro-
deretur, universoque terrae globo excellentia nominis circumquaque
celebrandum, cuius mens semper caelestia (ignis instar) petitura esset,
cuiusque ignita eloquia flammatae menti consona deum nostrum (*qui*
10 *ignis comburens est*) totis viribus quandoque celebratura, sed statim ob-
tutibus hominum (ut illa evanuit) occulenda. Legimus quippe doc-
tissimorum sanctissimorumque hominum ortus insolita quandoque
signa aut praecessisse aut subsequuta fuisse, veluti eorum incunabula
infantium ab aliorum caetu divino nutu segregantia summisque rebus
15 gerendis natos indicantia. Sic (ut omittam reliquos) examen apium
Ambrosii magni ora lustravit, in eaque introgressum est, deinde exiens
altissimumque volans seque inter nubila condens, paternos aspectus
aliorumque qui aderant visus elusit. Quod praesagium Paulinus plu-
rifaciens scriptorum eius favos nobis indicasse disseruit, qui caelestia
20 dona enuntiarent & mentes hominum de terris ad caelum erigerent.

Forma autem insigni fuit & liberali: procera & celsa statura, molli
carne, venusta facie in uniuersum, albenti colore decentique rubore
interspersa, caesiis & vigilibus oculis, flavo & inaffectato capillitio, den-
tibus quoque candidis & aequalibus.

25 Sub matris imperio ad magistros disciplinasque delatus, ita ardenti
animo studia humanitatis excoluit ut breui inter poetas & oratores
tempestatis illius praecipuos (nec iniuria) collocandus esset. In dis-
cendo quidem celerrimus erat, prompto adeo ingenio praeditus, ut
audita semel a recitante carmina, & directo & retrogrado ordine mira
30 omnium admiratione recenseret tenacissimaque retineret memoria.
Quod caeteris contra evenire solet, nam qui celeri sunt ingenio natura
fieri saepe solet ut non multum memoria valeant; qui uero cum labore
percipiunt tenaciores perceptorum evadant.

Dum vero quartum & decimum aetatis annum ageret, matris iussu,
35 quae sacris eum initiari vehementer optabat, discendi iuris pontificii
gratia, Bononiam se transtulit. Quod cum biennium degustasset, meris

---

16 deinde] *04 V-06/7,* dein *96 96+ 98 06*

after the death of Pino Ordelafo, prince of Forlì, whom she had married long
ago, took the count of Montagano as her second husband.

There was an extraordinary apparition before his birth. Above the bedroom where his mother was giving birth there stood a circular flame, which soon disappeared, perhaps intended to suggest to us that the one who was coming forth among mortals at that very hour would, by the perfection of his understanding, closely resemble a global form and would rightly be acclaimed on all sides throughout the whole globe of the earth because of his surpassing fame, and that his mind (like fire) would strive toward the things of heaven, and that his fiery eloquence, corresponding to his flaming thoughts, would one day do its utmost to celebrate our God (*who is "a consuming fire"*), but that it would suddenly be hidden from the sight of men, just as that flame disappeared. Indeed, we read that the births of exceptionally learned and holy men were sometimes preceded or followed by extraordinary signs, as if God gave his nod of approval to set off their cradles from the general run of other infants and to indicate that they were born to perform great deeds. Thus, to omit other instances, a swarm of bees crawled over the mouth of the great Ambrose, entered it, and then went away, flying up high and hiding itself in the clouds, eluding the gaze of his father and the sight of the others who were present. Making much of this omen, Paulinus explained that it referred to the honeycombs of his writings, which announced heavenly gifts and raised up the minds of men from earth to heaven.

He was extraordinarily handsome, in an aristocratic way, well built and tall. His flesh was soft, his face altogether attractive, fair complexioned but blended with a becoming blush, his eyes blue-gray and alert, his hair blond and not done up in any affected style. Also his teeth were white and even.

By his mother's command he was given over to tutors to instruct him, and he pursued the humanities with such ardent enthusiasm that he was soon considered, and rightly so, to be one of the leading poets and orators of his time. Indeed he was extremely quick to learn, furnished with such a ready intelligence that when verses had been recited to him only once, he amazed everyone by repeating them either forward or backward, and he remembered them very retentively. With others that is frequently not the case, for nature often arranges it so that those who are quick to understand do not remember very well, whereas those who have to work hard to learn turn out to be better at retaining what they have learned.

And then, when he was thirteen years old, at the direction of his mother, who was very eager for him to take holy orders, he went to Bologna in order to learn canon law. When he had tried it out for two

id inniti traditionibus conspicatus, alio deflexit, non tamen absque bonae frugis foetura, quando iam puer & quidem tenellus ex epistolis
summorum pontificum, quas decretales vocant, epitomen quandam
seu brevarium compilaverit, quo omnes concisius quam fieri potuit
5   sanctionum illarum sententias conclusit—consummatis professoribus
opus non tenue.

Sed secretarum naturae rerum cupidus explorator, tritas has semitas
derelinquens, intellectus speculationi philosophiaeque, cum humanae
tum divinae, se penitus dedidit. Cuius enanciscendae gratia, non tan
10 tum italiae sed & galliarum litteraria gymnasia perlustrans, celebres
doctores tempestatis illius, more Platonis & Apollonii, scrupulosissime
perquirebat, operam adeo indefessam studiis illis impendens ut consummatus simul & theologus simul & philosophus imberbis adhuc & et
esset & haberetur.

15 Iamque septennium apud illos versatus erat, quando humanae
laudis & gloriae cupidus (nondum enim divino amore caluerat *ut palam
fiet*) Romam migravit, inibique ostentare cupiens quanta eum a summussoribus in posterum maneret invidia, nongentas de dialecticis &
mathematicis, de naturalibus divinisque rebus quaestiones proposuit,
20 non modo ex Latinorum petitas arculis Graecorumque excerptas
scriniis, sed ex Hebraeorum etiam mysteriis erutas Chaldaeorumque
arcanis atque Arabum vestigatas. Multa item de Pythagorae Trimegistique & Orphaei prisca & suboscura philosophia, *multa de Cabala
(hoc est secreta Hebraeorum dogmatum receptione), cuius & Origenes & Hi
25 larius ex nostris potissimum comminiscuntur, quaestionibus illis intexuit; multa
etiam de naturali magia, quam non parvo interstitio ab impia & scelesta separari edocuit, idque multorum testimonio elegantissime comprobavit. Nec duo &
septuaginta nova dogmata physica & metaphysica, propria inventa & meditata,
ad quascunque philosophiae quaestiones elucidandas accommodata defuerunt.*
30 *His novam per numeros philosophandi institutionem adnexuit,* cunctaque
simul publicis locis, quo facilius vulgarentur, affixit, pollicitus se soluturum eis impensas qui ex remotis oris disceptandi gratia Romam se
contulissent. Verum obtrectatorum simultate (quae semper velut ignis
alta petit) nunquam efficere potuit ut dies altercationis praestitueretur.
35 Ob hanc causam Romae annum mansit, quo tempore vitiligatores illi
palam eum & libero examine non audebant aggredi, sed strophis
potius & cuniculis sugillare clanculariisque telis suffodere, pestifera

---

37 clanculariisque] *96 96+ 98,* clancularisque *04 06* V-*06/7*

years, he saw that it was based simply on what was handed down from one to another, and he turned elsewhere, not, however, without reaping a good harvest, since even in these boyish and tender years he had compiled a sort of epitome or digest of the papal letters called decretals, summarizing as concisely as possible all the substance of those decisions—no small achievement even for seasoned professors.

Nevertheless, eager as he was to explore the secrets of nature, leaving these well-worn paths behind him, he committed himself deeply to intellectual speculation and to philosophy, both human and divine. In pursuit of such knowledge, he went from one center of learning to another, not only in Italy but also in France, very carefully seeking out the famous teachers of his time, as Plato and Apollonius had done, and he expended such unwearied effort in these pursuits that, even as a beardless youth, he both was and was recognized as a past master in theology and philosophy alike.

After he had spent seven years with these teachers, eager for human praise and glory (for he was not yet burning with the love of God, *as will become clear*), he went to Rome, and there, in his desire to boast of how much envy he would later arouse among the grumblers, he proposed 900 questions concerning dialectics and mathematics, concerning natural phenomena and theology, matters not only sought out from the coffers of Latin learning and plucked from the writing boxes of Greek erudition, but also rooted out from the mysteries of the Jews and tracked down in the arcana of the Chaldeans and the Arabs. Likewise he interlaced among these questions many points from the ancient and rather obscure philosophy of Pythagoras and Trismegistus and Orpheus, *many points from the Cabala (that is, the secret tradition of Hebrew doctrines), which, among our scholars, were most investigated by Origen and Hilary, many points also concerning natural magic, which he showed to be at no small remove from wicked and evil magic—a point he demonstrated very elegantly by the testimony of many authorities. For full measure, there were 72 new propositions on physics and mathematics, which he had himself discovered and thought out and which were adapted to throwing some light on certain philosophical questions. To these he added a new system of philosophizing by numerology.* And he put all of them up simultaneously in public places so that they would be more easily disseminated, promising to pay the expenses of those who came to Rome from faraway lands for the disputation. But because of his detractors' enmity (which like fire aims at what is above it), he could never arrange to get a day set for the disputation.

For this reason he stayed in Rome for a year, during which time those cavillers did not dare to attack him openly and in a free debate, but rather they tried to pummel him with tricks and underhanded plots and to pierce him with darts thrown from hiding places, corrupted as

corrupti invidia (ita enim arbitrati sunt plurimi) conabantur. Livorem
hunc vel hac ratione sibi maxime eum movisse existimatum est, quod
multi qui vel ambitione fortassis vel avaritia litterario negotio diu incu-
buerant notam sibi fore autumarent, si iuvenis ille, aggestis atavorum
5   opibus multaque doctrina *quasi fertilis ager* luxurians, in prima orbis
urbe, de naturalibus divinisque rebus deque multis per plura saecula
nostris hominibus non accessis periclitari doctrinam & ingenium non
vereretur; et cum nihil adversus doctrinam veris machinis moliri posse
animadverterent, attulisse eosdem in medium tormenta calumniae,
10   tredecimque ex nongentis quaestiones rectae fidei suspectas accla-
mavisse, quibus forte se iunxisse nonnullos qui quaestiones illas utpote
insuetas eorum auribus, ut pie ita fortasse parum erudite, & zelo fidei &
praetextu religionis incesserent. Quas tamen quaestiones non pauci, &
quidem celebrati theologiae doctores, ceu pias & mundas prius appro-
15   baverant eisdemque subscripserant. *Quorum coetu Bonfranciscus Re-*
giensis episcopus annumeratus est, vir omnigena doctrina acerrimoque iudicio
& morum gravitate praeclarus, qui Romae ad pontificem maximum ea tempes-
tate pro Ferrariensium duce agebat legatus. Adversus tamen eum blaterones illi
nihil attentarunt, cum forte ab eis labefactari eius famam non posse vererentur,
20   *quando quicquid tractasset correctioni matris ecclesiae & pontificis submisisset.*
At is famae istaec dispendia non perpessus, Apologiam edidit, varium
certe opus & elegans multaque rerum scitu dignarum cognitione refer-
tum, vigintique tantum noctibus elucubratum. Qua editione luce
clarius conspici datum est, non tam conclusiones catholicos potuisse
25   sensus recipere quam illos qui prius adlatraverant insolentiae & ru-
ditatis coarguendos esse, librumque ipsum & quae scripturus erat in
posterum matris ecclesiae *eiusque praesidis* sanctissimo iudicio chris-
tianissimi hominis more commisit. *Id enim vel expresse vel tacite fieri opor-*
tere persuasissimum est, quasi illud Augustini proferret: Errare possum, here-
30   *ticus esse non possum, quando alterum sit hominis proprium, alterum perversae*
& obstinatae voluntatis. Sed ubi *Innocentius octavus* pontifex maximus
accepit *per editionem Apologiae* interpretatas conclusiones illas, *quae prius*
calumniis infestatae fuerant, in catholicum sensum & a nota criminis rele-
vatas, referentibusque nonnullis, quibus conclusionum examen de-
35   mandatum fuerat, decipulas opponi posse fidelibus si nonnullae quaes-
tionum illarum (crudae quidem & inexplicitae disceptandarum more

---

8 cum] *96 96+ 98 06 V-06/7 (errata),* eum *04 V-06/7 (text)*   27 praesidis] presidi *96*
96+ 98 04 06 V-06/7

they were by malignant envy (for that is what most people thought). It was considered that this envy was stirred up against him primarily for this reason: many who had long applied themselves to the business of learning out of either ambition or greed thought it would be a black mark against them if this young man, reveling in the accumulated wealth of his ancestors and rich with much learning *like a fertile field*, in the foremost city of the world, should not be afraid to venture his learning and intellect on questions about natural phenomena and theology and on matters not even approached by our scholars for many centuries. And when they noticed that they could not achieve anything against his learning with genuine instruments of siege, they brought out catapults of slander, proclaiming that 13 of the 900 questions were of dubious orthodoxy. Perhaps they were joined by some who, out of zeal for the faith and under the pretext of scrupulous devotion, assailed those questions, perhaps with more piety than learning, because they sounded strange to their ears. Nevertheless, the questions had been previously approved as pious and untainted and had been subscribed to by not a few scholars, among whom, indeed, were celebrated doctors of theology. *One of this number was Buonfrancesco, the bishop of Reggio, a man famous for his wide-ranging learning, his very penetrating judgment, and his solid character, who was in Rome at that time acting as ambassador to the pope from the duke of Ferrara. Against him, however, these babblers did not try anything, perhaps because they were afraid that they could do nothing to undermine his reputation, since he had submitted all his discussion to the correction of our mother the church and the pope.* But Pico, unwilling to suffer that loss to his reputation, published his *Apology,* certainly a wide-ranging and elegant work, filled with many insights about points worth understanding, a volume which he worked out in only twenty nights. This publication made it as clear as day not merely that his conclusions could be taken in an orthodox sense but also that those who had previously barked at him were guilty of insolence and ignorance; and, like a good Christian, he submitted the book itself and whatever he would write in the future to the most holy judgment of our mother the church *and the pope. For he was quite convinced that this should be done, either expressly or tacitly, in accordance with that saying of Augustine: "I can err but I cannot be a heretic, because the one belongs to the human condition, the other to a perverse and obstinate will."* But when the pope *Innocent VIII, by the publication of the "Apology,"* accepted those conclusions, *which had formerly been slanderously attacked,* as interpreted in an orthodox sense and relieved of any blot of wrongdoing, whereas some of those to whom the examination of the conclusions had been assigned reported that they could present a stumbling block to the faithful if some of them (which were posed in a bold and unqualified form, as is customary in

iacebant) passim vagarentur, libelli lectione quo continebantur inter-
dixit. Quae omnia per Alexandri sexti pontificis maximi, sub quo nunc
vivimus, Diploma (quod breve nominant) liquido visuntur: *quod cum*
apologia ipsa impressoribus tradere exarandum duximus. Verum in ipso apolo-
5 *giae calce, quod postea pontifex auctoritate praestitit,* quibus ille poterat
rationibus antea factitaverat. *Obsecraverat quippe amicos & inimicos, doctos*
& indoctos, ut Apologiam legerent, libellum vero ipsum conclusionum inex-
plicitarum praeterirent illectum, quando in eo plurima continerentur quae non
passim vulganda triuiis sed secreto congressu inter doctos & paucos
10 disputanda susceperat, *scolasticamque exercitationem more academiarum*
meditatus, multa veterum philosophorum, Alexandri scilicet & Averrois
aliorumque quamplurium impia dogmata proposuisset, quae semper publice &
privatim asseruerat, professus fuerat, praedicaverat non minus a verae rectae-
que philosophiae quam a fidei semitis declinare. Atque in hunc modum de libello
15 *illo nongentarum conclusionum verba faciens, apologeticum opus conclusit:*
"*Qui ergo me oderunt, ideo illa non legant quia nostra sunt; qui me amant, ideo*
non legant quia ex illis quae mea sunt cogitare plurima possent quae non sunt
nostra."
    Caeterum immensa dei bonitate, quae ex malis etiam bona elicit,
20 effectum esse (quemadmodum *mihi* rettulit) iudicabat, ut calumnia illa
falso a malevolis irrogata veros errores corrigeret, eique in tenebris
aberranti (ut quantum exorbitasset a tramite veritatis contueri posset)
ceu splendidissimum iubar illucesceret. Prius enim & gloriae cupidus &
amore vano succensus muliebribusque illecebris commotus fuerat.
25 Feminarum quippe plurimae ob venustatem corporis orisque gratiam,
cui doctrina amplaeque divitiae & generis nobilitas accedebant, in eius
amorem exarserunt, ab quarum studio non abhorrens, parumper via
vitae posthabita in delicias defluxerat. Verum simultate illa exper-
rectus, diffluentem luxu animum retudit & convertit ad Christum at-
30 que feminea blandimenta in supernae patriae gaudia commutavit, ne-
glectaque aura gloriolae quam affectaverat, dei gloriam & ecclesiae
utilitatem tota cepit mente perquirere adeoque mores componere ut
posthac vel inimico iudice comprobari posset.
    Cumque de ipso gloriosa statim fama & per vicinas & per remotas
35 oras volitare occepisset, plures ex philosophis qui eruditissimi habe-
bantur ad eum, tanquam ad mercaturam bonarum artium (*ut inquit*
Cicero), confluebant, vel ob commovenda litteraria certamina vel,

disputations) were to gain wide currency, the pope forbade the reading of the pamphlet which contained them. All of this is made perfectly clear by a document (called a brief) issued by Pope Alexander VI, our present pope. *This breve we thought it proper to be given to the printers to set up together with the "Apology."* But at the end of the Apology itself, Pico had earlier given every reason he could to support *what the pope later effected by authority. In fact, he earnestly begged friends and enemies alike, learned and unlearned, to read the Apology but to leave unread the pamphlet containing those unqualified conclusions, since it included many things* which he had brought up not so that they could be bruited about on every street-corner but so that they could be discussed in a private, small gathering of learned men. *He noted that, having in mind a scholastic exercise in the manner of the schools, he had proposed many impious teachings of ancient philosophers, namely Alexander and Averroes and many others, which he had always asserted, professed, and proclaimed, both publicly and privately, to deviate not only from the path of true and correct philosophy but also from the paths of the faith. And speaking of that pamphlet of 900 conclusions, he concluded his apologetic work as follows: "Therefore, let those who hate me avoid reading them because they are mine. Let those who love me avoid reading them because from those things which are mine they could conceive of many things that are not."*

Nevertheless, God's immense kindness, which draws good out of evil, brought it about, as Pico judged and as he himself said *to me,* that the slander wrongly inflicted on him by malevolent men set him on the straight and narrow after his wanderings and, as he was straying in the darkness, shone upon him a dazzling beam of light so that he could see how far he had deviated from the path of truth. For previously he had been eager for glory and inflamed by illusory love and aroused by the enticements of women. Certainly, his attractive body and handsome face, together with his learning, his great wealth, and his noble family, caused many women to fall passionately in love with him, and he did not shrink from their advances but departed for a while from the way of life and indulged in the pleasures of loose living. But when that strife had brought him to his senses, he checked his impulse toward sensual indulgence and turned to Christ and exchanged the blandishments of women for the joys of his heavenly homeland; and neglecting the breath of paltry glory which he had pursued, he began to set his mind completely on the glory of God and the welfare of the church and to change his morals so thoroughly that afterward even an enemy could think well of him.

And as his glorious reputation quickly began to fly abroad through countries far and near, many of those philosophers who were thought to be most learned flocked to him as if he were a marketplace of the arts and sciences (*to use Cicero's phrase*), either to engage in intellectual de-

quibus inerat rectior mentis sententia, ad audienda tenendaque recte vivendi salubria dogmata, quae tanto magis expetebantur quanto ab homine doctissimo pariter & nobilissimo profluebant, qui quandoque deuios mollitudinis voluptariae anfractus sectatus fuerat. Videntur
5 enim ad disciplinam morum auditorum mentibus inserendam ea plurimum habere momenti quae & suapte natura sint bona & a preceptore converso ad iustitiae semitas ex distorto & obliquo libidinum calle proficiscantur.

Elegiaco carmine amores luserat, quos quinque exaratos libris, religionis causa ignibus tradidit. Multa itidem rhythmis lusit Hetruscis, quae pari causa par ignis absumpsit.

Sacras deinde litteras ardentissimo studio complexus, *statim in templo dei ceu frugum primitias, octavum tunc & vigesimum annum agens, de operibus sex dierum Geneseos & die quietis heptaplum obtulit, opus quippe & perfec-*
15 *tum ingenio & elaboratum industria, cum sublimibus philosophorum dogmatis tum profundissimis nostrae christianae theologiae mysteriis refertissimum, septemplicique varia enarratione connexum, septemnario capitum numero cuilibet septemnae expositioni conserto, libri nomini maxime quadrans. Quod tamen ob erutas e naturae gremio res & difficiles divinarum quaestionum euolutiones*
20 *atque ob prophetae reconditissima sensa sermonisque elegantiam, non se passim philosophiae & eloquentiae rudibus offert, sed pretiosae illius & rarae supellectilis usus paucis paratur. Quod & ipse animadvertens, in eiusdem proemii calce mentionem de hac re non illepidam fecit.*

Cum primum sacras degustavit litteras, non tantum veram sapientiam sed &
25 *veram eloquentiam invenisse letabundus exultabat. Multaque ut omittam ab eo testamenti novi allata preconia, Pauli epistolas oratorum omnium scriptionibus eloquentia praestare dicebat, Tullii etiam ipsius Demosthenisque, primarii (ut inquit ille) dicendi artificis, lucubrationes nominatim citans, non quod essent, ut illae, calamistris inustae & corrasis undique fucis & concinnis constipatae, sed*
30 *quod veram et solidam & redolerent & saperent eloquentiam, veris sententiis vera arte suffultam, essentque (ut dicam breuius) Aegyptiorum opibus non consulto suffarcinatae. Omnia porro veteris legis eloquia consummatissimae scientiae & sapientiae plena praedicabat. Quod etsi cum alii tum Augustinus in libro de doctrina christiana luculenter ostenderit, Septimiusque Tertulianus,*
35 *Eusebius Pamphili, & Cassiodorus affirment grammaticos, rhetores, oratores, philosophosque omnes priscos eloquentiae & doctrinae suae fluenta ex divinarum scripturarum fontibus epotasse, ipse tamen aliis id muneris rationibus*

---

2 expetebantur] *98 04 06 V-06/7,* expectebantur *96 96+*   3 pariter &] *96 96+,* & pariter *98 04 06 V-06/7*   5 inserendam] *96 96+ V-06/7 (errata),* inferendam *98 04 06 V-06/7 (text)*   30 quod veram] ut veram *96 96+ 98 04 06 V-06/7* et solidam] *96 (text),* ut solidam *96 (errata) 96+,* solidam *98 04 06 V-06/7*

bates or else—and this was true of those whose mental outlook was
more sound—to hear and to cling to his wholesome teachings about
how to live well, which were desired all the more because they issued
from a man unmatched in both learning and nobility, who had at one
time followed the tortuous byways of sensuous indulgence. For it seems
that moral teachings take firmest root in the hearers' minds if they are
both good in their own right and also come from a teacher who has
returned to the path of righteousness from the crooked and wandering
track of pleasure.

He had amused himself by writing love elegies, arranging them in
five books, but for the sake of religion he committed them to the fire.
Likewise, he threw off many poems in Italian verse, which were con-
sumed by the same fire for the same reason.

After that, having ardently embraced the study of holy scripture, *at
the age of twenty-seven he immediately offered in the temple of God as his first
fruits his "Heptaplus" on the works of the six days of creation and on the day of
rest, a work both perfect in conception and elaborately worked out in detail,
extraordinarily rich both in the loftiest doctrines of philosophy and in the deepest
mysteries of our Christian theology, organized in a sevenfold pattern of varied
disquisition, with seven chapters woven into each of the seven expositions, in full
accord with the name of the book. But nevertheless, because of the secrets
searched out of nature's bosom and the difficult discussion of theological ques-
tions and because of the quite recondite meanings of the prophet and the elegance
of his speech, Pico does not always address those ignorant of philosophy and
eloquence, but rather he provides the use of those precious and rare utensils for
the few. He notes this point himself, mentioning it, not without wit, at the end of
the proem of the book.*

*As soon as he had sampled holy scripture he was delighted and overjoyed to
find in it not only true wisdom but also true eloquence. To pass over the many
encomia he bestowed on the New Testament, he said that Paul's epistles surpass
the writings of all orators in eloquence, specifically mentioning the lucubrations
even of Cicero and of Demosthenes himself, the prince of orators (as he called
him), not because Paul's writings, like those of the others, are prinked with
curling irons or layered with cosmetics scraped together and elegantly applied
everywhere, but because they breathe and savor of true and sound eloquence,
based with true art on true substance, and (to put it briefly) are unselfconsciously
crammed with the riches of the Egyptians. He also proclaimed that all the
declarations of the Old Testament are full of the most consummate knowledge
and wisdom. And although this point is clearly made by Augustine, among
others, in his book On Christian Instruction, and although Septimius Ter-
tullian, Eusebius Pamphili, and Cassiodorus affirm that all the ancient gram-
marians, rhetoricians, orators, and philosophers drank the draughts of their
eloquence and learning from the fountains of holy scripture, nevertheless Pico*

prosequebatur, quarum partem in heptapli celebratissimis exordiis inque ipso
secundae expositionis proemio videre operaeprecium est.

   Inter tot iuges divinae legis evolutiones, secundo anno ab heptapli editione
opusculum etiam de ente & uno decem capitibus distinctum absolvit, breue
5 *quidem corpore sed amplum viribus, sed altissimis & philosophorum dogmatis*
& theologicis sensibus undequaque respersum, quo superius ente non esse unum
sed sibi invicem respondere aequalique esse ambitu ostendit, controversiamque
super ea re a Platonis Aristotelisque sectatoribus habitam recensuit, asseverans
Academicos illos qui contrarium contenderunt verum Platonis dogma non asse-
10 *quutos, sensuumque prorsus communionem inter Aristotelem & Platonem de*
uno & ente, sicut & de reliquis in universum, etsi verba dissiderent, demons-
traturus erat non defuisse. Vltimo quoque operis capite totam disputationem ad
institutionem vitae & morum emendationem non minus ingeniose quam reli-
giose convertit. Adversum quod opus Antonius Faventinus, egregius alioquin
15 *philosophus, nonnulla quatuor epistolis obiectamenta protulit, quarum tribus*
ipse respondit, quartae vero, vel quia fideliter delata non fuit, vel quia ex
praescriptis responderi posse putavit, vel alia quapiam de causa quae iusta
tamen credenda est, mentionem (quod sciverim) non habuit. Cui nos postquam
decessit e vita, ne falsa vel latrandi maleuolis vel sinistri aliquid credendi
20 *rudibus praeberetur occasio, respondendi munus obivimus, illudque potissimum*
curavimus, ut ex praecedentibus ipsius sententiis fuisse magna ex parte respon-
sum monstraremus. Vidimus etiam nonnulla Platonica vernaculo sermone ab eo
digesta, in quibus multa ad priscorum theologiam enodandam facientia, multa
in aenigmatibus & scirpis abstrusa sapientum sensa reserantia, deprehendun-
25 *tur. Quae forsan maius otium nacti latina reddere tentabimus, ne tanti hominis*
supereminens doctrina hisce de rebus, maxime pervia quibusque vulgi ante ora
feratur.

   Hactenus de perfectis lucubrationibus, quas ante mortem emiserat, veluti
nuntios & anteambulones praeclarorum operum quae conceperat & pro-
30 *cudebat. Vetus enim testamentum interpretamenti iam facibus illuminarat, id*
ipsum muneris ut nouo praestaret accinctus, nec eos tantum quos litterae series
ferre poterat sensus protulerat, sed in his locis quae tres alios divinorum elo-
quiorum proprios latura fuerant superaedificabat. Graecisque & Hebraeis ex-
emplaribus nostrorum codicum discordes sententias conferebat, sed hoc po-
35 *tissimum in eius mente consitum fuit, hoc de universis propositis quae in*
commentandi genere conceperat altius insedit: ut aliorum dogmata non ad-
duceret, utpote quae iam haberentur, legerentur, noscerentur, sed sua prorsus

---

1 celebratissimis] celebratissimae *96 96+ 98 04 06 V-06/7*   23 in] *96 96+; om. 98 04*
06 V-06/7   33 fuerant] fuerat *96 98 04 06 V-06/7*, fuera/t *96+*

himself pursued the point with many other arguments, some of which are in the famous exordium of the Heptaplus and in the proem of its second exposition and will repay the effort of examining them.

Amidst such intensive and continuous examination of the divine law, in the second year after the publication of "Heptaplus" he also completed the opusculum "Being and Unity," divided into ten chapters. The body of the work is short, to be sure, but it is very powerful, everywhere replete with very profound philosophical teachings and theological insights. In this work he showed that unity is not superior to being but that they are coextensive and correspond equally to each other; and he traced the controversy on this point between the followers of Plato and those of Aristotle, asserting that those Academics who held the contrary view did not fully understand Plato's true teaching, and he would show that the complete agreement between Plato and Aristotle concerning unity and being, as on all other matters, could be established, even if their words differ. Moreover, in the last chapter of the work, he turned the whole discussion, with no less wit than religious devotion, to ethical instruction and the improvement of morals. Against this work Antonio Faventino, an outstanding philosopher in other respects, issued some objections in four epistles, to three of which Pico himself replied, but of the fourth he made no mention (as far as I know), either because it was not faithfully delivered to him, or because he thought it could be answered by what he had already written, or for some other reason, which we should assume was adequate. After he had departed from this life, I undertook the task of replying to it, lest those of ill will should falsely have an opportunity to carp or the uninformed might wrongly have an occasion to believe something was underhanded about it, and I was mainly concerned to show that it was mostly answered by what Pico himself had previously said. I also saw some Platonic material that he had assembled in the vernacular. It includes much that explicates the theology of the ancients, much that unfolds the meaning of wise men which has been drawn out into puzzles and knotty enigmas. Perhaps when I have more leisure, I will try to translate this into Latin, so that the superlative teaching of such a great man concerning these matters will not be completely open to everyone and exposed to the gaze of the masses.

So much for the discourses that he finished and published before his death, messengers and heralds, as it were, of the extraordinary works that he had conceived and was hammering out. For he had illuminated the Old Testament with the torches of a commentary. He was girded to perform the same task for the New Testament: and he had not only brought out the meaning which the literal events could bear but in these places he also added as a superstructure those points that would bring in the other three senses proper to holy scripture. In Greek and Hebrew copies he compared the places where the meaning disagrees with our codices. But this especially was his underlying intention, this was his most basic aim in all the commentaries he undertook: not to adduce the teachings of others, since they were already possessed, read, understood, but rather to

inventa & meditata dissereret, ut propriis, non alienis facultatibus famelicas
veritatis animas pro virili saturaret.

    Post haec Hebraico idiomate pollens, de veritate translationis Hieronymi
adversus Hebraeorum calumnias libellum edidit, necnon defensionem pro .lxx.
5 *interpretibus quantum ad psalmos attinet adversus eosdem. Libellum item de*
vera temporum supputatione conscripsit.

    Postremo ad debellandos septem hostes ecclesiae animum appulerat. Qui enim
nec Christo nec illius paret ecclesiae & (quod est sequens) eius est hostis, aut
impius existens nullum recipit credendum dogma; siue falsis inseruit idolis
10 *subque hisce simulacris demones adorat; seu Mosaicam perditissimorum*
Iudaeorum ritu legem colit; nefandumue Maomethem sequitur, detestandis il-
lius placitis mancipatus; aut christianam auditu tantum non operibus & mente
sincera vitam vivens euangelica documenta pervertit, Catholicaeque ecclesiae
non consentiens obstinato corde recalcitrat; vel non casta fide sed variis adulte-
15 *rata prophanataque superstitionibus evangelia suscipit; aut, licet solida nitida-*
que ac constanti fide receperit, operibus adversatur,—hos itaque septem, quasi
duces sub quibus reliqui velut gregarii continentur, propriis eorum armis con-
flicturus, ad congressum citaverat. Adversus impios philosophos, qui nullae
religionis iugo colla depressi nullique addicti numini naturales tantum rationes
20 *adorant, eisdem rationibus dimicabat. Veteris testamenti sententiis propriisque*
Iudaicae scholae auctoramentis validissime contra Hebraeos praeliabatur. Cum
Maumethanis, Alcorano nixus, pedem contulerat. Idolorum cultores & multis
vulneribus & ui non multa prostrauerat. Superstitionibus vanis irretitos, eos
praesertim qui divinatricem colunt astrologiam, & verae philosophiae & pecu-
25 *liaribus rationibus astrologorum acriter taxauerat, duodecimque iam libris, &*
quidem absolutissimis, ex tredecim ad hoc destinatis eorum deliria insectatus
fuerat. Demum hydromantiam, geomantiam, pyromantiam, haruspicinam, &
caetera id genus inania sigillatim explodere destinarat. Sed in prophetantes
astrologos cuneum ex professo direxerat totisque viribus arietem temperaverat,
30 *quando eorum dogmatis futilibus quidem & nullius momenti superstitiones*
caeterae suis erroribus fulcimenta aucupentur, vel inspectae geneseos momenta
trutinantes, vel in eligendis horis aut hexagonos aut trigonos aspectus (quos
benignos vocant) conciliantes, & eiusmodi reliqua, quibus nec insanus Orestes
accederet. Nec contentus astrologiam omnem funditus evertisse, ut ostenderet
35 *nostri temporis astrologis, graecae potissimum linguae ignaris, vanissimam*
omnium professionum astrologiam perversis translationibus vaniorem (si dici

---

4 .lxx.] *96 96+,* sexaginta *98 04 06,* septuaginta *V-06/7*   28 explodere destinarat]
V-06/7 (errata), exploserat *96 96+ 98 04 06 V-06/7 (text)*

discuss only what he himself had discovered and thought out, so that with his own talents, not those of others, he could nourish to the best of his ability souls hungry for truth.

After this, when he had become expert in Hebrew, he brought out a little book on the faithfulness of Jerome's translation, aimed at the calumnies of the Jews, and he also put forth against the same adversaries a defense of the Septuagint translation, insofar as it applies to the Psalms. He also wrote a little book about the accurate reckoning of chronology.

Afterwards he applied his mind to refuting the seven enemies of the church. For among those who do not obey either Christ or his church and consequently are hostile to it, one group wickedly refuses to believe any dogma. Another serves false idols and worships devils in the form of these images. Another cultivates the law of Moses in the manner of the most wicked Jews. Another follows the impious Mohammed and is enslaved by his detestable prescriptions. Another who lives a Christian life only by hearing about it and not by his works and genuine devotion perverts the teaching of the gospel and with obstinacy and recalcitrance opposes the Catholic church. Another does not accept the gospel with a pure faith but adulterates and profanes it with superstitions. Another, even though he accepts it with a sound, shining, and firm faith, counters it in his deeds. And so he challenges these seven to an encounter, the leaders, as it were, under whom the others are enlisted and grouped, intending to fight them with their own weapons. Against the impious philosophers who will not bend their necks under the yoke of religion or recognize any divinity but rather worship only natural reason, he fought with arguments also drawn from reason. He battled vigorously against the Jews, using passages from the Old Testament and their own authorities from the Hebrew scholarly tradition. He had faced up to the Mohammedans, relying on the Koran. He had laid low the worshipers of idols with many wounding blows and not much effort. Whoever is entangled in vain superstitions, especially those who cultivate judicial astrology, he had assailed sharply with the arguments of true philosophy and the arguments peculiar to the astrologers themselves, and in the twelve books he completely finished (of the thirteen to be devoted to this subject), he had assaulted their mad delusions. Finally he had set out to explode one by one divination by water or by geometric figures or fire or entrails and other such nonsense. But he had especially driven his phalanx against the astrologers who make predictions and aimed his battering ram at them with full force, since from their doctrines, futile and pointless as they are, other superstitions seek to find support for their errors, weighing the significance of sightings taken at birth or plotting triangular or hexagonal aspects (which they call favorable) for choosing times to do something, and all the rest of such things, which Orestes even in his madness never came to. And not content with completely overthrowing all of astrology, in order to show the astrologers of our times, who are mostly ignorant of the Greek language, that their astrology, the most empty of all professions, has been rendered even more empty (if that is possible) by

*potest) effectam, Ptolomaei fructus, quos Centiloquium vulgo nuncupant, inter
scribendum adversus eosdem quasi aliud agens e Graeco in Latinum sermonem
vertit, & elegantissima expositione honestauit. Quo in libro plura (ut ita dix-
erim) errata quam verba vulgata illa translatione contineri demonstrat, quam*

5   *tamen semper in arcanis veluti pretiosum thesaurum custodierunt eiusdem cul-
tores ignaui. De Christi fide perperam sentientes nec matris ecclesiae parentes
imperio, quos usitatiori vocabulo nominamus haereticos, & novo instrumento &
rationibus egregia obiurgatione incessiuerat. Nonaginta fere haereses in pro-
patulo habentur, verum ille cuncta rimatus ducentas inuenit, quas sigillatim*

10 *non modo eliminare & profligare proposuerat, sed & pariter docere qua ex parte
philosophiae non rite percepta suos errores traxissent aut furcillassent. In chris-
tianos postremo quorum fides sine operibus visitur vehementer inuectus fuerat,
necnon diligenter exploraverat qui fieri posset, ut ignem in meditullio terrae
constitutum homines credant, quo perpetuo datura sunt poenas damnatorum*

15 *corpora caeteraque id genus tam animae quam corporis inexcogitata supplicia,
immensa quoque deitatis visae gaudia quibus animae corporibus iunctae bean-
tur, atque dictis ecclesiae quae ad credendum compellunt obaudientes non sint,
& nihilominus passim debacchentur in vitia diuitiisque incumbant cumulandis,
nihilque minus formidetur ab eis quam poenae aut affectetur quam regnum dei.*

20 *Pro morborum item qualitate idoneam opem admovere tentabat, tetros scilicet
morbos & suapte natura impuros acribus acerbisque medicaminibus inurere, ea
vero vulnera quae minori infecta malitia depravataque forent cicatricemque
obducere desiderarent lenibus placabilibusque fovere, adeptis vero valitudinem
& recidiva metuentibus saluberrimas potiones celebrataque antidota preparare.*

25   *Multa alia opera fuerat exorsus quibus sperari poterat futurum, ut philoso-
phiae studia in universum eliminatis erroribus explosaque barbarie reflorerent.
Inter haec potissimim Platonis & Aristotelis numerabatur Concordia, quam iam
coeptam breui perfecturus erat si vita comes paucis adhuc annis superfuisset. Ita
enim philosophiam ab incunabilis lactando nutriverat & ad usque nostra tem-*

30 *pora perduxerat adultam, ut nostrae tempestatis philosopho nil amplius aut in
Graecis aut in Latinis aut in barbaris codicibus desiderandum esset. Citasset
udum Thaletem, ignitum Heraclitum, circumfusumque atomis Democritum;
Orpheus item & Pythagoras priscique alii eius ope & gratia in academiam
convenissent. Postremo philosophiae principes, Plato scilicet, fabularum vela-*

35 *mentis mathematicisque involucris constipatus, & Aristoteles, vallatus motibus,
dextera data fidem futurae amicitiae sanxissent. Inter Averroim quoque & Avi-
cennam, inter Thomam & Scotum, qui iam diu conflictaverant, si non pacem in*

---

17 non] 96 96+ 98 04 06 V-06/7, *but sense requires that it be omitted, and I have done so in the
translation. Or perhaps* inobaudientes non *is the correct reading.*   36 sanxissent]
V-06/7 *(errata),* sanxisset 96 96+ 98 04 06 V-06/7 *(text)*

wrongheaded translations, he translated from Greek into Latin the work of Ptolemy called Centiloquium, working it in by the by as he wrote against them and clearing its reputation by a very elegant exposition of it. He shows that the current translation of that book contains more errors than words (so to speak), although its lazy devotees have always kept it hidden away in secret places as if it were a precious treasure. Those who have wrong opinions about the faith of Christ and refuse to obey the authority of our holy mother the church, to whom we usually apply the term heretic, he had assailed and upbraided with remarkable force, using both the New Testament and arguments drawn from reason. Almost 90 heresies are commonly recognized, but by close scrutiny he found 200, which he had set out not only to eradicate and put to flight one after the other, but also to show from which part of philosophy, wrongly understood, they derive and prop up their errors. Finally, he had vehemently attacked Christians whose faith is clearly without works and had diligently explored how it can be that they believe in the fire that has been placed in the bowels of the earth, where the bodies of the damned will be punished forever, and believe in other such unimaginable afflictions of both soul and body, and also in the immense joy of the beatific vision that blesses bodies and souls joined together, and obediently accept the pronouncements of the church about what must be believed, and nevertheless lead utterly dissolute lives, obsessed with heaping up riches, fearing anything but the pains of hell and striving for anything but the kingdom of God. Likewise, for every kind of disease he tried to provide a suitable remedy: namely, to use sharp and bitter remedies to burn out grave and inherently corrupt diseases, but to treat with lighter and less drastic medications those wounds which are not so maliciously infected or depraved and which tend to form a healthy scar, and also to prepare very healthful potions and renowned antidotes for those who have regained their health but fear a recurrence of the disease.

He had undertaken many other works that he hoped would revitalize philosophical studies by turning all errors out of doors and hissing barbarism off the stage. Chief among the number of these was the Reconciliation of Plato and Aristotle, which he had already begun and would shortly have finished if a few more years of life had remained to him. For he had suckled and nourished philosophy from its infancy and had brought it to maturity in our own times, so that a philosopher of our era would have had to seek no further in the Greek or Latin or barbarian codices. He would have called up Thales soaked with water, Heraclitus burning with fire, and Democritus surrounded by atoms; Orpheus likewise, and Pythagoras, and the other ancients, with his help and on his behalf, would have gathered in the academy. Finally the princes of philosophy, namely Plato, swathed in his myths and attended by mathematical involutions, and Aristotle, walled in by motions, would have shaken hands as a sign of future friendship. Moreover, between Averroes and Avicenna, between Thomas and Scotus, who have fought for so long, he would have obtained, if not total peace, at

universum, in multis tamen impetrasset inducias, quando in eorum pluribus
controversiis, si quispiam dissidentia verba rimetur attentius & exactius libret,
scrupulosiusque vestigans, cutem deserens, introrsum ad imas latebras profun-
daque penetralia mente pervadat, unionem sensuum in disseparatis pugnan-
5 *tibusque verbis citra ambiguitatem comperiet. Neotericorum turba, partim pro*
meritis partim pro culpis, & honorata fuisset & taxata. Totus igitur deo dicatus
ecclesiam quibus poterat armis defendebat, atque latitantem (ut aiunt) e De-
mocriti puteo veritatem educebat, & ignorantiae gramen inexpugnabile, quo
multorum mentes prefocantur, subnascentesque pernitiosas herbas abrumpebat
10 *penitus & detruncabat. Sed mors adveniens tot tantarumque vigiliarum la-*
borem & excultae lucubrationis partum inanem fere reddidit, hocque potis-
simum fuit in causa, ut plurimas, quamquam magna ex parte exasciatas &
dedolatas, imperfectas commentationes dereliquerit, quod scilicet sibi ipsi tan-
tum, non autem nobis scribebat. Nam sicut celeri in commentando ingenio, ita
15 *veloci in scribendo manu fuit, et cum antea pulcherrimos litterarum characteres*
deliniaret, factum erat, ut ex usu nimiae in commentando velocitatis vix eorum
quae exarabat capax existeret. Huc etiam & illuc scribere solitus erat, vetusta
interdum supervenientibus novis oblitterans. Ea propter exoleta quaedam &
20 *dispuncta repperi, quaedam saltim & vellicatim exarata, omnia denique adeo*
confusa & inordinata ut sylvae aut farragines putarentur. Ex libro septemplici
quem adversus hostes ecclesiae praetitulaverat, pars illa quae divinaculos astro-
logos genethliacosque potissimum insectatur ab incude (ut dici solet) ad limam
perducta fuit, quam non parvo tamen labore nec mediocri cura ab exemplari
25 *liturato et pene discerpto deprompsimus. Quo in opere summum philosophum,*
summum theologum, summum oratorem, acerrimum Christi ecclesiae propug-
natorem, incomparabili praeditum ingenio, quod in cunctis ipsius commenta-
tionibus cernitur, se demonstrat. Quaedam item minutula, non tornata adhuc,
apud me comperi: interpretationem dumtaxat dominicae orationis, regulasque
30 *bene viuendi circiter quinquaginta, breves profecto nimis & inexplicitas, quas in*
multa capita si vixisset deducturus omnino fuerat. Duas quoque ad deum depre-
catorias, quarum unam rhythmis Hetruscis, elegiaco metro alteram, qua gravi-
oribus defatigatum quandoque studiis animum cantando ad lyram mulcere
posset, composuerat. Primis enim adolescentiae annis genus omne musicae artis
35 *adeo excoluerat, ut excogitata per ipsum modulamina notataeque debitis concen-*
tibus harmoniae celebres haberentur. Plurima quoque in eius scriniis quanquam
inordinata pervidimus, ex quibus tamen utile aliquid, praesertim psalmorum
enarrationem, compilari posse putaverim. Sed & epistolae circiter .l. diversis
editae temporibus, tum familiares, tum doctrinales, tum adhortatoriae emersere,

least a truce on many points, since in most of their controversies, if one examines very closely the words of their disagreements and weighs them very carefully, and if one investigates them in minute details, mentally penetrating beyond the skin to the hidden depths within and the farthest inner recesses, he will undoubtedly find an agreement in meaning behind the disparate and conflicting words. He would have honored or censured the crowd of modern philosophers according to their merits or their faults. And thus in his complete devotion to God he defended the church with all the weapons at his disposal, and he drew up the truth hidden in the well of Democritus (as they say), and he tore out and completely extirpated the deadly creeping shoots and the impenetrable underbrush of ignorance, in which the minds of many have suffocated. But the arrival of death made all but vain the labors of so many nights of intensive study and thwarted the birth of such exquisite lucubration, and the main reason why he left behind so many intellectual undertakings which were laid out and rough-hewn but not completed is this: that he wrote for himself alone but not, however, for us. For just as his mind was quick in thinking things through, so his hand was swift in writing them down. And whereas in his early years his handwriting was beautifully formed, it happened that as his thought processes became extremely swift, he was hardly able to keep up with what he had worked out. For he ordinarily wrote helter-skelter, crossing out the old version and substituting something new. For that reason I found some things reworked and deleted, some things sketchily and fleetingly worked out, and in the end everything so confused and disordered that it seemed like a medley or miscellany. Of the seven-part book to which he had given the preliminary title "Against the Enemies of the Church," the part which mainly attacked the judicial astrologers and casters of horoscopes had been carried through from the anvil to the file (as they say), and yet I have brought it forth, with no small labor and more than a modicum of effort, from a blotted and almost shredded copy. In this work he shows himself to be a consummate philosopher, a consummate theologian, a consummate orator, a very acute defender of the church of Christ, furnished (as can be seen in all his intellectual endeavors) with an incomparable intellect. Likewise I found in my possession some very short pieces, not completely rounded out: a bare interpretation of the Lord's Prayer and about fifty rules for living well, extremely brief and undeveloped, which he would have drawn out, to be sure, into many chapters had he lived. Also he composed two prayers begging mercy from God, one in Italian verse, the other in elegiac meter; by singing these with a lute accompaniment, he could sometimes soothe his mind when it was worn out by serious study. For from the early years of his youth he cultivated all kinds of musical composition so well that melodies he composed, with the harmonies marked for a suitable accompaniment, became famous. In his writing chests I also looked through some other disordered material from which I would think something useful might be compiled, especially a commentary on the Psalms. Moreover, about fifty epistles, written at various times, some personal, some instructional, some hortatory, turned up, together

una cum oratione quam Romae, si disputare contigisset, habiturus fuerat: quae
non tam iuvenis quartum & vigesimum annum nondum nati perspicacissimum
ingenium & doctrinam uberrimam redolet (quod & cunctae ipsius scriptiones
faciunt) quam fertilissimae ipsius eloquentiae locupletissimum nobis testimo-
5   *nium praebet.*

   Stilo quidem valde probando usus est semper, non ascito sed ingenuo, multi-
formi etiam pro rerum varietate, qui etsi totum (ut aiunt) Isocratis myrothecion
consumpserit, munditiae tamen & decorae maiestatis ornamenta servauit. Nam
et celebrata illa dicendi genera, quorum tria Gellius, Macrobius quattuor enar-
10 *rat, ex commentationibus ipsius nec impendio colliguntur. Ibi copiosum in quo*
Cicero dominari fertur, breve quod Salustio ascribitur, siccum Frontoni datum,
pingue & floridum in quo Plinium & Symmachum lascivisse prodiderunt. At
forte copiam hanc Brutus non vocasset elumbem nec Salustius immoderatam.
Siccitatem quoque Frontonis humectatam, Salustii brevitatem elongatam, flori-
15 *dam pinguedinem Plinii latiori in campo deportatam non difficile recto iudicio*
orator deprehendet. Adde his Livii lacteum fontem forte sine Patavinitate (ut ille
inquit), adiectis flosculis plurimis Apulei. Verum non hic in mutuata a Graecis
philosophia se exercuit, non in Atticis noctibus, non in fictis saturnalibus ad
laudandam prope Vergilii Aeneidem fabricatis, non in Romana historia, non in
20 *mera historia naturae altissimis difficilibusque speculatibus vacua, sed in ad-*
miranda illa mundi fabrica, in incessendis sacrosanctae catholicae ecclesiae
hostibus desudavit, in eliminandis astrologis fatigatus est, in theologicis quaes-
tionibus excutiendis, in Aristotelis & Platonis concordia laboravit, in enar-
randa sacra eloquia incubuit, in commonendis & adhortandis amicis navavit
25 *operam. Verum hanc de qua agimus eloquentiam tantum aberat, ut affectaret, ut*
eos potius damnaret qui pigmentata lenocinia scrupulosius exquirentes omnes
ingenii vires in vestigandis vocabulorum originibus accommodabant. Quae
omnia plurimos eo propensius in eius admirationem convertere, quod inter
eorum litteras diu & propensissime versatus esset qui latinas litteras eloquentiae
30 *floribus refertas non sunt professi. Patiantur haec aequo animo nimii antiqui-*
tatis amatores, nam haec etsi concisius compendiosiusque tamen eo forte verius,
quo me doctiores & Hermolaus Barbarus & Baptista Carmelita & Marsilius
Ficinus & Matheus Bossus & plerique alii doctissimi & eloquentissimi viri
prodidere.

35 Bibliothecas amplas, tam Latinorum quam Graecorum incredibili
celeritate & perlegit & excerpsit, *nullasque (si modo facultas data) commen-*
tationes illectas praeteriit. De priscis ecclesiae doctoribus tantum cogni-
tionis adeptus fuerat quantum credere difficile est, etiam in eo qui in

with an oration that he would have delivered at Rome if the disputation had taken place. Written when he was a youth not yet twenty-four years of age, it is not only instinct with brilliant intelligence and abundant learning (as indeed all his writings are) but it also gives very abundant evidence of the great riches of his eloquence.

Certainly the style he employed was always most worthy of approval, not farfetched but natural, also quite varied according to his subject matter; even if he used up the whole ointment box of Isocrates (as they say), he still kept his ornamentation within a fitting combination of neatness and majesty. For those famous levels of style (which Gellius discussed under three headings, Macrobius under four) are easily discoverable in his treatises. There we find the copious style in which Cicero is said to be dominant, the pithy style which is attributed to Sallust, the dry style assigned to Fronto, the lavish and florid style in which, according to ancient tradition, Pliny and Symmachus indulged. But perhaps Brutus would not have called this copiousness of Pico spineless, nor would Sallust have called it immoderate. An orator of good judgment will also easily discern that Fronto's dryness has been moistened, Sallust's pithiness has been expanded, the floral lavishness of Pliny has been spread out on a wider landscape. To these add Livy's fountain of milk, perhaps without his Patavianism (as he called it) and throw in also many of the flowerets of Apuleius. But Pico did not indulge in philosophical exercises borrowed from the Greeks, not in Attic nights, not in imagined Saturnalia made up more or less to praise Virgil's Aeneid, nor in Roman history, nor in mere natural history devoid of profound difficulties and insights, but rather he labored mightily in wonderment at the structure of the universe and in assault against the enemies of the holy Catholic church; he wore himself out in driving away the astrologers; he worked at sifting through theological questions, at reconciling Plato and Aristotle; he devoted himself to explaining holy scripture; he assisted his friends with advice and exhortation. But this eloquence of his that we are discussing was so far from being affected that he condemned those who overanxiously seek out painted and meretricious ornaments and apply all their energies to tracing out precedents for diction. All of this caused many to admire him all the more readily because he was for a long time very much taken up with writers who made no claims to a style replete with the flowers of eloquence. In saying these things I hope that those who love antiquity only too well will bear with me, for although these ideas of mine are put rather concisely and briefly, yet they may well be the truer for all that, being what those more learned than I, such as Hermolao Barbaro and Baptista Mantuano and Marsilio Ficino and Matteo Bosso and many other most learned and eloquent men, have published about him.

He perused and excerpted whole libraries of Latin and Greek books with incredible speed *and left unread no treatises to which he had access.* He had acquired so much knowledge of the ancient fathers of the church that it would be hard to believe, even of a person who had spent his

ipsis solum evolvendis totum vitae tempus consumpsisset. De neotericis
vero theologis, qui eo stilo sunt usi quem Parisiensem vulgo nuncu-
pant, tantum iudicii apud eum residebat *ut si quis ex improviso abstrusam*
illorum cuiuspiam maleque explicitam quaestionem enucleandam petiisset,
5   tanta ingenii fertilitate adaperiebat, tanta solertia reserabat, ut diceres
doctoris illius universa dicta prae oculis & *innumerato* habuisse, *cunctas-*
que pari modo familias agnoverat, cunctas schedas excusserat, nec uni illorum
sic addictum credas (qui nostris hominibus mos est) ut caeteros aspernaretur.
Ipse enim a teneris sic institutus fuit, sic animatus, ut in illis veritatem quaereret
10 *parique honore, quousque illa elucesceret inventa, quoscunque veneraretur,*
priuata affectione nudatus. Quid tamen de singulis sentiret qui in universum
famosiores habentur, in Apologiae proemio, cum de barbaris, Graecis, Latinis-
que philosophis proprietates peculiaresque laudes retulerit, videre datur.
Thomam vero Aquinatem, quando inter loquendum de his philoso-
15 phis theologisue qui gallico more disceptando scripsere mentio fieret,
prae omnibus laudare consueverat, utpote solidiori prae aliis veritatis
basi nitentem. *Eum quoque in heptaplo nostrae theologiae splendorem nomi-*
nat. De hoc percunctatus creberrime, & a me ipso, idem respondit. Nec oppo-
situm suadere cuiquam debent nonnulla quae in eius apologetico continentur
20 *disputanda, alioquin Thomae opinionibus ex professo adversantia, cum iuvenis*
admodum esset gloriaeque tunc cupidus in urbe celebratissima, Gorgiae Leon-
tini more, quascunque tutando partes, famam aucuparetur. Adde quod ex decem
millibus propositionum tribus tantum aut quatuor non consentire, sed & adver-
sari id non convincunt.
25 Disceptandi porro peritissimus fuit frequentemque & impensis-
simam operam litterariis agonibus, dum ferveret animus, impendit. *Eo*
obiectante facile Scoti acumen & vigilantiam, Francisci acrimoniam, copiam &
multitudinem Aureoli deprehendere potuisses, nec deesse nodos illos, multi-
plicibus flexionibus complicitos nec tam titillantibus argutiis quam gravitate
30 *subnixos. Eo respondente Thomae fortitudinem & robur, Alberti amplitudinem*
conspexisses. Verum his conflictibus nuntium pridem remiserat: &
magis atque magis id muneris in dies perosus fuerat adeoque detrac-
tabat, ut Herculi Estensi Ferrariensium Duci & internunciis et se ipso
enixissime postulanti, ut dum generalis Praedicatorum fratrum syno-
35 dus Ferrariae celebraretur, disceptare non aegre ferret, diu obsequi
reluctatus fuerit, multis tamen rogatibus annuens principi illi, cuius
amor in ipsum non mediocris exstiterat, morem gessit. Vnde datum est

---

8 addictum] *96 98 04 06 V-06/7*, adiectum *96+*   22 partes] partis *96 96+ 98 04 06*
V-06/7

whole lifetime in studying nothing else. As for modern theologians who follow the style commonly called Parisian, he had such a deep discernment about them *that if someone asked him to explicate extemporaneously an abstruse, unqualified question posed by one of them,* he laid it bare with such intellectual amplitude, he opened it up with such adroitness that you would say he had before his very eyes *and ready at hand* all the sayings of that theologian, *and he knew all the branches equally well, he had investigated all their papers, nor would you think that he was so committed to any one of them as to scorn the others (as is the custom nowadays). For in accord with his earliest education and his own inclination, he sought truth in them too, and once it was found, he venerated its source with the same reverence, wherever it might shine from, without any personal preferences. As for what he thought about the individual scholastics who are generally better known, it can be seen in the preface of his Apology, where he gives the special qualities and merits of barbarian, Greek, and Latin philosophers.*

But whenever in the course of conversation these philosophers *or theologians* who dispute in the French manner were mentioned, he regularly praised Thomas Aquinas above all the others as more solidly based than the others on a foundation of truth. *In the Heptaptlus he also calls him the splendor of our theology. He was frequently asked about him, also by me, and he always made the same reply. Nor should anyone be persuaded of the contrary by some of the disputatious matter in his Apology, which in other respects professedly opposes the opinions of Thomas, since he was still young then and eager for glory and was pursuing fame in the most illustrious city by defending either side of an argument in the manner of Gorgias of Leontini. Moreover, out of thousands of propositions they show that he disagreed with only three or four, but they do not prove that this amounts to opposition.*

Then, too, he was very skilled in disputation, and while his temperament was still fiery he expended an enormous amount of effort in scholarly contests. *When he was making objections, you could have easily discerned the sharpness and vigilance of Scotus, the keenness of Franciscus, the amplitude and multiplicity of Aureolus, nor would you have noted any deficiency in those knotty points, tied together with many twists and turns, but relying not so much on titillating subtleties as on weighty substance. When he replied to objections, you could have seen the vigor and strength of Thomas, the amplitude of Albert.* But he had long ago turned his back on such conflicts, and day by day he grew to hate this employment more and more, and he rejected it to such a degree that when Ercole d'Este, the duke of Ferrara, most earnestly requested, both through intermediaries and in person, that he condescend to enter into disputation at the general chapter of the Dominicans, which was to be held in Ferrara, for a long time he refused to comply, but finally he agreed, yielding to the many entreaties of that prince, whose love for him was by no means small. On

ambigi solertiorne an eloquentior, doctior an humanior appareret. *Ex
ore quidem disceptantis talis semper animi patebat alacritas ut de re comi &
placida potius quam subacida & difficili altercari videretur,* quapropter qui
ab ore pendebant audientes in mirum eius amorem excitabantur. Sed
5   frequens ei adagium inerat, munus id esse dialectici, non philosophi.
Aiebat item eas disputationes prodesse, quae placido animo ad ves-
tigandam perquirendamque veritatem priuatis in locis semotisque ar-
bitris exercebantur, at illas obesse plurimum, quae in propatulo fie-
bant, ad ostentandam doctrinam vel ad captandam vulgi auram atque
10 imperitorum applausum, vixque posse fieri omnino censebat, ut hono-
ris cupidini, qua frontiuagi illi disputatores exagitantur, inseparabili
vinculo annexum non sit illius cum quo disputatur desiderium infa-
miae confusionisque, letale vulnus animae venenumque charitatis mor-
tiferum. Latuit eum nihil omnino quod pertineret ad captiunculas
15 cavillasque sophistarum *& Suiseticas quisquilias quae calculationes vocan-
tur; hae mathematicae commentationes sunt, subtilioribusne dixerim an mo-
rosioribus excogitationibus naturalibus applicatae. Verum etsi in eis esset eru-
ditus ac eiusmodi scriptiones legisset quas forte ad plenum non novit Italia
(nulla enim tam invia & inaccessa litterarum reperiri poterant quae illius
20 vestigio lustrata abunde explorataque non essent)* odisse tamen & detestari
videbatur, valere *meo iudicio* earum communem usum animadvertens,
ad sociorum parandam infamiam *labefactandamque in replicando memo-
riam,* veritati vero inueniendae, cui indefessam operam navandam arbi-
trabatur, aut nihil aut parum conducere.
25   Sed ne plura consecter lectoremque detineam, comprehendam
brevi. Enituit aliquis eloquentia, sed inscitia rerum naturae secretarum
dehonestatus est. Alius peregrinas linguas, sed universa philoso-
phorum decreta non calluit. Priscorum alius inventa perlegit, non nova
dogmata concinnavit. Scientiae ab altero hominum tantum & humanae
30 gloriae causa, non christianae rei publicae emolumento, & divinae &
humanae, quaesitae sunt. Ille vero cuncta haec pari studio ita com-
plexus fuerat ut turmatim & coacervatim in eum confluxisse videren-
tur, nec ut multi qui non aliquo uno excellentes omnium participes
sunt, sed in omnibus usqueadeo profecerat scientiis, ut quamlibet ex
35 his in ipso considerasses, eam sibi propriam & peculiarem elegisse

---

12 annexum] annexus *96 96+ 98 04 06 V-06/7*   20 explorataque] *V-06/7 (errata),*
explorata *96 96+ 98 04 06 V-06/7 (text)*

that occasion one could wonder whether he showed more quickness or eloquence, more learning or kindness. *When he disputed, his countenance revealed such a cheerful mind that he seemed to be debating about some friendly and peaceful matter, not a somewhat rancorous and difficult point.* Consequently the audience, which hung on his every word, was wonderfully moved to love him. He frequently referred to the proverb that this is the function of a dialectician, not a philosopher. He also used to say that the only profitable disputations were those conducted privately and without spectators, with a peaceful frame of mind and for the sake of tracking down and seeking out the truth, but that much harm is done by disputations held openly in order to make a display of learning and to catch at the favor of the mob and the applause of the ignorant; and he thought it hardly possible at all to prevent the eager pursuit of honor, which motivates these boldly bobbling disputers, from being inextricably linked with a desire to disgrace and confound their opponents, a deadly wound to the soul and a lethal poison to charity. Nothing at all escaped him of the deceptive fallacies and cavils of the sophists *or of the Swinesheadical swill called "calculations" (mathematical contrivances applied to speculations about natural science—it would be hard to say whether they are more subtle or more captious). But though he was expert in these matters and had read more of such writings perhaps than is fully known in all of Italy (for no treatises could be so out of the way or inaccessible that he did not track them down and explore them thoroughly),* nevertheless it was apparent that he clearly hated and detested them, noting (*in my judgment*) that as they are commonly used they serve only to ruin the reputations of colleagues *and to wear down the memory by responses,* but that they contribute little or nothing to the discovery of truth, to which he thought our energies should be indefatigably devoted.

But so as to detain the reader no longer by pursuing these matters further, I will sum up briefly. One person has shone in eloquence but has been disgraced by ignorance of the secrets of nature. Another has excelled in foreign languages but not in all the doctrines of the philosophers. Another was very well read in the discoveries of the ancients but inept in assimilating modern doctrines. Another has pursued learning, both human and divine, merely to gain the favor of men and for the sake of human glory, not in order to benefit the Christian community. But he had embraced all these pursuits with equal eagerness, so much so that they seemed to flow together and to be mustered around him and heaped upon him, and that not as happens with many who excel in no one branch of learning but know something of all of them, but rather he had become so proficient in all branches that, whichever one you might have considered, you would have concluded that he had singled it out as his own special area. Moreover, this was all the more

iudicavisses. Haec quoque eo admirabiliora erant, cum a se ipso vi ingenii & ueritatis amore quasi absque praeceptore assequutus esset, ut quasi de ipso illud quod de se dicebat Epicurus possimus proferre: se sibi ipsum scilicet fuisse magistrum.

5   Ad quos mirabiles effectus tam parvo temporis spatio producendos, quinque ego causas convenisse repperi: incredibile ingenium; tenacissimam memoriam; facultates amplas, quibus ad coemendos tum nostrae tum graecae tum barbarae linguae libros adiutus est (septem quippe aureorum nummum milia *rettulisse mihi memoria repeto* in asciscendis sibi *usque ad diem illam* omnifariae litteraturae voluminibus erogasse); iuge & infatigabile studium; contemptionem postremo terrenarum rerum. *Hunc igitur si prisca illa aetas Laconum tempore protulisset, si Aristoteli credimus, divinum illum virum appellauisset.*

   Sed virtutes intellectus iam (*ut arbitror*) relinquendae videntur, &
15 nunc praeclarae eius animae partes quae actiones spectant prosequendae, exactissimique mores in publicum educendi sunt, ut flammatus ipsius in deum animus innotescat, ut erogatae in egenos divitiae collaudentur, ut his *qui tandem divinae legi sunt addicti* referendi gratias in bonorum omnium auctorem quam cumulatissime paretur occasio.

20   Triennio igitur priusquam diem obiret, ut posthabitis dominandi curis in alta pace degere posset, securus quo sceptra caderent, cuncta patrimonia quae Mirandulae Concordiaeque possidebat, hoc est tertiam partem earum, mihi nescio an dono an venditione tradidit. *Quod factum postea Maximilianus Augustus, qui nobis est rex & dominus (ut ita*
25 *dixerim) immediatus (neque enim alium tot saeculis quot est exaedificata Mirandula atque Concordia nisi qui successive in regali imperialive Romanorum throno consideret recognovimus) caesarea liberalitate firmauit.* Quicquid autem ex hoc negotio pecuniarum acceperat partim pauperibus elargitus est, partim in emendis agris unde & ipse & eius familiares alerentur
30 exposuit, *nominatimque Corbulas in agro Ferrariensi multis aureorum milibus nummum* sibi comparauerat. Multa itidem vasa argentea preciosasque supellectilis partes in pauperum usus distribuit. Mensa mediocri contentus fuit, retinente tamen nonnihil lautitiae prioris quantum ad fercula & ad vasa argentea pertineret. Diebus singulis preces ad deum
35 suis horis effundebat. Pauperibus semper, si qui occurrerant, pecunias tribuebat; nec eo contentus, Hieronymo Beniuenio civi Florentino litterato homini, quem pro magna in ipsum charitate proque morum integritate dilexit plurimum, demandaverat ut propriis pecuniis semper subveniret egenis, nuptum quoque virgines traderet, eique statim,
40 ut erogatos nummos quam primum restituere posset, renuntiaret. Id

---

25 alium] *V-o6/7 (errata)*, alium ut *96 96 + 98 04 06 V-o6/6*   33 lautitiae] *96 96 + 98 04 V-o6/7*, laetitiae *06*

amazing in that he achieved it on his own by the power of his intellect and his love of truth, without any mentor (as it were), so that in some fashion we could apply to him what Epicurus said of himself: namely, that he was his own teacher.

Five causes I have discovered that combined to enable him to achieve such marvelous results in such a short period of time: incredible intelligence; a most retentive memory; ample financial resources, which helped him to buy books in Latin, Greek, and barbarous languages (*for I remember he once told me that up to that day* he had spent 7,000 gold coins in acquiring volumes on all sorts of subjects); continuous and indefatigable study; and finally, contempt for earthly affairs. *If such a man as this had lived in the time of the ancient Spartans, they would have called him, if we may believe Aristotle, a god-man.*

But it is time, *I think*, to leave behind us the excellencies of his mind; and now I must pursue the splendid qualities of his soul that pertain to deeds, and I must make public the most finished virtues of his character so that his fiery devotion to God may shine forth, so that he may be extolled for the riches he distributed to the poor, and finally, so that *those who are devoted to the law of God* may have very ample occasion to offer thanks to the source of all good things.

And so, three years before he died, in order to put aside the cares of governance and to live his life in full peace and quiet, with no concern about where the scepters of power might land, he handed over to me— it would be hard to say whether by sale or by gift—all of his patrimony in Mirandula and Concordia, that is to say, one third of those estates. *This action was afterwards confirmed with imperial generosity by Emperor Maximilian, who is our king and (so to speak) immediate lord (for during all the centuries since the founding of Mirandula and Concordia we have never recognized anyone who did not sit by succession on the royal and imperial throne of the Romans).* Whatever money he received from this transaction he partly donated to the poor, partly used to buy lands to support himself and his household, *and specifically he paid many thousands of gold coins for Corbola in the territory of Ferrara.* He also distributed much silver plate and valuable household furnishings for the support of the poor. He was content with a moderate table, retaining, nevertheless, something of the former elegance of his silver plate and the courses of his meals. Every day at his fixed hours he poured forth his prayers to God. To poor people, if he encountered any, he always gave money. And not content with that, he required that Girolamo Benivieni, a well-read citizen of Florence for whom he had great affection because of his moral integrity and his great charity toward himself, should always help the poor and provide dowries for virgins with his own money, and should immediately inform him of what he had spent so that he could

enim muneris ei delegaverat, quo facilius, veluti fido internuntio, pau-
perum civium calamitates & miserias quae ipsum latuissent relevare
quiret.

Dedit & saepius (quod silentio praetereundum non puto) de corpore
5   proprio elemosynas. Scimus plerosque (ut verbis utar Hieronymi) por-
rexisse egentibus manum, sed carnis voluptate & illecebris superatos.
At ipse propriam carnem, diebus illis potissimum qui Christi cruciatus
& mortem nostrae salutis gratia representant, in summi illius beneficii
memoriam delictorumque expiationem caedebat, *meisque oculis saepius*
10 *(cuncta in dei gloriam redeant) flagellum vidi.*

Vultu hilari semper erat & placido adeoque miti natura ut nunquam
se fuisse turbatum *multis etiam audientibus testatus sit.* Recolo mihi inter
loquendum dixisse, in nullum eventum (ut res pessime cederent) ira
commoueri posse credere, nisi scrinia quaedam deperirent quibus elu-
15 cubrationes eius & vigiliae reconditae stipabantur, sed cum animadver-
teret pro deo optimo maximo eiusque ecclesia laborare eisdemque om-
nia opera, studia, actionesque dedicavisse & id fieri minime posse nisi
aut eo iubente aut permittente, confidebat se non contristatum iri. O
felicem mentem, quae iam nullis posset adversis deprimi, nullis quoque
20 commodis (*ut palam fiet*) extolli! Non illum certe universae philosophiae
peritia, non Hebraeae non Chaldaeae Arabicaeque linguae (ultra La-
tinam & Graecam) cognitio tumidum reddiderant. Non amplae di-
uitiae, non generis nobilitas inflauerant, non corporis pulchritudo &
elegantia, non magna peccandi licentia in mollem illam & spatiosam
25 multorum viam revocare poterant. Quid igitur poterat esse tam admi-
rabile quod illius quiret mentem pervertere? Quid (*inquam*) supra illum
esse poterat, qui (ut verbis Senecae utar) supra fortunam erat, cum
illam, sive secundis flatibus tumidam sive adversis reflatibus humilem,
aliquando contempserit, ut eius mens Christo & supernae patriae ciui-
30 bus spiritali glutino copuletur.

Quod vel hoc argumento liquido percipitur: quod dum ecclesiae officia &
dignitates, a plerisque nostri temporis (proh dolor!) licitatas aucti-
onatasque, non paucos videret expetere, flagitare, suspirare, enix-
issime mercari, ipse a duobus regibus *per internuntios oblatas (testes adsunt*
35 *gravissimi, testis ego) se sacris initiari nolle respondens* repudiavit; alter vero
quidam, cum saeculi dignitates & amplos reditus se daturum spon-

repay him. He delegated this responsibility to him so that he could more easily, through a faithful intermediary, alleviate the calamities and miseries of poor citizens which might be unknown to himself.

Also (and I think this should not be passed over in silence) he frequently gave alms out of his own body. We know of many who (to use the words of Jerome) have extended their hands to the poor but have been overcome by the pleasures and allurements of the flesh. But he himself, especially on those days which bring before us the suffering and death that Christ endured for our salvation, beat his own flesh in memory of that boundless benefit and in expiation for his sins (*and with my own eyes—may all redound to the glory of God!—I have often seen the whip*).

His countenance was always cheerful and peaceful, and by temperament he was so gentle *that he testified, in the hearing of many persons,* that he had never been upset. I recall that in a conversation with me he once said that, no matter how badly things might turn out, he did not believe he could be moved to anger, unless some of the boxes in which the lucubrations and fruits of his nightly studies were packed up and stored should be destroyed; but when he considered that he labored for almighty God and his church and had devoted to them all his works, studies, and actions, and that such a thing clearly could not occur without either the decree or the permission of God, he trusted he would not be saddened by it. O blessed mind, which could no longer be cast down by any adversity nor (as will become clear) be elated by any prosperity! Certainly he had not become proud because of all his philosophical learning or his knowledge of Hebrew, Chaldean, and Arabic (besides Latin and Greek). His abundant riches and noble birth had not puffed him up; the beauty and elegance of his body, the ample opportunities he had to commit sins had not called him back to that broad highway of self-indulgence trodden by the many. What could be so marvelous that it could pervert his mind? What, *I say,* could be beyond him who was (to use Seneca's words) beyond Fortune, since he scorned her in any case, whether her sail was swollen with favorable winds or drooping in the counterblasts of adversity, so that his mind might be spiritually linked and fused with Christ and the citizens of our heavenly homeland?

That this was so can be clearly seen from the following evidence. While he was aware that not a few seek out, solicit, long for, zealously purchase ecclesiastical offices and dignities, which nowadays are often enough (alas and alack!) bought and sold to the highest bidder, he himself refused such offices when they were offered to him *by two kings through their intermediaries, replying that he did not wish to enter into holy orders (to this there are very reliable witnesses, and I myself witnessed it also).* When another person promised that he would give him secular dignities and ample

disset si regem eius adiret, *conspicatus angulum non relinqui in quem se conderet ademptaque esse cuncta suffugia,* tale illi dedit responsum, ut intelligeret se non dignitates aut divitias expetere, sed potius, ut deo & studiis vacare posset, illas neglegisse. *Ferrariae quoque cum ex amicis*
5 *quidam Pandulpho Collenutio Pisaurensi, iurisconsulto, perspicacis ingenii viro, et multifariae lectionis quo amico familiarissime utebatur, suassissent, ut eum adduceret quibuscunque rationibus posset ad cardinalatus dignitatem petendam, vel certe si eam pontifex offerret (quod multis futurum videbatur) amplectendam, idque Pandulphus subhaesitans pertentasset (quippe qui non*
10 *ignarus esset omnia illum malle quam huiusmodi honoribus commisceri), ipse, qua erat animi magnitudine, responderi protinus propheticum illud per epistolam iussit "non sunt cogitationes meae cogitationes vestrae,"* contemplans *forte de bonis ecclesiae, quorum pars maxima pauperibus hereditario iure debetur, magnificos ducere apparatus non oportere. Sanctissimorum item homi-*
15 *num exempla ante oculos posita (Ambrosii scilicet, Augustini, Martini, caeterorumque) qui episcopatus dignitatem oblatam effugerunt diuque id muneris antequam obirent detractaverunt. Quid quod et non modo ab cardinalatu ipso, sed & ab suprema summi pontificii potestate sanctissimum Celestinum se abdicasse legerat, ipsumque totius christianae reipublicae humeris onus excussisse*
20 *(onus vere, cum subeuntibus maximum paretur praemium, invitis scilicet & parendi tantum iuvandique gratia illud amplectentibus)?* Persuassimum erat viro philosopho non esse laudis cumulasse diuitias, *non quaesisse honores,* sed renuisse, et umbratilem renuendo gloriam veram adipisci, quae semper virtutes ceu comes individua & assecla comitatur.
25 Humanam gloriam vel pro nihilo habebat, aiebatque saepius famam vivis nonnihil, mortuis minime profuturam, tantumque propriam aestimasse doctrinam *agnovimus,* quantum utilitati ecclesiae & eliminandis explodendisque adversis erroribus conduceret. Quinetiam ad eam perfectionis metam pervenisse *percepimus,* ut scilicet parum cura-
30 ret si eius commentationes non sub proprio nomine publicitus ederentur, dum tamen id ipsum quod sub Pici nomine facturae fuerant afferrent hominibus emolumenti, minimumque aliis amplius affici libris praeterquam veteri nouoque testamento, aetatisque residuum in eis semper volvendis consumere statuisse, nisi publica eum stimularet
35 utilitas, cum videret tot et tanta quae conceperat & parturierat passim ab omnibus non efflagitari modo *sed & immatura exigi.*
Minutulumque quantulumcunque devoti vel seniculi vel aniculae

---

24 comes] *96 96+ 98 04 V-06/7,* omnes *06*   26 nonnihil] non nihil *96 96+ 98 04 06*
V-06/7

income if he would come to the court of his king, *since Pico saw that there would be no nook or cranny left for him to hide in and that all means of escape would be taken from him,* he gave the envoy to understand that he did not seek dignities or riches but rather he neglected them in order to have time for God and his own studies. *Moreover, when some of his friends at Ferrara persuaded Pandolfo Collenuccio of Pesaro (a lawyer, a man of acute intelligence and wide reading, and a close friend of his) to induce him by whatever arguments he could muster to seek the dignity of the cardinalate or at least to accept it if the pope offered it to him (which many thought he would), and when Pandolfo had hesitantly broached the subject with him (for he was not unaware that he would prefer almost any fate to becoming entangled in such honors), Pico, with his customary highmindedness, commanded that a return letter be immediately sent to him with that saying of the prophet, "my thoughts are not your thoughts," having in mind perhaps that the property of the church, most of which ought to belong to the poor by right of inheritance, should not be used to provide magnificent panoply. Likewise he had before his eyes the example of very holy men (such as Ambrose, Augustine, Martin, and others) who fled from the dignity of the episcopate when it was offered to them and refused that office for a long time before agreeing to accept it. What if he had read that the most holy Celestine had renounced not only the cardinalate but also the supreme power of the papacy and had shaken from his shoulders the burden of the whole Christian community (a burden indeed, though it brings a very great reward to those who undertake it unwillingly, that is, embrace it for the sake of obedience and service)?* He was fully persuaded that it is not praiseworthy for a man of philosophy to accumulate riches *or to seek honors,* but rather to renounce them and by renouncing the shadowy image of glory to gain its true substance, which always accompanies virtue as an inseparable companion and attendant.

He thought nothing of human glory, and he often said that fame is of some use to the living but of none at all to the dead, and *we recognized that* he valued his own learning only insofar as it contributed to the welfare of the church and to the banishment and confutation of the errors directed against her. Indeed *we perceived that* he had reached such heights of perfection that he cared little if his thoughts were not published under his own name, as long as they profited mankind as much as if they had been published under the name of Pico, and that he was ultimately little affected by any other books but the Old and New Testaments, and that he had determined to spend the rest of his life doing nothing but studying them, except that he was spurred on by the public good when he saw that the many great things he had conceived and begun to bring forth were not only in demand by everyone everywhere *but were also sought for even before they were ripe.*

The devout feeling toward God of some little old man or woman,

affectum in deum pluris quam omnem eius humanarum divinarum-
que rerum notitiam faciebat, admonebatque saepissime familiares in-
ter loquendum, ut animadverterent quantum labant nutentque mor-
talia, quamque caducum & fluxum quod vivimus, quam firmum &
5   stabile quod sumus futuri, sive scilicet detrudamur ad inferos sive su-
bleuemur ad caelos, hortabaturque ut ad deum amandum converterent
& incitarent mentes, quod opus preponderaret cuicunque quam in hac
vita habere possemus cognitioni. Hoc etiam in libello ipso de ente &
uno luculentissime est exsecutus, quando ad Angelum Politianum, cui
10   librum nuncupavit, in ipsa disputatione conversus haec verba effatus
fuerit: "Sed vide, mi Angele, quae nos insania teneat: amare deum
dum sumus in corpore plus possumus quam vel eloqui vel cognoscere.
Amando plus nobis proficimus, minus laboramus, illi magis obsequimur.
Malumus tamen semper per cognitionem nunquam invenire quod
15   querimus, quam amando possidere id quod non amando frustra etiam
inveniretur." *Illud quoque divi Francisci, "Tantum scit homo quantum ope-*
ratur," illius in ore frequens fuerat.

Caeterum liberalitas sola in eo modum excessit, tantumque aberat ut
aliquid curae terrenis rebus apponeret, ut etiam incuriositatis naevo
20   macularetur. Ab amicis quoque saepius admonitum comperimus, ut in
totum divitias non contemneret, asseverantibus id sibi probro dari cum
vulgatum foret, sive id verum sive falsum, furti dispensatoribus prae-
buisse occasionem. Nihilominus mens illa, quae semper contemplandis
perscrutandisque totius naturae consiliis inhaerebat, demittere se fa-
25   cile non poterat ad haec infima abiectaque pensiculanda. *Memini, dum*
Ferrariae cum eo obversarer, obsonatorem pagella quadam oblata expensarum
approbationem expetere. Quo viso mirabundus exstiti, percunctatusque illum
mentemne ad id quod retroactis temporibus neglexerat apposuisset. Respondit
familiares non modo ab eo efflagitasse sed exegisse ut id subiret officii, quibus ut
30   *morem gereret factitaverat, tantum vero curae quantum prius habuisse.* Quine-
tiam dum eius dispensator primarius eum interpellasset, ut eius pecu-
niarum quas per multos annos contractaverat dispunctionem fieri
iuberet, *quo securius menti suae consuleret,* atque eiusmodi libros coram
attulisset, talia eidem verba respondisse *percepimus:* "Scio me quam
35   saepissime abs te & potuisse & posse fraudari. Quapropter libratione
expensarum harum opus non est. Si tibi debeo, quamprimum nummos
exsolvam. Si mihi debes, vel in presentia, si potes, vel in posterum, si
non adest facultas, debita relue."

---

3 labant] laborant *96 96+ 98 04 06 V-06/7; it should perhaps be emended to* laborent
5–6 sublevemur] *V-06/7 (errata),* subleuamur *96 96+ 98 04 06 V-06/7 (text)*   26 obso-
natorem] *96 96+ 98 04 06 V-06/7 (text),* opssonatorem *V-06/7 (errata)*   29 familiares]
V-06/7 (errata), familiaris *96 96+ 98 04 06 V-06/7 (text)*

however tiny and inconsequential it might seem, he valued more highly than all his knowledge of things human and divine; and in conversation he often advised his friends to notice how all mortal things totter and falter, how fleeting and evanescent is the life we now live, how fixed and unchanging the life we will live, whether we are thrust down to hell or lifted up to heaven, and he exhorted them to change their thinking and to rouse their minds to the love of God—an achievement far more important than any knowledge we can have in this life. He also made this point most lucidly in his little book "On Being and Unity," when in the course of the discussion he turned to Angelo Politiano, to whom the book is dedicated, and said: "But Angelo, my friend, see how insane we are: while we are in our bodies we can love God better than we can speak of him or know him. By loving him we gain more, we labor less, we obey him better. But we prefer never to find what we seek through knowledge than to possess through love what it would be useless to find without love." *He also often repeated that saying of St. Francis: "A man knows only as much as he puts into practice."*

But in generosity alone he went beyond the mark, and he was so far from paying any attention to earthly concerns that he was flecked with the mole of carelessness. I learned that his friends also often advised him not to scorn riches totally, arguing that it could be held against him if it were bruited about, whether truly or falsely, that he had provided an opportunity for his stewards to steal from him. Nevertheless, that mind of his, which was intent on contemplating and scrutinizing the whole range of nature's secrets, did not find it easy to come down to the consideration of these mean and lowly matters. *I remember that when I was staying with him at Ferrara, his butler offered him a certain account sheet and asked him to approve it. When I saw this I was amazed, and I asked him whether he was paying attention to matters that in former times he had neglected. He replied that those close to him had not only begged but even demanded that he fulfill this duty, which he had undertaken to do in order to humor them, but that he cared as little about it as he had before.* Indeed, when his chief steward asked him to order an audit of the money he had handled for him over a period of many years, *so that he could have some peace of mind about it,* and when he had brought the books to him, *I heard him* reply in these words: "I know that you have very often had and now have the power to cheat me. Hence there is no need of a balance sheet for these expenses. If I owe you anything, I will pay it as soon as possible. If you owe me, discharge the debt now if you can, or if you lack funds, do it later."

Amicos vero semper multa indulgentia tractavit, quibuscum hor-
tatoriis ad benevivendum locutionibus uti solebat. Hominem novi qui,
dum eius doctrina fretus & fama secum loqueretur & haberetur sermo
de moribus, duobus tantum ipsius verbis commotum ut via vitiorum
5   deserta mores reformaverit. Verba fuerunt eiusmodi: "si Christi mor-
tem nostri amore perpessam prae oculis haberemus, propriam quoque
identidem cogitando caveremus a uitiis." Modestiam & comitatem in
eos admirabilem exhibuit, quos non a viribus aut fortuna probatos sibi
devinciendos duxerat sed & a moribus & doctrina. *Eos tamen qui quan-*
10   *tulumcunque pollerent litteris, vel saltem bonarum artium studiis navos aptos-*
que inspiceret, diligere consueuerat. Similitudo namque amoris est causa,
& erga sapientem virum (ut, *teste Philostrato,* Apollonius inquit) affinitas
quaedam est. *Scientiam quoque perficere hominem qua homo est, perfectum*
vero bonitatem consequi, super aliosque probos esse diligendos non ambigitur.
15   Caeterum nihil ei intolerabilius quam (ut verbis Horatii utar) su-
perba ciuium potentiorum limina. Militiam quoque saeculi & coni-
ugale vinculum perosus fuerat, interrogatusque inter iocandum quid
ei, ad alterum subeundum onus ferendumque & necessitate cogente &
optione data, levius videretur, haesitabundus aliquantulum nutabun-
20   dusque necnon pauxillum subridens, coniugium respondit, cui non
tantum esset & servitutis annexum & periculi quantum militiae.
Libertatem enim supra modum dilexerat, quam & natura sic affecta
& philosophiae studia suggesserant, vagumque ob id plurimum ex-
titisse illum *autumo* nec propriam sibi unquam sedem delegisse, *licet*
25   *Florentiae saepius & Ferrariae quandoque commoraretur. Quarum alteram*
ciuitatem sibi quasi domicilium praestituisse putaverim, quod scilicet in ea post
Bononiam primum litterarum studia coluerat, illiusque princeps eum mirifice
diligeret, quadamque veluti affinitate coniunctus, utpote ex cuius ego sorore,
scilicet Blancha Maria Estensi, natus sim, nec etiam longe nimis esset a patria,
30   *quando triginta tantum passuum milibus ab Mirandula orientem solem versus*
Ferraria distet. Alteram, sive aeris amoenitate sive plurium amicorum suauitate
sive ingeniorum subtilitate dilexit plurimum & incoluit, quos inter litterario
amore duos sibi potissimum devinxit: Angelum scilicet Politianum, virum
Graece Latineque doctissimum necnon variarum litterarum floribus refertum
35   *ac prope vindicem Romanae linguae; alterum Marsilium Ficinum Floren-*
tinum, hominem omnifaria litteratura redolentem sed maximum ex his qui nunc
vivunt Platonicum, cuius opera in Academicis sibi vendicandis usus fuerat.
Exterioris latriae cultus non multum diligens fuerat; non de eo lo-

---

2–5 Hominem . . . reformauerit] *The construction in this sentence is mixed: either* qui *must be*
omitted or commotum *changed to* commouebatur.   10 navos] *96 96+ 98 04 V-06/7,*
vanos *06*   34 floribus] *V-06/7 (errata),* florum *96 96+ 98 04 06 V-06/7 (text)*

As for his friends, he treated them with great kindness, commonly addressing them with exhortations to lead good lives. I know a man who, relying on his learning and fame, spoke with him and conversed about morality, and was so moved by just two of his points that he abandoned his evil ways and reformed his character. His words were as follows: "If we kept before our eyes the death Christ suffered out of love for us and also kept constantly in mind our own death, we would avoid vices." He displayed admirable modesty and affability with persons whom he chose to bind to himself because they were recommended not by power or fortune but by good character and learning. *But he was especially inclined to love those who had some scholarly proficiency, however little, or whom he saw to be at least suited and apt for the pursuit of true learning.* For likeness is a cause of love, and (as Apollonius said, *according to Philostratus) we feel a certain affinity for a wise man. Also there is no doubt that knowledge perfects man as man, that a perfect man achieves goodness, and that the upright, above all others, are worthy of love.*

But nothing was more intolerable to him than (in the words of Horace) the proud thresholds of powerful citizens. He also loathed worldly competition and the marital bond, and once in merry conversation, when he was asked which of the two burdens would seem lighter to take upon himself and bear up under if he had to take one and were given his choice, he hesitated in uncertainty for a while and, smiling a bit, replied that he would choose marriage, since there is less of both servitude and danger in marriage than in worldly offices.

For he loved his freedom beyond measure, both because of his natural temperament and because of his philosophical studies, and *I say that this is the main reason why he mostly wandered from place to place and never chose his own permanent residence, although he often stayed in Florence and sometimes in Ferrara. The latter city, I think, provided him a sort of dwelling place because it was there that, after Bologna, he first pursued his scholarly studies and because its prince was marvelously fond of him and was linked to him in a sort of affinity by marriage, since I am the son of his sister, Bianca Maria d'Este, and it is also not very far from his patrimony, since Ferrara is only thirty miles away from Mirandola toward the east. For the other city he had a special fondness and he resided there either because of its pleasant air or because of the enjoyment of many friends or their refined intelligence. Among them he associated most closely with two because of their love of learning: Angelo Politiano, a man most learned in Latin and Greek, replete with the flowers of varied literary culture, the vindicator almost of the Roman language; and the other was Marsilio Ficino of Florence, a person redolent of wide-ranging scholarship, but especially the greatest Platonist now living, whose writings he made use of in vindicating the Academics.*

He did not much favor the cultivation of exterior worship; I am not

quimur quem observandum praecipit ecclesia (gestasse hunc quippe *prae oculis eum vidimus*) sed de his caerimoniis mentionem facimus quas nonnulli, posthabito vero cultu dei, qui in spiritu & veritate colendus est, prosequuntur & provehunt. At internis affectibus ferventissimo

5 deum amore prosequebatur. Interdum etiam alacritas illa animi propemodum elanguescebat & decidebat, maiori quandoque nixu vires assumens, adeoque in deum exarsisse illum *memini*, ut cum Ferrariae in pomario quodam de Christi amore colloquentes longis spatiaremur ambulacris, in eiusmodi verba proruperit: "Tibi haec dixerim, in ar-

10 canis recondito; opes quae mihi reliquae sunt, absolutis consummatisque elucubrationibus quibusdam, egenis elargiar & crucifixo munitus, exsertis nudatisque pedibus, orbem peragrans per castella, per urbes, Christum predicabo." Accepi postea illum mutavisse propositum, et Praedicatorum ordini se addicere statuisse. *Interim eorum quae conceperat*

15 *operum quaeque inchoaverat maturabat editionem.*

Sed millesimo quadringentesimo nonagesimo quarto anno redemptionis nostrae, dum ipse secundum & trigesimum aetatis annum impleret, Florentiaeque moraretur, insidiosissima correptus est febre, quae adeo in humores & viscera grassata est ut nullum non medicamen-

20 torum genus adhibitum contempserit, eumque omnino naturae satisfacere intra tertium decimum diem coegerit.

Sed quemadmodum in infirmitate se gesserit, licet eo tempore ab eo procul essem, narrare tamen non desinam quae ab gravissimis testibus qui aderant acceperim. Quale illud: cum post sumptum eucharistiae sacramentum

25 sigillum ei crucifixi Christi offeretur, ut inde plenos amoris haustus ob ineffabilis illius passionis nostrae salutis gratia memoriam, priusquam exhalaret animam, sumere posset, fortissimum dumtaxat aduersus quaecunque adversa munimen validissimumque contra iniquos daemones propugnaculum, interrogantique mox seniori an firmiter crederet

30 veram esse illam dei veri verique hominis imaginem, qui qua deus est ante tempus & aeuum ab ipso patre deo cui aequalis in omnibus genitus esset, deque spiritu sancto qui & deus est, ab ipsoque & patre (quae tria unum sunt) coeterne manante, in utero Mariae semper virginis conceptus esset in tempore, qui famem, qui sitim, qui labores,

35 aestus, vigilias perpessus esset, qui demum pro contractis ab Adae semine sordibus nostris abluendis *proque reseranda ianua coeli*, maxima qua genus humanum charitate complectabatur, preciosissimum sanguinem & sponte & libentissime in ara crucis effudisset, caeteraque id

---

33 manante] *96 96+ V-06/7 (errata),* manente *98 04 06 V-06/7 (text)*

speaking of what the church requires us to observe (indeed he performed that, *as I saw with my own eyes*), but I mean those ceremonies which some follow and promote to the neglect of the true worship of God, who should be worshiped in spirit and in truth. But he pursued God with interior feelings of the most burning love. Sometimes even that eagerness of his mind almost languished and died down; at other times he gathered his powers with a greater effort, and *I remember* that he burned with such love of God that, when we were walking along the long paths between the trees in an orchard in Ferrara, speaking of the love of Christ, he burst forth in these words: "If I tell you these things, keep them secret. Once I have finished and perfected some literary labors, I will give my remaining wealth to the poor, and, armed with a crucifix, shoeless and barefoot, wandering through the world from village to village and from city to city, I will preach Christ." I later learned that he had changed his mind and decided to join the Dominican order. *In the meantime he was bringing to fruition and publishing the works that he had conceived and begun.*

But in the fourteen hundred and ninety-fourth year of our redemption, when he had completed the thirty-second year of his life, while he was staying in Florence, he was seized by a very dangerous fever, which so assaulted his bodily fluids and inner organs that it scorned any kind of medication that was applied, and at any rate within thirteen days it forced him to pay his debt to nature.

But concerning how he conducted himself in his sickness, even though I was far away from him at that time, I will not neglect to declare what I heard from most reliable witnesses who were present. Such as the following. When he had received the sacrament of the eucharist and the sign of Christ crucified was held up before him, so that from it, before he breathed out his soul, he could drink in full draughts of love by remembering his ineffable passion for the sake of our salvation—the strongest armament of all against any kind of adversity and a most poweful weapon against the wicked demons—and when the priest went on to ask him whether he firmly believed that this is the true image of true God and true man, who insofar as he was God was begotten before all time and ages by God the Father, to whom he is equal in all things, and who was conceived in time within the womb of Mary ever virgin by the Holy Spirit, who is also God and who proceeds coeternally from Christ and the Father (all three being one), the same Christ who suffered hunger, thirst, labor, heat, sleeplessness, and who finally poured out his most precious blood most willingly and eagerly on the altar of the cross in order to wash away our filth, contracted from the seed of Adam, *and to open the gates of heaven* through the boundless love he felt for the human race, and other matters customarily recounted on such occasions, he replied that he

genus recenseri quandoque solita, non modo se credere sed & certum
esse responderit. *Et item illud:* cum Alberto Pio sororis filio *quem nomi-*
navimus inter huius vitae initia, iuveni & ingenio & bonarum artium
studiis & moribus conspicuo, eadem ratione *qua Alexander ex Aphro-*
5   *disiade & Themistius in auscultatoriorum librorum proemio* fortitudinem e
physicis contemplationibus sumi contra mortis metum declaravit (*quam*
mox sententiam usurpavit Auerrois), conanti (*inquam*) Alberto mortis con-
finia reddere placabiliora in hunc modum verba reddiderit: non illa
dumtaxat ratione pacari animum, non finem mortis cruciatibus poni,
10   sed hac potissimum, quod dei sui offensis terminus iam poneretur,
quando breviusculum vitae eius tempus crebriores in deum offensas
non contenturum arbitraretur. *Et illud praeterea:* quando pluribus *ex*
Praedicatorum collegio probatissimis testibus & Alberto ipso paulo ante
citato revelaverit caeli reginam ad se nocte adventasse, miro fra-
15   grantem odore, membraque omnia febre illa contusa confractaque
refovisse, seque morti omnino non concessurum promisisse, hilari
placidoque ore in strato dum aegrotaret iacuisse compertum est; atque
inter mortis aculeos quos sustinebat, quasi coelos sibi patefactos cer-
neret loqui solitum; salutantesque omnes & operam suam (*ut moris est*)
20   pollicentes blandissimo ab eo sermone & receptos & exosculatos. Ab
servis item omnibus, si cui molestus forte fuisset, ignosci sibi postulasse
certiores facti sumus, quibus ante acto anno testamento caverat victum
aliis *& tegumentum* dum viverent, aliis pecunias pro meritis erogari.
Haeredes Florentini xenodochei pauperes instituit, eorum dumtaxat
25   quae moveri non poterant; mobilium vero, Antonium Mariam fratrem.
  Quanta vero molestia eius obitus infimos & summos omnium gradus
affecerit, testes sunt Italiae principes, urbes, & populi; *testes hi reges quos*
supra citavimus. Testis iterum Caroli Galliarum regis benignitas &
gratia, silentio non praetereunda. Cui cum Florentiam adventanti, ut
30   inde Romam peteret Neapolitanum regnum expugnaturus, gravi eum
laborare aegretudine nuntiatum fuisset, duos statim medicos ad eum,
legatorum etiamnum fungentes officio, visitatum & opitulatum ipse
transmiserit, litterasque *quas & vidimus & legimus* propria subscriptas
manu dedit, plenas & humanitatis & earum pollicitationum quas &
35   magnanimi regis benivolentissimus animus & praeclarae virtutes ae-
grotantis exigebant. *Ei quippe tum fama notissimus erat, tum quadam fami-*
liaritate coniunctus. Nam ab eo in Galliis, dum Parisios inviseret, honorifice
exceptus fuerat. Enimvero qui eum dum vixit toti orbi & multis saeculis admi-

---

8–9 non . . . poni] *The text seems to be corrupt; perhaps we should read* quod finem mors
cruciatibus poneret, *and I have so translated it.*   15 confractaque] *96 96+,* contractaque
98 04 06 V-06/7

not only believed these things but was certain of them. *And likewise the following.* When Alberto Pio, his sister's son, *whom we mentioned at the beginning of this Life,* a young man outstanding for his intelligence, good scholarship, and character, employed the same argument *set forth by Alexander of Aphrodisias and Themistius in the proem of his book "The Listeners,"* that physical considerations offer strength against the fear of death *(an idea later used by Averroes),* when *(I say)* Alberto Pio in this way tried to render the approach of death more peaceful, Pico replied in this way: that his mind was not soothed merely by the argument that death puts an end to suffering but rather by the argument that his offenses against God would now come to an end, since he considered that the little bit of time left in his life would not contain very many offenses against God. *And moreover the following incident.* When he revealed to many very upright witnesses *from the Dominican convent* and to the aforementioned Alberto Pio that the queen of heaven had come to him at night, giving off a marvelous fragrance, refreshing all his limbs, which were bruised and broken by the fever, and that she promised him that he would not yield at all to death, it was well established that his countenance was cheerful and peaceful as he lay on his sickbed, and that, as he sustained the darts of death, he regularly spoke as if he saw the heavens opened up to him, and that he received, kissed, and spoke very courteously to all those who greeted him and promised their assistance *(as is the custom).* Likewise *we were truly informed that* he asked forgiveness from all his servants, if by chance he had dealt harshly with any of them. The year before he had made provision for them in his will, bequeathing to some food *and clothing* as long as they lived, to others money to be paid them according to their deserts. The poor in the hospital at Florence he made the heirs of his landed property, but his movable goods he bequeathed to his brother Antonio Maria.

How deeply his death distressed those of all ranks, high and low, has been testified by the princes, cities, and people of Italy, *and by those kings whom we mentioned above.* So too the testimony of the kindness and favor shown by Charles, king of France, should not be passed over in silence. When he arrived in Florence on his way to Rome in order to conquer the kingdom of Naples, and when he was informed of the grave illness of Pico, he immediately sent two physicians, who also functioned as ambassadors, to visit and assist him, and he sent a letter signed by his own hand *(we have seen it and read it),* filled with kindness and such promises of assistance as were requisite to the most benevolent mind of the magnanimous king and the illustrious virtues of the sick man. *Indeed, Pico was very well known to him by reputation and also bound to him by a kind of familiarity. For when he was in France, visiting Paris, he had been honorably received by him. Certainly, just as the king, while Pico was alive, had*

*randum praestitit, ita eius obitum non minus celebrem & inauditum celebrari
decrevit.*

    *Quocirca ea in presentiarum referenda puto quae meis auribus hausi, dum
Florentiae, quo illius infirmitate percepta, licet non tempestive, me contuleram,*
5 in aede sacra quae Sanctae Reparatae dicitur, Hieronymum Sa-
vonarolam Ferrariensem, ex Praedicatorum ordine virum & theologiae
consultissimum & praeclarissimum famatissimumque sanctimonia,
sacras habentem ad Florentinum populum contiones *audirem. Sed prius
sacrarum litterarum ignaros Apulei verbis admonere consilium est, ne crassis*
10 *auribus & obstinato corde ea putent mendacia, quae auditu noua vel uisu rudia
vel certe supra captum cogitationis ardua videantur, quae si paulo altius explo-
raverint, non modo compertu evidentia verum etiam factu facillima sentient.*

    *Is igitur e pulpito declamitans, quae sum dicturus cunctis qui aderant insin-
vauit:* "Arcanum tibi, O Florentia, pandendum est, quod equidem ita
15 verum est quam *prouerbium illud apud te frequens* Ioannis euangelium.
Subticuissem profecto, sed ad dicendum compellor, & qui mihi prae-
cipere potest, ut haec palam facerem imperavit. Neminem porro ves-
trum puto fuisse qui Ioannem Picum Mirandulam non noverit. Magnis
ille a deo beneficiis magnisque gratiis cumulatus, *multifariaque preditus
20 disciplina fuerat. Nulli forte mortalium tam celebre obtigit ingenium.* Mag-
nam in eo iacturam fecit ecclesia. Arbitrarer, si diutius ei vitae spatium
prorogatum fuisset, cunctos qui octingentis ab hinc annis decessere, ob
scriptionum monumenta quae reliquisset, excelluisse. Hic mecum ob-
uersari solitus erat, secreta palam facere, ex quibus noveram internis
25 eum locutionibus a deo ad religionem citari, unde afflatibus hisce obse-
qui cupiens non semel obtemperare proposuerat. Verum divinis bene-
ficiis male gratus vel ab sensibus euocatus detractabat labores (delicatae
quippe temperaturae fuerat), vel arbitratus eius opera religionem indi-
gere differebat ad tempus. Hoc tamen non ut verum sed ut a me
30 coniectatum & presumptum dixerim. Ob id duobus ei annis flagellum
interminatus sum, si opus quod ei deus patrandum proposuerat negli-
genter exsequeretur. Rogabam (fateor) deum identidem ut caesus ali-
quantulum viam quae ex alto eidem ostensa fuerat tandem capesseret.
Non hoc quaesivi quo perculsus est, non hoc putaveram, at id deo
35 decretum fuit ut vitam hanc relinqueret praeclaraeque coronae in
caelis preparatae partem amitteret *famamque & nominis celebritatem, quae*

---

27 evocatus] *V-06/7 (errata),* vocatus *96 96+ 98 04 06*

warranted that he was a man to be admired by the whole world and for ages to come, so too he determined to solemnize his decease as no less famous and astounding.

Therefore, I think I should relate in this document what I heard with my own ears when in the city of Florence, whither I betook myself after I learned of his infirmity (although I did not arrive in time), I heard a holy sermon preached to the people of Florence in the church called Santa Reparata by Girolamo Savonarola of Ferrara, a member of the Dominican order and a very learned theologian, most illustrious and famous for his holiness. *But those ignorant of holy scripture I have determined to admonish in the words of Apuleius, lest in their crude ears and obstinate hearts they consider as mendacious things that seem strange to hear or peculiar to see or certainly so difficult as to be beyond the grasp of their thoughts, whereas if they examined them more deeply, they would think them not only evident from personal experience but also easy of accomplishment.*

Thus, as he declaimed from the pulpit to all who were present, he worked his way into what I am about to relate: "O Florence, I must reveal to you a mystery that is nevertheless as true as *The gospel of John so frequently on your lips.* Indeed I would have kept silent, but I am compelled to speak and have been ordered to reveal these things by one who has the power to command me. And so, there is no one of you, I am sure, who did not know Giovanni Pico della Mirandola. God heaped great benefits and graces upon him, *and he was furnished with learning of many kinds. Perhaps no mortal has ever had such an illustrious intellect.* In him the church has suffered a great loss. I would think that, if his lifetime had been extended over a longer period, he would have surpassed all who have passed away over the past 800 years, because of the writings he would have left behind him as a monument. This man regularly conversed with me and revealed his secrets, whence I know that God had summoned him to join a religious order, and he more than once desired and decided to comply with this inspiration. But, ungrateful for God's benefits, he either shunned these labors because he was called away by sensuality (for he was of a voluptuous temperament), or he temporarily postponed them because he thought the religious life needed his present endeavors. I would not say this is true, but I presume and conjecture it was so. For this reason I threatened him for two years with punishing strokes of the whip if he failed to carry out the work that God had set before him to achieve. I asked God repeatedly (I confess it) to strike him somewhat so that he would finally enter upon the road that had been shown to him from on high. I did not seek the blow that has struck him down—I was not thinking of that—but it was decreed by God that he should leave this life behind and lose part of that shining crown prepared for him in heaven *and that he should not fully achieve the*

ad summum cummulum si vixisset fuerat habiturus, ad plenum non asse-
queretur. Verum benignissimus iudex clementissime erga ipsum se
habuit. Atque ob eleemosynas larga & effusissima manu pauperibus
elargitas & orationes quae ad deum instantissime effusae sunt, effec-

5   tum est ut nec eius anima in sinu patris adhuc super caelos exultet nec
ad inferos deputata perpetuis tormentis crucietur, sed purgatorio igni
ad tempus mancipata temporarias paenas luat. Quod in hac parte li-
bentissime dixerim, ut qui eum noverunt, & hi potissimum qui eius
beneficiis cumulati fuere, suffragiis adiuvent." Haec & plura alia vir dei

10 clara voce asseuerauit, se addens non latuisse ob mendacia eiusmodi, si
qua miscerentur, verbi dei precones dignos effici de quibus aeternum
sumeretur supplicium, necnon adiciens diebus aliquot haec sibi in uni-
versum fuisse comperta, sed propter verba quae virginem dixisse sibi
aegrotus affirmaverat, nutabundum stetisse formidasseque diu, ne ille

15 demonum opera fuisset ilusus, quando ob eius mortem virginis pol-
licitatio frustraretur, verum tamen innotuisse sibi defunctum ae-
quivocatione mortis deceptum, cum illa de secunda & aeterna locuta
fuisset, hic de prima & temporaria credidisset.

Quod si quis dixerit hominem hunc vel hypocrisi fuisse mentitum vel fantas-

20 *matis ludificatum vel daemonum praestigiis circumventum, is (nisi aut male de*
fide sentiens aut mentis emotae sit) fateatur necesse est, deum multifarie felici-
tatem eorum miseriamque qui animam effudissent, viventibus & revelasse iam
& revelare posse, eodemque temporis spatio eos quibus haec palam fiunt certiores
reddere, se non a visis aut spectris illudi, sed vera esse quae aut mente aut oculis

25 *cernant & videant. Tantae vero & doctrinae & auctoritatis virum, tantae*
probitatis & prudentiae, quorum in Aristotelis philosophiam compendiaria the-
oremata, monitiones publicae, praeclarissima interpraetamenta in sacra elo-
quia, futurorum contingentium praedictiones quae evenisse ad lineam omnis
fere novit Italia, sanctissimaque vitae conversatio testatissimam pridem fecere

30 *fidem, in principe templo tam celebratae urbis, haec ut vera, ut inconcussa*
tenenda, tot milibus hominum veritate non comperta pronuntiasse, nemo nisi
malevolus infitiabitur. Adde quod, *dum nonnihil super id negotii sciscitarer,*
virum qui sermoni interfuerat adiisse concionatorem *audivi,* ac eidem,
ut ea plus haberent roboris quae vulgauerat, rettulisse defunctum val-

35 latum igne sibi apparuisse & professum ingratitudinis adhuc paenas
dare.

---

3 larga] 96 96+ 98 04 V-06/7, largas 06   14 nutabundum] V-06/7 (errata), nuta-
bundus 96 96+ 98 04 06 V-06/7 (text)   29 fere] 96 96+ 98 04 06 V-06/7 (errata), vere
V-06/7 (text)

reputation and celebrity that he would have possessed in superabundance if he had lived. But the most benign judge acted most mercifully toward him. And because of the alms which he had distributed to the poor with an open and most generous hand and because of the prayers which were poured forth to God most fervently, the result was that his soul does not yet exult above the heavens in the bosom of the father, nor is it allotted to hell to suffer eternal torments, but rather it is consigned for a while to the fires of purgatory to suffer temporal punishment. I have said this most willingly for this reason, so that those who knew him, and especially those upon whom he has heaped benefits, may help him with their prayers and good deeds." These things and more the man of God asserted with a loud and clear voice, adding that he was not unaware that the heralds of God's word, if they intermingled any such lies, made themselves deserving of eternal punishment. He also added that he had known all this for some days, but because of the words which the sick man affirmed the Virgin had spoken to him, he had wavered for a long time out of fear that Pico had been deluded by the efforts of the demons, since the Virgin's promise concerning his death was unfulfilled, but then it dawned on him that the dead man had been deceived by an ambiguity in the word "death," since she had spoken about the second and eternal death, whereas he had thought she meant the first and temporary death.

But if anyone should say that this man was telling lies out of hypocrisy or was the victim of illusory visions, or was deceived by the trickery of demons, such a person (unless he is unorthodox in belief or out of his mind) will have to confess that in various ways God both has revealed and still can reveal to the living the happiness or the misery of those who have breathed out their souls; and at the same time he can certify to those who have the revelations that they are not deceived by visions or specters but rather that what they see with their eyes or perceive with their minds is in fact true. But that a man of such great learning and authority, of such integrity and prudence, a man whose absolute trustworthiness has been long since confirmed by his compendious theorems on Aristotle's philosophy, by his public admonitions, by his brilliant interpretations of holy scripture, by his predictions of future contingencies, which (as is known almost all over Italy) were exactly fulfilled, and by his very holy way of life, that such a man should announce these things to thousands of people as true and unassailably indisputable without having verified them—and that in the principal church of such a famous city—no one will dispute except out of ill will. Moreover, *while I was making some inquiries about this matter, I heard that* a man who had been present at the sermon came up to the preacher and told him, to lend more force to what he had divulged, that the dead man had appeared to him surrounded by flames and had acknowledged that he was still being punished for his ingratitude.

Quinetiam monacha quaedam, multis praeclara vaticiniis quaeque ipsi dum
viveret multa futura praedixit quae ad amussim evenere, inter reliqua hoc unum
protulit biennio antequam e vita migrasset, eum liliorum tempore opera &
hortatu fratris Hieronymi (de quo mentionem fecimus) Praedicatorum fratrum

5   *collegio se dicaturum, eodemque tempore Florentinam quandam familiam*
(quam Pactiam nuncupant) tunc exulantem ad patriam redituram. Complures
ad quos haec fama pervenerat, super hac liliorum nomenclatura demirabantur,
loqui eam arbitrantes de verno tempore quo lilia florescunt. Sed lilium hoc
Galliarum regem exstitisse compertum est talibus utentem insignibus, qui pridie

10   *quam ille religionem voveret (ita enim voverat antequam moreretur) & qua-*
triduo postquam extorris illa familia se contulit in urbem patriam, magno co-
mitatu Florentiam ingressus est, iter per Hetruriam faciens, Neapolitanum
regnum vi & armis in ditionem vindicaturus.

Verum antequam finem faciam praefari iterum paucula in calce operis non

15   *inutile puto. Videor enim mihi videre ad revelationes has veluti ad lunae um-*
bram baubantes molossos, quibus adhuc offula (prioribus fortasse non contentis)
obicienda est, ne frustra latratibus aera verberent. Video item dementibus excuti
risum. Video his qui sciolos se arbitrentur summoueri ludum, qui forte ob post-
habitum religionis ingrediendae salubrum afflatum igne torqueri animas non

20   *debere contendent, nec divino afflatos spiritu tempestate nostra reperiri homines,*
qui Christi colloquiis perfruantur. At si peccata non morte sed venia digna
purgatorio igni esse plectenda arbitrarentur, iustos etiam paenas dare non
mirarentur. Item si servum qui voluntatem domini sciens non adimplevit, teste
veritate, multis vapulaturum non ignoraverint, hunc qui dei voluntatem no-

25   *verat & implere distulit, etsi a noxis quibusque aliis fuisset immunis, supplicia*
luere non extasim paterentur. Alia ex parte rudem & insulsam eorum astutiam
mirari satis non possum, qui cum Christum pro hominibus mortuum credant,
eosdem homines alloqui eundem facile posse non credant, vehementiorique argu-
mento, virginis matris angelorumque beatorumve hominum spirituum affatibus

30   *participes eosdem mortales homines non posse fieri. Animadvertendum eis pro-*
fecto foret inferiora omnia per superiora gubernari, Dionysio etiam Areopagita
teste, in libro de Hierarchia caelesti, separatisque mentibus inferioris gradus &
naturae, quibus hominum cura demandata est, per superiores mentes (quae
iterum vel a supremis vel ab ipso deo divina mysteria hauriunt) illuminari,

35   *hominesque diuino afflatos spiritu easdem revelationes accipere, hominum mul-*
titudini cum expedit patefaciendas. Sacrosancta haec divinitatis lex (quod ab
eodem Dionysio libro caelestis Hierarchiae edocemur) ut per prima sequentia ad

---

18–19 posthabitum . . . afflatum] *96 (errata) 96+ V-06/7 (errata)*, non persolutum reli-
gionis votum *96 (text)*, non posthabitum . . . afflatum *98 04 06 V-06/7 (text)*   24 igno-
raverint] *96 96+ V-06/7 (errata)*, ignorauerit *98 04 06 V-06/7 (text)*   26 paterentur]
96 (errata) 96+ V-06/7 (errata), pateretur *98 04 06 V-06/7 (text)*, proderetur *96 (text)*

And what is more, a certain nun, famous for many prophecies, and who had predicted to Pico while he was alive many future events that were fulfilled to the letter, foretold this one thing, among others, two years before he departed from this life: that in the time of the lilies, through the endeavors and exhortation of Fra Girolamo (whom we mentioned before), Pico would join the convent of the Dominicans and that at the same time a certain Florentine family named Pazzi, who were then in exile, would return to their homeland. Very many who heard the news of this prediction were nonplussed by this mention of lilies, thinking that she was speaking of the spring, when lilies bloom. But it was discovered that this lily was the king of France, who uses it in his coat of arms, for the day before Pico took religious vows (for he did so before he died) and four days after that exiled family traveled to their home city, the king entered Florence with a great retinue, journeying through Tuscany, intending to claim by force of arms dominion over the kingdom of Naples.

But before I conclude, I think it will be not without use to say beforehand a little something once more at the end of my work. For I seem to see some who object to these revelations, like hunting hounds baying at the shadow of the moon, to whom we must still throw a sop (perhaps they are not content with what they got before) lest they should beat the air in vain with their barking. I also see some laughing like idiots. I see that some who think they are smart can hardly suppress their mockery, contending perhaps that neglecting a salutary inspiration to enter a religious order is no justification for tormenting souls by fire and that nowadays no one can be found who is inspired by the divine spirit and enjoys conversations with Christ. But if they should reckon that not mortal but venial sins deserve to be punished by the fires of purgatory, they would not be surprised that the righteous also suffer punishment. Likewise, if they are not unaware that a servant who knows his master's will and does not carry it out will receive many lashes (and Truth himself testifies to this), then they should not be dumbfounded at the idea that someone who knows the will of God and puts off obeying it should be punished for doing so, even if he is immune from punishment on all other grounds. On the other hand, I cannot but marvel at the crude and insipid cleverness of those who believe that Christ died for mankind but that he cannot easily speak to that same mankind, and a fortiori, those same mortal men cannot be made to share in the inspirations of the Virgin Mother, of the angels, and of the spirits of blessed souls. Certainly they should notice that everything lower is governed by something higher, on the authority of Dionysius the Areopagite in his book "The Celestial Hierarchy," and that the separate spirits of lower rank and nature to whom the care of mankind is delegated are illuminated by superior spirits, who in turn drink in the divine mysteries either from those above them or from God himself, and that persons inspired by the divine spirit receive those same revelations when it is expedient that they be manifested to mankind at large. This is the sacred law of the deity (as we are taught by the same Dionysius in his book "The Celestial Hierarchy"): by the first things those that follow are lifted up

augustissimam lucem subvehantur. Ignari proculdubio sunt divinarum lit-
terarum, insolentis quoque & pervicacis ingenii, nam in illis conspici datur
divina futura mysteria non tantum per bonos sed per scelestos homines & pseu-
doprophetas quandoque patefacta. Quid prohibet huic fidem habere qui & doc-
5   *trina & tot virtutibus pollet multaque iam futura, quae nunc evenere, praedixit,*
& hoc non somniculose testatus sed asseveranter affirmans. Adde quod Aris-
totelis philosophia his non reclamet & Platonica suffragentur, licet pro gravi
testimonio nisi scripturae divinae auctoritatem non acceperim, sed extraria haec
quandoque citare non absurdum est, ut malevolorum tela in auctores maiore vi
10   *quam venerint revertantur.*

    Verum ad nosmet ipsos iam redeundum est, quibus non tam moerendum est
quod talem amisimus quam quod habuimus & habemus gratias agendum regi
cui vivunt omnia, quippe qui mortalis vitae munere perfunctus, diuque
cum habitantibus cedar, quos luce non pauca perfuderat, conversatus,
15   inaccessibile & infinitum supernae patriae lumen iamiam ingrediens,
ineffabili divinitate, nobis etiam in dies laturus opem, sine fine fruetur.

FINIS

Ioannes Picus Mirandula Ioanni Francisco ex fratre nepoti, salutem in
eo qui est vera salus

20   Discedenti tibi a me plurimas statim ad malum oblatas occasiones
quae te perturbent & arrepto bene vivendi propositio adversentur, non
est, fili, quod admireris, sed neque quod doleas aut expavescas. Quan-
tum illud potius esset miraculum si tibi uni inter mortales sine sudore
via pateret ad caelum, quasi nunc primum & fallax mundus et malus
25   demon esse desineret, aut quasi tu in carne adhuc non esses, quae
concupiscit adversus spiritum &, nisi saluti nostrae vigiles perspex-
erimus, Circeis ebrios poculis in prodigiosas brutorum species *ille-*
cebrosa deformat.

    Sed et gaudendum tibi esse affirmat Iacobus scribens, "Gaudete,
30   fratres, cum in tentationes varias incideritis," nec immerito quidem.
Quae enim spes gloriae si nulla sit spes victoriae, aut victoriae locus quis
esse potest ubi pugna non est? Vocatur ad coronam qui provocatur ad

---

7 suffragentur] *96 96+ 98 04 06 V-06/7; perhaps it should be emended to* suffragetur
14 cedar] *96 98 04 06 V-06/7,* eedar *96+*   18 ex fratre nepoti] *96+ 98 04 06*
E-95+, nepoti *96 E-99 E-00 E-02 E-04 E-07+ E-08 E-09*   24 quasi nunc] *96 98 04 06*
E-95+ E-99 E-00 E-02 E-04 E-07+ E-08 E-09, quasi *96+*   30 immerito quidem] *96*
E-95+ E-99, immerito quod *96+ 98 06 E-00 E-02 E-04 E-07+ E-08 E-09,* immerito *04*

to the most majestic light of all. Undoubtedly they are ignorant of holy scripture, and their dispositions are impudent and obstinate, for in scripture we see that God's prophecies are sometimes manifested not only by good persons but sometimes by evildoers and pseudoprophets. What stands in the way of believing a person who is outstanding both for learning and for many virtues and who has foretold many events that have now come to pass, especially when he bears witness to this not in some vague, dreamy fashion but affirms it emphatically? Moreover, the philosophy of Aristotle does not outlaw such things and Platonism concurs with them, although for such grave testimony I would accept no authority except that of holy scripture, but it is not absurd to cite such extraneous authorities sometimes, so that the darts of the wicked may be thrown back at them with greater force than they had when they were first thrown.

But to come back to ourselves, we should not so much mourn that we have lost such a man as give thanks to the king for whom all things live that we have had him and have him, a man namely who has finished the duties of mortal life and having associated for a long time with those who dwell in darkness, on whom he cast no little light, is now about to enter the inaccessible and infinite light of our heavenly homeland, whence he will also help us day after day, and where he will enjoy ineffable divinity without end.

THE END

Giovanni Pico della Mirandola to his nephew Gianfrancesco,
his brother's son, salutations in him who is truly salvation

The fact that, when you left me, many disturbing occasions of sin immediately presented themselves to you and set themselves against the resolution you took to lead a good life should not surprise you, my son, nor even sadden or frighten you. How much more miraculous would it be if you alone among mortals, without any sweating about it, should have the road to heaven open to you, as if now for the first time the deceptive world and the wicked devil had ceased to exist or as if you yourself were not still in the flesh, which lusts against the spirit and which, unless we look to our salvation alertly, will make us drunk with the cups of Circe and *alluringly* deform us into unnatural kinds of beasts.

But James asserts that you should even rejoice, writing: "Rejoice, brothers, when you fall into various temptations," and for good reason indeed. For what hope is there for glory if there is no hope for victory, or what room can there be for victory where there is no battle? He is called to the crown who is called out to the battle, and especially to a

pugnam, atque ad eam praesertim in qua nemo vinci potest invitus, neque aliis nobis ut vincamus viribus opus est quam ut vincere ipsi velimus. Magna christiani felicitas, quando & in eius arbitrio posita est victoria, & omni vincentis uoto omnique expectatione maiora futura
5 sunt praemia.

Dic (quaeso), fili carissime, estne aliquid in hac vita ex his quorum libido terrenas agitat mentes pro quo adipiscendo non multi prius subeundi labores, multa indigna & misera tolleranda sint? Bene actum secum putat mercator si post decennem navigationem, post mille in-
10 commoda, mille vitae discrimina rem sibi comparaverit paulo uberiorem. De militia saeculi nihil est quod ad te scribam, cuius miserias ipsa satis te docuit, et docet, experientia. In principum gratia promerenda, in aequalium amicitiis conciliandis, in honoribus ambiendis, quae moles molestiarum, quantum anxietatis, quantum sit sol-
15 licitudinis, ex te ego discere potius possum quam te docere, qui meis libris, meo otiolo, contentus, a pueris usque intra fortunam vivere didici, & quantum possum apud me habitans nihil extra me ipsum suspiro vel ambio. Ergo terrena haec caduca, incerta, vilia, & cum brutis quoque nobis communia, sudantes etiam et anhelantes vix conse-
20 quemur; ad caelestia atque divina, quae nec oculus vidit neque auris audivit neque cor cogitavit, somniculosi & dormientes & propemodum inviti *a diis* trahemur, quasi sine nobis aut deus regnare aut caelestes illi cives beati esse non possint? Profecto si terrena felicitas otiosis nobis compararetur, posset aliquis laborem detrectans malle mundo servire
25 quam deo, sed si nihil minus quam in via dei, immo longe magis, in peccatorum via fatigamur (unde illa vox damnatorum, "Lassati sumus in via iniquitatis"), non potest non extremae esse dementiae ibi nolle potius laborare ubi a labore itur ad mercedem, quam ubi a labore itur ad supplicium. Mitto quanta sit illa pax quantaque felicitas animi, nil
30 conscire sibi, nulla pallescere culpa, quae proculdubio voluptatibus omnibus quae possideri vel optari possint in vita longe praeponderat. Quid enim optabile in voluptatibus mundi, quae dum quaeruntur fatigant, cum acquiruntur infatuant, cum amittuntur excruciant? Dubitas, fili, impiorum mentes perpetuis curis non agitari? Verbum est
35 dei, qui nec falli potest nec fallere, "Cor impii quasi mare feruens, quod quiescere non potest." Nihil enim illis est tutum, nihil pacatum; omnia metum, omnia curas, intentant omnia mortem. Hisne igitur in-

---

16 intra] 96 96+ 98 04 06 E-95 + E-99 E-04 E-07 + E-08, extra E-00 E-02 E-09   32 voluptatibus] 96 96+ 98 04 06 E-95 + E-99 E-00 E-02 E-04 E-07+ E-09, voluntatibus E-08   34 non agitari? Verbum] 96 96+ 98 04 06 E-99 E-00 E-02 E-04 E-08 E-09, agitari: non verbum E-95 +, agitari? verbum E-07 +

battle in which no one can be defeated against his own will, nor do we need any other strength to win except that we ourselves wish to win. Great indeed is the happiness of a Christian, since the victory lies within his own choice and the rewards will be beyond all the wishes and all the expectations of the victor.

Tell me, I beg you, my dearest son, of all the things which earthlings covet with such mental turmoil, is there any that can be acquired without much labor, without bearing many indignities and miseries? A merchant thinks life has treated him well if, after a ten years of sailing, after a thousand adversities, after a thousand dangers to his life, he makes a little profit. Concerning worldly offices there is nothing I can write to you, since experience has taught you and still teaches you enough about the wretchedness of it. What a mass of misery, anxiety, and worry there is in earning the favor of princes, in keeping up the friendship of your peers, in striving for honors, this I can learn from you better than I can teach it to you, since from my childhood onward I have learned to live within my lot, content with my books and the little leisure I have, and insofar as I can I dwell within myself, neither yearning nor striving for anything outside myself. And so, shall we, with all our panting and sweating, barely gain any of these earthly, evanescent, uncertain, worthless goals, which are also common to us and the beasts? And shall we in our drowsiness, sleepiness, and almost reluctance be dragged *by the gods* to the heavenly and the divine, to that which neither ear has heard nor heart imagined, as if without us neither God could reign nor the citizens of heaven be happy? Certainly if we could gain earthly happiness at our leisure, a person who wished to avoid work could well prefer to serve the world rather than God; but if we are worn out on the road of sinners no less, nay more, than on the road of God (whence that saying of the damned, "We are weary on the road of wickedness"), it can be nothing but utter madness not to choose to work where work leads to a reward and to choose instead to work where work leads to torment. I leave aside the great happiness and peace of mind that come from a clear conscience, devoid of fear and guilt, for that undoubtedly far outweighs all the sensuous pleasures that can be obtained or desired in this life. For what is desirable about worldly pleasures, which weary us as we seek them, make us into fools when we gain them, torment us when we lose them? Do you doubt, my son, that the minds of the wicked are continuously agitated by anxiety? The word of God, who can neither deceive nor be deceived, is this: "The heart of the wicked man is like a raging sea which can never be calm." For nothing is safe for them, nothing peaceful; all things assault them with fear, all things assail them with anxiety, all things threaten them with death. And shall we, then, envy such people? Shall we emulate them? And

videbimus? Hos emulabimur? & *obliti propriae dignitatis*, obliti patriae patrisque caelestis, horum nos ipsi, cum liberi simus nati, ultro mancipia faciemus, & una cum illis misere viventes, morientes miserius, miserrime tandem aeternis ignibus affligemur? O caecas hominum mentes! O pectora caeca! Quis non videat vel luce clarius haec omnia esse ipsa veritate veriora? nec tamen facimus quae facienda esse cognoscimus, sed haeremus adhuc, nequicquam caeno cupientes avellere plantam.

Occurrent tibi, fili, (ne dubita) in his praesertim locis in quibus habitas innumera singulis horis impedimenta quae te a proposito sancte beneque vivendi deterreant & nisi caveas agant in praeceps. Sed inter omnia exitialis illa est pestis versari inter eos dies & noctes quorum vita non solum omni ex parte illecebra est peccati, sed tota in expugnanda virtute posita, sub imperatore diabolo, sub vexillis mortis, sub stipendiis Gehennae militat adversus caelum, adversus dominum, & adversus Christum eius. Tu autem clama cum propheta, "Dirumpamus vincula eorum & proiiciamus a nobis iugum ipsorum." Hi sunt enim quos tradidit deus in passiones ignominiae & in reprobum sensum, ut faciant ea quae non conveniunt, plenos omni iniquitate, plenos invidia, homicidiis, contentione, dolo, malignitate, detractores deo odibiles, contumeliosos, superbos, elatos, inventores malorum, insipientes, incompositos, sine affectione, sine foedere, sine misericordia. Qui cum iustitiam dei quotidie videant, non intelligunt. Tamen quoniam qui talia agunt digni sunt morte, non solum qui ea faciunt sed etiam qui consentiunt facientibus, tu igitur, fili, noli illis placere quibus ipsa displicet virtus, sed illud apostoli tibi semper sit ante oculos, "Oportet deo magis placere quam hominibus," & illud, "Si hominibus placerem, Christi servus non essem." Invadat te sancta quaedam ambitio, & dedigneris eos tibi vitae esse magistros qui te potius praeceptore indigeant. Longe enim decentius ut ipsi tecum bene vivendo homines esse incipiant, quam ut tu velis per omissionem boni propositi cum illis turpiter obbrutescere. Tenet me (Deum testor) aliquando extasis quasi & stupor quidam cum mecum incipio studia hominum aut (ut dixerim significantius) meras insanias nescio an cogitare potius quam dolere, mirari an deplorare. Magna enim profecto insania evangelio non credere, cuius veritatem sanguis martyrum clamat, apostolicae resonant voces, prodigia probant, ratio confirmat, mundus testatur, elementa loquun-

---

3–4 & . . . affligemur] & . . . affligamur *96 96+ 98 04 06 E-99 E-95+ E-04 E-08*, ut . . . affligamur *E-00 E-02 E-07+ E-09; grammar requires either* ut . . . affligamur *or* & . . . affligemur *shall we forget our own dignity,* forget our fatherland and our father in heaven, and, though we are freeborn, willingly enslave ourselves to them, and together with them lead a miserable life, die a more miserable death, and finally suffer the most miserable torments of eternal fire? O the blind minds of men! O the blind hearts! Who cannot see as clear as daylight that all this is truer than truth itself? And yet we do not do what we know should be done, but rather we are stuck in the mire, without even wanting to pull our foot out.

Have no doubt of it, my son, every hour of the day you will encounter, especially in the places where you dwell, innumerable obstacles which will deter you from fulfilling your resolution to lead a good and holy life and which, if you are not careful, will cast you into the abyss. But among all of them, the most deadly plague is to be conversant day and night with those whose way of life in every respect is not only an enticement to sin but is also completely devoted to the defeat of virtue, as they fight under their commander the devil, under the banner of death, for the wages of Gehenna, battling against heaven, against the Lord, and against his Anointed. But as for you, cry out with the prophet: "Let us break their chains and let us cast their yoke off of us." For these are those whom God has given over to shameful passions and to wicked perceptions, so that they do what is not fitting, full of all iniquity, full of envy, murder, strife, deceit, malice, backbiters, odious to God, contemptuous, proud, high and mighty, devisers of evil, foolish, disordered, without affection, without trust, without mercy. Though they see the justice of God every day, they do not understand it. Nevertheless, since those who do such things deserve to die, not only those who do them but also those who concur with what they do, therefore, my son, do not please those whom virtue displeases, but always keep before your eyes that saying of the apostle, "It is right to please God more than men," and also, "If I should please men, I would not be a servant of Christ." Be taken over by a sort of holy ambition, and scorn to accept as masters to teach you how to live those who actually need you as their teacher. For it is far more fitting that they should begin to be human by living well with you than that you should be willing to become a shameful brute together with them by abandoning your good resolution. As God is my witness, I sometimes find myself dumbfounded and almost out of my mind when I begin to consider (or should I say lament?) and to marvel at (or should I say deplore?) the pursuits of mankind, or (to speak more accurately) their downright madness. For it is truly madness not to believe the gospel, the truth of which is proclaimed by the blood of martyrs, resounded by the voice of the apostles, proved by miracles, confirmed by reason, witnessed by the world, spoken of by the elements, confessed by the devils. But it is a far

tur, daemones confitentur. Sed longe maior insania, si de evangelii
veritate non dubitas, vivere tamen quasi de eius falsitate non dubitares.
Nam si illa sunt vera, difficillimum esse divitem ingredi regnum cae-
lorum, quid cumulandis quotidie divitiis inhiamus? Et si illud est
5   verum, quaerendam gloriam non quae ex hominibus sed quae ex deo
est, cur de iudiciis hominum semper pendemus, deo placere nemo est
qui curet? Et si firma in nobis est fides futurum aliquando ut dominus
dicat, "Ite maledicti in ignem aeternum," et rursus, "Venite benedicti
possidete regnum paratum vobis a constitutione mundi," cur nihil mi-
10 nus aut timemus quam Gehennam aut speramus quam regnum dei?
Quid possumus aliud dicere quam multos esse nomine christianos, sed
re paucissimos?
     Tu vero, fili, contende intrare per angustam portam nec quid multi
agant attende, sed quid agendum ipsa tibi naturae lex, ipsa ratio, ipse
15 deus ostendet. Neque enim aut minor tua erit gloria si felix eris cum
paucis, aut levior paena si miser eris cum multis. Erunt autem duo
praecipue praesentissima tibi remedia adversus mundum & Satanam,
quibus quasi duabus alis de lacrimarum valle tolleris in altum, ele-
emosyna scilicet atque oratio. Quid enim possumus sine auxilio dei?
20 aut quomodo ille auxiliabitur non invocatus? Sed & invocantem te certe
non audiet qui invocantem prius pauperem non exaudisti. Neque enim
decet ut te deus hominem non contemnat qui prius homo hominem
contempsisti. Scriptum est, "In qua mensura mensi fueritis remetietur
vobis," & alibi, "Beati misericordes quoniam misericordiam conse-
25 quentur."
     Cum autem te ad orationem invito, non ad eam invito quae in multi-
loquio est sed quae in secreto mentis recessu, in penetralibus animi,
ipso affectu loquitur deo & in lucidissima contemplationis tenebra
mentem patri non praesentat modo sed unit ineffabilibus quibusdam
30 modis, quos soli norunt experti, nec curo quam longa sit oratio tua sed
quam efficax, quam sit ardens, interrupta potius suspiriis quam per-
petua quadam serie dictionum numeroque diffusa. Si tua tibi salus est
cordi, si tutus a diaboli laqueis, a mundi procellis, ab inimicorum in-
sidiis, si deo gratus, si felix tandem esse desideras, fac nulla praetereat
35 dies qua vel semel Deum tuum per orationem non adeas et prostratus
ante eum humili piae mentis affectu illud non de summis labris sed de
imis visceribus clames cum propheta, "Delicta iuventutis meae & igno-
rantias meas ne memineris, sed secundum misericordiam tuam memen-

---

22 non contemnat] 96 96+ 98 04 06 E-95 + E-99 E-00 E-04 E-07 + E-08, contemnat E-02
E-09; homo hominem] 96 96+ 98 04 06 E-95 + E-00 E-99 E-04 E-07 + E-08, hominem
E-02 E-09   29 unit] 96 96+ 98 04 06 E-95 + E-99 E-00 E-04 E-07 + E-08, vult E-02
E-09

greater madness to have no doubt about the truth of the gospel and yet
to live as if you had no doubt about its falsity. For if it is true that it is very
difficult for a rich man to enter into the kingdom of heaven, why do we
long every day to pile up riches? And if it is true that we should not seek
the glory that comes from men but that which comes from God, why do
we always hang upon the judgments of men, while no one takes pains to
please God? And if we firmly believe that one day the Lord will say, "Go,
ye cursed, into eternal fire," and again, "Come, ye blessed, take posses-
sion of the kingdom which has been prepared for you from the foun-
dation of the world," why is hell the least of our fears and the kingdom
of God the least of our hopes? What can we say except that many are
Christians in name but very few in fact?

But you, my son, strive to enter by the narrow gate and pay no
attention to what the many do, but rather heed what the law of nature,
the law of reason, and God himself will show you is to be done. For your
glory will not be any less if you are happy with the few, nor will your
punishment be any lighter if you are miserable with the many. But two
remedies will be especially efficacious against the world and Satan; by
them you will be lifted up on high, as if with two wings, above this vale of
tears: almsdeeds and prayer. For what can we do without God's help?
Or how will he help us if he is not called upon to do so? But certainly he
will not hear you when you call on him if beforehand you have not
heard the poor man calling on you. For it is not fitting that God should
not scorn you as a man if you as a man have scorned another man. It is
written, "With the same measure by which you have measured out, it
will be measured out to you in turn," and elsewhere, "Blessed are the
merciful, for they shall obtain mercy."

But when I urge prayer upon you, I do not recommend the sort that
consists in saying many words but rather the kind which speaks to God
with feeling, in the inward recesses of your mind and the inner cham-
bers of your heart, and which in the brightest darkness of contempla-
tion not only presents your mind to the Father but unites it with him in
a sort of ineffable way known only to those who have experienced it;
nor do I care how long but rather how effectual your prayer is, how
ardent, broken off with sighs rather than stretched out in a sort of
endless series of multiplied words. If you care about your salvation, if
you wish to be safe from the snares of the devil, from the storms of this
world, from the plots of your enemies, if you want to be pleasing to
God, and finally if you desire to be happy, let no day pass by without
praying to your God at least once; and, prostrate before him, with the
humble disposition of a pious mind, not with mere lip service but from
the bottom of your heart, cry out with the prophet, "Do not remember
the sins of my youth and my foolishness but according to your mercy, O

to mei propter bonitatem tuam, domine." Suggeret tibi cum spiritus
qui interpellat pro nobis, tum ipsa necessitas singulis horis quid petas a
deo tuo; suggeret & sacra lectio, quam ut, omissis iam fabulis nugisque
poetarum, semper habeas in manibus etiam atque etiam rogo. Nihil

5 deo gratius, nihil tibi utilius facere potes, quam si non cessaveris litteras
sacras nocturna versare manu, versare diurna. Latet enim in illis cae-
lestis vis quaedam viva & efficax quae legentis animum, si modo illas
pure humiliterque tractaverit, in divinum amorem mirabili quadam
potestate transformat.

10 Sed epistolae iam fines excessi, trahente me ipsa materia & mira
quadam charitate, qua te cum semper, tum ex ea praesertim hora sum
prosequutus qua sanctissimi tui propositi factus sum certior. Illud
postremo te admonitum velim de quo hic etiam, cum mecum eras,
tecum saepe locutus sum, ut duo haec nunquam obliviscaris: & filium

15 dei pro te esse mortuum, & te quoque etiam si diu vixeris breui esse
moriturum. His quasi geminis stimulis, altero quidem timoris, amoris
altero, urge equum tuum per breve stadium momentaneae vitae ad
praemia felicitatis aeternae, quando nullum alium finem praefinire
nobis aut debemus aut possumus quam ut perpetua utriusque hominis

20 pace infinito bono sine fine fruamur. Vale & deum time. *Ferrariae, xv
Maii. Mcccclxxxxii.*

Ioannes Picus Mirandula Andreae Corneo *Urbinati,* salutem

*Quas proxime ad me dedisti litteras tuas idibus Octobris accepi. Quas scribis
dedisse prius non pervenerunt. Rescripsissem illico si accepissem, ita sum ad*

25 *scribendum impiger & in hoc munere, sive studio sive natura, minime cessator.
Non tamen erat quod verereris silentio etiam diuturnio amicitiam nostram posse
labefactari. Perpetuus amicus sum ego, non temporarius. Et firma satis non est
amicitia si qua, velut tibicines, has litterarum sibi vicissitudines postulet, quae
(ut Plauti dixerim verbo) quasi nutantem infirmusculamque furcillent.*

30 *Sed ut ad ea veniam quae scribis,* adhortaris me tu ad actuosam vitam &
ciuilem, frustra me & in ignominiam quasi ac contumeliam tam diu
philosophatum dicens, nisi tandem in agendarum tractandarumque
rerum palaestra desudem. Et equidem, mi Andrea, oleum operamque
meorum studiorum perdidissem, si ita essem nunc animatus ut hac tibi

35 parte accedere & assentiri possem. Exitialis haec illa est & monstrosa
persuasio quae hominum mentes invasit, aut non esse philosophiae

---

3 fabulis] *96 96+ 98 04 06 E-95+ E-99 E-00 E-02 E-04 E-07+ E-08,* famulis *E-09*
16 amoris] *96 96+ 98 04 06 E-95+ E-99 E-00 E-04 E-07+ E-08,* mortis *E-02 E-09*
26 verereris] *96 96+ E-99 E-00 E-04 E-08,* uereris *98 04 06 E-95+ E-02 E-09,* vetereris
E-07+ 35 & monstrosa] *96 96+ 98 04 06 E-95+ E-99 E-00 E-02 E-04 E-08 E-09,*
monstrosa *E-07+*

lord, remember me because of your goodness." What to ask of your God will be suggested both by the Spirit who intercedes for us and by your needs themselves from hour to hour; they will also be suggested by your reading of holy scripture, which I beg you over and over again to have always in your hands, putting aside the fables and follies of the poets. Nothing you can do will be more pleasing to God and more useful to you than never to cease turning the pages of holy scripture, by night and by day. For there is hidden within them a certain heavenly force, living and efficacious, which, as long as they are treated purely and humbly, has a certain marvelous power to transform the reader's mind into the love of God.

But I have already exceeded the bounds of a letter, led on by my subject and by a certain wonderful charity that I have felt for you always, but especially from the hour when I learned of your most holy resolution. Finally I want to remind you of what I often said to you also when you were here with me, that you should never forget two things: that the son of God died for you and that you also, however long you may live, must die before long. With these two spurs, the one of fear, the other of hope, urge on your mount through the short race of this brief life toward the reward of eternal happiness, since we neither ought nor are able to set ourselves any other goal than to enjoy infinite goodness forever with perpetual peace both of body and soul. Farewell and fear God. *Ferrara, May 15, 1492.*

Giovanni Pico della Mirandola to Andrea Corneo *of Urbino,* greetings

On October 15 I received the last letter you sent me. You write that you sent an earlier one, but it has not arrived. If I had received it I would have replied immediately, so diligent am I in writing, and in that duty, whether by nurture or nature, I am hardly a procrastinator. But there was no reason for you to be afraid that silence, even a long one, would impair our friendship. I am a constant, not a temporary, friend. And no friendship is sufficiently firm if it needs such exchanges of letters as pillars (so to speak) to prop it up, as if it were (in the words of Plautus) ramshackle and ready to fall down.

But to come to the subject of your letter, you urge me to take up an active and political life, saying that it is pointless and something of a disgrace and a reproach to me that I have philosophized such a long time if I do not now at last work up a sweat on the wrestling mat where practical affairs are handled and conducted. And indeed, my friend Andrea, I would have wasted the time and effort of my studies if I could now be of a mind to assent and agree with you on this point. This is a deadly and monstrous notion that has taken over the minds of men: that noblemen

studia viris principibus attingenda, aut summis labiis ad pompam potius ingenii quam animi cultum vel otiose etiam delibanda. Omnino illud Neoptolemi habent pro decreto, aut nil philosophandum aut paucis. Pro nugamentis & meris fabulis iam illa accipiuntur sapientum
5 dicta, firmam & solidam felicitatem in bonis animi esse, extraria haec corporis vel fortunae aut parum aut nihil ad nos attinere.

    Sed inquies, "ita volo Martham amplectaris ut Mariam interim non deseras." Hac tibi parte non repugno, nec qui id faciunt damno vel accuso, sed multum abest ut a contemplandi vita ad ciuilem transisse
10 error non sit, non transisse pro flagitio aut omnino sub culpae nota vel criminis censeatur. Ergo vitio alicui vertetur quod virtutem ipsam virtutis gratia, *nil extra eam quaerens*, perpetuo affectet & prosequatur, quod divina mysteria, naturae consilia perscrutans, hoc perfruatur otio, caeterarum rerum despector & negligens, quando illa possunt
15 sectatorum suorum vota satis implere? Ergo illiberale aut non omnino principis erit non mercennarium facere studium sapientiae? Quis aequo animo haec aut ferat aut audiat? Certe nunquam philosophatus est, qui ideo philosophatus est ut aliquando aut possit aut nolit philosophari. Mercaturam exercuit ille, non philosophiam.

20   Scribis appetere tempus ut me alicui ex summis Italiae principibus dedam. Adhuc illam philosophantium de se opinionem non nosti, qui iuxta Horatium se regum reges putant, mores pati & servire nesciunt. Secum habitant & sua contenti animi tranquillitate sibi ipsis ipsi supersunt. Nihil extra se quaerunt; quae in honore sunt apud vulgus inho-
25 nora sunt apud illos; et omnino quaecunque vel humana sitit libido vel suspirat ambitio negligunt & contemnunt. Quod cum omnibus, tum illis dubio procul faciendum est, quibus se ita indulsit fortuna ut non modo laute & commode sed etiam splendide vivere possint. Magnae istae fortunae sublimant quidem & ostentant, sed saepe uti ferox equus
30 & sternax sessorem excutiunt. Certe semper male habent et vexant potius quam vehunt. Aurea illa optanda mediocritas quae nos uti mannus vehat aequabilius & imperii patiens nobis vere seruiat, non dominetur.

    In hac ego opinione perstans, cellulam meam, mea studia, meorum
35 librorum oblectamenta, meam animi pacem, regiis aulis, publicis negotiis, vestris aucupiis, curiae favoribus antepono. Nec mei huius litterarii

---

8 Hac tibi] *96 96+ E-95+ E-99 E-00 E-02 E-04 E-07+ E-08 E-09,* tibi *98 04 06*   11 quod] *96+ E-95+,* & *96 98 04 06 E-99 E-00 E-02 E-04 E-07+ E-08 E-09*   24–25 inhonora] *96 96+ 98 04 06 E-95+ E-00 E-07+ E-08,* in honora *E-99 E-04,* in honore *E-02 E-09*   30 vexant] *96 96+ 98 04 06 E-95+ E-99 E-00 E-02 E-04 E-07+ E-09,* vexent *E-08*   31 vehunt] vehant *96 96+ 98 04 06 E-95+ E-99 E-00 E-02 E-04 E-07+ E-08 E-09 (the indicative is required here unless* & *is emended to* ut *and vexant to* vexent)   32 mannus] *96 E-00,* mañus *96+ 98 06 E-99 E-04 E-08,* manus *04 E-95+ E-02 E-07+ E-09*

either should have nothing to do with philosophy or should sip it a little at their leisure for the sake of showing off their wits rather than cultivating their minds. People consider the idea of Neoptolemus as taken altogether for granted, that philosophy should be studied not at all or only briefly. They consider as trifles and mere fables the dicta of wise men: that firm and solid happiness lies in the goods of the mind and that the external goods of the body or of fortune have little or no relevance to us.

But you will say, "I want you to embrace Martha without deserting Mary." On this point I will not oppose you, nor will I condemn or accuse those who do so, but it is one thing to say that it is not wrong to move from a contemplative life to a political one and quite another to say that not to do so should be considered disgraceful or indicative of guilt and altogether reprehensible. Shall we, then, brand someone as deficient if he perpetually loves and follows virtue for its own sake, *seeking nothing extraneous,* and employs his leisure in investigating the mysteries of God and the secrets of nature, looking down on and neglecting other concerns, since the contemplative life can satisfactorily fulfill the wishes of its followers? Shall the pursuit of wisdom, then, be completely unworthy of a free man or a prince unless we make it mercenary? Who could bear or hear such things with equanimity? Certainly no one has engaged in philosophy if he has done so only in order to be someday merely able or unwilling to engage in it. He has engaged in commerce, not in philosophy.

You write that it is time for me to commit myself to some great Italian prince. You still do not know the opinion philosophers have of themselves: according to Horace they think they are the kings of kings; they do not know how to patiently obey and serve. They dwell within themselves and, content with their own peace of mind, they are more than sufficient unto themselves. They seek nothing outside themselves; what is honorable to the mob is dishonorable to them; the things which human passion thirsts after or which ambition sighs for they utterly neglect and scorn. All philosophers should do this, but undoubtedly those whom fortune has kindly enabled to live not only elegantly and comfortably but even lavishly. Indeed such a great fortune raises a man up and shows him off, but often, like a fierce and skittish horse, it throws its rider. Certainly it treats them badly and does not so much carry them as harry them. We should choose the golden mean, which, like a pony, carries us along more evenly and responds patiently to our commands, truly our servant and not our master.

Persisting in this belief, I prefer my little cell, my studies, the pleasures of my books, my peace of mind, to the courts of kings, public business, that bird-catching of yours, favor at court. And as the fruit of

otii illos fructus expecto, ut in rerum publicarum aestu atque tumultu
iacter & fluctuem, sed ut quos parturio tandem pariam liberos & quod
felix faustumque sit dedam aliquid in publicum, si non doctrinam,
ingenium saltem & diligentiam quod oleat. Et ne credas nostrae indus-
5 triae & laboris quicquam remissum, scito me, post multam assiduis
indefessisque lucubrationibus navatam operam, Hebraicam linguam,
Chaldaicamque didicisse & ad Arabicae evincendas difficultates nunc
quoque manus applicuisse. Haec ego principis viri & existimavi semper
& nunc existimo.

10   *Sed haec ut vere ita severe dixerim. Equidem principes istos excellentissimos,*
inprimisque magnanimum Barri Ducem Ludovicum, ita colo & veneror ut ex
Italiae principibus neminem magis. Illi me multum multis de causis debere
intelligo, & nihil est tam grave, nihil tam arduum quod (mihi si detur facultas)
demerendi hominis causa facturus non sim. Sed quae illorum est amplitudo &
15 *mea tenuitas ut ego ipsis non egere non possim, ita egere ipsi aut mea opera aut*
meo istuc adventu nullo modo possunt. Romam propediem proficiscar, inibi
hiematurus nisi vel repens casus vel nova intercidens fortuna alio me traxerit.
Inde fortasse audies quid tuus Picus in vita umbratili et sellularia contemplando
profecerit aut quid tandem (dicam enim quanquam arrogantius) quid (inquam),
20 *quando tu illi istuc accedenti doctorum copiam polliceris, aliorum operae indiget*
in re litteraria. Romae & ubiubi terrarum fuero, habebunt principes isti cui
imperent, quem velut trusatilem (ut inquit Plautus) molam pro arbitrio uersent.

    Quod scribis de re uxoria, nec temere nec de nihilo dictum existimo. Sed Davus
sum, Oedippus non sum, nec si sim esse volo. Id quicquid est, si videtur, latius
25 *explica; sin minus esto Harpocrates. Ego ut sese res dant, in arma consilium*
capio.

    Rhythmos meos Etruscos non est quod desideres. Iamdudum amatoriis lusibus
nuntium remisimus, alia meditantes. Sed hoc te quoque monitum volo, Lauram
tuam, si eam esses editurus, supprimas adhuc aliquot dies. Nam forsan paulo
30 *mox legent nostri homines de amore (vide quid dicam) quae nondum legerunt, et*
tu annotare plurima poteris quae ad rem tuam plurimum facient.

    De Alibrana, quanquam dignus non est de quo verba faciam, haec tamen
dixerim, benemerito illum domino male gratiam rettulisse. Nec est quod fugam
suam in quemquam alium quam in se ipsum reiiciat aut deriuet, quando meis
35 *domesticis (quod negare ille non potest) non minus fere quam mihi debet. Sed*
non primum nunc, ut tu nosti, aut fidem fefellit aut dominum ludificatus est.

---

33 benemerito] benemeritum 96 96+ 98 04 06 E-95+ E-99 E-00 E-02 E-04 E-07+
E-08, bene meritum E-09   35 ille non potest] 96 96+ 98 04 06 E-95+ E-99 E-00 E-02
E-04 E-08 E-09, ille E-07+

my scholarly leisure I do not expect to be tossed and turned in the maelstrom and tumult of public affairs but rather to give birth to the book-children with which I am in labor and to publish something felicitous and propitious, something that savors, if not of learning, at least of intelligence and diligence. And lest you think I have been at all remiss in my industry and labor, hear this: having expended much energy in continual and unwearied studying, I have learned Hebrew and Chaldee, and now I have also set my hand to overcoming the difficulties of Arabic. I have always considered, and I still do consider, these to be the proper pursuits of a nobleman.

But I grant the severity of my verity. Certainly I cherish and venerate those most excellent princes, and especially Luigi, duke of Bari, none more among the princes of Italy. I understand that I owe him much for many reasons, and there is nothing so weighty, nothing so arduous which, if it were in my power, I would not do to oblige him. But their power is so great and mine so slender that there is no way that I could not be in need of them, and so too they cannot be in any need at all of my endeavors or my going to them. Very soon I am going to set out for Rome, to spend the winter there, unless some unexpected event or new contingency takes me elsewhere. From there perhaps you will hear what your Pico has accomplished by contemplation in his shadowy and sedentary life or you may learn (I will say it, however arrogantly), you may learn (I say), since you promise him that when he gets there he will find an abundance of learned men, to what degree he needs the help of others in matters of scholarship. In Rome, and wherever on earth I may be, those princes of yours will have me at their command; they can turn me at will, like a handmill (as Plautus says).

As for what you write about your marital concerns, I am confident that you do not say it frivolously or without good reason. But I am Davus, not Oedipus, and even if I were, I do not wish to be. Whatever it is, explain it more fully, if you wish. If not, play Harpocrates about it. And according to the circumstances I will decide on a strategy.

There is no reason for you to want my Italian verse. I have long since said farewell to amatory sports, having other things in mind. But let me also tell you this: if you are about to publish your Laura, withhold it for a few more days. For before long we Italians will be reading something about love that we have never read before (notice what I am saying) and you will be able to note down many things very relevant to your subject matter.

Concerning Alibrana, though he does not deserve that I should speak of him, nevertheless I would say this: he has been ungrateful to a master who deserved well of him. Nor is there any reason for him to put off or blame his flight on anyone but himself, since he is almost as deeply in debt to my servants as he is to me (which he himself cannot deny). But, as you know, this is not the first time that he has acted in bad faith and made sport of his master. I know what he said

Scio quid postquam etiam auffugit in me ille & de me [dixerit], sed non curat
culicem elephas. Et condonatum tibi volo quicquid antehac levis homo peccarit,
sed ne abutatur in posterum patientia mea, ne qualem se mihi ille immerito
praestitit, talem me ego illi tandem praestare cogar.

5   *Quod amicum illum tuum cui in amore res male cessit, apud Florianum*
nostrum excusaveris, ex officio fecisti. Habet ille quidem & ex historiis & ex
poetis, ex ipsa etiam philosophia unde se a nota criminis vendicet; habet unde
magnorum se hominum praeiudiciis (Davidis praesertim Salamonisque)
tutetur, ut Aristotelem taceam, qui dum nonnullas etiam meretrices saepe de-
10   *peribat suorum de moribus praeceptorum nil meminit, quando amatae feminae*
uti Cereri Eleusinae sacra fecit. Sed ille haec tutamenta & quasi propugnacula
sui facinoris non amplexatur modo vel amat, sed odit & reiicit & recusat;
iacturam queritur suam, non culpam deprecatur; dolet quod peccavit, non
defendit. Et mihi quidem vel hoc nomine videtur caeteris excusandus, quod ipse
15   *se nil excusat. Nihil homine imbecillius, nihil amore potentius. Hieronimi illa*
invicta & inconcussa mens, dum caelo tota inhaeret, puellarum choris intererat.
Quae illum pestis potuit vel infestare, quem non edomabit? Si hoc amor in eremo,
in humo collisis membris, in hebdomadarum potuit inedia, quid in pluma, in
umbra, in omni delitiarum affluentia non poterit? Accedit quod ille nunc primo
20   *cecidit, ruinae huius alioquin insolens & ignarus. De Neptuno conqueri potest*
qui semel tantum naufragium fecit. Si ad eundem iterum offenderit lapidem,
nemo manum porrigat, nemo misereatur. Nunc non excusari iure non potest,
quem ita facti paenitet, ut favore excusationis se dignum ipse non existimet. Sed
haec etiam nimis, quando amicus tuus huiusmodi facti memoriam non solum
25   *aliquo modo litteris tradi sed quod sequens vita eius faciat obliterari penitus*
cupit. Vale. Christophorus non aderat cum tuas accepi. Domino tuo et universae
Bonromeae familiae, quam & amavi semper & nunc plurimum amo, me non
vulgariter commendabis. Perusiae, xv Octobris, Mccclxxxvi anno gratiae.

1–2 me [dixerit]] me *96 96+ 98 04 06 E-95+ E-99 E-00 E-02 E-04 E-07+ E-08*
E-09   5 Florianum] *96 96+ 98 04 06 E-95+ E-99 E-00 E-02 E-04 E-08 E-09,* Floren-
tianum *E-07+*   28 Perusiae . . . gratiae] *96 96+ 98 04 06 E-95+ E-99 E-00 E-04*
E-07+ E-08 E-09, Perusiae . . . Mcccc.lxvxvi. . . . gratiae *E-02*

against me and about me after he ran away, but an elephant pays no attention to a gnat. And I want you to forgive the previous offenses of this fickle man, but let him not abuse my patience in the future, lest I should finally be forced to treat him as he has (quite unfairly) treated me.

You did your duty when you pleaded with our friend Floriano to excuse that friend of yours who had bad luck in his love affair. Indeed he has precedents from history and the poets and even philosophy to vindicate himself from any blame of wrongdoing; he has great men as precedents to defend himself, especially David and Solomon, to say nothing of Aristotle, who forgot all about his moral precepts on those many occasions when he fell head over heels for some wenches or even whores, and sacrificed to his mistress as if she were the Eleusinian Ceres. But this friend of yours not only does not embrace or cherish such defenses and ramparts (as it were) for his wrongdoing, but rather he hates and rejects and refuses them; he complains of his loss, he does not extenuate his guilt; he is sorry for his sin, he does not defend it. Indeed, it seems to me that others should excuse him precisely because he does not excuse himself. Nothing is weaker than man, nothing stronger than love. That most invincible and unshakable mind of Jerome, while it was entirely set on heaven, was present at the dances of the girls. If that plague could assail even him, who is there that it will not conquer? If love could do this to a hermit, whose limbs were crushed to the ground, who fasted for weeks, what can it not do among feather-pillows in the shadows, in the full flush of voluptuousness? Then too, this is the first time he has fallen, having no other experience or knowledge of such a catastrophe. Someone who has suffered only one shipwreck can complain against Neptune. If he stumbles again on the same stone, let no one give him a helping hand, let no one take pity on him. As it is, it is not right not to excuse him, since he is so sorry for what he has done that he does not consider he deserves the favor of being excused. But I have said too much already, since your friend not only does not want the memory of his deed committed to a letter in any way at all but rather desires that his life from now on should blot it out completely. Farewell. Cristoforo was not here when I received your letter. To your master and to the whole Borromeo family, to whom I have always been and still am deeply devoted, give my regards in no ordinary fashion. Perugia, October 15, in the year of grace 1486.

Ioannes Picus Mirandula *Ioanni* Francisco Pico nepoti, salutem

Felix es, fili, quando non solum id tibi tribuit deus ut bene vivas, sed
ut bene vivens a malis tamen ob id maxime quia bene vivis interim male
audias. Aequa enim laus a laudatis laudari et improbari ab improbis.
5   Sed non propterea te felicem appello quia haec tibi calumnia gloriosa
est, sed quia dominus Iesus, qui verax (immo ipsa veritas) est, futuram
affirmat mercedem nostram copiosam in caelis cum maledixerint nobis
homines & dixerint omne malum adversus nos mentientes propter
eum. Apostolica, *si nescis*, haec dignitas est, dignum haberi qui pro
10   evangelico nomine ab impiis infameris, quando apostolos legimus
apud Lucam gaudentes a conspectu abiisse concilii quia digni habiti
essent quibus pro nomine Iesu contumelia irrogaretur. Gaudeamus
igitur & nos si tanta apud deum gloria digni sumus ut eius gloria in
ignominia nostra manifestetur. Et si quid a mundo durum patimur ac
15   molestum, dulcissima illa domini vox nos consoletur: "Si vos mundus
odio habet, scitote quia priorem me vobis odio habuit." Si mundus
illum odio habuit per quem factus est mundus, nos vilissimi homun-
ciones, et si flagitia nostra pensitemus, dignissimi omnibus probris,
usqueadeo, si quis detrahat, si quis maledicat, aegre feremus ut ne ille
20   maledicat male agere ipsi incipiamus? Excipiamus haec potius alacres
maledicta & si non ea felicitas nostra est ut pro virtute, pro veritate,
quemadmodum olim heroes nostri, verbera, vincula, carceres, gladios
sustineamus, satis nobiscum bene actum putemus si vel convitia homi-
num improborum, detractiones, odia patiamur, ne omni nobis me-
25   rendi occasione sublata, praemii etiam spes reliqua nulla sit. Si bene
viventem te homines laudent, porro virtus haec tua quatenus quidem
virtus est similem te Christo facit, sed quatenus laudata est facit dis-
similem, qui praemium suae virtutis ab hominibus mortem crucis ac-
cepit, propter quod & deus, ut inquit apostolus, exaltavit eum & dedit
30   illi nomen quod est super omne nomen. Optabilius igitur crucifigi a
mundo ut exalteris a deo quam exaltari a mundo ut iudiceris a deo. Ille
enim crucifigit ad vitam, hic exaltat ad gloriam; ille exaltat ad casum,
hic iudicat ad Gehennam. Denique si tibi mundus applaudit, fieri vix
potest ut virtus quae tota sursum erecta solum deum debet habere cui

---

18 omnibus probris, usqueadeo] *96*, omnibus probris usque adeo *E-04*, omnibus us-
queadeo probris *98 04 06*, omnibus probris usque a deo *96+ E-00 E-95+ E-07+*, om-
nibus probaris usqueadeo *E-08*, omnibus probris / usque a deo *E-99 E-02*
E-09   21 pro virtute, pro veritate] *96 96+ 98 04 06 E-95+ E-99 E-02 E-04 E-08*
E-09, pro veritate pro virtute *E-07+*

Giovanni Pico della Mirandula to his nephew *Giovanni* Francesco Pico, greetings

You are blessed, my son, when God grants you not only the grace to live well but also, while you are living well, to be in bad repute now and then among the wicked precisely because you live well. For it is equally praiseworthy to be praised by the good and to be reproved by the reprobate. But I do not call you blessed because you have this slander as a source of your glory, but because our lord Jesus, who is truthful, nay Truth itself, affirms that our reward in heaven will be abundant when men speak evil of us and say all sorts of evil against us, lying because of him. *In case you do not know it,* it is a dignity befitting an apostle for you to be held worthy of defamation by the impious because of the gospel, since we read in Luke that the apostles left the presence of the council rejoicing that they were considered worthy to be objects of contempt because of the name of Jesus. Therefore, let us also rejoice if we are worthy of such great glory in God's eyes that his glory is revealed in our ignominy. And if we suffer from the world anything hard or troublesome, let that most sweet saying of our lord console us: "If the world hates you, know that it hated me before you." If the world hated the maker of the world, shall we worthless human wretches (and if we consider our sins we are most worthy of all manner of reproof), if someone slanders us, if someone speaks evil of us, shall we take it so ill that we start to do evil ourselves in order to keep him from speaking evil of us? Rather let us accept this evil speech gladly, and if we do not have the happiness to endure for virtue and for truth blows, chains, prisons, swords, as our heroes once did, let us think we have been treated well enough if we suffer at least the reproaches of wicked men, their slander and hatred, lest all occasions of merit be taken from us, leaving us also no hope of reward. If men praise you for living well, then that virtue of yours, insofar as it is indeed virtue, makes you like Christ, but insofar as it is praised, it makes you unlike him, since the reward men gave him for his virtue was death on the cross, for which reason also God, as the apostle says, raised him up and gave him the name which is above all names. And so it is more desirable to be crucified by the world so that you may be raised up by God than to be raised up by the world so that you may be judged by God. For the world crucifies us to life, God raises us up to glory; the world raises us up for a fall, God judges us to Gehenna. Finally, if the world applauds you, it is hardly possible that your virtue, which should be entirely directed on high and should seek

placeat, blandienti se paulisper hominum gratiae non inclinet, & si de sua etiam integritate non perdit, perdit tamen de praemio, quod cum in terris incipit persolui ubi omnia sunt exigua, minus erit in caelo ubi omnia sunt immensa.

5 Felices contumeliae quae nos tutos reddunt ne aut iustitiae flos pestifero inanis gloriae flatu marcescat aut popularis rumusculi vano auctoramento aeternitatis stipendia nobis imminuantur. Amplectamur, fili, has contumelias & de sola ignominia crucis domini fideles servi sanctissima ambitione superbiamus. "Praedicamus," inquit
10 Paulus, "Christum crucifixum, Hebraeis quidem scandalum, gentibus stultitiam, nobis autem dei virtutem & sapientiam. Sapientia ista mundi stultitia est apud deum, & stultitia Christi illa est quae sapientiam vincit mundi, per quam placuit deo salvos facere credentes." Si insanos eos esse non dubitas qui virtuti detrahunt tuae, & christianam
15 vitam, hoc est sapientiam, insaniam vocant, cogita quanta tua esset insania, de insanorum iudicio a rectae vitae instituto dimoveri, cum error omnis emendatione tollendus, non imitatione augendus sit.

Hinniant illi, baubentur, allatrent; tu coeptum perge iter intrepidus, & de illorum nequitia atque miseria quantum ipse debeas deo per-
20 pende, qui sedentem in umbra mortis illuminavit & de illorum caetu translatum qui in densissimis tenebris devii huc illuc sine duce bacchantur, filiis lucis associauit. Sonet vox illa domini suauissima in auribus tuis semper: "Sine mortuos sepellire mortuos suos, tu me sequere." Mortui enim sunt qui deo non vivunt & in hoc temporariae mortis
25 spatio laboriosissime sibi aeternam mortem acquirunt. A quibus si petas quo tendant, quo sua studia, opera, curas referant, quem denique finem sibi praestituerint in cuius adeptione felices futuri sint, aut nihil omnino habebunt quod respondeant aut pugnantia secum controversaque sibi ipsis verba velut fanaticorum deliramenta loquentur. Neque
30 enim sciunt ipsimet quid agant sed more eorum qui fluminibus innatant male importatae consuetudinis vi quasi torrentis impetu feruntur, et hinc caecante eos nequitia, inde ad malum Satana exstimulante ruunt praecipites in omne facinus (caeci duces caecorum) donec improvisa eos occupet mors & dicatur eis, "Amice, hac nocte repetent animam tuam a te. Haec autem quae parasti, cuius erunt?" Tunc his

---

1 blandienti] *96 96+ E-95+ E-99 E-00 E-02 E-04 E-07+ E-08 E-09*, plaudienti *98 04 06*   2 tamen] *96 96+ E-95+ E-99 E-00 E-02 E-04 E-07+ E-08 E-09*, tamen non *98 04 06*   8–9 & de sola . . . superbiamus] *96 96+ 98 04 06 E-95+ E-99 E-00 E-04 E-07+ E-08, om. E-02 E-09*   21 huc illuc] *96 96+ 98 04 06 E-95+ E-99 E-00 E-02 E-04 E-08 E-09*, illuc *E-07+*   26 studia] *In the British Library copy of E-08 the rest of the text of this letter is lacking.*   32 caecante] *96 96+ 98 04 06 E-95+ E-99 E-00 E-02 E-04 E-09*, sequante *E-07+;* inde] *96 (errata), unde 96 (text) 96+ 98 04 06 E-95+ E-99 E-00 E-02 E-04 E-07+ E-09*   34 occupet] *96 96+ 98 04 06 E-95+ E-99 E-00 E-02 E-04 E-09*, aucupet *E-07+*

to please God alone, will not stoop a bit to the flattery and favor of men, and even if it loses nothing of its integrity, nevertheless it loses some of its reward, which, since it has begun to be paid on earth, where all things are meager, will be less in heaven, where all things are immense.

Blessed are the reproaches that protect us, keeping the flower of righteousness from withering in the pestilent blast of vainglory and preventing the wages of eternity from being lessened for us by the vain pay of popular gossip. Let us embrace these reproaches, my son, and let us like faithful servants, with a very holy ambition, take pride only in the ignominy of our lord's cross. "We preach," says Paul, "Christ crucified, to the Jews a stumbling block, to the gentiles folly, but to us the power and wisdom of God. The wisdom of this world is folly in the eyes of God, and the wisdom of the world is conquered by the folly of Christ, by which it has pleased God to save those who believe." If you have no doubt that those who disparage your virtue and call the Christian life (that is, wisdom) madness are themselves madmen, think how mad you would be to be drawn away from the right way of living by the judgment of madmen, since all delusions should be eliminated by correction, not reinforced by imitation.

Let them whinny, bay, bark at you; as for you, go forward fearlessly on the journey you have begun and, reflecting on their wickedness and misery, consider how much you owe God, who enlightened you when you were sitting in the shadow of death, removing you from that crowd of revelers who wander here and there with no guide in the deepest darkness, and brought you into the company of the sons of light. May that most sweet saying of our lord always resound in your ears: "Let the dead bury the dead, but as for you, follow me." For the dead are those who do not live for God and who expend enormous effort in this place of temporal death to gain for themselves eternal death. If you ask them where they are going, to what end they direct their studies, labors, pains, and finally what goal they have set for themselves that would make them happy if they achieved it, they will either say nothing at all in reply or they will speak in contradictions and say words that conflict with one another, like the babblings of madmen. For they themselves do not know what they are doing, but, like swimmers in a river, they are borne along by the force of perniciously naturalized customs, as if by the rush of the current; and, blinded on the one hand by their wickedness and on the other goaded toward evil by Satan, they rush headlong into all sorts of wicked deeds (the blind leading the blind) until death suddenly seizes them and they hear those words, "Friend, this night they will take back your soul from you. But these things you have prepared, whose will they be?" Then they will envy those whom they

invident quos despexerunt; laudant quos deriserunt: & imitari eos
vellent cum non possunt, quos dum poterant sequi, persequi malu-
erunt.

Obde igitur, fili carissime, auribus *ceras,* & quicquid dixerint, quic-
5   quid senserint homines de te pro nihilo habens, solum iudicium dei
specta, qui reddet unicuique secundum opera sua in revelatione sua de
caelo cum angelis virtutis suae, in flamma ignis faciens vindictam in eos
qui non noverunt deum nec paruerunt evangelio eius, "qui paenas," ut
ait apostolus, "dabunt in interitu aeternas a facie domini & a gloria
10 virtutis eius cum venerit glorificari in sanctis suis & admirabilis fieri in
omnibus qui crediderunt." Scriptum est, "Nolite timere qui corpus
possunt occidere, sed qui animam potest mittere in Gehennam."
Quanto minus hi tibi timendi sunt qui nec corpori tuo possunt nocere
nec animae, qui si nunc tibi detrahunt ex ratione viventi, nihil de-
15 trahent minus si relicta virtute vitiis obruaris, non quia illis vitium
displicet sed quia detrahendi vitium illis semper placet. Fuge, si tua
salus tibi est cordi, fuge quantum potes eorum consuetudinem & ad te
ipsum rediens saepe in abscondito ora clementissimum patrem,
clamans cum propheta, "Ad te, domine, levavi animam meam; *deus*
20 *meus,* in te confido; non erubescam etiam si irrideant me inimici mei,
etenim universi qui sperant in te non confundentur; confundantur
iniqua agentes supervacue; vias tuas, domine, demonstra mihi &
semitas tuas edoce me; dirige me in veritate tua & doce me, quia tu es
deus salvator meus & in te sperabo tota die." Fac item cogites semper
25 instantem mortem, et punctum scilicet esse quod vivimus & adhuc
puncto minus, tum quam sit malus antiquus hostis qui nobis regna
mundi promittit ut nobis regna caelorum eripiat, quam falsae volup-
tates quae ideo nos amplectuntur ut strangulent, quam dolosi honores
qui nos sublimant ut deinde praecipitent, quam letales divitiae, quae
30 quanto nos magis pascunt tanto magis venenant; quam breve, incer-
tum, umbratile, falsum, imaginarium est omne illud quod haec omnia
simul, etiam si ex voto affluant, nobis praestare possunt, quam magna
his et promissa & parata sunt qui contemptis praesentibus illam sus-
pirant patriam cuius rex divinitas, cuius lex charitas, cuius modus ae-
35 ternitas. His atque similibus cogitationibus animum occupa, quae susci-
tent dormientem, tepescentem accendant, uacillantem confirment &
tendenti ad caelum divini amoris alas exhibeant, ut cum ad nos veneris

---

5 senserint] *96 96+ 98 04 06 E-95 + E-99 E-00 E-04 E-07,* censerint *E-02 E-09*

despised, praise those whom they mocked, and, when they can no longer do so, they would like to imitate those whom they preferred to hunt down when they could have followed after them.

Stop up your ears, my dearest son, *with wax* and, paying no attention to whatever men say, whatever they think about you, look only to the judgment of God, who will render unto each according to his works when he is revealed from the heavens among the angels of his might, taking vengeance with flames of fire on those who have not acknowledged God nor obeyed his gospel, "who," the apostle says, "will be punished to their everlasting destruction by the face of our lord and the glory of his might when he comes to be glorified in his saints and to be made marvelous in all who believed." It is written, "Do not fear those who can kill the body, but rather him who can send the soul to Gehenna." How much less should you fear those who can harm neither your body nor your soul, and who, if they now revile you because you live according to reason, would do so no less if you abandoned virtue and rushed into vice, not because they are displeased with vice but because they are always pleased by the vice of reviling. Flee, if your salvation is dear to you, flee their company as much as you can, and, withdrawing within yourself, pray often in private to the most merciful father, crying out with the prophet, "To you, O lord, I have lifted up my soul; *my God,* I have confidence in you; I will not be put to shame even if my enemies mock me, for all who hope in you will not be confounded; let those be confounded who do evil deeds gratuitously; show me, O lord, your ways and teach me your paths; guide me in your truth and teach me, because you are God my savior and in you I will hope throughout the day." Likewise, see to it that you consider how death always presses upon us and that the period of our lives is a point in time and even less than a point, and then think how wicked is our ancient enemy, who promises us the kingdoms of the world in order to snatch from us the kingdom of heaven, how false are the pleasures which embrace us only to strangle us, how deceptive are the honors which raise us up on high so that they can then cast us down, how deadly are riches, which feed us the better to poison us, how short, uncertain, shadowy, false, imaginary is everything that all these things taken together can do for us, even if they flow in upon us just as we wish, how great are the things which are promised and prepared for those who scorn the things of the present and yearn for that homeland whose king is the deity, whose law is charity, whose measure is eternity. Occupy your mind with such thoughts and others like them, which will arouse you when you are asleep, inflame you when you are lukewarm, steady you when you waver, and lend you wings for your flight to the heaven of

(quod magno omnes desiderio expectamus) non solum quem volumus sed & qualem volumus te videamus. Vale & deum ama quem timere olim coepisti. *Bigus te salutat.* Ferrariae, ii Iulii, Mcccclxxxxii.

[In Psalmum 15 Commentarius]

5   CONSERVA me domine.

Siquis perfectus vult recognoscere statum suum, unum habet periculum, ne de sua virtute superbiat. Ideo David loquens in persona iusti de statu incipit ab hoc verbo "conserva me," quod recte consideratum omnem amovet occasionem superbiae, nam qui potest aliquid ex se
10   acquirere potest & illud ex se sibi conservare. Qui ergo petit a deo conservari in statu virtutis significat per hoc quod nec a principio ipsam virtutem ex se acquisivit. Qui autem recordatur virtutem se consecutum non virtute propria sed virtute dei non potest de ea superbire sed magis humiliari coram deo, iuxta illud apostoli, "Quid habes quod
15   non accepisti? & si accepisti, quid gloriaris, quasi non acceperis?" Duo sunt ergo verba quae semper habere debemus in ore: alterum scilicet "Miserere mei, deus," cum scilicet recordamur peccatorum; alterum est "Conserva me deus," scilicet cum recordamur virtutum.

QVONIAM speravi in te.

20   Haec una res est quae facit nos a deo impetrare quod petimus: quum scilicet nos impetraturos speramus. Et si duas has conditiones observabimus, ut nunquam petamus *a deo* nisi ea quae nobis sunt salutaria, & ut id quod petimus ardenter petamus cum firma spe quod deus nos exaudiat, nunquam erunt irritae orationes nostrae. Quum igitur non
25   impetramus, est aut quod illud nobis est noxium (nescimus enim quid petamus, ut inquit Christus, & Iesus dixit, "Quicquid petieritis in nomine meo, dabitur vobis"; hoc enim nomen Iesus salvatorem significat & ideo nihil petitur in nomine Iesu nisi quod est ad salutem ipsi petenti) aut non exaudit quia, si bona petimus, non enim bene petimus, hoc est
30   cum parva spe (qui autem timide sperat, frigide petit; ideo dicebat Iacobus "Postulet autem in fide nihil haesitans").

DIXI domino, "deus meus es tu."

---

3 Mcccclxxxxii] *96 96+ 98 04 06 E-99 E-00 E-02 E-04 E-07+ E-09,* 1482 *E-95+*

divine love, so that when you come to us (which we are all very eagerly looking forward to) we may see not only you whom we wish for but also see you such as we wish you to be. Farewell, and love God, whom you began to fear some time ago. *Bigo sends you greetings.* Ferrara, July 2, 1492.

[Commentary on Psalm 15]

PRESERVE me, O lord.

If someone who is perfect wishes to examine his state, he faces one danger: that he should be proud of his virtue. That is why David, speaking in the role of the righteous man, starts off about his state with these words, "Preserve me," which, if they are rightly understood, remove all occasion for pride, for a person who can acquire something on his own can also preserve it for himself on his own. Therefore, anyone who asks God to preserve him in the state of virtue signifies by this that he did not originally acquire that virtue on his own. And so whoever remembers that he did not achieve his virtue by his own power but rather by God's power cannot be proud of it, but rather he should be humble before God, according to that saying of the apostle, "What do you have that you have not received? And if you have received it, why do you boast about it, as if you did not receive it?" Two sayings, therefore, we should always have on our lips: one is "Have mercy on me, O God," namely when we remember our sins; the other is "Preserve me, O God," namely when we remember our virtues.

BECAUSE I have hoped in you.

The one thing that causes us to obtain from God what we ask for is this: that we hope to obtain it. And if we observe these two conditions, that we never ask *God* for anything except what advances our salvation and that we make our petitions ardently and with firm hope that God will hear us, our prayers will never be in vain. Therefore, when we do not get something, it is either because it is harmful to us (for we do not know what we are asking for, as Christ stated, and Jesus said, "Whatever you ask in my name will be given to you"; for the name Jesus means "savior," and therefore nothing can be asked in the name of Jesus unless it advances the salvation of the person who asks for it), or he does not hear us because, if what we ask is good, we do not ask for it well, that is, we ask with little hope (for if our hope is fainthearted our prayer is feeble; that is why James said, "Then let him ask in faith and with no hesitation").

I SAID to the lord, "You are my God."

Postquam munivit se contra superbiam incipit describere statum
suum. Totus autem status iusti consistit in hoc verbo, "Dixi domino,
'deus meus es tu.'" Quod verbum licet videatur fere omnibus com-
mune, pauci tamen sunt qui illud possint vere dicere. Illud enim quis
5   habet pro deo quod habet pro summo bono, & illud habemus pro
summo bono quo solo habito, si caetera desint, putamus nos esse fe-
lices, & quod unum si desit, etiam si habeamus omnia alia bona, puta-
mus nos esse miseros. Dicit igitur avarus pecuniae "Deus meus es tu,"
quia etiam si ei desint honor & sanitas & virtus & amici, modo pecu-
10   niam habeat, contentus est. Et si habeat omnia illa bona quae diximus et
pecunia desit, putat se esse infelicem. Gulosus *item crapulae, et incon-
tinens* libidini, & ambitiosus *imperio sive* gloriae dicit "Deus meus es tu."
Vide igitur quam pauci possint dicere "Dixi domino, 'deus meus es tu,'"
quia ille solus hoc potest cui solus deus sufficit, ita ut si ei proponantur
15   omnia regna mundi & caelestia omnia & terrena bona, non tamen ut
illa consequeretur vel semel deum offenderet. In hoc igitur dicto con-
sistit totus status hominis iusti.
     QVONIAM bonorum meorum non eges.
     Reddit rationem propositi sui, quare scilicet soli domino dicat "Deus
20   meus es tu." Ratio autem quoniam solus deus bonis nostris non eget.
Nulla enim creatura est quae non indigeat aliis creaturis quam ea im-
perfectioribus, ut probant philosophi & theologi, quia si illae non es-
sent ista non esset, quia destructa una parte universi destruitur totum
universum. Destructo autem destruuntur omnes partes. Omnes autem
25   creaturae sunt partes unius universi. Cuius universi ipse deus non pars
est sed principium, nihil ab eo dependens. Nihil enim acquisiuit deus
ex hoc quod creavit mundum, & nihil perderet si totus mundus annihi-
laretur. Solus ergo deus bonorum nostrorum non eget. Debemus au-
tem erubescere illum habere pro deo qui bonis indiget nostris, qualis
30   est omnis creatura. Praeterea non debemus habere pro deo, hoc est pro
summo bono, nisi illud in quo est summum bonum. In nulla autem
creatura est omne bonum. Soli igitur domino debemus dicere, "Deus
meus es tu."
     SANCTIS qui sunt in terra eius.
35   Post deum maxime debemus amare illos qui sunt deo maxime con-
iuncti, quales sunt angeli & beati in patria. Ideo postquam dixit domino
"Deus meus es tu," subdit quod deus
     MIRIFICAVIT uoluntates suas.

---

23 ista non esset] ista non essent *96 96* + *98 04 06; or* ista *could be emended to* istae

After he has armed himself against pride, he begins to describe his state. Now the whole state of the righteous person is summed up in these words, "I said to the lord, 'You are my God.'" Though this statement may seem to be common to almost everyone, yet there are few who can say it truly. For a person takes as God what he takes to be the highest good, and we take as the highest good that which, if we have it alone, even if everything else is lacking, makes us consider ourselves happy, and which, if it alone is lacking, even if we have all other goods, makes us consider ourselves miserable. And so the miser says to his money, "You are my god," because, even if he lacks honor and health and virtue and friends, as long as he has money he is content. And if he should have all those goods we mentioned and lacks money, he considers himself unhappy. Likewise the glutton says *to his drunkenness and the incontinent* to his lust and the ambitious man to his *power or* glory, "You are my god." See, then, how few can say, "I said to the lord, 'You are my God,'" because the only one who can do this is the man to whom God alone is sufficient, so much so that if all the kingdoms of the world and all good things in heaven and on earth were offered to him, he would not offend God even once in order to get them. This saying, then, contains the whole state of the righteous man.

BECAUSE you do not need the good things I have.

He gives the reason for his resolution, namely why he says only to the lord, "You are my God." And the reason is that God alone does not need the good things we have. For there is no creature that does not need other creatures less perfect than itself, as the philosophers and theologians demonstrate, because if they did not exist it would also not exist, since if any part of the universe is destroyed, the whole universe is also destroyed. And if the universe is destroyed, so are all its parts. But all creatures are parts of one universe. God himself is not a part but the origin of that universe and does not depend on it at all. For God gained nothing by creating the world and would lose nothing if the whole world were annihilated. Therefore, only God does not need the good things we have. And so we should blush with shame to take as our god a thing that has need of the good things we have, as all creatures do. Furthermore, we should not take as God, that is, as the highest good, anything except that in which the highest good consists. But all good does not consist in any creature. Therefore, only to the lord should we say, "You are my God."

TO THE SAINTS who are in his land.

After God we ought to love most those who are closest to him, as are the angels and saints in their homeland. Therefore, after he said to the lord, "You are my god," he adds that God

HAS MADE his wishes marvelous.

Hoc est, mirabiles fecit amores eius & desideria eius erga sanctos qui sunt in terra eius, hoc est in caelesti patria, quae dicitur terra dei & terra uiuentium, & vere si consideremus quanta sit illius patriae felicitas quantaque huius mundi miseria, quanta ciuium illorum bonitas & cha-
5   ritas, desiderabimus semper hinc discedere ut illic habitemus. Haec autem & similia cum meditamur, illud semper curare debemus ne infructuosae sint meditationes nostrae. Sed ex qualibet meditatione aliquam semper acquirere uirtutem debemus, ut ex hoc videlicet de bonitate illius patriae superioris debemus acquirere uirtutem hanc, ut mortem
10   non solum fortiter feramus & patienter cum venerit hora nostra aut si pro fide Christi nobis obeunda sit, sed ultro etiam eam appetamus, cupientes scilicet ex hac valle miseriarum discedere ut in illa felici patria cum deo & sanctis eius regnemus. *Cum ergo iustus descripsit statum suum, qui totus est in affectu erga deum & diuina, despicitque ex alto* statum homi-
15   num malorum & dicit

MVLTIPLICATAE sunt infirmitates eorum.

Per infirmitates autem intelligit idola, & ita habet textus Hebraeus. Sicut enim bonus unum habet deum quem colit, ita mali multos habent deos & idola, quia multas scilicet voluptates, multa desideria vana, pas-
20   siones diversas quibus serviunt. Ideo autem multas quaerunt voluptates quia nullam inveniunt quae eos quietet, & ideo in circuitu impii ambulant, & subdit "postea acceleraverunt," quia scilicet post sua desideria praecipites ruunt & inconsiderate, unde edocemur ut non minus ipsi celeriter curramus ad virtutes quam ipsi currant ad vitium, nec
25   domino nostro minus diligenter ipsi serviamus quam ipsi serviant domino suo diabolo. Iustus autem considerans statum malorum proponit firmiter, sicut & nos semper debemus facere, nullo modo velle eos sequi & dicit

NON congregabo conventiculam eorum de sanguinibus nec memor
30   ero nominum.

Dicit autem de sanguinibus, tum quia idolatrae solebant collecto sanguine victimarum circa eum suas agere caerimonias, tum quia tota vita malorum relicta ratione sensualitatem sequitur, quae in sanguine sita est. Dixit autem quod non solum vult sacrificare idolis sed nec nomi-
35   nare ea, quod tamen dici & fieri potest, ostendens per hoc quod non solum homo perfectus debet abstinere ab illicitis voluptatibus sed etiam a licitis, ut magis totus feratur in caelum & contemplationi di-

---

21 impii] *04*, imperii *96 96+ 98 06*   22 accelerauerunt] acclamauerunt *96 96+ 98 04 06*   24 curramus] curremus *96 96+ 98 04 06*   34 vult] *perhaps we should read* non vult *or* nolit   35 tamen] tantum *96 96+ 98 04 06*

That is, he has made marvelous his love and his desire for the saints who are in his land, that is, in the heavenly homeland, which is called the land of God and the land of the living; and truly if we consider how great is the happiness of that homeland and how great is the misery of this world, how great the goodness and charity of those citizens, we will always desire to leave here in order to dwell there. Now when we meditate on these things and others like them, we should always take care that our meditations be not unfruitful. From any meditation, we should always gain some virtue, so that, for example, from this meditation on the goodness of that homeland on high we should gain this virtue: we should not only bear death bravely and patiently when our hour comes or if we must suffer death for the faith of Christ, but we should even be eager for it of our own accord, longing to leave this vale of misery and to reign in that happy homeland with God and his saints. *Thus, when the righteous man describes his state, which consists totally in a desire for God and the things of God, he both looks down from on high at the* state of evil men and he says

THEIR WEAKNESSES have been multiplied.

By their weaknesses he means idols, and that is what the Hebrew text has. For just as the good man has one God whom he worships, so too evil men have many gods and idols, namely because they have many pleasures, many vain desires, various passions which they serve. But the reason they pursue many pleasures is that they find none which gives them peace, and hence the wicked walk around in a circle; and he adds "afterwards they made haste," namely because they run headlong and thoughtlessly after their desires, whence we are taught to run no less swiftly toward virtue than they run toward vice and to serve our lord no less diligently than they serve their lord the devil. But the righteous man, considering the state of the wicked, resolves firmly, as we also ought always to do, by no means ever to choose to follow them, and he says

I WILL NOT frequent their gathering place of blood nor will I remember their names.

He speaks of blood both because idolaters were accustomed to collect blood and perform their ceremonies around it and because the whole life of wicked men abandons reason and follows sensuality, which is seated in the blood. He said, however, that he chooses not only not to sacrifice to idols but also not even to name them—though this can nonetheless be said and done—showing by this that a perfect person should abstain not only from illicit pleasures but also from licit ones, so as to be more completely carried up to heaven and to be more untram-

vinorum purius vacet. Et quia aliquis posset credere quod esset stultitia privare se omni voluptate, subdit

DOMINVS pars haereditatis meae.

Quasi dicat "non mireris si omnia alia relinquo ut deum possideam, in quo etiam alia *denique* bona possidentur." Debet haec esse vox cuiuslibet boni christiani, "Dominus pars haereditatis meae," quia nos christiani, quibus deus ipse pro haereditate promittitur, debemus erubescere aliquid praeter ipsum desiderare. Et quia posset videri alicui praesumptio audere haec sibi promittere, idem subdit

TV ES qui restituis haereditatem meam mihi.

Quasi dicat, "Domine deus meus, bene scio quod cum nihil sim respectu tui viribus meis non possum ascendere ad te possidendum. Sed tu es qui trahes me ad te per gratiam tuam, & tu es qui te ipsum dabis mihi possidendum." Consideret deinde iustus quanta sit haec felicitas, ut ei deus pro haereditate contigerit. Subdit

FVNES ceciderunt mihi in praeclaris.

Partes enim & sortes antiquitus per funes dividebantur, et quoniam multi sunt qui, licet ad hanc felicitatem sint vocati sicut sunt omnes christiani, ipsam tamen nihil faciunt, utpote pro levi saepe voluptate commutant, ideo subdit

HAEREDITAS mea praeclara est mihi.

Quasi dicat "Sicut ipsa est praeclara, ita ego eam praeclaram reputo, & omnia alia respectu eius (ut dicebat Paulus) sicut stercora reputo." Quoniam autem habere hoc lumen intellectus, ut homo cognoscat felicitatem sibi a deo datam, donum dei, & ideo subdit

BENEDICAM dominum qui tribuit intellectum.

Quoniam autem saepe homo iudicat secundum rationem servire deo, sensualitas autem & caro repugnant, tunc autem homo perfectus est ut non solum anima eius sed & caro in deum feruntur iuxta illud "Cor meum & caro mea exultaverunt in deum vivum," ideo subdit

ET VSQUE ad noctem increpuerunt me renes mei.

Id est, renes ipsi, in quibus maxima solet esse inclinatio ad concupiscentiam, non solum non inclinant me ad malum sed potius increpant, hoc est retrahunt etiam usque ad noctem, id est eousque ut etiam ipsi ultro proprium corpus affligant. Afflictio enim saepe per noctem solet designari. Ostendit deinde quae sit radix tantae priuationis et dicit

PROVIDEBAM deum semper in conspectu meo.

---

33 non solum non] non solum *96 96 + 98 04 06*

meled and free to contemplate the things of God. And because some-
one might think it is folly to deprive oneself of all pleasure, he adds

THE LORD is the share of my inheritance.

As if to say, "do not marvel that I leave all other things in order to
possess God, in whom *finally* other good things are also possessed."
This ought to be the saying of each and every good Christian, "The
lord is the share of my inheritance," because we Christians, to whom
God is promised as an inheritance, ought to be ashamed to desire
anything but him. And because someone might think it presumptuous
to dare to promise oneself these things, he adds

YOU ARE the one who restores my inheritance to me.

As if to say, "O lord, my God, I know very well that, since I am
nothing by comparison with you, I cannot by my own power rise to
possess you. But you are the one who will draw me to you by your grace,
and you are the one who will give yourself to be possessed by me." Then
let the righteous man consider how great a happiness it is that God
should fall to his lot by inheritance. He adds

THE ROPES have fallen to me in splendid places.

Shares and lots were divided up by ropes in ancient times, and be-
cause there are many who, though they are called to this happiness, as
are all Christians, yet take it so lightly that they often exchange it for
some slight pleasure, therefore he adds

MY INHERITANCE is splendid to me.

As if to say, "As it is illustrious in itself, so I consider it illustrious, and
by comparison with it, I consider all other things (as Paul said) to be like
dung." But because to have the understanding enlightened enough for
a person to recognize that happiness is given to him by God is itself a
gift of God, therefore he also adds

I WILL BLESS the lord, who has given me understanding.

But because a person, in accord with his reason, often decides to
serve God but his sensuality and flesh resist him, and he is perfect when
not only his soul but also his flesh is borne up to God, according to the
saying, "My heart and my flesh exulted in the living God," therefore he
adds

MY LOINS have upbraided me, urging me all the way to the night.

That is, my very loins, which are usually most strongly inclined to-
ward concupiscence, not only do not incline me to evil, but rather they
upbraid me, that is they even draw me back all the way to night, that is,
to such an extent that they even afflict their own body of their own
accord. For affliction is often signified by night. Then he shows what is
the root of such great privation, and says

I ALWAYS kept God in my sight.

Nam si quis deum semper haberet ante oculos pro regula omnium operationum suarum & in omnibus operationibus suis nec propriam utilitatem nec gloriam nec voluptatem quaereret sed solum ut deo placeret, brevi perfectus evaderet, & quia qui ita agit semper in om-
5 nibus prosperatur, ideo dicit
IPSE a dextris est mihi ne commovear.
Ostendit deinde quanta sit felicitas iusti viri, quia scilicet erit in aeternum felix & in anima & in corpore. Ideo subdit propter haec
LAEtatum est cor meum.
10 Id est, anima mea laeta est sciens post mortem sibi caelum esse paratum.
ET CARO mea requiescet in spe.
Id est, quamuis ipsa non laetetur quasi acceptura statim post mortem statum suum, requiescit tamen in sepultura cum hac spe quod resurget
15 in die iudicii cum anima sua immortalis & splendidissima, & *hoc totum* declarat in sequenti uersiculo. Nam quia dixerat quod anima laetabatur, subdit rationem.
QUIA non derelinques animam in inferno.
Et quia dixerat quod caro requiescebat in spe, subdit rationem,
20 dicens
NEC DABIS sanctum tuum videre corruptionem.
Quia scilicet quod fuit corruptibile resurget incorruptibile & quia Christus fuit primus qui intravit paradisum & nobis vitam aperuit & fuit primus qui resurrexit & resurrectio eius est causa nostrae resurrec-
25 tionis, ideo ista quae diximus de resurrectione principaliter de Christi intelliguntur, sicut declaravit Petrus apostolus, & secundario intelligi possunt de nobis inquantum sumus membra Christi, qui solus non vidit corruptionem quia corpus eius in sepulchro putrefactum non fuit. Quoniam igitur uia benevivendi ducit nos ad perpetuam vitam animae
30 & corporis, ideo subdit
NOTAS mihi fecisti vias vitae.
Et quia tota felicitas *huius vitae* consistit in aperta visione & fruitione dei, ideo subdit
ADIMPLEBIS me laetitia cum vultu tuo.
35 Et quia felicitas in aeternum durabit, ideo subdit
DELECTATIONES in dextera tua usque in finem.
Dicit autem "in dextera tua" quia felicitas nostra completur in visione & fruitione humanitatis Christi, qui sedet in dextera maiestatis in excelsis, iuxta illud Ioannis "Haec est tota merces ut videamus deum &
40 quem misisti Iesum Christum."

FINIS

---

9 LAEtatum] *o4*, Laetandum *96 96+ 98 o6*   18 derelinques] derelinquet *96 96+ 98 o4*
o6   22 scilicet] sive & *96 96+ 98 o4 o6*   30 ideo] *96 98 o4 o6*, non *96+*

For if anyone always kept God before his eyes as a rule for all his deeds and if in all his deeds he sought not his own advantage nor his glory nor his pleasure but only to please God, he would soon become perfect, and because anyone who does so is always successful in all things, therefore he says

HE IS at my right hand lest I be shaken.

Then he shows how great is the happiness of the righteous man, namely because he will be happy forever both in soul and in body. Therefore he adds, because of these things,

MY HEART has rejoiced.

That is, my soul is joyful, knowing that heaven is prepared for it after death.

AND MY FLESH will rest in hope.

That is, although it does not rejoice as if it were to achieve its status immediately after death, still it rests in the grave with this hope, that it will rise immortal and full of splendor on the day of judgment together with its soul, and he declares *all this* in the following verse. For, since he had said that the soul rejoiced, he adds the reason.

BECAUSE you will not abandon the soul in the underworld.

And because he had said that the flesh rested in hope, he adds the reason, saying

YOU WILL NOT LET your holy one see corruption.

Namely, because what was once corruptible will rise incorruptible and because Christ was the first to enter paradise and to open up life to us and was the first to rise, and since his resurrection is the cause of our resurrection, therefore what we have said about resurrection is understood principally of Christ's resurrection, as the apostle Peter made clear; and secondarily it can be understood of us insofar as we are members of Christ, who alone did not see corruption because his body did not putrefy in the grave. And so, because a good way of life leads us to the perpetual life of the soul and the body, therefore he adds

YOU HAVE MADE the ways of life known to me.

And because all the happiness *of this life* consists in the open sight and enjoyment of God, therefore he adds

WITH YOUR COUNTENANCE you will fill me with joy.

And because the happiness will last forever, therefore he adds

DELIGHTS are at your right hand all the way to the end.

He says "at your right hand" because our happiness consists in the sight and enjoyment of the humanity of Christ, who sits on high at the right hand of majesty, according to that saying of John, "This is our whole reward, that we see God and Jesus Christ, whom you sent."

THE END

Duodecim regulae Ioannis Pici Mirandulae, partim excitantes
partim dirigentes homines in spirituali pugna

Prima regula: si homini videtur dura via virtutis, quia continue
oportet nos pugnare adversus carnem & diabolum & mundum, recor-
5 detur quod quamcunque elegerit vitam etiam secundum mundum
multa illi aduersa, tristia, incommoda, laboriosa patienda sunt.

Secunda regula: recordetur quod in rebus mundi diutius pugnatur
& laboriosius & infructuosius, in quibus labor est finis laboris & tandem
paena aeterna.

10 Tertia regula: recordetur stultum esse credere ad caelum posse per-
veniri nisi per huiusmodi pugnam, sicut & caput nostrum Christus non
ascendit in caelum nisi per crucem, nec debet servi conditio melior esse
conditione domini.

Quarta regula: recordetur non solum non esse aegre ferendam hanc
15 pugnam sed optandam, etiam si nullum inde nobis praemium per-
veniret, solum ut conformemur Christo deo & domino nostro; & quo-
tiens resistendo alicui tentationi alicui ex sensibus tuis vim facis, cogita
cuinam parti crucis Christi conformis reddaris, ut quando gulae re-
sistens gustum affligis, recordare illum felle potatum & aceto. Quando
20 manus retrahis a rapina alicuius rei quae tibi placet, cogita manus illius
pro te ligno crucis affixas; & si resistis superbiae, recordare illum qui
cum in forma dei esset pro te formam serui accepisse & humiliatum
usque ad mortem crucis; & cum de ira tentaris, recordare illum qui
deus erat & omnium hominum iustissimus, cum se tamen videret quasi
25 latronem & illudi & conspui & flagellari & obprobriis omnibus affici &
cum latronibus deputari, nullum tamen unquam aut irae aut indigna-
tionis signum ostendit, sed patientissime omnia ferens omnibus man-
suetissime respondebat; & sic discurrendo per singula invenias nullam
esse passionem quae te Christo aliqua ex parte conformem non efficiat.

30 Quinta regula: quod in illis duodecim armis nec in quocunque alio
humano remedio confidas, sed in sola virtute Iesu Christi, qui dixit
"Confidite, ego vici mundum" et alibi "Princeps mundi huius eiicitur
foras"; quare & nos sola eius virtute confidamus & mundum posse
vincere & Diabolum superare. Et ideo debemus semper petere eius
35 auxilium per orationem & sanctorum suorum.

---

14 non solum non] non solum *96 96+ 98 04 06*   16 conformemur] *96 96+ 98*
04, confirmemur *06*

The twelve rules of Giovanni Pico della Mirandola, partly urging, partly directing men in their spiritual battle

The first rule: if the way of virtue seems hard to someone because we are required to fight continuously against the flesh, the devil, and the world, let him remember that, whatever sort of life he chooses, even by worldly standards, he will have to endure many adversities, griefs, difficulties, labors.

The second rule: let him remember that in the affairs of the world he fights longer and more laboriously and more fruitlessly, and the end result of his labor is labor and, finally, eternal punishment.

The third rule: let him remember that it is foolish to think one can reach heaven except by such a battle as this, just as our head, Christ, did not ascend to heaven except through the cross, and the condition of a servant should not be better than that of his lord.

The fourth rule: let him remember that he should not only not endure this battle unwillingly but should choose to bear it, even if we got no reward from it, for the sole purpose of being conformed to Christ, our God and our lord; and whenever in resisting any temptation you do violence to one of your senses, consider to which part of Christ's cross you are conforming yourself, as, for example, when you afflict your sense of taste to resist gluttony, remember that they gave him gall and vinegar to drink. When you hold back your hands from stealing something you like, consider that his hands were fixed to the wood of the cross for your sake; and if you resist pride, remember that, although he was by nature God, he accepted for your sake the nature of a servant and was brought low, even to the death of the cross; and when you are tempted to anger, remember that he who was God and the most righteous of all men, when he saw himself treated like a thief, mocked and spat upon, and scourged and subjected to all manner of insults and classed among thieves, he nevertheless did not ever show any sign of anger or outrage but bore everything with the greatest patience and answered everyone with the greatest mildness; and thus, running over the details one by one, you can discover that there is no suffering which may not render you conformed to Christ in some way.

The fifth rule: that you should not place your trust in those twelve weapons or in any other human remedy, but only in the power of Christ, who said, "Trust me, I conquered the world," and in another place, "The prince of this world has been cast out"; wherefore let us trust that by his power alone we, too, can both conquer the world and overcome the devil. And therefore we should always seek his help and that of his saints through prayer.

Sexta regula: recordare cum unam vicisti tentationem semper aliam esse expectandam, quia Diabolus semper circuit quem devoret; quare oportet semper servire in timore & dicere cum propheta "Super custodiam meam stabo."

5   Septima regula: ut non solum non vincaris a diabolo *quum te tentat,* sed ut vincas ipsum, & hoc est quando non solum non peccas, sed ex ea re unde te tentaverat occasionem sumis alicuius boni, ut si opus tuum bonum aliquod tibi offert, ut inde in vanam gloriam incidas, tu illud statim non ut opus tuum sed ut beneficium dei cogitans humilias te & 10 iudicas parum gratum te esse deo de beneficiis eius.

Octaua regula: ut quum pugnas, pugnes quasi vincendo, deinde perpetuam pacem habiturus, quia forte hoc tibi dabit deus ex gratia sua & diabolus amplius non redibit confusus de tua victoria; sed quum vicisti, geras te quasi mox pugnaturus ut in pugna semper victoriae & 15 in victoria semper sis memor pugnae.

Nona regula: ut quamvis te sentias undique benemunitum & paratum, semper tamen fugias occasiones peccandi, quia ut dicit sapiens "Qui amat periculum peribit in illo."

Decima regula: ut in tentationibus semper in principio occurras & 20 allidas parvulos Babylonis ad petram (*petra autem est Christus*), quia sero medicina paratur.

Vndecima regula: recordare quod licet in ipso conflictu tentationis amara videatur pugna, tamen longe dulcius est vincere tentationem quam ire ad peccatum ad quod te inclinat, et in hoc multi decipiuntur, 25 quia non comparant dulcedinem victoriae dulcedini peccati. Sed comparant pugnam voluptati & tamen homo qui milies expertus est quid sit cedere tentationi deberet semel saltem experiri quid sit vincere tentationem.

Duodecima regula: propterea quod tentaris ne credas te a deo derelictum aut deo parum gratum esse aut parum iustum & perfectum. 30 Memor sis quod postquam Paulus vidit diuinam essentiam patiebatur tentationem carnis, qua permittebat deus eum tentari ne de superbia tentaretur; in quo etiam homo debet advertere quod Paulus, qui erat vas electionis & raptus usque ad tertium caelum, tamen erat in periculo 35 ne de suis virtutibus superbiret, *sicut ipse dicit de se* "*Ne magnitudo revelationum extolleret me, datus est mihi stimulus carnis meae qui me collaphizet.*"

---

7 tuum] suum *96 96+ 98 04 06*   11 pugnes quasi] *96 98 04 06,* quasi *96+*   21 paratur] *96 98 04 06,* paratur quum mala per longas convaluere moras *96+* [*completing the quotation from Ovid, Remedia Amoris 91–92*]

The sixth rule: remember that when you have conquered one temptation you should always expect another, since the devil always prowls after someone to devour; that is why we should always serve with fear and say with the prophet, "I will stand on my guard."

The seventh rule: that you should not only not be conquered by the devil *when he tempts you,* but that you should conquer him, and this happens when you not only do not sin but, from the point on which he has tempted you, you take an occasion of doing something good, as, for example, if he presents to you some good deed of yours so that you may fall into vainglory, you should immediately think of it not as your deed but as a benefit from God, humbling yourself and judging yourself insufficiently grateful to God for his benefits.

The eighth rule: that when you fight you do so as if by conquering you will have have perpetual peace thereafter, because God will perhaps grant you this by his grace, and the devil, confounded by your victory, will not come back any more; but when you have conquered, that you conduct conduct yourself as if you will soon fight again, so that in battle you should always think of victory and in victory always of battle.

The ninth rule: that, however much you may think yourself well armed and prepared, still you should always flee all occasions of sin, since, as the wise man says, "Whoever loves danger will perish in it."

The tenth rule: that in temptations the very first thing you should always do is run up and smash the babes of Babylon against the rock (*and the rock is Christ*), because it is too late to apply the medicine.

The eleventh rule: remember that, although in the conflict with temptation the battle seems bitter, still it is far sweeter to conquer temptation than to commit the sin to which it inclines you, and on this point many are deceived, because they do not compare the sweetness of victory with the sweetness of sin. Rather they compare the battle with the pleasure, and yet a person who has experienced a thousand times what it is like to yield to temptation should experience at least once what it is like to conquer temptation.

The twelfth rule: just because you are tempted, do not think that God has abandoned you or that you are less pleasing to God or less righteous and perfect. Remember that after Paul saw the essence of God he suffered temptation of the flesh, with which God permitted him to be tempted lest he should be tempted to pride; here a person should also notice that Paul, who was a chosen vessel and was snatched up into the third heaven, was nevertheless in danger of taking pride in his virtues, *as he himself said about himself, "Lest the greatness of the revelations should lift me up, I have been given a goad in the flesh to buffet me."*

Quare super omnes tentationes homo debet maxime se munire contra
tentationem superbiae, quia radix omnium malorum superbia est, con-
tra quod unicum remedium est cogitare semper quod deus se humili-
avit pro nobis usque ad crucem & mors nos uel *invitos* eousque nos
5   humiliabit ut simus esca vermium.

Duodecim arma spiritualis pugnae quae in promptu
haberi debent cum peccandi libido mentem subdit

Voluptas brevis & exigua
Comites fastidium & anxietas
10   Iactura maioris boni
Vita somnus & umbra
Mors instans & improvisa
Suspitio impaenitentiae
Aeternum praemium, aeterna paena
15   Hominis dignitas & natura
Pax bonae mentis
Dei beneficia
Crux Christi
Testimonia martyrum & exempla sanctorum

---

20   Duodecim conditiones amantis

Amare unum tantum & contemnere omnia pro eo
Infelicem putare eum qui non est cum amato
Omnia pati ut cum illo sit, etiam mortem
Ornare se ut illi placeat
25   Esse cum illo quomodo potest, & si non re saltem cogitatione
Amare omnia quae ad eum attinent, *amicos omnes, domus, uestes,
imagines*
Cupere laudes nec posse pati aliquam eius ignominiam
De eo credere omnia summa idemque cupere ut omnes credant
30   Optare etiam pro eo pati aliquod incommodum & dulce esse illud
incommodum
Flere cum eo saepe, vel si absens ex dolore, vel si praesens ex
laetitia
Semper languere, semper ardere eius desiderio

Wherefore, above all temptations a person should most of all arm himself against the temptation to pride, because the root of all evil is pride, against which vice the only remedy is always to think that God humiliated himself for our sake even to the cross and that death will humiliate us, however *unwilling* we may be, even to be food for worms.

The twelve weapons in the spiritual battle, which should always be kept ready to hand when the urge to sin infiltrates the mind

The pleasure is brief and tiny
Its companions are disgust and anxiety
The loss of a greater good
Life is a sleep and a shadow
Death is pressing and unforeseen
The suspicion that you will not repent
Eternal reward, eternal punishment
The dignity and nature of man
The peace of a good conscience
God's benefits
The cross of Christ
The witness of the martyrs and the example of the saints

The twelve qualities of a lover

To love only one and to contemn all things for his sake
To consider unhappy anyone who is not with the beloved
To endure anything, even death, to be with him
To dress up in order to please him
To be with him if at all possible, and if not in fact at least in thought
To love everything which concerns him, *all his friends, houses, clothes, pictures*
To long to hear him praised and to be unable to bear that he should be dishonored in any way
In all things to believe the very best of him and to long that everyone else should believe so too
Even to choose to suffer some adversity for his sake and to think that adversity sweet
To weep with him often, either from sorrow when he is away or from joy when he is present
Always to pine away, always to burn with longing for him

Servire illi nihil cogitando de praemio aut mercede. Solemus au-
tem ad hoc induci praecipue ex tribus causis. Prima est quando
servitium ipsum per se est appetibile. Secunda quando ille cui
servimus est in se valde bonus & amabilis, sicut solemus dicere
"Servimus illi propter suas virtutes." Tertia est quando ille prius-
quam inciperes multa tibi beneficia contulit. Et haec tria sunt in
deo, quia pro servitio eius nihil noviter accipitur quod non sit
nobis bonum & quoad animam & quoad corpus, quia servire ei
non est aliud quam tendere ad eum, hoc est ad summum
bonum. Similiter ipse est optimus & pulcherrimus & sapien-
tissimus & habet omnes conditiones quae solent nos movere ad
amandum aliquem & serviendum ei gratis. Et in nos contulit
summa beneficia, cum nos & ex nihilo creaverit & per san-
guinem filii sui ab inferno redemerit.

Ioannis Pici Mirandulae Deprecatoria ad Deum

Alme deus, summa qui maiestate verendus
    Vere unum in triplici numine numen habes,
Cui *super excelsi flammantia moenia mundi*
    Angelici seruit *turba beata chori,*
Cuius & *immensum hoc oculis spectabile nostris*
    Omnipotens quondam dextra creavit opus,
Aethera qui torques, qui *nutu* dirigis orbem,
    Cuius ab imperio fulmina missa cadunt,
Parce precor miseris, nostras precor ablue sordes,
    Ne nos iusta tui paena furoris agat.
Quod si nostra pari pensentur debita lance
    Et sit iudicii norma severa tui,
Quis queat *horrendum viventis* ferre flagellum
    Vindicis & plagas sustinuisse *graves?*
Non ipsa iratae restabit machina dextrae,
    Machina *supremo* non peritura *die.*
Quae mens non primae damnata ab origine culpae?
    Aut quae non proprio crimine *facta nocens?*
At certe ille ipse es proprium cui parcere *semper*
    Iustitiamque pari qui pietate tenes,

---

17 numine] *96 96 + 98 04 06 E-99 E-00 E-02 E-04 E-7 + E-09; perhaps it should be emended
to* nomine

To serve him with no thought of recompense or reward. And there are three main reasons which ordinarily lead us to do so. The first is if the service is desirable in and of itself. The second is if he whom we serve is in and of himself extremely good and lovable, as we ordinarily say, "We serve him because of his virtues." The third is if, before you began to love him, he conferred many benefits on you. And these three reasons apply to God, because in return for serving him we receive nothing new that is not good for us, both in soul and in body, since to serve him is nothing else than than to tend toward him, that is, toward the highest good. Similarly, he is the best and the most beautiful and the wisest and has all qualities that usually move us to love someone and to serve him gratuitously. And he has conferred the greatest benefits on us, since he created us out of nothing and redeemed us from hell by the blood of his son.

A prayer to God for mercy, by Giovanni Pico della Mirandola

O bountiful God, terrible in the height of your majesty, whose three-fold divinity is truly one divinity, who are served *beyond the lofty, flaming walls of the world* by *the blessed multitude of the* angelic *choir,* who *long ago* created *with your omnipotent right hand* this *immense* work *which is visible to our eyes,* who turn the spheres, who control the world *with your nod, by whose command the thunderbolts are thrown down,* spare us wretches, I beg you, wash away our filth, I beg you, so that the just punishment of your anger may not strike us. But if our debts should be weighed with an exact scale and the standard of your judgment should be strict, who could bear the *horrible* scourge *of the living avenger* and endure his *heavy* strokes? The structure of the world will not resist your angry right hand, that structure which is not to perish utterly *on the last day.* What mind is not condemned from the beginning by original sin? Which is not *made guilty* by its own fault?

But surely you are the very one whose nature it is *always* to have pity, and who combines justice with equal mercy, who repays us with re-

Praemia qui ut meritis longe maiora rependis
 Supplicia admissis sic leviora malis,
Namque tua est nostris maior clementia culpis,
 Et dare non dignis res mage digna deo est,
40 Quanquam sat digni si quos dignatur amare,
 Qui quos non dignos invenit, ipse facit.
Ergo tuos placido miserans precor aspice vultu,
 Seu seruos mavis seu magis esse reos,
Nempe reos nostrae si spectes crimina vitae,
45 Ingratae nimium crimina mentis opus,
At tua si potius in nobis munera cernas,
 Munera praecipuis nobilitata bonis,
Nos sumus ipsa olim tibi quos natura ministros
 Mox fecit natos gratia sancta tuos.
50 Sed premit (heu) miseros tantae indulgentia sortis
 Quos fecit natos gratia, culpa reos.
Culpa reos fecit sed vincat gratia culpam,
 Vt tuus in nostro crimine crescat honor.
Nam tua sive aliter sapientia sive potestas
55 Nota suas mundo prodere possit opes,
Maior in erratis bonitatis gloria nostris,
 Illeque prae cunctis fulget amandus amor
Qui potuit caelo dominum deducere ab alto
 Inque crucem summi tollere membra dei,
60 Vt male *contractas patrio de semine* sordes
 Ablueret lateris sanguis & unda tui.
Sic amor & pietas tua, rex mitissime, tantis
 Dat mala materiam suppeditare bonis.
O amor, O pietas nostris bene provida rebus,
65 O bonitas servi facta ministra tui,
O amor, O pietas nostris male cognita saeclis,
 O bonitas nostris nunc prope victa malis,
Da precor huic tanto qui semper fervet amori
 Ardorum in nostris cordibus esse parem.
70 Da Satanae imperium, cui tot servisse per annos
 Paenitet, excusso deposuisse iugo.
Da precor extingui vesanae incendia mentis,
 Et tuus in nostro pectore vivat amor,
Vt cum mortalis perfunctus munere vitae
75 Ductus erit dominum spiritus ante suum,
Promissi regni felici sorte potitus,
 Non dominum sed te sentiat esse patrem.

FINIS

wards far beyond our merits, just as you assign punishments lighter than the sins we have committed, for your mercy is greater than our guilt and it is *more* worthy of God to give to the unworthy, though they are worthy enough if he deigns to love those whom, though unworthy when he finds them, he himself makes to be worthy. With mercy, therefore, and with a mild countenance look upon your own, I beg you, whether you prefer to take us as servants or as condemned criminals: criminals, namely, if you look at the offenses we have committed during our lives, offenses which are the work of exceedingly ungrateful minds, but if you examine instead the favors you have done us, favors crowned with preeminent benefits, we are those whom nature herself once made your servants and your holy grace soon made your children. But alas, the kindness of such a fate presses miserably upon us: whom grace made children, guilt made criminals. Guilt made us criminals, but let grace conquer guilt, so that your honor may be increased by our crime. For whether your wisdom on the one hand or your well-known power should be able to bring forth your riches to the world, your glory is greater in your kindness toward our transgressions, and that most lovable of all loves shines forth, the love which could bring the lord down from the heights of heaven and lift up on the cross the limbs of the most high God, so that the blood and water from your side might wash away the filth so wickedly *contracted from the seed of our father.* Thus your love and your pity, O most gentle king, make evil into the matter of such great good.

O love, O pity which looks out so well for our affairs, O goodness made the minister of your servant, O love, O pity, so little recognized in our times, O goodness, now almost overcome by our evil deeds, grant, I beg you, that the ardor of our hearts may be equal to this great, ever-burning love. Grant us release from the lordship of Satan, whom we are sorry we have served so many years, and let us cast off his yoke. Grant, I beg you, that the flames of our mad minds may be quenched and that your love may live in our hearts, so that when my spirit has finished the tasks of mortal life and is brought before its lord, *coming to possess the happy lot of the promised kingdom,* it may feel in you not a lord but a father.

THE END

APPENDIX B

Table of Corresponding Pages:
Pico (c. 1510), Merry Gest (c. 1516), Fortune Verses
(c. 1556), The English Works (1557), and The Yale Edition

APPENDIX B

Table of Corresponding Pages:

	Signatures in 1557 edition	Page numbers in Yale edition
	¶2v	3
	¶3	4
	¶3v	5
	¶4	6
	¶4v	9
	¶5	11

Folia in Merry Gest (c. 1516)	Signatures in 1557 edition	Page numbers in Yale edition
1	¶1	15
1v	¶1	17
2	¶1v	19
2v	¶1v	20
3	¶2	22
3v	¶2	24
4	¶2v	25
4v	¶2v	27

Signatures in Fortune Verses (c. 1556)	Signatures in 1557 edition	Page numbers in Yale edition
A1v		31
A2		32
A2v		32
	¶5v	33
	¶6	34
	¶6v	36
	¶7	37
	¶7v	39
	¶8	40
	¶8v	41
	XX8v	45
	YY1	46

Signatures in Pico (c. 1510)	Page numbers in 1557 edition	Page numbers in Yale edition
A_1	1	51
a_1	1	52
a_1v	2	53
a_2	2	54
a_2v	2	55
a_3	3	56
a_3v	3	57
a_4	3	57
a_4v	4	58
b_1	4	59
b_1v	4	60
b_2	5	61
b_2v	5	62
b_3	5	63
b_3v	6	64
b_4	6	65
b_4v	6	66
b_5	7	67
b_5v	7	68
b_6	8	69
b_6v	8	70
c_1	8	71
c_1v	9	72
c_2	9	72
c_2v	9	73
c_3	10	74
c_3v	10	75
c_4	10	76
c_4v	11	77
c_5	11	78
c_5v	11	79
c_6	12	80
c_6v	12	81
d_1	12	82
d_1v	13	83
d_2	13	84
d_2v	13	84
d_3	14	85
d_3v	14	86
d_4	15	87

Signatures in Pico (c. 1510)	Page numbers in 1557 edition	Page numbers in Yale edition
d_4v	15	88
d_5	15	89
d_5v	16	90
d_6	16	91
d_6v	16	91
e_1	17	92
e_1v	17	93
e_2	17	94
e_2v	17	95
e_3	18	96
e_3v	18	97
e_4	19	98
e_4v	19	98
e_5	19	99
e_5v	20	100
e_6	20	101
e_6v	20	102
f_1	21	103
f_1v	21	104
f_2	22	105
f_2v	23	106
f_3	23	107
f_3v	24	108
f_4	25	109
f_4v	25	110
f_5	26	111
f_5v	27	112
f_6	27	113
f_6v	28	114
g_1	29	115
g_1v	30	116
g_2	30	117
g_2v	31	118
g_3	32	119
g_3v	32	120
g_4	33	121
g_4v	34	122
	72	127
	73	129
	74	132

Page numbers in 1557 edition	Page numbers in Yale edition
75	134
76	136
77	138
78	141
79	143
80	145
81	147
82	150
83	154
84	156
85	158
86	160
87	163
88	165
89	167
90	168
91	169
92	170
93	171
94	173
95	174
96	175
97	176
98	177
99	178
100	179
101	181
102	181

GLOSSARY

GLOSSARY

The Glossary contains words and forms (not merely spellings) whose meanings are obsolete according to *The Oxford English Dictionary*. It also includes words or forms which might be puzzling because of their spelling or some other ambiguity. In general, if a word recurs more than twice, only the first instance, followed by "*etc.*," is given. Unusual forms of proper names are also included. Initial *v* when used as a vowel is alphabetized under *u;* consonantal *u* has not been distinguished from *v* in alphabetic sequence. The obsolete Middle English þ is alphabetized under *th*.

Abacuk *n.* Habakkuk 169/24
abieccion *n.* abasement 164/34
abiecte *adj.* degraded 68/9
accommodate *ppl. a.* suitable 135/29
accompt *n.* accounting 68/11
accompt *v.* esteem 52/26; consider 92/6
according *adj.* appropriate 83/3
accyon *n.* legal proceedings 21/203
adeption *n.* obtaining 91/17
adiuged *pp.* sentenced 74/18, 75/9
adnichilate *ppl. a.* reduced to nonexistence 97/8
adrad *ppl. a.* afraid 116/15
adventure, aventure *n. at a(d)venture* at random 36/141; 130/7. *See note on* 36/141
aduenturers *n. pl.* gamblers 107/17
aduertised *v. pp.* notified 128/15
advise *v.* look 39/219; *v. refl. the . . . advise* consider 110/16; *ppl. a.* **aduised** pondered 128/15
aduisedly *adv.* carefully 77/10
a ferde *adj.* afraid 21/202
affeccion *n.* attribute 159/21; disposition 162/29, 163/25; bodily state due to any influence 139/15; partiality 170/17
affect(e) *n.* feeling 83/10, 83/22; *n. pl.* 70/7
affection *n.* feeling 81/9; *n. pl.* 76/25 *etc.*
a flede *ppl. a.* escaped 28/416

after, aftir *prep.* according (to) 52/3 *etc.*
afore *prep.* before 89/7, 90/23
aftir *adv.* afterward 98/10, 98/19
againe, agayne *adv.* in return 24/297 *etc.*
against *prep.* toward 73/1
aggreued *ppl. a.* aggravated 162/34
agood *adv.* heartily 27/385
alacrite *n.* cheerfulness 70/9. *See note*
alaste *adv.* at last 33/61
all *adv.* entirely 68/2 *etc.*
allectiue *n.* enticement 80/23. *See note*
all redy *adv.* already 120/9
all waies *adv.* always 98/1–2
almes, almesse *n.* charity 63/21; *he gave alms of hys own body* he chastized himself 64/25
almes dede *n.* charity 82/27
a long *adv.* lengthwise 146/27
alway(e), alwei *adv.* always 15/2 *etc.*
amased *adj.* stupefied 28/413
amend *v. intr.* abandon one's faults 145/5
amyable *adj.* worthy to be loved 120/1
and, & *conj.* if 39/215 *etc.; and if* on condition that 162/32–33; if 172/4
Angel, Angelus Politianus *n.* Angelo Poliziano 67/17–18, 67/19
anon(e) *adv.* instantly 130/32, 159/4
apace *adv.* quickly 22/221, 22/237

apes *n. pl.* fools 38/206
appaled *v. pt.* dismayed 79/23
appertayneth *v.* belongs as an attribute 176/8
apply *v.* devote one's energy to 15/7
applye *v.* compare 108/13; *pt.* **appliede** ascribed 106/26
appointed, apointed *pp.* resolved 70/19; equipped 115/6
Arabies *n. pl.* Arabs 57/4
Araby *adj.* Arabic 88/7
araye *n.* clothing 22/223
argument *n.* subject 76/1
a ryght *adv.* truly 4/41
aryse *v.* advance, profit 16/36
asaie *n.* trial *putte it in a saie* make the experiment, try it 138/22–23
askyng *vbl. n.* petition 94/28
aspre *adj.* rough 133/29
assay *v.* put to the test 108/20; *pt.* **assaid, assaied** experienced 83/13, 140/21
associate *pp.* associated 91/9
astart *v.* escape 122/31
a strote *adj.* sticking out 176/20
attempt *v.* attack 57/17. *See note*
auayle *n.* advantage, profit 23/275
auoid *v.* vomit up 180/2
austen, Austine *adj.* Augustinian 23/272 *etc.*
auyse *v.* advise 28/427
await *n.* ambush 83/18; watchfulness 106/8
awaiward *adv.* away 141/21
axe *v.* ask 42/301 *etc.; pp.* **axed** asked 69/16
axis *n.* fever 70/24
ay(e) *adv.* always 10/30

bake *pp.* baked 22/217
balade *n.* stanzaic verse 114/2
balk *v. balk vp* belch 176/21. *See note*
bandes *n. pl.* bonds 81/2
bare *adj.* mere 129/29, 171/25
bare *v. pt. bare hyt out* carried on 21/178
barehed *adj.* bareheaded 161/5
baste *n.* bastardy 158/31. *See note*
bataile *n.* fighting 106/30
bate *n.* conflict 16/48
batylldore *n.* paddle used for laundry 27/392
baud *n.* bawd 175/7

bayte *n.* enticement 35/117
be *prep. be long space* for a long time 121/27
be *v. pp.* been 58/5 *etc.;* **bene** are 102/25, 115/5
beck vpon *v.* acknowledge with a bow 156/6
bedelem *adj. bedelem peple* lunatics 91/20. *See note*
behalf, bihalfe *n. in this (that) bihalfe* in this respect 74/20, 142/19
behauour *n.* behavior 71/4 *etc.*
behawor *n.* behavior 41/285. *See note*
beheste *v.* promise 21/204
behoofe *n.* benefit 171/29
bekith *v. pr. 3 s. bekith hym* warms himself 38/193
bekketh *v. pr. 3 s.* beckons 34/105
belly ioy *n.* bodily appetite 181/1
benefices *n. pl.* kindnesses 74/21
bere *v. refl. bere þe* behave 40/259; *the bere* conduct yourself 107/10
bereue, bereuyn *v.* deprive 116/31, deprive of 93/10 *etc.*
beshrewe *v.* bring evil upon, harm (oneself) 17/62; *I beshrewe your catte* I curse whatever plans you have for me 46/6. *See note*
besines, besynes, besynesse, busines(s), busynesse *n.* solicitude 63/23 *etc.;* public activities 87/23, 87/26; activity 91/16 *etc.*
besprent *ppl. a.* sprinkled 68/1
bestade *pp. woo bestade* surrounded by sorrow 116/14
bestowed *ppl. a.* employed 143/27
besy *adj.* elaborate 103/27
bet *pp. bet out* driven out 112/26
bewepte *adj.* tearstained 35/125
bigrace *v.* address as "your grace" 161/5
bisili, bisely *adv.* eagerly 59/28, 66/3
blandimentes *n. pl.* blandishments 59/16–17
blandisshing *vbl. n.* flattery 90/10
blode *n.* descendants 157/30
blow *v. blow vp his hart* make himself important 65/21–22
blunt *v. blunt forth* utter bluntly 137/4
bode *v. pt.* instructed 24/281; *pp.* bidden 61/5
bolte *n.* arrow 130/5

bond *adj.* enslaved 103/22

bondemen *n. pl.* slaves 80/11

Bononye *n.* Bologna 56/1

botyth *v. yt botith nott* it does no good 12/63

bought *v. pt.* redeemed 112/15

bounden, bownden *ppl. a.* secured 33/63; under moral obligation to 169/9

boystious *adj.* violent 91/22

brase *n.* pair 3/21

breake *v.* cut short 137/2

breke *v.* reveal 73/23; break up 27/379; *maters breke* disclose certain affairs 23/274 (*see note*); *pt.* **brake** broke 70/13; **broken** *broken hys mynde* revealed his thoughts 76/4

brennyng *adj.* burning 40/239

brent *ppl. a.* burnt 3/16

breuiary *n.* summary 56/5

brewes *n.* broth. *See note on* 176/21

bright *adj.* beautiful 12/67

brinkes *n. pl.* edges 148/2

brooke *v.* put up with 129/19

brosed *pp.* bruised 72/13

brotil(l), brotle, brotyll. *See* **brytill**

browes *n. pl. the browes to set vp* to be supercilious 31/21

brutissh *adj.* pertaining to animals 76/28–29. *See note*

bryng *v. bryng vp* bring into vogue 70/5

brytill, brotil(l), britle, brotyll *adj.* transitory 10/30 *etc. See note*

business(s), busynesse *n. See* **besines**

buskle *v.* start on a journey 149/2

but *conj. but if (yf)* unless 22/218 *etc.*

by *prep.* during 146/27

by and by *adv. phrase* immediately 67/2 *etc.*

byde *pp.* commanded 73/16

bynde *v.* require 42/308

bynding *vbl. n.* chaining 89/24

byrall *n.* beryl 130/29

by side *prep. by side that* in addition to the fact that 112/15

Caldaies *n. pl.* Chaldaeans 57/4

can *v.* know how to 167/3; *in . . . can skill* know about 130/6

canel *n.* channel 177/12

canker *n.* corruption 107/26

cankerd *adj.* tarnished 134/30

captions *n. pl.* sophisms 61/28. *See note*

carkas *n.* body 111/23

carued *pp.* cut 112/27

case *n. in case* into circumstances (in which) 37/179

cast *n.* aim 17/59; fortune 18/90

cast *v.* add 168/10, 168/26; *v. imp.* consider 104/25; *cast a way* waste 85/19; *pt.* **cast vp** vomited 77/5, 179/1; *pp.* reckoned 110/4; *pr. 3 s.* plants 106/22; *casteth theron, casteth . . . therto* sets one's affections on 171/4–5, 171/12–13

catchith *v. pr. 3. s.* attacks 107/26

catte *n. See* **beshrewe** 46/6

cauillations *n. pl.* quibbles 61/28

causeles *adj.* without cause 78/10

certes, certesse *adv.* certainly 18/89 *etc.*

certyne *adj.* fixed 69/24–25

certyne *adv.* certainly 23/275

chaldairs *n. pl.* Chaldeans, astrologers

chaldey *adj.* Aramaic 65/19, 88/6

charge *n.* care 63/22

chargeable *adj.* weighty, serious 4/56, 137/20

chaunge *v.* exchange 100/17

chayre *n.* throne 4/47

chepe *See* **good** *adv.*

chere *n.* expression 35/106 *etc.;* temperament 65/5; *make good chere* feast 177/7

chese *v. & v. imp.* choose 39/222 *etc.*

chiden *pp.* chided 101/12

chines *n. pl.* cracks 180/6

christen, chrysten *adj.* Christian 51/14

christen *n. euen christen* fellow Christian 153/29

circes *n.* Circe 78/5

circuit *n.* circle 98/18

ciuile *adj.* public 85/15. *See note*

clappes *n. pl.* blows 26/355; *after clappes* unexpected events 39/235

claue *v. pt. claue togyder* clung together 26/365

claw *v.* scratch 178/19, 178/22; *pr. 2. s.* **clawest** 148/1; *pt.* **clawed** 171/35; *vbl. n.* **clawing** 178/20

cledd *pp.* clad 51/12

clen(e) *adv.* wholly 11/47 *etc.*

clene *adj.* virtuous 58/9, 84/8, 115/7

clense *v.* purge 111/13; *vbl. n.* **clensing** expiation 65/2

clere *adj.* splendid 53/12

clere *adv.* clearly 80/14
clere *v.* illuminate 117/20
clerkes *n. pl.* learned men 31/2
cleued *v. pt.* held 68/7 *etc.; pr. 3. s.* **cleuith**
  stands fast 110/12
cloche *n. in my cloche* in my power, clutches
  25/335
cloute *v.* patch clumsily 146/17
coeternalli *adv.* with equal eternity 71/15
cognition *n.* understanding, knowledge
  58/12 *etc.*
cokstele *n.* a stick to throw at a cock 3/13.
  See note
comforteth *v. pr. 3 s.* encourages 76/10,
  88/20
commen *pp.* come 53/33
commendet *pp.* commended 88/27
commune *adj.* public 87/23
commune *v.* talk 68/26
communication *n.* conversation 67/8
communing *vbl. n.* communication 68/22
compace *n.* circle 98/18
compaced, compassed *pp.* surrounded
  5/74, 75/7
complexion, *n.* constitution 73/28
compnyed *pp.* accompanied 20/163
comprise *v.* comprehend 117/26
conceyte *n.* fancy article 117/5
concordia *n.* Concordia 64/1–2
condition *n.* quality 62/19; *n. pl.* **condi-
  tions** circumstances 69/2, 71/27; quali-
  ties 53/18 *etc.*
confounde *v.* defeat 5/76
conning, connying, cunnyng(e) *n.* knowl-
  edge 31/15; cleverness 67/4; learning
  57/24 *etc.*
connying, cunning *adj.* learned 49/4 *etc.;*
  clever 68/24 *etc.*
contenaunce *n.* countenance 72/15
contract *pp.* become infected with 106/20
contrari *adv.* in contrary fashion 55/18
conuenience *n.* correspondence 76/27–28
conuenient *adj.* appropriate 73/2, 81/5
conuersation *n.* conduct 75/14–15
conuersaunt(e) *adj.* engaged in 56/22;
  dwelling 80/18 *etc.;* on terms of intimacy
  with 73/23 *etc.;* present with 116/29,
  145/29
coost *n.* region 111/21
corne *n.* seed 132/28, 132/30
corse *n.* corpse 180/29, 180/32

cost *n.* effort 28/418
cote armour *n.* coat of arms 161/10
couenaunt *n.* mutual agreement 81/9
couetice, couityce, couetise, couetyse *n.*
  covetousness 57/22 *etc.*
counceill, counsell *n. in counsell* in private
  25/317; secret design 68/8; *of counceill in*
  privy to 76/4–5
course *n.* coursing 4/1. *See note*
courtese *adj.* courteous 73/6
cowpled *ppl. a.* tied 65/27
crop *n. crop and rote* totality 109/5. *See note*
crime, cryme *n.* accusation 58/1, 59/4; sin
  121/22
cure *n. do this cure* do this diligently
  22/218; *besy cure* anxious concern
  117/11 *(see note)*; amendment 168/30
cursed *ppl. a.* wicked 93/9
cuseth *v. pr. 3 s.* accuse 37/158. *See note*
customably *adj.* usually, customarily 51/10

daie *n. on a daie* one day 68/25
dalt *pp.* dealt 74/12
damoysell *n.* maiden 23/246. *See note*
danger *n.* haughtiness 35/129
darketh *v. pr. 3. s.* obscures 132/9
dawde *pt.* roused (from unconsciousness)
  26/356
dayntye *adj. dayntye stomaked* fussy about
  food 129/24–25
dead *n.* deed 180/22
deadly, dedly *adj.* mortal 71/31 *etc.*
deadly *adv.* in a way that entails spiritual
  death 182/10
debate *n.* contention 176/31
declare *v.* make clear 63/14; **declared** *pp.*
  made clear 58/25
decline *v.* deviate from 53/11, 86/14,
  86/16
dede *adj.* pallid 118/14
dedicate *pp.* dedicated 65/12
deface *v.* discredit 57/24
deforme *v. pr. 2 pl.* distort, debase 77/16
defye *v.* despise 33/72
degre(e) *n.* status (in society) 20/151,
  34/82, 79/5
deinties *n. pl.* luxuries 145/2
delice *n.* delight 10/24
delitiouse *adj.* exquisite 60/5
delyght *v. refl. me delyght* am delighted 3/26
demaunded *v. pt.* asked 71/11, 139/6

demeanour *n.* behavior 88/19
demed *pt.* considered 57/20; condemned 157/2
depart *v.* separate 139/9
departyn *v.* depart 111/16
dependants *n. pl.* appurtenances 178/14
depend therupon *v.* result from it 182/4
depose *v.* put down 109/2
deputed *pp.* consigned 74/17
dere *adj. See* **yere**
dere *adv.* dearly 113/2
derked *ppl. a.* obscured 132/15
descanted *v. pt.* commented on 88/16. *See note*
desirefull *adj.* desirable 90/4
despite, dispight, dispite *n.* contempt 38/183, 90/21; injury 134/14, 162/27
determineth *v. pr. 3 s.* settles 72/1–2, 98/26
deuice, devise *v.* provide 121/5; imagine 39/233
devide *v.* apportion 42/303
devise *v. See* **deuice**
devise, deuyse *n.* contriving 33/59; invention 175/13–14; *n. pl.* **deuises** desires 136/12
deuoyre *n.* endeavor 143/2
deuynatryce *adj.* divining, that which divines 10/26. *See note*
dewe *n.* rain 36/143
deynty *adj.* choice 64/9, 111/5
digne *adj.* worthy 49/10, 89/7
discomfortable *adj.* comfortless 101/19
dishoneste *n.* disgrace 68/3
dishonested *pp.* discredited 62/10
dispaire *v. refl. dispaire the* despair 108/24
dispence *v.* apportion 121/6
dispiteful *adj.* contemptuous 164/2
dispiteouse *adj.* cruel 110/18. *See note*
dispition *n.* disputation 67/17; *n. pl.* **dispitions** 56/21 *etc. See note on* 56/21
disport *n.* entertainment 111/4, 118/25
disposed vpon *ppl. a.* bestowed on 171/7
disseur(e) *v.* separate 111/23, 119/24
diuers *adj.* different 129/8 *etc.*; various 157/22; *divers qualifyed* having various qualities 147/19
do *v.* give 73/4
doctryne *n.* learning 57/25
dolor, dolour *n.* sorrow 116/16; physical suffering 140/23
dome *n.* the Last Judgment 129/4

done *v.* do 117/14
dopped *v. pt.* bobbed his head 22/228, 24/294
double, dowble *adj.* inconstant 37/170, 40/254
dowsy *adj.* stupid 35/128. *See note*
draffe *n.* refuse 131/10
draw *v.* tend 91/15
drawghtes *n. pl.* plans 39/214
dredefull *adj.* awe-inspiring 120/13, 122/16
driue, drive dryue *v.* carry out 17/59; *driue forth* pass time 157/12, 166/33
drye *adj.* not accompanied by bloodshed 163/9
ducatis *n. pl.* ducats, gold coins 63/7
dyght *v. pt.* placed 18/113; *pp.* dressed 22/225
dysherited *pp.* deprived of inheritance 161/8
dystres *n.* pressure 107/16

edyfye *v.* build 11/42
eft *adv.* afterward 70/9 *etc.*
eft sone *adv.* again 113/9
egall *adj.* equal 112/4, 122/30
eight *adj.* eighth 6/95
eisell *n.* vinegar 104/28
eke *adv.* also 35/127 *etc.*
election *n.* choosing 69/18
elementes *n. pl.* simple substances of which all material bodies are compounded 147/19
embassiatours *n. pl.* ambassadors 73/3
encreace *n.* advancement 62/16
endeuere *v. refl. thi selfe endeuere* strive 119/22
enforce *v. refl. enforce himself* strive 135/19; *enforce thy self(e) (themselfe)* exert yourself (themselves) 82/18 *etc.; pr. 3 s.* **enforcith** strengthens 61/2; *pt.* **enforced** strove 57/18
engine, engyne *n.* cunning 40/241; stratagem 105/15; *engyne of all this world* universal frame 120/23. *See note on* 120/23
enhaunce *v.* raise up 65/17–18; *v. refl. hymself enhaunce* enrich himself 34/92; *pr. 3 s.* **enhaunceth** raises up 37/173
eni *pron.* any 64/11
enprynted *ppl. a.* printed 123/13
ensample *n.* example 118/21

enserche *v.* look for 32/54, 180/23; *pr. 3 s.*
  enserchith looks for 86/18
enserching *vbl. n.* seeking 61/18 *etc.*
enserchour *n.* seeker out 56/11
ensew(e), ensue *v.* seek after 17/57; *pr. 3 s.*
  ensueth follows 86/17 *etc.; pp.* **ensewed**
  92/4
entende *v.* attend 99/14
entent *n.* judgment 118/3; *to thentent yᵗ* in
  order that 63/17 *etc.*
enterpryse, entreprise *v.* meddle with
  15/10; attack 111/7
entreate *v.* treat (a matter) 135/31; *pp.* **en-
  treted, entreated** treated 68/22, 84/9
entremengled *ppl. a.* intermingled 55/6
entreting *vbl. n.* undertaking 85/18. *See
  note*
enueigleth *v. pr. 3 s.* deceives 143/24
Epicure *n.* Epicurus 62/26
equivocation *n.* ambiguity 75/3–4
ere *adv.* before 71/7
erst *adj. at erst* for the first time 78/1
erst *adv.* first 11/49
eschaped *v. pt.* escaped 54/25
Esop *n.* Aesop 159/21
espirituall *adj.* spiritual 105/24
estate, state *n.* position 12/66 *etc.;* moral
  condition 94/21 *etc.;* condition 102/10
  etc.; pomp 160/34; worldly prosperity
  160/29, 169/8; *cloth of estate* canopy (over
  a throne) 6/92; *pl.* **estates** persons of
  high position 87/5
eth(e) *adj.* easy 148/20 *etc.*
ether other *pron.* each other 175/24
Ethna *n.* Etna 158/27
euen christen *See* **christen** *n.*
euery *pron.* each 3/4; *euery chone* everyone
  29/434
euin *adv.* steadily 107/10
excepte *conj.* unless 137/2
excercised, exercised *pt.* engaged in
  86/27; *ppl.* accustomed 62/13
exciting *pr. pl.* arousing 103/18
exhibit *v.* provide 93/24
expensis *n. pl.* accounts 68/15
expowned *v. pt.* expounded 54/27
expugnation *n.* conquest 80/24
extolle *v.* lift up 108/27
extreme *n. extreme lippis* 85/25. *See note on*
  83/23

extremes *n. pl.* last moments 71/4
extremite *n.* outer point 83/23. *See note*
eyen *n. pl.* eyes 171/30 *etc. See also* **yeen**

faculte *n.* skill, occupation 15/11
fader *n.* father 52/19
failed *v. pt. subj.* were absent 78/2
fain, fayne *adv.* gladly 21/186 *etc.*
faine *v.* pretend 153/26; *pr. 3 s.* **fayneth**
  imagines 159/23
fained *ppl. a.* fictitious 156/25
fall *v.* descend to 15/19; *fall vnto* happen to
  100/8; *fall to* come to 100/11; befall
  115/20; *pr. 3 s.* **falleth** descends to
  15/17; *pt.* **fell** happened 19/127, 65/7;
  fill 76/8; *his mynde fill from it* he became
  averse to it 156/3–4; **fyll** came about
  17/73
falling *adj.* transitory 67/10
fantasie(s), fantasy(e) *n.* delusive imagina-
  tion 136/21, 146/30; an image im-
  pressed on the mind by an object of
  sense 139/20, 139/28; the faculty by
  which an object of perception is appre-
  hended 175/11
fantasye *v.* imagine 136/12
fare *v.* act 129/14, 131/8; *fare by* deal with
  144/14; *fare harde* get on badly 166/31
farrare, fer(r)are *n.* Ferrara 70/12 *etc.*
fassion *n.* appearance 156/25, 158/6
fast *adj.* retentive 63/5
fast *adv.* vigorously 26/365; firmly 55/20
fauoure *n.* beauty 59/10
faye *n.* faith 23/263
fayne *adj.* glad 19/117; *etc.;* obliged to
  145/32 *etc.*
fayre *adv.* completely 19/122
feithfull *adj.* believing 51/15–16
fele *v.* perceive 174/32; *pr. 3 s.* **feleth** per-
  ceives 132/17
fence *v.* protect 109/3; *pp.* **fenced** pro-
  tected 95/29; *ppl. a.* 107/14; *pr. ppl.*
  fencyng protecting 70/16
ferder *adj. comp. well ferder* more afraid
  26/352
fere, ferre *adv.* far 17/59, 40/261
fere *n.* companion 9/11, 12/61
fere *v.* frighten 80/19; *pp.* **ferde** frightened
  111/15
fer forth, ferforth, ferre forth *adv.* to a

certain degree 41/284; *so ferforth* to such an extent that 70/24, 101/16; *in so far forth (farreforth)* to the extent that 154/12 *etc.*

ferme *adj.* secure 67/11

feruent *adj.* intense 88/4

fet *v.* go in search of 128/33; *pp.* fetched 57/3, 128/30

ffees *n. pl.* goods 38/199

ffist *n.* power, control 39/224

fforseth *v. pr. 3 s.* cares 36/136

ffull *adj.* satisfied 39/217

fier *a fier on him,* inflamed with love for him 59/13

figure *n.* form 76/15, 111/27; **figures** *pl.* forms 76/19 *etc.*

fill *v. See* **fall**

find *v.* provide for 168/35

finders *n. pl.* devisers 81/8

finding, findying *vbl. n.* provision for 64/5, 169/33

fle *v.* avoid, shun 12/76

flesshly *adj.* material 123/7

fleying *vbl. n.* flying 54/24

flitting *pr. ppl.* changing from one habitation to another 69/24

flodes *n. pl.* rivers 91/21

floke *n.* company 37/174

floure, flowre *n.* preeminence 6/88; *to haue a goodly floure* to enjoy preeminence 20/149

flowred *v. pt.* gained distinction 62/10

flyght *n.* pursuit of game by a bird 4/28. *See note*

fobby *adj.* lacking muscle tone 179/6

folily *adv.* foolishly 144/17

folowen *v.* follow 99/5

folys *n. pl.* fools 61/22

fond *adj.* mad 132/18

fondely *adv.* foolishly 33/62

for *conj.* because 57/19; *conj. phr. for that* because 72/4 *etc.;* for by because of 144/11; *for by cause* because 98/16

for *prep.* because (of) 53/8 *etc.*

forboden *pp.* forbidden 58/29

force *n. no force* no matter 4/32; *he gaue no . . . force* he did not attach importance to 70/2

forced *v. pt.* cared 66/22

fordre *v.* help 23/260

foregrowen *adj.* overgrown 132/27

forethought *pp.* anticipated 161/31

foreweried *adj.* excessively wearied 179/27

forfare *v.* destroy 40/240

forlabored *v.* exhausted 79/16

former *adj.* first 142/11

forsaken *v.* forsake 99/4

forslouth, forslowth *v.* neglect 128/21; *pt.* **forslowthed** neglected 74/4

forther *v.* advance 34/86

forth warde *adv.* forward 91/24

fountain, fountayn(e) *n.* source 164/17 *etc.*

framing *vbl. n.* shaping 128/10

frappe *adj.* beaten (?) 28/402. *See note*

fre *adj.* generous 74/13

frekill *n.* spot 68/1

frered *v. pt.* played the part of a friar 22/236

fro *prep.* from 11/57 *etc.; him fro* from him 119/11; *þe fro* from you 40/254

from *prep.* absent from 147/15

fruition, fruytion *n.* enjoyment 103/4, 103/10

frushed *adj.* crushed 72/13

frustrate *pp.* frustrated 75/2

frute *n.* enjoyment 104/1

ful, full *adv.* very 19/145, 111/6; completely 149/22

fulfilled *pp.* completed 70/23

furnisheth *v. pr. 3 s.* embellishes 168/4

furth *prep.* forth 164/10, 164/11

fyft *adj.* fifth 63/10

gadered, gedered *pp.* gathered 78/26, 92/1

gadering *vbl. n.* gathering 63/8

gan *v. pt.* began (to) 21/199 *etc.*

gape *v. gape aftir* long for 82/7; *gape after* þe *wynde* desire something insubstantial 35/114; *pr. 3 s.* **gapeth** longs 172/15; *vbl. n.* **gaping aftir** longing for 120/3

garnisshe *v. garnisshe thi self* dress in elegant fashion 115/12; *pp.* **garnysshed** clothed elegantly 34/99. *See notes on* 34/99, 115/12

gate *v. pt.* got 20/152 *etc.*

gentiles *n. pl.* pagans 139/5

gere *n.* wealth 10/19, 158/2; clothing 19/135; armour 107/7; stuff 145/2

ghostly, gostly *adj.* spiritual 51/15 *etc.*

gife *v.* give 121/9
glade *n.* a gleam of hope 143/6
glasse *n.* mirror 115/16
glideth *v. pr. 3 s.* slips (away) 110/11. *See note*
glisters *n. pl.* enemas 179/30
glosse *n.* superficial luster 109/6. *See note*
godly *adv.* in a godly way 51/23
godwarde *adv.* toward God 63/15 *etc.*
gone *v.* go 29/431
good *adv. good chepe* very cheaply 64/3–4
good, goodes *n.* possessions, property 42/293 *etc.*
goost *n.* soul 111/22
gorbely *n.* person with a protuberant belly 179/1
gorbelyed *adj.* potbellied 175/29–30
gorge *n.* a second meal eaten before another is digested 178/34
gotin *pp. was gotin* had got 65/25
grace *n. with euyll grace* threateningly 25/329
grafe *n.* scion 158/30
graue *v.* engrave 114/11
grennys *n. pl.* snares 83/17
grete *v. pt.* greeted 24/295
gretter *adj. comp.* greater 78/18
greuous, grieuous *adj.* burdensome 129/32; causing great suffering 134/17
grief, grif *n.* physical pain 134/3 *etc.;* disease 145/23; *pl.* **griefes** wrongs or injuries that are the subject of a formal complaint 162/27
grieue *v.* bring harm or trouble to 134/8
grounde *n. brought to grounde* overthrown 5/77
grudge *n.* misgiving 110/13 *etc.;* grumbling 169/19, 169/27
grudge *v.* complain 104/15, 129/25; **grudgith** *pr. 3 s.* oppresses 79/23
gwerdon *n.* reward 119/20
gyse *n.* practice, custom 42/300
gyuen *v. pp. gyuen out* published 66/23

habitation *n.* residing 75/13
halynge *vbl. n.* pulling, tugging 26/367
hand *n. at our hand* near us 109/22
handkercher *n.* handkerchief 129/28

hap *v.* happen 150/26
haply, happeli, happely(e) *adv.* by chance 40/248, 107/5; perhaps 53/26 *etc.*
happe *n.* chance 33/65
harkeneth after *v. pr. 3 s.* inquires about 156/31–32
hast *adj.* hasty 172/34
hawke *v. hawke aftir* attempt to gain 87/24. *See note*
heale *n.* good health 141/30
hebrieus *n. pl.* Hebrews 57/4
hebriew *adj.* Hebrew 98/12
hedge *n. vnto the hard hedge* to the very end 21/179
hedling, hedlynge *adv.* headlong 28/407 *etc.*
helping *adj.* helpful 95/22
helth *n.* salvation 83/16
hepis *n. pl. by hepis* in large quantities, great numbers 62/17
hercules *n.* Ercole I d'Este, Duke of Ferrara 61/7
heuen warde, heuinwarde *adv.* toward heaven 93/24–25, 99/13–14
heuily *adv.* sorrowfully 171/35
Heuines, heuynes *n.* sorrow 65/16 *etc.*
hewe *n.* complexion 12/67
heynous *adj.* grievous 141/23
hight *v. pt. was* called 54/1
his *pron.* its 105/28, 110/11
hold(e) *v.* remember 55/21; *holde . . . in hande* keep in suspense 62/7; *pr. 3. s.* **holdith** possesses 67/19, 81/24; *pt.* **hold** helped 10/18; *pp.* **holden** considered 87/9; held 61/10, 61/20; *holden in* occupied with 59/9
hole *adv.* completely 56/12
holpe *v. pt.* helped 27/395; *pp.* **holpen** helped 63/7
homelye *adj.* familiar 156/5
honest *adj.* honorable 115/13
horsone *adj.* wretched, vile 26/342
horyloge *n.* hourglass 5/84
hote *adj.* ardent 115/19
houe *v.* wait 172/26; *pr. 3 s.* **hoveth** waits 35/123
howsolde *n. in howsholde with* familiar with 87/1
humanite *n.* classical scholarship 55/9
hyder *adv.* hither 24/285

hye *adj.* high 155/36
hyed *v. pt.* hastened 27/380

iapes *n. pl.* foolish acts 38/207; frauds 86/2
Ibent *pp.* inclined 117/33
iche *pron.* each 72/10
Iclensed *pp.* cleansed 122/19
Ieopard *v.* wager 107/18
Ieopardous *adj.* perilous 107/24, 111/11
Illudethe *v. pr. 3 s.* tricks 34/102
imaginacions *n. pl.* devices 175/11
impassyble *adj.* 141/7. *See note*
imperfite *adj.* imperfect 96/28
impugnation *n.* assault 58/5
in *prep.* on 71/21, 119/17
incogytable *adj.* unthinkable 143/3
incommodite *n.* disadvantage 116/6; *pl.*
   incommoditees afflictions 72/2, 78/24
incontinent *adv.* immediately 107/8
infatigable *adj.* tireless 56/17 *etc.*
in how much *adv. phr.* to the extent that
   181/23
Insampull *n.* example 9/6
insensibilite *n.* unconsciousness 81/25.
   See note
inspecable, inspekable *adj.* unspeakable
   75/19, 83/12
instant *adj.* urgent 61/11
instantly *adv.* urgently 74/15
institution *n.* ordering 91/1
in such wise *adv. phr.* in such a way 137/16
insyght *n.* knowledge 130/28
integrite *n.* virtue 64/14
intentife *adj.* attentive 142/5–6
interpretation *n.* commentary 94/1
into, in to *prep.* unto 70/10 *etc.*
inuencyon *n.* inventiveness 162/7–8; *pl.*
   inuentions discoveries 62/12
inward *adj.* inner 112/13
inwardnes *n.* inner part 83/23
Iohn frauncis *n.* Gianfrancesco Pico della
   Mirandola 70/11
iolle *n.* blow 27/390
Ipocrites, ypocrites *n.* hypocrites 153/25,
   155/25
irows, yrous *adj.* angry 77/1, 162/29
Iset *pp.* set 119/21
Iulya *n.* Julia 53/33
Iwrought *pp.* made 118/9
Iwys *adv.* certainly 103/28

kayes *n. pl.* keys 141/33
keuer *v.* cover 155/31
kind *adj.* grateful 73/27
kind, kynd(e) *n.* condition 131/33; *in his
   kynde* in its way 3/14; in itself 144/9–10,
   153/11
kindle *v.* inflame 93/22; *pp. kindled in* in-
   flamed by 56/24, 59/9
knaweth *v. pr. 3. s.* gnaws 178/33
knowlegeth *v. pr. 3. s.* acknowledges
   162/21
kysse *v. kysse yᵉ cup* to drink 16/29

laberous *adj.* laborious 108/15
lacketh *v. pr. 3. s.* is wanting 136/16; *pr. 2 s.
   subj.* **lacke** be in want 169/5; *pr. 3. s. im-
   pers. the lacketh* is lacking to you 169/10
lake *n.* den 169/25
langwished *n. pt.* weakened 70/9
Laodice *n.* Laodicea 154/19
late *adv.* recently 17/65, 37/175
laude, lawde *n.* praise 63/18 *etc.*
laweth *v. pr. 3 s.* laughs 38/206
laye *v. to laye . . . to pledge* to deposit in
   pawn 21/182
leife, liefe *adj.* beloved 117/8; acceptable
   165/2
leman *n.* mistress 172/16
lenger *adv. comp.* longer 62/7 *etc.*
lenght *n. on lenght* protractedly 83/15
lent *v. pt.* gave 27/389
lepry *n.* leprosy 147/33
lese *n.* group of three 38/191
le(e)se, leseth, lesith *v.* lose 32/46 *etc.*
lesing *vbl. n.* losing 80/1
let *n.* hindrance 172/6, 175/10
let, lette *v.* hinder 119/23; forbear 137/5,
   163/24; allow to remain 164/25; *pr. 3 s.*
   letteth prevents 144/9; *pt.* **letted** hin-
   dered 76/9 *etc.*
letred *ppl. a. wel letred* well educated
   64/14–15
leud(e) *adj.* common 156/11; vile 165/10;
   evil 176/30; ignorant 180/4
leudnes *n.* ignorance 180/5
leve *adj.* glad 41/276
leue *v.* stop 137/6
leve *v.* live 9/5, 10/24
leuer *adv.* rather 67/23 *etc.*
leuing *vbl. n.* abandoning 81/23

leyned *v.* was inclined toward 56/2

leysour *n. by leysour* by degrees 179/11

licorouse *adj.* fond of delicious food 110/1

life stringes *n. pl.* nerves 140/17

lift *pp.* lifted 67/12 *etc.*

light *adj.* wanton 172/16

lightsome *adj.* radiant with light 83/10

lightsomely *adv.* clearly 67/16

liketh, lyketh *v. pr. 3 s. hym lyketh* pleases him 169/22; likes 154/11; *pt.* **liked** *him liked* pleased him 60/23; *v. intr.* **liketh** pleases 119/8

list(e), lyst(e) *v.* desire 39/222 *etc.*; *impers* it pleases 33/70 *etc.*

litterature *n.* writing 63/9

loke *v. loke to what coost* to whatever region; 111/21; see to it 119/25

longith, longethe *v. pr. 3 s. longethe for, longethe to* belongs to 23/257, 53/2

long lien *ppl. a.* unused 128/30

lordshyp *n.* domain 52/1; *pl.* **lordeshippes** 63/21

lorel *n.* rogue 156/16

lose *adj.* loose 41/271

lothe *adj.* loathsome 33/79; reluctant 41/276

lothsomnes *n.* aversion 143/8

louely *adj.* lovable 120/8

lovely *adv.* in a loving way 39/229

louers *n. pl.* well-wishers 68/21

lowly *adv.* humbly 84/8

lucre *n.* money 85/12

luggynge *vbl. n.* pulling 26/366

lust(e) *n.* desire 132/18 *etc.*; vigor 150/13

lustely *adv.* cheerfully 31/21

lusty *adj.* vigorous 4/29, 26/362; hearty 19/141

lyke *adj.* likely 23/265, 39/218

lyking(e) *n.* sexual desire 131/4; pleasure 131/6

lynne *v.* cease 110/27

lyste *n.* ear 26/346

made *pp.* composed 127/7

magnyfye *v.* praise 12/77; *ppl. a.* **magnifyed, pp.** **magnyfyed** 5/65, 162/8

magrey, maugry *prep. maugry thy teeth* in spite of you 5/78; *magrey oure teth* in spite of ourselves 79/11

make *v.* compose (a work) 31/10; *make a pro(o)fe* establish the truth of 138/23, 138/30; *pr. 2 s.* **makeste for** assert 129/21; *ppl.* **making . . . into** reducing to 142/14

maner *adj. no maner* no kind of 157/4

maner *n. in maner* very nearly 174/31; *al maner* all kinds of 176/32

maner *n.* character 158/6; moderation 40/253; *in maner* in such a way 51/13 *etc.*

marchandise, marchaundyse *n.* buying and selling 16/37, 154/14; salable commodity 85/9

maschefe *n. with a maschefe* bad luck to you! 26/343. *See note*

mased *ppl. a.* amazed 35/119

matche *n.* companion 160/30; equal 162/20; *pl.* **matches** companions 160/32

mat(t)er *n.* material 122/23; *pl.* **matters** doings 176/21

may(e) *v.* can 67/20 *etc.*; *pr. 2 s.* **mast** can 84/3 *etc.*

maye *n.* maid 23/267

mayny *n.* multitude 173/4

meane, meanne *adj.* moderate 52/12 *etc.*

meane *n.* means 118/11, 137/1

meanely *adv.* moderately 52/14

measure, mesur(e) *n.* moderation 67/27; standard of measurement 93/21; *owt of mesure* excessively 34/99 *etc.*

meate, mete *n.* food 72/9 *etc.*

mede *n.* reward 120/5

mediocrite *n.* mean 87/18. *See note*

mend *v.* reform 154/4

merchaundise, marchandise *n.* commerce 86/27; transaction 110/19

mete *adj.* appropriate 58/25

mete *v.* measure 83/5; *pp.* **met, mette** measured 83/6, 100/12

metely *adj.* appropriate 61/16

metely *adv.* fairly 143/25, 160/25

might, mighten *v. pt.* could 53/22 *etc.*

minisheth *v. pt. 3 s.* reduces 132/10; *vbl. n.* **minishing** reduction 149/27

Mirandula *n.* Mirandola 52/1

mischiefe, mischefe *n.* wickedness 91/25, 109/5

mischieuous *adj.* having a harmful influence 153/14

misliketh *v. pr. 3 s.* dislikes 154/3
mo *n.* more 180/25
mokke *n.* mockery 37/177
more *adj. comp.* greater 141/8 *etc.*
most *adj. sup.* greatest 117/2
mote *v. pr.* may 28/420
moueable *adj. moueable goodes* personal
  property 72/19
mought *v. pp.* been able 68/14; *pt. subj.*
  might be able 142/18
mych *adv.* much 42/300
mynde *n.* purpose, intention 3/12
mynyssh(e) *v.* lessen 18/104, 115/10; *pp.*
  minisshed lessened 90/17
myrrour *n.* example 4/41
mys, mysse *of . . . mysse* fail to obtain
  114/22; *mys the effect* fail to achieve 95/17
myscheveth *v. pr. 3 s.* harms 37/174
myscontente *v.* disturb 19/140
mysshape *ppl. a.* misshapen 5/62
mystrystynge *ppl.* mistrusting 24/282

nameli, namely *adv.* especially 64/28; at
  any rate 138/4
nathles *adv.* nonetheless 150/3
necessite *n.* poverty 64/20
nede(s) *adv.* necesarily 103/24
nede *v. impers.* be necessary 68/15; **nedeth**
  me nedeth I need 6/96; is necessary 143/14
nedis *adv.* necessarily 79/19, 111/20
negard *n.* miser 96/9
neghe *v.* neigh 91/3
nere *adj. comp.* nearer 28/419
nere *adv.* never 155/20
nerely *adv.* with great care 144/31
nigardous *adj.* niggardly 173/35–174/1
nobles *n. pl.* nobles, gold coins 17/79
nolle *n.* top of the head 27/391
not *v.* know not 111/8
noþer *adv.* neither 40/256
no thing *adv.* not at all 108/24, 113/26
nought *adj.* valueless 19/115; immoral
  136/27; wicked 137/30, 154/26
nought *n.* sinful act 154/1
noughtely *adv.* in an evil manner 170/22
nowhither *adv.* nowhere 157/10–11
noyous *adj.* harmful 95/18; troublesome
  177/9
nycely *adv.* foolishly 129/26

nygh *adv.* near 59/26
nyl *v.* will not 116/24
nys *v. pr. 3 s.* is not 33/69

occasion *n.* opportunity 65/22; *pl.* **occa-
  sion(e)s** occurences 77/24, 78/7
occupied *pp.* used 170/18
odd *adj.* single 114/12
of *adv.* off 81/2 *etc.*
of *prep.* for 67/26 *etc.*; by 71/13 *etc.*; from
  71/14, 108/8; off 144/13 *etc.*; because of
  180/25; at 175/9; *of a chylde* from the
  time of childhood 79/4
office *n.* obligation 64/18; duty 181/2
on *pron.* one (person) 36/152
oppresse *v.* put an end to 4/56
opprobriouse *adj.* shameful 90/2. *See note*
or *conj.* before 17/67 *etc.*
ordeynance *n.* contriving 33/59
ostentation *n.* display 61/21
other, othir *pron. pl.* others 62/20 *etc.*
ouer *prep.* in addition to 55/17
ouer *v.* overcome 158/24. *See note*
ouer caste, over caste *v.* destroy 18/100;
  pp. 33/64
ouer commen *pp.* overcome 64/27
ouerloketh *v. pr. 3 s.* treats with contempt
  156/4
over þat *adv. phr.* moreover 34/86
ouerthrowe *v. ppl.* overthrown 26/350
ouertorne *v.* pervert 65/25
ought *pron.* anything 31/8, 68/16
ought *v. pt.* owed 21/197
out *prep. out all yᵉ way to mend* entirely astray
  from mending 154/12
outward *adj.* practical 85/18

pageant *n.* part in the drama of life
  156/22; *pl.* **pageauntes** pictures repre-
  sented in tapestry 3/4, 3/6 *etc. See note*
paining *n.* mortification 64/22
paleys *n.* palace 156/10
pampereth *v. pr. 3 s.* overindulges with rich
  food 175/30, 175/34
panting *ppl. a.* throbbing violently 140/3
pappes *n. pl.* breasts 175/10
paradeuenture, peraduenture *adv.* per-
  haps 54/7 *etc.*
parcase, percase *adv.* perhaps 137/19 *etc.*

parcell *n.* portion 42/291

parceyue *v.* perceive 158/9

pardee *interj.* indeed! 121/11

parfit(e), parfyt, perfit *adj.* fully accomplished 56/8 *etc.*

parson *n.* person 158/21

part(e) *v.* share 114/16, 171/23

parties *n. pl.* parts 97/4

partying *pr. ppl.* sharing 114/13

passe(n) *v.* pass away 110/28; surpass 130/23; *pr. 3 s.* **passeth** exceeds 130/2; *pt.* **passed** got beyond 134/21; *passed him* eluded him 61/27–8

passion *n.* affliction 147/17

passioned *ppl. a.* moved by passion 118/29. *See note*

pate *n.* head 17/68

patens *n. pl.* slippers 172/32

pax *n. See note on* 165/28

payne *v. refl. payne him self* exert himself 119/16

paynym *adj.* pagan 159/24

perced *pp.* deeply moved 69/1

pered *pp.* examined, looked at closely 22/233

perilous *adj.* greatly to be dreaded 147/27, 155/11–12

peruse *v.* recount in order 105/16. *See note*

peseable, pesybull *adj.* peaceful 80/7; harmonious 11/46

peuishe *adj.* foolish 4/31

phisik, physyke *n.* medical treatment 16/30 180/10

piked(e) *pp.* selected 57/2; *vbl. adj. to pikede* carefully dressed 55/8. *See note*

pistle *n.* epistle 145/7

piteous, pyteouse *adj.* compassionate 121/4, 122/13

placabilite *n.* mildness of disposition 65/4. *See note*

plaining *pr. ppl.* complaining 170/3

pledge *v.* pawn 21/182. *See* **laye** *v.*

plenteouse *adj.* possessing abundantly 57/25

plentuosly *adv.* plenteously 64/11

plentuouse *adj.* abundant 53/15

plesaunce *n.* pleasure 118/25

pletynge *pr. ppl.* pleading 16/45

plucketh *v. pr. 3 s.* afflicts 42/299

point *n.* piece of lace 117/6

pointe *n.* readiness 163/18. *See note*

poke *n.* sack 27/374

pompe *n.* boastful display 85/26

pondre *v.* weigh 120/21

populare *adj.* common 90/18

pore blinde, pore blynde *adj.* dimsighted 173/3 *etc.*

port *n.* style of living 160/34

portculiouse *n.* protection 71/10. *See note*

possede *v.* possess 67/24, 82/14

poticary *n.* apothecary 128/28

pottell *n.* half-gallon 181/12

pouder *n.* ashes 3/16

preace *n.* pressure 122/6; *put thi selfe in preace* enter into the thick of the fight 106/30

preace *v.* crowd 37/161

prece *n.* throng 38/188

prefir *v. prefir our selfe* present to ourselves 84/19

presence *n.* assembly 137/13

preuy, priuey, pryuey *adj.* secret 73/24 *etc.*

prik *n.* bull's-eye 66/21

priked *v. pt.* instigated 66/27

prikking *pr. ppl.* spurring 91/24

priuation *n.* deprivation 101/20

priuely *adv.* secretly 84/6.

proces *n. in proces* in the course of time 6/90

profited *v. pt.* made progress 62/20

promocyon *n.* the laying of information as to debt 20/169. *See note*

promotion *n.* advancement 90/17

pronostication *n.* prognostication 54/27

proofe *n.* experience 137/34; *putte in proofe* test 130/13

proper *adj.* own 153/23

propirly, proprely *adv.* appropriately 52/27, 87/12

prorogyd *pp.* extended 73/20

prouen *v.* prove 96/28

prouided *v. pt.* discerned 101/23

provisioun *n.* foresight 33/64

prouoked *pp.* challenged 78/13

prowde *adv.* proudly 40/259

prowle *v.* search for, gaze (?) 115/16. *See note*

punicion *n.* punishment 142/25

purchace, purchase *v.* acquire 91/13–14, 98/2

purchasing, purchasyng *vbl. n.* acquisition 52/8 *etc.*

purpose *v.* intend 70/17; *pt.* **purposed** put forward for discussion 57/1; intended 73/25

pursewed *v. pt.* persecuted 92/4

puruaye *n.* arrangement 18/107. *See note*

puruey *v.* contrive 116/30

put *v. pt. put vnto* imposed upon 135/16; *pr. 3 s.* **puteth** *puteth therto* adds to it 99/1

quart *n. in good quart* healthy 146/3

quere *n.* choir 180/32

queste *n.* inquest 180/20

qwenche *v.* extinguish 123/3; *ppl. a.* **quenched** extinguished 132/4

quik, quike *adj.* living 84/6 *etc.*; lively 55/7

quod *v. pt.* said 21/207 *etc.*

ragged *adj.* irregular 60/9

ragious *adj.* full of suffering 141/2; mad 161/27

ramping *adj.* ferocious 165/39

ransake *v. ransake vp* search through 173/21

rappes *n. pl.* blows 26/354

rathir *adv.* earlier 75/19

rauen *n.* robbery 105/2

rauenous *adj.* rapacious 77/2

raynes, reynis *n. pl.* kidneys 101/12, 101/13

reason *n. good reason* rational conduct 32/47

rebuke *n.* disgrace 81/4, 105/12

rebuke *v. pt.* repulsed 107/4

receite *n.* prescription 128/29 *etc.*

reconyng *n.* outcome 9/13. *See note*

recorde *v.* remember 104/12

reherce *v.* recount 53/24; *pr. ppl.* **rehersing** recounting 52/25; *pt.* **reherced** delivered 73/11

rekenyng *n.* cost 110/20; *bokęs of rekenyng* account books 68/12

rekkith *v. pr. 3 s.* cares 82/11

releue *v.* relieve 64/20

religion *n.* life under religious vows 73/25, 74/1

reliques *n. pl.* sacred remains 117/15

remenaunte *n.* remainder (of the human race) 158/10; remainder 174/24

renaying *vbl. n.* renunciation 66/15

renneth *v. pr. 3 s.* runs 41/271

rente *v. pt.* pulled 26/363

reprefe, repriefe *n.* reproach 89/11 *etc.*

reprouable *adj.* blameworthy 81/5, 89/1

reprouable *n.* those deserving reproof 32/39. *See note*

reproued *pp.* blamed 88/28–89/1

repugneth *v. pr. 3 s.* resists 101/5

repute, reputen *v.* esteem 87/13 *etc.*; *pt.* **reputed** valued 66/14, 89/7

require *v.* ask for 106/3

residewe *n.* remainder 66/26

resonable *adj.* endowed with reason 111/26

resort *v.* repair to 114/28; *pr. ppl.* **resorting from** issuing from 164/20

rest(e) *v.* arrest 21/205

reuell *v. intr.* make merry 118/24

rialty, ryalty *n.* royal power 156/3; kingdom 157/27; pomp 161/3

richess, rychesse *n.* wealth 59/12 *etc.*; *pl.* **richessis** riches 93/14

rif raf *n.* trash 176/4

right *adv.* very 51/1 *etc.*

rightwise *adj.* righteous 96/21

riot, ryot *n.* debauchery 181/29; *in riot* wildly 59/16

riseth, ryseth *v. pr. 3 s.* results 131/4, 133/3

rocke *n.* distaff 27/396

rode *n.* cross 120/10

rombeling *vbl. n.* tumult 87/26

rote *n.* cause 101/20

rought *v. pt. he rought not* he did not care 19/137

rowt *n. on a rowt* in a crowd 35/115

royleth *v. pr. 3 s.* strays 177/12

ruddis *n. pl.* reddish color 55/6. *See note*

rude *adj.* inexpert 53/20; irrational 108/12

rudenesse *n.* ignorance 58/16

rueth *v. refl. me rueth I* regret 123/1

rumble *v.* make a disturbance 27/372

ryfely *adv.* often, frequently 17/66

rynne *n.* run 91/24; *pr. 3 s.* **rynneth** runs 106/10, 110/28

sadde *adj.* heavy 26/371

sample *n.* confirmation 134/6

sathanas *n. poss.* Satan's 122/31

saue for, sauing *prep.* but for 136/9 *etc.*

sauour *v. intr.* be agreable 88/1

sawes *n. pl.* maxims 130/2

scante *adv.* scarcely 174/20

scantly *adv.* scarcely 172/17

schricheth *v. pr. 3 s.* cries in pain 32/42. *See note*

science *n.* knowledge 50/8; *pl.* **sciencis** knowledge 50/4 *etc.*

sclaundre *n.* slander 58/32

sclaundred *v. pt.* slandered 88/18

scolis *n. pl.* branches of univerity instruction 62/14

scripture *n.* inscription 4/49, 5/82

season *n.* period of time 74/19

secrete *adj.* private 68/22

secte *n.* group 39/208; *pl.* **sectes** kinds of people 31/3

secundarily *adv.* secondly 102/26

seke *adj.* sick 16/31

sely, syly *adj.* pitiful 121/17; helpless 123/6; pitiable 140/24, 155/34

semely *adj.* well-formed 55/4

semeth *v. impers. me semeth* it seems to me 149/23, 167/26

semyng *adj.* fitting 81/21

sende *v. sende betwene* exchange 51/5–6. *See note*

sense *n.* opinion 81/5

sensuall *adj.* perceptible by the senses 104/24. *See note*

sentence *n.* profitable utterance 31/8; meaning 139/18

sergeaunt *n.* one charged with the arrest or summons of offenders 17/65

serpentines *n. pl.* cannons 57/30. *See note*

serued *v. pt. they serued of nought but they* served only 62/2

seruile *adj.* ignoble 86/22

seruisable *adj.* willing to do service 120/2

sessions *n. pl.* periodic sittings of the justices of the peace 156/32

set, sette *v.* place in position 3/14; *set . . . by* esteem 66/19 *etc.; set at nought* place no value on 65/27 *etc.; sette in the way* put in a position to receive 159/3; *set more bi* place more importance upon 87/21; *set*

hand to set to work to 88/6; *set on* assail 91/26; *set to* add 129/34; *pp.* arranged 136/8

seuerynge *pr. ppl.* setting apart 54/19

seuyngly, suingly, suyngly *adv.* subsequently 100/18 *etc.*

shape *n.* beauty 34/96

sharping *pr. ppl.* sharpening 140/5. *See note on* 140/4–5

shede *v. pt. shede owt* poured out 71/22

shew *n. settith him owt to the shew* make him ostentatious 87/15

shew *v. shew out* proclaim 55/1; *pr. 3 s.* **shewith** proclaims 122/14; *pt.* **shewed** proclaimed 122/15

shift *n.* manner of livelihood 169/2 *etc.*

shifted out *v. pt.* clothed 157/21–22

shit *pp.* shut 131/30

shone *n. pl.* shoes 15/17

shorting *pr. ppl.* growing shorter 140/6

shrewd, shrewed *adj.* ill-disposed 42/299; vexatious 159/14

shrifte *n.* penance 143/8

shyned *pp.* illuminated 34/98. *See note*

Sicil *n.* Sicily 158/18

singuler *adj.* exceptional 72/27, 73/18

singulerly *adv.* particularly well 61/11, 64/15

sith(e), syth(e) *conj.* since 51/15 *etc.;* from (the time that) 149/20; *sith y* since 78/17

sitten *pp.* sat 176/34

sixt *adj.* sixth 5/71

slake *v.* become less energetic 138/26; *pp.* **slakked** slackened 88/3

sleight *adj.* slight 144/12, 156/1

sleightes *n. pl.* tricks 138/32

slenderly *adv.* inadequately 52/3

slipper, slypper *adj.* unstable 32/48 *etc.*

slouth *n.* sloth 129/15

slumbri *adj.* slumberous 79/11

smal *adj.* of the lower classes 109/11

smart *adj.* keen 119/1

smart *n.* pain 116/6

smater *v.* chatter 17/52

sondred *pp.* separated 119/5

sore *adj.* grievous 146/13

sore *adv.* bitterly 11/52, 36/153; sorely 25/326; keenly 51/24, 169/20; greatly 147/21 *etc.;* with great effort 147/22

sore *n.* illness 107/27 *etc.;* grievous condition 164/22 *etc.*

so that *conj.* as long as 68/23

sotle *adj.* cunning 105/20, 107/15

sottishlye *adv.* foolishly 136/10

soueragne, soueraigne, souereyne *adj.* paramount 71/20 *etc.*

soul priest *n. pore soul priest* a priest having the special function of praying for the souls of the dead 157/19

soused *pt. soused hym up* brought him to extremity 16/32

sow drunk *adj.* extremely drunk 153/20. *See note*

sowne *n. in sowne* in a swoon 26/349

sowne *v.* resound 91/10; *pr. 3 s.* **sowneth, sownith** tends 52/14, 117/23; proclaims 82/1

sowre *adj.* bitter 108/2. *See note*

space *n.* time 111/13, 121/27; *in space* in a certain length of time 5/86

sparing from *vbl. n.* withholding 171/24

spectacle *n.* example 53/18

spede *n.* profit 120/7

spede *v.* succeed 95/13

spilt *pp.* destroyed 120/19

sport *n. in sport* in jest 69/16

spotty *adj.* stained 71/19

spurrys *n. pl.* stimuli 84/17

squyrge *n.* a whip to drive a top 3/10, 3/24

stalk *v.* enter stealthily 118/15

stande, stonde, *v. stonde against* impede 77/25; *pt.* remained steadfast 113/9; *pr. 3 s.* **stondeth in, stondith in** consists of 83/8 *etc.; vbl. a.* **stondyng** *stondyng with* consonant with 58/14

starteth *v. pr. 3 s.* springs (up) 37/181

state *n.* See **estate**

stateli, stately *adj.* haughty 69/14, 81/8

steppes *n. pl.* degrees 53/11

stere, stire *v.* urge 83/7, 106/23; *pp.* **stered** stirred 139/23

sterte *v. pt.* sprang 26/358

stiked *v. pt.* hesitated 69/18

stipende *n.* soldier's pay 80/26

stithe *v. pr. 3 s.* rises up 37/164

stock *n.* tree stump 146/6

stok *n.* lineage, line of descent 54/1

stomak *n.* state of feeling 61/4. *See note*

stone *n.* kidney or gall-bladder disease 140/12, 147/32

store *n. in store* in reserve 42/290

straite, strayt, strayte, streight *adj.* tight-fitting 117/6; strict 120/20; narrow 133/29; confining 176/3, 176/5

strangury(e) *n.* a disease characterized by slow and painful urination 140/12, 179/12

straunge *adj.* foreign 62/11

strayte *adv.* immediately 20/156

strenkyth *n.* strength 54/14

stretchith *v. pr. 3 s.* applies 51/13

strongly *adv.* boldly 71/29, 98/4

stroyest *v. pr. 2 s.* destroy 32/39

study *n.* pursuit 86/26

subscribed *pp.* signed 58/9, 73/5

substance, substaunce *n.* wealth 18/104 *etc.*

subuerted *pp.* destroyed 97/3

suchwise *adv.* in such a way 75/8

suerely *adv.* firmly 55/21

suerte *n.* security 39/218, 40/250

suffice *v. refl. suffice them selfe* satisfy themselves 87/6–7

suffrages *n. pl.* prayers (for the dead) 74/22–3

suffre *v.* tolerate 86/24

summe *n.* summary 56/5

sumptious *adj.* magnificent 6/92

supped *v. pt. supped . . . vp* drank 19/122

supplanted *v. pt.* caused to fall 159/6

surceace *v. surceace of* cease from 84/29

sure *adj.* safe 83/17, 156/29

surely *adv.* with certainty 161/6

suretye *n.* certain knowledge 142/33

surmownten *v.* surpass 122/6

sustayne *v.* endure 116/5

sute *n. to fall in sute* to become involved in legal proceedings 16/42

swappe *n.* blow 28/403

swarue *v.* swerve 90/29

swerdes *n. pl.* swords 89/24

swetter *adj. comp.* sweeter 4/31

sye *v. pt.* saw 27/381

synglar *adj.* single 10/31

taber *n.* drum 176/20. *See note*

take *v.* betake 69/20; *imp. take . . . on hande* undertake 106/17; *pp.* carried 114/16; **taken** considered 59/27

tast *n.* taste 104/27, 110/1

taxe *v.* burden 42/303

teche *v.* teach 93/5 *etc.*

tedious *adj.* troublesome 141/15

tempered *ppl. a.* having the proper quality 147/19

temporall *adj.* transitory 91/3

tempt *pp.* tempted 105/4

tere *v. pt.* tore 26/363

terre *n.* tar 132/18

thagreuing *vbl. n.* the bringing of grief (upon) 143/32

than *adv.* then 69/5 *etc.*

thankles *adj.* unthanked 122/26

thare *adv.* there 35/125

that, yᵗ *pron.* what, that which 62/26 *etc.*

the *v.* prosper 15/14, 28/420

thedir, thyder *adv.* thither 61/12, 75/13

then *conj.* than 150/17

ther agayn *adv.* in comparison with 10/33

þerbe *adv.* thereby 40/245

there *adv.* where 28/425

ther fore *adv.* concerning it 74/6

therefre, therefro *adv.* from it 116/31, 117/22

thik *adj.* numerous 38/204

thin *pron.* your 92/5

thing *n. pl.* things 54/12 *etc.*

this *dem. pron. pl.* these 78/7

tho *dem. pron. pl.* those things 40/253

thorough, thorow *prep.* through 56/17, 57/12

thorowfare *n.* road 111/19

thou *conj.* though 107/10

though *conj. & though* even if 93/2 *etc.*

thought *v. impers. pt. hym thought* it seemed to him 19/114, 65/8; *them thought* it seemed to them 88/16

thrall *adj.* enslaved 103/22

thrall *n.* slave 39/216

thred, threde *adj.* third 64/1 *etc.*

thredly *adv.* thirdly 63/5, 120/2

threst *pp.* placed 105/11

thretened *v. pt.* threatened 74/3

thrust *n.* thirst 71/18

thryes *adv. well thryes* more than three times as much 18/85

thryfte *n.* prosperity 15/20; *euyll thryfte* bad luck 28/406

thryfty *adj.* prosperous 16/47, 17/77

time *n. on a time* once 68/10

to *prep.* for 128/9

to . . . warde *prep. to gadwarde* toward God 63/15 *etc.; to heuinwarde* toward heaven 93/24–5

to gedir, togyder *adv.* together 24/286 *etc.*

tokene *n.* sign 54/7; *pl.* **tokens** signs 54/17

tone *pron. the tone* the one (of two) 132/26 *etc.*

to pikede *pp. See* **piked(e)**

tormentry *n.* infliction of torment 142/15

toted *pt.* peered 22/233. *See note*

tother *pron. the tother* the other (of two) 130/27 *etc.*

totorned *pp.* changed violently 38/183

toty *adj.* tipsy 176/20

toward *adv.* near 141/22

towre *n.* watch tower 106/11

toye *n.* foolish trifle 36/133. *See note*

trace *v.* pursue 40/237

traines *n. pl.* trickery 138/32

translating *vbl. n.* removing 91/7

trauaile, travayle, trauel *n.* toil 35/127 *etc.;* struggle 108/15; hardship 133/33

trauaile *v. trauaile on* am in labor with 87/27; *pr. 3 s.* **trauaileth** exerts 142/19; *pt.* **trauailed, trauelled** was in labor 54/6, 135/8; *trauailed vppon* worked on 67/1

trayne *n.* trap 142/10

tree *n.* cross 105/7

trenches *n. pl.* tunnels 57/18. *See note*

trimegistus *n.* Hermes Trismegistus 57/6

tristith *v. pr. 3 pl.* trust 34/95

trot *n.* hag 16/27

trow(e) *v.* believe 145/21 *etc.; pr. ppl.* **trowynge** believing 31/14

trusse *v.* pack 42/304

tryacle *n.* medicinal compound used against malignant diseases 129/16, 129/26; any antidotal compound 132/18

trymme *v. refl. trymme the* dress yourself 107/7

twayn(e) *n.* two 84/16; *in twayne* in two 112/27

twich *n.* pang 79/23; *pl.* **twitches** throes 72/16

tyde *n. at a tyde* for a period of time 20/167

vnaduisedly *adv.* recklessly 98/22, 108/12

vncorteyse *adj.* discourteous 121/23

vncurable *adj.* incurable 148/4, 148/10

vndirtoke *v. pt.* understood 75/5

vndre *adv.* less than 121/7
vndrestonden *pp.* understood 76/16 *etc.*
vngracious *adj.* reprobated 158/30
vnieth *v. pr. 3 s.* joins 83/12
vniuersite *n.* universe 97/5 *etc. See note*
vnkindnes *n.* ingratitude 75/9
vnknowe *ppl. a.* unknown 60/28
vnknowe(n) *ppl. a.* strange 54/17 *etc.*
vnkunnyngly *adv.* inexpertly 53/28
vnprouided *ppl. a.* unforeseen 161/31
vnpurueid *adj.* unprepared 106/12
vnseparable *adj.* inseparable 66/16–17
vnto *prep.* until 77/5
vnware *adj.* unexpected 109/23, 111/1
vnware *adv.* unexpectedly 111/6
vppon *prep.* by means of 76/6
vpwarde *prep.* up 27/380
vre *n. bene . . . in vre* been experienced,
expert 22/215; *in vre* used to, accus-
tomed to 58/5; *putte in vre* put into prac-
tice 137/26–7
vse *n.* work 76/22; activity 108/6; habitual
practice 130/30
vse *v.* treat 86/8; *pr. 3 s.* **vsith** enjoys 86/19
vtter *v.* reveal 67/21
vttermoste *adv.* utmost 158/11

valour *n.* value 20/176
variance *n.* contention 176/31
vayne *n.* vein 112/26
verely, verily *adv.* truly 73/16 *etc.*
veri, very *adv.* genuinely 151/5; truly
13/183, 163/12
verteous *adj.* virtuous 50/5
vertously *adv.* virtuously 68/22
vertue *n.* power 90/22, 92/9, 92/12
very(e) *adj.* true 4/30 *etc.;* mere 86/2,
165/26; actual 139/28, 166/19; unqual-
ified 142/33
viage *n.* military expedition 73/1
viand(e) *n.* food 64/9 *etc.*
voice *n.* saying 89/14 *etc.*
voide *adj.* fruitless 95/16; devoid 115/2
vowsons *n. pl.* ecclesiastical appointments
172/25
voyde *v.* leave 37/160
vulgare *adj.* vernacular 60/13

wacche, watch(e) *n.* wakefulness 35/127;
vigilance 65/10 *etc.;* staying awake (for

devotional purposes) 71/18; (to study)
88/5
wageles *adj.* not receiving wages 119/28
waingloriouse *adj.* vainglorious 65/20–1.
See note
wais *n. no maner wais* in no way at all 117/28
waltrynge *pr. ppl.* rolling 27/383
walue *adv.* cloyingly 178/16. *See note on*
178/9–16
wamble *v.* turn (as in nausea) 131/8
wanne *v. pt.* gained 97/7
wanteth *v. pr. 3. s.* lacks 167/10; **wanted** *pp.*
lacked 62/11
wanton *adj.* frivolous 112/9; reckless
129/26; ill-mannered 137/7
warantise *n. on warantise* it can be guaran-
teed that 112/11
waraunt *v.* guarantee 32/40
warded *pp.* guarded 95/29
ware *n. pl.* goods, property 41/263
wark(e) *n.* work 58/11 *etc.; pl.* **warkes,**
warkis 51/23 *etc.*
warne *v.* caution 70/14, 84/13
waveryng *adj.* mutable 35/122
wax(e) *v.* become 4/45 *etc.; pr. 2 s.* **waxest**
become 93/23; *pr. 3 s.* **waxeth** becomes
131/31; *pt.* **waxed** became 26/341
way *n. out of the way* missing the point
86/12
weale, wele *n.* welfare 4/53, 128/3; happi-
ness 159/16
web *n.* a white film on the eye 155/14
well *adj.* happy 12/76
well *n.* spring 123/9
wene *v.* think 16/26 *etc.; pr. 2 s.* **weneste**
hope 34/100; *pr. 3 s.* **weneth** thinks
131/35 *etc.; pr. ppl.* **wenynge** thinking
16/36
were away *v. phr.* gradually diminish 155/14
which *rel. pron.* who 63/17 *etc.*
whither *rel. pron.* which 69/16
whithir *conj.* whether 66/22 *etc.*
wield *v.* carry 176/7
wight, wyght *n.* person 23/260, 34/90,
34/105
wilfully *adv.* voluntarily 80/10
willes *n. pl.* desires 97/18
wink *v.* close (eyes) 173/9
wirche *v.* make 117/14
wise, wyse *n.* manner, fashion 51/12 *etc.;*
pl. 121/2, 157/22

wit *v.* know 146/34

wit, witt, witte *n.* intellect 62/24 *etc.*; *pl.*
sensuall wittis senses 104/24

w⁹al *prep.* with 165/20

with all, withall *adv.* moreover 17/83 *etc.*

within *adj.* inner 108/7

withstode *v. pt.* impeded 76/9

witnes *n.* example 113/3, 113/6

witsafe, witsave *v.* vouchsafe 5/67, 11/41

wode, wood(e) *adj.* mad 26/341 *etc.;* raging
106/9

wolde *v. pt.* wished 17/81, 116/31; wanted
to 19/136, 21/186

wordis *n. pl.* utterances 95/5

worke *v.* perform 93/4

worship *n.* honor 10/16

worth *n. take all in worth* be content 12/60

wot(e) *v.* know 9/7 *etc.; pr. 2 s.* wottest
129/21; *pr. ppl.* woting knowing 136/16;
pr. 3 s. woteth knows 144/14; *subj. 3 pl.*
wit know 181/23; *inf.* wit learn from
146/34

wrak *v. goth to wrak* falls into ruin 38/189

wringeth *v. pr. 3 s.* pains 122/1

wroth(e) *adj.* angry 24/290 *etc.*

wrought *v. pt.* operated 68/24; *pp.* done
113/1

wynne *v.* obtain 98/4

wynnyng *n.* wealth 36/151

wyst *v. pt.* knew 21/188

wyte *adj.* white 16/22

yea *adv.* yes 134/9

yee, yen, yeen *n.* eye(s) 34/101 *etc.*

yeftis *n. pl.* gifts 51/6

yere *n. dere yere* year of dearth 180/13; *pl.*
years 56/2 *etc.*

yerth *n.* earth 157/12

yes *n. pl.* eyes 121/19

yet *adv.* as well 27/393

ypocrites *n. See* **Ipocrites**

yrous *adj. See* **irows**

yrryte *v.* provoke 137/4

ywis *adv.* assuredly 157/25

INDEX

INDEX

ADDENDA AND CORRIGENDA
TO VOLUMES 2, 3/2, 4, 5/2, 6/2, 7, 9, 11, 14/2, 15

ADDENDA AND CORRIGENDA TO VOLUMES 2, 3/2, 4, 5/2, 6/2, 7, 9, 11, 14/2, 15

Volume 2, *The History of King Richard III*

The Latin text in this volume has been superseded by a superior text in *CW 15*, which is keyed to the text in *CW 2*. The commentary of *CW 15*, together with its addenda and corrigenda, usually has a bearing on the texts in *CW 2*.

Volume 3/2, *Latin Poems*

Page 132, No. 59, line 2. Change "anino" to "animo"

Pages 323–24, note on 8/6,9. Add: See also Walther no. 1924.

Page 335, note on No. 21/2–7. Add: On the "great year" now see William Adler, *Time Immemorial: Archaic History and Its Sources in Christian Chronography from Julius Africanus to George Syncellus* (Washington, D.C., 1989), p. 51.

Page 364, note on No. 115/1–3. Add: More's suggestively volatile contrast between kings and tyrants as watchdogs and wolves has a precedent in Plato, *Republic* 416a, a passage also cited by Erasmus in *Institutio principis christiani, ASD 4/1*, 158, lines 683–85.

Page 387, note on 186/1–7. Add: For More's painterly joke cf. also Aelian, *Varia historia* 10.10.

Page 390, note on 195/8–9. Add: See the addition to the note on page 403 to No. 242/6, below.

Page 403, note on No. 242/6. Add: Perhaps influenced by More's joke about Brixius' mindless poetic effusions, Erasmus refers this Vergilian line to "raving prophets" in *Lingua, ASD 4/1*, 245; See also *CW 3/2*, Appendix C, Commentary at 632/2.

Page 418, line 2. Change "Schooldays" to "School Days"

Pages 421–22, note on 276/1–39. Add: See also Gilbert Tournoy, "Twee ongepubliceerde gedichten bij portretten van Erasmus en Thomas More," *Liber amicorum Prof. Dr. G. Degroote*, ed. Jozef Veremans (Brussels, 1980), pp. 159–62.

Page 476, footnote 2. Add: As M.-M. de la Garanderie has pointed out in a personal letter, Macrinus' commendatory verses on *Antimorus* (*CW* 3/2, 483/12–17) allude to the *Deloinus* of Brixius (ca. 1511), a poetic tribute to François Deloynes in which Brixius also praises Deloynes' daughter, "nomen / Anthos cui dedit" ("to whom a flower gave her name," Brixius, *Poemata duo* [Paris: N. de la Barre, 1520], sig. a₃v). Uncorrected copies of *Antimorus* give her name as "Floris," corrected copies as "Chloris"; the French name was probably closer to the former (unclassical) form, but it seems Brixius finally resorted to Ovid's equation (*Fasti* 5.195) of the near-cognate "Flora" in Latin and "Chloris" in Greek.

Page 477, footnote 1. Add: On *castigatio* see E. R. Curtius, *European Literature and the Latin Middle Ages*, trans. W. Trask (Princeton, 1973), p. 317.

Page 505, line 23. Change "Venus," to "Venus next to"

Page 505, line 24. Change "groves;" to "groves; and"

Page 571, footnote 2. Add: Rogers, nos. 96 and 97, are probably both parts of one letter in which 96 followed 97; it is possible that More there refers *inter alia*, to a copy of his own Latin history of Richard III, in which sensitive issues are treated in a way that could certainly cause More some difficulties.

Page 611, line 15. Change "triumphant" to "triumphing"

Page 613, line 1 (Latin). Move this line to the bottom of the Latin on page 612.

Page 613, line 4. Change "has laid it down" to "sets it aside"

Page 619, lines 16–17. Change "the barking of envious men" to "envious men's barking"

Page 633, lines 11–14. Change "as if . . . Brixius," to "as if chance had not licensed just such mockery of Ermolao Barbaro even by the most shocking barbarians, or of Thomas More's name by one Germanus Brixius,"

Page 639, line 3. Change "was first to catch fire" to "caught fire even sooner"

Page 655, lines 6–7. Change "since . . . fatherland" to "as if you wished to say that in my country"

Page 663. Add the following note: 600/17 **triste . . . praeludium**. Cf. Vergil, *Aeneid* 11.156–57.

Page 666. Add the following note: 604/20–21 **fictiones . . . pannos**. This division of topics corresponds to *CW* 3/2, 610/16–19 and 622/13–16.

Pages 667–68, note on 606/25–608/12, line 8. After "Galen" add "(*De fac. nat.* 2.2)"

Page 669, note on 608/30–610/1. Add: See also Plutarch, *Life of Camillus* 10.4 (134B).

Page 670, note on 612/1–2. Add: The two Cercopes brothers, who ended up transformed to apes in some versions of the story, tried to steal Hercules' club while he was sleeping; see V. Dasen, *Dwarfs in Ancient Egypt and Greece* (Oxford, 1993), pp. 188–94, and cf. 614/1–2.

Page 671, note on 614/1–2. Add: Cf. the addition, above, to the note on page 670 to 612/1–2.

Page 673, note on 616/3–6. Add: Cf. also Phaedrus 1.10.1–2.

Page 674, note on 618/7–8. Add: See also a citation of Ennius in Cicero, *De natura deorum* 1.35.97 ("simia quam similis turpissima bestia nobis"), and Allen, no. 1087, line 422 ("non minus ridicule poetas imitatur [sc. Brixius] quam hominem simia").

Page 676, note on 620/6. Add: Cf. also *CW 15*, Commentary at 16/24.

Page 678, note on 622/3. Add: Cf. *Carmina priapea* 12.13–15 on an old woman's pudendum, "qui tanto patet indecens hiatu, / barbato macer eminente naso, / ut credas Epicuron oscitari." Brixius' lies are *pudenda mendacia* (604/20; cf. 622/14–16 and *CW 5*, 142/3–4 and 438/10–16). Cf. also Cicero, *De natura deorum* 1.26.72, on the primeval void great "yawn" of Epicurus, with the *ingens inane* of Hythloday's fiction in *Utopia* (*CW 4*, 110/14) and the new addendum to *CW 5*, page 947, note on 434/2.

Page 682, note on 632/2. Change "no. 198" to "no. 195"

Page 686. Add the following note: 638/26 **Quasi . . . invidet.** Cf. Ovid, *Epistulae ex Ponto* 2.5.28–30.

Page 687, note on 644/6–7. Add: Cf. also Seneca, *Epistulae* 108.9–11, on the special efficaciousness of verse precepts.

Page 689. Add the following note: 648/8–9 **pugnos . . . tragaedias.** According to the grammarian Dionysius (*Grammatici Latini*, ed. W. Keil, *1*, 488), *luctus*, *exilia*, and *caedes* are among the prime subjects of tragedy.

Page 689, note on 648/20–21. Add: Cf. also Vergil, *Aeneid* 2.470–75, where the "snake" is the sinister Pyrrhus.

Page 691. Add the following note: 652/21 **amiculas . . . lusites.** Cf. Plautus, *Captivi* 1003: "quasi patriciis pueris coturnices dantur, quicum lusitent." More also employs the rare iterative verb *lusitare* ("to keep playing around") in *CW 15*, 272/5. Pliny (*Historia naturalis* 3.8) implicitly posits the same verb as a transition-form in alleging that *lusus* or *lyssa*, the "play" or the "madness" of Bacchic observance, is the source of the Latin *Lusitani* ("the Portuguese"), the same ethnic term More in *Utopia* applies to the ludic narrator Raphael Hythloday. Cf. also the addendum to *CW 5*, page 876, note on 64/19 *gloss*.

Page 691. Add the following note: 652/25 **scurrandi solertes in sua vicia ludunt ipsi.** Cf. Quintilian 6.3.82: "in se dicere non fere est nisi scurrarum."

Page 768, under "Barbaro, Ermolao." Change "630" to "632"

Volume 4, *Utopia*

Page 301, note on 48/31–32. Add: Cf. also the new addendum to *CW 15*, page 510, note on 36/14–15.

Page 301. Add the following note: 50/4 **Lusitanus**. See the new addendum to *CW 3/2*, page 691, note on 652/21.

Page 343, note on 74/21. Add: The name of the Polylerites is from Lucian *Quomodo historia conscribenda sit* 31; see *CW 3/2*, note on 600/20–604/24.

Page 385. Add the following note: 110/14 **ingens inane**. See the new addendum to *CW 3/2*, page 678, note on 622/3.

Page 430, note on 152/28. Add: Cf. also Plato, *Theaetetus* 149A–151D, echoed by Erasmus in *Adagia* (LB 2, 888F) on the empty imaginings of intellectual "wind-eggs" (*anemolia*), which Socratic midwifery, or *elenchos*, is supposed to sort out from true births; for related ideas see the new addendum to *CW 5*, page 876, note on 64/19 *gloss*, and Erasmus, *Parabolae*, *ASD 1/5*, 160, lines 14–15.

Volume 5/2, *Responsio ad Lutherum*

Page 862. Add the following note: 8/9 **quum nihil dicat, non taceat tamen**. Cf. Epicharmus, fr. 272: οὐ λέγειν δεινός, ἀλλὰ σιγᾶν ἀδύνατος ("not competent to speak, but unable to hold his tongue")

Page 872. Add the following note: 42/25–26 **scripturae . . . torquenti**. Cf. 2 Cor. 2:17, 4:2, terms applied to "adulterate" or adulterine uses of scripture by friars in particular in *CW 15*, 272/25–26. Cf. also Gregorius Magnus, *Moralia in Iob* 16.60 (*PL 75*, 1156), who applies the same terms more directly to self-pleasing heretics. More's long letter in response to an illiterate monk and his treatise responding to Luther, whom More fairly often belittles as "frater potator" or "Friar Tosspot," converge at a number of points: see *CW 15*, index, "More: Works: *Responsio ad Lutherum*."

Page 876. Add the following note: 64/19 *gloss* **Vanitatis omnis antistes**. This description of Luther anticipates More's gloss of "Luther" or "Luder" at 584/12–22 as "Lud-Herr," "ludens herus," or "mocking-master." Cf. new addenda to notes on *CW 5*, page 890, note on 126/33; page 913, note on 240/9 *gloss; CW 5*, page 913, note on 434/2; *CW 3/2*, page 678, note on 622/3; *CW 3/2*, page 691, note on 652/21; *CW 4*, page 430, note on 152/28; *CW 15*, page 510, note on 36/14–15; and *CW 15*, page 524, note on 72/25.

Page 890. Add the following note: 126/33 **mendaciorum patri diabolo**. John 8:44.

Page 896, note on 142/3–4. Add: Cf. also the new note on *CW 5*, 438/10–16.

Page 901. Add the following note: 172/34 **ineffabiliter.** Perhaps we should read "infallibiliter."

Page 902. Add the following note: 176/32 **ecclesia malignantium.** Ps. 25:5.

Page 902. Add the following note: 180/12 **meientis mulae.** Catullus 97.8.

Page 903. Add the following note: 184/15 **euanescas . . . tuis.** Cf. Rom. 1:21.

Page 908. Add the following note: 212/28 **bene . . . deprauat.** See *CW 15*, note on 40/24–27.

Page 913. Add the following note: 240/9 *gloss* **nugarum sator.** This gloss answers Luther's "nugigerulus" (from Plautus, *Aul.* 525) used at *CW 5*, 240/7 (cf. 244/23); both are terms not unlike More's own coinage "Hythlodaeus," which can be rendered "Dealer in nonsense." Cf. also the biblical (Acts 17:18) *spermologos* (variously rendered as *verborum sator* and *seminiverbius*) and the new addendum to page 876, note on 64/19 *gloss*.

Page 914. Add the following note: 244/30–31 **non tantum meiere fas est.** Juvenal 1.131.

Page 915, note on 258/11–12. Add: Actually a verbatim citation of Virgil, *Georg.* 2.491–92.

Page 922, note on 310/12. Add: The rest of the sentence is from Terence, *Ad.* 184; cf. *CW 15*, note on 20/12–13.

Page 944. Add the following note: 414/8–9 *gloss* **extra controuersiam.** More appears to be playing on this phrase's two possible meanings, "beyond dispute" and "beside the point"; for the latter, see *CW 15*, note on 20/17.

Page 947. Add the following note: 434/1 **obscuratur cor insipiens.** Cf. Rom. 1:21.

Page 947. Add the following note: 434/2 **uertigine rotantur haeretici.** Cf. 1 Sam. 25:29 and *CW 5*, 490/16–17, with the new addendum to page 967, note on 598/16–17. For More, passages like these make Luther's self-enclosed, circular reasoning both the proof and the punishment of his heresy. Is a warning against something similar implicit in Hythloday's own involuted invention, the cipher Utopia, captiously misconceived in Book I of *Utopia* as a kind of material proof? Cf. also Gregorius Magnus, *Moralia in Iob* 16.65 (*PL* 75, 1159), *ad* Job 16:65:

> Super faciem ergo aquae levis est is quem quilibet erroris ventus cum venerit impellit. Unde bene quoque . . . "Deus meus, pone illos ut rotam . . ." [Ps. 82:14]. Ut rota quippe ponuntur iniqui, quia, in circuitu laboris missi, dum ea quae ante sunt negligunt, et ea quae deserenda sunt sequuntur, ex posterioribus elevantur, et in anterioribus cadunt . . . dum nulla subnixi sunt ratione gravitatis, elevantur ut corruant, et saepe eo se alicuius meriti existere aestimant, quo eos in alta flatus erroris portat.

Page 947. Add the following note: 434/21–438/26 **VERUM . . . inuisum**. For a detailed discussion of this bizarre, resonant passage see D. Kinney, "Heirs of the Dog: Cynic Selfhood in Medieval and Renaissance Culture," in *The Cynics: The Cynic Movement in Antiquity and Its Legacy*, ed. R. B. Branham and M.-O. Goulet-Cazé (Berkeley, 1996), 322–28.

Page 947, note on 438/4. Add: Donatus on Terence, *Andria* 597, actually links *irritare* and *hirrire*, a verb echoing a rabid dog's snarling.

Page 948. Add the following note: 438/10–16 **nec . . . patere**. For similar phrases linking impudent rhetoric with sexual exposure see the new addendum to page 678, note on *CW 3/2*, 622/3.

Page 952. Add the following note: 490/16–17 **rotari . . . hereticos**. See the new addendum to *CW 5*, page 947, note on 434/2.

Page 965, note on 584/21. Add: For a recent translation with commentary see ps.-Albertus Magnus, *Women's Secrets*, ed. and tr. H. R. Lemay (Albany, 1992).

Page 967. Add the following note: 598/16–17 **circumfereris . . . doctrinae**. Cf. Eph. 4:14, also echoed at *CW 5*, 618/23, with the similar formulas at 434/2 and 490/16–17.

Page 970. Add the following note: 618/23 **omni . . . circumferri**. See the new addenda to *CW 5*, page 592, note on 490/16–17, and *CW 5*, page 967, note on 598/16–17.

Page 972. Add the following note: 644/3–9 **postquam . . . altissimo**. Cf. *CW 15*, 278/6–11, and Commentary.

Page 981. Add the following note: 692/1 **precor, uanus ut uates fiam**. Cf. Juvenal 6.638, "nos utinam vani."

Volume 6/2, *A Dialogue Concerning Heresies*

Page 536, running head. Change "INTROD" to "INTRODUCTION"

Page 658, note on 192/8–9, line 2. Change "(F686)" to "(F696)"

Volume 7, *Letter to Bugenhagen, Supplication of Souls*, and *Letter against Frith*

Page xx, footnote 1, line 2. Change "Major" to "Mayor"

Page xxiv, footnote 2, lines 4–5. Change "Langland" to "Longland"

Page xciv, footnote 3. Change ὡϛδιὰ to ὡς διὰ

Page clxii, footnote 1. Omit: "and in his collation . . . instead of a_1"

Page 308, note on 72/16–16. Change "*Moreana 33*" to "*Moreana 23*"

Page 526. Change "Francastoro" to "Fracastoro"

Page 530. Change "Langland" to "Longland"

Page 532. Change "J. E. B. Major" to "J. E. B. Mayor"

Page 532. Under "Marius, Richard" add: 313

Page 532. Before "Martin, John, clvii" add: Martha, St., 147

Page 532. Change "More, John" to "More, John (chronicler)"

Page 538. Change "Saulnier, Verdum" to "Saulnier, Verdun"

Volume 9, *The Apology*

Page 328, note on 40/25. Add: There can be no reasonable doubt that More's "Father Alphonse, the Spaynish frere" is Alphonsus de Villa Sancta, confessor to Katherine of Aragon. The two works of his named in the original note were both compiled at the command of Katherine and dedicated to her. Alphonsus must have been a familiar figure at court, and well known to More. See Maria Dowling in *Bulletin of the Institute of Historical Research,* 57 (1984), 52n.

Page 393, note on 170/35. Add: Cf. Chaucer, *The Canterbury Tales,* Prologue to "The Cook's Tale," I (A), line 4355. More uses Chaucer to translate Horace.

Volume 11, *The Answer to a Poisoned Book*

Page lxxxv, footnote 1. Change "the Commentary at 13/1–10" to "149/16–17

Pages 236–37, note on 7/19–21. In penultimate paragraph, line 4, change "*Men*" to "*Mean*"

Page 263, note on 97/21–22. Add: See also Rogers, page 450, lines 376–77

Pages 276–77, note on 136/33–137/2. In last sentence change "*Works*" to "*Work*"

Page 280, note on 163/31–169/5, six lines from bottom. Change "feats" to "feasts"

Page 315, note on 18/4–5. In penultimate last line change "Flessman" to "Flesseman"

Volume 14/2, *De Tristitia Christi*

Page 724, line 1. Change "cuidad" to "ciudad"

Page 926, note on 361/1. Change "quickly." to "quickly.'"

Page 1006, note on 35/3. Change "6:13" to "6:12"

Page 1012, note on 113/3–7. Add: See new addendum on *CW 15*, page 598, note on 292/2–3, below.

Page 1020, note on 201/8. Change "3:9" to "3:29"

Page 1026, note on 263/9. Add: See Jerome, *Commentarii in Isaiam prophetam*, book 17, on Isa. 63:17 (*PL 24*, col. 619C): "Est enim tristitia quae ducit ad vitam, et est tristitia quae ducit ad mortem."

Page 1036, note on 347/4. Add: On the origin of this word-play in the fourth-century cosmographer Ethicus, see Michael J. Heath, "Renaissance Scholars and the Origins of the Turks," *Bibliothèque d'Humanisme et Renaissance, 41* (1979), 456–57. Erasmus exploited it in *De Bello Turcico* (1530), *ASD 5/3*, 38.

Page 1060, note on 615/6–8. Change "angustiam" to "angustam"

Volume 15, *In Defense of Humanism* and *Historia Richardi Tertii*

Page ix, line 3. Change "objectives" to "objections"

Pages xxxi–xxxii, footnote 6. Add: On the dedicatee of More's *Pico* see also *CW 1*, xl. From the terms of the "Lambeth" Joyce Lee's will, in which children named Edward and "Dame Joisse" are mentioned, it seems clear that the "Lambeth" Joyce Lee named by Rogers was in fact Edward's mother, not his sister; but his sister "Dame Joisse" may indeed be the dedicatee of More's treatise. For additional details on Lee see P. Bietenholz, *Contemporaries of Erasmus F-M* (Toronto, 1986), pp. 312–14.

Page lv, footnote 3. Add: For Erasmian parallels together with a useful discussion, see U. Langer, *Divine and Poetic Freedom in the Renaissance: Nominalist Theology and Literature in France and Italy* (Princeton, 1990), esp. pp. 13–14.

Page lvii, footnote 3. Add: Cf. also the passage from Gregorius Magnus cited in the new addendum to *CW 5*, page 947, note on 434/2.

Page cxxvii, footnote 1. Change "1625" to "1633"

Page cxxx, footnote 2. Add: On the editorial and textual issues address in the paragraphs, see my essay "On Transposing a Context: Making Sense of More's Humanist Defenses," in *Editing Texts from the Age of Erasmus: Papers Given at the Thirtieth Annual University of Toronto Conference on Editorial Problems*, ed. Erika Rummel (Toronto, 1996), pp. 39–48.

Page cxlv, footnote 1. Add: On the tally of Edward IV's daughters, see the new addendum to page 607, note on 314/4–20.

Pages cl–cli, footnote 3. Add: For a more recent treatment of Grafton's authorial-editorial procedure, see E. J. Devereux, "Empty Tuns and Unfruitful Grafts: Richard Grafton's Historical Publications," *Sixteenth-Century Journal, 21* (1990), 33–56.

Page cliii, footnote 1. Add: On this argument and linked textual issues, see my forthcoming article "The Tyrant Being Slain: Afterlives of More's *History of Richard III,*" in *History, Language, and the Politics of Renaissance Prose,* ed. Neil Rhodes, Medieval & Renaissance Texts and Studies (Binghamton, forthcoming). Ben Jonson appears to have made careful use of More's Latin (in the 1565 text) as well as his English; for the English see *CW 3/2,* 579, footnote 5; and for the Latin see Robert C. Evans, "More's *Richard III* and Jonson's *Richard Crookback* and *Sejanus,*" *Comparative Drama,* 24 (1990), 97–132, a discussion based largely on notes in a Canterbury Cathedral Library holding which was once Jonson's personal copy of *1565.* There are German and Russian translations of More's (English) *History* by Hans P. Heinrich (Munich, 1984) and (along with More's *Epigrammata*) by M. L. Kasparov et al. (Moscow, 1973).

Page 19, line 13. Change "only the ones who" to "only those stir up these tragedies who"

Between pages 53 and 54. The caption for the four Holbein drawings should read "(all enlarged)"; the enlargements resulted from a printer's error.

Page 57, line 13. Change "more difficult to understand" to "more intellectually challenging than a most complete mastery of all sacred scripture"

Page 135, line 25. Change "won" to "wins"

Page 209, line 32. Change "life-style" to "manner of life"

Page 219, line 10. Change "life-style" to "conversation"

Page 275, line 31. Change "life-style and conduct" to "way of life and conversation"

Page 293, line 8. Change "vagabond life-style" to "vagabond conversation"

Page 314, variant at lines 12–17. Change "p. oooo" to "p. cxliv"

Page 321, line 23. Change "his case . . . weight" to "his cause or his partisan following prevailed to the point"

Page 322, line 21. After "inferior /" add "habitu corporis exiguo /"

Page 322, variant at line 21. Change to read: inferior / habitu corporis exiguo /] *A H 1565,* inferior. *P*

Page 323, line 26. Change "His limbs" to "Slight of stature, his limbs"

Page 338, variant at line 16. Change "agnotorum *A*" to "agnotorum *changed to aquotorum A; see* the addendum to page 612, note on 338/16."

Page 347, line 7. Change "exists" to "exits"

Page 367, line 5. Enclose "fear" in square brackets.

Page 373, running head. Change "SANTUARY" to "SANCTUARY"

Page 430, line 7. As Germain Marc'hadour has suggested, change "puluere" to "pulueri" and add variant "pulueri] *1565,* puluere *P A*"

Page 484, line 23. Change "mensis tempore" to "mensis eiusdem"

Page 484, variant at line 23. Change to read: "23   mensis eiusdem] mensis eiusdem *with no space preceding in P,* the   day of the same moneth *1557*L; see new addendum to 484/23, *below.*"

Page 485, line 26. Change "a month later" to "the   day of the same month"

Page 498, note on 6/16–17. Add: *Morosi senes,* or "peevish old men," were a standard comic type, best exemplified by the "heavy father" Demea in Terence's *Adelphoe;* see Marvin T. Herrick, *Comic Theory in the Sixteenth Century* (Urbana, 1964), pp. 155–57.

Page 500, note on 12/19–21. Add: and Erasmus, *De recta pronuntiatione (Opera omnia, 1,* 914F–915B). Cf. also J. E. Sandys, *A History of Classical Scholarship,* 3 vols. (Cambridge, 1908), *1,* 5–11.

Page 501, note on 14/15–16. Add: Cf. also *CW 15,* pp. lxvii and lxxxiv, as well as an epistle attributed to St. Basil (*Epistulae* 41, *PG 32,* 345B), treating Scripture as "good letters" *par excellence.*

Page 502, note on 16/24. Add: Cf. also *CW 3/2,* Commentary at 620/6, and *CW 15,* 56/25–58/5.

Page 502, note on 18/2. Add: See also the elder Seneca, *Controversiae* 3, praef. 13.

Page 506. Add the following note: 24/21–24 **Nam . . . aucupari.** Cf. Erasmus, *De recta pronuntiatione (Opera omnia, 1,* 922F).

Page 509, note on 30/1–5. Add: Cf. also Plautus, *Bacchides* 447–48, another comic-retributive inversion of hierarchy.

Page 509. Add the following note: 30/10–13 **Pater erit . . . proponi?** Cf. Niccolò Perotti, *Cornucopiae* (Venice, Aldus, 1499), sig. y₂v: "Est enim aenigma quaestio velata, siue (ut Quintilianus [8.6.52] ait) obscura allegoria, ut Mater me genuit eadem mox generatur a me, quod de glacie dicitur, quae ex aqua concrescit, et mox in aquam effluit rursus . . . "

Page 510, note on 36/14–15. Add: Cf. also Erasmus, *Adagia* no. 91 (*Opera omnia,* 2, 179C), citing Aristophanes, *Clouds* 359, where the poet calls Socrates "the high priest of most subtle nonsense." Cf. also More's "Hythloday" ("learned in trifles") in *Utopia*, as well as *CW 15*, 388/4–5 and 422/22, with the new addendum to *CW 5*, page 876, note on 64/19 *gloss*.

Page 511. Add the following note: 40.10–14 **Quod . . . competit.** Cf. Seneca, *Epistulae* 29.1–3, against the *promiscua libertas* of Cynic street-preachers; Dorp does worse in attempting to home in on quite the wrong target.

Page 512. Add the following note: 42/14–16 **seria . . . numeranda**. Cf. Vergil, *Eclogues* 7.17–18.

Page 515, note on 54/12. Add: as well as *CW 15*, 378/10–13.

Page 515, note on 54/14–16. Add: Cf. also Gregory the Great, *Moralia* 20.18 (*PL 76*, 147).

Page 516, note on 56/14. Add: As Germain Marc'hadour has remarked in a personal letter on this passage, More appears to treat scripture as both harder and easier than standard scholastic debate; More would probably have been quick to contrast substantive and contrived intellectual difficulty. See Pope John XXII's quite similar criticism of then-current scholastic debates; an excerpt from the pope's 1317 comment is cited in J. Enders, *Rhetoric and the Origins of Medieval Drama* (Ithaca and London, 1992), p. 97.

Page 517, note on 58/13–20. Add: and Ps. 35:7 ("iudicia tua abyssus multa"), which Augustine directly applies to the meaning of Scripture after glossing "abyssus" as "profunditas quaedam impenetrabilis" in *Enarrationes in psalmos* 41.13, *PL 36*, 473.

Page 523, note on 72/5–6. Add: But for both of the phrases here given in capital letters cf. 2 Sam. 19:33: "Veni mecum, ut requiescas securus [*al.*, secure]."

Pages 523–24, note on 72/8–9. Add: Cf. Allen, no. 176, line 6, and no. 181, lines 52–53.

Page 524, note on 72/25. Add: Cf also *CW 15*, lvii, footnote 3, and the new addendum to that note, above.

Page 525, note on 76/15–19. Add: Just how bold *is* More's statement? Compare the subtitle of John Milton's 1649 justification for the overthrow and execution of King Charles I, *The tenure of kings and magistrates, proving, that it is lawfull, and hath been held so through all ages, for any, who have the power, to call to account a tyrant, or wicked king, and after true conviction, to depose, and put him to death; if the ordinary magistrate have neglected, or deny'd to do it. . . .*

Page 530, note on 92/21–22. Add: For related appeals to the wisdom of "hastening slowly" see *CW 3/2*, 590, footnote 2, and the note on *CW 15*, 174/2–3.

Page 537, note on 106/24–25, line 3. Change "Herman" to "Francis"

Page 545, note on 130/26. Add: Cf. Erasmus, *De civilitate morum puerilium* (*Opera omnia, 1,* 1041D).

Page 546, note on 134/29–30. Add: On the respect due the Host see Erasmus, *De civilitate morum puerilium* (*Opera omnia, 1* 1037D); on the Host as Christ's *verum corpus* see more generally M. Rubin, *Corpus Christi: The Eucharist in Late Medieval Culture* (Cambridge, 1991), esp. pp. 63–67, 153–55.

Page 547. Add note on 136/12–14 **rusticos . . . provolare.** Cf. Augustine, *Confessions* 8.8, *PL 32,* 757.

Page 547. Add the following note: 136/16 **deuotam inscitiam.** On "saintly simplicity" see Peter Damian, *Opuscula* 45 (*PL 145,* 695–706) and cf. St. Bernard, Ep. 53.3 (*CSEL 64,* 447).

Page 547, note on 136/26. Add: Cf. Erasmus, *De civilitate morum puerilium* (*Opera omnia, 1,* 1041D).

Page 547, note on 136/30–31. Add: and Quintilian 10.1.26.

Page 549, note on 142/3–4. Add: cf. also Erasmus, *Adagia* no. 3401 (*Opera omnia,* 2, 1171).

Page 555, note on 164/16–17. Add: Cf. also Ovid, *Fasti* 4.627–28, on the *Mutinensia arma* subdued by Octavius in 43 B.C. Because Erasmus' defenders so often cast Lee as a puppet of murmuring slanderers, there may be a pun here linking Mutina's name with "mut(t)ire" ("to mutter," "to murmur").

Page 555, note on 166/8. Add: Cf. also Erasmus, *Enchiridion,* Holborn, p. 36.

Page 557, note on 170/26. Change "work" to "word"

Page 557. Add the following note: 172/5–6 **laus . . . tuae.** Cf. Horace, *Epistles* 2.1.9–10.

Page 558, note on 174/2–3. Add: as well as *CW 15,* 216/10–19, and the notes on 26/22–24, 130/17–19, and 258/17–20.

Page 560, note on 184/22–23. Add: citing Terence, *Andria* 426–27, 636.

Page 561. Add the following note: 188/10–11 **tractandae . . . artifex.** Cf. *CW 15,* 398/6.

Page 562. Add the following note: 192/24–26 **laetus . . . exige.** Cf. Tiresias' advice to Menippus in *CW 3/1,* 4/39–43/1.

Page 562, note on 194/14–15. Add: Cf. also Erasmus, *Adagia* no. 391 (*Opera omnia,* 2, 179C).

Page 564. Add note on 202/18–22 **Quis . . . inuexit.** Cf. St. Paul's reproach to the newly self-righteous Galatians (Gal. 3:1): "Quis vos fascinavit?" ("Who has bewitched you?"). More reiterates this charge of self-righteous "bewitchment" at *CW 15,* 267/6–20, 274/11–22, 290/10–21, 292/16–24, and 306/3–

5. Cf. also 202/7–8 and Erasmus' *Paraphrases* and *Annotations* on Gal. 3:1 for a discussion of the term "fascinavit" in relation to both common sleight-of-hand (or *praestigium*) and malignant or "envious" bewitchment.

Page 566, note on 208/1–3. Add: But see also *CW 15*, 450/11–12.

Page 566. Add note on 208/1–2 **concinnantes mendacia**. Cf. Augustine, *Enarrationes in psalmos* 65.7 (*PL 36*, 792), referring (as here) to false witness.

Page 567, note on 208/2–3. Add: Cf. also *CW 5*, 48/9.

Page 567. Add note on 210/17 **singulari . . . teste**. For the legal limitations of a solitary witness see the note in *CW 15*, 208/3–8, and Varro, *De lingua Latina* 5.180; Jerome, *Adversus Rufinum* 2.24 (*PL 23*, 468); and *Codex Iustinianus* 4.20.9.

Page 569, add new note on 210/18 **fictus**. Cf. Cicero, *Pro Caecina* 25.71: "fictus testis."

Page 569. Add note on 210/24–25 **Nec nova . . . calumnia**. Cf. Plautus' cynical summary of an old lecher's conduct in *Asinaria* 943: "neque nouum neque mirum fecit neque secus quam alii solent."

Page 571, note on 214/23–24. Add: For very similar wordplay in Greek, see the epistle to Julian the Apostate attributed to St. Basil, *Epistolae* 41 (*PG 32*, 348A).

Page 572, note on 216/10–13. Add after "*WA 10/2*, 89" (end of line 21): [cf. *WA* 2, 447].

Page 572, note on 216/15. Add: For a parallel appeal to Matt. 10:16 and the notion of "prudent simplicity" see *CW 15*, 258/25–260/6.

Page 573. Add note on 218/6 **insuetiora vocabula**. Cf. 1 Tim. 6:20 and Erasmus' note in *Opera omnia, 6*, 947C–948B.

Page 582, note on 252/2, line 7. Change "clost" to "close"

Page 584, note on 258/17. Add: Cf. *CW 15*, 92/16–22 and 174/2–3 with notes, for related variations on the notion of "hastening slowly."

Page 585, note on 260/5–6. Add: and Erasmus, *Ratio verae theologiae*, Holborn, p. 236. Erasmus parallels Aldus' trademark (the dolphin and anchor, emblematic of "hastening slowly") with Froben's insignia (the serpent and the dove, emblematic of prudent simplicity) in *Adagia* no. 1001 (*Opera omnia, 2*, 400D). Cf also *CW 15*, 216/13–19, for a closely related appeal to a different verse, Rom. 10:2.

Page 587, note on 264/17–20. Add: Indeed, there are a number of quite striking parallels between 264/8–21 and *Lingua*, 320–25, which seems almost an expanded paraphrase of More's own complaints.

Page 590, note on 272/26. Add: Cf. also the new note on *CW 5*, 42/25–26.

Page 590. Add note on 274/17–19 **quo . . . sui**. See also Erasmus, *Adagia* no. 292 (*Opera omnia*, 2, 147C), quoting Plato, *Laws* 5, 731E.

Pages 591–92, note on 278/12–13. Add: Cf. also *CW* 5, 208/11–12, and Commentary.

Page 593, note on 282/7–9. Add: For the "third degree of lunacy" see ps.-Dioscorides, *Alexipharmacon* 14, cited by Erasmus in *Adagia* no. 2401 (*Opera omnia*, 2, 826B).

Pages 595–96, note on 286/12–15. Add: See also the essays collected in *The Dogma of the Immaculate Conception: History and Significance*, ed. Edward D. O'Connor (South Bend, 1958).

Page 597, note on 288/21. Add: Cf. 290/23.

Page 597, note on 290/23. Add: Cf. 288/21.

Page 598, note on 292/2–3. Add: A description of humility as the "foundation" of the virtues is quite common in medieval sources; a composite word-search in the *Patrologia Latina*–Online yielded over fifty pertinent texts in that archive alone. This description offsets a still more common treatment of pride as the basis of sin, and makes suitable didactic sense of the fact that humility is not included among the three prime Christian virtues of faith, hope, and charity; for connections between this account of humility and the "root" of the Tree of Life viewed as the Cross cf. Jennifer O'Reilly, *Studies in the Iconography of the Virtues and Vices in the Middle Ages* [Ph.D. thesis (Nottingham) 1972] (New York, 1988), esp. 135–37, with additional references. For the suggestion that humility is the "foundation" of a monastic profession in particular see most notably John Cassian, *De coenobiorum institutis* 6.18 (*PL 49*, 288), with the notes of Alardus Gazaeus.

Page 598, note on 294/4–10. Add: Cf. also Quintilian 12.1.29.

Page 600, note on 300/18–19. Add: as well as Augustine, *De symbolo ad catechumenos* (*PL 40*, 646), and Gregorius Magnus, *Moralia in Iob* 5.22 (*PL 75*, 703). Erasmus links a similar opposition between faintheartedness and impetuosity with the notion of "hastening slowly"; see *Adagia* no. 1001 (*Opera omnia*, 2, 397C–401D), and the note on *CW 15*, 316/20–23.

Page 601, note on 300/20–22. Add: Cf. also the passage from Gregorius Magnus in the new note on *CW 5*, 490/16–17.

Page 602, note on 306/10–11. Add: A similar phrase from Cicero (*In Verrem* 1.4.10, "metuo . . . ne quid arrogantius apud tales viros videar dicere") could be cited as a typical specimen of the "disarming" figure *correctio* (Heinrich Lausberg, *Handbuch der literarischen Rhetorik*, 2nd ed., 2 vols., Munich, 1973, *1*, 388; cf. the note on *CW 15*, 202/16). Three different versions of the versatile opening line "Vereor ne . . . " are cited in B. Haureau, *Initia operum scriptorum latinorum medii potissimum aevi . . .* , 8 vols. (Turnhout, 1973–1974), *8*, 544.

Page 603, note on 308/10–12. Add: Erasmus likens his own emendation of Scripture to sweeping rubbish out of a sanctuary in *Capita argumentorum* (*Opera omnia, 6,* **4).

Page 607, note on 314/4–20. Add: See *CW 1*, pp. cx–cxi and Commentary at 12/72, concerning a parallel omission in a pre-1505 text of one of More's poems; this recurrent omission suggests that one stratum of More's *History* may well date from considerably before the traditional date, 1513.

Page 607, note on 316/11–16. Change "note" to "notes" and add: 324/13–14, 324/20–26, 340/12, 364/19–27, 402/11–12, 424/8–10, 428/28–29, 446/19–22, 448/10, and 482/12–13.

Page 608, note on 316/20–23. Add: See also the notes on *CW 15*, 300/18–19, 360/4–7, and 478/21.

Page 609, note on 320/7–14. Change "334/14–15" to "334/14–17"

Page 609, note on 320/22–23. Add: Parliament makes a very similar claim for its own power to crown a new king in *Titulus regius* (1484), ratifying King Richard's accession (*Rotuli Parliamentorum,* 6 vols. [London, 1767–1777], *6,* 240–42); the *Titulus* was suppressed by the Tudors. It frequently provides parallels with Buckingham's oration at *CW 15,* 454/22–468/14. On the *Titulus* see M. A. Hicks, *Richard III: The Man Behind the Myth* (London, 1992), pp. 82–85, 88–95.

Page 609, note on 322/10–11. Add: In Erasmus' *Lingua* (*ASD 4/1,* 334), not wives but harlots are indicted as sowers of discord; in More's history, conversely, Edward's queen seems to help stir up trouble, while his mistress "Jane" Shore plays the peacemaker (428/88–430/8).

Page 609, note on 322/17–18. Add: Ovid (*Fasti* 4.472) credits Romulus with tears much like Edward's upon his brother's death, though, according to myth, Romulus actually murdered his brother; cf. also the phrasing at *CW 15,* 350/3. Romulus' Cainlike *putsch* dominates St. Augustine's account of the founding of Rome and more generally the "City of Man"; see the note on *CW 15,* 334/14–17, and cf. R. Quinones, *The Changes of Cain* (Princeton, 1991).

Page 609. Add the following note: 322/21 **habitu corporis exiguo.** *P* alone lacks this phrase ("slight of stature" in English); thanks to Alistair Fox for first noting this scribal omission.

Page 610. Add the following note: 322/23–24 **eiusmodi . . . solet.** Cf. Erasmus, *Parabolae, ASD 1/5,* 274, lines 878–79.

Page 610, note on 322/25–28. Add: Cf. further Pliny, *Naturalis historia,* 7. 45–47, where breech-birth is pronounced inauspicious, but caesarean birth (at least from a dead mother!) is declared to bode well for the offspring.

Page 610. Add the following note: 322/26 **obstetricante ferro.** More perhaps got the image of the sword or knife (*ferrum*) as a midwife from a short poem in *The Greek Anthology* (*AP* 9.311) on a hunting-bitch who gives birth to her pups by caesarean delivery: "Artemis is no longer the kind mistress of birth; / instead, Ares serves females as midwife." Cf. *CW 15*, 324/2–3, and Shakespeare's contentious description of Richard III's mother: "From forth the kennel of thy womb hath crept / a hell-hound that doth hunt us all to death . . . "(*Richard III*, 4.4.47–48; cf. *3 Henry VI*, 3.2.174–81, 5.6.70–77). Milton's Sin (*Paradise Lost* 2.653–56) borrows something from Shakespeare's description as well as from Spenser's personified Error (*Faerie Queene* 1.1.15); by way of these echoes in Shakespeare and Milton, More's image may well have helped give rise to Karl Marx's description of violence per se as the "[male] midwife of history" ("*Die* Gewalt . . . *der* Geburtshelfer" [emphasis added; *Das Kapital* (1867), part 7, chapter 24 (28)]).

Page 610, note on 326/15–18. Add: and Horace, *Epistles* 2.1.63.

Page 611, note on 332/24–26. Add: Cf. also Gal. 3:20 and Erasmus' preface to the *Adagia* (*Opera omnia*, 2, 6F).

Page 611. Add the following note: 328/23 **ipsius sanguine fedus sanciretur.** Cf. Servius on Vergil, *Aen.* 1.61, 8.641; Servius claims that the term *foedus* ("treaty") refers to the "foul" (*foeda*) death of the beast killed to clinch the alliance or truce, with the implicit wish that whoever breaks faith would then die the same sort of foul death as the beast, specified as a *pig*, either male or female; for the boar as Richard's own heraldic device see the new note below on 414/11–16, and for Richard's own fatal faith-breaking see the old and new notes on 390/6–9 and 464/26–466/1. Cf. also George Wither, *A Collection of Emblemes* (London, 1635), 38 ("SI SCIENS FALLO").

Page 612, note on 334/14–17. Add: Cf. also *CW 15*, 320/7, 322/3, 394/16–17, and 330/25–332/2, along with the new addendum to page 609, note on 322/17–18.

Page 612. Add the following note: 338/1–4 **licenter . . . audacia refrenaretur.** Cf. Isidore, *Etym.* 5.20 ("QVARE FACTA EST LEX"): "Factae sunt autem leges ut earum metu humana coerceatur audacia, tutaque sit inter inprobos innocentia, et in ipsis inpiis formidato supplicio refreneter nocendi facultas." The prince is dispatched to the Welsh as a kind of living law, an arrangement then badly abused by the Woodvilles and Richard's rival faction alike; see the following lines in *CW 15*. The same passage from Isidore may find another ironic echo in *CW 15*, 386/23–26; cf. also 378/11–13, where the wildness initially assigned to the Welsh is ironically brought home to London.

Page 612. Add the following note: 338/10–11 **praetextum . . . fecit.** Cf. Augustine, *Enarrationes in psalmos* 64.9, *CCSL 39*, 832: "quam multi aliorum defectione cupiunt sublimari!" This has a parallel in Chrysippus' standard Stoic description of envy; see Plutarch, *De stoic. rep.* 25, 1046b = Frag. 418, *Stoicorum veterum fragmenta*, ed. Hans F. A. von Arnim, 4 vols. (Leipzig, 1903–24), *3*, 102.

Page 612, note on 338/16. Add: A new look at a microfilm copy of *A* with corrector's dots under "agnotorum" and a "q" clearly penned in the margin makes it clear that the reading preferred in that text (in which "n" and "u" generally look interchangeable) is the seemingly meaningless "aquotorum"; it seems likely that the reading that gave rise to these various textual corruptions was a tendentious pun ("Aquatorum" = "Watered-down," "Water-bearers"), a replay of a late fifteenth-century quibble on "Rivers" (*Great Chronicle of London*, ed. A. H. Thomas and I. D. Thornley, London, 1938, p. 208) applied to the queen's entire family and not just the Earl Rivers More mentions, the queen's eldest brother. Cf. also *CW* 2, Commentary at 47/29, on the queen's own supposed derivation from a witch/water-nymph, Melusina. Femininity and fluidity may also be linked in the way this text foregrounds the charming incontinent "Jane" Shore, represented as giving her name to the sewer or "Shore-Ditch" of London at the end of Part 2 of Thomas Heywood's *Edward IV*, a late sixteenth-century play quite dependent on More's English *History*.

Page 612, note on 340/2. Add: Another possible reading is "promotionem." The problem is partly to find a term that goes as well with *immoderatam* in Latin as "advauncement" goes with "immoderate" in English; here, at least, English serves as the template.

Page 614. Add the following note: 350/3 **quod . . . illachrimauit**. For a highly ironic half-parallel see *CW 15*, 322/17–18 and the new addendum thereon.

Page 615. Add the following note: 362/19–20 **maiusque . . . queat**. Cf. Cicero, *Pro Rabirio Postumo* 15: "Serpet hoc malum—mihi credite!—longius, quam putastis."

Page 616, note on 368/6. Add: Cf. also Erasmus, *Adagia* no. 465 (*Opera omnia*, 2, 207F).

Page 616, note on 368/12–13. Add: Cf. *CW 15*, 430/23–24.

Page 617, note on 378/10–13. Add: Cf. also the new addendum to page 619, note on 394/18–20.

Page 617. Add the following note: 386/9 **efflictim . . . amat**. Cf. 396/13–15 and Erasmus, *Adagia* no. 3691 (*Opera omnia*, 2, 1120E–1121A): "ut lupus ovem [*sc.* amat]." Erasmus refers the adage to self-serving, feigned lovers, "although such love is more truly hatred."

Page 618. Add the following note: 388/4–5 **callidis . . . ineptias**. See the new addendum to *CW 15*, page 510, note 36/14–15.

Page 619, note on 394/16–17. Add: As Jacques Chomarat notes in his review of this version of More's Latin history, one can get an acceptable alternative meaning by emending the *1565* text as follows: " . . . liberique per pulsos regno atque adeo vita parentes ad imperium affectant" (" . . . and the children aspire to the throne by depriving their parents of power, and even of life"). This may be one more case in which *1565* keeps—and garbles—an early authorial variant.

Page 619, note on 394/18–20. Add: and Erasmus, *Moriae encomium, ASD 4/3,* 192, Commentary at lines 234–35.

Page 620, note on 402/14–15. Add: But the ominous irony here is that now the common people get right what their princes get wrong; Erasmus calls such reversals portents of disaster for humanity (*Parabolae, ASD 1/5,* 232, lines 154–58).

Page 620, note on 406/14–412/7. Add: Cf. also the new addendum to *CW 15,* page 621, 410/7, and Henry A. Kelly, "English Kings and the Fear of Sorcery," *Mediaeval Studies, 39* (1977), 206–38, esp. 233–34, noting that the same Tower allegation of witchcraft occurs in the 1514 MS. recension as well as in the later printed versions of Polydore Vergil's *Anglica historia.*

Page 621. Add the following note: 408/6–9 **Quae . . . tollere.** On the legal issues in this captious but crucial exchange, which may be More's invention, see my article "The Tyrant Being Slain: Afterlives of More's *History of Richard III,*" in *History, Language, and the Politics of Renaissance Prose,* ed. Neil Rhodes, Medieval & Renaissance Texts and Studies (Binghamton, forthcoming). The fundamental Statute of Treasons (1352) includes plotting the death of the king or his heir or actually killing the chancellor or certain other high officials among forms of the most serious crime of high treason; see the translation from the original French in A. R. Myers, ed., *English Historical Documents, 1327–1485* (Oxford, 1969), p. 403.

Page 621, first note on 408/27. Add: The same new note on "Shore's wife" also appears in *CW 8/3,* 1829.

Page 621. Add the following note: 410/7 **mulierem libidinis haud magiae famosam.** This is not a very stable distinction, especially given the frequency of love-magic charges in Richard's own era; cf. the addition, above, to the note on *CW 15* 406/14–412/7, along with Chaucer's "Friar's Tale" 4–5, *Canterbury Tales* III (D), 1304–05: "In punysshynge of fornicacioun, / Of wicchecraft, and eek of bawderye . . . "

Page 622. Add the following note: 414/11–16 **aprum . . . gestamen.** On the earlier and later meanings of Richard's boar-emblem see "The Tyrant Being Slain," n. 19, and the new notes on *CW 15,* 328/23 and 482/22–24; see also W. Schouwink, *Der wilde Eber in Gottes Weinberg* (Sigmaringen, 1985), and M. Kearney, *The Role of Swine Symbolism in Medieval Culture: Blanc Sanglier* (Lewiston, 1991).

Page 622. Add the following note: 416/26 **forte . . . nomine.** On this ghostly attendant named Hastings see Walter H. Godfrey et al., *The College of Arms, Queen Victoria Street* (London, 1963), pp. 265–66, under the name "Hastings Pursuivant." Such a person ("pursuivant" = "herald-attendant") is actually attested in other connections, but only More makes him uncannily shadow his master so close to his downfall; for a better attested example of such ironic doubling, which may well have suggested this dire duplication of Hastings in More's text, see Godfrey, pp. 106, 238, on a "Norroy" or "Blaunche Senglier pursuivant" alias "John More," or perhaps John More's son (!), who bore Richard's dead body from Bosworth. For two earlier missions of the Blanc Sanglier herald, see P. W. Hammond and Anne F. Sutton, eds., *Richard III: The Road to Bosworth Field* (London, 1985), pp. 128–29.

Page 622, note on 418/29–22. Add: More also tersely reiterates the argument of 416/23–418/22 (now applied to the traitor Judas) in *CW 14*, 457/4–8.

Page 622, note on 420/19–21. Add: For the medical metaphor cf. Ovid, *Metamorphoses* 1.190–91.

Page 622, note on 422/8. Add: Cf. the note at 318/3–8.

Page 622. Add the following note: 422/22 **solertem . . . stulticiam**. See the new addendum to page 510, 36/14–15.

Page 622, note on 424/1. Add: The stated punishment of "Jane" Shore for flagrant immorality has no lack of close parallels in England and France; see M. C. Mansfield, *The Humiliation of Sinners: Public Penance in Thirteenth-Century France* (Ithaca and London, 1995), esp. pp. 114, 341. But the most telling historical parallel for Richard III's purposes was, no doubt, the forced penance of Eleanor Cobham, upstart wife of King Henry VI's uncle Humphrey of Gloucester. She was charged with using both love-magic and treasonably life-threatening witchcraft; see the resonantly equivocal account of her punishment in *An English Chronicle . . . Written Before the Year 1471*, ed. J. S. Davies (London, 1856), p. 60. See also R. A. Griffiths, "The Trial of Eleanor Cobham: An Episode in the Fall of Humphrey Duke of Gloucester," *Bulletin of the John Rylands Library, 51* (1968), 381–99. Both shamed women eventually figured in the Tudor *Mirror for Magistrates;* see G. Schmitz, *The Fall of Women in Early English Narrative Verse* (Cambridge, 1990), pp. 105–26.

Page 623. Add the following note: 426/5 **mundi muliebris**. For this technical phrase for feminine portable property (literally, "women's world") see Seneca, *Quaestiones naturales* 1.17.10, and Ulpian, *Digesta* 34.2.25.10.

Page 623, note on 426/21–428/1. Add: See also Lucian, *Menippus* 15. For paired life-and-death images like these two antithetical views of "Jane" Shore in the arts of More's day see K. Cohen, *The Metamorphosis of a Death Symbol: The Medieval Transi Tomb* (Berkeley and Los Angeles, 1973), esp. pp. 84–85, nn. 1–2. What we have in this double ("anamorphic") perspective on worldly attainment and grace may be close to a Morean rebus or cipher; for some resonant puns linking More and *memento mori* see *CW 3/2*, Commentary at 278/3–6, 9–10, and on Morean anamorphosis see Stephen Greenblatt, *Renaissance Self-Fashioning: From More to Shakespeare* (Chicago and London, 1980), p. 16.

Page 623. Add the following note: 428/8–430/8 **nemo . . . insculpimus**. See the new addendum to *CW 15*, page 609, note on 322/10–11.

Page 624. Add the following note: 430/23–24 **neque miserabatur . . . reuerebatur**. Cf. *CW 15*, 368/12–13 and note.

Page 624. Add the following note: 434/8–9 **ieiunum laudis principem**. Cf. Erasmus, *Parabolae, ASD 1/5*, 142, lines 678–80: "Vt qui vehementi laborant fame, nec est quod edatur, suis ipsorum artubus vesci coguntur, ita quidam prae fame gloriae, seipsos laudare cogunt, si desit a quo laudentur."

Page 625, note on 440/21–22. Add: with no. 18203 and Boethius, *Consolatio philosophiae* 2, prose 6.

Page 625. Add the following note: 440/23–25 **sustinere . . . reges**. Duchess Cecily's case here for princely eugenics is an ironic echo of Plutarch *De liberis educandis* 1.2 (*Moralia* 1d), concerning the Spartans' high-minded rebuke of *their* king for his choice of a mate, a short queen who would breed merely "kinglets" (*basiliskoi;* cf. More's "regulos" in the variants to *CW 15*, 440/25). Of course it is the duchess–queen mother herself who both breeds and, by this dispute, helps to promote the best known of all basilisk-kinglets, Richard III.

Page 626, note on 444/17–19. Add after "796–98": Cf. also the wolf to the watchdog in Phaedrus 3.7.27: "regnare nolo, liber ut non sim mihi." A similar contrast between watchdogs and wolves, kings and tyrants, is borrowed from Plato's *Republic* 416a in *CW 3/2*, no 115, and in Erasmus' *Institutio principis christiani, ASD 4/1*, 158, lines 683–85. Erasmus also points out (at 152, lines 502–03) that the most abject servitude is not deference to others but enslavement to ungoverned passions, of which lust for power is traditionally the most tyrannous of all. Cf. the note on *CW 15*, 334/14–17; Tacitus, *Annales* 15.53, *Historia* 1.36 ("omnia serviliter pro dominatione"), and the new addendum to page 630, note on 480/18–20, and the note on 484/17–18.

Pages 626–27, note on 448/7–8. Add: Cf. *CW 2*, lxix, footnote 2, for a striking convergence between Polydore's manuscript account of Hasting's death and the account in Hall's version of More's *History*.

Page 627, note on 452/2–3. Add: More here apparently makes Shaw allude to the feast of the Nativity of St. John, which fell on June 24, two days after his sermon; see *CW 2*, Commentary at 67/13–15.

Page 627. Add the following note: 454/16 **plurium . . . scirent**. Cf. Ovid, *Metamorphoses* 6.580, on the bearer of Philomela's disguised message to Procne: "nescit, quid tradat in illis."

Page 627, note on 454/22–468/14. Add: Much of Buckingham's speech may actually be based on the *Titulus regius* of 1484 (suppressed by the Tudors), in which Parliament ratified the stage-managed petition formally recognizing

Richard's accession to the throne; see also the new addendum to page 609, note on 320/22–23.

Page 628, note on 458/3–19. Add: on Cook see M. A. Hicks, *Richard III and His Rivals* (London and Rio Grande, 1991), chapter 23, "The Case of Sir Thomas Cook, 1468."

Page 628. Add the following note: 462/18 **suapte**. Jacques Chomarat suggests that we read "sua parte"; we may also construe "-pte" as the common emphatic Latin suffix, with a feminine noun like "natura" or "parte" understood.

Page 628. Add the following note: 464/26–466/1 **sanguine . . . firmatum**. Jacques Chomarat prefers to read "sanguini" ("for whose blood [or "line"] the succession was secured"). The literal meaning of the ablative phrasing ("*with* whose blood the succession was settled by law") seems to hint that the father as well as the son was at bottom a natural-born scapegoat, an *enemy* of peace whose blood had to be shed to restore it; cf. *CW 15*, 328/22–23, and the various puns on "blood" in the (only loosely) parallel English in *CW 2*, 73. Indeed More's entire text in this sense "scapegoats" Richard, or does so on one level, at least; on another, it also exposes the typical partisan ploys that, like Richard, it uses to form such a scapegoat, and thereby in no less basic ways it can even be said to revive and reorient the question of Richard's real guilt or real innocence. For a comparable though more strictly secular way of reframing this question see J. Burckhardt, *Judgements on History and Historians*, tr. H. Zohn (Boston, 1958), pp. 77–79.

Page 629. Add the following note: 472/7–8 **audiri . . . apibus**. Cf. Vergil, *Aeneid* 12.587–92. Seneca speaks of swarms breaking up when beehives lose their sovereign (*De clementia* 1.19.2, cited by Erasmus in *Institutio principis christiani, ASD 4/1*, 156).

Page 630, note on 480/18–20. Add: On Christian kingship as "administratio," not "imperium," see Augustine, *De civitate dei* 5.12, cited by Erasmus, *Institutio principis christiani, ASD 4/1*, 159. Cf. also Bracton, 2:33 ("Attribuat igitur rex legi, quod lex attribuit ei, videlicet dominationem et potestatem. Non est enim rex ubi dominatur voluntas non lex") and the new addendum to page 626, note on 444/17–19.

Page 630. Add the following note: 482/7–9 **receptam . . . ceremonijs**. Cf. Erasmus, *Adagia* no. 1388 (*Opera omnia*, 2, 548F–549A): "sacra haec non aliter constant."

Page 631. Add the following note: 482/17–20 **si quis . . . turbare**. Cf. Lucian, *Piscator* 33, where, however, a flogging is wished on unworthy impersonators (of gods or philosophers) as contrasted with Lucian, who exposes them.

Page 631. Add the following note: 482/22–24 **quosdam . . . pericula**. Cf. Phaedrus 1.29.1–3 on an ass mocking a boar (a beast which became Richard III's own heraldic insignia) by comparing his own penis to the boar's snout:

> Plerumque stulti risum dum captant levem,
> gravi distringunt alios contumelia,
> et sibi nocivum concitant periculum. . . .

Page 631, note on 484/18–21. Add after "Hades": For Hercules' role in such contexts as a spectral deterrent resembling a death's head or a gorgon, see C. Faraone, *Talismans and Trojan Horses: Guardian Statues in Ancient Greek Myth and Ritual* (New York and Oxford, 1992), pp. 58–59.

Page 631. Add the following note: 484/23 **mensis**. The correct reading after this word is not "tempore" but rather "eiusdem." I misread *P* at first because this word in *P* is both heavily and ambiguously abbreviated (using a sign that *P*'s scribe also sometimes employs to abbreviate words like "ijsdem" and "quibusdam") and because *P* lacks the space before "mensis" that we can restore on the basis of Rastell's close rendering of this bit of Latin in *1557*[L] (for which see the new variant supplied above, keyed to this passage). More thus left a small gap in the Latin for a date he had yet to pin down; see the comparable gaps noted on pp. cxliv–cxlvi. Unlike both Fabian's *Chronicle* and *The Great Chronicle of London*, both *P* and *1557*[L] (possibly for dramatic effect) thus misleadingly place Richard's coronation sometime late in June 1583, even earlier than the actual date (July 6). Of course, More's English history omits this section.

Page 657, under "Vienne." Change "581" to "582"